ALIV
CHRIST

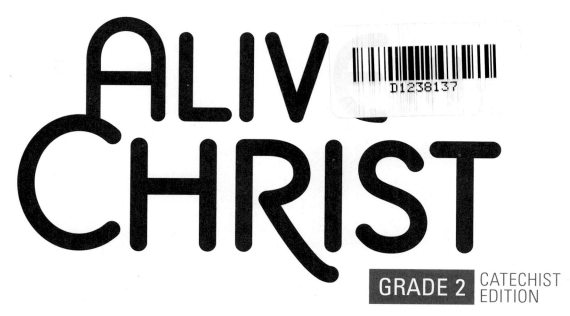

GRADE 2 CATECHIST EDITION

Sacraments of Penance and Eucharist

aliveinchrist.osv.com

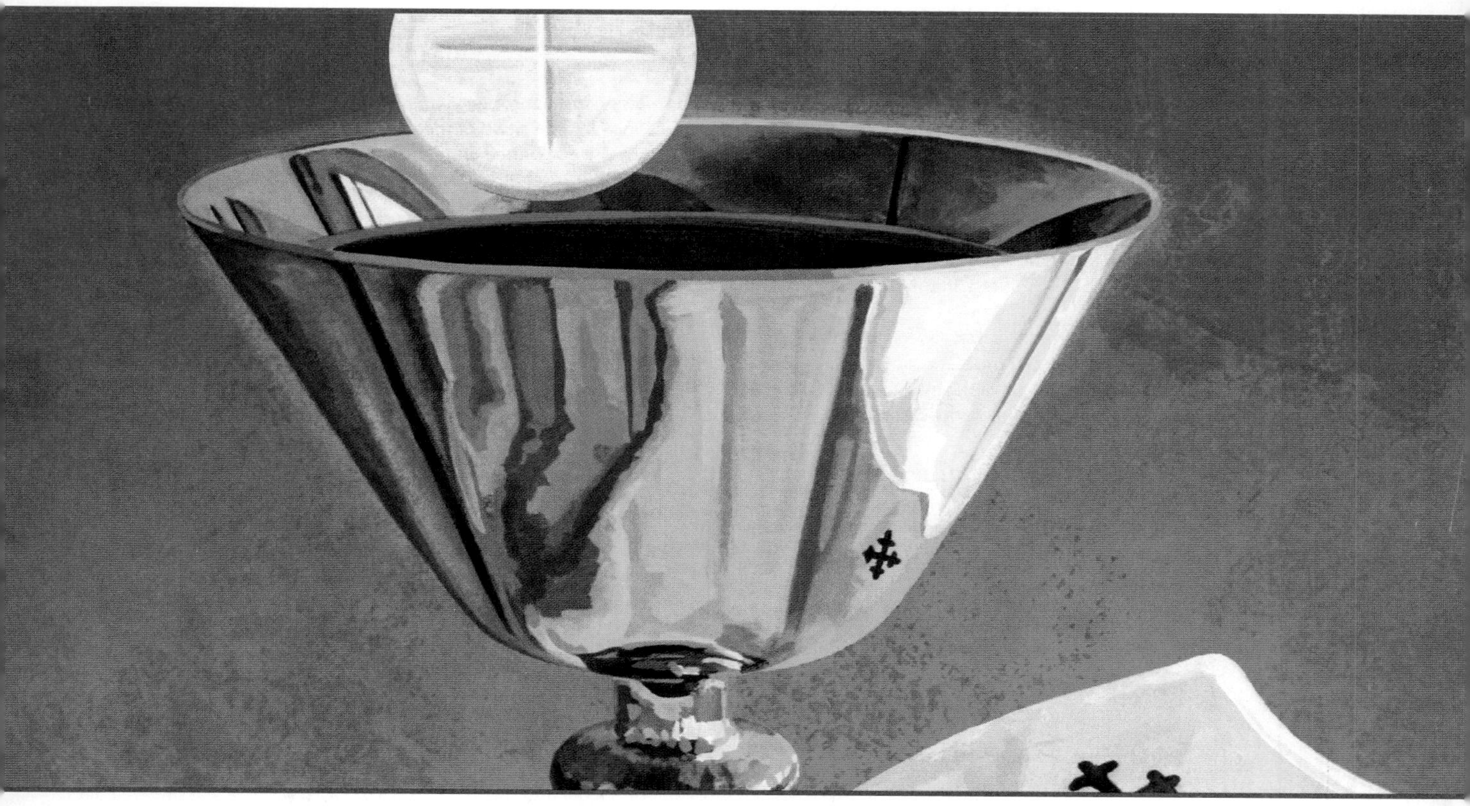

Our Sunday Visitor

The Subcommittee on the Catechism, United States Conference of Catholic Bishops, has found the doctrinal content of this manual, copyright 2014, to be in conformity with the *Catechism of the Catholic Church*.

Nihil Obstat
Rev. Fr. Jeremiah L. Payne, S.Th.L.
Censor Librorum, Diocese of Orlando

Imprimatur
✠ Most Rev. John Noonan
Bishop of Orlando
April 30, 2013

Alive in Christ Parish Grade 2 Catechist Edition
ISBN: 978-1-61278-023-8
Item Number: CU5113
2 3 4 5 6 7 8 015016 18 17 16 15 14
Webcrafters, Inc., Madison, WI, USA; September 2014; Job#118185

Table of Contents

About *Alive In Christ*

Student Lessons

Vision and Philosophy

“I am the way and the truth* and the life… I am the resurrection and the life.”

John 14:6, 11:25

“Jesus Christ not only transmits the word of God: he is the Word of God. Catechesis is therefore completely tied to him. Thus what must characterize the message transmitted by catechesis is, above all, its 'christocentricity'.”[1]

General Directory for Catechesis, 98

Jesus Christ at the Center

Welcome to ***Alive in Christ***. Christ is at the center of our faith, our Church, our catechesis. ***Alive in Christ*** is intentional in its focus on the life, mission, and saving work of Jesus Christ. This lays a foundation for a relationship with Jesus, who continually leads us to his Father's love and calls us through the Spirit to share in the divine life through his Church (see *Catechism of the Catholic Church*, 426).

Mirroring the Divine Pedagogy

The catechetical process of ***Alive in Christ*** mirrors the divine pedagogy—the gradual and relational way God teaches us so that we can know him and his truth, be guided by the Holy Spirit to respond with faith and love, and accept the gift of new life in Christ.

In this unique and effective pedagogy, each lesson encourages a personal and ongoing relationship with God, beginning with God's invitation through Sacred Scripture and leading children to reflect on his Word, deepen their understanding of our Sacred Tradition, and respond with a lived faith within the home and among friends, within the Church and in the community.

Building Knowledge of, and Reverence for, Sacred Scripture

Sacred Scripture from the *New American Bible Revised Edition* is foundational to every lesson in ***Alive in Christ***. Scripture from both the Old Testament and New Testament is presented in a variety of ways that encourage children to listen to the voice of God in his written Word and learn about the people and stories of the Bible. Each lesson offers several distinct encounters with Sacred Scripture, giving children the opportunity to pray with, reflect on, study, and apply God's Word to their lives.

Comprehensive Presentation of Catholic Teaching

Alive in Christ provides an authentic and comprehensive presentation of the essentials of the Catholic faith and has been found by the United tates Conference of Catholic Bishops' Subcommittee n the Catechism to be in conformity with the *Catechism of the Catholic Church*.

ollowing a systematically organized scope and sequence, key themes f Catholic teaching are repeated each year, through a grade-level focus, uilding on the child's knowledge of the faith at each developmental stage. This presentation of Catholic teaching—coupled with a purposeful mphasis on Catholic practices, images, and models of faith—promotes a common language of faith and builds a vibrant Catholic identity.

Developmentally Responsive and Appropriate

reated by a team of experts in catechesis, theology, and child psychology, *live in Christ* incorporates the most trusted research on how children learn and communicate. Definitions, activities, questions, and reading passages have been reviewed for developmental appropriateness. Targeted on-page nteractions help children more effectively learn or reinforce lesson content.

opics are presented at important developmental "windows"—ages when research in child development tells us that learning about a particular topic would be most effective. Illustrations, Catholic art, and photos emphasize cripture and visually present the chapter objectives in ways children can nderstand and relate to.

Complete and Purposeful Approach to Prayer and Worship

very grade level intentionally incorporates each of the five forms of prayer mentioned in the *Catechism*—blessing and adoration, petition, intercession, hanksgiving, and praise (see CCC, 2626–2643). Children learn about and pray hese basic prayer forms and are introduced to traditional prayers and evotions of the Church. They are taught how to talk with God in their own words and listen silently as he speaks to them. Each grade level also presents many opportunities to deepen children's understanding of the feasts and easons of the Church year and how we celebrate the Paschal Mystery hrough them.

Putting Faith into Practice

Alive in Christ presents and effectively implements the six fundamental tasks of catechesis (see *General Directory for Catechesis*, 84–85). Exercises, features, and questions throughout the text prompt children to relate knowledge of our Catholic faith with their life experience. Every chapter has on-page activities for immediate application as well as concrete suggestions for children to live out the faith at school, at their parish, and in their homes and communities.

Each lesson's Our Catholic Life section provides practical examples of the ways we worship, live, pray, and serve together as Catholics. It introduces children to Catholic figures who stand as models of heroic virtue in everyday life. Every lesson has connections to the Catholic social tradition, and each grade level provides catechesis on the seven major themes of the Church's Social Teaching.

Practical Ways to Involve Families in Their Children's Faith Formation

The "Family + Faith" page and an extensive website give parents the tools they need to know what their children are learning, talk about the faith, and recognize how they can more consciously live the faith in their daily family life.

On each lesson's take home page, parents will find information about children's developmental understanding, discussion prompts, and resources for family prayer. Taking into consideration the aims of the New Evangelization, each page includes an opportunity for adult reflection on their own relationship with Jesus and the Church.

Online resources offer multimedia tools to foster family interaction and reinforce the lesson at home.

A Commitment to Support Both New and Experienced Catechists

Alive in Christ Catechist Editions empower catechists with easy-to-use and effective tools for lesson planning, teaching and reinforcing faith concepts, and growing in their own relationship with Christ and his Church.

The key concepts and chapter objectives are fully explained and conveniently located at the beginning of each lesson along with background information to strengthen catechist understanding and nurture personal faith. A clear, concise, wraparound lesson plan leads the catechist page-by-page through the effective three-step process with integrated background on Sacred Scripture and doctrine, teaching tips, and connections to music, liturgy, and Catholic Social Teaching.

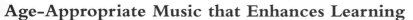

Extensive Online Resources for Catechists and Families

Alive in Christ provides catechists and leaders comprehensive program level resources and unit, chapter, and seasonal specific tools and activities. Online support includes lesson planning tools, catechist formation, custom test building and eAssessments, connections to the Sunday readings, and the option to share lesson plans via social media.

This extensive site provides children and families access to web-based assessments, interactive games and reviews, and articles and resources targeted specifically to adults—all to support faith sharing and continued learning in the home.

Age-Appropriate Music that Enhances Learning

With the knowledge that music is a means for forming children in Sacred Scripture, Church teachings, and Catholic Identity, *Alive in Christ* integrates multiple music options into every lesson. A variety of music from OCP (Oregon Catholic Press), John Burland, Dr. Jo Ann Paradise, and other sources is tied to chapter objectives and themes.

Music is suggested at point-of-use in the Catechist Edition, with multiple song suggestions for each chapter. Many prayer pages feature a song to be used within the prayer service. Music can be sampled and downloaded.

Also, we now have an all-new music component, *Songs of Scripture: Deepening Children's Understanding of the Word of God*, which features songs that teach, reinforce, and unfold the meaning of Scripture stories presented in the Student Book.

Alive in Christ Development Team

Greg Erlandson
President and Publisher

Beth McNamara
General Manager

Sabrina Magnuson
Associate Publisher

Dr. Jo Ann Paradise   Dr. Joseph White

Ana Arista   Heidi Busse   David Dziena   Dr. Hosffman Ospino   Denise Utter

Alive in Christ Structural Framework

Alive in Christ follows a systematic Scope and Sequence organized around key themes of Catholic teaching that repeat each year within a grade-level focus, building on the child's knowledge of the faith at each developmental stage.

This organizational structure takes into account research in child development that tells us at which age learning about a particular topic is most effective. These developmental "windows" help us to understand when the spiritual, cognitive, emotional, sociological, moral, and physical abilities of a child are "ripe" for learning. Included in the sequence, then, is a sensitivity to when children are ready to learn. A grade-level focus based within the structural framework of the seven essential themes allows for optimal learning.

The seven essential, foundational themes of the faith— Revelation, Trinity, Jesus Christ, The Church, Morality, Sacraments, and Kingdom of God—provide the structural framework that organizes the content of the grade. Progressing from first to sixth grade, the child deepens understanding as he or she is presented content that is theologically precise and developmentally appropriate.

As you study the Scope and Sequence, you will see how the objectives across grades move the learner to examine and appropriate a greater knowledge of our Catholic faith and how those objectives help to form a vibrant Catholic Identity.

Grade Level Focus	
1: Jesus Christ	"For through faith you are all children of God in Christ Jesus." **Galatians 3:26**
2: Sacraments of Penance and the Eucharist	"This is my body, which will be given for you; do this in memory of me." **Luke 22:19**
3: The Church	"I am the vine, you are the branches. Whoever remains in me and I in him will bear much fruit…" **John 15:5**
4: The Moral Life	"This is my commandment: love one another as I love you." **John 15:12**
5: The Seven Sacraments	"The water I shall give will become in him a spring of water welling up to eternal life." **John 4:14**
6: The Word of God in the Old Testament	"Your word is a lamp for my feet, / a light for my path." **Psalm 119:105**

Go to **aliveinchrist.osv.com** for an overview of the developmental windows for each grade level focus and full program Scope and Sequence.

Program Scope and Sequence

This graphic gives a visual image of the scope and sequence as a second grader in your group will experience it. The circles on the outside name the foundational themes that are the framework (unit structure) for every grade level. The child is holding key developmental factors or "windows" that lead to the grade level focus (for more on this, see page CE29). No matter what unit you are teaching, some component of the grade level focus is being treated.

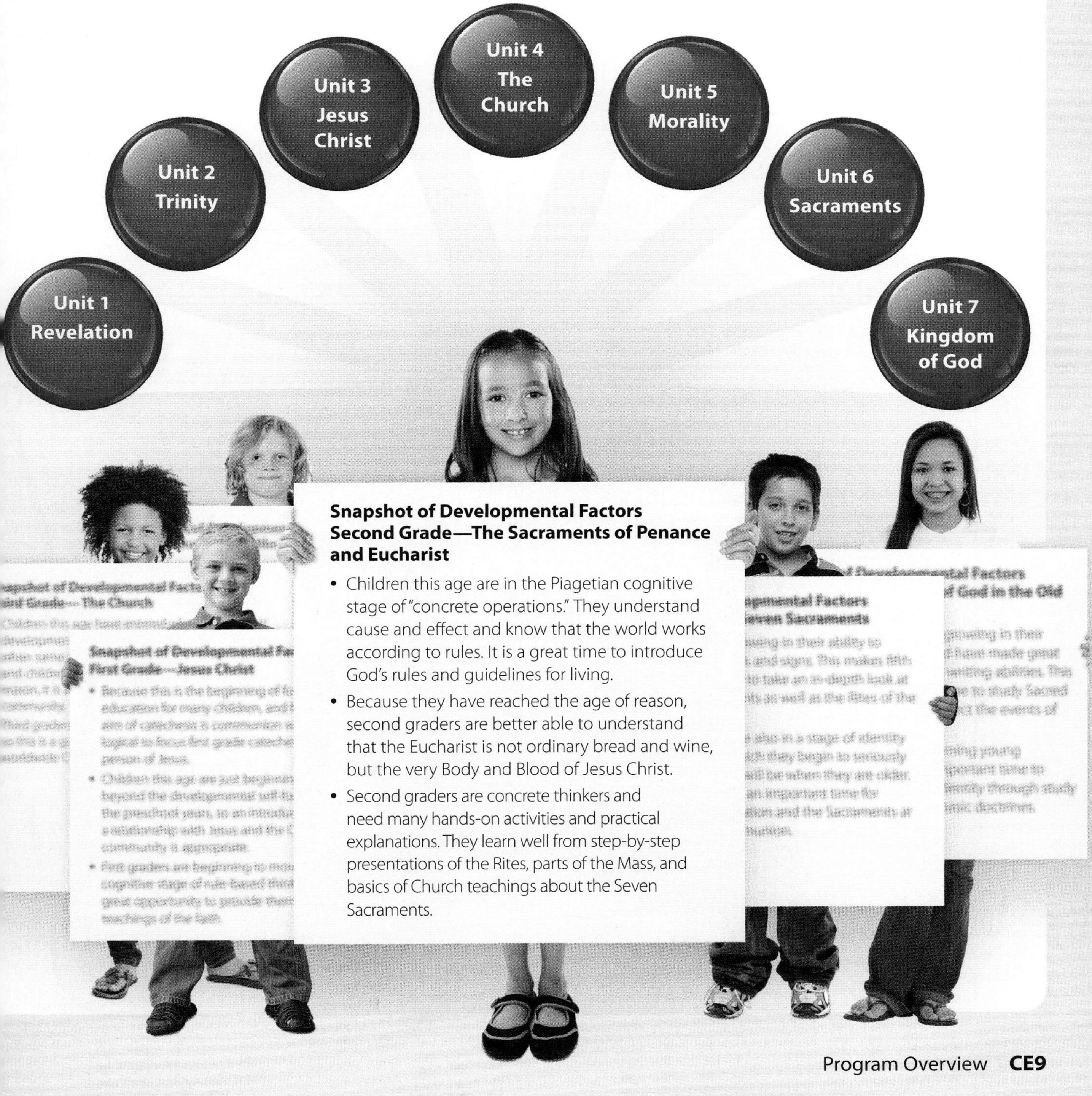
Unit 1 Revelation
Unit 2 Trinity
Unit 3 Jesus Christ
Unit 4 The Church
Unit 5 Morality
Unit 6 Sacraments
Unit 7 Kingdom of God
Snapshot of Developmental Factors Second Grade—The Sacraments of Penance and Eucharist
• Children this age are in the Piagetian cognitive stage of "concrete operations." They understand cause and effect and know that the world works according to rules. It is a great time to introduce God's rules and guidelines for living.
• Because they have reached the age of reason, second graders are better able to understand that the Eucharist is not ordinary bread and wine, but the very Body and Blood of Jesus Christ.
• Second graders are concrete thinkers and need many hands-on activities and practical explanations. They learn well from step-by-step presentations of the Rites, parts of the Mass, and basics of Church teachings about the Seven Sacraments.

Alive in Christ Parish Edition Program Components

Student Books Grades 1–6

Student Books follow a seven unit structure with a grade level focus on a foundational topic in our Catholic faith. They are the perfect tool to teach children to know, love, and live their Catholic faith through Sacred Scripture, doctrine, prayer, practices of the faith, and seasonal celebrations.

Catechist Editions Grades 1–6

The Catechist Editions help to build confident, capable, and successful catechists with comprehensive background and lesson preparation pages, timed wrap around lesson plans, optional activities, and point of use information. They are spiral bound and conveniently sized to match the Student Book.

People of Faith Collection Grades 1–6

This beautifully illustrated collection of Saints, Blesseds, and Venerables are connected to specific chapters. Children will learn about models of our Catholic faith while deepening their relationship with God and the Church.

Music Resources

Catechists are provided options for developmentally appropriate music that enhances learning. *Alive in Christ* integrates music into each step of the lesson. A variety of music from Oregon Catholic Press is tied to chapter objectives and themes.

A unique, all new music component, ***Songs of Scripture: Deepening Children's Understanding of God's Word***, features songs by John Burland and Dr. Jo Ann Paradise that teach, reinforce, and unfold the meaning of Scripture stories presented in the Student Book.

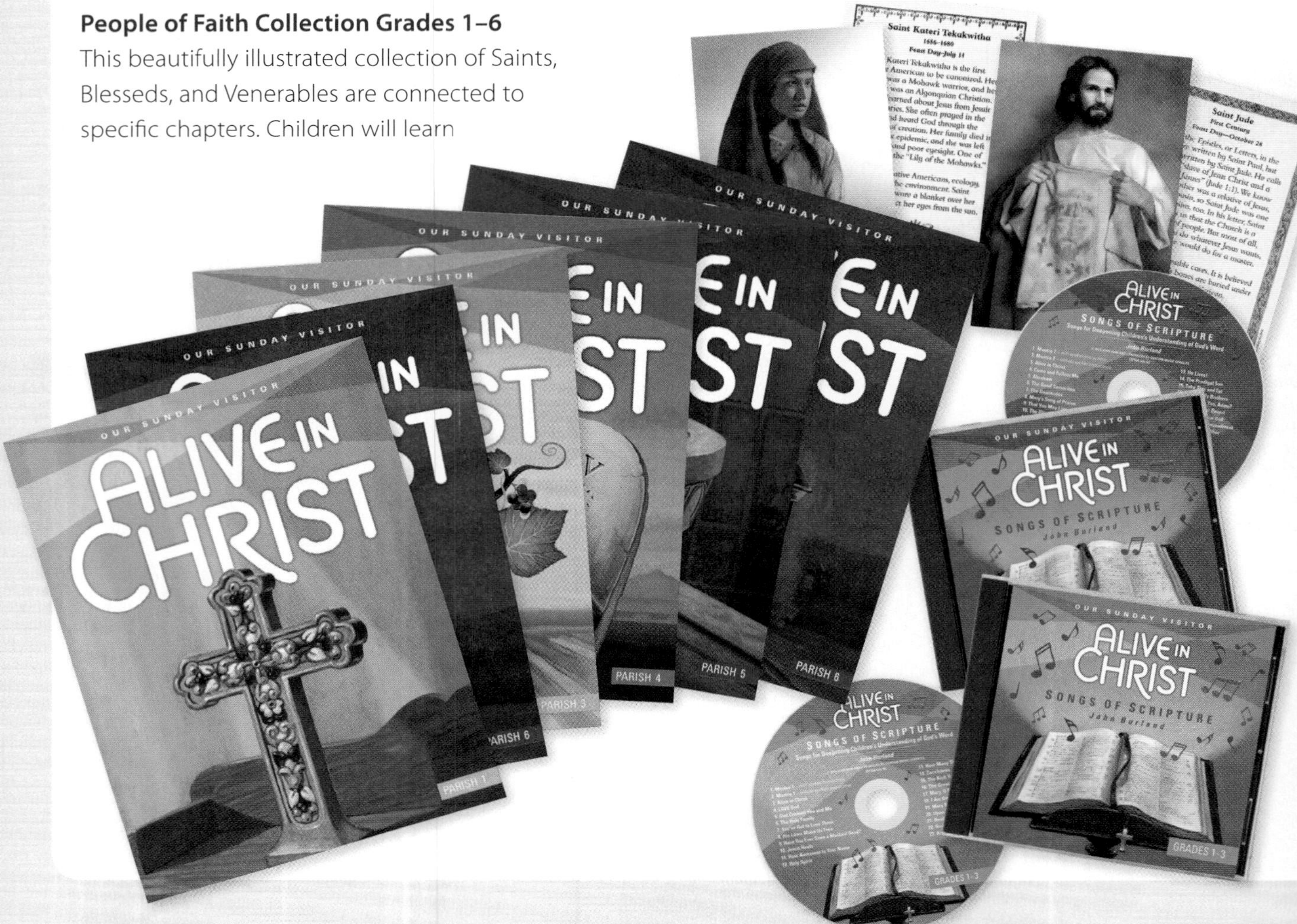

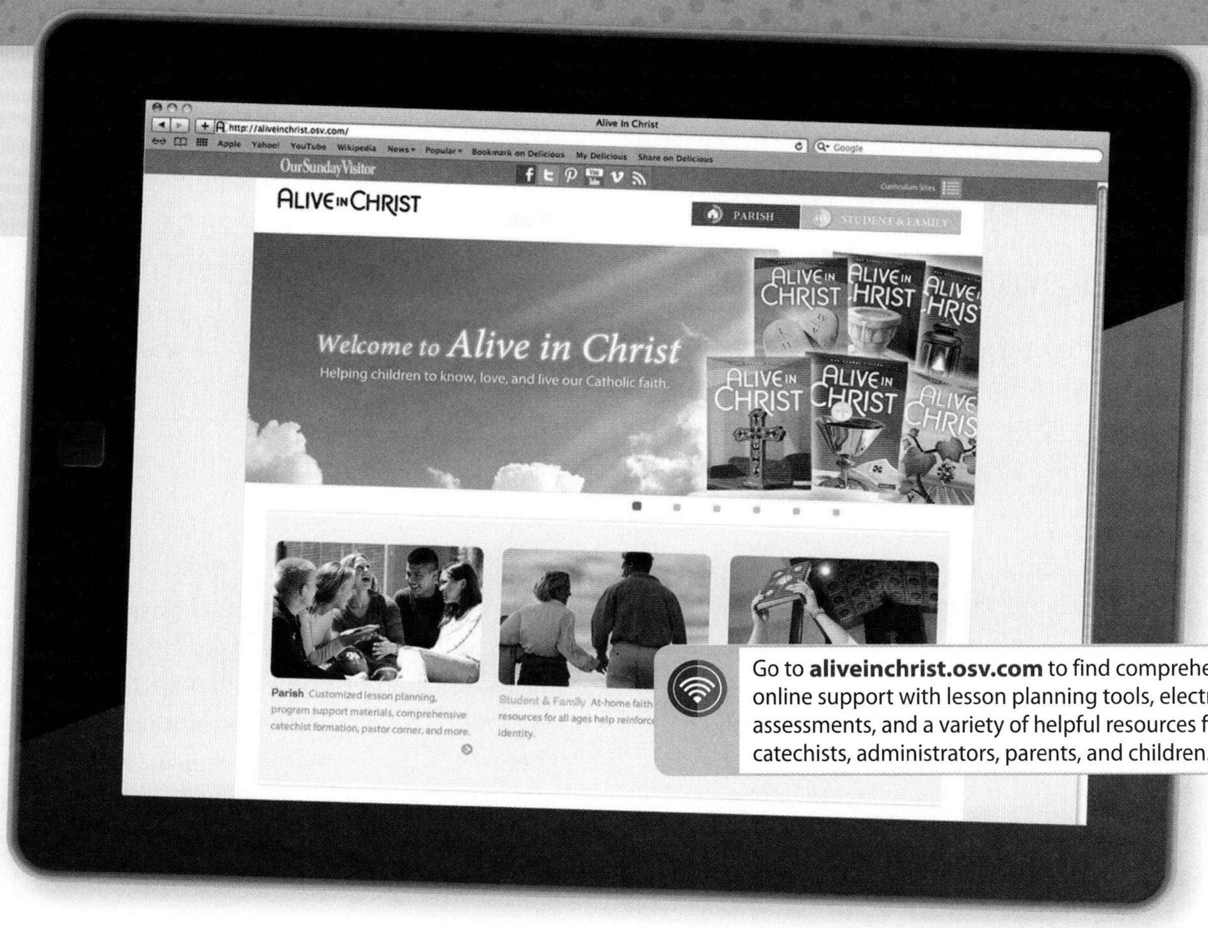

Go to **aliveinchrist.osv.com** to find comprehensive online support with lesson planning tools, electronic assessments, and a variety of helpful resources for catechists, administrators, parents, and children.

Online Resources for the Catechist

- Online lesson planning helps catechists to plan using chapter, seasonal, or Catholic Social Teaching lessons
- Share lesson plans via social media such as Facebook & Twitter
- Unit- and chapter-specific tools, assessments, activities, and multimedia resources
- Build a Custom Test allows catechists to build, print, and distribute tests using a bank of multiple choice, matching, fill in the blank, and long answer questions
- Assign eAssessments to children for completion online
- Catechetical formation and professional development tools are designed to help catechists hone their skills and grow in the knowledge of God's love
- Sample and download chapter-specific music to enhance catechetical learning or for prayer

Online Resources for the Student & Family

- Interactive Reviews offer children an opportunity for web-based assessment, preparation, and practice
- At-home faith formation resources for all ages help reinforce Catholic identity
- Faith-sharing features and resources geared to parents, children, and families encourage continued learning at home via games, multimedia activities, Lectionary-connected resources, social media interaction, and topical articles
- Sample and download chapter-specific music to enhance catechetical learning or for prayer

Online Resources for the Leader

- Program-level tools and resources provide directors, administrators, and leaders with higher-level materials from correlations to in-service models
- Sample and download chapter-specific music to enhance catechetical learning or for prayer

Responding to Your Vocation

"Give thanks to the Lord for the gift of your vocation, through which Christ has called you from among other men and women to be instruments of his salvation. Respond with generosity to your vocation and your names will be written in heaven."

— Pope Saint John Paul II, *Guide for Catechists*, 37

These words, taken from a talk by Pope Saint John Paul II to the catechists of Angola, are both awe inspiring and challenging! You have been called, he said, called by Christ from among other men and women. Have you ever wondered why you responded to the talk of the pastor or DRE that spoke about the need for catechists? Why did the bulletin article that outlined the responsibilities of a catechist stir your heart and prompt you to respond? Who gave your name to the catechetical leader in your parish?

No matter how the invitation came, it was Christ who called you. And by the power of the Holy Spirit, you, like Mary, responded, "Yes!" The vocation to catechesis, like all vocations, first comes from the grace of Baptism, is strengthened in Confirmation, and is sustained by the Eucharist and Penance. "The Church awakens and discerns this divine vocation and confers the mission to catechize….This personal call of Jesus Christ and its relationship to him are the true moving forces of catechetical activity. 'From this loving knowledge of Christ springs the desire to proclaim him, to "evangelize" and to lead others to the "Yes" of faith in Jesus Christ'[2]" (GDC, 231).

You have been called by Christ and been given the mission by his Church to be instruments of his work. Take a moment and ponder that statement. With so many responsibilities and demands on our time, we might sometimes lose sight of this, and being a catechist becomes just one of the many things we must do each week. This cannot be so. Every time you gather with your children, you take your place in the long line of those who have for 2,000 years held the sacred duty of bringing others into "communion, in intimacy, with Jesus Christ" (*Catechesi Tradendae*, 5).

Your Role as Catechist

To support and nurture children in their baptismal call to a lifetime of growing closer to and more like Jesus, the Church sets out some essential instructions. In order to provide a presentation of the "entire treasure of the Christian message" while adapting it to the "capacity of those being catechized" (GDC, 112), a catechist must do several things.

Teach the comprehensive course of study outlined by the United States Conference of Catholic Bishops' Subcommittee on the Catechism. In ***Alive in Christ***, you find these doctrines and practices presented in the objectives of the lesson. (See GDC, 112.)

Respect the developmental level of your children by understanding how they learn. (See GDC, 112.)

Use various methods as they are a "sign of life and richness" that will address multiple learning styles and special needs (GDC, 148).

Model a Catholic life through your own behaviors and practices, for the "charism given to [the catechist] by the Spirit, a solid spirituality and transparent witness of life constitutes the soul of every method" (GDC, 156).

Proclaim with joy and enthusiasm that "God so loved the world he sent his only Son" (John 3:16). In the words of Pope Benedict XVI, "Today too, there is a need... to rediscover the joy of believing and the enthusiasm for communicating the faith" (*Porta Fidei*, 7).

As you accept this sacred and challenging vocation, be assured that the Holy Spirit will lead and guide you in handing on our Catholic faith to the next generation. Let the love of God pour through so that they see in you the image and heart of our loving God.

The Task of Catechesis

As Jesus Formed His Disciples

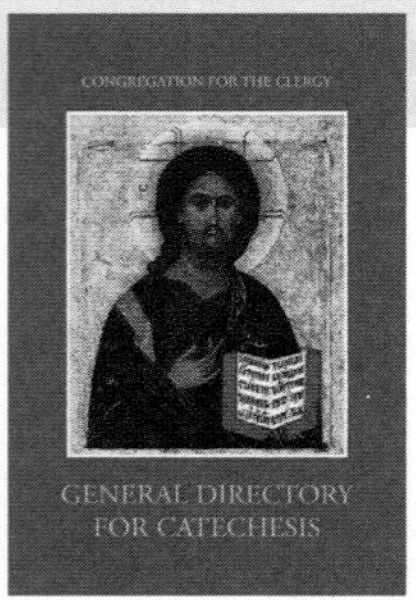

General Directory for Catechesis

There are six fundamental tasks in the ministry of catechesis. These six tasks are named and treated in the *General Directory for Catechesis* (see GDC , 85), and later in the *National Directory for Catechesis* (see NDC, 20). Each of these tasks corresponds to an aspect of faith in Jesus. The following are the six tasks of catechesis.

Promoting Knowledge of the Faith

We cannot live a faith we do not know. For this reason, studying the teachings of Jesus and his Church is an essential task of catechesis. The U.S. Bishops' Subcommittee on the Catechism and the conformity review process direct what is to be contained in this comprehensive presentation of the faith. According to the *National Directory for Catechesis*, this task of catechesis is a response to the individual's desire that God plants in the heart of every person to know. This desire comes naturally when individuals have had opportunities to encounter Christ and his message and have experienced an initial conversion. ***Alive in Christ*** begins each lesson by giving children an opportunity to meet God in his Word and to wonder about his life and love, followed by a process of helping them to know more about him through Sacred Tradition—the teaching of the Church. In this way, we help children frame questions that drive their desire to know more.

Liturgical Education

This task relates to learning about the ways in which the Church worships and celebrates, including the Seven Sacraments, the Order of Mass, and the liturgical year. According to the *General Directory for Catechesis*, liturgical education includes teaching about the form and the meaning of liturgical celebrations, but also means helping individuals prepare their minds and hearts to enter into these mysteries of our faith. As you use ***Alive in Christ***, you will teach your students about the liturgy both through the doctrine presented in the core chapters as well as through seasonal activities and prayerful experiences that echo the words and rhythms of our liturgical celebrations.

Moral Formation

This task of catechesis involves forming the consciences of learners through the moral teachings of Jesus and his Church and fostering understanding of what it means to live these teachings in one's daily life. Morality in the Christian life involves standards and guidelines, but it is more than learning a list of rules. Morality is about discipleship. As you use ***Alive in Christ***, you will find opportunities to challenge children to apply what they have learned about the Ten Commandments, Jesus' command to love as he has loved, and the Beatitudes to situations at home and school and in the community.

Teaching to Pray

When catechesis is permeated by a climate of prayer, ne assimilation of the entire Christian life reaches its ummit" (GDC, 85). The "climate of prayer" in catechesis nvites individuals into an ever deeper relationship with iod. Teaching to pray is more than merely "teaching rayers"; it involves fostering an understanding of prayer s conversation with God—helping children learn how o talk with God in their own words as well as how to sten to God.

his task of catechesis involves teaching the traditional rayers of the Church and the various forms and xpressions of prayer mentioned in the *Catechism of the atholic Church*. ***Alive in Christ*** incorporates experiences f all five forms of prayer. You will also have opportunities o help children speak to God in their own words.

Education for Community Life

his task of catechesis relates to developing an nderstanding of what it means to be a part of ne Christian community, including respecting the uthority and structure of the Church as well as living ut Jesus' New Commandment to love one another s he has loved us. "Catechesis prepares the Christian o live in community and to participate actively in the fe and mission of the Church" (GDC, 86). Catechesis hould prepare us to live and work with one another, oth within the Church and in society as a whole. The bishops write that catechesis should encourage a spirit of simplicity and humility, a special concern for the poor, particular care for the alienated, a sense of fraternal correction, common prayer, mutual forgiveness, and a fraternal love that embraces all these attitudes. (See GDC, 86.) Various chapter features, as well as the "Live Your Faith" sections on Catholic Social Teaching will assist you in this task of catechesis.

Missionary Initiation

While only some may be called to other lands to minister in Christ's name, by Baptism, all are called to live in such a way that we serve as witnesses of the faith to those who are around us. This task of catechesis prepares the learner to share his or her faith with others. ***Alive in Christ*** helps to form children in the language of the Catholic faith and the behaviors and practices of the faith. Forming them in a vibrant Catholic identity gives them the skills necessary to be strong witnesses of the faith. This is reinforced in the tools we provide the parents in the Family + Faith page, as it equips the parents to talk about faith with their children.

Our bishops state, "all efforts in evangelization and catechesis should incorporate these tasks" (NDC, 20). In this way, we pay attention to several different dimensions of faith, with the ultimate goal of helping children grow into deeper communion with Christ so that they live as disciples in faith, word, and deed.

Unique and Effective Pedagogy

The Divine Pedagogy

As catechists, we always hold two realities: the "what" and the "how" of catechesis. What do we want our children to know and love about our faith and how do we best communicate the treasure of our faith?

We use the word *pedagogy* to speak about the art, science, or profession of teaching. In other words, pedagogy is the "how" of faith formation. We are called to hand on the truths of our faith by echoing God's own way of teaching us his truths. The *General Directory for Catechesis* tells us that,

> "Catechesis, as communication of divine Revelation, is radically inspired by the pedagogy of God, as displayed in Christ and in the Church. [It is the Church's mission to be] a visible and actual continuation of the pedagogy of the Father and of the Son."
>
> GDC, 143, 141

Jesus the Teacher

Each lesson in ***Alive in Christ*** mirrors the divine pedagogy—the gradual and relational way God teaches us so that we can know him and his truth, be guided by the Holy Spirit to respond with faith and love, and accept the gift of new life in Christ. Even as we teach others, God remains active in their hearts, bringing growth to the seeds of faith that are planted there.

Here are five important characteristics of the divine pedagogy that are at the heart of each lesson of *Alive in Christ*.

The pedagogy of God is invitational and person-centered.
God initiates a relationship with each person. He does so by first creating us with a desire to know him and the capacity to respond to him. The ultimate invitation to relationship comes in Jesus. Pope Saint John Paul II tells us that the purpose of all catechesis is to bring people into intimacy with Jesus.

As God enters into dialogue with us, we are called to follow this example by providing catechesis that it is rooted in interpersonal relationships and involves a process of dialogue. (See GDC, 143.) God also meets us where we are and accommodates for our particular needs. Therefore, effective catechesis should be developmentally appropriate and should make allowances for adapting to special needs.

God's pedagogy is incarnational.
Dei Verbum points out the "inner unity" of deeds and words in God's plan of revelation: "the deeds wrought by God in the history of salvation manifest and confirm the teaching and realities signified by the words, while the words proclaim the deeds and clarify the mystery contained in them" (2).

From speaking the universe into existence, to his promise to Noah and his covenants with Abraham and Moses, to the Word made flesh in Jesus Christ, it is evident that God's Word becomes action.

An effective pedagogy should make the faith come to life through hands-on activities and applications and multisensory teaching methodologies. It should give learners clear ways to go out and live the Gospel they have received.

The pedagogy of God is familial and communal.
God reveals himself as a communion of persons—Father, Son, and Holy Spirit—and creates human beings to be in communion with one another.

Effective catechesis should build community among the children, involve parents and families as primary catechists, and connect children to the larger parish community. Connecting the families to the life of the parish, particularly through participation in the Sunday Eucharist, is vital in building up the Body of Christ.

God's pedagogy is structured and comprehensive.
In salvation history, God reveals himself to humanity gradually as people are able to understand. One revelation builds upon the next, until Revelation reaches its fullness in the Person of Jesus Christ. Effective catechesis also presents key truths of the faith gradually as the learner is able to receive them.

The pedagogy of God is perpetual.
We read in **Isaiah 55:11**, "So shall my word be / that goes forth from my mouth; / It shall not return to me empty, / but shall do what pleases me, / achieving the end for which I sent it." God's truths are handed on through the generations in the forms of Sacred Scripture and Sacred Tradition, which is the living memory of the Church. God's covenants do not end, but come to greater fulfillment and realization.

A catechesis based on the divine pedagogy prepares the learner to share the Gospel with others, in word and deed, so that the Good News of salvation is handed on to others and to future generations.

Three-Step Catechetical Process

Invite

Alive in Christ's catechetical methodology mirrors the divine pedagogy by following a three-step process of **Invite**, **Discover**, and **Live**. This process encourages a personal and ongoing relationship with the Holy Trinity.

1. **The Invite Step** begins the lesson with God's invitation through Sacred Scripture. Children open their minds and hearts to what God is saying to them in Scripture, reflect on it, and transition to the Discover step and chapter objectives.

2. **The Discover Step** helps form Catholic identity through the study of Scripture, knowledge of Church teaching, and an understanding of Catholic practices. It presents the doctrine of the lesson in developmentally appropriate language and images. Charts, on-page questions, and gold star activities prompt children to interact directly with the page, and aid in understanding and retention. With large on page activities, children are given the opportunity to process and reinforce what they have learned and apply it to their own lives and the experience of the Church.

3. **The Live Step** helps children relate knowledge of the faith and the ways we worship, live, pray, and serve together as Catholics. Children are given the tools to connect their faith to everyday life and to deepen their relationship with God and the Church through the prayer experiences at the end of each lesson.

If you follow this three-step process, you will in fact mirror the divine pedagogy by offering children the opportunity to know God and his truth through Sacred Scripture and Sacred Tradition. You will inspire them to be open to the Holy Spirit so that they will respond in faith and love and accept the gift of new life in Christ!

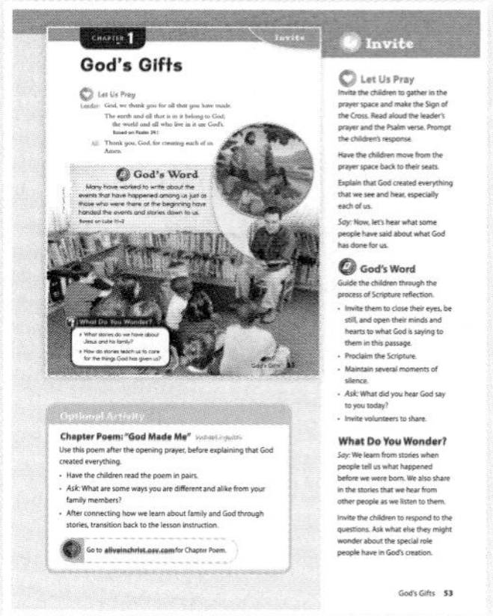

As a catechist, during the **Invite** step you:

- Call the children together to begin in **prayer**.
- Prepare the children to hear the **Word of God**.
- Guide the children through the **Scripture reflection** process, proclaiming God's Word and inviting quiet thought. (See CE22 for a full description of the Scripture reflection process.)
- After proclamation of the Scripture, allow time (governed by what is developmentally appropriate) for sacred **silence**.
- Invite children **to share** what they have experienced, what they felt God was saying to them or what he wanted them to know in a special way today. Assure them sharing is voluntary.
- Prompt continued thought about God's Word and move to chapter objectives by using the "**What Do You Wonder**" questions.

Discover

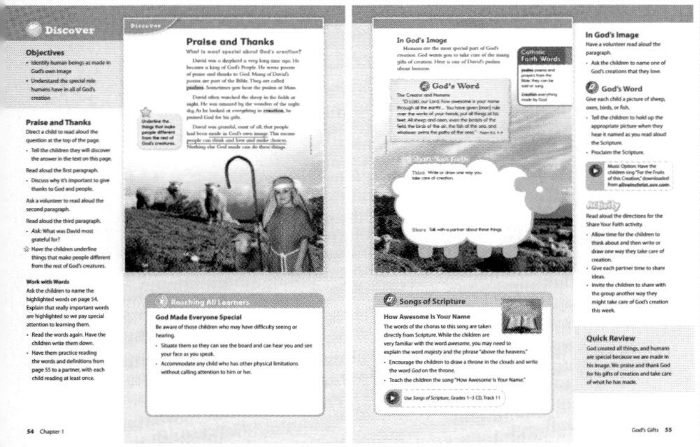

As a catechist, during the **Discover** step you:

- Teach the **objectives** of the lesson, which are identified in the Catechist Edition in two places: the overview Lesson Plan in the catechist background section and in the top left-hand corner of each Discover spread. The Quick Review, highlighted in the bottom right hand corner of the Discover spread, allows you to check that you have fully covered the objectives.
- Follow the **instruction** in the vertical side columns, which walks you through the entire lesson. Note that the activities are an integral part of the lesson. They emphasize the essential elements of Church teaching and help the children apply those truths to worship, prayer, and daily life.
- Present the **Catholic Faith Words**, which are highlighted in the text and called out in the side boxes. These words build a common language of faith and are explained with precise theological language that is developmentally appropriate.
- Use the **boxes** framed in green at the bottom of the page that provide additional Scripture and doctrinal background, optional activities, quick tips, ways to adapt for special needs, suggestions for including music, and more.

Live

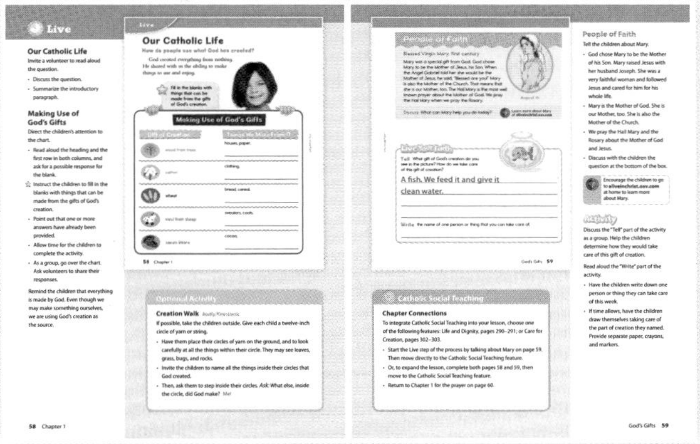

As a catechist, during the **Live** step you:

- Guide the children through a graphic organizer, chart, or reflection activity to **synthesize** what they have learned in the chapter.
- Hold up the Communion of Saints, and introduce the children to a **Saint**, **Blessed**, or **Venerable** whose life exemplifies the content of the lesson. What better way to encourage faith-filled living than through Catholic heroines and heroes?
- Give the children the opportunity through a closing **activity** to relate their knowledge of the faith to their lives, and invite them to commit themselves more deeply to what it means to be Catholic with concrete action and future steps.
- Conclude with a **prayer celebration**. Make sure to leave time at the end of the lesson to pray with the children. If the prayer calls for it, you may want to assign parts a week ahead of time.
- Send home the **Family + Faith** page. As the children live their faith primarily in the circle of their families, this page is an excellent resource to connect the children's learning with their home and to form their parents in faith.

Unique and Effective Pedagogy

Lesson Preparation

Alive in Christ Catechist Editions give you everything you need for lesson planning, teaching and reinforcing faith concepts, and growing in your own relationship with Christ and his Church.

Each chapter has catechist-specific content provided in the planning and background pages. These are the five pages that provide scriptural, doctrinal, and methodological background and formation. You will also find pages that address the different ways children process, understand, and learn lesson content at any given grade level.

Catechist Background easy-to-understand theological background on the chapter content. The Reflect questions help connect faith concepts with the catechist's own life experience.

Key Concept for each lesson is clearly stated at the start of each chapter.

Doctrinal Content correlates to paragraphs from the *Catechism of the Catholic Church*.

Tasks of Catechesis relate lesson components to one of the six Tasks of Catechesis as outlined in the *National Directory for Catechesis*.

Catechist's Prayer offers a moment of reflection for the catechist before planning each lesson.

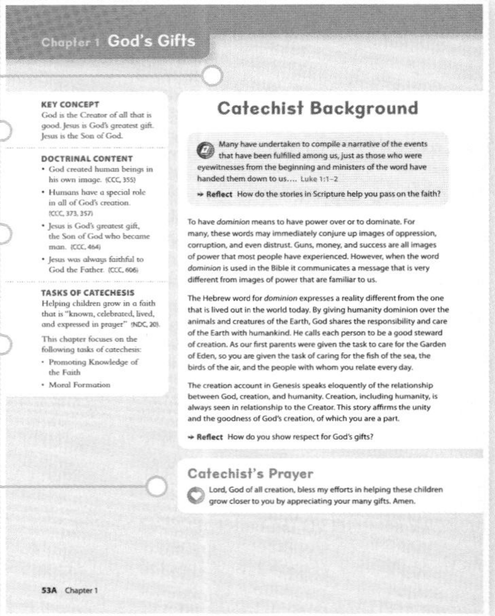

Chapter 1 God's Gifts

KEY CONCEPT
God is the Creator of all that is good. Jesus is God's greatest gift. Jesus is the Son of God.

DOCTRINAL CONTENT
- God created human beings in his own image. (CCC, 355)
- Humans have a special role in all of God's creation. (CCC, 373, 357)
- Jesus is God's greatest gift, the Son of God who became man. (CCC, 464)
- Jesus was always faithful to God the Father. (CCC, 606)

TASKS OF CATECHESIS
Helping children grow in a faith that is "known, celebrated, lived, and expressed in prayer" (NDC, 20).

This chapter focuses on the following tasks of catechesis:
- Promoting Knowledge of the Faith
- Moral Formation

Catechist Background

Many have undertaken to compile a narrative of the events that have been fulfilled among us, just as those who were eyewitnesses from the beginning and ministers of the word have handed them down to us.... Luke 1:1–2

→ **Reflect** How do the stories in Scripture help you pass on the faith?

To have *dominion* means to have power over or to dominate. For many, these words may immediately conjure up images of oppression, corruption, and even distrust. Guns, money, and success are all images of power that most people have experienced. However, when the word *dominion* is used in the Bible it communicates a message that is very different from images of power that are familiar to us.

The Hebrew word for *dominion* expresses a reality different from the one that is lived out in the world today. By giving humanity dominion over the animals and creatures of the Earth, God shares the responsibility and care of the Earth with humankind. He calls each person to be a good steward of creation. As our first parents were given the task to care for the Garden of Eden, so you are given the task of caring for the fish of the sea, the birds of the air, and the people with whom you relate every day.

The creation account in Genesis speaks eloquently of the relationship between God, creation, and humanity. Creation, including humanity, is always seen in relationship to the Creator. This story affirms the unity and the goodness of God's creation, of which you are a part.

→ **Reflect** How do you show respect for God's gifts?

Catechist's Prayer

Lord, God of all creation, bless my efforts in helping these children grow closer to you by appreciating your many gifts. Amen.

53A Chapter 1

Timed Lesson Plan clearly stated chapter objectives, step-by-step instructions, and a suggested time frame to complete each step of the lesson.

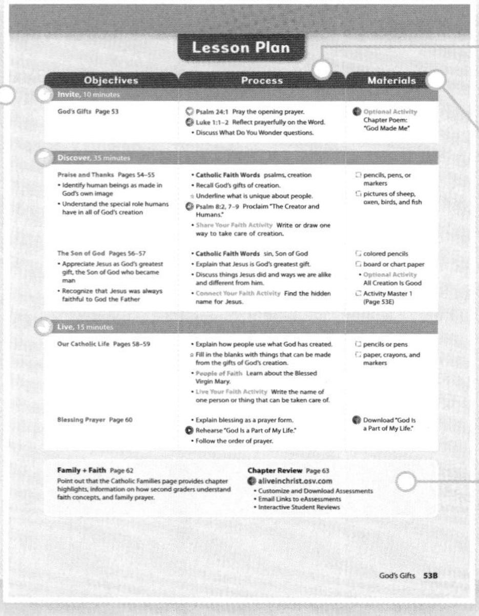

Lesson Plan

Objectives	Process	Materials
Invite, 10 minutes		
God's Gifts Page 53	Psalm 24:1 Pray the opening prayer. Luke 1:1–2 Reflect prayerfully on the Word. • Discuss What Do You Wonder questions.	Optional Activity Chapter Poem: "God Made Me"
Discover, 35 minutes		
Praise and Thanks Pages 54–55 • Identify human beings as made in God's own image • Understand the special role humans have in all of God's creation	• Catholic Faith Words psalms, creation • Recall God's gifts of creation. Underline what is unique about people. Psalm 8:2, 7–9 Proclaim "The Creator and Humans." • Share Your Faith Activity Write or draw one way to take care of creation.	pencils, pens, or markers pictures of sheep, oxen, birds, and fish
The Son of God Pages 56–57 • Appreciate Jesus as God's greatest gift, the Son of God who became man • Recognize that Jesus was always faithful to God the Father	• Catholic Faith Words sin, Son of God • Explain that Jesus is God's greatest gift. • Discuss things Jesus did and ways we are alike and different from him. • Connect Your Faith Activity Find the hidden name for Jesus.	colored pencils board or chart paper • Optional Activity All Creation Is Good Activity Master 1 (Page 53E)
Live, 15 minutes		
Our Catholic Life Pages 58–59	• Explain how people use what God has created. Fill in the blanks with things that can be made from the gifts of God's creation. • People of Faith Learn about the Blessed Virgin Mary. • Live Your Faith Activity Write the name of one person or thing that can be taken care of.	pencils or pens paper, crayons, and markers
Blessing Prayer Page 60	• Explain blessing as a prayer form. Rehearse "God Is a Part of My Life." • Follow the order of prayer.	Download "God Is a Part of My Life."

Family + Faith Page 62
Point out that the Catholic Families page provides chapter highlights, information on how second graders understand faith concepts, and family prayer.

Chapter Review Page 63
aliveinchrist.osv.com
- Customize and Download Assessments
- Email Links to eAssessments
- Interactive Student Reviews

God's Gifts 53B

Process Column notes prayer, Scripture, activities, and Catholic Faith Words in each step.

Materials Column materials and online resources needed for the lesson.

Family + Faith / Chapter Review reminders to share chapter content with families and directs catechists to various opportunities for review and assessment.

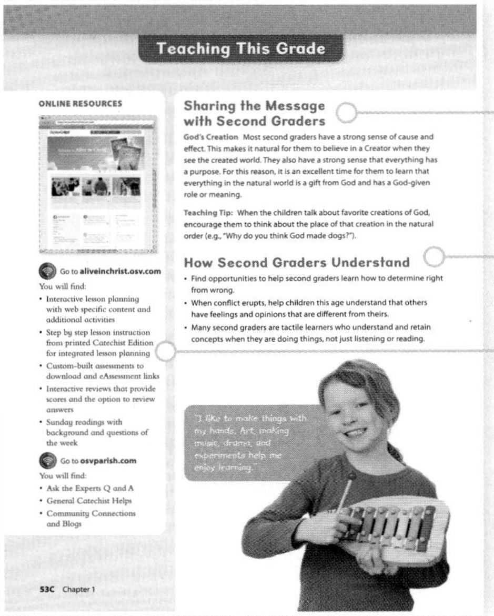

Teaching This Grade

ONLINE RESOURCES

Go to **aliveinchrist.osv.com**

You will find:

- Interactive lesson planning with web specific content and additional activities
- Step by step lesson instruction from printed Catechist Edition for integrated lesson planning
- Custom-built assessments to download and eAssessment links
- Interactive reviews that provide scores and the option to review answers
- Sunday readings with background and questions of the week

Go to **osvparish.com**

You will find:

- Ask the Experts Q and A
- General Catechist Helps
- Community Connections and Blogs

Sharing the Message with Second Graders

God's Creation Most second graders have a strong sense of cause and effect. This makes it natural for them to believe in a Creator when they see the created world. They also have a strong sense that everything has a purpose. For this reason, it is an excellent time for them to learn that everything in the natural world is a gift from God and has a God-given role or meaning.

Teaching Tip: When the children talk about favorite creations of God, encourage them to think about the place of that creation in the natural order (e.g., "Why do you think God made dogs?").

How Second Graders Understand

- Find opportunities to help second graders learn how to determine right from wrong.
- When conflict erupts, help children this age understand that others have feelings and opinions that are different from theirs.
- Many second graders are tactile learners who understand and retain concepts when they are doing things, not just listening or reading.

"I like to make things with my hands. Art, making music, drama, and experiments help me enjoy learning."

53C Chapter 1

Sharing the Message offers insight on the relationship between the lesson objectives and the child's developmental level of understanding of those topics.

How Grade Level Children Understand provides background on where children this age typically are in terms of cognitive, social, spiritual, and emotional development.

Online Resources are clearly labeled throughout the Catechist Edition and direct you to downloads, lesson planning tools, interactive reviews, eAssessments, and more.

Chapter Story or poem provides an opportunity to extend the Invite step of the process with additional life experience connections.

NCEA IFG: ACRE Edition correlates the lesson objectives to the domains of *NCEA Information for Growth: Assessment of Children/Youth Religious Education* (2013) and helps catechists measure children's understanding and appropriation of lesson content.

Catholic Social Teaching identifies which principles of Catholic Social Teaching/Live Your Faith pieces connect to this chapter and provides direction for how to integrate them into the Live step of the process. These connections are also noted at point of use in the bottom band of the lesson plan.

Music Options are provided to enhance catechetical learning and the prayer celebration. These options are also called out at point of use in the wraparound lesson plan.

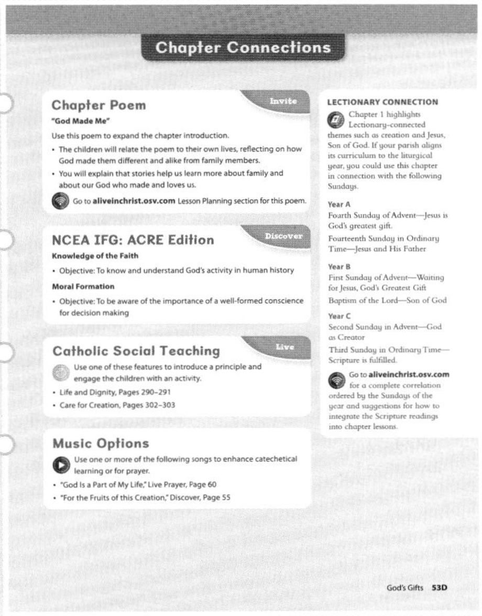

Chapter Connections

Chapter Poem

Invite

"God Made Me"

Use this poem to expand the chapter introduction.

- The children will relate the poem to their own lives, reflecting on how God made them different and alike from family members.
- You will explain that stories help us learn more about family and about our God who made and loves us.

Go to **aliveinchrist.osv.com** Lesson Planning section for this poem.

NCEA IFG: ACRE Edition

Discover

Knowledge of the Faith

- Objective: To know and understand God's activity in human history

Moral Formation

- Objective: To be aware of the importance of a well-formed conscience for decision making

Catholic Social Teaching

Live

Use one of these features to introduce a principle and engage the children with an activity.

- Life and Dignity, Pages 290–291
- Care for Creation, Pages 302–303

Music Options

Use one or more of the following songs to enhance catechetical learning or for prayer.

- "God Is a Part of My Life," Live Prayer, Page 60
- "For the Fruits of this Creation," Discover, Page 55

LECTIONARY CONNECTION

Chapter 1 highlights Lectionary-connected themes such as creation and Jesus, Son of God. If your parish aligns its curriculum to the liturgical year, you could use this chapter in connection with the following Sundays.

Year A

Fourth Sunday of Advent—Jesus is God's greatest gift.

Fourteenth Sunday in Ordinary Time—Jesus and His Father

Year B

First Sunday of Advent—Waiting for Jesus, God's Greatest Gift

Baptism of the Lord—Son of God

Year C

Second Sunday in Advent—God as Creator

Third Sunday in Ordinary Time—Scripture is fulfilled.

Go to **aliveinchrist.osv.com** for a complete correlation ordered by the Sundays of the year and suggestions for how to integrate the Scripture readings into chapter lessons.

God's Gifts 53D

New American Bible Revised Edition

Sacred Scripture

"For in the sacred books, the Father who is in heaven meets His children with great love and speaks with them; and the force and power in the word of God is so great that it stands as the support and energy of the Church...."

Dei Verbum, 21

Sacred Scripture from both the Old Testament and New Testament is at the heart of ***Alive in Christ***. The children are invited to understand the importance of Sacred Scripture, as a font of Divine Revelation and the guide for their lives. The Word is always given prominent visual importance to highlight its significance, with a parchment background, an icon, and a logo. Children are led to know, love, and be formed by God's Word.

Scripture in the Catechetical Process

The children always **pray** with Scripture in the opening prayer of the Invite step and often in the prayer experience in the Live step.

The practice of Scripture **reflection** is an essential element in the Invite step of every lesson and the means by which we enter into the divine pedagogy.

Children are formed by this practice of reflecting on Scripture and being open to the Word of God personally speaking to them. Listening with the ear of the heart and reflecting on Scripture prepares children for practices such as *Lectio Divina*.

Sacred Scripture is **studied** in the Discover step as children learn about God's action throughout salvation history and see how Scripture is a source of Church teaching. Key Scripture accounts are presented in multiple grade levels to encourage biblical literacy, familiarity, and understanding.

Throughout the Discover and Live steps, the children **apply** the Word of God to their lived experience and acquire the behaviors and practices of a Catholic life.

Scripture Reflection

Step 1: Begin by using the directions provided on the Invite page of the lesson or you may use the recorded preparation, titled "Mantra," included in both the *Songs of Scripture* CDs.

Step 2: Help the children enter into sacred space by prominently displaying the Bible, lighting or turning on a candle, and guiding them to become quiet and still.

Step 3: Read the passage in a slow and steady voice, one complete sentence at a time.

Step 4: Ask the question, "What did you hear God say to you today?" This reflection is critical in providing the children an opportunity to encounter God through his Word. It prepares the child to receive and respond in faith to God's personal invitation.

Sacred Tradition

Vhat is necessary for the children to know so that they will develop a vibrant Catholic dentity and be able to express their faith with competence, understanding, and love?

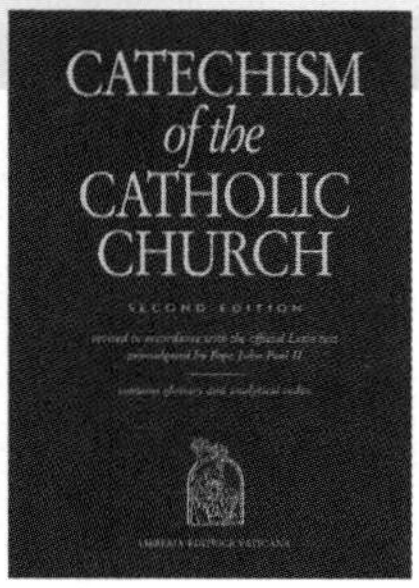

Catechism of the Catholic Church

'he Church guides us, teaching that the catechetical message has "a 'comprehensive ierarchical character,'[3] which constitutes a vital synthesis of the faith" (GDC, 114). The ruths of the faith are organized in a hierarchy around the mystery of the most Holy 'rinity, in a Christ-centered (or *Christocentric*) perspective.

> "The mutual connections between dogmas, and their coherence, can be ound in the whole of the Revelation of the mystery of Christ.[4] 'In Catholic loctrine there exists an order or "hierarchy" of truths, since they vary in their elation to the foundation of the Christian faith.'[5]"
>
> CCC, 90

n other words, some truths are so basic and oundational to what we believe as Catholics that they nust be presented first, and then other related truths an be better understood.

'o help us know what is basic and foundational, the JSCCB's Subcommittee on the Catechism has identified he truths of the faith deemed essential to the formation of children. ***Alive in Christ*** has been found to be in onformity with the *Catechism of the Catholic Church*.

n salvation history, God has revealed himself to people n a systematic and gradual way, showing us more of imself as we are capable of understanding. (See GDC, 38 and CCC 54–65.) Our catechesis models this divine edagogy and includes all of the foundational elements of the faith, presenting them in a gradual and systematic vay as the learner is ready to hear them.

Alive in Christ organizes the foundational truths around even key themes of Catholic teaching that repeat each 'ear within a grade level focus.

Systematic and Comprehensive

The content of Sacred Scripture and Sacred Tradition are systematically presented in precise theological language in the **lesson objectives** of each lesson. The objectives are found on your Lesson Plan and at point of use where they are presented to the children.

Important **Catholic Faith Words** are highlighted in every chapter with definitions that grow as children's understanding does, and their repetition across grades helps to promote the common language of faith.

Each **Unit Opener** summarizes key concepts being presented and identifies *Catechism of the Catholic Church* references for each of these faith statements.

At the back of each Student Book, the **Our Catholic Tradition** reference section reinforces the faith basics presented in the lessons. It is referenced in your lesson plan with specific instructions on how to integrate the content into the lesson.

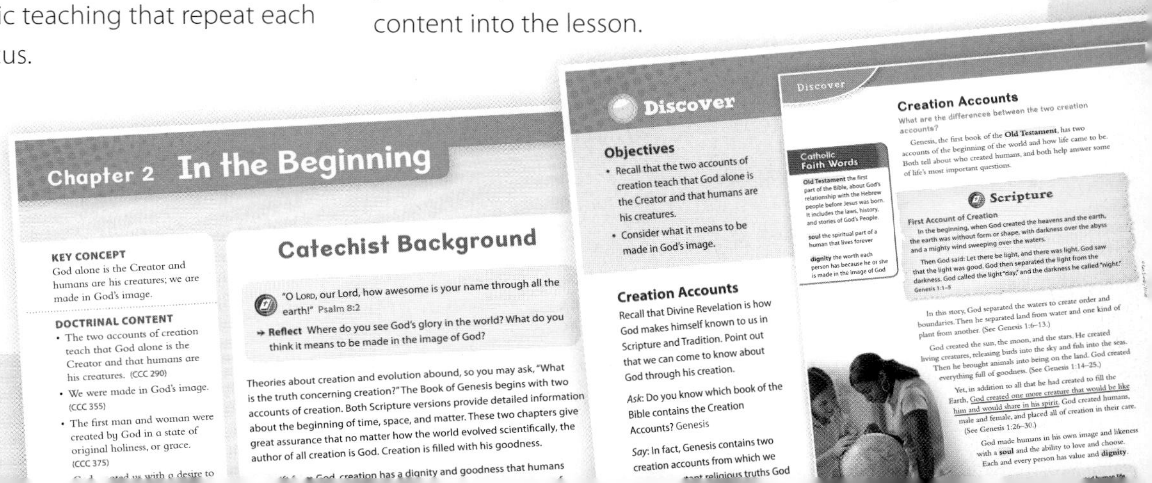

Developmental Appropriateness

The Theory Behind It

At one point or another in your family life and your ministry as a catechist, you've likely found yourself explaining to a child, "It's not just what you say, it's how you say it." The message is as important as the delivery. You can't separate the *what* from the *how*. Similarly, doctrine and method are not two ends of a spectrum. They are interdependent. In catechesis, you can't have one without the other. And it goes a step further, for it's not just *what* we teach, and how we teach it, but *how* the learner receives it.

"Consequently catechesis starts out with…the integral structure of the Christian message, and proceeds to explain it in a manner adapted to the capacity of those being catechized" (GDC, 112).

When we teach things in a theologically accurate way, and in a manner sensitive to where the children are developmentally, we provide the best chance that they will appropriate the content—process and understand it in a way that has meaning to them and that they can then apply to their own lives.

According to the National Association for the Education of Young Children (NAEYC), *developmental appropriateness* includes multiple components.

1. It is important to know how children develop and learn at particular ages and stages and to create learning environments that are responsive to these general needs.
2. Because every child is unique, knowing the individual children and how they learn best is essential.
3. It is important to know what is culturally appropriate for different ages and stages of development.

The Practice of It

Alive in Christ provides you with carefully selected topics and activities that meet the developmental level of the children you are teaching as well as tips for addressing individual needs. The program includes prayers, Saints, activities, and stories that represent the

Presentation of Text

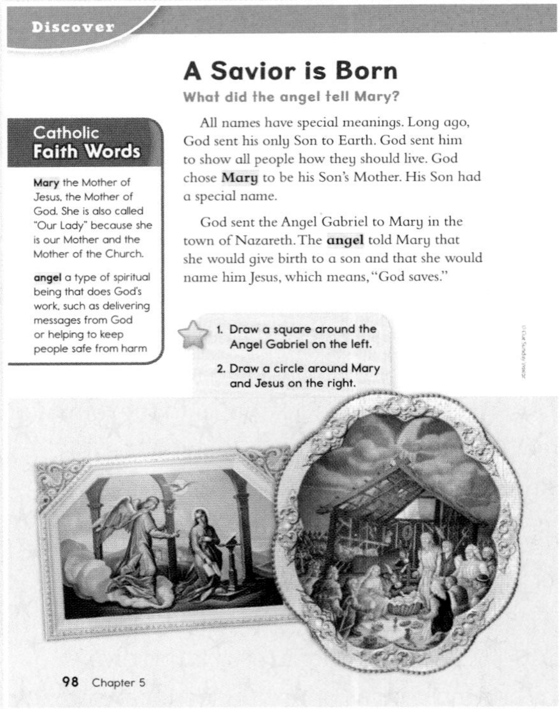
Discover

A Savior is Born

What did the angel tell Mary?

All names have special meanings. Long ago, God sent his only Son to Earth. God sent him to show all people how they should live. God chose **Mary** to be his Son's Mother. His Son had a special name.

God sent the Angel Gabriel to Mary in the town of Nazareth. The **angel** told Mary that she would give birth to a son and that she would name him Jesus, which means, "God saves."

Catholic Faith Words

Mary the Mother of Jesus, the Mother of God. She is also called "Our Lady" because she is our Mother and the Mother of the Church.

angel a type of spiritual being that does God's work, such as delivering messages from God or helping to keep people safe from harm

1. Draw a square around the Angel Gabriel on the left.
2. Draw a circle around Mary and Jesus on the right.

98 Chapter 5

- Information is sequenced and organized in smaller "chunks" to make reading and understanding faster and easier.
- Sentences are shorter in length for younger grades.
- Fonts and type sizes are set with consideration given to the reading level of the child.
- Words are defined consistently at point-of-use and highlighted for easy identification.
- Terms and concepts are introduced, reinforced, and then further defined in advanced ways as they develop across grades.

diversity of cultures found in our Church and introduces hese traditions at developmentally-appropriate times.

live in Christ takes into account the experience level of today's children with various topics and how they are ısed to receiving and processing those topics. So, the eries is developmentally appropriate not just in what kids learn at particular ages, but how they learn it.

As a catechist, you can feel confident that you are giving the children the most precise presentation of Church teaching in the most developmentally appropriate way. That's what excellent catechesis is all about.

Jse of Visuals

CHAPTER 3

Invite

God's Commandments

Let Us Pray

Leader: Loving Father, you made us to know you and your desire for us.

"I delight to do your will, my God; your law is in my inner being!" Psalm 40:9

All: O God, help us to learn how to listen for your voice so that we will know how to follow you. Amen.

Scripture

"When [Moses] looked, although the bush was on fire, it was not being consumed. . . . When the LORD saw that he had turned aside to look, God called out to him from the bush: Moses! Moses! He answered, 'Here I am.' God said: Do not come near! Remove your sandals from your feet, for the place where you stand is holy ground." Exodus 3:2b, 4–5

What Do You Wonder?

- How does God speak to people today?
- How do the Ten Commandments help you to know God and what he wants for you?

God's Commandments 73

- Fine art, illustrations, and photos advance in detail and sophistication as grades progress.
- Graphic organizers, charts, and callouts are used to present content in easy to track and access formats.
- Captions are used to aid in learning, and the content and purpose of captions advance as the grades do.
- The text-to-art ratio is intentional and customized for each grade level.

Teaching Strategies

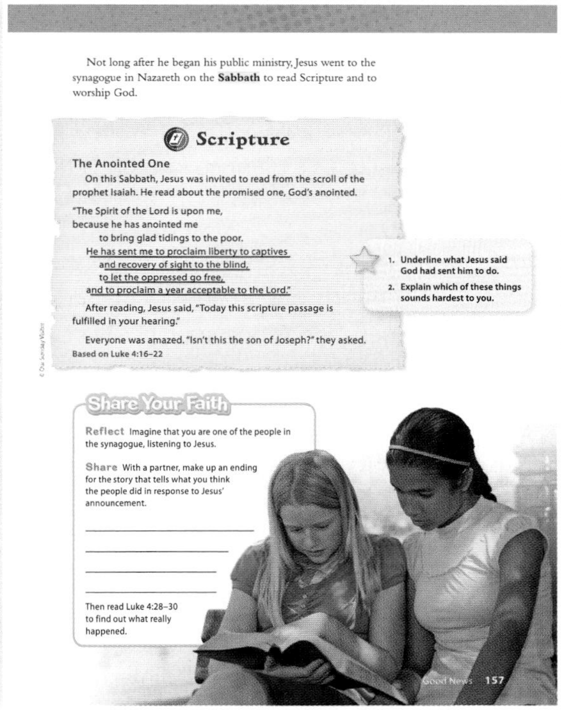
Not long after he began his public ministry, Jesus went to the synagogue in Nazareth on the **Sabbath** to read Scripture and to worship God.

Scripture

The Anointed One

On this Sabbath, Jesus was invited to read from the scroll of the prophet Isaiah. He read about the promised one, God's anointed.

"The Spirit of the Lord is upon me,
because he has anointed me
to bring glad tidings to the poor.
He has sent me to proclaim liberty to captives
and recovery of sight to the blind,
to let the oppressed go free,
and to proclaim a year acceptable to the Lord."

After reading, Jesus said, "Today this scripture passage is fulfilled in your hearing."

Everyone was amazed. "Isn't this the son of Joseph?" they asked.
Based on Luke 4:16–22

1. Underline what Jesus said God had sent him to do.
2. Explain which of these things sounds hardest to you.

Share Your Faith

Reflect Imagine that you are one of the people in the synagogue, listening to Jesus.

Share With a partner, make up an ending for the story that tells what you think the people did in response to Jesus' announcement.

Then read Luke 4:28–30 to find out what really happened.

Good News 157

- Questions focus reading, prompt reflection, and reinforce learning.
- On-page activities and teaching strategies incorporate dynamic, interactive learning methods.
- Chapter Reviews use multiple formats to accommodate different learning styles.
- The Catechist Edition includes a Teaching This Grade page that gives details on how children at this age might understand lesson objectives.
- Ideas for customizing content are found in the Reaching All Learners boxes in some chapters.

The Use of Images

"In order to communicate the message entrusted to her by Christ, the Church needs art."

—*Letter of Pope Saint John Paul II to Artist* (1999), 12

While educational research assures us that children make meaning through the interplay of text and images (Carney and Levine, 2002), any adult who has spent time with a young child knows that verbal and visual both tell the story. For hundreds of years, the Church has used sacred art and stained glass windows to teach Catholic doctrine and provide a physical presentation of the truths of our faith. Jesus often used images when he preached, giving his disciples a glimpse into his Father's mystery and the Kingdom.

Alive in Christ mirrors the divine pedagogy through its use of photos, illustrations, and images of fine art, stained glass, and statues—each one specifically selected for this program.

Educational research (Carney and Levine, 2002) and our own experience tell us that photos, illustrations, and art closely tied to text

- improve the reader's learning and recall
- direct the child's attention to what's most important on the page
- make the text more understandable and memorable
- help the child connect and apply what's been learned to their lived experience.

In ***Alive in Christ*** lessons, developmentally appropriate visuals—Scripture illustration, fine art, stained glass, statues, icons, photos, and accompanying captions—meet lesson objectives and build Catholic identity.

You will find historically accurate, child friendly Scripture and Saint illustrations that grow in sophistication and detail as grades advance. This promotes a common visual language of faith and builds a vibrant Catholic identity.

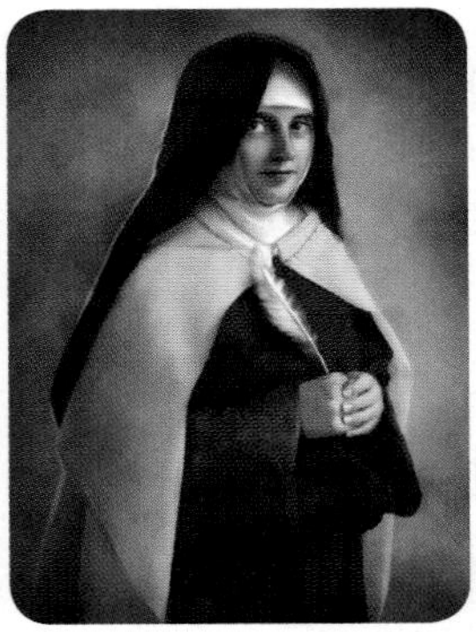

Grade 2 **Grade 6**
Saints Thérèse of Lisieux and Teresa of Ávila

Grade 1 **Grade 3**
The Sacred Heart of Jesus in statue and fine art

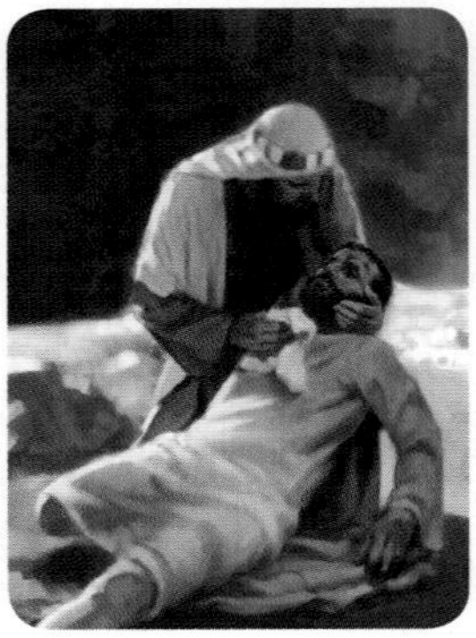

Grade 2 **Grade 5**
The Parable of the Good Samaritan

The Role of Music

The use of music in *Alive in Christ* is both intentional and purposeful. The music has been chosen to form children in the lesson content and Catholic identity. It is age appropriate and includes children's voices. It has both a formative and an informative purpose.

Long-term Retention

It has been demonstrated that the repeated rehearsal of information has a positive effect on long-term retention. Activities from the arts, such as music integrated into classroom content, can be used as prompts to recall information. Combining music with movement further enhances a child's learning. We "encode" information through both verbal and motor activity. In other words, when we sing and move, we are learning in both our bodies and our minds.

Sustain Attention

Music and movement also sustain attention. Translating material into actions (role-playing a song) helps learners not only recall a story but can also help them connect that story to a concept they have learned. Besides, moving to music is a universal response, and, with the proper disposition, can enhance prayer.

Emotional and Spiritual Connection

Music can also affect us on an emotional level. Who of us has not been moved by a song to feel something deep within our hearts? Music has helped form us as Catholics throughout the ages and has enabled us to both experience God's presence and respond to him from the depths of our being.

Moral Formation

- Objective: To be aware of the importance of a well-formed conscience for decision making

Catholic Social Teaching Live

Use one of these features to introduce a principle and engage the children with an activity.

- Life and Dignity, Pages 290–291
- Care for Creation, Pages 302–303

Music Options

Use one or more of the following songs to enhance catechetical learning or for prayer.

- "God Is a Part of My Life," Live Prayer, Page 60
- "For the Fruits of this Creation," Discover, Page 55

First Sunday of Advent—Waiting for Jesus, God's Greatest Gift

Baptism of the Lord—Son of Go

Year C

Second Sunday in Advent—God as Creator

Third Sunday in Ordinary Time—Scripture is fulfilled.

Go to **aliveinchrist.osv.com** for a complete correlation ordered by the Sundays of the year and suggestions for how to integrate the Scripture readings into chapter lessons.

Music options are integrated into every lesson and can be used to celebrate prayer or enhance learning. You will find these options both at point of use in the wraparound and on the Chapter Connections page in the box titled, "Music Options."

Play chapter-specific music to enhance catechetical learning or for prayer. Go to **aliveinchrist.osv.com** to sample and download.

Songs of Scripture Music CDs

To support the commitment to Sacred Scripture, an all-new, original resource, *Songs of Scripture Deepening Children's Understanding of God's Word*, by John Burland and Jo Ann Paradise, unfolds one of the Scripture passages in each unit. Activities for these songs are found in bottom-band boxes in the Catechist Edition.

Go to **aliveinchrist.osv.com** to order the *Songs of Scripture* CDs and for more information.

Reaching All Learners

"Growth in faith is related to human development and passes through stages. Individuals develop as human beings and faithful followers of Christ in different ways and according to their own pace...The Church's catechesis—and even more so, the catechist—must take into consideration all the human factors of a particular age level in order to present the Gospel message in a vital and compelling way."

NDC, 48

Benefitting from the work of educators in the past decades, religious educators now have new tools in providing children the fullness of the faith in developmentally appropriate ways.

Not only must we teach the faith related to children's level of human development, we must also meet the individual needs of our children. When working with any group of children, it does not take long to realize that they learn in different ways. Many have written about how to best provide strategies to address different learning styles. Dr. Howard Gardner's research on Multiple Intelligences provides particular insight. His theory looks at eight different ways people learn. Applying his theory to your planning will help you reach each child with the Good News of salvation.

Throughout *Alive in Christ*, a variety of teaching strategies are employed within the lesson process. Working with words and reading Scripture (Verbal/Linguistic), using photos and illustrations to prompt discussion (Visual/Spatial), and listening to, singing, and reflecting on songs (Musical) are just a few examples. Additional features, such as Reaching All Learners and Optional Activities, address various methods to help students with different learning styles and abilities connect with the lesson.

Go to **aliveinchrist.osv.com** for additional resources on meeting the challenges of providing for special needs in your faith formation sessions.

Multiple Intelligences

Verbal/ Linguistic	This learning occurs best through reading, writing, telling stories, and discussing ideas.
Logical/ Mathematical	This learning occurs best through problem solving, analyzing, and applying logic.
Musical	This learning occurs best through singing, listening to music, and remembering melodies.
Bodily/ Kinesthetic	This learning occurs best through physically moving, dancing, acting, and making things.
Visual/Spatial	This learning occurs best through looking at pictures, drawing, and creating.
Interpersonal	This learning occurs best through sharing about one's feelings, talking with others, and collaborating with others on tasks.
Intrapersonal	This learning occurs best through working alone and reflecting.
Naturalist	This learning occurs best through exploring nature and living things.

Ieaching Second Graders

econd grade is an exciting year in children's catechesis. It is customarily the year in vhich children begin to celebrate two important Sacraments—Reconciliation and ucharist—that they will continue to celebrate throughout their lives. What a blessing ɔ introduce young souls to these two great gifts!

₹ule-Based Thinking

:hildren this age are in the Piagetian cognitive stage of :oncrete operations." They understand cause and effect nd know the world works according to rules. Therefore, his is a great time to introduce God's rules and uidelines for living. They will need some help seeing ow to connect the Commandments and Beatitudes to neir daily lives. When second graders learn about God's ules, they also become aware of the areas in which they ave not followed God's will for their lives. It's important hat we present the idea of sin honestly, but we can do his in a way that helps them to feel good, rather than ad, about themselves. God created each person to do ood, and we fall short of that at times, but through his race and mercy we are forgiven and strengthened to o better next time.

Growing in Holiness

lelp children this age understand that growing in oliness—becoming the people God made us to be—is process. It is a journey, and we need to be committed ɔ going ever forward. Avoid oversimplified statements ke "Nobody's perfect," or "God doesn't expect us to do verything right." In reality, God *does* call us to goodness 1 every moment. Remember, Jesus said, "Be perfect, ıst as your heavenly Father is perfect" **(Matthew 5:48)**. :'s important for children this age to know that we vere made for good things, and God is always ready ɔ forgive us our sins and help us grow.

Aultisensory Methods Help vith Learning Abstract Concepts

ecause they organize their own thinking according to ules, second graders usually have a good memory for facts. They can learn even more if we teach them using memory devices such as rhymes and music. Second graders usually enjoy singing and poetry.

Because they have reached the age of reason, second graders are better able to understand that the Eucharist is not ordinary bread and wine, because Jesus taught us that it was his Body and Blood. We can help them understand that this is true and explain that Jesus gave this gift to us, his followers. In other words, they learn the "rule" about this and it forms their idea of what the Eucharist is. They still struggle with abstract ideas like transubstantiation, but will grow in their understanding as they continue to learn about their faith and celebrate the Eucharist with their Church family.

Second graders are concrete thinkers and need many hands-on activities and practical explanations. Our approach to teaching the Sacraments should be step-by-step and very concrete. This is a good time to learn the steps of the Rites, parts of the Mass, and the basics of what the Church teaches about the Sacraments. Also, second graders are better able to apply principles of Christian living when we role-play good decision making and loving actions. Look for ways for them to practice what they are learning.

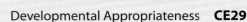

Living and Learning Together

In the *General Directory for Catechesis* we are told that the "childhood religious awakening which takes place in the family is irreplaceable"[6] (226). The role of the catechetical leader and the catechist in the parish is to help form and support families in this sacred journey.

The Family + Faith page gives families the tools they need to talk about faith and more consciously live the faith in their homes and daily lives. The resources on this page are invaluable in providing adults the practical help they need to grow in faith themselves and to nurture the faith of their children.

Your Child Learned This section summarizes key Catholic teaching covered in the chapter and introduces families to the Scripture and Person of Faith presented.

Children at This Age This feature helps families understand the relationship between the content presented and the child's developmental level of understanding. It provides a look at the content through the eyes of the child and equips parents with a perspective that is necessary in order to nurture their child's faith.

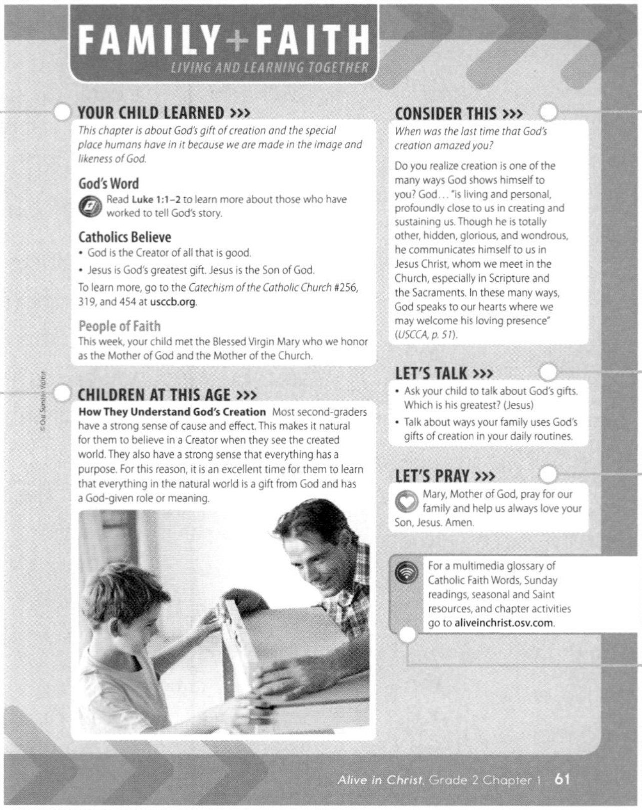

FAMILY+FAITH
LIVING AND LEARNING TOGETHER

YOUR CHILD LEARNED >>>

This chapter is about God's gift of creation and the special place humans have in it because we are made in the image and likeness of God.

God's Word

Read **Luke 1:1–2** to learn more about those who have worked to tell God's story.

Catholics Believe

- God is the Creator of all that is good.
- Jesus is God's greatest gift. Jesus is the Son of God.

To learn more, go to the *Catechism of the Catholic Church* #256, 319, and 454 at **usccb.org**.

People of Faith

This week, your child met the Blessed Virgin Mary who we honor as the Mother of God and the Mother of the Church.

CHILDREN AT THIS AGE >>>

How They Understand God's Creation Most second-graders have a strong sense of cause and effect. This makes it natural for them to believe in a Creator when they see the created world. They also have a strong sense that everything has a purpose. For this reason, it is an excellent time for them to learn that everything in the natural world is a gift from God and has a God-given role or meaning.

CONSIDER THIS >>>

When was the last time that God's creation amazed you?

Do you realize creation is one of the many ways God shows himself to you? God… "is living and personal, profoundly close to us in creating and sustaining us. Though he is totally other, hidden, glorious, and wondrous, he communicates himself to us in Jesus Christ, whom we meet in the Church, especially in Scripture and the Sacraments. In these many ways, God speaks to our hearts where we may welcome his loving presence" (*USCCA*, p. 51).

LET'S TALK >>>

- Ask your child to talk about God's gifts. Which is his greatest? (Jesus)
- Talk about ways your family uses God's gifts of creation in your daily routines.

LET'S PRAY >>>

Mary, Mother of God, pray for our family and help us always love your Son, Jesus. Amen.

For a multimedia glossary of Catholic Faith Words, Sunday readings, seasonal and Saint resources, and chapter activities go to **aliveinchrist.osv.com**.

Alive in Christ, Grade 2 Chapter 1 61

Consider This Through the use of targeted questions that encourage reflection, adults are given the opportunity to reflect on the experience and inform that experience with the teaching of the Church.

Let's Talk Adult-specific questions or directions help to facilitate discussion with the child about the lesson content.

Let's Pray This provides families with a short prayer that incorporates the key concept of the lesson.

Go to **aliveinchrist.osv.com** The Family + Faith page sends adults to aliveinchrist.osv.com so that families can reinforce and assess their learning, as well as find suggestions for family discussions and ways to apply faith to family life.

The **aliveinchrist.osv.com** Student/Family pages extend learning, foster family faith sharing, and provide session plans and tools for home-based catechesis.

Catholic Social Teaching

Pope Saint John Paul II reminded us that one of the fundamental tasks of the Christian family is to remember that the family is always at the service of God's Kingdom. While the family is to "guard, reveal, and communicate love," it does so knowing that their love is not only to be shared within itself, but meant to be shared with the world (*Familiaris Consortio*, 17). We are called to reach out past our family to build relationships of love and justice in our neighborhoods, communities, and beyond.

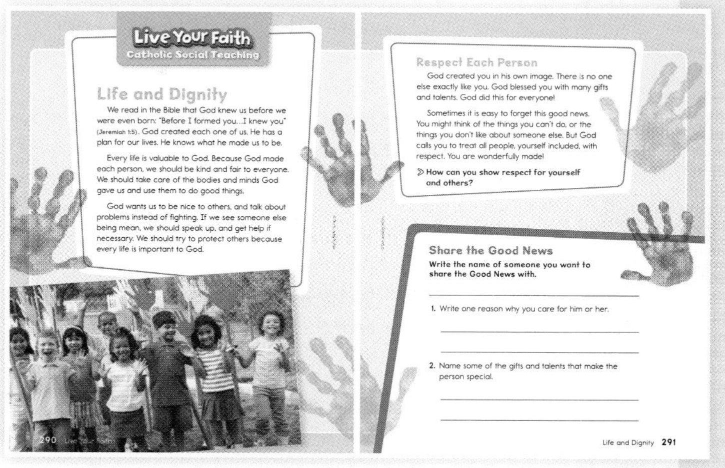

Live Your Faith
Catholic Social Teaching

Life and Dignity

We read in the Bible that God knew us before we were even born: "Before I formed you...I knew you" (Jeremiah 1:5). God created each one of us. He has a plan for our lives. He knows what he made us to be.

Every life is valuable to God. Because God made each person, we should be kind and fair to everyone. We should take care of the bodies and minds God gave us and use them to do good things.

God wants us to be nice to others, and talk about problems instead of fighting. If we see someone else being mean, we should speak up, and get help if necessary. We should try to protect others because every life is important to God.

290 Live Your Faith

Respect Each Person

God created you in his own image. There is no one else exactly like you. God blessed you with many gifts and talents. God did this for everyone!

Sometimes it is easy to forget this good news. You might think of the things you can't do, or the things you don't like about someone else. But God calls you to treat all people, yourself included, with respect. You are wonderfully made!

» How can you show respect for yourself and others?

Share the Good News

Write the name of someone you want to share the Good News with.

1. Write one reason why you care for him or her.

2. Name some of the gifts and talents that make the person special.

Life and Dignity 291

Each grade level of ***Alive in Christ***, presents the seven principles of Catholic Social Teaching, articulated by the United States Conference of Catholic Bishops. In this **Live Your Faith** component, the scriptural and doctrinal foundations of the principles help the children connect their faith to a life of peace and justice. While peace and justice are taught in many of the core chapters, the seven principles are intentionally treated in Live Your Faith.

You can use these Catholic Social Teaching features in a variety of ways. Every core chapter and seasonal lesson has a Catholic Social Teaching connection integrated into the lesson plan. A **bottom band box** will provide you with suggestions on how to incorporate the Live Your Faith component with the lesson. Combining these components with the seasonal lessons can help your children connect how Catholics worship with how Catholics live.

Your catechetical leader may choose to schedule these components so that all the children will be focusing on the same principle at the same time. If you schedule your own sessions, you may choose to combine several of the principles and present them at one time.

This presentation of Catholic teaching builds a vibrant Catholic identity and prepares us to evangelize the world through faith and action as we work in service of God's Kingdom.

Using This Feature

Lesson Connection

Use this feature to enhance, or in place of, the Live section of the following chapters:

Chapter 1, page 53 | **Chapter 5**, page 97
Chapter 3, page 73 | **Chapter 12**, page 175
Chapter 4, page 87 | **Chapter 20**, page 267

Use this feature after the Discover section, before the Live prayer begins in the following seasonal lessons:

Ordinary Time: All Saints, page 15
Christmas, page 25 | **Easter, We Rejoice**, page 43

Grade 1 Scope and Sequence

Unit	Chapter		Lesson Concepts
1 REVELATION	CHAPTER 1	Created by God	• The Bible is God's Word written by humans. We learn about God from the Bible. • God made humans to be his friends, to know and love him. • God made everything. All of his creation is good.
	CHAPTER 2	God's Gifts for Us	• God created the world to show his love. • All of creation is God's gift to us, and his Son, Jesus, is his greatest gift. • People use God's gifts in the world to make things we need. • Thanksgiving is showing God we are grateful for all that he's given us.
	CHAPTER 3	Made to Care	• The image of God is the likeness of God that is in all human beings because we are created by him. • Humans are the most special part of creation. God gave us the ability to think and make choices. • God gave Adam and Eve the responsibility to be caretakers of his creation. • Each of us is responsible for treating all of creation with care and respect.
2 TRINITY	CHAPTER 4	The Holy Trinity	• God asks us to be friends with one another, to be nice, and to help each other when in need. • Jesus is the Son of God who shows us the way to his Father. • God the Father loves us so much he sent his only Son to be with us. • The Holy Trinity is God the Father, God the Son, and God the Holy Spirit, the one God in three Divine Persons.
	CHAPTER 5	The Holy Family	• Signs of love are expressed in families. • Jesus is the Son of God and a human being. • The Holy Family is the name of the human family of Jesus, Mary, and Joseph. • Jesus grew up with Mary and Joseph in Nazareth, praying and learning.
	CHAPTER 6	About the Bible	• Jesus told stories like the Lost Sheep to show us how God watches over and guides us, always welcoming us back. • A parable is a short story Jesus told about everyday life to teach something about God. • The Bible is the Church's holy book. • The two parts of the Bible are the Old Testament and the New Testament.
3 JESUS CHRIST	CHAPTER 7	Jesus the Healer	• Blessed Mother Teresa is an example of how we are to share God's love by caring for the sick. • Jesus' healings showed God the Father's power and love. • Faith is the gift of believing and trusting in God so much that we do what he asks us to do.
	CHAPTER 8	Jesus Teaches Love	• A Commandment is a law that God made for people to obey. • Jesus taught the Great Commandment to love God above all else and to love others the way you love yourself.
	CHAPTER 9	Jesus Teaches Us to Pray	• Prayer is talking to and listening to God. • We need prayer to get close to God. • The Lord's Prayer is the prayer Jesus taught his followers to pray to God the Father.
4 THE CHURCH	CHAPTER 10	Responding to God	• Noah said "yes" to God, and God promised to always keep him safe. The rainbow is a sign of that promise. • Jesus invites everyone to God's Kingdom—the world of love, peace, and justice that is in Heaven and is still being built on Earth. • The Church shares Jesus' message about God's love. • The Church is a community of baptized people who believe in God and follow Jesus.
	CHAPTER 11	The Church's Guide	• A guide helps us and shows us the way. • The Holy Spirit is the Third Divine Person of the Holy Trinity. • Jesus promised us that the Holy Spirit would guide the Church. • Saint Thérèse loved God very much and worked for him through her little jobs. She called this "The Little Way."

Go to **aliveinchrist.osv.com** for complete program Scope and Sequence.

Sacred Scripture	Catechism of the Catholic Church	Tasks of Catechesis	Catholic Faith Words	People of Faith	Catholic Social Teaching
You Created Me Psalm 139:13–15; The Garden of Eden Genesis 2:7–22	105–106, 355, 299	Promoting Knowledge of the Faith, Education for Community Life	Bible, creation	Bl. Fra Angelico	Life and Dignity, Care for Creation
God Was Pleased Genesis 1:11–31; The Story of Creation Genesis 1:6–25	293–294, 299, 312, 2402, 2637	Promoting Knowledge of the Faith, Teaching to Pray	Jesus, praise, thanksgiving	St. Nicholas	Dignity of Work, Care for Creation
Humans in Charge Genesis 1:27–31; Take Care of What I've Given You Genesis 1:26–30	357, 356, 373, 2415	Promoting Knowledge of the Faith, Education for Community Life	image of God	St. Albert the Great	Life and Dignity, Care for Creation
Go and Make Disciples Matthew 28:19–20; The Way to the Father John 14:8–9	1822, 1844, 426, 1698, 422, 253–254	Promoting Knowledge of the Faith, Education for Community Life	God the Father, Son of God, Holy Trinity	St. Patrick	Life and Dignity, Rights and Responsibilities
Joseph's Dream Matthew 2:19–23; The Boy Jesus Luke 2:51–52	1656–1657, 423, 1655, 532–533	Promoting Knowledge of the Faith, Education for Community Life	Mary, Holy Family	Sts. Zechariah, Elizabeth, and John	Life and Dignity, Call to Community
Jesus' Parables Matthew 13:34–35; The Parable of the Lost Sheep Luke 15:3–6; The Good Shepherd John 10:14–15	605, 546, 104, 138, 120	Promoting Knowledge of the Faith, Moral Formation	Old Testament, New Testament	St. Paul of the Cross	Life and Dignity, Option for the Poor
Jesus Preached and Healed Matthew 9:35; Have Faith Luke 8:40–56	2447, 1503, 1814	Promoting Knowledge of the Faith, Education for Community Life	faith	St. Louise de Marillac	Option for the Poor, Human Solidarity
The Most Important Commandment Mark 12:28–31; The Greatest Commandment Luke 10:25–28	2056, 2055	Moral Formation, Education for Community Life	Commandment, Great Commandment	St. Thomas of Villanova	Life and Dignity, Dignity of Work
When You Pray Matthew 6:6–8; How to Pray Ephesians 5:18–20	2559, 2565, 2759	Promoting Knowledge of the Faith, Teaching to Pray	prayer, Lord's Prayer	St. Ephrem the Hymnist	Life and Dignity, Call to Community
Noah Built an Ark Hebrews 11:7; Noah Says "Yes" Genesis 6:14–22, 7:1–10, 9:17; The Parable of the Great Feast Luke 14:16–23	2569, 543, 737, 782	Promoting Knowledge of the Faith, Education for Community Life	Kingdom of God, Church	Bl. Mary Theresa of Jesus	Call to Community, Rights and Responsibilities
Live in and Follow the Spirit Galatians 5:22–23, 25; Jesus Promises the Holy Spirit John 14:26	729, 243, 747, 1477	Promoting Knowledge of the Faith, Education for Community Life	Holy Spirit	St. Rose of Lima	Rights and Responsibilities, Dignity of Work

Grade 1 Scope and Sequence

Unit	Chapter		Lesson Concepts
4	CHAPTER 12	Friends of God	• Saints are heroes of the Church who loved God very much, did his work on Earth, and are now with him in Heaven. • Holy means unique and pure; set apart for God and his purposes. • We are part of the family of Saints, connected to the Saints who lived before us and to those who believe in Jesus now.
5 MORALITY	CHAPTER 13	Disciples Serve	• Jesus washed his disciples' feet to show us how to serve and love one another. • Jesus asks us to have a kind, giving heart when we serve and help others. • A disciple is a follower of Jesus who believes in him and lives by his teachings. • Serving others is a way to serve God.
	CHAPTER 14	Making Choices	• The Ten Commandments are God's laws that tell people how to love him and others. • Free will is being able to choose whether to obey God or disobey God. • God created us with free will because he wants us to make good choices. • All choices have consequences, or results, that can show love and respect or hurt others.
	CHAPTER 15	Showing Sorrow	• Sin is the choice to disobey God on purpose and do what you know is wrong. It is not an accident or a mistake. • The consequences of sin are hurting your friendship with God and others. • God wants us to be close to him and will always forgive us when we say we are sorry. • Jesus wants us to be sorry for our sins and turn to God our forgiving Father.
6 SACRAMENTS	CHAPTER 16	Jesus the Savior	• Adam and Eve chose to bring sin into the world. Their disobedience is called Original Sin. • God did not stop loving people because of their sin. • God sent his Son, Jesus, to be our Savior and bring people back to him. • Jesus died for all people to save them, giving his life so that people could have new life with God.
	CHAPTER 17	Holy Signs	• The Seven Sacraments are special signs and celebrations that Jesus gave his Church. • The Sacraments celebrate that Jesus is still with us, sharing his life and love. • Every Sacrament has words and actions we do and things God does that we can't see that bring us life.
	CHAPTER 18	We Are Welcomed	• Baptism is the Sacrament that brings new life in God and makes the person a member of the Church. • Grace is God's gift of sharing in his life and help. • In Baptism, a person is immersed, or has water poured over him or her in the name of the Father, Son, and Holy Spirit. • The baptized person is anointed, receives a white garment, and is given the light of Christ.
7 KINGDOM OF GOD	CHAPTER 19	We Give Thanks	• The Last Supper is the meal Jesus shared with his disciples the night before he died. • The Eucharist is the Sacrament in which Jesus himself, and the bread and wine become his Body and Blood. • The Mass is the gathering of Catholics to worship God and celebrate the Eucharist. • In the Mass we hear God's Word, give thanks for his gifts, and receive Jesus in Holy Communion.
	CHAPTER 20	Forever with God	• Heaven is living and being happy with God forever. • God desires for everyone to be happy with him forever. • Following Jesus and obeying God's laws are how we live in love now and forever.
	CHAPTER 21	God's Kingdom	• We pray for the coming of God's Kingdom, working together with God as he builds his Kingdom. • By being forgiving, treating others with respect, and helping those who are hungry and in need, Jesus showed us how to work for the Kingdom. • When we are kind, share, play fair, and include others, we are spreading peace.

Go to **aliveinchrist.osv.com** for complete program Scope and Sequence.

Sacred Scripture	Catechism of the Catholic Church	Tasks of Catechesis	Catholic Faith Words	People of Faith	Catholic Social Teaching
Love Your Enemies Matthew 5:44–45; Martha and Mary Luke 10:38–42	823, 228, 825, 946–948	Promoting Knowledge of the Faith, Missionary Initiation	Saint, angel, holy	St. Dominic	Call to Community, Rights and Responsibilities
The Greatest Among You Matthew 23:11–12; The Washing of the Disciples' Feet John 13:2–17	1337, 1823, 618, 1816	Education for Community Life, Missionary Initiation	serve, disciple	V. Fr. Solanus Casey	Option for the Poor, The Dignity of Work
Do This and You Will Live Luke 10:25–28; God's Commandments Deuteronomy 10:12–13	2067, 1731, 1743, 1739	Promoting Knowledge of the Faith, Moral Formation	Ten Commandments, obey, free will	St. Frances Cabrini	Call to Community, Rights and Responsibilities
Seventy-Seven Times Matthew 18:21–22; The Forgiving Father Luke 15:11–32	1850, 1849, 1431–1432, 1427	Promoting Knowledge of the Faith, Moral Formation	sin	St. Dismas	Rights and Responsibilities, Option for the Poor
Do Not Be Afraid Matthew 28:5–6; Jesus Lives Luke 23–24	402–404, 410, 457, 613	Promoting Knowledge of the Faith, Moral Formation	Original Sin, Resurrection	St. Josephine Bakhita	Option for the Poor, Human Solidarity
I Am in My Father John 14:20; The Advocate John 14:18–19	1084, 1131, 1123	Promoting Knowledge of the Faith, Liturgical Education	Seven Sacraments	Mary	Human Solidarity, Care for Creation
Go Into the Whole World Mark 16:15–16; People Everywhere Believe Acts 8:4–12	1213, 1996, 1239, 1241	Promoting Knowledge of the Faith, Liturgical Education	Baptism, grace, godparents	St. Moses the Black	Rights and Responsibilities, Human Solidarity
For the Forgiveness of Sins Matthew 26:26–28; The Last Supper 1 Corinthians 11:23–25	610, 1333, 1329–1330, 1346–1347	Promoting Knowledge of the Faith, Liturgical Education	Last Supper, Eucharist, Mass, Holy Communion	Pope Saint John XXIII	Call to Community, Human Solidarity
God's Kingdom Is Not Something You Can See Luke 17:20–21; Together Always John 14:1–3	1024, 1045, 1693	Moral Formation, Teaching to Pray	Heaven	St. Emily de Vialar	Option for the Poor, Human Solidarity
Do Justice, Love Goodness, and Walk Humbly Micah 6:8; Starting Small Matthew 13:31–32	2818, 2831–2832, 2304	Moral Formation, Education for Community Life	peace	St. Pedro Calungsod	Call to Community, Option for the Poor

Grade 2 Scope and Sequence

Unit	Chapter		Lesson Concepts
1 REVELATION	CHAPTER 1	God's Gifts	• God created human beings in his own image. • Humans have a special role in all of God's creation. • Jesus is God's greatest gift, the Son of God who became man. He is always faithful to God the Father.
	CHAPTER 2	God's Promise	• God gives all people the ability to choose. • Original Sin is the first sin committed by Adam and Eve. • Jesus is the Savior because he led people who were lost through sin back to God; Jesus is the Good Shepherd.
	CHAPTER 3	The Word of God	• God tells us about himself through the Bible. • The Bible is God's Word written down by humans. • Jesus tells stories that help us know and love God the Father. • The Old and New Testaments are the two parts of the Bible, also called Scripture.
2 TRINITY	CHAPTER 4	God the Father	• God the Father is the First Divine Person of the Holy Trinity. • Jesus taught us that God the Father loves and cares for us. • We rely on God the Father, praying to him and trusting he will provide what we need.
	CHAPTER 5	God the Son	• The Angel Gabriel announced to Mary that she would be the Mother of the Son of God, the Savior, Jesus. • The Holy Family of Jesus, Mary, and Joseph lived in Nazareth where Jesus grew up, learning and praying. • Jesus is both the Son of God and a human being. • The Baptism of the adult Jesus by John the Baptist was the beginning of his public teaching.
	CHAPTER 6	God the Holy Spirit	• The Holy Trinity is one God in three Divine Persons. • The Holy Spirit is the Third Divine Person of the Holy Trinity who helps and guides us as Jesus promised. • Jesus is the Son of God who became man, the Second Divine Person of the Holy Trinity. • The Holy Spirit helped the Apostles understand and spread Jesus' teachings and he remains with the Church today.
3 JESUS CHRIST	CHAPTER 7	God's Commandments	• The Ten Commandments are God's laws that teach us to love him and others. • The Great Commandment sums up all of God's laws, telling us to love God above all else and others the way you love yourself. • Jesus told the parable of the Good Samaritan to help us understand that loving God means loving our neighbor. • Jesus gave us a New Commandment to teach us to love as he loves.
	CHAPTER 8	Choose to Do Good	• When we make bad choices that hurt our relationship with God and others, God forgives us if we are truly sorry. • Sin is a free choice to do what we know is wrong. Mistakes and accidents are not sins. • Both venial and mortal sins harm our relationship with God, but in different ways. • Conscience is an ability given to us by God that helps us make choices about right and wrong.
	CHAPTER 9	God's Mercy	• We learn about God's mercy in the story of the Prodigal Son. • The virtues can help us say no to temptation and choose what is good. • Mercy is kindness and concern for those who are suffering; God has mercy on us even though we are sinners. • It's important to ask God and others for forgiveness, and to be forgiving.
4 THE CHURCH	CHAPTER 10	The Sacraments	• The Seven Sacraments are special signs and celebrations that Jesus gave his Church that allow us to share in God's life and work. • Jesus continues to share his life and love with us in the Sacraments. • Baptism, the first Sacrament received, makes a person a child of God and member of the Church, taking away Original Sin and all personal sin. • The Sacraments of Initiation—Baptism, Confirmation, Eucharist—celebrate our membership into the Catholic Church.
	CHAPTER 11	Seek Forgiveness	• An examination of conscience is a prayerful way of thinking about how we have followed the Ten Commandments, Beatitudes, and Church teachings. • Contrition is being sorry for your sins and wanting to live better. • In the Sacrament of Penance and Reconciliation, God's forgiveness for sin is given through the Church. • The Sacrament includes confession, penance, contrition, and absolution.

Go to **aliveinchrist.osv.com** for complete program Scope and Sequence.

Sacred Scripture	Catechism of the Catholic Church	Tasks of Catechesis	Catholic Faith Words	People of Faith	Catholic Social Teaching
Handing Down the Stories Luke 1:1–2; The Creator and Humans Psalms 8:2, 7–9	355, 373, 357, 464, 606	Promoting Knowledge of the Faith, Moral Formation	psalms, creation, sin, Son of God	Blessed Virgin Mary	Life and Dignity, Care for Creation
The Sinner Who Repents Luke 15:7; The Garden of Eden Genesis 2:15–17; 3:1–6, 23; The Good Shepherd John 10:11–14	1730–1731, 389, 397, 457, 754	Promoting Knowledge of the Faith, Moral Formation	Original Sin, Savior	St. Cristóbal Magallanes Jara	Call to Community, Human Solidarity
Jesus Among the Crowds Luke 6:17–18; The Great Flood Genesis 6–9; Jesus Teaches Matthew 4:23–25	104, 105, 546, 120	Promoting Knowledge of the Faith, Missionary Initiation	Bible, Old Testament, New Testament	St. Luke	Life and Dignity, Rights and Responsibilities
Trust in the Father Luke 12:29–31; Rely on God Matthew 6:25–32	254, 322, 2779–2781, 2590	Promoting Knowledge of the Faith, Teaching to Pray	Saint, God the Father, prayer, trust	Bl. Julian of Norwich	Life and Dignity, Care for Creation
My Beloved Son Luke 3:21–22; Announcing Jesus' Birth Luke 1:26–38; 2:1–11; The Boy Jesus in the Temple Luke 2:41–52; Baptism of Jesus Matthew 3:13–17	430, 514–515, 723–724, 535	Promoting Knowledge of the Faith, Liturgical Education	Mary, angel, Holy Family	St. Peter	Life and Dignity, Human Solidarity
Risen Jesus Appears to Disciples Luke 24:49; The Promise John 14: 15–26; The Spirit Comes Acts 1:4–5, 8; 2:2–3	683–684, 258–259, 253–255, 767–768	Promoting Knowledge of the Faith, Liturgical Education	Holy Spirit, Holy Trinity, disciples, Pentecost, Apostles	St. Arnold Janssen	Call to Community, Rights and Responsibilities
Moses on the Mountain Exodus 24:12; Love the Lord Your God Luke 10:27; The Parable of the Good Samaritan Luke 10:29–37	1962, 2055, 1465, 546, 1970	Promoting Knowledge of the Faith, Moral Formation	Ten Commandments, Great Commandment, parable, New Commandment	St. Elizabeth of Hungary	Rights and Responsibilities, Option for the Poor
Peter Hears the Rooster Mark 14:69–72; Peter Denies Jesus John 18:17–18, 25–27	1441, 1849, 1777–1778, 1854–1855	Promoting Knowledge of the Faith, Moral Formation	free will, mortal sin, venial sin, conscience	St. Thérèse of Lisieux	Rights and Responsibilities, The Dignity of Work
Forgive Seventy-Seven Times Matthew 18:21–22; The Prodigal Son Luke 15:11–32	1439, 270, 2447, 1810, 1459	Moral Formation, Education for Community Life	virtues, temptation, mercy	St. Jane de Chantal	Call to Community, Human Solidarity
Jesus Heals a Blind Man Luke 18:35–43; The Commissioning of the Apostles Matthew 28:19–20	1113, 1116, 1127–1128, 1212, 1213	Promoting Knowledge of the Faith, Liturgical Education	Seven Sacraments, Baptism, grace, Sacraments of Initiation	St. Pius X	Option for the Poor, Care for Creation
Whose Sins You Forgive John 20:21, 23; The Woman Who Was Forgiven Luke 7:36–39, 44–50	1779, 1432, 1422, 1423–1424	Liturgical Education, Moral Formation	examination of conscience, contrition, Sacrament of Penance and Reconciliation, confession, penance, absolution	St. Benedict-Joseph Labre	Call to Community, Human Solidarity

Grade 2 Scope and Sequence

Unit	Chapter		Lesson Concepts
4	CHAPTER 12	The Church Year	• The liturgy is the public prayer of the Church. • The Church year celebrates the life, Death, Resurrection, and Ascension of Jesus. • The seasons of the Church year are Advent, Christmas, Ordinary Time, Lent, The Three Days (Triduum), and Easter. • Easter celebrates Christ's Resurrection and is the greatest feast of the Church year.
5 MORALITY	CHAPTER 13	Welcome in the Kingdom	• By the things he said and did, Jesus included those often left out and showed that God welcomes everyone. • The story of Zacchaeus is an example of Jesus welcoming someone who had faith and was willing to repent. • Jesus has a great love for children, and welcomed them along with all others into his Kingdom. • The Kingdom of God is the world of love, peace, and justice that God has in Heaven and wants for us on Earth.
	CHAPTER 14	Share the Good News	• The Gospel message is the Good News of God's Kingdom and his saving love. • In his parable of the Vine and Branches, Jesus teaches us that we need to stay connected to him in order to have life. • The Holy Spirit strengthened the Apostles to share what Jesus had taught them. • Many people in our parish share Jesus' message and work together with God as he builds his Kingdom.
	CHAPTER 15	Ways to Pray	• Jesus taught us to pray the Lord's Prayer, which we also call the Our Father. • There are five basic forms of prayer: blessing, petition, intercession, thanksgiving, and praise. • Prayer is important to deepen our friendship with God, and we can pray in many ways and at different times. • Sacramentals are blessings, objects, and actions that remind you of God and are made sacred through the prayers of the Church.
6 SACRAMENTS	CHAPTER 16	Gather to Worship	• The Eucharist is the Sacrament in which Jesus Christ shares himself and the bread and wine become his Body and Blood. • The Mass is another name for the celebration of the Eucharist. • The assembly is all those gathered for Mass. We take part by praying, singing, and using actions to worship God. • The Introductory Rites gather and unite us, preparing our hearts to hear God's Word.
	CHAPTER 17	Listen to God's Word	• Jesus used stories as a way to help us understand more about God and his Kingdom. • The first main part of the Mass is the Liturgy of the Word during which we hear readings from both the Old and New Testaments. • We listen to the deacon or priest proclaim the Gospel reading and give a homily to help us understand and apply God's Word. • This part of the Mass ends with the Creed and Prayer of the Faithful.
	CHAPTER 18	Remembering Jesus' Sacrifice	• The Mass is a memorial celebration of Jesus' Death, Resurrection, and Ascension. • Jesus' Death on the Cross is a sacrifice and gift that saves all people from the power of sin and everlasting death. • The Liturgy of the Eucharist is the second main part of the Mass in which Jesus Christ gives us the gift of himself, and we receive his Body and Blood in Holy Communion. • In the consecration, through the power of the Holy Spirit and the words and actions of the priest, the gifts of bread and wine become the Body and Blood of Jesus Christ.
7 KINGDOM OF GOD	CHAPTER 19	Supper of the Lamb	• The story of the Loaves and the Fish helps us understand what Jesus gives us in Holy Communion. • Before receiving Communion, we pray together the Lord's Prayer and offer each other a sign of peace. • Through the Eucharist, Jesus' followers are united with him and one another. • Jesus Christ is really and truly present with us in the Eucharist, so we receive Holy Communion with reverence and adore him in the reserved Blessed Sacrament.
	CHAPTER 20	Go Forth!	• In the Concluding Rites of the Mass, we are blessed and sent out to proclaim the Good News and give honor to God by the way we live. • As the Apostles were called to share the Good News, the Church's mission is to share Jesus' message of love and the Kingdom. • All members of the Church share in her mission, and some serve as missionaries who travel far away to spread the Good News.
	CHAPTER 21	A Feast for Everyone	• Heaven is life and happiness forever with God. • The story of the Wedding Feast is compared to God's invitation and our response. • The Eucharist is spiritual food that helps us to live with Jesus forever. • We are called to say "yes" daily to God.

Go to **aliveinchrist.osv.com** for complete program Scope and Sequence.

Sacred Scripture	Catechism of the Catholic Church	Tasks of Catechesis	Catholic Faith Words	People of Faith	Catholic Social Teaching
The Holy Family Celebrates Passover Luke 2:41–42	1069–1070, 1171, 1163–1164, 1169	Liturgical Education, Education for Community Life	liturgy, worship, Resurrection	Pope Saint Victor	Life and Dignity, Human Solidarity
Let the Children Come Luke 18:15–17; Zacchaeus the Tax Collector Luke 19:1–10; Blessing of the Children Matthew 19:13–15	542–543, 2412, 526, 559, 2818–2819	Promoting Knowledge of the Faith, Education for Community Life	faith, peace, Kingdom of God	St. Brigid of Kildare	Option for the Poor, The Dignity of Work
Jesus' Disciples Receive a Mission Mark 16:15–16; The Vine and the Branches John 15:4–5	541, 787, 746–747, 941–942	Education for Community Life, Missionary Initiation	Gospel, proclaim, parish	Bl. Mother Teresa of Calcutta	Rights and Responsibilities, The Dignity of Work
The Lord's Prayer Luke 11:1–4; How to Pray Matthew 6:5–9	2759, 2644, 2565, 1668, 1671	Liturgical Education, Teaching to Pray	Lord's Prayer, blessing, petition, intercession, thanksgiving, praise, sacramentals	St. Alphonsus Liguori	Human Solidarity, Care for Creation
The Road to Emmaus Luke 24:30–32; The Community Gathers Acts 2:42–47	1323–1324, 1382, 1346, 1348–1349	Education for Community Life, Liturgical Education	Eucharist, Mass, assembly	St. Tarcisius	Call to Community, The Dignity of Work
The Parable of the Yeast Luke 13:18–21; The Mustard Seed Matthew 13:31–32	2613, 1154, 131–132, 1349, 1184, 1346	Promoting Knowledge of the Faith, Liturgical Education	Liturgy of the Word, homily, creed, Prayer of the Faithful	St. Paul	Call to Community, Care for Creation
Give God His Due Matthew 6:24; The Rich Young Man Matthew 19:21–22	1330, 616–617, 1408, 1142, 1411	Liturgical Education, Education for Community Life	sacrifice, Last Supper, Liturgy of the Eucharist, consecration	Bl. Imelda Lambertini	Option for the Poor, Human Solidarity
The Bread of Life John 6:30–35; The Feeding of the Five Thousand Luke 9:10–17	1335,1365, 1369–1370, 1374	Liturgical Education, Moral Formation	Holy Communion, Real Presence, reverence, Blessed Sacrament, Tabernacle	V. Pierre Toussaint	Call to Community, Option for the Poor
Paul Proclaims the Kingdom Acts 28:30–31; Peter Preaches Acts 10:42–48	1332, 849, 851–852	Missionary Initiation, Education for Community Life	mission, missionaries	St. Anthony Claret	Life and Dignity, The Dignity of Work
Jesus Knocks Revelation 3:20; The Wedding Feast Matthew 22:2–10 and Luke 14:16–23	326, 1329, 1391, 143	Promoting Knowledge of the Faith, Moral Formation	Heaven	St. Mary Magdalen de Pazzi	Option for the Poor, The Dignity of Work

Grade 3 Scope and Sequence

Unit	Chapter		Lesson Concepts
1 REVELATION	CHAPTER 1	The Creator's Work	• God created human beings in his image and likeness. • Creation is a gift from God that shows his goodness; it is the work of the Holy Trinity. • Humans have the responsibility to care for all of creation, especially each other.
	CHAPTER 2	The Church Gathered	• The Bible is the Word of God written in human words. It is the holy book of the Church. • The Church is the community of all baptized people who believe in God and follow Jesus. • The Church helps us understand God's Word, teaches us about God's love, and gathers us to honor and worship God.
	CHAPTER 3	Families Teach Love	• Families teach us how to care for, respect, and help one another. • We honor Mary as the Mother of God, the greatest of Saints, and our Mother, too. • The Hail Mary begins with the words Elizabeth used to greet Mary. • The Catholic family is the domestic Church where we experience love and learn about God and how we pray and live as Catholics.
2 TRINITY	CHAPTER 4	The Holy Trinity	• A mystery is a truth that is difficult to perceive or understand with our senses, but is known through faith and through signs. • Jesus teaches us about God his Father and the Holy Spirit. • God the Father, God the Son, and God the Holy Spirit are a perfect communion of love. • The Creed is a statement of the Church's beliefs.
	CHAPTER 5	The Church Celebrates	• At the Last Supper Jesus celebrated the Passover with his Apostles. • Liturgy is the public prayer of the Church. It includes the Seven Sacraments and forms of daily prayer. • Catholics are required to attend Mass on Sundays and Holy Days of Obligation. • The Blessed Sacrament is the Holy Eucharist, especially the Body of Christ, which is kept in the Tabernacle.
	CHAPTER 6	Pray Always	• In the Lord's Prayer, Jesus taught his followers to pray to God the Father. • Daily prayer is important. We can pray using traditional prayers and our own words, out loud or silently, and at any time. • The five basic forms of prayer are blessing and adoration, praise, petition, intercession, and thanksgiving.
3 JESUS CHRIST	CHAPTER 7	The Good News	• The Gospel message is the Good News of God's Kingdom and his saving love. • The four Gospel books in the New Testament are about Christ's life, teaching, Death, and Resurrection. • The Kingdom of God is the world of love, peace, and justice that is in Heaven and is still being built on Earth. • In his miracles and parables, Jesus shows us that God's Kingdom is here and yet to come fully.
	CHAPTER 8	The Paschal Mystery	• Jesus offered the greatest sacrifice: he gave his life to save us from sin so that we could have new life with God in Heaven. • The Resurrection is the event of Jesus being raised from Death to new life by God the Father through the power of the Holy Spirit. • The Paschal Mystery is the mystery of Jesus Christ's suffering, Death, Resurrection, and Ascension. • The Church celebrates the Paschal Mystery in each of the Seven Sacraments.
	CHAPTER 9	The Body of Christ	• With the help of the Holy Spirit, members of the Church continue Jesus' work here on Earth. • The Church is the Body of Christ of which Christ is the head. • All the baptized use their gifts and talents to serve others. • Stewardship is the way we appreciate and use God's gifts, including our time, talent, and treasure and the gift of creation.
4 THE CHURCH	CHAPTER 10	Church Leaders	• The Apostles are the twelve disciples Jesus chose to be his closest followers to share in his work and mission in a special way. • Peter was the leader of the Apostles and first Pope, head of the entire Church. • The bishops are successors of the Apostles. • The Pope, bishops, priests, and deacons lead, guide, and make the Church holy.
	CHAPTER 11	One and Holy	• The Marks of the Church are the four characteristics that identify Christ's Church: one, holy, catholic, and apostolic. • Pentecost is the feast that celebrates the coming of the Holy Spirit fifty days after Easter. • The Holy Spirit continues to unify the Church and make her holy. • The Communion of Saints is everyone who believes in and follows Jesus, people on Earth and in Purgatory and Heaven.

Go to **aliveinchrist.osv.com** for complete program Scope and Sequence.

Sacred Scripture	Catechism of the Catholic Church	Tasks of Catechesis	Catholic Faith Words	People of Faith	Catholic Social Teaching
You Formed Me Psalm 139:13–15; The Creation of the World Genesis 1:1–23	355, 293, 292, 2415	Promoting Knowledge of the Faith, Moral Formation	creation, Holy Trinity, image of God	St. Rabanus Maurus	Life and Dignity, Care for Creation
Jesus Prays John 17:20–23; Helping One Another Acts 2:42–47	105–106, 1213, 2030, 942, 1816	Promoting Knowledge of the Faith, Education for Community Life	Bible, Church, Sacred Tradition	St. Francis of Assisi	Call to Community, Human Solidarity
Those Who Hear and Act on the Word of God Luke 8:19–21; Mary Visits Elizabeth Luke 1:39–56	1657, 2207, 963, 435, 2676, 2204	Promoting Knowledge of the Faith, Education for Community Life	Visitation, Mary, domestic Church	Bls. Luigi and Maria	Life and Dignity, Call to Community
This Is How We Know 1 John 4:13–14, 16; The Father and the Spirit John 14:6–7, 16–17	237, 240, 2780, 850, 187	Promoting Knowledge of the Faith, Education for Community Life	mystery, Incarnation, creed, Apostles' Creed	St. John of Matha	Call to Community, Human Solidarity
They Were Hungry Mark 6:34–42; The Last Supper Luke 22:14–20	2097, 1339–1340, 1069–1070, 1389, 1379	Promoting Knowledge of the Faith, Liturgical Education	Seven Sacraments, Last Supper, liturgy, Nicene Creed, Tabernacle, Blessed Sacrament	St. Mary MacKillop	Call to Community, Rights and Responsibilities
Pray Quietly Matthew 6:5–6; The Lord's Prayer Matthew 6:9–13; Praying Well Matthew 6:5–8	2765, 2659, 2644	Teaching to Pray, Liturgical Education	prayer, Lord's Prayer, blessing, adoration, praise, petition, intercession, thanksgiving	St. Gertrude the Great	Life and Dignity, Human Solidarity
The Woman and the Lost Coin Luke 15:8–10; The Rejection at Nazareth Luke 4:16–21; The Mustard Seed Mark 4:30–32	125, 120, 127, 2818–2819, 546	Promoting Knowledge of the Faith, Moral Formation	Gospel, Messiah, Kingdom of God, miracle, parable	St. Isaac Jogues	Life and Dignity, Rights and Responsibilities
No Greater Love John 15:12–13; Mary Meets Jesus John 20:11–18	619, 623, 648, 571, 1113	Promoting Knowledge of the Faith, Liturgical Education	sacrifice, Resurrection, Ascension, Paschal Mystery	St. Mary Magdalene	Life and Dignity, Human Solidarity
Gifts of the Spirit 1 Corinthians 12:4–7; Those Who Helped Matthew 25:31–40	1287–1288, 792, 791, 1937, 2402	Education for Community Life, Liturgical Education	parish, Body of Christ, stewardship	Bl. Joseph Vaz	Call to Community, Option for the Poor
Jesus Sent Out the Twelve Matthew 10:5–10; Peter and Jesus Matthew 16:15–19, 26:69–75, John 21:15–17	551, 552, 861–862, 939	Education for Community Life, Liturgical Education	Pope, bishop, Magisterium, Apostolic Succession	St. Gregory the Great	The Dignity of Work, Care for Creation
Jesus Preached Peace Ephesians 2:19–21; The Coming of the Spirit Acts 2:1–12	811, 731, 2623–2625, 960–962	Education for Community Life, Liturgical Education	Marks of the Church, one, holy, catholic, apostolic, Pentecost, Saint, Communion of Saints	Sts. Perpetua and Felicity	Call to Community, Human Solidarity

Grade 3 Scope and Sequence

Unit	Chapter		Lesson Concepts
4	CHAPTER 12	Catholic and Apostolic	• Saint Paul was one of the first to take the message of Jesus across many countries, establishing Church communities and writing them letters that became part of the New Testament. • All Church members participate in her mission to announce the Good News of God's Kingdom to people of all nations. • The Church is catholic because she is everywhere and welcomes everyone. • The Church is apostolic because Jesus gave his Apostles the mission of sharing his Good News with people all over the world.
5 MORALITY	CHAPTER 13	Choose Love	• The Story of Joseph in the Old Testament shows us to forgive and love. • Jesus teaches us to love our enemies. • The Beatitudes are teachings of Jesus that show the way to true happiness and tell how to live in God's Kingdom. • Jesus' New Commandment is for his disciples to love one another as he has loved us.
	CHAPTER 14	Live in the Light	• Vocation is God's plan for our lives, the purpose for which he made us. • Virtues are good spiritual habits that make you stronger and help you do what is right and good. • The Theological Virtues of faith, hope and charity are gifts from God that help us live in relationship with the Holy Trinity. • Virtues grow over time with our practice and openness to God's grace.
	CHAPTER 15	Help with Choices	• Conscience is an ability given to us by God that helps us make choices about right and wrong. • The Precepts of the Church are some of the minimum requirements given by Church leaders for deepening our relationship with God and the Church. • The Holy Spirit and the teachings of the Church help us to make good choices. • In the Sacrament of Penance and Reconciliation, we receive God's forgiveness and the grace to help us change.
6 SACRAMENTS	CHAPTER 16	Sacraments of Initiation	• People of all ages can be baptized into the Church. • The Sacraments of Initiation celebrate membership into the Catholic Church: Baptism, Confirmation, and Eucharist. • Baptism removes Original Sin, forgives personal sin, and gives new life in Christ. Confirmation seals and completes Baptism. • In the Eucharist, Jesus Christ shares himself with us, giving us the gift of his Body and Blood.
	CHAPTER 17	Sacraments of Healing	• In the Sacraments of Healing, God's forgiveness and healing are given to those suffering physical and spiritual sickness. • In Penance and Reconciliation, we confess our sins to a priest who forgives in the name of Christ and his Church. • In the Anointing of the Sick, the priest prays that God will send his healing love to the person who is being anointed.
	CHAPTER 18	Sacraments at the Service of Communion	• Sacraments at the Service of Communion celebrate people's commitment to serve God and the community and help build up the People of God. • Holy Orders is the Sacrament in which baptized men are ordained as deacons, priests, or bishops to lead and serve the Church. • Matrimony joins a baptized man and a baptized woman in Christian marriage to serve God by loving and serving each other and any children God gives them.
7 KINGDOM OF GOD	CHAPTER 19	The Church Through Time	• A covenant is a sacred promise or agreement between God and humans. • God established a covenant with Abraham, and from that came the beginning of God's People. • As the Son of God, Jesus fulfills God's promise and his covenant extends to all people. • The first Christians faced difficult times, but they tried to be faithful to him and to the covenant, and the Church grew.
	CHAPTER 20	The Work of the Church	• The Church continues Jesus' work on Earth through her worship, teaching, care for others, and work for peace and justice. • The Church is a sign of God's Kingdom and helps people share in the love of the Holy Trinity. • By our Baptism, we are called to participate in the Church's mission to share the Good News and serve God and others.
	CHAPTER 21	Everlasting Life	• Jesus' Resurrection is proof of his promise of eternal life. • The Particular Judgment is the individual judgment by God at the time of a person's death when God decides where that person will spend eternity according to his or her faith and works. • The Last Judgment is God's final triumph over evil, when Christ will come again and bring the Kingdom of God to its fullness. • The last book of the Bible, Revelation, ends with John's vision of a new creation, God's everlasting Kingdom.

Go to **aliveinchrist.osv.com** for complete program Scope and Sequence.

Sacred Scripture	Catechism of the Catholic Church	Tasks of Catechesis	Catholic Faith Words	People of Faith	Catholic Social Teaching
Do Everything in the Name of Jesus Colossians 3:16–17; Doing God's Work 1 Corinthians 3:5–9	849, 856, 863, 830–831, 869	Education for Community Life, Missionary Initiation	evangelization, mission, missionaries	St. Elizabeth Ann Seton	Option for the Poor, The Dignity of Work
Pray for Those Who Mistreat You Luke 6:27–28, 31; The Story of Joseph Genesis 37–45; Love of Enemies Matthew 5:43–47	312, 1825, 1716, 1970–1971	Promoting Knowledge of the Faith, Moral Formation	Beatitudes, mercy, New Commandment	St. Peter Canisius	Life and Dignity, Option for the Poor
The Light of the World John 8:12; Your Light Must Shine Matthew 5:14–16	1877, 1803, 1813, 1830	Promoting Knowledge of the Faith, Moral Formation	vocation, virtues, Theological Virtues, faith, hope, charity	St. Genevieve	Rights and Responsibilities, Care for Creation
You Know My Thoughts Psalm 139:23–24; Saul and Jesus Acts 9:1–30	1777, 2041, 1783–1785, 1422–1423	Promoting Knowledge of the Faith, Moral Formation	grace, conscience, Precepts of the Church, sin	St. Pio of Pietrelcina	Rights and Responsibilities, The Dignity of Work
A People Chosen by God 1 Peter 2:9–10; Many Are Baptized Acts 2:38–41	1247, 1250, 1212, 1217, 1323	Promoting Knowledge of the Faith, Liturgical Education	Sacred Chrism, Sacraments of Initiation, Real Presence, Eucharist	St. John the Baptist	Life and Dignity, Call to Community
All Were Healed Matthew 14:34–36; Jesus Gives New Life Luke 8:40–42, 49–56	1421, 1424, 1517	Promoting Knowledge of the Faith, Liturgical Education	Sacraments of Healing	St. Marianne Cope	Rights and Responsibilities, The Dignity of Work
Called to Be Free Galatians 5:13–14; Servants of Christ 1 Corinthians 3:21–4:2	1534, 1536, 1601	Liturgical Education, Moral Formation	vows, priest, deacon, Sacraments at the Service of Communion	St. Jean-Baptiste de La Salle	Call to Community, Human Solidarity
They Lived Together Acts 2:42; I Will Be Your God Genesis 17:1–19	56-58, 72, 73, 706, 2471–2472	Promoting Knowledge of the Faith, Liturgical Education	covenant, proclaim, faithful	St. Clement of Rome	Rights and Responsibilities, Human Solidarity
Be Happy 2 Corinthians 13:11; The Commissioning of the Twelve Matthew 10:5–14	759, 763, 2044–2046	Moral Formation, Missionary Initiation	justice, peace	St. Peter Claver	Rights and Responsibilities, The Dignity of Work
Whoever Knows Jesus Has Life 1 John 5:11–12; The New Heaven and the New Earth Revelation 21:1–4; Alpha and Omega Revelation 22:13	655, 1022, 1038–1040, 1044–1045	Promoting Knowledge of the Faith, Moral Formation	Heaven, Hell, Purgatory, Last Judgment	St. Joseph	Life and Dignity, Rights and Responsibilities

Endnotes:

1. Cf. CCC 426-429; CT 5-6; DCG (1971) 40.
2. CCC 429.
3. Cf. CT, 31; CT 31 which expounds the integrity and organization of the message; cf. DCG (1971) 39 and 43.
4. Cf. Vatican Council I: DS 3016: *nexus mysteriorum*; LG 25.
5. UR 11.
6. CT 68.

Opening Lesson
&
Church Year Feasts and Seasons

Feasts and Seasons at a Glance

KEY CONCEPT
The key concept for each lesson is clearly stated at the start of each chapter.

DOCTRINAL CONTENT

- The doctrinal content for each chapter will be found in this section. It will show how the chapter correlates to paragraphs from the *Catechism of the Catholic Church.*

TASKS OF CATECHESIS
The six tasks of catechesis are outlined in the *National Directory for Catechesis.* The relevant tasks of catechesis for a chapter will be found in this section.

Catechist Background

For through faith you are all children of God in Christ Jesus. For all of you who were baptized into Christ have clothed yourselves with Christ. Galatians 3:26–27

→ **Reflect** In what ways do I see myself as a child of God?

The Catechist Background includes a short essay that provides easy-to-understand theological background on the chapter content for both novice and experienced catechists.

The catechetical process of ***Alive in Christ*** mirrors the divine pedagogy—the gradual and relational way God teaches us so that we can know him in his truth, be guided by the Holy Spirit to respond with faith and love, and accept the gift of new life in Christ. Each lesson encourages this personal and ongoing relationship, beginning with God's invitation through Sacred Scripture. This leads children to reflect on his Word, deepen their understanding of our Sacred Tradition, and respond with a lived faith within the home and in the community.

Alive in Christ incorporates the most trusted research on how children learn and communicate. Topics are presented at important developmental "windows"—ages when research in child development tells us that learning about a particular topic would be most effective. For example, because they have reached the age of reason, second graders are better able to understand that the Eucharist is not ordinary bread and wine, because Jesus taught us that it was his Body and Blood. In Chapter 18, they will learn that at Mass, we receive Christ's Body and Blood in Holy Communion. We remember Jesus' sacrifice and give thanks for it.

→ **Reflect** Throughout your life, how has God invited you to know him and love him?

Catechist's Prayer

Lord, thank you for calling me to the ministry of catechesis. It is a great privilege and an awesome responsibility to echo your Word to others. Draw me closer to you, so that I may teach your wisdom and mirror your love by word and example. Amen.

A New Year

Let Us Pray

Leader: Loving God, you share your Word with us in the Bible. Thank you for inviting us to be your children.

"Enter, let us bow down in worship;
let us kneel before the LORD who made
us." Psalm 95:6

All: Thank you, God, for sharing your life and love with us. We want to listen to your Word and live in your love.

God's Word

For through faith you are all children of God in Christ Jesus. For all of you who were baptized into Christ have clothed yourselves with Christ.
Galatians 3:26-27

What Do You Wonder?

- What does it mean to be God's children?
- How does God invite us to know and love him?

Invite

Ask the children how they feel when they are invited somewhere. Point out the *Invite* heading on the page. Explain that each lesson begins with an invitation to learn about God.

Let Us Pray

Introduce the children to the prayer space and invite them into it. Lead them in the Sign of the Cross. Read aloud the leader's prayer and the Psalm verse. Prompt the children's response.

God's Word

Guide the children in reflecting on Scripture.

- Invite them to close their eyes and concentrate on the message in this passage.
- Proclaim the Scripture.
- Pause for several moments.
- *Ask:* What message did you hear in these words?
- Invite volunteers to share.

Have the children move from the prayer space back to their seats.

What Do You Wonder?

Point out the picture and ask why the children are happy. Explain that being a child of God makes people happy. Read aloud the questions and invite responses. Ask what else they wonder about God.

Catechist Background

Reflecting on Scripture

Each chapter in ***Alive in Christ*** begins with a focus on Sacred Scripture. On the *Invite* page, the children are called to open their minds and hearts to God's message.

- The Psalm verse and New Testament excerpt set the theme for the chapter. The passage from Galatians is especially appropriate for this opening lesson, as it relates to being alive in Christ through the Sacrament of Baptism.
- For more information on the use of Sacred Scripture throughout the chapters, refer to page CE22.

Discover

Objectives

- Chapter objectives relating to this Discover section are clearly stated here
- Begin to understand what is going to be learned this year, especially about the Sacraments of Penance and Reconciliation

Second Grade

Ask the children to explain what the word *discover* means.

Point out that the Discover pages in this book will help them find out important things about their faith.

Explain that the children will use this book to learn about God.

- Have the children investigate the book by looking at the table of contents.
- Let them preview the illustrations and headings.
- Ask the children to report on what they will learn. Point out the icons on the page and invite the children to speculate on what they signal. Use the text to expand on their responses.
- As you define the icons, reinforce the importance of Scripture, prayer, and songs in learning about God. Call attention to the photograph.
- Explain that the gold stars in the book will give them directions.

☆ Have the children underline two things in the text that they will do this year.

Second Grade

What's going to happen this year?

This year is all about learning, loving, and celebrating our Catholic faith!

When you see [Bible icon], you know it's a story or reading from the Bible. Through Bible stories you will discover that Jesus the Son shares God's love and mercy.

When you see [prayer icon], you know it's time to pray. Each time you are gathered together, you can listen to and talk to God in prayer. You will grow closer to Jesus as you pray and get to know his teachings.

When you see [music icon], you will sing songs to praise God and celebrate our faith. You'll explore the Church's feasts and seasons and meet many Saints, our heroes of the Church.

☆ Underline two things you will do this year.

The gold star above begins an exercise to help you learn what's being taught. You may underline, circle, write, match, or draw.

Quick Tip

Lesson Structure

The chapters in this book will all follow the same three-step process:

- *Invite* begins with prayer that includes Sacred Scripture and calls the children to be open to God's Word.
- *Discover* presents Scripture, Church teachings, and Catholic practices with developmentally appropriate language and art and contains activities to reinforce and apply learning.
- *Live* connects the children's faith knowledge with the ways that Catholics worship, live, pray, and serve in community. It also contains the concluding prayer for the chapter.
- For more information on the lesson process, see pages CE18–CE19.

Special Signs and Celebrations

A big part of this year is learning about the **Seven Sacraments**. The Sacraments are special signs and celebrations that Jesus gave his Church. Important words like this are **highlighted** in yellow so you don't miss them.

You'll discover how the Church celebrates God's love and forgiveness in the Sacrament of Reconciliation. You will explore the different parts of the Mass and learn how Jesus gives himself to us in the Eucharist.

Everything you learn and do in class will help you take part in parish celebrations in new ways.

Catholic Faith Words

In this box you will see the **highlighted** words again and their definitions.

Seven Sacraments special signs and celebrations that Jesus gave his Church. They allow us to share in God's life and work.

Share Your Faith

When you see these fun green words, you know it's time for an activity!

Think What is something you know about Church celebrations?

Share Talk in a small group about how you learned this. Write one new thing you learned from your group.

____

____

Catechist Background

Focus on Second Graders

Alive in Christ presents key themes of Catholic teaching in a developmentally appropriate sequence. For more information on how the series framework supports faith development, see pages CE8–CE9.

- The Grade 2 focus is on the Sacraments of Penance and the Eucharist.
- This year's lessons have been designed to address the children's need for hands-on activities and practical explanations.
- For more information on the abilities and perspectives of the children you are teaching, see pages CE9 and CE29.

Special Signs and Celebrations

Read aloud the first three paragraphs to explain what the children will learn about this year. Emphasize that sacramental celebrations are happy times in the Church.

Work with Words

Point out the term *Seven Sacraments* in the first paragraph and the Catholic Faith Words treatment. Tell the children that important words will be highlighted in the text.

Write the terms *Reconciliation, Mass,* and *Eucharist* on the board or on chart paper. Tell the children that they will learn about these celebrations this year.

Activity

Point out the Share Your Faith feature.

- Explain that this feature and others like it will help them think about their faith and share it.
- Read aloud the directions.
- Allow time for the children to reflect silently on Church celebrations. Then have them share their ideas with a group of classmates.

Quick Review

This book will teach about the Seven Sacraments. It contains Scripture, prayers, songs, and activities to help us learn.

Discover

Objectives

- Learn that the Bible is the inspired Word of God written by humans
- Be able to explain the content of the Gospels

God's Word

Explain that we use words to share important ideas. God also uses words to teach us.

Read aloud the first two paragraphs to show the importance of God's Word.

- Tell the children that the Bible is a collection of books that were written at many different times and by many different people. The Bible tells about God and his People.
- Read aloud the text to acquaint the children with the Old and New Testaments. Emphasize that the Old Testament tells about the time before Jesus was born. Point out that the New Testament teaches about the time after Jesus was born.
- ☆ Read aloud the names of the people on the Bible pages. Have the children circle familiar names. If time permits, have the children tell what they know about these people.

Discover

God's Word

Where can you find stories about God?

Catholic Faith Words

Bible the Word of God written down by humans

The **Bible** is the Word of God written down by humans. It is one great book, made up of many small books. In fact, the word Bible means "books." The books of the Bible are divided into two parts: The Old Testament and the New Testament.

Another name for the Bible is Scripture, which means "writing." We hear readings from Scripture during Mass and the other Sacraments.

☆ Circle the names of the people you have heard of.

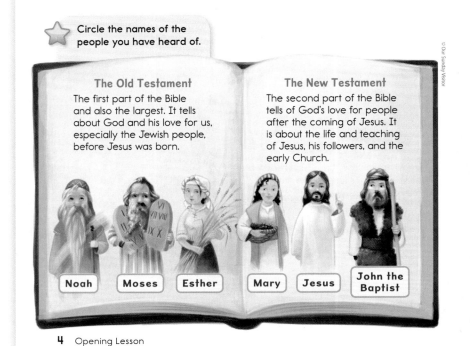

The Old Testament
The first part of the Bible and also the largest. It tells about God and his love for us, especially the Jewish people, before Jesus was born.

The New Testament
The second part of the Bible tells of God's love for people after the coming of Jesus. It is about the life and teaching of Jesus, his followers, and the early Church.

Liturgy Link

Bible Readings

The Old Testament and New Testament are the core of the Liturgy of the Word. However, the priests, deacons, and readers do not read directly from the Bible; they read from the Lectionary and Book of Gospels, which contain passages from the Bible.

- Typically, the first reading on a Sunday is from the Old Testament, followed by a responsorial Psalm. The next reading is usually from a New Testament Epistle, and the last is always from the Gospels.

Go to **aliveinchrist.osv.com** for Sunday readings, Scripture background, questions of the week, and seasonal resources.

The Gospels

The New Testament begins with four very special books called Gospels. The word Gospel means, "Good News." These four books of the Gospels tell of the Good News Jesus brought of the Kingdom of God and his saving love.

- The Gospel according to Matthew
- The Gospel according to Mark
- The Gospel according to Luke
- The Gospel according to John

The Gospels are filled with stories about Jesus, the words of Jesus, words other people said about Jesus, and stories that Jesus told.

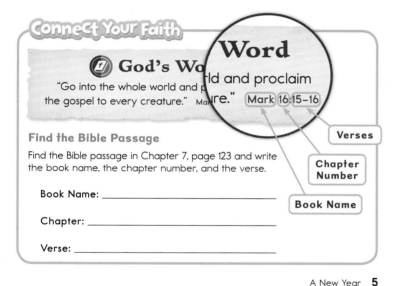

Connect Your Faith

God's Word

"Go into the whole world and proclaim the gospel to every creature." Mark 16:15–16

Verses

Chapter Number

Book Name

Find the Bible Passage

Find the Bible passage in Chapter 7, page 123 and write the book name, the chapter number, and the verse.

Book Name: ____________________

Chapter: ____________________

Verse: ____________________

The Gospels

Invite a volunteer to read aloud the first paragraph.

- Emphasize that the Gospels tell the story of Jesus' life on Earth. The Gospels are named after four of Jesus' followers: Matthew, Mark, Luke, and John.
- Point out that the readings we hear during Mass are from both the Old and New Testaments. The Gospel that we hear at Mass is always from one of the four Gospels.

Activity

Explain that the Bible is a very big book. To help people find different parts in it, it is divided into books. The books are named with words. The books are divided into chapters, and the chapters contain verses.

We can find any part of the Bible if we know its book, chapter, and verse.

- Have the children complete the activity. Walk among them as they work and give assistance as needed.

Quick Tip

Sacred Tradition

Part of the richness of the Catholic faith resides in Sacred Tradition, handed down through two millennia of Church history.

- Every lesson in this book presents truths of the faith.
- At the back of the book, the Our Catholic Tradition reference section expands on the lesson contents. Your lesson plans will contain specific references to this reference section when appropriate. You may want to have the children explore this section. For more on Sacred Tradition, see page CE23.

Quick Review

The Bible tells the story of God and his People. The Gospels are part of the Bible and tell about Jesus' life on Earth.

Our Catholic Life

Point out the *Live* heading on the page.

- Explain that each chapter in this book has a section that will help the children live as good Catholics.

Read aloud the first paragraph.

Grow as a Follower of Jesus

Invite volunteers to read aloud the six bullet points.

- Discuss why following each point will make us good Catholics.
- Reinforce that the children will learn about each of these ways to grow during this school year.

People of Faith

Read aloud this paragraph. Tell the children that they will learn about Saints and other holy people in this feature.

Activity

Have the children complete the activity. Invite volunteers to share how they hope to be a Person of Faith this year.

Our Catholic Life

What does it mean to be Catholic?

Each chapter in your book has an Our Catholic Life section. This section shows you in a special way what it means to be Catholic. Words, pictures, and activities help us grow closer to Jesus and the Church.

Grow as a Follower of Jesus

- know more about our faith
- understand and take part in the Sacraments
- live as Jesus calls us to
- talk and listen to God in prayer
- be an active member of the Church
- help others know Jesus through our words and actions

People of Faith

Look for this box, where you will meet People of Faith, holy men and women who loved God very much and did his work on Earth.

Live Your Faith

Be a Person of Faith! Draw yourself in the picture frame.

Tell how you can be a Person of Faith this year.

Catechist Background

Six Tasks of Catechesis

As a catechist, you are charged with six fundamental tasks as contained in the *National Directory for Catechesis*.

- Each of these tasks corresponds to an aspect of faith in Jesus. They are: Promoting Knowledge of the Faith, Liturgical Education, Moral Formation, Teaching to Pray, Education for Community Life, and Missionary Initiation.
- For more information on these tasks, refer to pages CE14–CE15.

Let Us Pray

Pray Together

Every chapter has a prayer page, with lots of different ways to pray. You may listen to God's Word read from the Bible, pray for the needs of others, call on the Saints to pray for us, and praise God the Father, Son, and Holy Spirit in words and songs.

Gather and begin with the Sign of the Cross.

Leader: Blessed be God.

All: Blessed be God forever.

Leader: Let us pray.

Bow your heads as the leader prays.

All: Amen.

Leader: A reading from the holy Gospel according to John.

Read John 6:35–38.

The Gospel of the Lord.

All: Praise to you, Lord Jesus Christ.

Sing "Alive in Christ"

We are Alive in Christ
We are Alive in Christ
He came to set us free
We are Alive in Christ
We are Alive in Christ
He gave his life for me
We are Alive in Christ
We are Alive in Christ

Let Us Pray

Pray Together

Read the first paragraph aloud to the children.

- Explain that every chapter will end with prayer.

Prepare

Assume the role of Leader.

Show the children where their responses are on the page.

Rehearse "Alive in Christ," downloaded from **aliveinchrist.osv.com**.

Gather

Lead the children into the prayer space.

- Lead the Sign of the Cross.
- Invite the children to be still and listen to the reading.

Pray

Follow the order of prayer on the student page.

As you read the Scripture, emphasize the words identifying Jesus as the Bread of Life.

Conclude by processing around the room with the children singing "Alive in Christ."

Songs of Scripture

Songs for Deepening Children's Understanding of God's Word

In addition to all of the chapter-specific songs available for download, a program component, *Songs of Scripture: Songs for Deepening Children's Understanding of God's Word* by John Burland and Dr. Jo Ann Paradise helps celebrate faith and support catechesis.

- Two CDs, Grades 1–3 and Grades 4–6, offer songs that teach, reinforce, or unfold the meaning of Scripture stories.
- These and other songs are available through **aliveinchrist.osv.com** and are searchable by grade and chapter level.

Family + Faith

Distribute the page to the children or parents/adult family members.

Point out the chapter highlights, insights on how second graders understand concepts, the opportunity for the adults to reflect on their own experience and faith journey, and the family prayer.

Your Child Learned is a summary of the Catholic teaching that was covered in the chapter and introduces families to the Scripture and the Person of Faith that was presented.

Children at This Age helps parents become aware of how their child comprehends what was taught and suggests ways to help the child gain a deeper understanding of the material.

Consider This invites parents to ponder some of their own experiences and listen as the Church speaks to their personal journey of faith.

Let's Talk offers parents developmentally appropriate questions that lead to discussion of the week's lesson.

Let's Pray provides a short family prayer based on the Person of Faith featured in the lesson.

Online Resources offers multimedia tools to encourage family interaction and reinforce the lesson at home.

FAMILY + FAITH

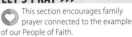

LIVING AND LEARNING TOGETHER

YOUR CHILD LEARNED >>>

This page is for you, the parent, to encourage you to talk about your faith and see the many ways you already live your faith in daily family life.

God's Word

In this section, you will find a Scripture citation and a summary of what your child has learned in the chapter.

Catholics Believe

- Bulleted information highlights the main points of doctrine of in the chapter.

Here you will find chapter connections to the *Catechism of the Catholic Church*.

People of Faith

Here you meet the Saint, Blessed, or Venerable featured in People of Faith.

CHILDREN AT THIS AGE >>>

This feature gives you a sense of how your child, at this particular age, will likely be able to understand what is being taught. It suggests ways you can help your child better understand, live, and love their faith.

How They Understand the Lessons Your second-grader has begun to understand that he or she is not the only person in the world. He or she can learn to see things from perspectives other than their own which means they are beginning to develop empathy and compassion.

At age seven or eight most children are capable of making moral choices. You can help your child develop morally by giving them good examples and clear moral guidelines. With that your child will be able to choose between right and wrong.

At this age children love to celebrate. Many like music and find comfort in ritual. Try singing some hymns at home with them and using gestures when you pray as a family. Don't hesitate to do spontaneous prayer with your child or to have them lead family prayer.

CONSIDER THIS >>>

This section includes a question that invites you to reflect on your own experience and consider how the Church speaks to you on your own faith journey.

LET'S TALK >>>

- Here you will find some practical questions that prompt discussion about the lesson's content, faith sharing, and connections with your family life.
- Ask your child to share one thing they've learned about their book.

LET'S PRAY >>>

This section encourages family prayer connected to the example of our People of Faith.

Holy men and women, pray for us. Amen.

For a multimedia glossary of Catholic Faith Words, Sunday readings, seasonal and Saint resources, and chapter activities go to **aliveinchrist.osv.com**.

Optional Activity

Explore the Student Book

In addition to what is presented in this opening lesson, there are many other features that help you present the Catholic faith to the children. Ask them to find the following features in their books.

- The Church Year: Children learn about Church feasts and seasons.
- Unit Openers: Preview the doctrinal theme with photos and art that convey the richness of our Catholic Tradition.
- Catholic Social Teaching/Live Your Faith: Introduce the children to important teachings of Jesus and the Church that help us live Jesus' New Commandment to love as he loved.

Check out the activities and resources available for the seasons of the Church Year at the following websites.
Go to **aliveinchrist.osv.com** and click on the Resource Library tab and select a season.
Go to **teachingcatholickids.com** and click on the current month's newsletter.

Ordinary Time: Mother of Mercy

LESSON OBJECTIVES

- Understand Mary's compassion
- Identify ways of showing compassion during Ordinary Time

ENVIRONMENT

Crucifix
Marian statue
Prayer table
Battery-powered or electric candle
Bible or Lectionary
White cloth

- Place the prayer table in a central location.
- Cover the table with the white cloth and arrange the statue, candle, and Bible or Lectionary on top of the table.
- Light the candle before beginning the ritual.
- Allow plenty of space around the prayer table for the children.
- Consider furnishing flowers for the prayer table.

MUSIC OPTIONS

Go to **aliveinchrist.osv.com** to sample and download,
"Mary, Our Mother"
"Hail Mary"
"Yes, We Will Do What Jesus Did"

CATHOLIC SOCIAL TEACHING

- **Option for the Poor**, Pages 296–297
- **Care for Creation**, Pages 302–303

Catechist Background

On the third day there was a wedding in Cana in Galilee, and the mother of Jesus was there. Jesus and his disciples were also invited to the wedding. When the wine ran short, the mother of Jesus said to him, "They have no wine." … [She] said to the servers, "Do whatever he tells you." **John 2:1–3, 5**

➔ **Reflect** Do you sometimes find it challenging to do what Jesus tells you?

Stories of Mary from the early Church portray her as a person of compassion and mercy. She went to visit her cousin Elizabeth when she found out that Elizabeth was pregnant. During the Wedding at Cana, Mary urged Jesus to help when the wine ran out. It was Mary who stayed at the foot of the cross when Jesus was dying and held him in her arms when he was taken down from the Cross.

As prayers to Mary, such as the Hail Mary or the *Memorare*, developed, they affirmed her qualities of compassion and mercy. In them we petition Mary to be with us at the hour of death. We proclaim that it has never been known that anyone who sought her intercession was left unaided. In the Litany of the Blessed Mother, we pray to Mary as Comforter of the Afflicted.

On September 24th, the Church celebrates the Feast of Our Lady of Mercy. This feast developed during the Middle Ages to commemorate the apparition of Our Lady of Mercy to Saint Peter Nolasco. In this vision, Mary appeared carrying two bags of coins for use in ransoming Christian captives. As a result, the Order of Mercy was founded to liberate Christians imprisoned by the Moors.

➔ **Reflect** How do you show mercy toward others in your daily life?

Catechist's Prayer

God the Father, make me a person of compassion and mercy such as the Blessed Mother so that I may serve as a good example for the children in my care. In Jesus' name. Amen.

Ordinary Time

Invite

Mother of Mercy

Let Us Pray

Leader: Mother of Mercy, pray for us that we show kindness and mercy when it is needed.

The LORD is kind and merciful.

Based on Psalm 103

All: Amen.

God's Word

Mary was at a wedding feast in Cana. Jesus and his friends were there too. Mary saw that there was no more wine for the guests. She told Jesus, "They have no wine." Jesus asked his mother how this affected him. His time had not yet come. But Mary turned to the servants and said, "Do whatever he tells you."

Based on John 2:1–5

What Do You Wonder?

- What would have happened if the food or drinks had run out?
- Why did Mary want to help?

9

Lectionary Connection

John 2:1–11

This Gospel reading is proclaimed on the Second Sunday in Ordinary Time, Year C.

- Mary's role in this story is one of intercession with Jesus, her son. When she sees the problem that has arisen, she has compassion on the hosts and asks Jesus to act.
- Mary has a similar role with us today. As Mother of God and our Mother, she intercedes for us with God.

Invite

Let Us Pray

Invite the children to gather in the prayer space and make the Sign of the Cross. Pray the leader's prayer and the Psalm verse. Prompt the children's response.

Have the children move out of the prayer space and back to their seats.

Say: We know that God is kind and shows us mercy. He wants us to be kind and merciful too. Let's listen to how Mary showed mercy at a wedding.

God's Word

Guide the children through the process of Scripture reflection.

- Invite them to close their eyes, be still, and open their minds and hearts to what God is saying to them in this passage.
- Proclaim the Scripture.
- Maintain several moments of silence.
- *Ask:* What did you hear God say to you today?
- Invite volunteers to share.

What Do You Wonder?

Say: Mary was paying attention to what other people needed and she knew Jesus would help if she asked him.

Invite the children to respond to the questions. Ask what else they might wonder about ways they can be kind and helpful to others.

Discover

Ordinary Time

Invite volunteers to read aloud the facts about Ordinary Time from the green box in the side column.

Read aloud the introduction.

Mary's Example

Say: Mary shows us how to live as God's children.

- Ask the children what they know about Mary. Possible responses: She is Jesus' Mother; she said "yes" to God; an angel visited her.

Invite a volunteer read aloud the paragraph.

- Review the definition of *mercy* from the text.
- Invite the children to share examples of times they received mercy from others. Possible responses: a sibling helped them do something difficult; a parent forgave them
- Ask one of the children to read aloud the caption on the page.

Music Option: Have the children sing "Hail Mary," downloaded from **aliveinchrist.osv.com**.

Ordinary Time

- This season of the Church year comes twice, after Christmas and for a longer time after Easter.
- During this time, we learn more about Jesus' teachings so we continue to grow as his disciples.
- We also honor Mary and the Saints.

Ordinary Time

Ordinary Time occurs twice in the year. The Church celebrates the words and works of Jesus.

In Ordinary Time the priest wears green. The church is decorated in green, too.

There are many feasts of Mary during Ordinary Time. The Church color for Mary's feasts is white.

Mary's Example

Mary is the Mother of Jesus. She is the greatest of Saints. The Church honors Mary with different titles. One of these titles is Mary, Our Lady of Mercy—to show mercy means to be forgiving and loving to others. Mary is an example of love, kindness, and forgiveness.

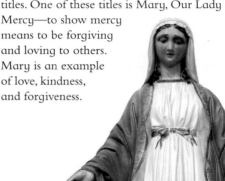

Mary is the Mother of God and our Mother, too. She loves us and welcomes us with open arms.

Optional Activity

Showing Mercy *Visual/Spatial*

Second graders are quite merciful individuals if given the opportunity.

- Ask the children to think of a time they saw someone in need.
- Invite them to draw a picture of how they responded (visited someone in the hospital, shared their toys).
- Have them share their drawing and the story behind it with the rest of the group.

Acting Out of Love

Mary's actions showed love. She stayed with her cousin Elizabeth who was going to have a baby. She searched for her Son, Jesus, when he was lost in Jerusalem. Mary stayed at the Cross when Jesus died. She forgave those who hurt him, as Jesus did. Mary shows us how to love and forgive others.

Showing Mercy

Merciful people think of what others need and try to help. God is merciful. He forgives us when we sin. Jesus shows us how to be merciful, too. Many of his stories in the Gospels are about being merciful.

- ➔ **How has Jesus shown his mercy to us?**
- ➔ **How has someone shown mercy to you? How can you show mercy to others?**

Underline the way that Mary showed mercy to others after Jesus' Death.

Activity

Act Out a Mercy Prayer Make gestures to go with this mercy prayer. Show what the words mean. Say the mercy prayer every morning.

Jesus, have mercy on me.
Mary, help me show mercy to others today. Amen.

Catechist Background

Cultural Connection: Marian Devotion

There have been miraculous visions of Mary with black or brown skin, dating as early as the twelfth century. There are many different images of Mary around the world.

- Our Lady of Guadalupe (Mexico) and Our Lady of Jasna Gora (Czestochowa, Poland) are examples.
- Today there is a return to this art form and devotion reflecting a movement to inculturation. Some darker skinned portrayals of Mary are also probably more accurate, since she was a Middle-Eastern woman.

Acting Out of Love

Have a volunteer read aloud the paragraph.

- ☆ Have the children underline how Mary showed mercy to others after Jesus' Death.
- Allow time for the children to search for the words and underline them.

Showing Mercy

Read aloud the paragraph.

- Ask the questions following the text.
- Together brainstorm answers to the questions.
- List the children's responses on the board or on chart paper.

Activity

Read aloud the instructions.

- Allow the children to work in pairs as they decide the best gestures for the prayer.

Music Option: While the children work on the activity, play "Yes, We Will Do What Jesus Did," downloaded from **aliveinchrist.osv.com**.

- Ask volunteer-pairs to demonstrate their prayer gestures for the rest of the group.
- Remind the children that this mercy prayer is a meaningful prayer to pray each morning.

People of Faith

Invite the children in your group to take turns reading a line of the chart until all 21 chapters, names, and feast days have been read.

- Ask them to each choose one of the people of faith listed to research from home.
- Encourage the children to bring back their findings to share with the group at a later date.

Tell the children they will learn more about Mary as they complete the lessons in this book, especially when they get to Chapter 5.

People of Faith

Mary

Saint Peter

Pierre Toussaint

Chapter	Person	Feast Day
1	Blessed Virgin Mary	August 15
2	Saint Cristóbal Magallanes Jara	May 21
3	Saint Luke	October 18
4	Blessed Julian of Norwich	May 13
5	Saint Peter	June 29
6	Saint Arnold Janssen	January 15
7	Saint Elizabeth of Hungary	November 17
8	Saint Thérèse of Lisieux	October 1
9	Saint Jane Frances de Chantal	August 21
10	Saint Pius X (Giuseppo Sarto)	August 21
11	Saint Benedict-Joseph Labré	April 17
12	Pope Saint Victor	July 28
13	Saint Brigid of Kildare	February 1
14	Blessed Mother Teresa of Calcutta	September 5
15	Saint Alphonsus Liguori	August 1
16	Saint Tarcisius	August 15
17	Saint Paul	July 25
18	Blessed Imelda Lambertini	May 13
19	Venerable Pierre Toussaint	July 25
20	Saint Anthony Claret	October 24
21	Saint Mary Magdalene de Pazzi	July 22

Catholic Social Teaching

Lesson Connections

To integrate Catholic Social Teaching into your lesson, choose one of the following features: Option for the Poor, pages 296–297; or Care for Creation, pages 302–303.

- To expand the lesson, complete page 12, then move to the Catholic Social Teaching feature.
- Return to the prayer on page 13.

Let Us Pray

Hail Mary

Gather and begin with the Sign of the Cross.

Leader: A reading from the holy Gospel according to Luke.

Read Luke 1:39–42, 45.

The Gospel of the Lord.

All: Praise to you, Lord Jesus Christ.

Bow your heads and pray the Hail Mary together.

Leader: Hail, Mary, full of grace, the Lord is with thee. Blessed art thou among women and blessed is the fruit of thy womb, Jesus.

All: Holy Mary, Mother of God, pray for us sinners, now and at the hour of our death. Amen.

Leader: Go forth to love and serve the Lord, as Mary did throughout her life.

All: Thanks be to God.

Sing "Mary, Our Mother"

Mother of Jesus, be with us every day.
We want to stay close to you always.
You are our mother.
We are your children.
Guide us in every way each day.
Guide us in every way.

Live

Let Us Pray

Hail Mary

Set up a crucifix, picture, or other image of Mary in the prayer space.

You will be the leader.

Rehearse with the children "Mary, Our Mother," downloaded from **aliveinchrist.osv.com**.

Invite the children to gather around the image of Mary.

Follow the order of prayer on the student page.

Have the children sing "Mary, Our Mother" as they process back to their seats.

Liturgy Link

Liturgical Colors

The liturgical color during Ordinary Time is green, a symbol of hope.

- For the celebrations of some Saints' days and feast days, the color may change.
- For the Feast of Our Lady, the color white is worn. White is a symbol of light, innocence, purity, joy, and triumph.

Distribute this page to the children or parents/adult family members.

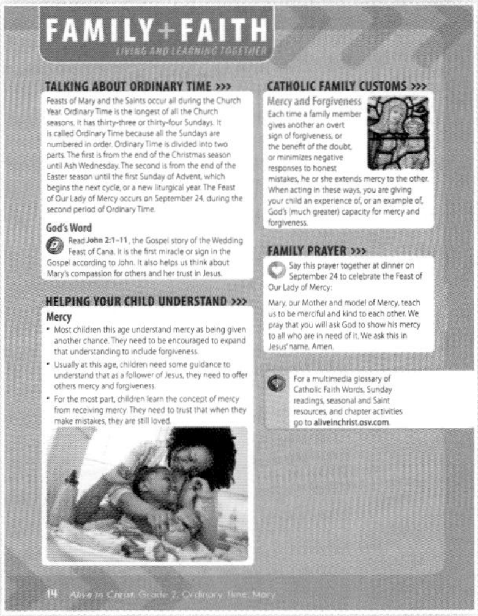

FAMILY+FAITH
LIVING AND LEARNING TOGETHER

TALKING ABOUT ORDINARY TIME >>>

Feasts of Mary and the Saints occur all during the Church Year. Ordinary Time is the longest of all the Church seasons. It has thirty-three or thirty-four Sundays. It is called Ordinary Time because all the Sundays are numbered in order. Ordinary Time is divided into two parts. The first is from the end of the Christmas season until Ash Wednesday. The second is from the end of the Easter season until the first Sunday of Advent, which begins the next cycle, or a new liturgical year. The Feast of Our Lady of Mercy occurs on September 24, during the second period of Ordinary Time.

God's Word

Read **John 2:1–11**, the Gospel story of the Wedding Feast of Cana. It is the first miracle or sign in the Gospel according to John. It also helps us think about Mary's compassion for others and her trust in Jesus.

HELPING YOUR CHILD UNDERSTAND >>>

Mercy

- Most children this age understand mercy as being given another chance. They need to be encouraged to expand that understanding to include forgiveness.
- Usually at this age, children need some guidance to understand that as a follower of Jesus, they need to offer others mercy and forgiveness.
- For the most part, children learn the concept of mercy from receiving mercy. They need to trust that when they make mistakes, they are still loved.

CATHOLIC FAMILY CUSTOMS >>>

Mercy and Forgiveness

Each time a family member gives another an overt sign of forgiveness, or the benefit of the doubt, or minimizes negative responses to honest mistakes, he or she extends mercy to the other. When acting in these ways, you are giving your child an experience of, or an example of, God's (much greater) capacity for mercy and forgiveness.

FAMILY PRAYER >>>

Say this prayer together at dinner on September 24 to celebrate the Feast of Our Lady of Mercy:

Mary, our Mother and model of Mercy, teach us to be merciful and kind to each other. We pray that you will ask God to show his mercy to all who are in need of it. We ask this in Jesus' name. Amen.

For a multimedia glossary of Catholic Faith Words, Sunday readings, seasonal and Saint resources, and chapter activities go to **aliveinchrist.osv.com**.

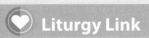

14 Alive in Christ, Grade 2, Ordinary Time: Mary

LESSON OBJECTIVES

- Understand that All Saints Day is a special occasion when the Church honors all women and men in Heaven whose lives were transformed by God's loving grace
- Reflect on baptismal mission

ENVIRONMENT

Statues or pictures of Saints
Prayer table
Battery-powered or electric candle
Bible or Lectionary
Green cloth

- Place the prayer table in a central location.
- Cover the table with the green cloth and arrange the statues, candle, and Bible or Lectionary on top of the table.
- Turn on the candle before beginning the ritual.

MUSIC OPTIONS
Go to **aliveinchrist.osv.com** to sample and download,
"Litany of Saints"
"Sing a Song to the Saints"
"We Gather Around Your Throne"
"When the Saints Go Marching In"

CATHOLIC SOCIAL TEACHING

- **Life and Dignity**, Pages 290–291
- **The Dignity of Work**, Pages 298–299

Catechist Background

We know that all things work for good for those who love God, who are called according to his purpose. Romans 8:28

➜ **Reflect** Do you feel you have a calling according to his purpose?

When a child is asked the question, "What do you want to be when you grow up?" the response is not usually "a Saint." For many of us the word *Saint* has the connotation of someone set apart, someone extraordinary. The Feast of All Saints celebrated on November 1st gives us a different perspective. On All Saints Day, we celebrate the extraordinary Saints who have been canonized, but also those who are enjoying eternal life in Heaven who probably never thought of themselves as Saints.

All Saints Day is an ancient feast day. Originally Christians celebrated the martyrdom of Saints on the anniversary of their martyrdom. When martyrs increased during the persecutions of the late Roman Empire, local dioceses instituted a common feast day in order to ensure that all martyrs, known and unknown, were properly honored.

Soon the meaning of the word *Saint* began to change. It became clear that some Christians lived lives of extraordinary, or heroic, virtue. They were examples of how to live. Others struggled to live by Gospel principles and even with their flaws were examples of Christian discipleship.

All Saints Day reminds us that Saints are not celebrities who distance themselves from us by fame or extraordinary actions. If the New Testament can be a standard, they are the forgiven who know God's grace and act on it—they are the Saints of daily life, in classrooms, emergency rooms, soup kitchens, and retirement communities.

➜ **Reflect** Who will you remember on All Saints Day?

Catechist's Prayer

Lord of All, let me portray the Saints as your blessed ones to these little ones. Help me to give them a vision of what they can be with your help. Amen.

Called to Be Saints

Let Us Pray

Leader: Dear Jesus, you are always with me. You help me to be a child of the light. You guide me to make right choices. Thank you.

"The LORD is my shepherd;
there is nothing I lack." Psalm 23:1

All: Amen.

God's Word

We know that for those who love God, all things work together for good. Those whom God created were made in the image of his Son, in order that he might be the first born within a large family.
Based on Romans 8:28–29

What Do You Wonder?

- In what ways are you like Jesus?
- How does Jesus care for you?

Lectionary Connection

Romans 8:28–29

This reading is proclaimed on the Seventeenth Sunday in Ordinary Time, Year A.

- God has a plan for each of our lives. First and foremost, he plans for us to be his sons and daughters, and to live out faithfully the call we have received. God desires each one of us to be Saints.
- When we love God and serve him faithfully, we can be sure that God can make something good out of all things that happen, even very difficult circumstances. The Saints show us great examples of this in the way they trusted God and persevered even in the face of suffering.

Invite

Let Us Pray

Invite the children to gather in the prayer space and make the Sign of the Cross. Read aloud the leader's prayer and have a volunteer read aloud the Psalm verse. After the prayer, have the children return to their seats.

Explain that we know that God is always with us. He will always help us to become more like Jesus.

Say: Let's listen to what Saint Paul tells the Romans about those who love God.

God's Word

Guide the children through the process of Scripture reflection.

- Invite them to close their eyes, be still, and open their minds and hearts to what God is saying to them in this passage.
- Proclaim the Scripture.
- Maintain several moments of silence.
- *Ask:* What did you hear God say to you today?
- Invite volunteers to share.

What Do You Wonder?

- *Say:* Saint Paul's words remind us that God our Father wants us to be like his Son, Jesus, and no matter what happens, God will take care of us.
- Invite the children to respond to the questions. Ask what else they might wonder about becoming like Jesus.

Discover

Remembering Our Saints

Invite several volunteers to read aloud the paragraphs.

- *Ask:* Who do we honor on the Feast of All Saints? All people in Heaven

☆ Have the children underline the mission that the baptized members of the Church share.

- Next, have them circle what it means.
- Ask volunteers to share what they underlined and circled.

Point out the photo on the student page. Ask the children to share what they think is happening here.

Remembering Our Saints

The Feast of All Saints, on November 1, honors all people who are in Heaven. We do not know the names of all those who are in Heaven. But the Church sets aside this day to celebrate everyone enjoying God's presence forever.

1. Underline the mission that the baptized members of the Church share.
2. Circle what it means.

We know that Baptism makes a person a member of the Church. Everyone who is baptized shares a mission to be children of the light.

This means you love God above all things and that you share his love with everyone. It also means you share the Good News of Jesus.

God calls you to do your mission for your whole life. When someone who has lived like a child of the light dies in God's grace, that person joins God in Heaven forever. We are happy for all those in Heaven. We call them Saints.

We don't know the names of all of the Saints. Many of them are our relatives who lived before us. The Church honors these Saints on All Saints' Day. On that day, we remember that we want to be like them. The Saints care about us. They will pray with us and for us if we ask them to.

Catholic Social Teaching

Lesson Connections

To integrate Catholic Social Teaching into your lesson, choose one of the following features: Life and Dignity, pages 290–291; or The Dignity of Work, pages 298–299.

- To expand the lesson, complete page 16, then move to the Catholic Social Teaching feature.
- Return to the prayer on page 17.

Let Us Pray

Giving Thanks

Gather and begin with the Sign of the Cross.

Leader: Let us pray.
Lord God, you bless us with the gift of life.

All: We give you thanks.

Leader: You gave us all the gifts of creation.

All: We give you thanks.

Leader: You made us your children, your holy People.

All: We give you thanks.

Leader: You invite us to love you by loving others.

All: We give you thanks.

Leader: You have given us your Spirit.

All: We give you thanks.

Leader: Dear God,
You have given us everything.
We bless your name.
We thank you.

All: Sing "Litany of Saints"
Pray for us. Pray with us.
Help us to share God's love.

Live

Let Us Pray

Giving Thanks

Set up images of Saints in the prayer space. Prepare the environment with the candle and other items.

Ask one of the children to be the leader. Allow him or her time to practice.

Have the children rehearse "Litany of Saints," downloaded from **aliveinchrist.osv.com**.

Invite the children to gather in the prayer space.

Follow the order of prayer on the student page.

- Before the closing prayer, allow a few volunteers to add their own brief prayers of thanks.
- Prompt the group response.

Conclude the celebration by singing with the children "Litany of Saints."

Liturgy Link

Liturgical Colors

Green is used during Ordinary Time because it is symbolic of life and growth.

- Ordinary Time occurs during the Earth's growing seasons, when green is the prevalent color in nature.
- During Ordinary Time, we, too, grow into the hope of our calling as Christians.

Distribute this page to the children or parents/adult family members.

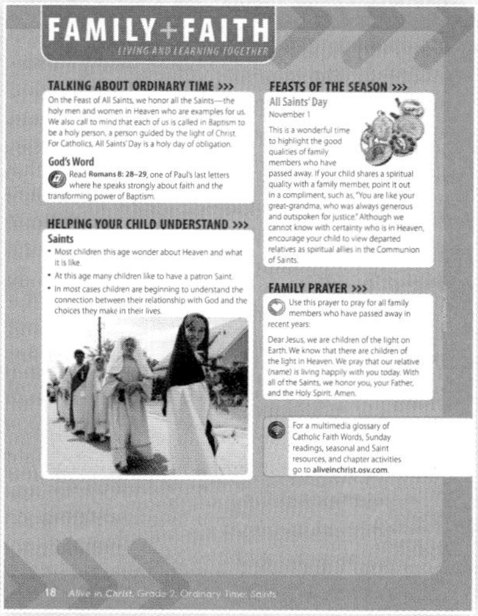

FAMILY+FAITH
LIVING AND LEARNING TOGETHER

TALKING ABOUT ORDINARY TIME >>>
On the Feast of All Saints, we honor all the Saints—the holy men and women in Heaven who are examples for us. We also call to mind that each of us is called in Baptism to be a holy person, a person guided by the light of Christ. For Catholics, All Saints' Day is a holy day of obligation.

God's Word
Read **Romans 8: 28–29**, one of Paul's last letters where he speaks strongly about faith and the transforming power of Baptism.

HELPING YOUR CHILD UNDERSTAND >>>
Saints
- Most children this age wonder about Heaven and what it is like.
- At this age many children like to have a patron Saint.
- In most cases children are beginning to understand the connection between their relationship with God and the choices they make in their lives.

FEASTS OF THE SEASON >>>
All Saints' Day
November 1
This is a wonderful time to highlight the good qualities of family members who have passed away. If your child shares a spiritual quality with a family member, point it out in a compliment, such as, "You are like your great-grandma, who was always generous and outspoken for justice." Although we cannot know with certainty who is in Heaven, encourage your child to view departed relatives as spiritual allies in the Communion of Saints.

FAMILY PRAYER >>>
Use this prayer to pray for all family members who have passed away in recent years:
Dear Jesus, we are children of the light on Earth. We know that there are children of the light in Heaven. We pray that our relative (name) is living happily with you today. With all of the Saints, we honor you, your Father, and the Holy Spirit. Amen.

For a multimedia glossary of Catholic Faith Words, Sunday readings, seasonal and Saint resources, and chapter activities go to **aliveinchrist.osv.com**.

18 Alive in Christ, Grade 2, Ordinary Time: Saints

LESSON OBJECTIVES

- Recognize that Advent is a time of waiting and preparing our hearts
- Discover ways to prepare for Christ's coming

ENVIRONMENT

Prayer table
Purple cloth
Advent wreath
Bible

- Battery-powered candles in colored sleeves
- Cover the prayer table with the purple cloth.
- Place the Advent wreath in the center of the prayer table.

MUSIC OPTIONS

Go to **aliveinchrist.osv.com** to sample and download,
"Candles of Advent"
"God of Mercy"
"Kyrie"
"Prepare the Way"
"Stay Awake"

CATHOLIC SOCIAL TEACHING

- **Call to Community**, Pages 292–293
- **Rights and Responsibilities**, Pages 294–295

Catechist Background

John [the] Baptist appeared in the desert proclaiming a baptism of repentance for the forgiveness of sins. … this is what he proclaimed: "One mightier than I is coming after me. … I have baptized you with water; he will baptize you with the holy Spirit." **Mark 1:4, 7–8**

➜ **Reflect** What does being baptized by the Holy Spirit mean to you?

For centuries the People of God waited for the coming of a savior. They wondered what this savior would bring and how they might be changed by his coming. In the years leading up to the birth of Christ, God prepared his People through the ministry of the prophets who heralded his coming and awakened expectation in their hearts.

Each year, the Church prepares to celebrate Christ's coming during Advent—the four weeks before Christmas. The Advent season also marks the beginning of the liturgical year. Through Scripture, music, and ritual actions, the worshipping assembly renews the ancient expectations and promises of the Messiah. The color purple, which symbolizes that the hearts of the gathered community are in preparation, adorns the sanctuary and is the color of the vestments worn by the priest. By sharing in Advent celebrations, the faithful renew their sense of desire to see and know Christ when he comes again.

The celebration of Advent takes place both communally and in people's hearts. It is a time for reflection and preparation, not only remembering Christ's first coming, but preparing for his Second Coming at the end of time.

➜ **Reflect** How will you prepare your heart for Christ's coming this Advent?

Catechist's Prayer

Faithful God, Advent arrives as the sun rises, and we know you will keep your promises. Let me instill anticipation in the children paired with blessed assurance that you are faithful. Amen.

Change Our Hearts

Let Us Pray

Leader: Lord, God, send your Holy Spirit
to help us see your path more clearly.
"...prepare the way of the LORD!" Isaiah 40:3
Through Christ, our Lord.

All: Amen.

God's Word

The Jewish people were waiting for the Messiah to come. Many had turned away from God. John the Baptist said to them, "Turn back to God. Be sorry for your sins. Change your hearts." Based on Mark 1:1–8

What Do You Wonder?

- What does it means to change your heart?
- What words or actions tell someone that you are sorry?

Lectionary Connection

Mark 1:1–8

This Gospel reading is proclaimed on the Second Sunday of Advent, Year B.

- In the beginning of this passage, Mark points out the strength of the response to John's call for the people to acknowledge their sin and turn back to God.
- John challenged those who heard him to receive baptism by water as a symbolic submission to God, but he also pointed to the baptism of the Spirit that was to come through the Messiah.

Invite

Let Us Pray

Invite the children to gather in the prayer space and make the Sign of the Cross. Pray the first part of the leader prayer, and have a volunteer pray aloud the verse from Isaiah.

Have the children move out of the prayer space and back to their seats.

Say: In today's reading, we will hear John the Baptist ask the people to change their hearts.

God's Word

Guide the children through the process of Scripture reflection.

- Invite them to close their eyes, be still, and open their minds and hearts to what God is saying to them in this passage.
- Proclaim the Scripture.
- Maintain several moments of silence.
- *Ask:* What did you hear God say to you today?
- Invite volunteers to share.

What Do You Wonder?

Say: God wants us to be happy. He wants our hearts to be joyful. He wants us to know how wonderful he is and how great our lives can be if we follow him.

Invite the children to respond to the questions. Ask what else they might wonder about changing their hearts.

Discover

Preparing

Invite a volunteer to read the facts about Advent from the purple box in the side column.

- Ask the children to share anything else they know about Advent.

Invite a volunteer to read aloud the three paragraphs on the page.

☆ Instruct the children to use a purple marker or crayon to underline the copy in the text that states what we prepare for during Advent.

Without reading the caption, ask the children to describe what they see in the photograph on the page.

- After a few responses, invite a volunteer to read aloud the caption.
- Share with the group the information on Las Posadas from the Catechist Background box below.

Music Option: Play or sing with the children "God of Mercy," "Kyrie," or "Prepare the Way," downloaded from **aliveinchrist.osv.com**.

Discover

Preparing

Advent

- The season of four weeks before Christmas.
- During this time, we prepares to celebrate the coming of Jesus.

Advent is the first season of the Church year. During the four weeks of Advent, the whole Church prepares to celebrate Jesus' coming again in glory.

Purple is the Advent color. The priest wears purple colors. The church has purple decorations.

The color purple reminds you to change your heart for Jesus' Second Coming. It reminds you to ask for God's forgiveness and mercy.

☆ **Using a purple marker or crayon, underline what we prepare for during Advent.**

Las Posadas is a celebration in Mexico that honors Mary and Joseph's journey to Bethlehem before Jesus' birth.

Catechist Background

Cultural Connection: Las Posadas

This is a Mexican Advent custom.

- From December 16–24, families dressed as the Nativity figures go from house to house, looking for an "inn," or *posada*.
- The parade stops at several houses and is turned away. At the last stop, the doors are flung open and all are invited to enter. Then the party begins.

Closer to God

Sometimes you may forget that God is near. You may make choices that draw you away from God. Advent is a good time to remember God's love for you. It is a time to draw closer to him.

➻ **What is one way you would like to grow closer to Jesus during Advent?**

Activity

Fill the Manger Inside the manger, write one way you will show your love for others during Advent. Decorate the manger to make a soft bed for Baby Jesus.

Closer to God

Have a volunteer read aloud the paragraph.

Read aloud the question at the end of the text.

- Invite the children to respond.
- Write their responses on the board or on chart paper.
- Remind them that they do not have to share this information. The question could just be used for personal reflection.

Activity

Ask a volunteer to read aloud the directions.

- Provide the children with crayons, colored pencils, or markers to decorate the manger.

Music Option: While the children work on the activity, play "Stay Awake," downloaded from **aliveinchrist.osv.com**.

- Encourage volunteers to share what they wrote inside the manger.

Optional Activity

Filling the Manger *Bodily/Kinesthetic*

Provide a manger or cradle to which the children may add straw.

- Set the manger or cradle in an accessible place.
- Cut long strips of paper and place them next to the cradle with a pencil or pen.
- Throughout Advent encourage the children to write on the strips of paper about ways they have shown love. Have them place their papers in the manger.
- Be sure to add your own strips of paper as well.

Prayer for God's Mercy

Let Us Pray

Tell the children that this is a prayer of petition, an asking prayer. In this prayer, we ask for God's mercy and forgiveness.

Prepare

Ask the children when they have heard the words "Lord, have mercy."

- Help the children identify the words as part of the Mass.

Prepare the environment with the Bible and other items.

You will be the leader.

Rehearse with the children "Candles of Advent," downloaded from **aliveinchrist.osv.com**.

Invite the children to gather in the prayer space around the Advent wreath and Bible.

Pray

Follow the order of prayer on the student pages.

Prayer for God's Mercy

This is a prayer of petition. A prayer of petition is an asking prayer. In this prayer we ask for God's mercy and forgiveness.

Let Us Pray

Gather and begin with the Sign of the Cross.

Leader: Our help is in the name of the Lord.

All: Who made Heaven and Earth.

Leader: Lord, you came to gather all peoples in peace. Lord, have mercy.

All: Lord, have mercy.

Leader: Lord, you came to show us how to be holy. Christ, have mercy.

All: Christ, have mercy.

Leader: Lord, you will come again in glory to save your people. Lord, have mercy.

All: Lord, have mercy.

Leader: May God have mercy on us, forgive us our sins, and bring us to everlasting life.

All: Amen.

Catholic Social Teaching

Lesson Connections

To integrate Catholic Social Teaching into your lesson, choose one of the following features: Call to Community, pages 292–293; or Rights and Responsibilities, pages 294–295.

- To expand the lesson, complete pages 20–21, then move to the Catholic Social Teaching feature.
- Return to the prayer on pages 22–23.

Listen to God's Word

Leader: A reading from the holy Gospel according to Mark.

Read Mark 1:14–15.

The Gospel of the Lord.

All: Praise to you, Lord Jesus Christ.

Pray Around the Advent Wreath

Sit in silence before the Advent wreath. Think of a way you will change your heart during Advent.

Leader: Glory be to the Father, and to the Son, and to the Holy Spirit:

All: as it was in the beginning, is now, and ever shall be, world without end. Amen.

Go Forth!

Leader: Let us go forth to love and serve the Lord by showing kindness to one another.

All: Thanks be to God.

Sing "Candles of Advent"

Listen to God's Word

Have the children stand.

- Proclaim the Gospel.
- Prompt the children to respond at the conclusion of the reading.
- Pause for a few moments of silence.

Pray Around the Advent Wreath

Invite the children to sit around the Advent wreath.

- Light the appropriate number of candles.
- Reflect, with the children, on how you will change your heart.
- Lead the children in the Glory Be.

Go Forth!

Conclude the celebration by having the children sing "Candles of Advent" as they process around the room.

Liturgy Link

The Advent Wreath

Using an Advent wreath as part of our spiritual preparation for Christmas is a long-standing Catholic tradition.

- The circle of the wreath symbolizes the eternity of God and the everlasting life found in Christ. The four candles represent the four weeks of Advent.
- The custom of lighting a candle each week enables Christians to mark the anticipation and joy of the coming of Christ.

Distribute this page to the children or parents/adult family members.

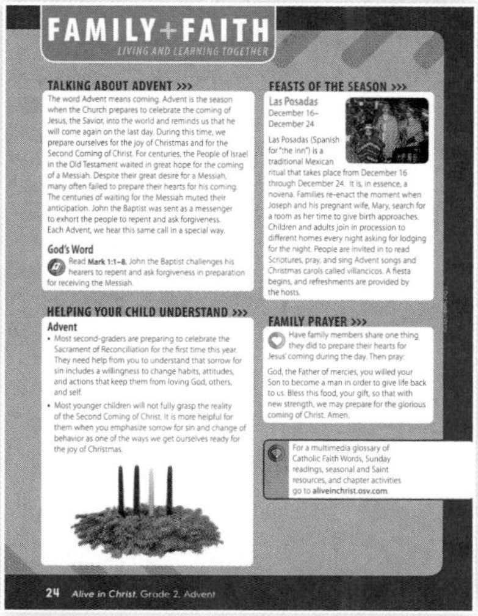

FAMILY + FAITH
LIVING AND LEARNING TOGETHER

TALKING ABOUT ADVENT >>>

The word Advent means coming. Advent is the season when the Church prepares to celebrate the coming of Jesus, the Savior, into the world and reminds us that he will come again on the last day. During this time, we prepare ourselves for the joy of Christmas and for the Second Coming of Christ. For centuries, the People of Israel in the Old Testament waited in great hope for the coming of a Messiah. Despite their great desire for a Messiah, many often failed to prepare their hearts for his coming. The centuries of waiting for the Messiah muted their anticipation. John the Baptist was sent as a messenger to exhort the people to repent and ask forgiveness. Each Advent, we hear this same call in a special way.

God's Word

Read **Mark 1:1–8.** John the Baptist challenges his hearers to repent and ask forgiveness in preparation for receiving the Messiah.

FEASTS OF THE SEASON >>>

Las Posadas
December 16–December 24

Las Posadas (Spanish for "the inn") is a traditional Mexican ritual that takes place from December 16 through December 24. It is, in essence, a novena. Families re-enact the moment when Joseph and his pregnant wife, Mary, search for a room as her time to give birth approaches. Children and adults join in procession to different homes every night asking for lodging for the night. People are invited in to read Scriptures, pray, and sing Advent songs and Christmas carols called villancicos. A fiesta begins, and refreshments are provided by the hosts.

HELPING YOUR CHILD UNDERSTAND >>>

Advent

- Most second-graders are preparing to celebrate the Sacrament of Reconciliation for the first time this year. They need help from you to understand that sorrow for sin includes a willingness to change habits, attitudes, and actions that keep them from loving God, others, and self.
- Most younger children will not fully grasp the reality of the Second Coming of Christ. It is more helpful for them when you emphasize sorrow for sin and change of behavior as one of the ways we get ourselves ready for the joy of Christmas.

FAMILY PRAYER >>>

Have family members share one thing they did to prepare their hearts for Jesus' coming during the day. Then pray:

God, the Father of mercies, you willed your Son to become a man in order to give life back to us. Bless this food, your gift, so that with new strength, we may prepare for the glorious coming of Christ. Amen.

For a multimedia glossary of Catholic Faith Words, Sunday readings, seasonal and Saint resources, and chapter activities go to **aliveinchrist.osv.com**.

24 *Alive in Christ*, Grade 2, Advent

Christmas: Glory to God

LESSON OBJECTIVES

- Describe Christmas as a season to celebrate God's Glory
- Recognize that we are called to bring the Good News to others

ENVIRONMENT

Prayer table
White cloth
Battery-powered or electric candle
Manger scene
Bible or Lectionary

- Create a worship space that is conducive to kneeling.
- Place the cloth on the table.
- Arrange the manger scene, candle, and Bible or Lectionary on top of the table.

MUSIC OPTIONS

Go to **aliveinchrist.osv.com** to sample and download,
"Away in a Manger"
"Gifts"

CATHOLIC SOCIAL TEACHING

- **Life and Dignity**, Pages 290–291
- **Care for Creation**, Pages 302–303

Catechist Background

Blessed be the God and Father of our Lord Jesus Christ, … he destined us for adoption to himself through Jesus Christ, … for the praise of the glory of his grace that he granted us in the beloved. Ephesians 1:3, 5, 6

→ **Reflect** Do you think your life is in accord with the favor of his will?

The waiting is finally over. Born in a stable to a poor family, Jesus, the Messiah, comes to us—God incarnate. We rejoice and sing Glory to God in the Highest! The Church celebrates the season of Christmas beginning with the celebration of Christ's birth on December 25th and ending on the Feast of the Baptism of the Lord in January.

The Christmas liturgy sings the glory of the night when the angels appeared to the shepherds in the region of Bethlehem and proclaimed the Good News that the Messiah was born. The Scripture and hymns of the liturgy reflect the joy the shepherds felt when they returned from seeing Jesus—praising God's holy name. The gathered assembly meets Christ in the Word of God and, filled with joy, they celebrate the arrival of the Messiah. All go forth from the Christmas liturgies to spread the Good News just as the shepherds did.

The liturgy of the season goes on to celebrate the Feast of the Epiphany—the celebration that Jesus came to reveal himself to all people—the Feast of the Holy Family, and the Feast of the Baptism of the Lord.

The Son of God became man to win our salvation. After his Death and Resurrection, he sent the Holy Spirit and is still with us in his Church. The Christmas season continues to celebrate the light of Christ found in the People of God.

→ **Reflect** How can you share this Good News with those around you?

Catechist's Prayer

Almighty God, let my life be a living example to these children on how to share the Good News through my words and actions. Amen.

Glory to God

Let Us Pray

Leader: Dear God, we are so happy you sent us your Son, Jesus. Thank you. We want to be as loving and kind as he was. We want to give you glory.

"May God be gracious to us and bless us;
may his face shine upon us." Psalm 67:2

All: Amen.

God's Word

Blessed be the God and Father of our Lord Jesus Christ, who has blessed you in Christ with every blessing. God chose you before the world was created. He wants you to be holy and loving. He adopted you as his children through Jesus Christ. God wants you to give him glory. Based on Ephesians 1:3–6

What Do You Wonder?

- What kind of blessings does God give you?
- How do children give glory to God?

Lectionary Connection

Ephesians 1:3–6

This reading is proclaimed on the Second Sunday after Christmas, in all three cycles of the Church year.

- God has given us so many different blessings. We glorify God for the many great things he has done.
- God's most important gift to us is his Son, Jesus, through whom he gave us the opportunity to become his children as well.

Invite

Let Us Pray

Invite the children to gather in the prayer space and make the Sign of the Cross. Pray the complete leader's prayer, including the Psalm verse.

Have the children move out of the prayer space and back to their seats.

Say: God's greatest gift to us was to send his Son to live among us. Jesus became one of us so we would know how to give God glory. As Saint Paul says in today's reading, God has given us many blessings.

God's Word

Guide the children through the process of Scripture reflection.

- Invite them to close their eyes, be still, and open their minds and hearts to what God is saying to them in this passage.
- Proclaim the Scripture.
- Maintain several moments of silence.
- *Ask:* What did you hear God say to you today?
- Invite volunteers to share.

What Do You Wonder?

Say: In this reading, Saint Paul says that because Jesus was born, lived, died, and rose, we are all joined to him in Baptism. In Baptism, God our Father adopts us as his children. What a wonderful blessing.

Invite the children to respond to the questions. Ask what else they might wonder about giving glory to God.

Season of Christmas

Ask the children to share some of the things they do to celebrate Christmas.

- Write their responses on the board or on chart paper.
- Go over some of their traditions and add religious practices as needed to the list.
- Discuss their feelings and excitement about Christmas.

Invite a volunteer to read aloud the paragraph.

Glory to God

Read aloud the paragraph.

☆ Instruct the children to underline the best gift God has given to the world.

- Allow enough time for the children to reread or scan the text and underline the sentence.
- Verify that everyone understands that Jesus is the best gift.

Invite the children to describe what they see in the illustration at the bottom of the page.

Music Option: Have the children sing "Gifts," downloaded from **aliveinchrist.osv.com**.

Season of Christmas

Christmas is a joyful season. It lasts from the Feast of Christmas on December 25 until the Feast of the Baptism of Jesus. During this season, the priest wears white or gold vestments. You can see the Christmas Nativity scene in church for the whole season. You'll also hear about all the things that happened to Jesus as a young child.

☆ Underline the best gift God has given to the world.

Glory to God

The Church celebrates the birth of Jesus at Christmas. We remember that Jesus is the best gift God gave to the world. God sent an angel to tell some men who watch sheep (shepherds) that Jesus the Savior was born. The angel told them to go to a stable to find him. Then the angels sang a song of praise to God.

Catechist Background

Kneeling

This posture is an expression of submission, adoration, and humility.

- Kneeling can be an expression of devotional piety. It is a posture often used in private prayer.
- In the prayer celebration for this lesson, when the children kneel before the Nativity scene, it is an expression of our adoration and reverence of the Christ Child.

Share the Good News

The angel shared the Good News about Jesus with the shepherds. At Mass, we sing what the angels sang that first Christmas:

> "Glory to God in the highest,
> and on earth peace to people
> of good will." Based on Luke 2:8–14

Like us, the shepherds in the fields were people of faith. They believed what the angel told them about Jesus. After they saw the Baby Jesus, they shared the Good News with others.

➔ **What other Good News about Jesus do you know? Who can you tell?**

Activity

Welcome Baby Jesus
Draw how your family welcomes Jesus at Christmas.

Share the Good News

Read aloud the first paragraph and the Scripture from Luke.

- Have a volunteer read aloud the last paragraph.
- Talk about what the shepherds saw and what they did after that night.

Read aloud the questions.

- Invite the children to respond.
- Write their responses on the board or on chart paper.

Activity

Ask a volunteer to read aloud the directions.

- Provide art materials and allow enough time for the children to draw.
- Ask volunteers to share how their family welcomes Jesus at Christmas.

Optional Activity

Draw and Share *Visual/Spatial*

Provide each child with a piece of paper, a pencil, and some crayons.

- Read aloud Luke 2:8–14. Ask the children to draw a picture of the story.
- Prompt them by asking them to think about what the shepherds saw.
- Encourage the children to retell the story through their artwork.
- Hang the children's artwork in the prayer space.

Celebrate Christmas

Let Us Pray

Explain that this prayer is a celebration of the Word and an act of praise and thanksgiving.

Prepare

Set up a Nativity scene in the center of the prayer table, and turn on the battery-powered or electric candle.

Prepare the environment with the Bible and other items.

You will be the leader.

Rehearse with the children "Away in a Manger," downloaded from **aliveinchrist.osv.com**.

Invite the children to gather in the prayer space around the prayer table.

Pray

Follow the order of prayer on the student pages.

Leader's prayer: God, our Father, thank you for the gift of your Son and our brother Jesus. Help us spread the Good News of Christmas with joy.

Listen to God's Word

Have the children stand while you proclaim Luke 2:8–14.

- Invite the children to kneel before the Nativity scene.

Celebrate Christmas

This prayer is a celebration of the Word and an act of praise and thanksgiving. It is a moment of prayer with the Church, using the Scriptures.

Let Us Pray

Gather and begin with the Sign of the Cross.

Leader: Blessed be the name of the Lord.

All: Now and forever.

Leader: Let us pray.

Bow your heads as the leader prays.

All: Amen.

Listen to God's Word

Leader: A reading from the holy Gospel according to Luke.

Read Luke 2:8–14.

The Gospel of the Lord

All: Praise to you, Lord Jesus Christ.

Come forward and pray before the Nativity scene.

Leader: God, our Father, we thank you for the gift of Jesus, your Son.

All: We praise you, we bless you,we thank you.

Catholic Social Teaching

Lesson Connections

To integrate Catholic Social Teaching into your lesson, choose one of the following features: Life and Dignity, pages 290–291; or Care for Creation, pages 302–303.

- To expand the lesson, complete pages 27–28, then move to the Catholic Social Teaching feature.
- Return to the prayer on pages 28–29.

Leader: We thank you for all the gifts of creation.

All: We praise you, we bless you,we thank you.

Leader: We ask your blessing on all your people.

All: We praise you, we bless you,we thank you.

Go Forth!

Leader: Go forth to sing of God's glory and to share his peace with others.

All: Thanks be to God.

Sing "Away in a Manger"

Away in a manger, no crib for a bed,
the little Lord Jesus laid down his sweet head.
The stars in the sky looked down where he lay,
the little Lord Jesus, asleep on the hay.

Be near me, Lord Jesus, I ask thee to stay
close by me forever, and love me I pray.
Bless all the dear children in thy tender care,
and take us to Heaven to live with thee there.

Away in a manger, no crib for a bed,
the little Lord Jesus, asleep on the hay.

Verse 1, Little Children's Book for Schools and Families, ca. 1885; verse 3, Gabriel's Vineyard Songs, 1892, alt. Music: William James Kirkpatrick, alt.

29

- Tell the children to respond "We praise you, we bless you, we thank you" after each of your short prayers.

Go Forth!

Have the children stand.

- Pray the concluding prayer.

Sing with the group "Away in a Manger."

- Have the children return to their seats.

Liturgy Link

Symbols

The liturgical color for the season of Christmas is white—the color symbolizing new life, light, and joy.

- The empty manger in the Nativity scene, now filled, becomes a symbol of joy and hope.
- It is customary to make a visit to the Nativity scene in the church during the Christmas season.

To share more on the colors of the seasons with the children, have them turn to page 315 in the Our Catholic Tradition section of the Student Book.

Distribute this page to the children or parents/adult family members.

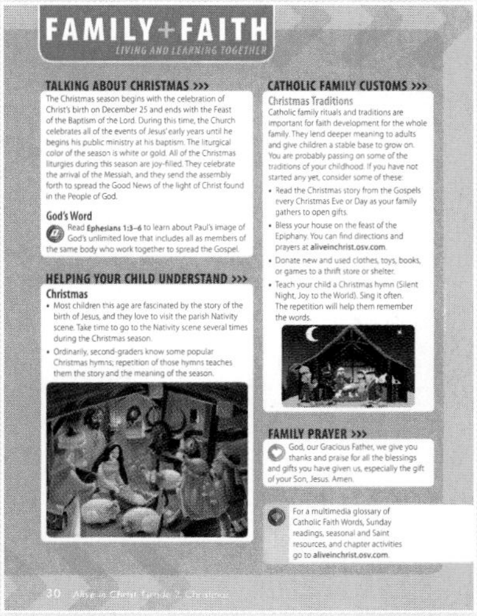

FAMILY+FAITH
LIVING AND LEARNING TOGETHER

TALKING ABOUT CHRISTMAS >>>

The Christmas season begins with the celebration of Christ's birth on December 25 and ends with the Feast of the Baptism of the Lord. During this time, the Church celebrates all of the events of Jesus' early years until he begins his public ministry at his baptism. The liturgical color of the season is white or gold. All of the Christmas liturgies during this season are joy-filled. They celebrate the arrival of the Messiah, and they send the assembly forth to spread the Good News of the light of Christ found in the People of God.

God's Word

Read **Ephesians 1:3–6** to learn about Paul's image of God's unlimited love that includes all as members of the same body who work together to spread the Gospel.

HELPING YOUR CHILD UNDERSTAND >>>

Christmas

- Most children this age are fascinated by the story of the birth of Jesus, and they love to visit the parish Nativity scene. Take time to go to the Nativity scene several times during the Christmas season.
- Ordinarily, second-graders know some popular Christmas hymns; repetition of those hymns teaches them the story and the meaning of the season.

CATHOLIC FAMILY CUSTOMS >>>

Christmas Traditions

Catholic family rituals and traditions are important for faith development for the whole family. They lend deeper meaning to adults and give children a stable base to grow on. You are probably passing on some of the traditions of your childhood. If you have not started any yet, consider some of these:

- Read the Christmas story from the Gospels every Christmas Eve or Day as your family gathers to open gifts.
- Bless your house on the feast of the Epiphany. You can find directions and prayers at **aliveinchrist.osv.com**.
- Donate new and used clothes, toys, books, or games to a thrift store or shelter.
- Teach your child a Christmas hymn (Silent Night, Joy to the World). Sing it often. The repetition will help them remember the words.

FAMILY PRAYER >>>

God, our Gracious Father, we give you thanks and praise for all the blessings and gifts you have given us, especially the gift of your Son, Jesus. Amen.

For a multimedia glossary of Catholic Faith Words, Sunday readings, seasonal and Saint resources, and chapter activities go to **aliveinchrist.osv.com**.

Lent: Teach Me Your Ways

LESSON OBJECTIVES

- Explain that Lent is a time to learn from Jesus
- Discuss ways of following Jesus' path of love

ENVIRONMENT

Prayer table
Purple cloth
Willow branch or broken pots
Cross
Bible or Lectionary

- Place the prayer table at the center of your prayer space.
- Drape the purple cloth on the table and decorate it with the branches, broken pots, and the cross.

MUSIC OPTIONS
Go to **aliveinchrist.osv.com** to sample and download,
"These Ashes"
"God of Mercy"
"Lord, Teach Me Your Ways"
"Kyrie"

CATHOLIC SOCIAL TEACHING

- **Option for the Poor**, Pages 296–297
- **Human Solidarity**, Page 300–301

Catechist Background

For we are his handiwork, created in Christ Jesus for the good works that God has prepared in advance, that we should live in them. Ephesians 2:10

➔ **Reflect** Do you treat your body as God's precious handiwork?

Overscheduling, responsibilities, and financial needs are just a few things that can get in the way of a relationship with God—if one allows them. Lent, which means springtime, is a forty-day journey that includes fasting, prayer, and penance. Its destination is conversion, a change of heart. During this period, we are called to focus on our relationship with God—to deepen it and also to evaluate it. During Lent, the Church focuses on turning away from sin and back toward Christ and his will.

The Church celebrates the forty days of Lent beginning with Ash Wednesday. The spirit of repentance is reflected in the color purple used for the liturgical vestments and in the environment created for liturgy. The assembly listens to the Word and is reminded of Christ's works and unconditional love. The Alleluia is neither said nor sung during the Lenten season. These practices remind the community of their constant need for God and their hunger for the joy of the Risen Christ.

Lent is also a time of intense preparation for those who will receive the Sacraments of Initiation at the Easter Vigil and for the baptized to reflect on their baptismal promises, which they will renew at the Easter Vigil or on Easter morning.

➔ **Reflect** What Lenten practices are most helpful to you?

Catechist's Prayer

God of Mercy, let the children in my care see my earnest change of heart to turn back to you, be absorbed in your teachings, and be unceasingly in prayer. Amen.

Teach Me Your Ways

Let Us Pray

Leader: Lord, God, send your Holy Spirit
to guide our actions and make them loving.

"Let the words of my mouth be acceptable,
the thoughts of my heart before you."
Psalm 19:15a

Through Christ, our Lord.

All: Amen.

God's Word

We are the work of God's hands, created in Jesus Christ. God made us to lead a life of good works.
Based on Ephesians 2:10

What Do You Wonder?

- What does God's handiwork look like?
- What kinds of good works can children do?

Lectionary Connection

Ephesians 2:10

This reading is proclaimed on the Fourth Sunday of Lent, Year B.

- This reading reminds us that God created us for a special purpose.
- Lent is a time to refocus on the truths that we are created by God and to renew our commitment to the "good works" he has planned for us.

Invite

Let Us Pray

Invite the children to gather in the prayer space and make the Sign of the Cross. Have one volunteer read aloud the leader prayer and another read the Psalm verse.

Have the children move out of the prayer space and back to their seats.

Explain that we ask God to send the Holy Spirit to help us think good thoughts and to do right actions.

Say: We always want to remember that God made us to show his goodness. In our reading today Saint Paul tells the Ephesians how special God's children are.

God's Word

Guide the children through the process of Scripture reflection.

- Invite them to close their eyes, be still, and open their minds and hearts to what God is saying to them in this passage.
- Proclaim the Scripture.
- Maintain several moments of silence.
- *Ask:* What did you hear God say to you today?
- Invite volunteers to share.

What Do You Wonder?

Say: In this reading, we heard that we are God's special creations, God's handiwork.

Invite the children to respond to the questions. Ask what else they might wonder about being God's creation.

Discover

Love and Sacrifice

Say: During Lent, the Church sets aside time for us to think about how we can grow in our relationship with God. We ask God to help us see what we need to change to be more like him.

Invite a volunteer to read the facts about Lent from the purple box in the side column.

Invite three volunteers to each read aloud one of the paragraphs.

☆ Have the children underline the things that the Church does during Lent.

- Allow time for them to reread or scan the text and underline the answers.
- Invite volunteers to share what they underlined.

Point out the photo at the top of the page.

- Ask the children to share what they believe is happening in the picture.

Discover

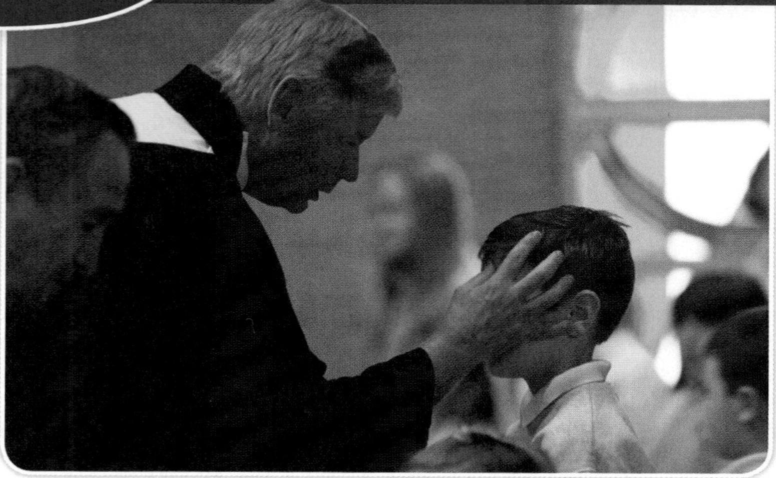

Love and Sacrifice

Lent is a season to change our hearts. It begins on Ash Wednesday, and it lasts forty days. The priest wears purple during Lent, and the church is decorated in purple.

The forty days of Lent are a good time to think about God's loving kindness to all people. When the people had turned from God, he sent them a Savior. No matter how many times we sin, God still invites us back into friendship with him.

Each day during Lent, the whole Church reads and listens to stories of God's love. We hear the stories of the works of Jesus. We hear about his sacrifice to save us from our sins. As we listen, we try to think of ways that we can be more loving to others.

Lent
- The season of forty days during which the Church gets ready for Easter.
- A time of prayer, good actions, and sorrow for sin.
- Lent begins with Ash Wednesday.

☆ Underline the things that the Church does during Lent.

Catechist Background

Mardi Gras

The phrase *Mardi Gras* is French for "Fat Tuesday," the day before Ash Wednesday.

- Mardi Gras actually comes from the tradition called *Shrovetide*—a time to confess sins.
- People would wear dark clothing, abstain from meat, and avoid celebrations.
- The days before Ash Wednesday were an opportunity to engage in one last celebration.

Love God and Others

You are learning many stories about Jesus. As you learn these stories, you will find new ways to follow him. Jesus teaches us to remember one very important thing: Love God above all things, and love your neighbor as you love yourself.

➔ **What is one way you could love your neighbor as much as you love yourself?**

Activity

Unscramble the Message Unscramble the words to find one very important thing Jesus teaches us.

OLVE OGD
VELO RUYO
GBEHRONI

L O V E G O D.
L O V E Y O U R
N E I G H B O R

Love God and Others

Read aloud the paragraph.

- Encourage the children to share some of the things they are learning about Jesus. Ask them to name the most important thing Jesus teaches us. Love God above all things, and love your neighbor as you love yourself.
- Have a volunteer read aloud the question.
- Invite the children to respond.
- Write their responses on the board or on chart paper.

Ask: How are the children in the photo showing love for their neighbor?

- Allow the children to describe what they see.

Activity

Ask a volunteer to read aloud the directions.

- You might want to walk around the room and offer assistance to anyone who appears to be struggling with unscrambling the words.
- Ask volunteers to share how they solved the puzzle.

Optional Activity

Friendship Mural *Visual/Spatial*

Prepare the children for the activity by talking about what it means to be Jesus' friend.

- Place a large blank piece of paper on the wall.
- Distribute crayons and markers to the children and invite them to use the paper to write words or draw pictures about friendship with Jesus.
- Keep the mural up throughout the lesson, and encourage the children to add to it.

Celebrate Lent

Let Us Pray

Explain to the children that this prayer includes a signing prayer. A signing prayer is a ritual prayer of action where the Sign of the Cross is traced on your body.

Prepare

Set up the prayer table and turn on the candle.

Prepare the environment with the Bible and other items.

You will be the leader.

Rehearse with the children "These Ashes," downloaded from **aliveinchrist.osv.com**.

Invite the children to gather in the prayer space around the Bible.

Pray

Follow the order of prayer on the student pages.

Listen to God's Word

Proclaim the Gospel.

Celebrate Lent

This prayer includes a signing prayer. A signing prayer is a ritual prayer of action where the Sign of the Cross is traced on your body.

Let Us Pray

Gather and begin with the Sign of the Cross.

Leader: O Lord, open my lips.

All: That my mouth shall praise you.

Leader: Lord Jesus, you have shown us the way to the Father.

All: Lord, have mercy.

Leader: Lord Jesus, you have given us the truth.

All: Christ, have mercy.

Leader: Lord Jesus, you lead us to everlasting life.

All: Lord, have mercy.

Leader: May almighty God have mercy on us, forgive us our sins, and bring us to everlasting life.

All: Amen.

Listen to God's Word

Leader: A reading from the holy Gospel according to John.

Read John 3:16–17.

The Gospel of the Lord.

Catholic Social Teaching

Lesson Connections

To integrate Catholic Social Teaching into your lesson, choose one of the following features: Option for the Poor, pages 296–297; or Human Solidarity, pages 300–301.

- To expand the lesson, complete pages 32–33, then move to the Catholic Social Teaching feature.
- Return to the prayer on pages 34–35.

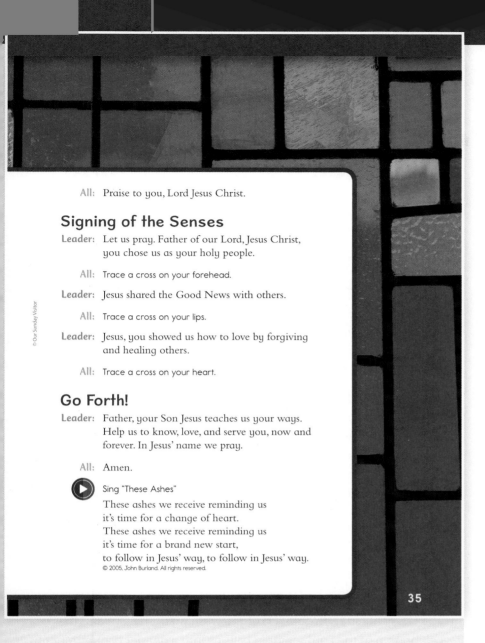

All: Praise to you, Lord Jesus Christ.

Signing of the Senses

Leader: Let us pray. Father of our Lord, Jesus Christ, you chose us as your holy people.

All: Trace a cross on your forehead.

Leader: Jesus shared the Good News with others.

All: Trace a cross on your lips.

Leader: Jesus, you showed us how to love by forgiving and healing others.

All: Trace a cross on your heart.

Go Forth!

Leader: Father, your Son Jesus teaches us your ways. Help us to know, love, and serve you, now and forever. In Jesus' name we pray.

All: Amen.

Sing "These Ashes"

These ashes we receive reminding us
it's time for a change of heart.
These ashes we receive reminding us
it's time for a brand new start,
to follow in Jesus' way, to follow in Jesus' way.

Signing of the Senses

Tell the children to watch you and follow along by tracing the movements after each of your short prayers.

- Lead the children in the prayer.
- Model the actions for the children.

Go Forth!

Pray the final blessing.

Conclude by processing around the room with the children singing "These Ashes."

Liturgy Link

Signing of the Senses

The ritual action for this prayer celebration is similar to the ritual used by the celebrant during the Liturgy of the Word at Mass.

- The signing of the senses is also done during the Rite of Acceptance into the order of catechumenate.
- The cross, whether in ritual or in symbol, is a primary symbol of Lent.

Distribute this page to the children or parents/adult family members.

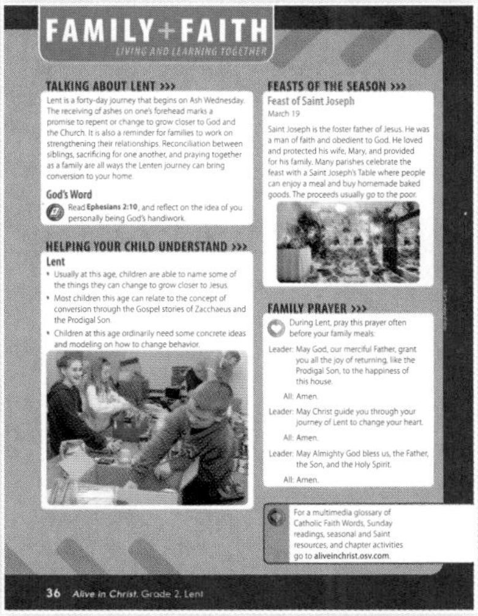
FAMILY + FAITH
LIVING AND LEARNING TOGETHER

TALKING ABOUT LENT >>>

Lent is a forty-day journey that begins on Ash Wednesday. The receiving of ashes on one's forehead marks a promise to repent or change to grow closer to God and the Church. It is also a reminder for families to work on strengthening their relationships. Reconciliation between siblings, sacrificing for one another, and praying together as a family are all ways the Lenten journey can bring conversion to your home.

God's Word

Read **Ephesians 2:10**, and reflect on the idea of you personally being God's handiwork.

HELPING YOUR CHILD UNDERSTAND >>>

Lent

- Usually at this age, children are able to name some of the things they can change to grow closer to Jesus.
- Most children this age can relate to the concept of conversion through the Gospel stories of Zacchaeus and the Prodigal Son.
- Children at this age ordinarily need some concrete ideas and modeling on how to change behavior.

FEASTS OF THE SEASON >>>

Feast of Saint Joseph

March 19

Saint Joseph is the foster father of Jesus. He was a man of faith and obedient to God. He loved and protected his wife, Mary, and provided for his family. Many parishes celebrate the feast with a Saint Joseph's Table where people can enjoy a meal and buy homemade baked goods. The proceeds usually go to the poor.

FAMILY PRAYER >>>

During Lent, pray this prayer often before your family meals.

Leader: May God, our merciful Father, grant you all the joy of returning, like the Prodigal Son, to the happiness of this house.

All: Amen.

Leader: May Christ guide you through your journey of Lent to change your heart.

All: Amen.

Leader: May Almighty God bless us, the Father, the Son, and the Holy Spirit.

All: Amen.

For a multimedia glossary of Catholic Faith Words, Sunday readings, seasonal and Saint resources, and chapter activities go to **aliveinchrist.osv.com**.

36 *Alive in Christ*, Grade 2, Lent

LESSON OBJECTIVES

- Explore how, during Holy Week, we remember Jesus' dying and rising
- Understand the importance of the Cross

ENVIRONMENT

Prayer table
Red cloth
Cross or crucifix
Bible or Lectionary

- Place the prayer table in the center of the room.
- Cover the table with a red cloth and place the cross in the center of the table.

MUSIC OPTIONS

Go to **aliveinchrist.osv.com** to sample and download,
"We Remember (The Three Days)"
"Were You There?"

CATHOLIC SOCIAL TEACHING

- **Call to Community**, Pages 292–293
- **Human Solidarity**, Pages 300–301

Catechist Background

Jesus cried out in a loud voice, "Father, into your hands I commend my spirit"; and when he had said this he breathed his last. The centurion who witnessed what had happened glorified God and said, "This man was innocent beyond doubt." Luke 23:46–47

→ **Reflect** How do you remember the Paschal Mystery during Holy Week?

Lent ends and the Triduum begins at sundown on Holy Thursday and continues through Evening Prayer on Easter Sunday. Think of the Triduum as three days of sacred remembrance. This is not merely a remembrance of the events of Jesus' Passion and Resurrection as a historical event; it is a remembrance of the Paschal Mystery as it has been experienced throughout all of salvation history until now.

During these three days, the Church fasts and prays with anticipation and hope. Although the Easter Vigil is the center and high point of the Triduum, each day has its own liturgical actions and symbols which draw the assembly more deeply into the mystery of faith. Holy Thursday begins as a rich, colorful feast and ends in somber silence. The Holy Thursday celebration of the washing of the feet and the celebration of the Lord's Supper calls us into a deeper commitment to service and to doing the things that Jesus did.

On Good Friday, the church is devoid of decoration, and the prominent symbol is the Cross. During the Good Friday liturgy, which is not a Mass but a three-part celebration including proclamation of Scripture and Holy Communion, the assembly processes forward to venerate the Cross and to continue to celebrate the salvation won by the sacrifice of Christ.

→ **Reflect** What are some ways you reverence the Cross in your own life?

Catechist's Prayer

Spirit of Jesus, help me influence the children's understanding of your sacrifice and your suffering for us so that they might fully experience the Triduum as a solemn, deeply passionate time. Amen.

The Three Days

Let Us Pray

Leader: Lord, God, you are always taking care of us.
Even when we forget, you are there.
Help us to remember your love.
Through Christ, our Lord.

"But I trust in you, LORD;
I say, 'You are my God.'
My destiny is in your hands." Psalm 31:15–16a

All: Amen.

God's Word

"Jesus cried out in a loud voice, 'Father, into your hands I commend my spirit'; and when he had said this he breathed his last. The centurion who witnessed what had happened glorified God and said, 'This man was innocent beyond doubt.' When all the people who had gathered for this spectacle saw what had happened, they returned home beating their breasts." Luke 23:46–48

What Do You Wonder?

- Why did Jesus die?
- Why did the people let Jesus die?

Lectionary Connection

Luke 23:46–48

This reading is taken from a portion of the Gospel proclaimed on Palm Sunday, Year C.

- This passage is often used to show that Jesus willingly gave up his own life.
- The grace with which Jesus gives his life is evidence to the centurion that he is an innocent man.

Invite

Let Us Pray

Invite the children to gather in the prayer space and make the Sign of the Cross. Read aloud the leader's prayer. Ask a volunteer to pray the Psalm verse. Prompt the children's response.

Have the children move out of the prayer space and back to their seats.

Say: We just prayed a prayer of trust in God our Father. In today's reading, listen for Jesus' prayer of trust.

God's Word

Guide the children through the process of Scripture reflection.

- Invite them to close their eyes, be still, and open their minds and hearts to what God is saying to them in this passage.
- Proclaim the Scripture.
- Maintain several moments of silence.
- *Ask:* What did you hear God say to you today?
- Invite volunteers to share.

What Do You Wonder?

Say: In the reading, Jesus hands his life over to his Father. The soldier who watched him realized he was innocent, and so did some of the people. They could see he was very close to his Father.

Invite the children to respond to the questions. Ask what else they might wonder about Jesus' Death.

Discover

We Remember

Say: Starting on Palm, or Passion, Sunday, we begin the holiest week of the Church Year.

Invite a volunteer to read aloud the first paragraph and the Scripture quote from Matthew.

- Have another volunteer read aloud the rest of the text.
- Instruct the children to circle the three special days during Holy Week.
- Invite volunteers to share what they circled.

Point out the photo on the bottom of the page and ask a volunteer to read aloud the caption.

- Ask the children if any of them have seen this procession before. Allow them to share their experience.
- Share your own experience.

Discover

We Remember

The Church sets aside a whole week to remember Jesus' dying and rising. It is called Holy Week. It begins on Passion Sunday and ends on the evening of Easter Sunday. The first days are part of Lent. On Palm Sunday, the people welcomed Jesus with the words,

"Hosanna to the Son of David!" Matthew 21:9

There are three very special days in Holy Week. These days are called the Easter Triduum.

Circle the three special days during Holy Week.

- Holy Thursday
- Good Friday
- Holy Saturday

Members of the assembly carry the Cross during a procession on Good Friday.

Quick Tip

Serve Our Enemies

Sometimes it is difficult to show mercy and compassion toward those who are not friends.

- Encourage the children to "carry a cross" for someone who isn't necessarily their friend.
- This may include offering a smile, a helping hand, or a prayer for that person.

Good Friday

On Good Friday, the Church remembers the day that Jesus died on a Cross. He died to save all people from sin and everlasting death. On this day, people walk up in a procession to honor the holy Cross. They bow or kneel before the Cross. Sometimes they touch or kiss it. They do this to thank Jesus for giving his life for us.

Helping Others

Jesus carried his Cross to the place where he would die. He loved all people so much he was willing to die for them. When we do something that is difficult in order to help others, sometimes we say that we are "carrying a cross," too. We are willing to think of their needs.

➔ **What is something you have done for others, even though it was hard?**

Activity

Make a Cross Decorate the cross. Think of a time when you had to do something difficult. Touch the cross and say a prayer. Ask Jesus to help you, and he will!

Good Friday

Have a volunteer read aloud the paragraph.

- *Ask*: What are some ways people honor the Cross? Walk in a procession, bow or kneel before the cross; they touch or kiss it.

Helping Others

Talk about the meaning of "carrying a cross." Explain that when we carry a cross for others, we are carrying a burden or doing something that might be difficult to help them out.

Read aloud the question.

- Invite the children to respond.
- Write their responses on the board or on chart paper.

Activity

Ask a volunteer to read aloud the directions.

- Give the children time to decorate the cross and say a prayer.

Music Option: Have the children sing "Were You There?" downloaded from **aliveinchrist.osv.com**.

Catechist Background

The Veneration of the Cross

This ritual was introduced into the Latin liturgy around the seventh century.

- It had its origin in the Church of Jerusalem.
- Kissing the foot of the Cross was a part of this ancient tradition that is an element of Good Friday liturgy today.

Honor the Cross

Let Us Pray

Explain to the children that this celebration includes a Prayer of the Faithful, which is a prayer of petition. We also pray a ritual prayer of honoring the Cross.

Prepare

Set up the prayer table and light the candle.

- Prepare the environment with the cross and other items.
- You will be the leader.

Have the children rehearse "We Remember (The Three Days)," downloaded from **aliveinchrist.osv.com**.

Invite the children to gather in the prayer space around the cross.

Pray

Follow the order of prayer on the student pages.

Leader's prayer: Lord, we praise and thank you for the gift of your Death and Resurrection. We honor your Cross as a sign of your love for us and for the world.

Prayer of the Faithful

Pray the intercessions with the children.

Live

Honor the Cross

This celebration includes a Prayer of the Faithful, which is a prayer of intercession. We also pray a ritual prayer of honoring the Cross.

Let Us Pray

Gather and begin with the Sign of the Cross.

Leader: O Lord, open my lips.

All: That my mouth shall speak your praise.

Bow your heads as the leader prays.

Leader: Let us pray.

All: Amen.

Prayer of the Faithful

Leader: Let us pray for the holy People of God.

All: Lord, guide your Church.

Leader: Let us pray for our bishop, for all bishops, priests, and deacons, and for all who work in ministry in our Church.

All: Holy Spirit, guide our leaders.

Leader: Let us pray for all in our parish who are preparing for Baptism.

All: Lord, make them members of your family.

40

Catholic Social Teaching

Lesson Connections

To integrate Catholic Social Teaching into your lesson, choose one of the following features: Call to Community, pages 292–293; or Solidarity of the Human Family, pages 300–301.

- To expand the lesson, complete pages 38–39, then move to the Catholic Social Teaching feature.
- Return to the prayer on pages 40–41.

Procession to the Cross

Fold your hands and pray silently to Jesus. Walk up slowly and in silence to honor the Cross. Bow deeply and touch the foot of the Cross.

All: Sing "We Remember (The Three Days)"

We remember; we give thanks.
We remember.
God's love is everlasting.
All thanks and praise to God.

Go Forth!

Leader: We believe that by his dying
Christ destroyed death forever.
May he give us everlasting life.

All: Amen.

Leader: May almighty God bless us,
the Father, the Son, and the Holy Spirit.

All: Amen.

41

Procession to the Cross

Direct the children to move in procession to the cross. Have the children individually reverence the cross.

- Model the actions for the children.

Go Forth!

Pray the final blessing.

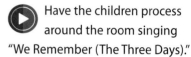

Have the children process around the room singing "We Remember (The Three Days)."

Liturgy Link

Liturgical Color

Black was once used as the liturgical color for Good Friday because it symbolized mourning and the absence of light.

- Today, the color red is used on Good Friday. Red is also used for feasts of martyrs and for Pentecost.
- The cross is a symbol of the sacrifice Jesus made and his victory over Death.

Distribute this page to the children or parents/adult family members.

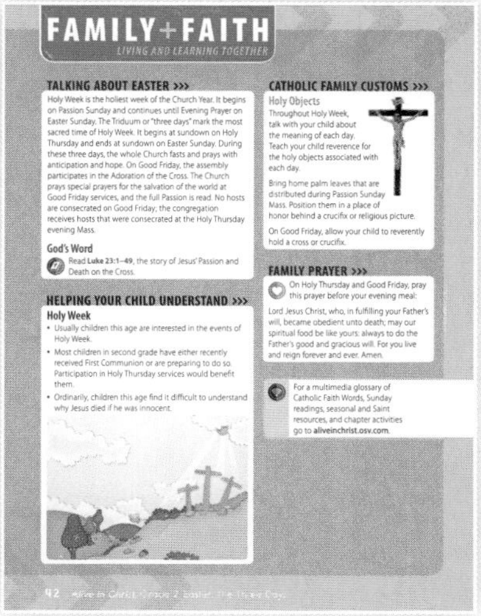
FAMILY+FAITH
LIVING AND LEARNING TOGETHER

TALKING ABOUT EASTER >>>

Holy Week is the holiest week of the Church Year. It begins on Passion Sunday and continues until Evening Prayer on Easter Sunday. The Triduum or "three days" mark the most sacred time of Holy Week. It begins at sundown on Holy Thursday and ends at sundown on Easter Sunday. During these three days, the whole Church fasts and prays with anticipation and hope. On Good Friday, the assembly participates in the Adoration of the Cross. The Church prays special prayers for the salvation of the world at Good Friday services, and the full Passion is read. No hosts are consecrated on Good Friday; the congregation receives hosts that were consecrated at the Holy Thursday evening Mass.

God's Word

Read **Luke 23:1–49**, the story of Jesus' Passion and Death on the Cross.

HELPING YOUR CHILD UNDERSTAND >>>

Holy Week

- Usually children this age are interested in the events of Holy Week.
- Most children in second grade have either recently received First Communion or are preparing to do so. Participation in Holy Thursday services would benefit them.
- Ordinarily, children this age find it difficult to understand why Jesus died if he was innocent.

CATHOLIC FAMILY CUSTOMS >>>

Holy Objects

Throughout Holy Week, talk with your child about the meaning of each day. Teach your child reverence for the holy objects associated with each day.

Bring home palm leaves that are distributed during Passion Sunday Mass. Position them in a place of honor behind a crucifix or religious picture.

On Good Friday, allow your child to reverently hold a cross or crucifix.

FAMILY PRAYER >>>

On Holy Thursday and Good Friday, pray this prayer before your evening meal:

Lord Jesus Christ, who, in fulfilling your Father's will, became obedient unto death; may our spiritual food be like yours: always to do the Father's good and gracious will. For you live and reign forever and ever. Amen.

For a multimedia glossary of Catholic Faith Words, Sunday readings, seasonal and Saint resources, and chapter activities go to **aliveinchrist.osv.com**.

42

Easter: We Rejoice

LESSON OBJECTIVES

- Discover Jesus' Easter message
- Explain that Easter is a season of joy

ENVIRONMENT

Prayer table
White cloth
Large, white, battery-powered or electric candle
Bible or Lectionary

- Place the prayer table at the center of the room.
- Cover the prayer table with the white cloth.
- Place the candle and the Bible or Lectionary on the table.

MUSIC OPTIONS

Go to **aliveinchrist.osv.com** to sample and download,
"Easter Alleluia"
"Alleluia"
"New Life"
"This Is the Day"

CATHOLIC SOCIAL TEACHING

- **Life and Dignity**, Pages 290–291
- **Care for Creation**, Pages 302–303

Catechist Background

On the evening of that first day of the week, when the doors were locked, ... Jesus came and stood in their midst and said to them, "Peace be with you." ... The disciples rejoiced when they saw the Lord." **John 20:19, 20**

→ **Reflect** Do you let Jesus bring you peace?

The celebration of the Easter season includes the fifty days following the Triduum. The Easter liturgies reflect the joy of salvation. The Alleluia is sung once again to express whole-heartedly the joy of the Body of Christ. The assembly renews their baptismal promises in the sprinkling rite. The Gospels unpack the meaning of the Easter event and help the assembly celebrate that God has invited us into the Paschal Mystery of Jesus.

In the *Rite of Christian Initiation of Adults*, the term *mystagogia* is used as a name for this season. Mystagogia means to "uncover the mysteries." The Rite explains that these eight weeks are a time for the newly baptized and the assembly to share the Eucharist, reflect on the Sunday readings, and do acts of service as a means to more fully uncover the mystery and meaning of their Baptism. In this season, the Church celebrates as the People of God who have received the extravagant gift of salvation, a people who have received new life and Good News—a reason to rejoice!

In the events after the Resurrection, Jesus' followers did not always recognize him or the meaning of his being raised from the dead. The depth of that understanding would come with the coming of the Holy Spirit. Perhaps you do not always recognize the meaning of your own Baptism. The whole Easter season is meant to be a time when you can do that.

→ **Reflect** How does your Baptism make a difference in the way you live your daily life?

Catechist's Prayer

Risen Jesus, remind me that this celebration is not one day, but a whole season of joy and gratitude for your sacrifice and your victory over death. Help me to express the joy and gratitude with these children. Amen.

Easter

Invite

We Rejoice

Let Us Pray

Leader: Lord, God, send your Holy Spirit,
that we will see and hear the Risen Christ
as he guides us to right and loving actions.

"Make known to me your ways, LORD;
teach me your paths." Psalm 25:4

Through Christ, our Lord.

All: Amen.

God's Word

On Easter Sunday evening, the disciples were together in a house. They had the doors locked because they were afraid of the Jews. All of a sudden, Jesus came and stood among them and said, "Peace be with you." He showed them his hands and his side and the disciples rejoiced. Jesus said to them again, "Peace be with you. As the Father has sent me, so I send you."
Based on John 20:19–21

What Do You Wonder?

- Why were the disciples so afraid?
- How do we experience Jesus' peace in our lives?

43

Lectionary Connection

John 20:19–21

The reading is taken from a portion of the Gospel proclaimed on the Second Sunday of Easter, in all three cycles of the Church year.

- The disciples were hiding in the upper room after Jesus' Death, but were filled with joy when Jesus appeared to them.
- Twice Jesus says, "Peace be with you." Jesus' Resurrection brings us peace and dispels our fear, just as it did for the disciples.

Invite

Let Us Pray

Invite the children to gather in the prayer space and make the Sign of the Cross. Ask a strong reader to pray the leader's part and the Psalm verse. Prompt the children's response.

Have the children move out of the prayer space and back to their seats.

Say: When Jesus came to the disciples after his Resurrection, he gave them a message about acting as he had acted.

God's Word

Guide the children through the process of Scripture reflection.

- Invite them to close their eyes, be still, and open their minds and hearts to what God is saying to them in this passage.
- Proclaim the Scripture.
- Maintain several moments of silence.
- *Ask:* What did you hear God say to you today?
- Invite volunteers to share.

What Do You Wonder?

Say: In today's reading, Jesus wishes the disciples peace. He tells them his Father will now send them out.

Invite the children to respond to the questions. Ask what else they might wonder about experiencing Jesus' peace.

A Joyful Season

Say: Jesus' blessing of peace helps the disciples change from being afraid to being joyful.

Invite two volunteers to read aloud the paragraphs.

Ask: What do we celebrate in the Easter season? The Resurrection of our Lord

☆ Direct the children to underline the length of time that the Church celebrates Easter.

- Invite a volunteer to share the answer.

> Music Option: Have the children sing "Alleluia," "New Life," or "This Is the Day," downloaded from **aliveinchrist.osv.com**.

Point out the photo at the bottom of the page.

- Ask the children to share their impressions of it.
- Call on a volunteer to read aloud the caption.
- Encourage the children to share some of their family's Easter traditions.

A Joyful Season

Underline the length of time that the Church celebrates Easter.

The whole Church joyfully celebrates the Resurrection of the Lord. The priest wears white vestments. We celebrate Easter for fifty days.

Easter is always in the spring in the northern half of the world. It is the most joyful season in the Church year. We sing Alleluia and ring bells.

After God the Father raised Jesus to new life, Jesus met with his followers several times. They were so happy to see him again! Then Jesus returned to his Father in Heaven. But he promised to send the Holy Spirit to be with them always.

Many parishes include an Easter egg hunt for children during the celebration of Easter Sunday.

Catholic Social Teaching

Lesson Connections

To integrate Catholic Social Teaching into your lesson, choose one of the following features: Life and Dignity, pages 290–291; or Care for Creation, pages 302–303.

- To expand the lesson, complete page 44, then move to the Catholic Social Teaching feature.
- Return to the prayer on page 45.

Let Us Pray

Celebrate Easter

Gather and begin with the Sign of the Cross.

Leader: Light and peace in Jesus Christ, Alleluia.

All: Thanks be to God, Alleluia.

The Lord's Prayer and Peace

Leader: Let us pray in the words that Jesus taught us.

All: Our Father . . .

Leader: May the God of light and peace fill our hearts and lives.

All: Amen.

Leader: Let us offer to each other a sign of the peace of Christ.

Offer one another a sign of peace.

Leader: Go in peace, Alleluia.

All: Thanks be to God, Alleluia.

Sing "Easter Alleluia"

Liturgy Link

Easter Symbols

White, the symbol of the light of Christ, rejoicing, and the Resurrection, is the color used during the Easter season.

The Paschal Candle is lit from the Easter fire at the Easter Vigil and then at every Mass during Easter to remind us that Christ is risen and among us.

Let Us Pray

Celebrate Easter

Prepare the environment with the candle and other items.

You will be the leader.

Have the children rehearse "Easter Alleluia," downloaded from **aliveinchrist.osv.com**.

Invite the children in the prayer space around the prayer table.

Follow the order of prayer on the student page.

- Invite the children to raise their hands in the *orans* (arms out, palms up) position while praying the Lord's Prayer.

Conclude by processing around the room with the children singing the refrain for "Easter Alleluia."

Distribute this page to the children or parents/adult family members.

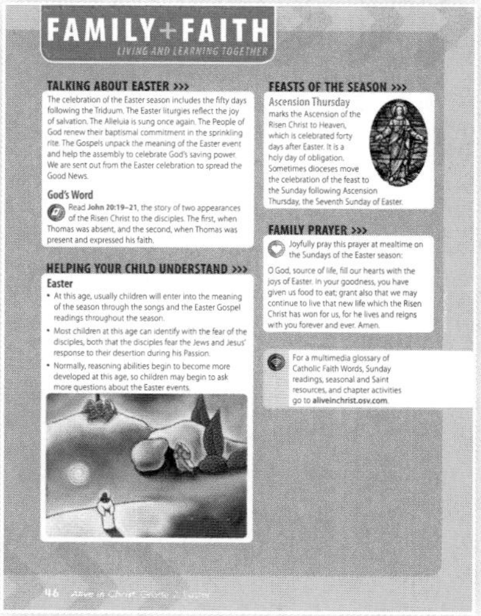

FAMILY+FAITH
LIVING AND LEARNING TOGETHER

TALKING ABOUT EASTER >>>

The celebration of the Easter season includes the fifty days following the Triduum. The Easter liturgies reflect the joy of salvation. The Alleluia is sung once again. The People of God renew their baptismal commitment in the sprinkling rite. The Gospels unpack the meaning of the Easter event and help the assembly to celebrate God's saving power. We are sent out from the Easter celebration to spread the Good News.

God's Word

Read **John 20:19–21**, the story of two appearances of the Risen Christ to the disciples. The first, when Thomas was absent, and the second, when Thomas was present and expressed his faith.

HELPING YOUR CHILD UNDERSTAND >>>

Easter

- At this age, usually children will enter into the meaning of the season through the songs and the Easter Gospel readings throughout the season.
- Most children at this age can identify with the fear of the disciples, both that the disciples fear the Jews and Jesus' response to their desertion during his Passion.
- Normally, reasoning abilities begin to become more developed at this age, so children may begin to ask more questions about the Easter events.

FEASTS OF THE SEASON >>>

Ascension Thursday marks the Ascension of the Risen Christ to Heaven, which is celebrated forty days after Easter. It is a holy day of obligation. Sometimes dioceses move the celebration of the feast to the Sunday following Ascension Thursday, the Seventh Sunday of Easter.

FAMILY PRAYER >>>

Joyfully pray this prayer at mealtime on the Sundays of the Easter season:

O God, source of life, fill our hearts with the joys of Easter. In your goodness, you have given us food to eat; grant also that we may continue to live that new life which the Risen Christ has won for us, for he lives and reigns with you forever and ever. Amen.

For a multimedia glossary of Catholic Faith Words, Sunday readings, seasonal and Saint resources, and chapter activities go to **aliveinchrist.osv.com**.

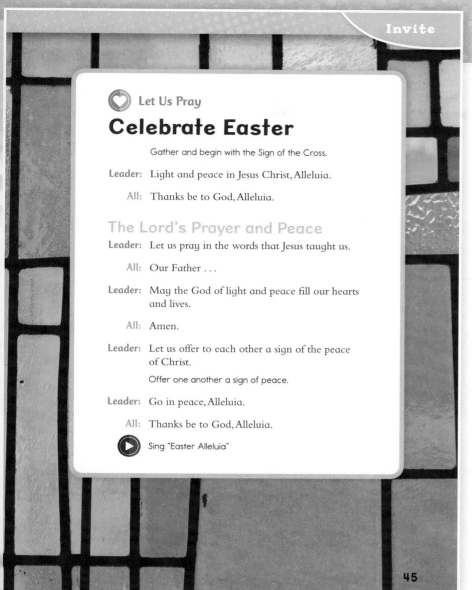

LESSON OBJECTIVES

- Describe the Pentecost event
- Show that the Holy Spirit helps us spread the Good News

ENVIRONMENT

Prayer table
Red cloth
Fresh flowers
Battery-powered or electric white candle
Bible or Lectionary

- Place the prayer table in the center of the space.
- Place the cloth on the table.
- Arrange the flowers, candle, and Bible or Lectionary on the table.

MUSIC OPTIONS

Go to **aliveinchrist.osv.com** to sample and download,
"Come to Us, Holy Spirit"
"Come to Us, Spirit of Jesus"
"Come, Holy Ghost"
"The Holy Spirit"

CATHOLIC SOCIAL TEACHING

- **Call to Community**, Pages 292–293
- **Human Solidarity**, Pages 300–301

Catechist Background

When the time for Pentecost was fulfilled, ... suddenly there came from the sky a noise like a strong driving wind, and it filled the entire house in which they were. Then there appeared to them tongues as of fire, which parted and came to rest on each one of them. And they were all filled with the holy Spirit and began to speak in different tongues... Acts 2:1–4

➔ **Reflect** How have you experienced the Holy Spirit in your life?

The Feast of Pentecost marks the end of the Easter season. The coming of the Holy Spirit at Pentecost completed the work of Christ's Passover and opened a new enthusiasm and ability on the part of the Apostles and disciples to proclaim the Gospel to all people. The story of the first Pentecost shows how people from many different places, who spoke a variety of languages, heard the Good News, believed in Jesus, were baptized, and formed the beginnings of the early Church.

The occasion for the large gathering of people in Jerusalem at that time was the Jewish celebration of the Feast of Pentecost, also called the Feast of Weeks. For the Jewish people, this feast celebrated two things: thanks for a successful harvest and the revelation of the Torah to Moses on Mount Sinai. By the early New Testament period, the feast had gradually lost its association with agriculture and had become associated with the celebration of God's creation of his People and their religious history.

Just as in the Old Testament, the images of wind and fire at Pentecost signify the manifestation of God's presence. It is this presence and power that transformed the disciples into courageous preachers and teachers; today, it continues to transform us and to bring more people into the Church.

➔ **Reflect** In what ways do you want to be transformed by the Holy Spirit?

Catechist's Prayer

Come Holy Spirit, fill the children's hearts with your love and guidance. Guide me to be the leader and example you want me to be for them. Amen.

Pentecost

Let Us Pray

Leader: Come Holy Spirit,
come in power and light to show us
how to live for God alone.

"May the glory of the LORD endure
forever;
may the LORD be glad in his works!"
Psalm 104:31

All: Amen.

God's Word

When the day of Pentecost had come, they were all together in one place. And suddenly from Heaven there came a sound like the rush of a violent wind, and it filled the entire house where they were sitting. Divided tongues, as of fire, appeared among them, and a tongue rested on each of them. All of them were filled with the Holy Spirit and began to speak in other languages, as the Spirit gave them ability.
Based on Acts of the Apostles 2:1–4

What Do You Wonder?

- What would it have been like to be in the room with the disciples?
- Why do you think they began to speak in other languages?

Lectionary Connection

Acts 2:1–4

This reading is proclaimed on Pentecost Sunday, in all three cycles of the Church year.

- The Holy Spirit comes and shows forth his power in the form of a noise like a strong wind and tongues of fire.
- The disciples, filled with the Holy Spirit, began to speak in various tongues, and all of those present heard them in their own languages.

Invite

Let Us Pray

Invite the children to gather in the prayer space and make the Sign of the Cross. Read aloud the leader's prayer and the Psalm verse. Prompt the children's response.

Have the children move out of the prayer space and back to their seats.

Say: Jesus asked God the Father to send the Holy Spirit to share his power with the Apostles and Mary. He sends the Holy Spirit to help us as well.

God's Word

Guide the children through the process of Scripture reflection.

- Invite them to close their eyes, be still, and open their minds and hearts to what God is saying to them in this passage.
- Proclaim the Scripture.
- Maintain several moments of silence.
- *Ask:* What did you hear God say to you today?
- Invite volunteers to share.

What Do You Wonder?

Say: In today's reading, we hear that the Holy Spirit came in a rush of wind and tongues of fire. He came with power. Wonderful things can happen with the guidance and strength of the Holy Spirit!

Invite the children to respond to the questions. Ask what else they might wonder about the Holy Spirit.

Discover

The Power of the Spirit

Say: The power of the Holy Spirit changed the Apostles, just like it can change us.

Invite volunteers to read the paragraphs.

- *Ask:* How many days after Easter was the coming of the Holy Spirit at Pentecost? fifty days

Activity

Read aloud the directions.

- Allow the children to work in pairs to discuss and answer the questions.
- Invite volunteers to share their responses.

Discover

The Power of the Spirit

The Holy Spirit came to the followers of Jesus on Pentecost, fifty days after Easter. They were gathered in a room together. They missed Jesus. Jesus had gone to be with his Father in Heaven. They were not sure what to do.

Then the Holy Spirit came in wind and fire. Jesus' followers were filled with joy and hope. They went out of the room and began to tell the Good News of Jesus.

Everyone understood their words, and many were baptized that day.

Activity

Write the Gifts Answer the questions to remember Pentecost.

How did the Holy Spirit come to Jesus' followers?

Wind and Fire

What were Jesus' followers filled with when the Holy Spirit came to them?

Joy and Hope

48 The Church Year

Catholic Social Teaching

Lesson Connections

To integrate Catholic Social Teaching into your lesson, choose one of the following features: Call to Community, pages 292–293; or Solidarity of the Human Family, pages 300–301.

- To expand the lesson, complete page 48, then move to the Catholic Social Teaching feature.
- Return to the prayer on page 49.

Let Us Pray

Celebrate the Spirit

Gather and begin with the Sign of the Cross.

All: Sing "Come to Us, Holy Spirit"

Come to us Holy Spirit
So we can know God's love
Come to us Holy Spirit
So we can know God's love

Pray the Sign of the Cross together and bow your heads as the leader prays.

Leader: May the Lord bless us and keep us.

All: Amen.

Leader: May the Lord's face shine upon us.

All: Amen.

Leader: May the Lord look upon us with kindness, and give us peace.

All: Thanks be to God, Alleluia, Alleluia.

Liturgy Link

Pentecost

The Pentecost liturgy celebrates the coming of the Holy Spirit on the disciples and his work in the mission and ministry of the people.

- Red is the liturgical color for Pentecost, and all Masses of the Holy Spirit, in memory of the tongues of fire at Pentecost.

Let Us Pray

Celebrate the Spirit

Set up flowers in the prayer space. Prepare the environment with the candle, Bible, and other items.

You will be the leader.

Rehearse with the children "Come to Us, Holy Spirit," downloaded from **aliveinchrist.osv.com**.

- Invite the children to gather in the prayer space.

Follow the order of prayer on the student page.

Begin by singing with the children "Come to Us, Holy Spirit."

Play the song again at the conclusion of the celebration, when the children process back to their seats.

Distribute this page to the children or parents/adult family members.

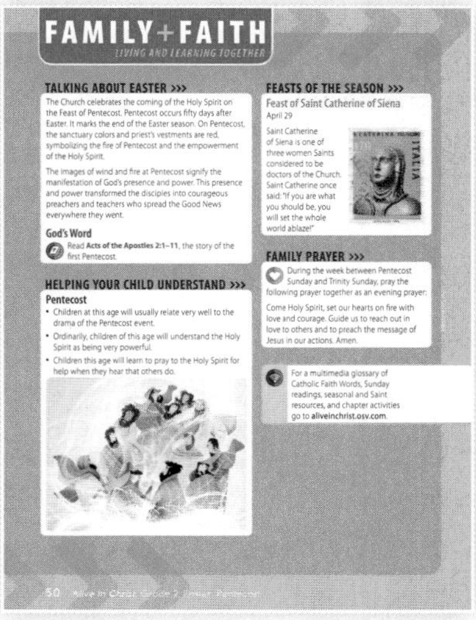

FAMILY + FAITH
LIVING AND LEARNING TOGETHER

TALKING ABOUT EASTER >>>

The Church celebrates the coming of the Holy Spirit on the Feast of Pentecost. Pentecost occurs fifty days after Easter. It marks the end of the Easter season. On Pentecost, the sanctuary colors and priest's vestments are red, symbolizing the fire of Pentecost and the empowerment of the Holy Spirit.

The images of wind and fire at Pentecost signify the manifestation of God's presence and power. This presence and power transformed the disciples into courageous preachers and teachers who spread the Good News everywhere they went.

God's Word

Read **Acts of the Apostles 2:1–11**, the story of the first Pentecost.

HELPING YOUR CHILD UNDERSTAND >>>

Pentecost

- Children at this age will usually relate very well to the drama of the Pentecost event.
- Ordinarily, children of this age will understand the Holy Spirit as being very powerful.
- Children this age will learn to pray to the Holy Spirit for help when they hear that others do.

FEASTS OF THE SEASON >>>

Feast of Saint Catherine of Siena
April 29

Saint Catherine of Siena is one of three women Saints considered to be doctors of the Church. Saint Catherine once said: "If you are what you should be, you will set the whole world ablaze!"

FAMILY PRAYER >>>

During the week between Pentecost Sunday and Trinity Sunday, pray the following prayer together as an evening prayer:

Come Holy Spirit, set our hearts on fire with love and courage. Guide us to reach out in love to others and to preach the message of Jesus in our actions. Amen.

For a multimedia glossary of Catholic Faith Words, Sunday readings, seasonal and Saint resources, and chapter activities go to **aliveinchrist.osv.com**.

50

Core Chapters

Units At A Glance

UNIT 1

Revelation

Our Catholic Tradition

- God gave us many gifts. His gifts tell us about what he is like. (CCC, 41)
- We can learn about God's gifts and his love from the Bible. (CCC, 105)
- Adam and Eve turned away from God. God continued to love them anyway. (CCC, 410)
- Jesus, God's only Son, is God's greatest gift. He is our Savior. He brings us back into friendship with God the Father. (CCC, 430, 452)

How does Jesus help us find our way to God the Father?

Learning more about God through his gifts of creation.

Unit 1 Overview

Chapter 1

The children will:

- identify human beings as made in God's own image
- understand the special role humans have in all of God's creation
- appreciate Jesus as God's greatest gift, the Son of God who became man
- recognize that Jesus was always faithful to God the Father

Songs of Scripture
"How Awesome Is Your Name"

Catholic Social Teaching: Live Your Faith

- Life and Dignity, Pages 290–291
- Care for Creation, Pages 302–303

Chapter 2

The children will:

- appreciate that God gives all people the ability to choose
- recognize Original Sin as the first sin committed by Adam and Eve
- begin to understand our need for a savior
- recognize Jesus as Savior because he led people who were lost through sin back to God
- identify Jesus as the Good Shepherd

Catholic Social Teaching: Live Your Faith

- Call to Community, Pages 292–293
- Solidarity of the Human Family, Pages 300–301

Chapter 3

The children will:

- recognize that God tells us about himself through the Bible
- relate the words *Bible* and *Scripture*
- identify the Bible as God's Word written down by humans
- learn that Jesus tells stories that help us know and love God the Father
- distinguish between the Old Testament and New Testament
- begin to develop an understanding of the need for the Word of God in our lives

Catholic Social Teaching: Live Your Faith

- Life and Dignity, Pages 290–291
- Rights and Responsibilities, Pages 294–295

Preview Unit Theme

Ask: What is the unit theme?

Summarize that the unit focus is on Revelation.

Have four volunteers each read aloud one of the bullets under the Our Catholic Tradition heading.

Have the children study the photos and illustration. Ask volunteers to describe what they see.

Ask: What do these images say about the unit theme?

After some discussion, explain that the children will learn about all these things in the next three chapters of this unit.

KEY CONCEPT
God is the Creator of all that is good. Jesus is God's greatest gift. Jesus is the Son of God.

DOCTRINAL CONTENT
- God created human beings in his own image. (CCC, 355)
- Humans have a special role in all of God's creation. (CCC, 373, 357)
- Jesus is God's greatest gift, the Son of God who became man. (CCC, 464)
- Jesus was always faithful to God the Father. (CCC, 606)

TASKS OF CATECHESIS
Helping children grow in a faith that is "known, celebrated, lived, and expressed in prayer" (NDC, 20).

This chapter focuses on the following tasks of catechesis:
- Promoting Knowledge of the Faith
- Moral Formation

Catechist Background

Many have undertaken to compile a narrative of the events that have been fulfilled among us, just as those who were eyewitnesses from the beginning and ministers of the word have handed them down to us.... Luke 1:1–2

➔ **Reflect** How do the stories in Scripture help you pass on the faith?

To have *dominion* means to have power over or to dominate. For many, these words may immediately conjure up images of oppression, corruption, and even distrust. Guns, money, and success are all images of power that most people have experienced. However, when the word *dominion* is used in the Bible it communicates a message that is very different from images of power that are familiar to us.

The Hebrew word for *dominion* expresses a reality different from the one that is lived out in the world today. By giving humanity dominion over the animals and creatures of the Earth, God shares the responsibility and care of the Earth with humankind. He calls each person to be a good steward of creation. As our first parents were given the task to care for the Garden of Eden, so you are given the task of caring for the fish of the sea, the birds of the air, and the people with whom you relate every day.

The creation account in Genesis speaks eloquently of the relationship between God, creation, and humanity. Creation, including humanity, is always seen in relationship to the Creator. This story affirms the unity and the goodness of God's creation, of which you are a part.

➔ **Reflect** How do you show respect for God's gifts?

Catechist's Prayer

Lord, God of all creation, bless my efforts in helping these children grow closer to you by appreciating your many gifts. Amen.

Lesson Plan

Objectives	Process	Materials
Invite, 10 minutes		
God's Gifts Page 53	**Psalm 24:1** Pray the opening prayer. **Luke 1:1–2** Reflect prayerfully on the Word. • Discuss What Do You Wonder questions.	**Optional Activity** Chapter Poem: "God Made Me"
Discover, 35 minutes		
Praise and Thanks Pages 54–55 • Identify human beings as made in God's own image • Understand the special role humans have in all of God's creation	• **Catholic Faith Words** psalms, creation • Recall God's gifts of creation. ☆ Underline what is unique about people. **Psalm 8:2, 7–9** Proclaim "The Creator and Humans." • **Share Your Faith Activity** Write or draw one way to take care of creation.	☐ pencils, pens, or markers ☐ pictures of sheep, oxen, birds, and fish
The Son of God Pages 56–57 • Appreciate Jesus as God's greatest gift, the Son of God who became man • Recognize that Jesus was always faithful to God the Father	• **Catholic Faith Words** sin, Son of God • Explain that Jesus is God's greatest gift. • Discuss things Jesus did and ways we are alike and different from him. • **Connect Your Faith Activity** Find the hidden name for Jesus.	☐ colored pencils ☐ board or chart paper • **Optional Activity** All Creation Is Good ☐ Activity Master 1 (Page 53E)
Live, 15 minutes		
Our Catholic Life Pages 58–59	• Explain how people use what God has created. ☆ Fill in the blanks with things that can be made from the gifts of God's creation. • **People of Faith** Learn about the Blessed Virgin Mary. • **Live Your Faith Activity** Write the name of one person or thing that can be taken care of.	☐ pencils or pens ☐ paper, crayons, and markers
Blessing Prayer Page 60	• Explain blessing as a prayer form. Rehearse "God Is a Part of My Life." • Follow the order of prayer.	Download "God Is a Part of My Life."

Family + Faith Page 62

Point out that the Catholic Families page provides chapter highlights, information on how second graders understand faith concepts, and family prayer.

Chapter Review Page 63

aliveinchrist.osv.com

- Customize and Download Assessments
- Email Links to eAssessments
- Interactive Student Reviews

ONLINE RESOURCES

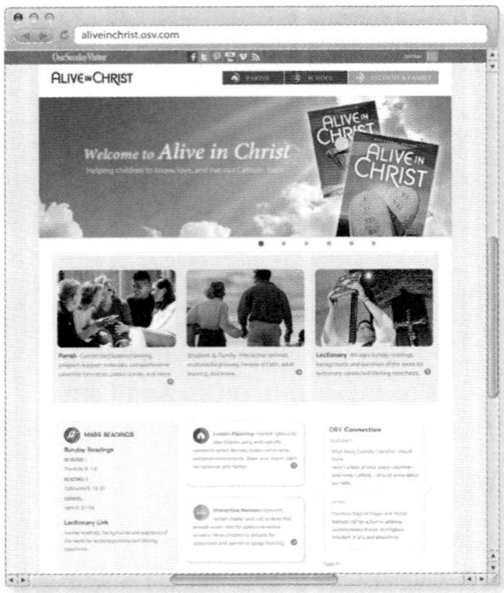

Go to **aliveinchrist.osv.com**

You will find:

- Interactive lesson planning with web specific content and additional activities
- Step by step lesson instruction from printed Catechist Edition for integrated lesson planning
- Custom-built assessments to download and eAssessment links
- Interactive reviews that provide scores and the option to review answers
- Sunday readings with background and questions of the week

Go to **osvparish.com**

You will find:

- Ask the Experts Q and A
- General Catechist Helps
- Community Connections and Blogs

Sharing the Message with Second Graders

God's Creation Most second graders have a strong sense of cause and effect. This makes it natural for them to believe in a Creator when they see the created world. They also have a strong sense that everything has a purpose. For this reason, it is an excellent time for them to learn that everything in the natural world is a gift from God and has a God-given role or meaning.

Teaching Tip: When the children talk about favorite creations of God, encourage them to think about the place of that creation in the natural order (e.g., "Why do you think God made dogs?").

How Second Graders Understand

- Find opportunities to help second graders learn how to determine right from wrong.
- When conflict erupts, help children this age understand that others have feelings and opinions that are different from theirs.
- Many second graders are tactile learners who understand and retain concepts when they are doing things, not just listening or reading.

"I like to make things with my hands. Art, making music, drama, and experiments help me enjoy learning."

Chapter Connections

Chapter Poem

Invite

"God Made Me"

Use this poem to expand the chapter introduction.

- The children will relate the poem to their own lives, reflecting on how God made them different and alike from family members.
- You will explain that stories help us learn more about family and about our God who made and loves us.

Go to **aliveinchrist.osv.com** Lesson Planning section for this poem.

NCEA IFG: ACRE Edition

Discover

Knowledge of the Faith

- Objective: To know and understand God's activity in human history

Moral Formation

- Objective: To be aware of the importance of a well-formed conscience for decision making

Catholic Social Teaching

Live

Use one of these features to introduce a principle and engage the children with an activity.

- Life and Dignity, Pages 290–291
- Care for Creation, Pages 302–303

Music Options

Use one or more of the following songs to enhance catechetical learning or for prayer.

- "God Is a Part of My Life," Live Prayer, Page 60
- "For the Fruits of this Creation," Discover, Page 55

LECTIONARY CONNECTION

Chapter 1 highlights Lectionary-connected themes such as creation and Jesus, Son of God. If your parish aligns its curriculum to the liturgical year, you could use this chapter in connection with the following Sundays.

Year A

Fourth Sunday of Advent—Jesus is God's greatest gift.

Fourteenth Sunday in Ordinary Time—Jesus and His Father

Year B

First Sunday of Advent—Waiting for Jesus, God's Greatest Gift

Baptism of the Lord—Son of God

Year C

Second Sunday in Advent—God as Creator

Third Sunday in Ordinary Time—Scripture is fulfilled.

Go to **aliveinchrist.osv.com** for a complete correlation ordered by the Sundays of the year and suggestions for how to integrate the Scripture readings into chapter lessons.

Name ______________________ Date ____________

All Creation Is Good

Color the pictures of God's creation. Write the name of the gift on the lines below the pictures.

CHAPTER 1

Invite

God's Gifts

Let Us Pray

Leader: God, we thank you for all that you have made.

The earth and all that is in it belong to God;
the world and all who live in it are God's.
Based on Psalm 24:1

All: Thank you, God, for creating each of us. Amen.

God's Word

Many have worked to write about the events that have happened among us just as those who were there at the beginning have handed the events and stories down to us.
Based on Luke 1:1–2

What Do You Wonder?

- What stories do we have about Jesus and his family?
- How do stories teach us to care for the things God has given us?

Optional Activity

Chapter Poem: "God Made Me" *Verbal/Linguistic*

Use this poem after the opening prayer, before explaining that God created everything.

- Have the children read the poem in pairs.
- *Ask:* What are some ways you are different and alike from your family members?
- After connecting how we learn about family and God through stories, transition back to the lesson instruction.

Go to **aliveinchrist.osv.com** for Chapter Poem.

Invite

Let Us Pray

Invite the children to gather in the prayer space and make the Sign of the Cross. Read aloud the leader's prayer and the Psalm verse. Prompt the children's response.

Have the children move from the prayer space back to their seats.

Explain that God created everything that we see and hear, especially each of us.

Say: Now, let's hear what some people have said about what God has done for us.

God's Word

Guide the children through the process of Scripture reflection.

- Invite them to close their eyes, be still, and open their minds and hearts to what God is saying to them in this passage.
- Proclaim the Scripture.
- Maintain several moments of silence.
- *Ask:* What did you hear God say to you today?
- Invite volunteers to share.

What Do You Wonder?

Say: We learn from stories when people tell us what happened before we were born. We also share in the stories that we hear from other people as we listen to them.

Invite the children to respond to the questions. Ask what else they might wonder about the special role people have in God's creation.

Objectives

- Identify human beings as made in God's own image
- Understand the special role humans have in all of God's creation

Praise and Thanks

Direct a child to read aloud the question at the top of the page.

- Tell the children they will discover the answer in the text on this page.

Read aloud the first paragraph.

- Discuss why it's important to give thanks to God and people.

Ask a volunteer to read aloud the second paragraph.

Read aloud the third paragraph.

- *Ask:* What was David most grateful for?

☆ Have the children underline things that make people different from the rest of God's creatures.

Work with Words

Ask the children to name the highlighted words on page 54. Explain that really important words are highlighted so we pay special attention to learning them.

- Read the words again. Have the children write them down.
- Have them practice reading the words and definitions from page 55 to a partner, with each child reading at least once.

Praise and Thanks

What is most special about God's creation?

David was a shepherd a very long time ago. He became a king of God's People. He wrote poems of praise and thanks to God. Many of David's poems are part of the Bible. They are called **psalms**. Sometimes you hear the psalms at Mass.

David often watched the sheep in the fields at night. He was amazed by the wonders of the night sky. As he looked at everything in **creation**, he praised God for his gifts.

☆ Underline the things that make people different from the rest of God's creatures.

David was grateful, most of all, that people had been made in God's own image. This means people can think and love and make choices. Nothing else God made can do these things.

Reaching All Learners

God Made Everyone Special

Be aware of those children who may have difficulty seeing or hearing.

- Situate them so they can see the board and can hear you and see your face as you speak.
- Accommodate any child who has other physical limitations without calling attention to him or her.

In God's Image

Humans are the most special part of God's creation. God wants you to take care of the many gifts of creation. Here is one of David's psalms about humans.

Catholic Faith Words

psalms poems and prayers from the Bible; they can be said or sung

creation everything made by God

God's Word

The Creator and Humans

"O LORD, our Lord, how awesome is your name through all the earth!... You have given [man] rule over the works of your hands, put all things at his feet: All sheep and oxen, even the beasts of the field, the birds of the air, the fish of the sea, and whatever swims the paths of the seas." Psalm 8:2, 7–9

Share Your Faith

Think Write or draw one way you take care of creation.

Share Talk with a partner about these things.

In God's Image

Have a volunteer read aloud the paragraph.

- Ask the children to name one of God's creations that they love.

God's Word

Give each child a picture of sheep, oxen, birds, or fish.

- Tell the children to hold up the appropriate picture when they hear it named as you read aloud the Scripture.
- Proclaim the Scripture.

Music Option: Have the children sing "For the Fruits of this Creation," downloaded from **aliveinchrist.osv.com**.

Activity

Read aloud the directions for the Share Your Faith activity.

- Allow time for the children to think about and then write or draw one way they take care of creation.
- Give each partner time to share ideas.
- Invite the children to share with the group another way they might take care of God's creation this week.

Songs of Scripture

How Awesome Is Your Name

The words of the chorus to this song are taken directly from Scripture. While the children are very familiar with the word *awesome*, you may need to explain the word *majesty* and the phrase "above the heavens."

- Encourage the children to draw a throne in the clouds and write the word *God* on the throne.
- Teach the children the song "How Awesome Is Your Name."

Use *Songs of Scripture*, Grades 1–3 CD, Track 11

Quick Review

God created all things, and humans are special because we are made in his image. We praise and thank God for his gifts of creation and take care of what he has made.

Discover

Objectives

- Appreciate Jesus as God's greatest gift, the Son of God who became man
- Recognize that Jesus was always faithful to God the Father

The Son of God

Ask a volunteer to read aloud the question.

- List the children's answers on the board or on chart paper.

Read aloud the first two paragraphs. Then discuss with the children how Jesus is different from humans.

Ask a volunteer to read aloud the last paragraph.

- Reinforce that Jesus is the Son of God. He is God's greatest gift to us, and he is both human and Divine.
- Discuss the question at the end of the page.

Work with Words

Direct the children to the box on the top of the page, and have a volunteer name the two highlighted words.

- As you slowly read aloud the definitions, have the children circle unfamiliar words.
- Walk around the room to get a sense of the words the children find to be unfamiliar, and then clarify as needed.

To reference the Holy Trinity, which will be taught in later chapters, go to page 304 in the Our Catholic Tradition section of the Student Book.

Discover

The Son of God

Why is Jesus God's greatest gift?

David knew that God is the Creator of everything that is good. But David was born too soon to know about God's greatest gift.

God's greatest gift is his Son, Jesus. Jesus is man and God, human and divine. He was human, just like all of us, except in one way. He never disobeyed God the Father. Jesus did not commit **sin**.

Jesus learned about his Jewish faith and how to pray from his family. He listened to Mary, his Mother, and Joseph, his foster father. Jesus did what they asked him to do.

➔ **What are some other things that Jesus might have done that you also do?**

Catholic Faith Words

sin a person's choice to disobey God on purpose and do what he or she knows is wrong. Accidents and mistakes are not sins.

Son of God a name for Jesus that tells you God is his Father. The Son of God is the Second Divine Person of the Holy Trinity.

Optional Activity

Activity Master 1: All Creation Is Good

Distribute copies of the activity master found on catechist page 53E.

- Have the children color the pictures of God's creation and write the name of each gift.
- As an alternative, you may wish to send this activity home with the children.

Chapter 1 Activity Master

Name ______ Date ______

All Creation Is Good

Alike But Different

While he was on Earth, Jesus saw interesting things every day, just as you do. He enjoyed the flowers, the birds of the air, and the fruit trees. He learned to do new things, just like you.

Jesus is human. He is also divine, which means he is God. Jesus is the **Son of God** who became man. That is why you look to Jesus to learn more about God his Father.

➔ **In what ways are you and Jesus alike? How are you different?**

Connect Your Faith

Find the Hidden Word Color the X's red. Color the O's blue, green, or yellow to find a name for Jesus that you have heard.

Alike But Different

Explain that Jesus lived a very long time ago and that he was human just like us except for one thing: Jesus never committed sin.

Have two volunteers read aloud the first and second paragraphs, respectively.

Have the children discuss the question at the end of the text.

- Use a board or chart paper to illustrate with two columns: *How I'm like Jesus*, and *How I'm different from Jesus*.
- Be sure that the main difference between us and Jesus is mentioned. He did not sin.

Activity

Read aloud the directions for the Connect Your Faith activity.

- Provide the children with colored pencils to complete the activity.
- After everyone is through, have them share with the group what the picture reveals.

Encourage the children to study the illustration and photo on these two pages and share with the group what they see.

Quick Review

Jesus is the Son of God. He is both God and man. He is like us in all ways except he did not sin.

Catechist Background

Cultural Awareness: Diversity

One of the unique things about our planet is that the harmony, which exists in the created world, results from the diversity of beings and from their relationships.

Help the children understand that diversity in our world is good and intended by God. Just as all flowers are not the same, all people are different, but all are beautiful.

To reinforce, invite the children to name some examples of diversity in nature (e.g., ocean creatures, insects, stars, and planets).

Live

Our Catholic Life

Invite a volunteer to read aloud the question.

- Discuss the question.
- Summarize the introductory paragraph.

Making Use of God's Gifts

Direct the children's attention to the chart.

- Read aloud the heading and the first row in both columns, and ask for a possible response for the blank.
- ☆ Instruct the children to fill in the blanks with things that can be made from the gifts of God's creation.
- Point out that one or more answers have already been provided.
- Allow time for the children to complete the activity.
- As a group, go over the chart. Ask volunteers to share their responses.

Remind the children that everything is made by God. Even though we may make something ourselves, we are using God's creation as the source.

Our Catholic Life

How do people use what God has created?

God created everything from nothing. He shared with us the ability to make things to use and enjoy.

☆ Fill in the blanks with things that can be made from the gifts of God's creation.

Making Use of God's Gifts

Gift of Creation	Things We Make From It
wood from trees	houses, paper, ________
cotton	clothing, ________
wheat	bread, cereal, ________
wool from sheep	sweaters, coats, ________
cacao beans	cocoa, ________

Optional Activity

Creation Walk *Bodily/Kinesthetic*

If possible, take the children outside. Give each child a twelve-inch circle of yarn or string.

- Have them place their circles of yarn on the ground, and to look carefully at all the things within their circle. They may see leaves, grass, bugs, and rocks.
- Invite the children to name all the things inside their circles that God created.
- Then, ask them to step inside their circles. *Ask:* What else, inside the circle, did God make? Me!

People of Faith

Blessed Virgin Mary, first century

Mary was a special gift from God. God chose Mary to be the Mother of Jesus, his Son. When the Angel Gabriel told her she would be the Mother of Jesus, he said, "Blessed are you!" Mary is also the Mother of the Church. That means that she is our Mother, too. The Hail Mary is the most well known prayer about the Mother of God. We pray the Hail Mary when we pray the Rosary.

August 15

Discuss: What can Mary help you do today?

Learn more about Mary at **aliveinchrist.osv.com**

Live Your Faith

Tell What gift of God's creation do you see in the picture? How do we take care of this gift of creation?

A fish. We feed it and give it clean water.

Write the name of one person or thing that you can take care of.

Catholic Social Teaching

Chapter Connections

To integrate Catholic Social Teaching into your lesson, choose one of the following features: Life and Dignity, pages 290–291; or Care for Creation, pages 302–303.

- Start the Live step of the process by talking about Mary on page 59. Then move directly to the Catholic Social Teaching feature.
- Or, to expand the lesson, complete both pages 58 and 59, then move to the Catholic Social Teaching feature.
- Return to Chapter 1 for the prayer on page 60.

People of Faith

Tell the children about Mary.

- God chose Mary to be the Mother of his Son. Mary raised Jesus with her husband Joseph. She was a very faithful woman and followed Jesus and cared for him for his whole life.
- Mary is the Mother of God. She is our Mother, too. She is also the Mother of the Church.
- We pray the Hail Mary and the Rosary about the Mother of God and Jesus.
- Discuss with the children the question at the bottom of the box.

Encourage the children to go to **aliveinchrist.osv.com** at home to learn more about Mary.

Activity

Discuss the "Tell" part of the activity as a group. Help the children determine how they would take care of this gift of creation.

Read aloud the "Write" part of the activity.

- Have the children write down one person or thing they can take care of this week.
- If time allows, have the children draw themselves taking care of the part of creation they named. Provide separate paper, crayons, and markers.

Live

Let Us Pray
Blessing Prayer

Explain that blessings can either praise God or ask for God's care for a person, a place, a thing, or an action.

Prepare

Tell the children that today they will be praying a prayer of blessing.

You will be the leader.

Rehearse "God Is a Part of My Life," downloaded from **aliveinchrist.osv.com**.

Gather

Lead the children into the prayer space.

Pray

Begin by leading the children in the Sign of the Cross.

- Follow the order of prayer on the student page.

Conclude by processing with the children around the room singing the refrain for "God Is a Part of My Life."

Live

Let Us Pray

Blessing Prayer

Gather and begin with the Sign of the Cross.

Leader: Bless God
All: Oh, God, bless

Leader: The wonderful Earth where we live and play.
All: Bless God

Leader: The sun and moon that light our way.
All: Bless God

Leader: The trees and plants both large and small.
All: Bless God

Leader: The birds that fly, the fish in the sea.
All: Bless God

Leader: The people just like you and me.
All: Bless God

Leader: The gift of Jesus, your own Son.
All: Bless God

Leader: Sent to bless us, everyone.

All: Sing "God Is a Part of My Life"
God is a part of my life.
God is a part of my life.
God is a part of my life;
I rejoice, I rejoice, I rejoice.

Liturgy Link

The Sign of the Cross

Remind the children that the Sign of the Cross is the way we begin prayers. The Sign of the Cross is a reminder that God is three Divine Persons in one God. It also reminds us that we are baptized in the name of the Father, and of the Son, and of the Holy Spirit.

- To review the Sign of the Cross in Latin, the official, universal language of the Church, turn to page 320 in the Our Catholic Tradition section of the Student Book.

Go to **aliveinchrist.osv.com** for Sunday readings, Scripture background, questions of the week, and seasonal resources.

FAMILY + FAITH

LIVING AND LEARNING TOGETHER

YOUR CHILD LEARNED >>>

This chapter is about God's gift of creation and the special place humans have in it because we are made in the image and likeness of God.

God's Word

Read **Luke 1:1–2** to learn more about those who have worked to tell God's story.

Catholics Believe

- God is the Creator of all that is good.
- Jesus is God's greatest gift. Jesus is the Son of God.

To learn more, go to the *Catechism of the Catholic Church* #256, 319, and 454 at **usccb.org**.

People of Faith

This week, your child met the Blessed Virgin Mary who we honor as the Mother of God and the Mother of the Church.

CHILDREN AT THIS AGE >>>

How They Understand God's Creation Most second-graders have a strong sense of cause and effect. This makes it natural for them to believe in a Creator when they see the created world. They also have a strong sense that everything has a purpose. For this reason, it is an excellent time for them to learn that everything in the natural world is a gift from God and has a God-given role or meaning.

CONSIDER THIS >>>

When was the last time that God's creation amazed you?

Do you realize creation is one of the many ways God shows himself to you? God… "is living and personal, profoundly close to us in creating and sustaining us. Though he is totally other, hidden, glorious, and wondrous, he communicates himself to us in Jesus Christ, whom we meet in the Church, especially in Scripture and the Sacraments. In these many ways, God speaks to our hearts where we may welcome his loving presence" (*USCCA*, p. 51).

LET'S TALK >>>

- Ask your child to talk about God's gifts. Which is his greatest? (Jesus)
- Talk about ways your family uses God's gifts of creation in your daily routines.

LET'S PRAY >>>

Mary, Mother of God, pray for our family and help us always love your Son, Jesus. Amen.

For a multimedia glossary of Catholic Faith Words, Sunday readings, seasonal and Saint resources, and chapter activities go to **aliveinchrist.osv.com**.

Family + Faith

Distribute the page to the children or parents/adult family members. Point out the chapter highlights, insights on how second graders understand concepts, the opportunity for the adults to reflect on their own experiences and faith journey, and the family prayer.

Chapter 1 Review

A Work with Words Write the correct words from the Word Bank to complete each sentence.

Word Bank
creation
psalms
gift
sin
care

1. All that God has made is called **creation**.
2. You can **care** for creation.
3. Jesus did not **sin**.
4. David wrote **psalms** of praise and thanks to God.
5. Jesus is God's greatest **gift**.

B Check Understanding Draw a line from the words ending in Column A to the best ending in Column B.

Column A	Column B
6. Jesus is human and	God is the Father of Jesus
7. The name Son of God tells you that	Mary and Joseph
8. God created everything from	Creator
9. David knew that God is the	the Son of God
10. Jesus learned how to pray from	nothing

Go to **aliveinchrist.osv.com** for an interactive review.

Chapter Review

Use Catechist Quick Reviews to highlight lesson concepts.

A Work with Words
Direct the children to fill in the blanks with the correct answer from the Word Bank.

B Check Understanding
Direct the children to draw a line from the words in Column A to the best ending in Column B.

Go to **aliveinchrist.osv.com** to prepare customized and downloadable assessments, send eAssessments, and assign interactive reviews.

KEY CONCEPT

God sent his beloved Son, Jesus, to bring all people back into his friendship. Jesus is the Savior and the Good Shepherd.

DOCTRINAL CONTENT

- God gives all people the ability to choose. (CCC, 1730–1731)
- Original Sin is the first sin committed by Adam and Eve. (CCC, 389, 397)
- Jesus is the Savior because he led people who were lost through sin back to God. (CCC, 457)
- Jesus is the Good Shepherd. (CCC, 754)

TASKS OF CATECHESIS

Helping children grow in a faith that is "known, celebrated, lived, and expressed in prayer" (NDC, 20).

This chapter focuses on the following tasks of catechesis:

- Promoting Knowledge of the Faith
- Moral Formation

Catechist Background

I tell you, in just the same way there will be more joy in heaven over one sinner who repents than over ninety-nine righteous people who have no need of repentance. Luke 15:7

→ **Reflect** Why does our turning back to God bring him such joy?

The Parable of the Lost Sheep can be found in the Gospel according to Matthew, as well as in the Gospel from Luke. Luke also includes the two parables of The Lost Coin and The Prodigal Son in his writings, which further illustrate Christ's concern for the lost and God's great love for the repentant sinner. These parables lead up to Jesus' proclamation about the coming of the Kingdom and the revelation of the Savior. In this way, Luke highlights Jesus' call to look out for one another.

Whether a lost sheep, a coin, or a father's son, Jesus' message in the Gospel according to Luke is clear. Despite one's failings, God's love is abundant. Jesus' followers struggled in their daily lives with many of the same issues and decisions by which you are challenged today: finding the resources to feed yourself and your family, taking care of children, doing the work it takes to survive, and living together in community.

Confronted by these daily trials, many flounder, sink into despair, or lose their way when things don't work out as planned. Christ's Parable of the Lost Sheep is a reminder that he is searching for you along the winding and confusing pathways of life and awaits you at the end with open arms. God reminds you of his everlasting love.

→ **Reflect** When have you experienced God's loving presence?

Catechist's Prayer

Lord, I need your help to be the best catechist I can be. Help me use the talents you have given me to lead these children to know, love, and serve you. Amen.

Lesson Plan

Objectives	Process	Materials
Invite, 10 minutes		
God's Promise Page 63	**Psalm 78:70–71** Pray the opening prayer. **Luke 15:7** Reflect prayerfully on the Word. • Discuss What Do You Wonder questions.	**Optional Activity** Chapter Story: "A Trip to the Zoo"
Discover, 35 minutes		
Free to Choose Pages 64–65 • Appreciate that God gives all people the ability to choose • Recognize Original Sin as the first sin committed by Adam and Eve	• **Catholic Faith Words** Original Sin • Recall what choice Adam and Eve made. **Genesis 2:15–17; 3:1–6, 23** The Garden of Eden • **Share Your Faith Activity** Write or draw one way to obey God at school and at home.	☐ pencils, crayons, or markers
God Sends a Savior Pages 66–67 • Begin to understand our need for a savior • Recognize Jesus as Savior because he led people who were lost through sin back to God • Identify Jesus as the Good Shepherd	• **Catholic Faith Words** Savior • Discuss why Jesus came into the world. • Explain the need for a Savior. **John 10:11–14** Proclaim "The Good Shepherd." ☆ Underline what shepherds do and discuss how Jesus is like a shepherd. • **Connect Your Faith Activity** Fill in the blanks to find the name Good Shepherd.	☐ board or chart paper • **Optional Activity** Follow the Shepherd ☐ Activity Master 2 (Page 63E)
Live, 15 minutes		
Our Catholic Life Pages 68–69	• Discuss having the freedom to choose. ☆ Read bad choices and indicate a better choice. • **People of Faith** Learn about Saint Cristóbal Magallanes Jara. • **Live Your Faith Activity** Circle the good actions that lead to God.	☐ pencils, pens, or markers ☐ board or chart paper
Prayer of Praise Page 70	• Have volunteers practice the parts. Rehearse "Jesus, Shepherd." • Follow the order of prayer.	Download "Jesus, Shepherd."

Family + Faith Page 71

Point out that the Catholic Families page provides chapter highlights, information on how second graders understand faith concepts, and family prayer.

Chapter Review Page 72

aliveinchrist.osv.com

- Customize and Download Assessments
- Email Links to eAssessments
- Interactive Student Reviews

ONLINE RESOURCES

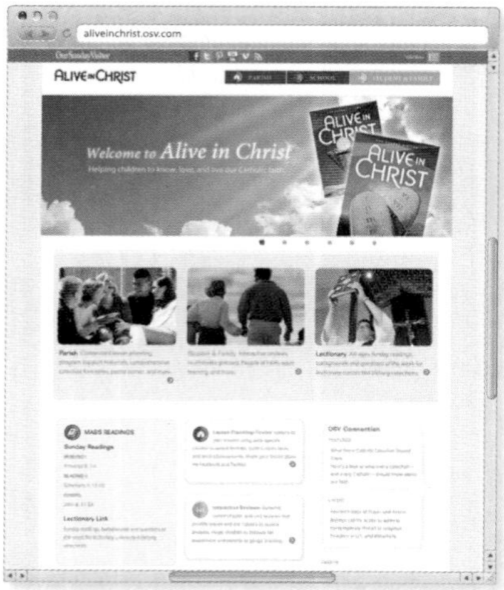

Go to **aliveinchrist.osv.com**

You will find:

- Interactive lesson planning with web specific content and additional activities
- Step by step lesson instruction from printed Catechist Edition for integrated lesson planning
- Custom-built assessments to download and eAssessment links
- Interactive reviews that provide scores and the option to review answers
- Sunday readings with background and questions of the week

Go to **osvparish.com**

You will find:

- Ask the Experts Q and A
- General Catechist Helps
- Community Connections and Blogs

Sharing the Message with Second Graders

God's Plan Just as there is a purpose for everything God made, there is a plan for each of our lives. God gives each of us free will because actions cannot truly be good or loving if they are not done freely. As second graders learn about God's plan for their lives, they will also understand that there are times when they stray from God's plan. It's important for them to know that God will help them become what he made them to be and that God always provides us a way back to him.

Teaching Tip: It's not too soon to encourage children to think about the plans God has for them. Instead of asking them what they want to do when they grow up, ask them what they think God has planned for them.

How Second Graders Understand

- Telling stories and allowing role-play are helpful teaching tools; acting out a story helps children understand it.
- Challenge second graders. It makes them feel grown up.

"Remind me that you love me anyway, even when I make mistakes."

Chapter Connections

Chapter Story

Invite

"A Trip to the Zoo"

Use this story to expand the chapter introduction.

- Children will relate their own experiences of getting or feeling lost like the child in this story.
- Have the children work in pairs to create an ending to the story.
- Encourage the children to share their endings with the group.

Go to **aliveinchrist.osv.com** Lesson Planning section for this story.

NCEA IFG: ACRE Edition

Discover

Knowledge of the Faith

- Objective: To know and understand God's activity in human history

Moral Formation

- Objective: To be aware of the importance of a well-formed conscience for decision making

Catholic Social Teaching

Live

Use one of these features to introduce a principle and engage children with an activity.

- Call to Community, Pages 292–293
- Solidarity of the Human Family, Pages 300–301

Music Options

Use one or more of the following songs to enhance catechetical learning or for prayer.

- "Jesus, Shepherd," Live Prayer, Page 70
- "My Shepherd," Discover, Page 67
- "The King of Love, My Shepherd Is," Discover, Page 67

LECTIONARY CONNECTION

Chapter 2 highlights Lectionary-connected themes such as Jesus, the Good Shepherd; and Jesus, Son of God. If your parish aligns its curriculum to the liturgical year, you could use this chapter in connection with the following Sundays.

Year A

Fourteenth Sunday of Easter—The Good Shepherd

Eleventh Sunday in Ordinary Time—Saved by Christ

Year B

Seventh Sunday in Ordinary Time—Jesus is the Son of God

Thirty-third Sunday in Ordinary Time—Jesus is God's Son

Year C

Fourth Sunday of Easter—Jesus is the Good Shepherd

Fifteenth Sunday in Ordinary Time—Jesus is the Son of God

Go to **aliveinchrist.osv.com** for a complete correlation ordered by the Sundays of the year and suggestions for how to integrate the Scripture readings into chapter lessons.

Name ______________________________ Date ____________

Follow the Shepherd

Jesus is the Good Shepherd. Circle the sheep below that are following the Good Shepherd. Draw an *X* on the sheep that are not following Jesus.

CHAPTER 2

God's Promise

Let Us Pray

Leader: God, we thank you for showing us how to live.

God chose his servant David.
He took David from the sheepfolds.
From tending sheep, God brought him
to shepherd Jacob and his People, Israel.
Based on Psalm 78:70–71

All: Thank you, Father, for sending faithful people to help us know the way. Amen.

God's Word

Jesus said, "I tell you, in just the same way there will be more joy in heaven over one sinner who repents than over ninety-nine righteous people who have no need of repentance." Luke 15:7

What Do You Wonder?

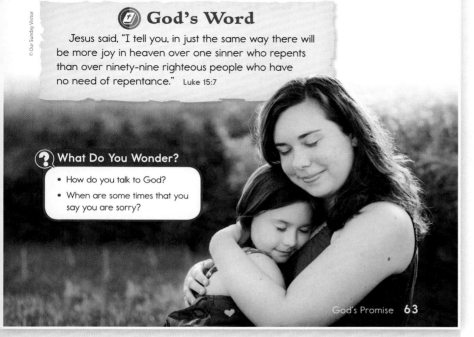

- How do you talk to God?
- When are some times that you say you are sorry?

Invite

Let Us Pray

Invite the children to gather in the prayer space and make the Sign of the Cross. Have a volunteer read aloud the leader's prayer. You will read the Psalm verse. Prompt the children's response.

Have the children return to their seats. Explain that God puts people into our lives at different times to show us how to live. But Jesus is different.

Say: Let's listen to hear what Jesus says about turning to God.

God's Word

Guide the children through the process of Scripture reflection.

- Invite them to close their eyes, be still, and open their minds and hearts to what God is saying to them in this passage.
- Proclaim the Scripture.
- Maintain several moments of silence.
- *Ask:* What did you hear God say to you today?
- Invite volunteers to share.

What Do You Wonder?

Say: Jesus is telling us that we need someone to show us the way. Sometimes we go in the wrong direction and we need to turn back to God. Jesus helps us do this.

Invite the children to respond to the questions. Ask what else they might wonder about God's love, even when we make bad choices.

Optional Activity

Chapter Story: "A Trip to the Zoo" *Verbal/Linguistic*

Use after the opening prayer, before explaining that God gives us help.

- *Ask:* How many of you have visited a zoo before?
- After the children respond to the question, invite them to listen to "A Trip to the Zoo."
- Have the children work in pairs to create an ending to the story.
- *Say:* When we feel lost, we ask trusted adults for help. We ask Jesus to help us find our way to the Father.

Go to **aliveinchrist.osv.com** for Chapter Story.

Discover

Objectives

- Appreciate that God gives all people the ability to choose
- Recognize Original Sin as the first sin committed by Adam and Eve

Free to Choose

Ask a volunteer to read the question.

Explain that the first book of the Bible tells about a choice made by Adam and Eve.

God's Word

Proclaim the first two paragraphs of the Scripture story.

- *Ask:* What were the names of the first two people? Adam and Eve
- *Ask:* Did God give Adam and Eve freedom to eat from all the trees in the garden? yes, except one
- *Ask:* What did God tell Adam and Eve not to do? Do not eat from one of the trees.

Tell the children to read the remaining text on this page.

- Discuss with the children what the serpent said to Eve. If you eat that fruit, you will be like God.

To talk with the children about what we can do if we are sorry for going against God's will, reference the Sacrament of Reconciliation, which will be covered in Chapter 11. You'll find helpful information on page 314 in the Our Catholic Tradition section of the Student Book.

Our first parents, called Adam and Eve, in the Garden of Eden.

Free to Choose

What choice did Adam and Eve make?

God gives all people the freedom and ability to choose. The first book of the Bible tells a story about a choice made by Adam and Eve.

God's Word

The Garden of Eden

God put Adam and Eve in a garden called Eden. They had all they needed to live and be happy.

God told Adam and Eve that they were free to eat from all the trees in the garden, except one. God said, "When you eat from that tree, you will surely die."

Satan, a fallen angel and enemy of God and his People, disguised himself as a serpent and said to the woman, "This is not true. If you eat that fruit you will be like God."

Scripture Background

Genesis 2:15–17; 3:1–6, 23

The Story of Adam and Eve in Genesis uses figurative language, but tells about the state of Original Holiness and goodness in which God created man and woman.

- Genesis also tells of an event that took place at the beginning of the human race—the first choice to disobey God.
- No one knows for sure what the specific choice was, but Scripture reveals the truth that sin came into the world because of human desire and action, not by God's doing.

Eve saw the tree's fruit and ate some. She gave some to Adam. He ate it, too.

Adam and Eve chose to do what they knew God did not want them to do. So God sent them away from the Garden of Eden.

Based on Genesis 2:15–17; 3:1–6, 23

Catholic Faith Words

Original Sin the first sin committed by Adam and Eve and passed down to everyone

God gave Adam and Eve a choice. Instead of doing what he asked them to do, they chose to disobey God. This is called **Original Sin**.

➔ **What happened to Adam and Eve when they chose to disobey God?**

Share Your Faith

Think Write or draw one way you can obey God at school and one way you can obey God at home.

Share Share your answer with a partner.

The Garden of Eden,

continued

Have the children continue reading the Scripture story on this page.

- Point out that Adam and Eve freely chose to eat the fruit, even though they knew that God had told them not to eat it.
- Explain that *original* means first. Since Adam and Eve committed the first sin, that sin is called *Original Sin*. Point out the Catholic Faith Words box and read aloud the definition.
- *Ask:* What did Adam and Eve lose when they chose to disobey God?
- Encourage volunteers to share responses. The Garden of Eden

Activity

Read aloud the directions for the activity.

- Ask the children to think about what God wants them to do.
- Invite them to share their thoughts.
- Allow the children time to draw their pictures.
- Ask volunteers to share their work.

Optional Activity

Making Choices *Interpersonal/Intrapersonal*

Discuss ways to make better choices.

- Organize the group into two teams.
- Have one team name good choices children their age can make, such as taking good care of their pets.
- Have the other team name some poor choices that children may make, such as not using good manners.
- If time allows, give the children an opportunity to act out their better choices.

Quick Review

God made all humans with the ability to choose. Adam and Eve, chose to disobey God. Their sin is called Original Sin.

Discover

Objectives

- Begin to understand our need for a savior
- Recognize Jesus as Savior because he led people who were lost through sin back to God
- Identify Jesus as the Good Shepherd

God Sends a Savior

Begin the lesson by engaging the children with the question.

- Ask a volunteer to read aloud the question.
- List the children's answers on the board or on chart paper.

Ask a volunteer to read aloud both paragraphs.

- *Ask:* Why did Jesus, the Son of God, come into the world? to save all people
- *Ask:* What are some ways you can show God you love him?
- Write all responses on the board or on chart paper.

Work with Words

Ask the children to place their finger on the word *Savior*, and have a volunteer read the definition from the Catholic Faith Words box.

- *Ask:* How did Jesus help people understand he was the Savior? He led people back to God the Father.

God Sends a Savior

How does Jesus save and lead us?

God did not turn away from Adam and Eve. Instead, God promised to send a **Savior**. God promised that the Savior would lead all people back to friendship with him.

God kept his promise. He sent his own Son to be the Savior of all people. Jesus came into the world to save all people and lead them to God. Jesus wanted people to love God and to be happy with God again.

Catholic Faith Words

Savior a title for Jesus, who was sent into the world to save all people lost through sin and to lead them back to God the Father

Catechist Background

Shepherds

The chief work of shepherds is to find food and water for their flock and to keep it safe.

- There are many images of Jesus carrying a lamb over his shoulders. Search for and provide an example for children to view.
- Often shepherds carry a newborn lamb until it is strong enough to walk on its own.

Jesus, the Good Shepherd

Jesus wanted the people to understand he is the Savior. Jesus told a story to show that he is like a shepherd and his followers are like sheep. Shepherds care for their sheep and lead them to grass and water. Shepherds make sure their sheep do not get lost.

Underline what shepherds do. Talk about how Jesus is like a shepherd.

God's Word

The Good Shepherd

Jesus said, "I am the good shepherd. A good shepherd lays down his life for the sheep. A hired man, who is not a shepherd and whose sheep are not his own, sees a wolf coming and leaves the sheep and runs away, and the wolf catches and scatters them...he...has no concern for the sheep. I am the good shepherd, and I know mine and mine know me." John 10:11–14

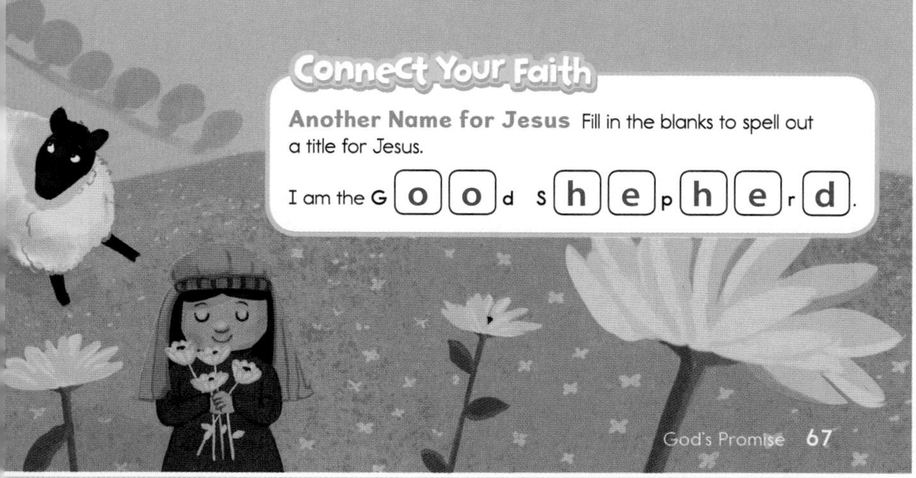

Connect Your Faith

Another Name for Jesus Fill in the blanks to spell out a title for Jesus.

I am the G o o d S h e p h e r d.

Jesus, the Good Shepherd

Have a volunteer read the opening paragraph.

God's Word

Proclaim the Scripture story.

- *Ask:* What is happening in the picture?
- After some discussion on the illustration, explain the chief work of shepherds is to find food and water for their flock and to keep it safe.
- Have the children go back to the opening paragraph and underline what shepherds do. Then facilitate a discussion about how Jesus is like a shepherd.

Music Option: Have children sing "My Shepherd," or "The King of Love, My Shepherd Is," downloaded from **aliveinchrist.osv.com**.

Activity

Read aloud the directions for the Connect Your Faith activity.

- Ask the children to think about other names they have learned for Jesus. Then have them complete the activity.
- Encourage the children to share their sentences.

Optional Activity

Activity Master 2: Follow the Shepherd

Distribute copies of the activity found on catechist page 63E.

- Tell the children to circle the sheep that are following the Good Shepherd, and draw an *X* on those that are not.
- As an alternative, you may wish to send this activity home with the children.

Chapter 2 Activity Master

Name ____ Date ____

Follow the Shepherd

Jesus is the Good Shepherd. Circle the sheep below that are following the Good Shepherd. Draw an X on the sheep that are not following Jesus.

63E Alive in Christ, Grade 2 Chapter 2

Quick Review

After Adam and Eve sinned, God promised to send a savior. God the Father sent his own Son, Jesus, to lead people back to him. Jesus is our Savior and the Good Shepherd.

Live

Our Catholic Life

To engage the children, have them describe how humans are different from robots.

After a brief discussion, point out that God gave each of us freedom to choose.

- *Ask:* What happens when you make a choice?
- Write the words *responsible* and *consequence* on the board or on chart paper.
- Explain that the children will be learning more about how we are responsible for what we do and how our actions have consequences.

Read aloud the two paragraphs.

☆ Tell the children they will be drawing a line from each bad choice on the left to the good choice on the right.

- Invite a volunteer to read aloud each bad choice in the left column, pausing to allow the group to find the good choice that can be made instead.

Our Catholic Life

What happens when you make a choice?

You were created in God's image. God gave you the freedom to make choices. You are responsible for the choices you make.

Every time you make a choice, things happen. All choices have results, or consequences. Good choices have good consequences for you and for others. Bad choices can have bad consequences for you and may hurt others.

☆ Draw a line from the bad choice on the left to the good choice on the right.

Bad Choices	Good Choices
Goofing off at school and not doing your homework	Taking care of your belongings
Making fun of others	Working hard and paying attention in class
Skipping your chores or letting someone else do them	Praying every day
Being careless with what you have been given	Helping out at home without being asked
Not taking time to talk to God	Treating all people with kindness

Quick Tip

Vocabulary: Responsible

Share with the children that they must explain their actions and accept what happens (consequences) because of them.

- Write the word *responsible* on the board or on chart paper.
- Underline the first two syllables of the words (re spons).
- Remind the children that the word *response* means "answer."
- Tell the children that being responsible for their choices means answering for what they do.

People of Faith

Saint Cristóbal Magallanes Jara, 1869–1927

Saint Cristóbal Magallanes Jara grew up in Mexico. When he was a boy, he was a shepherd. Later, as a priest, he tried to be like Jesus, the Good Shepherd. He took care of the people in his village by building schools, starting a newspaper, and training men to become priests. He was arrested on his way to say Mass at a farm. Some people thought that he was trying to rebel against the government. He wasn't, but he was killed anyway. Before he died, Saint Cristóbal forgave the people who killed him.

May 21

Discuss: How was Saint Cristobal like Jesus?

Learn more about Saint Cristóbal at **aliveinchrist.osv.com**

Live Your Faith

Circle Good Actions

Circle the actions that lead to God.

Praying

Being kind

Telling a lie

Write one good action that you will do this week.
I will...

______________________________.

Catholic Social Teaching

Chapter Connections

To integrate Catholic Social Teaching into your lesson, choose one of the following features: Call to Community, pages 292–293; or Solidarity of the Human Family, pages 300–301.

- Start the Live step of the process by talking about Saint Cristóbal Magallanes Jara on page 70. Then move directly to the Catholic Social Teaching feature.
- Or, to expand the lesson, complete both pages 69 and 70, then move to the Catholic Social Teaching feature.
- Return to Chapter 2 for the prayer on page 70.

People Of Faith

Tell the children about Saint Cristóbal Magallanes Jara.

- Though he wrote and preached against rebellion, he was falsely accused of being a rebel.
- Saint Cristóbal was arrested on his way to Mass.
- He gave away his belongings to his executioners, gave them absolution, and without a trial, was martyred.
- His last words were "I die innocent."
- Read aloud the paragraph on Saint Cristóbal.
- Have a volunteer read aloud the Discuss question.
- Ask volunteers to share their thoughts.

Encourage the children to go to **aliveinchrist.osv.com** at home to learn more about Saint Cristóbal Magallanes Jara.

Activity

Read aloud the directions.

- Remind the children that good actions lead to God.
- *Ask:* What good action is a better decision than telling a lie? telling the truth
- Have the children write a good action they will do this week.

Let Us Pray

Prayer of Praise

Tell the children that a prayer of praise includes saying something that means the Lord is great! Explain that this prayer is a reminder that Jesus, the Good Shepherd, always cares for us.

Prepare

Choose volunteers for the four leaders' parts. Practice the parts with the leaders.

- Point out that today's prayer celebration is based on one of the most often quoted Psalms from the Bible.

Rehearse with the children "Jesus, Shepherd," downloaded from **aliveinchrist.osv.com**.

Gather

Invite the children to come to the prayer space with their books. Lead them into the prayer space.

Pray

Follow the order of prayer on the student page.

Conclude by singing with the children the refrain for "Jesus, Shepherd." Have the children continue singing as they return to their seats.

Live

Let Us Pray

Prayer of Praise

Gather and begin with the Sign of the Cross.

Leader: The Lord is my shepherd.
I have all that I need.

All: The Lord is my shepherd.
I have all that I need.

Leader: You lead me to green pastures.
You guide me on the right path.

All: The Lord is my shepherd.
I have all that I need.

Leader: I am not afraid.
Your rod and staff give me courage.

All: The Lord is my shepherd.
I have all that I need.

Leader: Your goodness and kindness follow me
all the days of my life.

All: The Lord is my shepherd.
I have all that I need.

Based on Psalm 23

Sing "Jesus, Shepherd"
You are the shepherd,
we are the sheep.
Come, Good Shepherd,
lead us home.

70 Chapter 2

Liturgy Link

Psalm 23

This is one of the most often quoted Psalms from the Bible.

- Traditionally the word *shepherd* has also been used to refer to the leaders of the Church, such as bishops and pastors, but it can also be applied to parents, teachers, and catechists.
- Because this Psalm is about God's love and care, part of the Psalm is often used in the funeral liturgy.

Go to **aliveinchrist.osv.com** for Sunday readings, Scripture background, questions of the week, and seasonal resources.

FAMILY + FAITH

LIVING AND LEARNING TOGETHER

YOUR CHILD LEARNED >>>

This chapter introduces our need for Jesus, our Savior, who shows us the way to his Father.

God's Word

Read **Luke 15:7** to see how God rejoices when people turn to him.

Catholics Believe

- God sent his beloved Son, Jesus, to bring all people back into his friendship.
- Jesus is the Savior and the Good Shepherd.

To learn more, go to the *Catechism of the Catholic Church* #457–458 at **usccb.org.**

People of Faith

This week, your child met Saint Cristóbal Magallanes Jara, a Mexican priest who was martyred on false charges of encouraging a revolt.

CHILDREN AT THIS AGE >>>

How They Understand God's Plan Just as there is a purpose for everything God made, there is a plan for each of our lives. God gives each of us free will because actions cannot truly be good or loving if they are not done freely. As your child learns about God's plan for his or her life, he or she will also understand that there are times when we stray from God's plan. It's important for children to know that God will help them become what he made them to be and that God always provides us a way back to himself.

CONSIDER THIS >>>

When have you ever regretted something you've said or done?

At times, we all do things that are insensitive or downright hurtful. We sin and need to be redeemed. "In our churches, we behold Jesus nailed to the Cross, an image that reminds us of his painful sacrifice to bring about the forgiveness of all our sins and guilt. . . . Each time we see the crucifix, we can reflect on the infinite mercy of God, who saves us through the reconciling act of Jesus" (*USCCA, p. 243*).

LET'S TALK >>>

- Ask your child what he or she thinks it means to be responsible for your choices.
- Talk about how to react when someone thinks you have done something you didn't.

LET'S PRAY >>>

Saint Cristóbal, ask Jesus to watch over our family as a shepherd watches over his sheep. Amen.

For a multimedia glossary of Catholic Faith Words, Sunday readings, seasonal and Saint resources, and chapter activities go to **aliveinchrist.osv.com**.

Family + Faith

Distribute the page to the children or parents/adult family members. Point out the chapter highlights, insights on how second graders understand concepts, the opportunity for the adults to reflect on their own experiences and faith journey, and the family prayer.

Chapter 2 Review

A **Work with Words** Write the letter of the correct word or words from the Word Bank to complete each sentence.

Word Bank
a. Savior
b. Original Sin
c. Shepherd
d. Jesus
e. friendship

1. The choice of Adam and Eve to disobey God is called [b].
2. God promised to send a [a].
3. The Savior God sent was [d].
4. Jesus is the Good [c].
5. Jesus brings people back into [e] with God.

B **Check Understanding** Fill in the circle beside the correct answer.

6. You were created in ____ image.
   - ○ your friend's ○ your own ● God's
7. God gave you the ____ to make choices.
   - ○ responsibility ● freedom ○ plan
8. All choices have results, or ____.
   - ● consequences ○ freedom ○ responsibility
9. ____ are responsible for the choices you make.
   - ○ The Saints ○ Others ● You
10. Jesus is like a shepherd and his ____ are sheep.
    - ○ friends ● followers ○ parents

Go to **aliveinchrist.osv.com** for an interactive review.

Chapter Review

Use Catechist Quick Reviews to highlight lesson concepts.

A **Work with Words**
Read the words in the Word Bank. Have the children write the letter that corresponds to the correct word.

B **Check Understanding**
Explain to the children that they will be filling in the circle of the correct answer.

Go to **aliveinchrist.osv.com** to prepare customized and downloadable assessments, send eAssessments, and assign interactive reviews.

Chapter 3 The Word of God

KEY CONCEPT
God tells his People about himself through the Bible. The Bible is God's inspired Word written by humans.

DOCTRINAL CONTENT

- God tells us about himself through the Bible. (CCC, 104)
- The Bible is God's Word written down by humans. (CCC, 105)
- Jesus tells stories that help us know and love God the Father. (CCC, 546)
- The Old Testament and New Testament are the two parts of the Bible, also called Scripture. (CCC, 120)

TASKS OF CATECHESIS
Helping children grow in a faith that is "known, celebrated, lived, and expressed in prayer" (NDC, 20).

This chapter focuses on the following tasks of catechesis:

- Promoting Knowledge of the Faith
- Missionary Spirit

Catechist Background

And he came down with them and stood on a stretch of level ground. A great crowd of his disciples and a large number of the people… came to hear him and to be healed of their diseases. Luke 6:17–18

➔ **Reflect** How do you listen for Jesus' direction?

The early prophets and writers of the Scriptures were inspired by God to share his message. These writings were collected and edited over time, becoming a part of the collection of sacred books known as the Bible. It is divided into the Old Testament and the New Testament. This holy book contains the story of Hebrew and Christian peoples. The Bible proclaims the Word of God that Christ came to tell.

Jesus listened to the stories of his faith as they were read aloud in the synagogue. The stories of the Hebrew people were important to Jesus. The Bible is important for us, too. Listening to the Scriptures can help you know who you are as a Christian. Reading the Bible can enable you to grow in your relationship with Christ. It can help you recognize the way God is calling you to share his message.

You will be more compelled to tell others of the Bible's richness as you read and learn more about your faith. The more time you spend with Scripture, the deeper will be your yearning to share God's Word.

➔ **Reflect** How can you share God's Word with others this week?

Catechist's Prayer

Loving Father, bless the children in my group as they listen to the words of your Son, Jesus. Open their hearts to hear the Good News of your love. Guide them in your ways as they go forth to live as Jesus' disciples. Amen.

Lesson Plan

Objectives	Process	Materials
Invite, 10 minutes		
The Word of God Page 73	**Psalm 119:89** Pray the opening prayer. **Luke 6:17–18** Reflect prayerfully on the Word. • Discuss What Do You Wonder questions.	**Optional Activity** Chapter Story: "Share Stories"
Discover, 35 minutes		
Learning about God Pages 74–75 • Recognize that God tells us about himself through the Bible • Relate the words *Bible* and *Scripture* • Identify the Bible as God's Word written down by humans	• **Catholic Faith Words** Bible, Old Testament • Talk about God's love for his People. **Genesis 6–9** Proclaim "The Great Flood." ☆ Color in the sign of God's promise to Noah. • Describe the first part of the Bible. • **Share Your Faith Activity** Think of one thing known about God.	☐ pencils or pens ☐ crayons or markers
Jesus' Message Pages 76–77 • Learn that Jesus tells stories that help us know and love God the Father • Distinguish between the Old Testament and the New Testament • Begin to develop an understanding of the need for the Word of God in our lives	• **Catholic Faith Words** New Testament **Matthew 4:23–25** Proclaim "Jesus Teaches and Heals." • Point out that God gave each of us freedom to choose. ☆ Underline things that Jesus said and did and circle reasons that people followed Jesus. • **Connect Your Faith Activity** Write three words that tell about Jesus.	☐ pencils or pens
Live, 15 minutes		
Our Catholic Life Pages 78–79	• Discuss ways to learn about and share God's love. ☆ Write one way to learn about God's love and one way to share his love. • **People of Faith** Learn about Saint Luke. • **Live Your Faith Activity** Draw part of a Bible story about God's love.	☐ pencils or pens ☐ crayons or markers • **Optional Activity** Bible Fun ☐ Activity Master 3 (Page 73E)
Pray with God's Word Page 80	Rehearse "Your Words Are Spirit and Life." • Follow the order of prayer.	☐ Bible and decorative pillow Download "Your Words Are Spirit and Life."

Family + Faith Page 81

Point out that the Catholic Families page provides chapter highlights, information on how second graders understand faith concepts, and family prayer.

Chapter Review Page 82

aliveinchrist.osv.com

- Customize and Download Assessments
- Email Links to eAssessments
- Interactive Student Reviews

Teaching This Grade

ONLINE RESOURCES

Go to **aliveinchrist.osv.com**

You will find:

- Interactive lesson planning with web specific content and additional activities
- Step by step lesson instruction from printed Catechist Edition for integrated lesson planning
- Custom-built assessments to download and eAssessment links
- Interactive reviews that provide scores and the option to review answers
- Sunday readings with background and questions of the week

Go to **osvparish.com**

You will find:

- Ask the Experts Q and A
- General Catechist Helps
- Community Connections and Blogs

Sharing the Message with Second Graders

The Bible The Bible is God's Word. At first, second graders might have trouble understanding how Scripture is the Word of God, but was written down by human beings. They might think that God somehow delivered the Bible as a book to humankind or literally dictated what was written. Over time they will understand better that the Holy Spirit inspired people of faith to write down what is in the Bible, and that Scripture reflects the culture and personalities of the writers while still transmitting God's message at its core.

Teaching Tip: When looking at a Scripture verse with the children, mention the person who is traditionally believed to have written the book (e.g., Luke for the Acts of the Apostles). Be sure to reiterate that God helped this person write in such a way that it communicated God's message.

How Second Graders Understand

- Give second graders a chance to volunteer. If they know the answer to a question, they will respond enthusiastically. This will build confidence and a love of learning.
- Remember that children this age are hurt and embarrassed easily, so they do not like being asked to respond when they are not sure of the answer.
- Children this age like structure, and it confuses them when rules are not established and enforced.

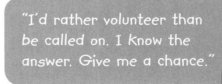

"I'd rather volunteer than be called on. I know the answer. Give me a chance."

Chapter Connections

Chapter Story

Invite

"Share Stories"

Use this story to expand the chapter introduction.

- Explain that a family website is a personal place on the Internet where family members can share their stories and pictures.
- Partner the children together so they can share their family stories if there is enough time.

Go to **aliveinchrist.osv.com** Lesson Planning section for this story.

NCEA IFG: ACRE Edition

Discover

Knowledge of the Faith

- Objective: To know and understand basic Catholic teaching about the Incarnate Word Jesus Christ as the way, truth, and life

Missionary Spirit

- Objective: To be aware of how cultures are transformed by the Gospel

Catholic Social Teaching

Live

Use one of these features to introduce a principle and engage children with an activity.

- Life and Dignity, Pages 290–291
- Rights and Responsibilities, Pages 294–295

Music Options

Use one or more of the following songs to enhance catechetical learning or for prayer.

- "Your Words Are Spirit and Life," Live Prayer, Page 80
- "Jesus Is the Word," Discover, Page 75
- "We Hear God's Word," Discover, Page 77

LECTIONARY CONNECTION

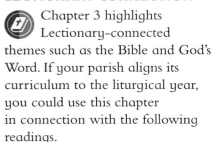

Chapter 3 highlights Lectionary-connected themes such as the Bible and God's Word. If your parish aligns its curriculum to the liturgical year, you could use this chapter in connection with the following readings.

Year A

Fifteenth Sunday in Ordinary Time—Triumph of God's Word

Feast of the Assumption of Mary—Keep the Word of God

Year B

Twenty-first Sunday in Ordinary Time—The Bible is God's Word.

Twenty-second Sunday in Ordinary Time—God's Word

Year C

Fourth Sunday in Ordinary Time—The Bible is God's Word.

Feast of the Assumption of Mary—Keep the Word of God.

Go to **aliveinchrist.osv.com** for a complete correlation ordered by the Sundays of the year and suggestions for how to integrate the Scripture readings into chapter lessons.

Name ______________________ Date ______________

Bible Fun

Stories of God's love can be found in the places listed in the Word Bank. Search for the words from the Word Bank in the puzzle below and circle them.

Word Bank

Scripture	Bible	New Testament
Word of God	Gospels	Old Testament

W	R	T	Y	B	I	B	L	E	N	O	Q
O	L	D	T	E	S	T	A	M	E	N	T
R	G	O	S	P	E	L	S	R	W	T	X
D	B	L	S	C	R	I	P	T	U	R	E
O	Q	L	P	U	B	V	D	L	E	L	P
F	M	J	K	L	G	B	F	R	S	M	N
G	O	W	R	T	I	P	G	H	T	L	P
O	Z	H	G	F	D	S	A	K	L	P	B
D	Q	A	D	S	Z	R	T	P	M	Y	T
N	E	W	T	E	S	T	A	M	E	N	T

The Word of God

Let Us Pray

Leader: Your Word, O God, teaches us each day.

"Your word, LORD, stands forever,
it is firm as the heavens." Psalm 119:89

All: Thank you, God, for your Word. Amen.

God's Word

"And he came down with them and stood on a stretch of level ground. A great crowd of his disciples and a large number of the people … came to hear him and to be healed of their diseases." Luke 6:17–18

What Do You Wonder?

- What does Jesus say to you?
- How will you listen for Jesus?

Invite

Let Us Pray

Invite the children to gather in the prayer space and make the Sign of the Cross. Ask a volunteer to read aloud the leader's prayer and the Psalm verse. Prompt the children's response.

Have the children move from the prayer space back to their seats.

Explain that God's Word is what we hear and read in the Bible.

Say: Let's listen to hear how people followed Jesus.

God's Word

Guide the children through the process of Scripture reflection.

- Invite them to close their eyes, be still, and open their minds and hearts to what God is saying to them in this passage.
- Proclaim the Scripture.
- Maintain several moments of silence.
- *Ask:* What did you hear God say to you today?
- Invite volunteers to share.

What Do You Wonder?

Say: Jesus spoke to the people that were around him and told them how to live. Jesus speaks to us; we only need to listen and to follow.

Invite the children to respond to the questions. Ask what else they might wonder about stories from the Bible or how God speaks to us today.

Optional Activity

Chapter Story: "Share Stories" *Verbal/Linguistic*

Use this story after the opening prayer, before the explanation of God's Word in the Bible.

- Read aloud the story and then ask the children to share a favorite family story.
- After connecting personal stories with the stories in the Bible, transition back to the lesson instruction.

Go to **aliveinchrist.osv.com** for Chapter Story.

Discover

Objectives

- Recognize that God tells us about himself through the Bible
- Relate the words *Bible* and *Scripture*
- Identify the Bible as God's Word written down by humans

Learning about God

Gather the children in the story circle with their books.

- Ask a volunteer to read the opening question and the first paragraph.

God's Word

Direct the children to look at the picture of Noah and the ark.

- Proclaim the Scripture story.
- *Ask:* Do you know what a promise is? When have you made a promise to someone? Do you think it is important to keep promises? Why?
- Discuss God's promise to Noah.
- *Ask:* What does the rainbow represent? God's promise to Noah that God would not destroy the world with water again.

☆ Have the children color in the sign of God's promise.

Explain that God took care of Noah and his family. Reinforce Divine Help by reading aloud the paragraph on page 318 of the Our Catholic Tradition section in the Student Book.

Learning about God

Where is God's Word written?

God wants people to believe in him and to love him. He wants you to remember his special love. Here is a story about God's love for his People.

God's Word

The Great Flood

Once God told Noah to build a large boat called an ark. He told Noah and his family to put all different kinds of animals on the ark, too. A great flood came, and the rains poured down for forty days. Noah's family and the animals were safe on the ark.

Then the rains stopped and the sun came out. Noah praised God for saving his family. God promised that he would always take care of his People. The rainbow was a sign of God's promise. Based on Genesis 6–9

Color in the sign of God's promise to Noah.

Optional Activity

Rainbows *Visual/Spatial*

Have the children make rainbows to remember God's promise.

- Prior to gathering, cut paper plates in half, and then cut a semicircle out of the center. Draw lines to divide the colors of the rainbow.
- Give each child half of a paper plate and have him or her color the rainbow.
- Paste cotton balls to represent clouds.

The Bible

You can find stories of God's love in a special book called the **Bible**. The Bible is the Word of God written in human words. God guided the human writers to write about him and his saving actions. In the Bible, God tells you about himself and his plan for you. Another name for the Bible is Scripture.

The Bible has two parts. The **Old Testament** is the first part of the Bible. It is about the friendship between God and his People before the birth of Jesus. In this part of the Bible, there are history books, law books, poetry, stories, and songs. The story of Noah's Ark is in the Old Testament.

Catholic Faith Words

Bible the Word of God written in human words. The Bible is the holy book of the Church.

Old Testament the first part of the Bible about God and his People before Jesus was born

Share Your Faith

Think What is one thing you know about God? Write it here.

____

____

Share Talk with a partner about how you learned this.

The Bible

Read aloud the first paragraph.

- Invite the children to put a finger on the word *Bible* and have a volunteer read the Catholic Faith Words definition.

Summarize the second paragraph.

- Have the children put a finger on the words *Old Testament* and have a volunteer read the Catholic Faith Words definition.
- Tell the children that the Old Testament was written before Jesus was born.

Music Option: Have the children sing "Jesus Is the Word," downloaded from **aliveinchrist.osv.com**.

Activity

Read aloud the directions for the Share Your Faith activity.

- Have the children write one thing they know about God.
- Invite them to share with a partner how they know this.

Quick Review

The Bible is also known as Scripture, and is God's Word to us. The Bible was written by humans, inspired by the Holy Spirit. The Old Testament is about God and his People before Jesus was born.

Catechist Background

Storytelling

Second graders love listening to Scripture stories. There are many ways you can help them understand that God speaks to us today in Scripture, and his message has meaning for us, no matter our age.

- Use songs, games, puzzles, and art projects to help the children understand the Scripture stories.
- Have the children act out the stories. You will find an honest and untainted approach that is likely close to how Jesus intended his stories to be understood.
- Model respect and reverence for the Bible to help the children develop a love of Sacred Scripture.

Discover

Objectives

- Learn that Jesus tells stories that help us know and love God the Father
- Distinguish between the Old Testament and the New Testament
- Begin to develop an understanding of the need for the Word of God in our lives

Jesus' Message

Have a volunteer read aloud the question.

- Discuss answers with the children.

Read aloud the first paragraph.

- *Ask:* Why did Jesus tell stories? to help people come to know God
- *Ask:* Why did Jesus do wonderful things on Earth? to show people God's love for them

God's Word

Proclaim the Scripture story.

- Lead a large group discussion. *Ask:* What would you do if you could have heard Jesus tell his stories in person?
- ☆ Instruct the children to underline things Jesus said and circle why people followed him.

Tell the children that during the year they will be learning many stories and teachings of Jesus.

Discover

The modern-day region of Galilee, Israel, where Jesus lived and taught.

Jesus' Message

When do you read or hear Bible stories?

Jesus knew the stories of God and his People. Jesus told many stories also. These stories helped people know and love God the Father. Jesus helped people love God by his actions, too.

God's Word

Jesus Teaches and Heals

Jesus went all around Galilee. He taught in the synagogues where the Jewish people studied Scripture and prayed. He told people about the Good News of God's Kingdom. He healed many people who were ill.

Jesus became well-known. People from different cities came to hear Jesus teach. They brought their friends who could not walk, and Jesus cured them. Large crowds followed Jesus wherever he went.

Based on Matthew 4:23–25

1. Underline things that Jesus said and did.
2. Circle the reasons that people followed Jesus.

Scripture Background

Matthew 4:23–35

The crowds that followed Jesus were made up of people from all walks of life, and Jesus welcomed them all. Many of Jesus' teachings emphasize acceptance, leaving the task of judging others to God.

Explain to the children that it is according to Jesus' teachings and God's will that we love one another, accepting all humans as part of God's family.

Read About Jesus

You can learn about Jesus by reading the **New Testament**. The New Testament is the second part of the Bible. It is about the life and teachings of Jesus and his followers. The first four books are called Gospels. There are also letters written by Jesus' followers to the new Christians.

Listen to God's Word

Every Sunday during Mass, you hear readings from the Old and New Testaments. You also hear God's Word when you read Bible stories with your family. You can read or act out some of these stories with family or friends. When you gather with others to learn about your faith and pray, you often hear Bible stories or psalms.

Catholic Faith Words

New Testament the second part of the Bible about the life and teachings of Jesus, his followers, and the early Church

Connect Your Faith

Write About Jesus Imagine you are talking to a group of younger children. What would you say to them about Jesus? Write three words that tell about him.

1. ______________________

2. ______________________

3. ______________________

Read About Jesus

Read aloud the first paragraph.

- Have the children put a finger on the words *New Testament* and read the paragraph.
- Invite a volunteer to read aloud the Catholic Faith Words definition.

Listen to God's Word

Ask a volunteer to read aloud the paragraph.

- Discuss the times the children read and hear Bible stories.

Music Option: Have the children sing "We Hear God's Word," downloaded from **aliveinchrist.osv.com**.

Activity

Read aloud the directions for the Connect Your Faith activity.

- Allow time for the children to come up with their three words.
- Encourage volunteers to share their words with the group.

Quick Review

Jesus shows people how to love God the Father through his words and actions. We learn about Jesus in the New Testament, the second part of the Bible.

Reaching All Learners

Visual Learners

Visual learners may need help understanding the information on pages 75–77.

- Use some books to compare the number of books in the Old Testament (46) and the New Testament (27). Arrange the books in two stacks.
- Another option is to use Bible story picture books to help the children discuss the content on the student pages.

Our Catholic Life

Invite a volunteer to read aloud the question and the first paragraph.

- Have the children give examples of ways they follow Jesus' example.

Have the children take turns reading the examples of "Ways to Learn about God's Love" in the chart.

☆ Ask the children to add to the chart one way they have learned about God's love.

Have the children take turns reading the examples of "Ways to Share God's Love."

- Ask them to write another way they share God's love.
- Encourage volunteers to share their responses.
- Ask volunteers for specific examples of when, how, and where they can do these things.
- In conclusion, *say:* When we find opportunities to practice the things Jesus taught us, we are sharing God's love by living as a reflection of God's love.

Our Catholic Life

How can you learn about and share God's love?

Jesus treated people kindly. He did not care if people were young, old, healthy, or sick. He cared for all people. Jesus teaches us how to live. You can learn about God the Father's love from Jesus. Then, you can share his love.

1. Write in one way you can learn about God's love this week.
2. Write in one way you will share God's love this week.

Ways to Learn about God's Love	Ways to Share God's Love
Read the Bible with our families.	Listen to our parents.
Gather with our parish to worship.	Treat people kindly.
Take part in religion class.	Tell others stories about Jesus.
Sing songs about Jesus.	Include everyone in our games.
1. ______________.	2. ______________.

Optional Activity

Activity Master 3: Bible Fun

Distribute copies of the activity found on catechist page 73E.

- Tell the children that they will search for words that describe where to find stories of God's love.
- As an alternative, you may wish to send this activity home with the children.

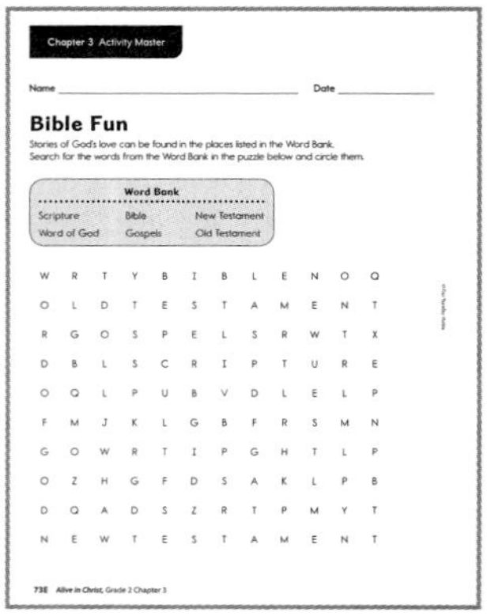

Chapter 3 Activity Master

Name ______________ Date ______________

Bible Fun

Stories of God's love can be found in the places listed in the Word Bank. Search for the words from the Word Bank in the puzzle below and circle them.

Word Bank		
Scripture	Bible	New Testament
Word of God	Gospels	Old Testament

W	R	T	Y	B	I	B	L	E	N	O	Q
O	L	D	T	E	S	T	A	M	E	N	T
R	G	O	S	P	E	L	S	R	W	T	X
D	B	L	S	C	R	I	P	T	U	R	E
O	Q	L	P	U	B	V	D	L	E	L	P
F	M	J	K	L	G	B	F	R	S	M	N
G	O	W	R	T	I	P	G	H	T	L	P
O	Z	H	G	F	D	S	A	K	L	P	B
D	Q	A	D	S	Z	R	T	P	M	Y	T
N	E	W	T	E	S	T	A	M	E	N	T

73E Alive in Christ, Grade 2 Chapter 3

People of Faith

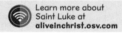

Saint Luke, first century

Saint Luke was a follower of Jesus. He learned about Jesus from Saint Paul and probably the Apostles and Mary. He wrote down their stories about Jesus in what became one of the Gospels. In his Gospel, Luke talks about Jesus' birth and also how Jesus cared for people who were poor, sick, and lonely. Luke traveled with Saint Paul. He wrote down stories about their trips in another book of the Bible called the Acts of the Apostles. Luke was also a doctor and a painter.

October 18

Discuss: What is your favorite story about Jesus?

Learn more about Saint Luke at **aliveinchrist.osv.com**

Live Your Faith

Draw a Bible Story Think about a time when you heard a Bible story about God's love. Draw part of that Bible story here.

Catholic Social Teaching

Chapter Connections

To integrate Catholic Social Teaching into your lesson, choose one of the following features: Life and Dignity, pages 290–291; or Rights and Responsibilities, pages 294–295.

- Start the Live step of the process by talking about Saint Luke on page 79. Then move directly to the Catholic Social Teaching feature.
- Or, to expand the lesson, complete both pages 78 and 79, then move to the Catholic Social Teaching feature.
- Return to Chapter 3 for the prayer on page 80.

People of Faith

Tell the children about Saint Luke.

- According to tradition, Saint Luke was a physician.
- He was born a Greek and Gentile.
- The Gospel according to Luke suggests that he had a great respect for Mary and for all women.
- Luke also is believed to be the author of the Acts of the Apostles.
- He remained with his friend, Saint Paul, until Paul's death.
- Read aloud the paragraph on Saint Luke.
- Discuss the question with the children.

Encourage the children to go to **aliveinchrist.osv.com** at home to learn more about Saint Luke.

Activity

Read aloud the directions for the Live Your Faith activity.

- Have the children share with a partner the Bible story they remember.
- If time allows, have the children retell the story and/or act it out.
- After the children draw part of the Bible story, post their drawings around the room for all to enjoy.

Let Us Pray

Pray with God's Word

Tell the children that when we pray with God's Word, we use Scripture as we pray.

Prepare

Locate a Bible. If possible, find one with larger print for the children to read.

- Arrange a place in the prayer space where you can enthrone the Bible, perhaps on a decorative stand or pillow.
- If you know that one of the children is a strong reader, have him or her read the passage from the Gospel of John. Allow the child time to look over the reading beforehand.
- You will be the leader.

Have the children rehearse "Your Words are Spirit and Life," downloaded from **aliveinchrist.osv.com**.

Gather

Lead the children into the prayer space.

- With Bible in hand, gather the children around you.

Pray

Begin by leading the children in the Sign of the Cross.

- Follow the order of prayer on the student page.

Conclude by processing with the children around the room singing "Your Words Are Spirit and Life."

Let Us Pray

Pray with God's Word

Gather and begin with the Sign of the Cross.

Leader: The Bible is God's holy Word.
It is as sure as the sky above.
It is as solid as the Earth below.
Let us listen, follow,
and honor
God's holy Word.

All: We will listen to
God's Word in the Bible.

Reader: Read John 1:1–2

All: We will live by God's good Word
in the Bible.

Follow the leader in a procession.
Then honor the Bible by bowing before it.

All: We will honor God's good Word in the Bible.

Sing "Your Words Are Spirit and Life"

Your words are spirit and life, O Lord:
richer than gold, stronger than death.
Your words are spirit and life, O Lord:
life everlasting.

Based on Psalm 19:8–11: Text and Music. © 1993 Bernadette Farrell, Published by OCP.

Liturgy Link

Song

Songs are an integral part of the liturgy because they invite everyone to participate in prayer and praise.

- Include familiar liturgical songs in your prayer experiences.
- Encourage the children to sing in loud, clear voices to show their love for God.

Go to **aliveinchrist.osv.com** for Sunday readings, Scripture background, questions of the week, and seasonal resources.

FAMILY + FAITH

LIVING AND LEARNING TOGETHER

YOUR CHILD LEARNED >>>

This chapter explains how the Old Testament and New Testament are the Bible, God's inspired Word.

God's Word

Read **Luke 6:17–18** to learn more about listening to God's Word.

Catholics Believe

- God tells his People about himself through the Bible.
- The Bible is God's Word written by humans.

To learn more, go to the *Catechism of the Catholic Church* #61, 69 at **usccb.org**.

People of Faith

This week, your child met Saint Luke, author of the Gospel of Luke and the Acts of the Apostles, which recounts the story of the early Church.

CHILDREN AT THIS AGE >>>

How They Understand the Bible As Catholics we believe that the Bible is God's Word. At first, your child might have trouble understanding how Scripture is the Word of God, but was written down by human beings. Children this age might think that God somehow delivered the Bible as a book to humankind or literally dictated each word that was written. Over time your child will understand better that the Holy Spirit inspired people of faith to write down what is in the Bible, and that Scripture reflects the culture and personalities of the writers while still transmitting God's message at its core.

CONSIDER THIS >>>

What gives you inspiration?

Did you know that "inspiration is the word used for the divine assistance given to the human authors of the books of Sacred Scripture? This means that guided by the Holy Spirit, the human authors made full use of their talents and abilities while, at the same time, writing what God intended. Sacred Scripture is inspired by God and is the Word of God. Therefore, God is the author of Sacred Scripture, which means he inspired the human authors, acting in and through them" (*USCCA, p. 26–27*).

LET'S TALK >>>

- Ask your child to name one thing he or she learned about the Bible.
- Share one of your favorite stories about Jesus and any family memories you have that include the Bible.

LET'S PRAY >>>

Saint Luke, help us to always listen to each other. Amen.

For a multimedia glossary of Catholic Faith Words, Sunday readings, seasonal and Saint resources, and chapter activities go to **aliveinchrist.osv.com**.

Family + Faith

Distribute the page to the children or parents/adult family members. Point out the chapter highlights, insights on how second graders understand concepts, the opportunity for the adults to reflect on their own experiences and faith journey, and the family prayer.

Chapter 3 Review

A Work with Words Write the letter of the word or words from the Word Bank to complete each sentence.

1. The Bible is **c** Word.
2. The New Testament tells about **b**.
3. The first part of the Bible is the **a**.
4. One name for the Bible is **e**.
5. The first four books of the **d** Testament are the Gospels.

Word Bank

a. Old Testament
b. Jesus
c. God's
d. New
e. Scripture

B Check Understanding Circle the correct answer.

6. The Old Testament tells about ____ and his Chosen People.
   Jesus | **(God)** | Adam
7. You can read the ____ to learn about God's love.
   newspaper | hymnal | **(Bible)**
8. When you ____ you share God's love.
   (are kind) | are unkind | steal
9. The New Testament is about Jesus' life and ____.
   (teachings) | friends | pets
10. You hear God's ____ when you read Bible stories.
   songs | laugh | **(Word)**

Go to **aliveinchrist.osv.com** for an interactive review.

Chapter Review

Use Catechist Quick Reviews to highlight lesson concepts.

A Work with Words Review the Word Bank with the children. Have them write the letter that corresponds to the correct word in the Word Bank.

B Check Understanding Have the children circle the correct answer.

Go to **aliveinchrist.osv.com** to prepare customized and downloadable assessments, send eAssessments, and assign interactive reviews.

UNIT 1 Unit Review

Use Catechist Quick Reviews in each chapter to highlight lesson concepts for this unit and prepare for the Unit Review.

Have the children complete the Review pages. Then discuss the answers as a group. Review any concepts with which the children are having difficulty.

A Work with Words Direct the children to complete each sentence with the correct word from the Word Bank.

B Check Understanding Tell the children to fill in the circle beside the correct answer.

Unit Review

UNIT 1

A Work with Words Complete each sentence with the correct word from the Word Bank.

Word Bank
Bible
Jesus
Savior
God
Creation

1. The Old and New Testaments make up the ___Bible___.
2. You are made in the image and likeness of ___God___.
3. God's greatest gift is ___Jesus___.
4. God promised to send a ___Savior___.
5. ___Creation___ is everything made by God.

B Check Understanding Fill in the circle beside the correct answer.

6. Who told the story of the Good Shepherd?
   - ○ Eve ○ John ● Jesus
7. What is the Word of God written in human words?
   - ○ a book ● the Bible ○ the Savior
8. Who wrote the psalms?
   - ● David ○ Mary ○ Jesus
9. Which part of the Bible is about Jesus?
   - ● New Testament ○ Psalms ○ Old Testament
10. Who guided the Bible writers?
    - ○ humans ○ Adam ● God

UNIT 1

Unit Review

Draw a line from Column A to the best ending in Column B.

Column A	Column B
11. Humans are	the holy book of the Church.
12. The Bible is	your choices.
13. You are responsible for	the most special part of God's creation.
14. You can learn about God by	all people.
15. Jesus cared for	reading the Bible.

C Make Connections Circle the correct answer.

16. ____ is the sin committed by Adam and Eve.

Old Sin   Original lie   **Original Sin**

17. ____ is the name of Jesus that tells you God is his Father.

Son of God   Christ   Good Shepherd

18. Choosing to disobey God on purpose is a ____.

sin   friend   teaching

19. The first four books of the New Testament are called ____.

Acts   Letters   **Gospels**

20. The ____ Testament tells about God and his People before Jesus was born.

New   **Old**   Original

Write the name or names that best answer the question.

21. I was a king of God's people. I wrote poems of praise and thanks to God. Who am I?

David

22. We lived in the Garden called Eden. We disobeyed God. Who are we?

Adam and Eve

23. I am the Good Shepherd. I lead God's People back to him. Who am I?

Jesus

24. I built an ark that saved my family from a flood. Who am I?

Noah

25. I guided the Bible writers. Who am I?

God the Holy Spirit

B Check Understanding,

Have the children draw a line from Column A to the best ending in Column B.

C Make Connections

16–20. Instruct the children to circle the correct answer.

21–25. Have the children write the name or names that best answer the questions.

Go to **aliveinchrist.osv.com** to prepare customized and downloadable assessments, send eAssessments, and assign interactive reviews.

UNIT 2

Trinity

Our Catholic Tradition

- There are three Divine Persons in the Holy Trinity. (CCC, 253)
- God the Father loves and cares for us. (CCC, 239)
- We can trust and rely on God the Father. (CCC, 322)
- Jesus, the Son of God, sets an example for us with his life and teachings. (CCC, 561)
- God the Holy Spirit guides the Church and helps us to be holy. (CCC, 747)

How does the Sign of the Cross remind us of the Holy Trinity?

Unit 2 Overview

Chapter 4

God the Father 87

The children will:

- name God the Father as the First Divine Person of the Holy Trinity
- understand that God loves and cares for us
- begin to develop a capacity to trust and rely on God the Father
- understand that prayer is talking and listening to God

Catholic Social Teaching: Live Your Faith

- Life and Dignity, Pages 290–291
- Care for Creation, Pages 302–303

Chapter 5

God the Son 97

The children will:

- recall that the Angel Gabriel announced to Mary that she would be the Mother of the Son of God, the Savior, Jesus
- connect that the Holy Family of Jesus, Mary, and Joseph lived in Nazareth where Jesus grew up, learning and praying
- identify Jesus as both the Son of God and a human being
- recall the baptism of Jesus as the beginning of his public teaching

Catholic Social Teaching: Live Your Faith

- Life and Dignity, Pages 290–291
- Solidarity of the Human Family, Pages 300–301

Chapter 6

God the Holy Spirit 107

The children will:

- define the Holy Trinity as one God in three Divine Persons
- Identify the Holy Spirit as the Third Divine Person of the Holy Trinity who helps and guides us
- identify Jesus as the Second Divine Person of the Holy Trinity
- Recognize the Holy Spirit's role in helping the Apostles understand and spread the teachings of Jesus
- understand that the Holy Spirit is with the Church today, helping us in many ways

Songs of Scripture
"Holy Spirit"

Catholic Social Teaching: Live Your Faith

- Call to Community, Pages 292–293
- Rights and Responsibilities, Pages 294–295

Preview Unit Theme

Ask: What is the unit theme?

Summarize the unit focus is on the Holy Trinity.

Have volunteers read aloud each of the bullets in Our Catholic Tradition.

Have the children study the photos and image. Ask volunteers to describe what they see. Ask them what these images say about the unit theme.

Ask: How does the Sign of the Cross remind us of the Holy Trinity?

After some discussion, explain that they will be exploring this question in the next three chapters.

KEY CONCEPT
God is our Father who created us and cares for us. We can trust in God because he loves us.

DOCTRINAL CONTENT

- God the Father is the First Divine Person of the Holy Trinity. (CCC, 254)
- Jesus taught us that God the Father loves and cares for us. (CCC, 322)
- We rely on God the Father, praying to him and trusting he will provide what we need. (CCC, 2779–2781)
- Prayer is talking and listening to God. (CCC, 2590)

TASKS OF CATECHESIS
Helping children grow in a faith that is "known, celebrated, lived, and expressed in prayer" (NDC, 20).

This chapter focuses on the following tasks of catechesis:

- Promoting Knowledge of the Faith
- Teaching to Pray

Catechist Background

Do not seek what you are to eat and what you are to drink, and do not worry anymore. All the nations of the world seek for these things, and your Father knows that you need them. Instead, seek his kingdom, and these other things will be given you besides. Luke 12:29–31

➔ **Reflect** How do you come to know God as God the Father?

The fatherhood of God is a frequent theme throughout the Scriptures. God reveals himself as the Father of the Israelite People, the Israelites as God's children. During the Egyptian sojourn, the description of God was broadened from *father* to *father* and *king*. In the New Testament, Jesus invites a more intimate relationship, calling his followers to address God as *Abba*, an affectionate term for *Father*.

Young children reach out to parents or caregivers for comfort and answers. Consumed with worry, afraid of the unknown, in need of answers, adult Christians seek someone to care for them, too. Jesus invites his followers to reach out to their heavenly Father. He summons them to pray to the Father for all they need and to trust in his loving care.

A good parent's love is steadfast. Good parents go to great lengths to protect their children and are willing to sacrifice themselves to meet their children's needs. God, our heavenly Father, loves each and every person with a love beyond that of any human parent. He loves his children unconditionally. He invites his children to rely on him, to trust in him as our loving Father. He invites them to experience the depth of his love.

➔ **Reflect** How can you be God's loving arms for others on this day?

Catechist's Prayer

O God our Father, sustain my spirit when I feel tired and am tempted to do less than my best. Give me the grace to continue with love and enthusiasm. Amen.

Lesson Plan

Objectives	Process	Materials
Invite, 10 minutes		
God the Father Page 87	**Psalm 2:7** Pray the opening prayer. **Luke 12:29–31** Reflect prayerfully on the Word. • Discuss What Do You Wonder questions.	**Optional Activity** Chapter Poem: "Parents"
Discover, 35 minutes		
Care for God's Children Pages 88–89 • Name God the Father as the First Divine Person of the Holy Trinity • Understand that God loves and cares for us	• **Catholic Faith Words** Saint, God the Father • Read about Father John Bosco and his home for boys. • Discuss how Jesus taught others about his Father's love. • **Share Your Faith Activity** Write one way to know God cares.	☐ pencils or pens
The Father's Love Pages 90–91 • Begin to develop a capacity to trust and rely on God the Father • Understand that prayer is talking and listening to God	• **Catholic Faith Words** prayer, trust • Talk about how we can always trust God. • Discuss the difference between a need and a want. **Matthew 6:25–32** Proclaim "Rely on God." ☆ Color the flowers and the birds that go with the Scripture story. • Explain that God always gives us what is best for us. • **Connect Your Faith Activity** Unscramble the words of the prayer Jesus taught his disciples.	☐ pencils or pens ☐ crayons or markers ☐ board or chart paper • **Optional Activity** Trusting God with Our Prayers ☐ Activity Master 4 (Page 87E)
Live, 15 minutes		
Our Catholic Life Pages 92–93	• Discuss what it means to have trust. ☆ Match people with the reasons they can be trusted. • **People of Faith** Learn about Blessed Julian of Norwich. • **Live Your Faith Activity** Find the message.	☐ pencils or pens
Asking Prayer Page 94	• Point out the response. Rehearse "People Worry." • Follow the order of prayer.	Download "People Worry."

Family + Faith Page 95

Point out that the Catholic Families page provides chapter highlights, information on how second graders understand faith concepts, and family prayer.

Chapter Review Page 96

aliveinchrist.osv.com

- Customize and Download Assessments
- Email Links to eAssessments
- Interactive Student Reviews

Teaching This Grade

ONLINE RESOURCES

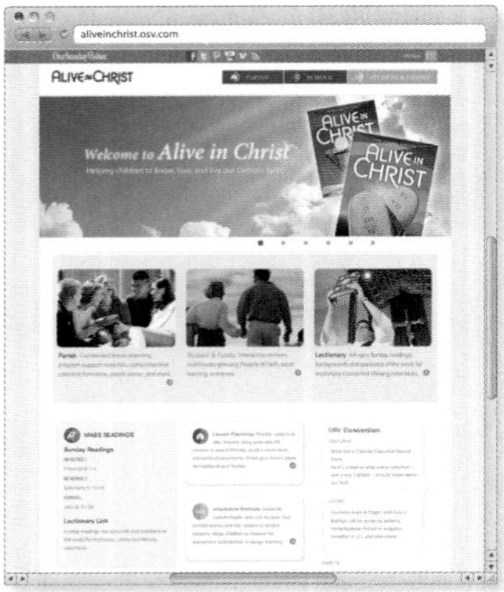

Go to **aliveinchrist.osv.com**

You will find:

- Interactive lesson planning with web specific content and additional activities
- Step by step lesson instruction from printed Catechist Edition for integrated lesson planning
- Custom-built assessments to download and eAssessment links
- Interactive reviews that provide scores and the option to review answers
- Sunday readings with background and questions of the week

Go to **osvparish.com**

You will find:

- Ask the Experts Q and A
- General Catechist Helps
- Community Connections and Blogs

Sharing the Message with Second Graders

God the Father God reveals himself as a loving father. Second graders who have good fathers in their lives will be able to relate to this and connect it with an understanding of God's love for us. Alternatively, if children have no father present, or if they have had negative experiences with a father figure, they might have difficulty integrating the concept of God as a father. Knowing how God intends for parents to care for their children can help with this understanding, and knowing God as the perfect Father can become a particular source of comfort and hope to these children.

Teaching Tip: If you had a loving, healthy relationship with your own father, talk about this when you discuss God the Father. It's important for children who don't have this experience to understand that God's plan for fatherhood is one of unconditional love and care.

How Second Graders Understand

- Children this age get excited about learning new things. Give them interesting activities to help them understand these concepts.
- Second graders like concrete things. Respond to questions like "How does God care for me?" in a way they can understand.
- Often, children this age are starting to become more aware of the needs of others. Let them work on activities with a partner.

"I like concrete things. It helps when you answer questions in a way that I can understand."

Chapter Connections

Chapter Poem

Invite

"Parents"

Use this poem to expand the chapter introduction.

- Discuss ways parents and others show love to children. Write the children's responses on the board or on chart paper.
- Explain that a family is made up of people who love and care for each other. Tell the children we are all part of God's family.

Go to **aliveinchrist.osv.com** Lesson Planning section for this poem.

NCEA IFG: ACRE Edition

Discover

Knowledge of the Faith

- Objective: To know and understand basic Catholic teaching about the Incarnate Word Jesus Christ as the way, truth, and life

Prayer

- Objective: To recognize and learn how to engage in Catholic forms of personal and communal prayer and ways of deepening one's spiritual life

Catholic Social Teaching

Live

Use one of these features to introduce a principle and engage the children with an activity.

- Life and Dignity, Pages 290–291
- Care for Creation, Pages 302–303

Music Options

Use one or more of the following songs to enhance catechetical learning or for prayer.

- "People Worry," Live Prayer, Page 94
- "Children of God," Discover, Page 90

LECTIONARY CONNECTION

Chapter 4 highlights Lectionary-connected themes such as God and love, asking and receiving, and Jesus' final instructions. If your parish aligns its curriculum to the liturgical year, you could use this chapter in connection with the following readings.

Year A

Seventeenth Sunday in Ordinary Time—God's Love for All

The Ascension of the Lord—Jesus' Final Instructions

Year B

Fifth Sunday in Ordinary Time—God's Love

Eighth Sunday in Ordinary Time—God will hold us close forever.

Year C

Seventeenth Sunday in Ordinary Time—Whoever asks receives.

Twenty-seventh Sunday in Ordinary Time—God as Father

Go to **aliveinchrist.osv.com** for a complete correlation ordered by the Sundays of the year and suggestions for how to integrate the Scripture readings into chapter lessons.

Name ______________________________ Date ______________

Trusting God with Our Prayers

Name some people, places, or problems that need prayers and that begin with the letters in the word *Father*. Trust God the Father to listen to your prayers.

____

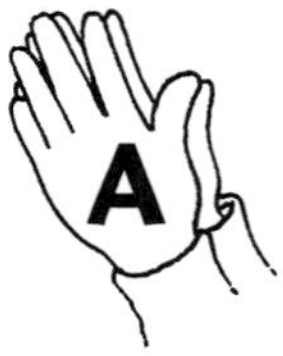

____

____

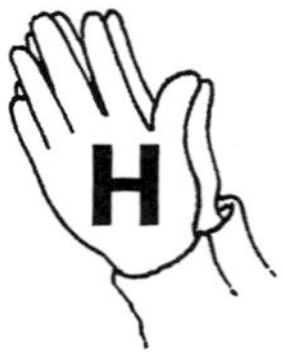

____

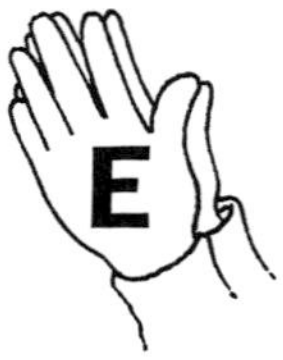

____

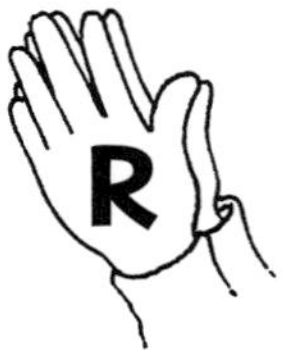

____

CHAPTER 4

Invite

God the Father

Let Us Pray

Leader: God, you call us to be your children.

God said to me: "You are my child;
today I have created you." Based on Psalm 2:7

All: God, please bless us today and every day. Amen.

God's Word

"Do not seek what you are to eat and what you are to drink, and do not worry anymore. All the nations of the world seek for these things, and your Father knows that you need them. Instead, seek his kingdom, and these other things will be given you besides." Luke 12:29–31

What Do You Wonder?

- How do you know God?
- Why do we call God our Father?

Optional Activity

Chapter Poem: "Parents" *Verbal/Linguistic*

Use this poem after the opening prayer, before talking about God as our Father.

- Have the children write a thank-you note to a family member. Invite them to give their notes to the people for whom they were written.
- After connecting family love with God the Father's love, transition back to the lesson instruction.

Go to **aliveinchrist.osv.com** for Chapter Poem.

Invite

Let Us Pray

Invite the children to gather in the prayer space and make the Sign of the Cross. Read aloud the leader's prayer and the Psalm verse. Prompt the children's response.

Have the children move from the prayer space back to their seats.

Explain that today we remember that God is our Father.

Say: Let's listen to how we should put God first in our lives.

God's Word

Guide the children through the process of Scripture reflection.

- Invite them to close their eyes, be still, and open their minds and hearts to what God is saying to them in this passage.
- Proclaim the Scripture.
- Maintain several moments of silence.
- *Ask:* What did you hear God say to you today?
- Invite volunteers to share.

What Do You Wonder?

Say: God, our Father knows what we need. If we trust in God, we don't need to worry.

Invite the children to respond to the questions. Ask what else they might wonder about God's life and love and how he shares them with us.

Discover

Objectives

- Name God the Father as the First Divine Person of the Holy Trinity
- Understand that God loves and cares for us

Care for God's Children

Ask a volunteer to read aloud the question.

- Allow time for the children to consider their answers before discussing.

Read aloud the first paragraph.

Saint John Bosco

Invite the children to sit in a circle.

- Read aloud the biography of Saint John Bosco.
- Point out the picture of Father John. Discuss how Father John helped children who were homeless.
- Explain that besides giving them a place to stay, Father John taught the children about the love of God.

Ask: What do you think Father John's home for the children was like?

- Invite the children to share their responses.

Work with Words

Point out that Father John told the children about God the Father, and after he died, he was named a Saint.

- Have two volunteers read aloud the definitions from the Catholic Faith Words box.

Care for God's Children

How does God care for you?

This is a story about a priest. He made a home for children who had no parents to love and care for them.

Catholic Faith Words

Saint a hero of the Church who loved God very much, led a holy life, and is now with God in Heaven

God the Father the First Divine Person of the Holy Trinity

Saint John Bosco

Lorenzo and Giovanni huddled alone in the shadows. They heard mothers and fathers calling for their children. Nobody called their names. Father John Bosco found the boys cold and in the dark. They told Father John that many other children lived alone on the streets.

"I will start a home for the children of the streets. I will teach them how to read, fix things, and pray," said Father John.

Father John helped many homeless children to feel loved. He taught them that God is everyone's Father. After he died, he was named a **Saint**.

➔ **What do you think Father John's home for children was like?**

Catechist Background

Holy People

The Church solemnly proclaims some holy men and women as Saints because they lived lives of heroic virtue. Their holiness makes them models of Christian life and intercessors with God on our behalf.

Feasts and Memorials of the Saints are opportunities to praise God for what he accomplished through these holy people. (See USCCA, p.176.)

God the Father

Father John Bosco treated the young children like they were his own. He showed them love and taught them about God, like Jesus did.

Jesus taught about his Father's great love. You call God "Father" because he created you and cares for you. He cares for everyone. **God the Father** loves you as a good parent does.

I will never forget you.
See, upon the palms of my hands
I have engraved you. Isaiah 49:15–16

Share Your Faith

Think Trace the outline of your hand. Write one way that you know God cares for you.

Share With a partner, talk about ways you can thank God.

God the Father

Have volunteers read aloud the first two paragraphs.

- Remind the children that Jesus taught people about his Father's love.
- Explain that God loves them even more than a good parent loves a child. Tell them that God will always care for them.
- Read the lines of Scripture from Isaiah.
- Explain that this passage is from the Old Testament. God made this promise before Jesus was born.

Ask: How do you know that God cares for you?

- Have the children discuss the question.

Activity

Read aloud the directions.

- Have the children trace their hand and write inside the outline one way they know God cares for them.
- Arrange the group into pairs. Have each pair talk about ways they can thank God.

Reaching All Learners

Helping Hands

Children with less developed motor skills may have difficulty tracing their hands.

- You may wish to pair these children with children who are more adept at motor skills so that one may assist the other in tracing.
- Their helpers may also assist them with writing inside the hand outline.
- Or, allow them to skip the tracing part of the activity and just write down their answer.

Quick Review

God the Father is the First Divine Person of the Holy Trinity. He loves us and cares for us more than a good parent does.

Discover

Objectives

- Begin to develop a capacity to trust and rely on God the Father
- Understand that prayer is talking and listening to God

The Father's Love

Ask: What does it mean to trust in God?

- List the children's answers on the board or on chart paper.

Read aloud the introduction.

- Discuss the difference between a need and a want. Stress that God always takes care of our needs.

God's Word

Proclaim the Scripture story.

- Ask the children to give examples of how their parents take care of them. They cook for them. They help them when they are sick.
- Ask volunteers to share ways that God cares for them.

☆ Have a volunteer read aloud the directions. Allow time for the children to draw and color.

Music Option: Have the children sing "Children of God," downloaded from **aliveinchrist.osv.com**.

Discover

The Father's Love

What does it mean to trust in God?

Jesus told people not to worry too much. He said that God the Father wants you to have everything you need.

God's Word

Rely on God

Do not worry about what you will eat or wear. Life is more important than food and clothing. Look at the birds in the sky. They do not plant their food; they do not gather grain, yet your heavenly Father feeds them. Are you not more important than they? Learn from the way the wild flowers grow. They do not work or spin, but they are beautiful. If God cares so much for the grass of the field, how much more will he take care of you? Do not worry. Your heavenly Father knows what you need. Based on Matthew 6:25–32

1. Color the flowers and the birds.
2. Draw yourself into the picture.

90 Chapter 4

Scripture Background

Heavenly Father

As Christians, we can call God Father because we are his adopted children by virtue of Baptism and the anointing of the Holy Spirit.

- This Scripture passage calls Christians to rely on God the Father for what they need.
- Jesus acknowledges that humans do have needs, but people should not become obsessed with meeting them. We need to trust God.

Turn to God in Prayer

Jesus told his followers to pray to the Father for whatever they might need. In your **prayer**, you will be speaking to God the Father as Jesus did. Sometimes we say God or Lord when we pray to God the Father.

Jesus knew that you can always **trust** God. You can be sure that God loves you and wants what is best for you. God, your loving Father, is always listening.

Catholic Faith Words

prayer talking to and listening to God

trust to believe in and depend on someone

Connect Your Faith

Pray to God Unscramble the words below to find the first lines of the prayer Jesus taught us.

ROU HERFAT,
OHW TRA NI
VANHEE,
WODLELAH EB
HTY MENA

O U R F A T H E R,
W H O A R T I N
H E A V E N,
H A L L O W E D B E
T H Y N A M E.

Turn to God in Prayer

Have a volunteer read aloud the two paragraphs.

- Remind the children that Jesus told us that we can call God our Father. Explain that God the Father always gives us what we need and what is best for us.
- Connect the experience with trusting God who wants only what is good for his People.
- To further discuss how Jesus taught us to pray to God the Father, have the children turn to page 320 of the Our Catholic Tradition section in the back of their books for the Lord's Prayer.

Activity

Read aloud the directions for the Connect Your Faith activity.

- If the children are having difficulty unscrambling the letters to find the words to the prayer, you might want to give them some hints.

Quick Review

Trust God; know that he will provide all that we need. We can talk and listen to God through prayer.

Optional Activity

Activity Master 4: Trusting God with Our Prayers

Distribute copies of the activity found on catechist page 87E.

- Tell the children in this activity, they will name people, places, or problems that need prayers.
- As an alternative, you may wish to send this activity home with the children.

Chapter 4 Activity Master

Name ____ Date ____

Trusting God with Our Prayers

F ____
A ____
T ____
H ____
E ____
R ____

Our Catholic Life

Read aloud the question at the top of the page.

- Discuss with the children what it means to have trust.

Read aloud the first paragraph.

- *Ask:* What does it mean to depend on someone? Who trusts you?

Read aloud the second paragraph

- *Ask:* Who can you always depend on? God
- Direct the children's attention to the chart. Invite a volunteer to read aloud the heading and each of the entries in the first column.
- Instruct the children to match the people named on the left with the important reason you can trust them on the right.
- Read aloud the heading and the entries in the second column.
- Allow time for the children to make the matches.
- When everyone is done, encourage volunteers to share their answers.

Our Catholic Life

What does it mean to have trust?

When you love or respect someone, you trust in him or her. You believe that the person will do what is best for you. You know you can depend on that person in good times and bad times.

Sometimes, people you trust may let you down, even though they do not mean to. That is because we are human. But you can always depend on God. You are his child. He is with you every day. You can trust God to love you and care for you.

Match the people on the left with one important reason you can trust them.

People in Your Life	You Can Trust Them
Family Members	to protect you
Friends	to love you and take care of you
Teachers	to help you grow closer to God
Crossing Guards and Police Officers	to help you learn
Members of Your Parish Family	to play fair and treat you kindly

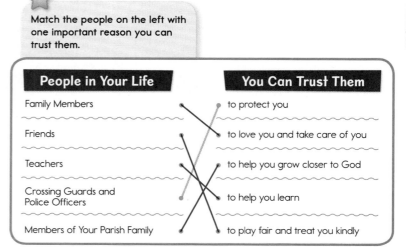

Optional Activity

Trust Walk *Bodily/Kinesthetic*

Arrange the children in pairs. Tell them they will be doing a trust walk to build trust with their partner.

- Tell one child in each pair to close his or her eyes and keep them closed. Ask the other child to lead their partner around the room, helping them avoid running into things.
- Connect the experience with trusting God who wants only what is best for his People.
- *Ask:* Why is it important to trust God? God cares for us. He created us and wants us to trust him to provide what we need.

People of Faith

Blessed Julian of Norwich, 1342–c.1430

May 13

Blessed Julian lived in a town in England called Norwich. She loved to pray. She prayed by talking to God like she talked to her mother or father. Julian said that the whole world was like a little nut in God's hand. When we pray, we don't have to worry because God will always take care of us. Even when we are unhappy, God watches over us. Julian said that we should ask God for help in all we do. She was the first woman to write a book in English. It was about God's love.

Discuss: How does God care for you?

Learn more about Blessed Julian at **aliveinchrist.osv.com**

Live Your Faith

Find the Message Circle the red letters. Then copy the circled letters in order on the lines below for a special message.

EGDFMO	KRNJLO	ACTYZW	XTOMNR	VKRCBY
CVGLLO	ZADRTW	VMISSL	NLLRST	CBAMMK
USEABC	CBAQVR	LMEDEO	PZFMMY	MNOHKU

DO NOT WORRY
GOD WILL TAKE
CARE OF YOU

Name one person you can share this message with.

Catholic Social Teaching

Chapter Connections

To integrate Catholic Social Teaching into your lesson, choose one of the following features: Life and Dignity, pages 292–293; or Care for Creation, pages 300–301.

- Start the Live step of the process by talking about Blessed Julian of Norwich on page 93. Then move directly to the Catholic Social Teaching feature.
- Or, to expand the lesson, complete both pages 92 and 93, then move to the Catholic Social Teaching feature.
- Return to Chapter 4 for the prayer on page 94.

People of Faith

Tell the children about Blessed Julian of Norwich.

- Julian believed that God loves and wants to save everyone.
- She didn't believe that God was angry, but that he was full of love and compassion.
- Blessed Julian wrote books about faith. In fact, she was the first woman to write a book in English. It was about God's love.
- She believed in the authority of the Church and that we should ask God for help in all we do.

Read aloud the final question and discuss the children's responses.

Encourage the children to go to **aliveinchrist.osv.com** at home to learn more about Blessed Julian of Norwich.

Activity

Read aloud the directions for the Live Your Faith activity.

- After the children have had time to complete the activity, ask a volunteer to read aloud the message.
- Allow other children to share who they would like to share this message with.

Let Us Pray

Asking Prayer

Explain that in an asking prayer, we ask God to help us and others.

Prepare

Point out that the response in today's prayer is the same as one we pray at Mass.

Today you will serve as the leader.

Rehearse with the children "People Worry," downloaded from **aliveinchrist.osv.com**.

Gather

Invite the children to come to the prayer space. Have them bring their books.

Pray

Begin by leading the children in the Sign of the Cross.

Follow the order of prayer on the student page.

If there is time, add specific prayers for the children in your group and/or people they may know in the parish.

Conclude by processing around the room with the children singing the refrain for "People Worry."

Let Us Pray

Asking Prayer

Gather and begin with the Sign of the Cross.

Leader: Let us pray for those who need God's help.

All: Lord, hear our prayer.

Leader: For people who have lost their homes, let us pray to the Lord.

All: Lord, hear our prayer.

Leader: For people who are far from their families, let us pray to the Lord.

All: Lord, hear our prayer.

Leader: For help to care for others as Jesus did, let us pray to the Lord.

All: Lord, hear our prayers.

Sing "People Worry"

People worry about this and that.
People worry about this and that!
But Jesus tells us, "Don't worry.
Don't worry about this and that!"

Liturgy Link

The Prayer of the Church

The Lord's Prayer is central to liturgical prayer. It is prayed at celebrations of Baptism, Confirmation, Eucharist, and the Anointing of the Sick, as well as the major hours of the Divine Office.

Early Christians who were Jewish converts prayed this prayer three times a day in place of the daily "Eighteen Benedictions" that were a traditional part of Jewish piety.

Go to **aliveinchrist.osv.com** for Sunday readings, Scripture background, questions of the week, and seasonal resources.

FAMILY + FAITH

LIVING AND LEARNING TOGETHER

YOUR CHILD LEARNED >>>

This chapter explores God the Father's love and the importance of prayer to deepen our relationship with him.

God's Word

Read **Luke 12:29–31** and see why God doesn't want us to worry.

Catholics Believe

- God is our Father who created us and cares for us.
- We can trust in God because he loves us.

To learn more, go to the *Catechism of the Catholic Church* #322, 2780–2782 at **usccb.org**.

People of Faith

This week, your child met Blessed Julian of Norwich who said that all "shall be well" for those who trust in God.

CHILDREN AT THIS AGE >>>

How They Understand God the Father God reveals himself as a loving father. Second-graders who have good fathers at home will be able to relate to this and connect it with an understanding of God's love for us. Alternatively, if a child has no father in the home, or if they have had negative experiences with a father figure, they might have difficulty integrating the concept of God as a father. Knowing how God intends for parents to care for their children can help with this understanding, and knowing God as a perfect Father can become a particular source of comfort and hope to these children.

CONSIDER THIS >>>

How important is trust in a relationship?

Without trust there is not even the possibility of relationship. Throughout the Old Testament there is a growing understanding of the special relationship between God and the Israelites as they learn to trust ever more deeply in the providential care of God. "Jesus' revelation of God as his Father flows from a profound awareness not only of that same providential care but also of an indescribable intimacy" (cf., e.g., Jn14) (*USCCA, p. 484–485*).

LET'S TALK >>>

- Ask your child to name people your family trusts. Discuss why.
- Share a time when you knew God was really there for you. Talk about how depending on and trusting in God made a difference for you or the family.

LET'S PRAY >>>

"All shall be well and all shall be well and all manner of thing shall be well." (Prayer of Blessed Julian of Norwich)

For a multimedia glossary of Catholic Faith Words, Sunday readings, seasonal and Saint resources, and chapter activities go to **aliveinchrist.osv.com**.

Family + Faith

Distribute the page to the children or parents/adult family members. Point out the chapter highlights, insights on how second graders understand concepts, the opportunity for the adults to reflect on their own experience and faith journey, and the family prayer.

Chapter 4 Review

A Work With Words Fill in the blank with the correct word from the Word Bank.

Word Bank
Trust
cares
Father
depend
Prayer

1. God ___cares___ for everyone.
2. Jesus taught you to call God the ___Father___.
3. ___Trust___ God.
4. ___Prayer___ is talking to and listening to God.
5. You can always ___depend___ on God.

B Check Understanding Complete each sentence in Column A with the letter of the correct word or words in Column B.

Column A	Column B
6. A [c] is a holy person who obeyed God.	a. respect
7. Jesus told people not to [e].	b. his Father's great love
8. Jesus taught about [b].	c. Saint
9. We love and [a] the people we trust.	d. best for you
10. God loves you and wants what is [d].	e. worry too much

Go to **aliveinchrist.osv.com** for an interactive review.

Chapter Review

Use Catechist Quick Reviews to highlight lesson concepts.

A Work with Words
Have the children write the word from the Word Bank to complete each sentence.

B Check Understanding
Have the children complete each sentence in Column A with the correct letter from Column B.

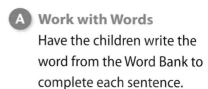

Go to **aliveinchrist.osv.com** to prepare customized and downloadable assessments, send eAssessments, and assign interactive reviews.

KEY CONCEPT

Jesus is the beloved Son of God, born of Mary. Jesus is the Savior of the world who showed us God the Father's love.

DOCTRINAL CONTENT

- The Angel Gabriel announced to Mary that she would be the Mother of the Son of God, the Savior, Jesus. (CCC, 430)
- The Holy Family of Jesus, Mary, and Joseph lived in Nazareth where Jesus grew up, learning and praying. (CCC, 514–515)
- Jesus is both the Son of God and a human being. (CCC, 723–724)
- The Baptism of the adult Jesus by John the Baptist was the beginning of his public teaching. (CCC, 535)

TASKS OF CATECHESIS

Helping children grow in a faith that is "known, celebrated, lived, and expressed in prayer" (NDC, 20).

This chapter focuses on the following tasks of catechesis:

- Promoting Knowledge of the Faith
- Liturgical Education

Catechist Background

After all the people had been baptized and Jesus also had been baptized and was praying, heaven was opened and the holy Spirit descended upon him in bodily form like a dove. And a voice came from heaven, "You are my beloved Son; with you I am well pleased." Luke 3:21–22

→ **Reflect** Do you ever wonder if you live for and like Jesus?

The name Jesus stems from the Hebrew word *Yeshua*, meaning "God saves." Christ comes from the Greek word *Christos*, which translates to "Messiah." Hence, the name Jesus Christ reveals who Jesus is and his mission. Yet, throughout his public ministry, there was great mystery surrounding Jesus' identity. When Jesus' disciples witnessed the calming of the storm by Jesus, they asked, "Who then is this whom even wind and sea obey?"(Mark 4:41). Jesus then turned this question on his Apostles, and Peter answered, "You are the Messiah" (Matthew 16:16). Jesus did not deny it but rather told his followers to keep this news quiet.

Jesus, the Son of God, understood his life's mission. He knew that he had been sent to repair sinful humanity's relationship with God and to reward humanity with eternal life. He understood the price that his mission would require. His willingness to die and his Resurrection both speak of and bring God's great love and power.

This love is all the greater in that Jesus was willing to die for all humans—not only the righteous, the strong, and the powerful, but also for the unrighteous, the weak, and the oppressed. His willingness to sacrifice his life is love beyond comprehension. His Resurrection is a mystery beyond human power. Jesus is Savior. He breaks the chains of oppression and personal sinfulness.

→ **Reflect** When have you felt Jesus' saving power and love?

Catechist's Prayer

Jesus, Son of God, throughout your life you led by your example. Help me use my words and actions to help these children grow in their love and understanding of you. Amen.

Lesson Plan

Objectives	Process	Materials
Invite, 10 minutes		
God the Son Page 97	**Psalm 103:13** Pray the opening prayer. **Luke 3:21–22** Reflect prayerfully on the Word. • Discuss What Do You Wonder questions.	**Optional Activity** Chapter Story: "Fun with Names"
Discover, 35 minutes		
A Savior Is Born Pages 98–99 • Recall that the Angel Gabriel announced to Mary that she would be the Mother of the Son of God, the Savior, Jesus • Connect that the Holy Family of Jesus, Mary, and Joseph lived in Nazareth where Jesus grew up, learning and praying	• **Catholic Faith Words** Mary, angel • Talk about the special meanings of names. ☆ Identify Jesus, Mary, and the Angel Gabriel. **Luke 1:26–38; 2:1–11** Proclaim "Announcing Jesus' Birth." • Discuss why Mary agreed to be the Mother of Jesus. • **Share Your Faith Activity** Write or draw part of the Scripture story.	• **Optional Activity** Jesus Comes to Us! ☐ Activity Master 5 (Page 96E) ☐ pencils or pens ☐ crayons or markers
The Holy Family Pages 100–101 • Identify Jesus as both the Son of God and a human being • Recall the baptism of Jesus as the beginning of his public teaching	• **Catholic Faith Words** Holy Family • Explain that Jesus is the Son of God. • Talk about the Holy Family. **Luke 2:41–52** Proclaim "The Boy Jesus in the Temple." **Matthew 3:13–17** Proclaim "Baptism of Jesus." • **Connect Your Faith Activity** Circle names for Jesus.	☐ pencils or pens ☐ board or chart paper
Live, 15 minutes		
Our Catholic Life Pages 102–103	• Discuss what Jesus teaches about loving God and others. ☆ Give examples of things to say to follow Jesus' teachings. • **People of Faith** Learn about Saint Peter. • **Live Your Faith Activity** Act out what Jesus might say in various situations.	☐ pencils or pens ☐ board or chart paper
Signing Prayer Page 104	• Teach the ASL sign for "Jesus." Rehearse "You Are God." • Follow the order of prayer.	☐ crucifix ☐ image of Jesus Download "You Are God."

Family + Faith Page 105

Point out that the Catholic Families page provides chapter highlights, information on how second graders understand faith concepts, and family prayer.

Chapter Review Page 106

aliveinchrist.osv.com

- Customize and Download Assessments
- Email Links to eAssessments
- Interactive Student Reviews

ONLINE RESOURCES

Go to **aliveinchrist.osv.com**

You will find:

- Interactive lesson planning with web specific content and additional activities
- Step by step lesson instruction from printed Catechist Edition for integrated lesson planning
- Custom-built assessments to download and eAssessment links
- Interactive reviews that provide scores and the option to review answers
- Sunday readings with background and questions of the week

Go to **osvparish.com**

You will find:

- Ask the Experts Q and A
- General Catechist Helps
- Community Connections and Blogs

Sharing the Message with Second Graders

Jesus, God's Son Second graders have often already heard many stories of Jesus. Because the Gospel stories offer few glimpses into Jesus' childhood (only infancy and age 12), it might be hard for the second grader to picture Jesus as a child his or her age. It's important for children this age to know that Jesus was at one time seven and eight years old, and that they can follow him in the choices they make right now. Their understanding of this will grow as you point out daily opportunities to be like Jesus through the choices the children make.

Teaching Tip: Drawing from what we know about Jesus, his nature, and his life, encourage the children at times to imagine how Jesus might have behaved as a second grader.

How Second Graders Understand

- Second graders are naturally curious. Encourage them to ask questions.
- Children this age can't always put what they're thinking into words. Let them draw pictures to help them explain their ideas.
- Young people often enjoy working and sharing with others. Allow them to occasionally work in a group.

"I can't always put my thoughts into words. Let me draw pictures to explain my ideas."

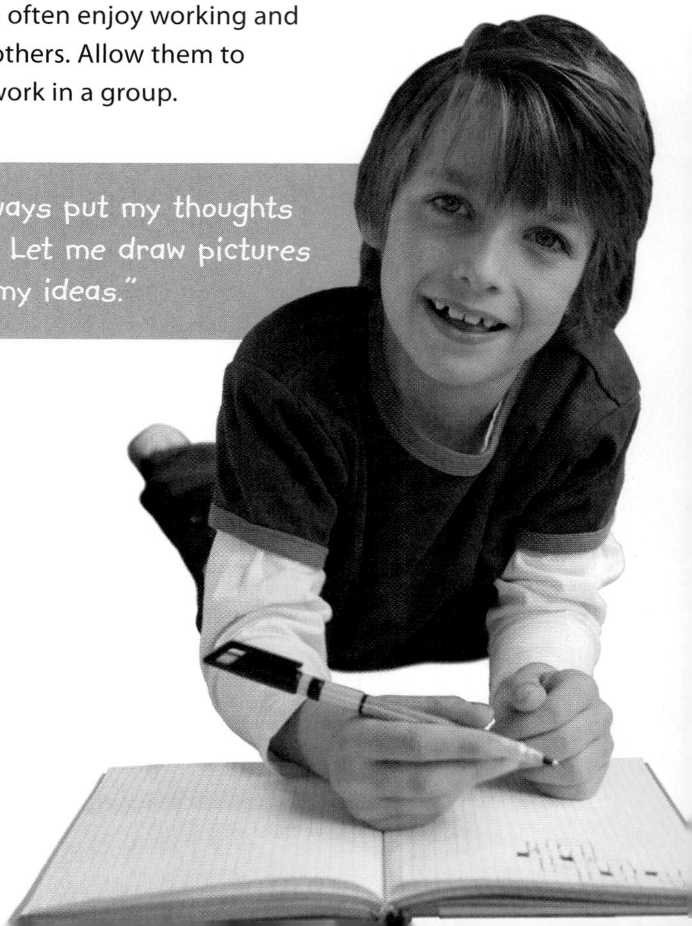

Chapter Connections

Chapter Story

Invite

"Fun with Names"

Use this story to expand the chapter introduction.

- Let the children work together in pairs.
- Have partners share and list names they both like.
- Invite pairs to share their lists with the large group.

Go to **aliveinchrist.osv.com** Lesson Planning section for this story.

NCEA IFG: ACRE Edition

Discover

Knowledge of the Faith

- Objective: To know and understand basic Catholic teaching about the Incarnate Word Jesus Christ as the way, truth, and life

Liturgical Life

- Objective: To know the Paschal Mystery of Jesus: in the Church's liturgical life—feasts, seasons, symbols, and practices and in the Sacraments as signs and instruments of grace

Catholic Social Teaching

Live

Use one of these features to introduce a principle and engage the children with an activity.

- Life and Dignity, Pages 290–291
- Solidarity of the Human Family, Pages 300–301

Music Options

Use one or more of the following songs to enhance catechetical learning or for prayer.

- "You Are God," Live Prayer, Page 104
- "Incarnate One," Discover, Page 98

LECTIONARY CONNECTION

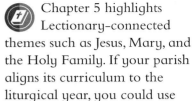

Chapter 5 highlights Lectionary-connected themes such as Jesus, Mary, and the Holy Family. If your parish aligns its curriculum to the liturgical year, you could use this chapter in connection with the following readings.

Year A

The Baptism of the Lord—Savior

The Most Holy Trinity—Belief in the Son Sent by the Father

Year B

Third Sunday of Advent—Jesus as Savior

Second Sunday of Easter—Son of God as Savior

Year C

Ninth Sunday in Ordinary Time—Jesus as Savior

Twelfth Sunday in Ordinary Time—Jesus as Savior

Go to **aliveinchrist.osv.com** for a complete correlation ordered by the Sundays of the year and suggestions for how to integrate the Scripture readings into chapter lessons.

Name ______________________________ Date ______________

Jesus Comes to Us!

Use your imagination! Then use pictures or words to rewrite the story of Jesus. In your story, Jesus is born in today's world. Let your story answer all or some of these questions.

- Where would Jesus live?
- What clothes would he wear?
- Where would he learn to pray?
- What great things would he do?

My Story of Jesus

CHAPTER 5

Invite

God the Son

Let Us Pray

Leader: God the Father, show us your Son.

As a father has compassion on his children,
so the Lord has compassion on those
who honor him. Based on Psalm 103:13

All: Thank you, God, for sending your Son
to show us the way to you. Amen.

God's Word

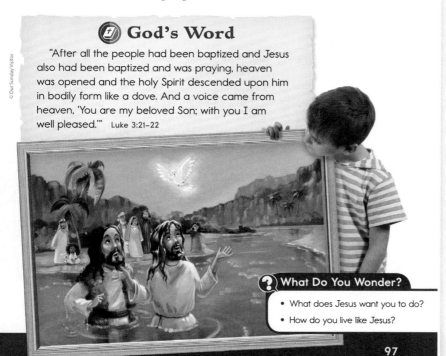

"After all the people had been baptized and Jesus also had been baptized and was praying, heaven was opened and the holy Spirit descended upon him in bodily form like a dove. And a voice came from heaven, 'You are my beloved Son; with you I am well pleased.'" Luke 3:21–22

What Do You Wonder?

- What does Jesus want you to do?
- How do you live like Jesus?

97

Optional Activity

Chapter Story: "Fun with Names" *Verbal/Linguistic*

Use this story after the opening prayer, before you tell the children that God sent his Son.

- Have the children list first names that they like.
- Point out how names can make us feel special and distinguish us from others.
- After connecting our names with the name of the Son of God, transition back to the lesson instruction.

Go to **aliveinchrist.osv.com** for Chapter Story.

Invite

Let Us Pray

Invite the children to gather in the prayer space and make the Sign of the Cross. Read aloud the leader's part. Then pray the Psalm verse and have the children repeat it after you. Prompt the children's response.

Have the children move out of the prayer space and back to their seats.

Explain that God sent his Son, Jesus, to lead us to Heaven.

Say: Let's listen to find out what God said about Jesus.

God's Word

Guide the children through the process of Scripture reflection.

- Invite them to close their eyes, be still, and open their minds and hearts to what God is saying to them in this passage.
- Proclaim the Scripture.
- Maintain several moments of silence.
- *Ask:* What did you hear God say to you today?
- Invite volunteers to share.

What Do You Wonder?

Say: God tells us that Jesus is his Son. God is pleased with him, and we should work to be like Jesus.

Invite the children to respond to the questions. Ask what else they might wonder about Jesus, the Son of God.

Discover

Objectives

- Recall that the Angel Gabriel announced to Mary that she would be the Mother of the Son of God, the Savior, Jesus
- Connect that the Holy Family of Jesus, Mary, and Joseph lived in Nazareth where Jesus grew up, learning and praying

A Savior is Born

Read aloud the introductory paragraph.

- Ask the children what special name they think God gave his Son. Jesus

Read aloud the second paragraph.

Work with Words

Direct the children to the Catholic Faith Words box, and have a volunteer name the two highlighted words.

- As you slowly read the definitions, have the children circle any unfamiliar words.
- Ask them where they heard the familiar words.

Direct the children to draw a square around the Angel Gabriel and draw a circle around Mary and Jesus.

Music Option: Have the children sing "Incarnate One," downloaded from **aliveinchrist.osv.com**.

A Savior is Born

What did the angel tell Mary?

All names have special meanings. Long ago, God sent his only Son to Earth. God sent him to show all people how they should live. God chose **Mary** to be his Son's Mother. His Son had a special name.

God sent the Angel Gabriel to Mary in the town of Nazareth. The **angel** told Mary that she would give birth to a son and that she would name him Jesus, which means, "God saves."

Catholic Faith Words

Mary the Mother of Jesus, the Mother of God. She is also called "Our Lady" because she is our Mother and the Mother of the Church.

angel a type of spiritual being that does God's work, such as delivering messages from God or helping to keep people safe from harm

1. Draw a square around the Angel Gabriel on the left.
2. Draw a circle around Mary and Jesus on the right.

Optional Activity

Activity Master 5: Jesus Comes to Us!

Distribute copies of the activity found on catechist page 97E.

- Have the children use pictures or words to write a story about Jesus.
- As an alternative, you may wish to send this activity home with the children.

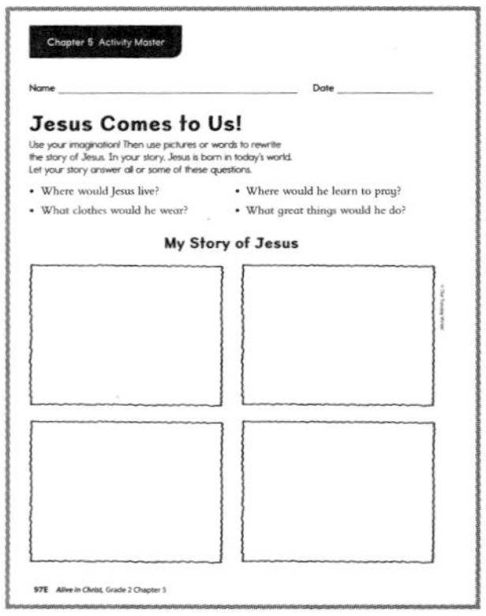
Chapter 5 Activity Master

Name Date

Jesus Comes to Us!

- Where would Jesus live?
- What clothes would he wear?
- Where would he learn to pray?
- What great things would he do?

My Story of Jesus

God's Word

Announcing Jesus' Birth

When the Angel Gabriel visited Mary he said, "He will be great and will be called Son of the Most High." Mary didn't understand how this could happen to her.

The angel said in reply, "The holy Spirit and the power of the Most High will come over you. Therefore the child to be born will be called holy, the Son of God." Mary told the angel, "May it be done to me as you say."

Months later, Jesus was born in Bethlehem. There were shepherds nearby caring for their flock. An angel of the Lord appeared to them in a great light. The shepherds were frightened.

The angel said, "Do not be afraid. Behold, I have Good News of great joy for all people. Today a savior has been born!" Based on Luke 1:26–38; 2:1–11

Share Your Faith

Think Write or draw your favorite part of the story inside the star.

Share Share with a partner.

Scripture Background

Annunciation

In the Gospel according to Luke, the writer says that Gabriel is the angel of the Lord with an important mission: to announce to Mary that God had selected her to bear his Son.

Tell the children that Gabriel's visit to Mary is called the *Annunciation* because he is announcing that she will be the Mother of the Son of God.

God's Word

Proclaim the first paragraph of the Scripture story.

- Tell the children that God named his Son *Jesus*.

Proclaim the second paragraph.

- Discuss with the children why they think Mary agreed to become the Mother of Jesus. because she wanted to do God's will; it was a special honor
- Organize the children into groups and have them role-play the Scripture events.

Ask: What is your favorite part of this story?

- Invite volunteers to share their responses.

Refer the children to Our Catholic Tradition, page 306 in the Student Book, for information on Mary and the Saints.

Activity

Read aloud the directions for the Share Your Faith activity.

- Provide the children with crayons or markers.
- When they are done, ask the children to share their work with a partner.

Quick Review

The Angel Gabriel announced to Mary that she would be the Mother of the Son of God. The Holy Family lived in Nazareth where Jesus grew up, learning and praying.

Discover

Objectives

- Identify Jesus as both the Son of God and a human being
- Recall the baptism of Jesus as the beginning of his public teaching

The Holy Family

Ask a volunteer to read the question.

- Record the children's responses on the board or on chart paper.

Read aloud the introductory paragraph, pointing out that Jesus, Mary, and Joseph are called the Holy Family. Tell the children that the Holy Family is a good role model for our own families.

God's Word

Ask the children to describe what is happening in the picture on this page.

- Invite three proficient readers to each proclaim a paragraph of the Scripture story.

Read aloud the final question and invite discussion.

The Holy Family

How did Jesus set an example for others?

Mary and Joseph brought Jesus back to Nazareth where he grew up. Together, they are called the **Holy Family**. Like most children, Jesus loved to learn and play. But Jesus was also very different, he was the Son of God.

Catholic Faith Words

Holy Family the name for the human family of Jesus, Mary, and Joseph

God's Word

The Boy Jesus in the Temple

When Jesus was twelve, Mary and Joseph took him to Jerusalem for a holy day. On their way home, Joseph and Mary noticed that Jesus was missing. They were very worried and went back to Jerusalem to find him.

They found Jesus sitting with wise teachers in the Temple. Jesus' questions and answers amazed everyone in the temple.

Jesus came back to Nazareth and obeyed his parents. He grew in age, in learning, and in holiness. Based on Luke 2:41–52

➔ **What is one thing Jesus might have told the wise teachers about God?**

Scripture Background

Jesus in the Temple

The part of the Temple where Jesus was speaking with the teachers was probably the portico or Temple classroom.

- This is the only Scripture reference we have to Jesus' activities at this age.
- The New Testament says that Jesus taught openly in the Temple or a synagogue.

Jesus Begins His Work

When Jesus was thirty years old, he went to see his cousin John. John wanted all sinners to turn toward God. He baptized them with water in the Jordan River.

God's Word

Baptism of Jesus

One day, Jesus asked John to baptize him. Jesus never sinned. But he wanted to set an example for others. After Jesus' baptism, the Holy Spirit came down on him in the form of a dove. Then a voice from Heaven said, "You are my beloved Son. I am pleased with you."

After this, Jesus taught about God his Father and shared his Father's love with everyone.

Based on Matthew 3:13–17

We learn about God the Father from the people in our families.

➔ **Who teaches you about God the Father?**

Connect Your Faith

Circle the Words Circle the names for Jesus and mark an X on the words that aren't. What's your favorite name for Jesus?

- Good Shepherd
- Savior
- John
- God the Son
- God the Cousin

____

Jesus Begins His Work

Read aloud the paragraph.

- Ask the children what John was doing. teaching sinners to turn to God; baptizing people

God's Word

Proclaim the Scripture story.

Explain that Jesus asked John to baptize him, not because Jesus was a sinner but because he wanted to set a good example for others.

Read aloud the question.

- Encourage the children to share their responses.

Ask a volunteer to read aloud the caption under the picture.

- Encourage volunteers to share what they see in the photo.

Activity

Read aloud the directions for the Connect Your Faith activity.

- Have the children complete the activity.
- Ask them to share their favorite name for Jesus.

Quick Tip

Graphic Organizer

Draw a graphic organizer on the board or on chart paper as you talk about the work of God the Father and God the Son.

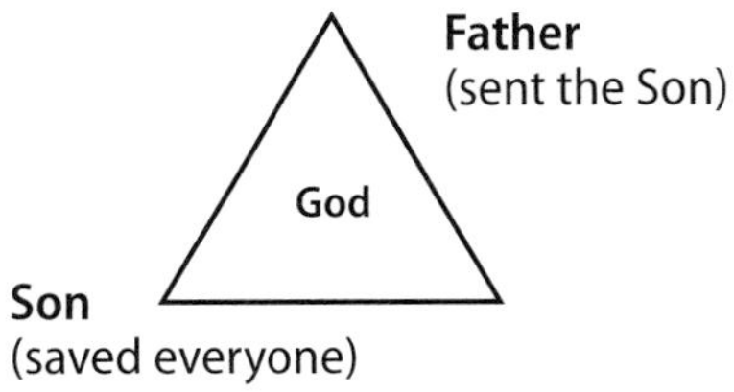

Quick Review

Jesus was both the Son of God and a human being. He began his Father's work by being baptized. After his baptism, Jesus taught about God the Father.

Live

Our Catholic Life

Ask: What does Jesus teach us about loving God and others?

- Discuss the children's responses.

Invite the children to listen as you read aloud the two paragraphs.

- Pause after reading the first sentence of the second paragraph. Point out that this is important for us to remember.

Say: Let's review the chart on this page to learn how to show our love for God and others.

- Read aloud the teachings of Jesus from the left column of the chart.
- Explain that the right column gives examples of what we can say to follow Jesus' teachings.

☆ Have the children complete the chart by filling in the blanks in the right column.

- When they are done, ask five children to each read aloud one of the things Jesus teaches and the corresponding example of things they can say.
- *Ask:* What are some other things Jesus teaches us?
- Write the children's responses on the board or on chart paper.

Our Catholic Life

What does Jesus teach us about loving God and others?

After his baptism, Jesus traveled throughout his country to remind others that God loved them. He taught them to love one another and to be good to others.

Jesus still teaches us today through the Bible, the Church, the Sacraments, and his followers. Listen carefully and you will learn how to show your love for God and others.

☆ Fill in the blanks with things you can say to follow Jesus' teachings.

What Jesus Teaches	Things You Can Say
Forgive other people.	I forgive you.
Be kind to others.	____________
Help people who are sick.	May I come visit you?
Share with others.	I'll share this orange with you.
Pray often.	____________

Reaching All Learners

Visual Learners

The children may benefit from seeing a visual representation of the events of Jesus' birth.

- Draw on the board or on chart paper a simple timeline. Work with children to complete the timeline with events from Scripture.
- Keep the timeline displayed so that the children may refer to it throughout the chapter.

People of Faith

Saint Peter, first century

Saint Peter was a fisherman with his brother Saint Andrew. Later, he was the leader of Jesus' followers. He knew that Jesus was the Son of God. But he also knew Jesus was a man. He ate with Jesus. He prayed with Jesus. He walked and talked with Jesus. He even went to parties with Jesus! Saint Peter knew that Jesus got tired and hungry. He knew when Jesus was happy and sad. But most of all, he knew that Jesus loved everyone. After Jesus died, Saint Peter told many people about Jesus. He is considered to be the first Pope.

June 29

Discuss: What do you think Jesus might have done for fun?

Learn more about Saint Peter at **aliveinchrist.osv.com**

Live Your Faith

Meet Jesus Choose one of the events shown and act out what Jesus might be saying. What would you say to Jesus if you were there?

Catholic Social Teaching

Chapter Connections

To integrate Catholic Social Teaching into your lesson, choose one of the following features: Life and Dignity, pages 292–293; or Human Solidarity, pages 300–301.

- Start the Live step of the process by talking about Saint Peter on page 103. Then move directly to the Catholic Social Teaching feature.
- Or, to expand the lesson, complete both pages 102 and 103, then move to the Catholic Social Teaching feature.
- Return to Chapter 5 for the prayer on page 104.

People of Faith

Tell the children about Saint Peter.

- Peter's birth name was Simon. Jesus renamed him Peter, which means "rock."
- He was married and lived with his mother-in-law when he first met Jesus.
- Peter made many missionary journeys.
- He died in Rome.

Read aloud the paragraph.

- Ask the Discuss question and encourage the children to share their thoughts.

Encourage the children to go to **aliveinchrist.osv.com** at home to learn more about Saint Peter.

Activity

Read aloud the directions for the Live Your Faith activity.

- Arrange the children in three small groups and assign each group one of the events. Give them time to rehearse their role-plays.
- Allow the small groups to act out their events in front of the rest of the children.
- *Ask:* What would you say to Jesus if you were there?

Let Us Pray
Signing Prayer

Prepare

Set up a crucifix and an image of Jesus in the prayer space.

You will be the leader.

Rehearse with the children "You Are God," downloaded from **aliveinchrist.osv.com**.

- Teach the children the ASL sign for "Jesus." (Tap each palm with the middle finger of the opposite hand. This represents the wounds of Christ.) Explain that they will use this in their prayer together.
- Point out to the children that just saying the name "Jesus" is a prayer all by itself. Say, "Wherever and whenever we want, we can pray just by saying Jesus' name with love." (See 2 Thessalonians 5:17—"Pray without ceasing.")

Gather

Invite the children to gather in the prayer space around the image of Jesus.

Pray

Follow the order of prayer on the student page.

Conclude by singing with the children "You Are God."

Let Us Pray

Signing Prayer

Gather and begin with the Sign of the Cross.

Leader: Father, you sent us your only Son, giving him "the name that is above every name" Philippians 2:9, the name that means "God saves." Accept our prayer of praise and thanks for

All: Sign and pray—Jesus,

Leader: the Redeemer who became one of us;

All: Sign and pray—Jesus,

Leader: who taught us in word and example;

All: Sign and pray—Jesus,

Leader: who suffered and celebrated with us;

All: Sign and pray—Jesus,

Leader: who died for us and rose to save us;

All: Sign and pray—Jesus,

Leader: in whose name we give glory to you, O God, now and forever.

All: Sing "You are God"

Jesus, you are God.
There is none like you.
Jesus, you are God,
and we worship you.

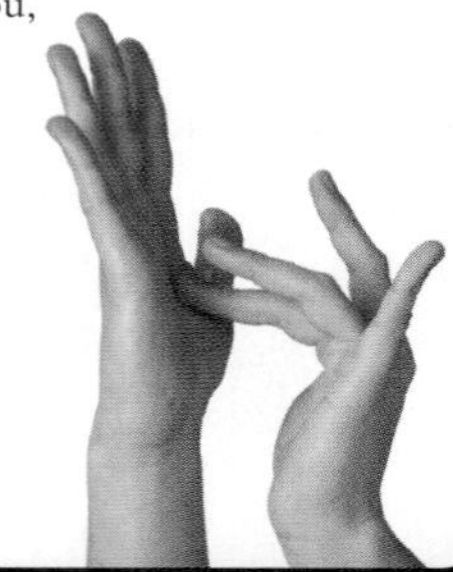

Liturgy Link

Singing

The musical tradition of the Church is one that can never be ignored. The combination of sacred music and words is an integral part of the celebration of the Eucharist and other liturgical celebrations.

- Include songs as part of your prayer services.
- Encourage the children to sing in loud, clear voices to show their love for God.

Go to **aliveinchrist.osv.com** for Sunday readings, Scripture background, questions of the week, and seasonal resources.

FAMILY + FAITH

LIVING AND LEARNING TOGETHER

YOUR CHILD LEARNED >>>

This chapter explores the Holy Family and Jesus' life on Earth.

God's Word

Go to **Luke 3:21–22** to read what happened at the baptism of Jesus.

Catholics Believe

- Jesus is the beloved Son of God born of Mary.
- Jesus is the Savior of the world who showed us God the Father's love.

To learn more, go to the *Catechism of the Catholic Church* #452–454 at **usccb.org**.

People of Faith

This week, your child met Saint Peter, who knew Jesus both as God and man.

CHILDREN AT THIS AGE >>>

How They Understand Jesus, God's Son Second-graders have often already heard many stories of Jesus. Because the Gospel stories offer few glimpses into Jesus' childhood (only infancy and age 12), it might be hard for your child to picture Jesus as a child his or her age. It is important for children this age to know that Jesus was also seven and eight years old, and that they can follow him in the choices they make right now. Their understanding of this will grow as you point out daily opportunities to be like Jesus through the choices your child makes.

CONSIDER THIS >>>

How is love made visible in your family?

The love visible in your family begins in the heart of God. "... Christ's command to love is the door to the supernatural order. At the same time, it encourages [us] to know that Jesus affirms the human good of each person. Together [we] must seek the same goals of mutual love united to Christ's love, the raising of a family and the continued growth of [our] relationship" (adapted from *USCCA, p. 286*).

LET'S TALK >>>

- Ask your child what stories about Jesus he or she heard this week (Jesus' birth, childhood, and baptism).
- Share what teaching of Jesus you remember learning about as a child and how it is still important to you today.

LET'S PRAY >>>

Saint Peter, pray for us that we may come to know and love Jesus as much as you did. Amen.

For a multimedia glossary of Catholic Faith Words, Sunday readings, seasonal and Saint resources, and chapter activities go to **aliveinchrist.osv.com**.

Family + Faith

Distribute the page to the children or parents/adult family members. Point out the chapter highlights, insights on how second graders understand concepts, the opportunity for the adults to reflect on their own experience and faith journey, and the family prayer.

Chapter 5 Review

A Work with Words Write the letter of the correct word or words from the Word Bank to complete the sentence.

1. Jesus is the c.
2. e told Mary about being the Mother of God's Son.
3. d is the Savior of the world.
4. b was Jesus' cousin.
5. Mary, Joseph, and Jesus are a.

Word Bank

a. the Holy Family
b. John
c. Son of God
d. Jesus
e. The Angel Gabriel

B Check Understanding Make a list of five things Jesus teaches us. Write the word that is missing from each teaching.

6. Forgive other people.
7. Be kind to others.
8. Help people who are sick.
9. Share with others.
10. Pray often.

Go to **aliveinchrist.osv.com** for an interactive review.

Chapter Review

Use Catechist Quick Reviews to highlight lesson concepts.

A Work with Words
Have the children write the letter that corresponds to the correct word or words in the Word Bank to complete each sentence.

B Check Understanding
Direct the children to write in the missing word from each teaching.

Go to **aliveinchrist.osv.com** to prepare customized and downloadable assessments, send eAssessments, and assign interactive reviews.

God the Holy Spirit

KEY CONCEPT
The Holy Spirit guides the Church and helps you to be a disciple. The Holy Trinity is one God in three Divine Persons.

DOCTRINAL CONTENT
- The Holy Trinity is one God in three Divine Persons. (CCC, 253–255)
- The Holy Spirit is the Third Divine Person of the Holy Trinity who helps and guides us as Jesus promised. (CCC, 683–684)
- Jesus is the Son of God who became man, the Second Divine Person of the Holy Trinity. (CCC, 258–259)
- The Holy Spirit helped the Apostles understand and spread the teachings of Jesus and is with the Church today, helping us in many ways. (CCC, 767–768)

TASKS OF CATECHESIS
Helping children grow in a faith that is "known, celebrated, lived, and expressed in prayer" (NDC, 20).

This chapter focuses on the following tasks of catechesis:
- Promoting Knowledge of the Faith
- Liturgical Education

Catechist Background

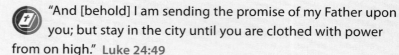

"And [behold] I am sending the promise of my Father upon you; but stay in the city until you are clothed with power from on high." Luke 24:49

→ **Reflect** How do you allow the Holy Spirit to guide you?

The word *Spirit* is translated from the Hebrew word *ruah*, which means "movement of air, wind, breathing." All of these meanings combine in an expression that makes the wind a sign of the breath of God or his Spirit. The Third Divine Person of the Blessed Trinity, the Holy Spirit, is often described as the spirit of love between the Father and the Son. In your own life, this love strengthens you to fulfill God's call.

Throughout the Old Testament, the Spirit of God is a companion of those who have a mission to fulfill. The actions of the Holy Spirit are present in the New Testament accounts of the Annunciation of the Lord and the Baptism of Jesus. He worked in Jesus' followers, too. After Jesus' close followers received the Holy Spirit, they went forth to preach the Good News. Today the Holy Spirit continues to act in the lives of Christ's followers.

The Holy Spirit is alive in the Body of Christ. He is working through people who have touched your life, people who have been instrumental in your own ministry as a catechist. They have used their gifts from the Holy Spirit to nurture new life in you, so that through the power of the Holy Spirit, you can continue the work of Jesus each time you serve another.

→ **Reflect** Who has helped you open up and respond to the Holy Spirit in your life?

Catechist's Prayer

Holy Spirit, help me as I teach the children you have entrusted to me. Bless each of them, their families, and their friends. Guide my words and actions that I may help them to grow closer to you. Amen.

Lesson Plan

Objectives	Process	Materials
Invite, 10 minutes		
God the Holy Spirit Page 107	**Psalm 143:10** Pray the opening prayer. **Luke 24:49** Reflect prayerfully on the Word. • Discuss What Do You Wonder questions.	**Optional Activity** Chapter Story: "Wind"
Discover, 35 minutes		
One in Three Pages 108–109 • Define the Holy Trinity as one God in three Divine Persons • Identify the Holy Spirit as the Third Divine Person of the Holy Trinity who helps and guides us • Identify Jesus as the Second Divine Person of the Holy Trinity	• **Catholic Faith Words** Holy Spirit, Holy Trinity • Talk about the effects of the Holy Spirit. ☆ Color around the image of the Holy Spirit. **John 14:15–26** Proclaim "The Promise." • Discuss the three Divine Persons of the Holy Trinity. • **Share Your Faith Activity** Color the circles to represent each Person of the Holy Trinity.	☐ pencils or pens ☐ colored pencils or fine-tipped markers ☐ board or chart paper • **Optional Activity** The Holy Trinity ☐ Activity Master 6 (Page 107E)
Guided by the Spirit Pages 110–111 • Recognize the Holy Spirit's role in helping the Apostles understand and spread the teachings of Jesus • Understand that the Holy Spirit is with the Church today, helping us in many ways	• **Catholic Faith Words** disciples, Pentecost, Apostles • Review what Jesus promised the disciples. ☆ Underline how the Holy Spirit came. **Acts 1:4–5; 8; 2:2–3** Proclaim "The Spirit Comes." • Discuss how the the Holy Spirit helps disciples. • **Connect Your Faith Activity** Circle the places where the Holy Spirit helps.	☐ pencils or pens
Live, 15 minutes		
Our Catholic Life Pages 112–113	• Discuss what it means to follow Jesus. ☆ Write or draw how you can follow Jesus. • **People of Faith** Learn about Saint Arnold Janssen. • **Live Your Faith Activity** Memorize the Prayer for the Holy Spirit.	☐ pencils or pens ☐ board or chart paper
Prayer for the Holy Spirit Page 114	• Choose a volunteer for the leader part. Rehearse "The Holy Spirit." • Follow the order of prayer.	Download "The Holy Spirit."

Family + Faith Page 115

Point out that the Catholic Families page provides chapter highlights, information on how second graders understand faith concepts, and family prayer.

Chapter Review Page 116

aliveinchrist.osv.com

- Customize and Download Assessments
- Email Links to eAssessments
- Interactive Student Reviews

Teaching This Grade

ONLINE RESOURCES

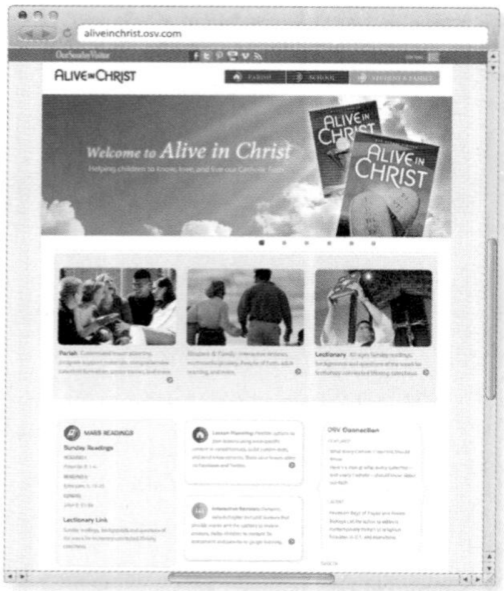

Go to **aliveinchrist.osv.com**

You will find:

- Interactive lesson planning with web specific content and additional activities
- Step by step lesson instruction from printed Catechist Edition for integrated lesson planning
- Custom-built assessments to download and eAssessment links
- Interactive reviews that provide scores and the option to review answers
- Sunday readings with background and questions of the week

Go to **osvparish.com**

You will find:

- Ask the Experts Q and A
- General Catechist Helps
- Community Connections and Blogs

Sharing the Message with Second Graders

God the Holy Spirit The Holy Spirit might still be difficult for a second grader to understand, but children this age are growing in their understanding that the Holy Spirit lives in their heart. Because cause and effect is so important to children this age, reflecting on the Gifts and Fruits of the Spirit can help second graders see the work of the Holy Spirit in their own lives.

Teaching Tip: Refer to the Fruits of the Spirit in Galatians 5:22. When you see one of these demonstrated in the session (e.g., a child who is joyful or someone who is being patient), point out that the Holy Spirit helps these characteristics to grow in our lives.

How Second Graders Understand

- Second graders are still dreamers. Most of what they know about God comes from what they imagine.
- Sometimes children this age have a hard time sitting still. Try to incorporate hands-on activities.
- At this point in their lives, some children like to take ownership of their tasks. Give them the opportunity to contribute individually and in groups.

"Sometimes I find it hard to sit still. Give me some hands-on activities."

Chapter Connections

Chapter Story

Invite

"Wind"

Use this story to expand the chapter introduction.

- Ask the children to draw a windy day. Have them discuss why the wind is blowing.
- Ask them if they can draw the Holy Spirit.
- Remind them that we can only draw how we see the Holy Spirit work.

Go to **aliveinchrist.osv.com** Lesson Planning section for this story.

NCEA IFG: ACRE Edition

Discover

Knowledge of the Faith

- Objective: To know and understand basic Catholic teaching about the Incarnate Word Jesus Christ as the way, truth, and life

Liturgical Life

- Objective: To know the Paschal Mystery of Jesus: in the Church's liturgical life—feasts, seasons, symbols, and practices and in the Sacraments as signs and instruments of grace

Catholic Social Teaching

Live

Use one of these features to introduce a principle and engage the children with an activity.

- Call to Community, Pages 292–293
- Rights and Responsibilities, Pages 294–295

Music Options

Use one or more of the following songs to enhance catechetical learning or for prayer.

- "The Holy Spirit," Live Prayer, Page 114
- "The Sign of the Cross," Live, Page 112
- "The Trinity," Live, Page 112
- "Come to Us, Spirit of Jesus," Live, Page 112

LECTIONARY CONNECTION

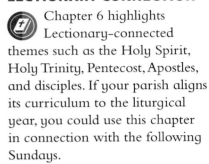

Chapter 6 highlights Lectionary-connected themes such as the Holy Spirit, Holy Trinity, Pentecost, Apostles, and disciples. If your parish aligns its curriculum to the liturgical year, you could use this chapter in connection with the following Sundays.

Year A

Sixth Sunday of Easter—Promise of the Paraclete

Pentecost Sunday—Descent of the Holy Spirit

Year B

Pentecost Sunday—Holy Trinity

Twenty-eighth Sunday in Ordinary Time—Holy Spirit

Year C

Sixth Sunday of Easter—The Advocate Will Teach

Pentecost Sunday—The Spirit dwells in you.

Go to **aliveinchrist.osv.com** for a complete correlation ordered by the Sundays of the year and suggestions for how to integrate the Scripture readings into chapter lessons.

Name ______________________________ Date ______________

The Holy Trinity

Use pictures or words to tell about each Divine Person of the Holy Trinity.

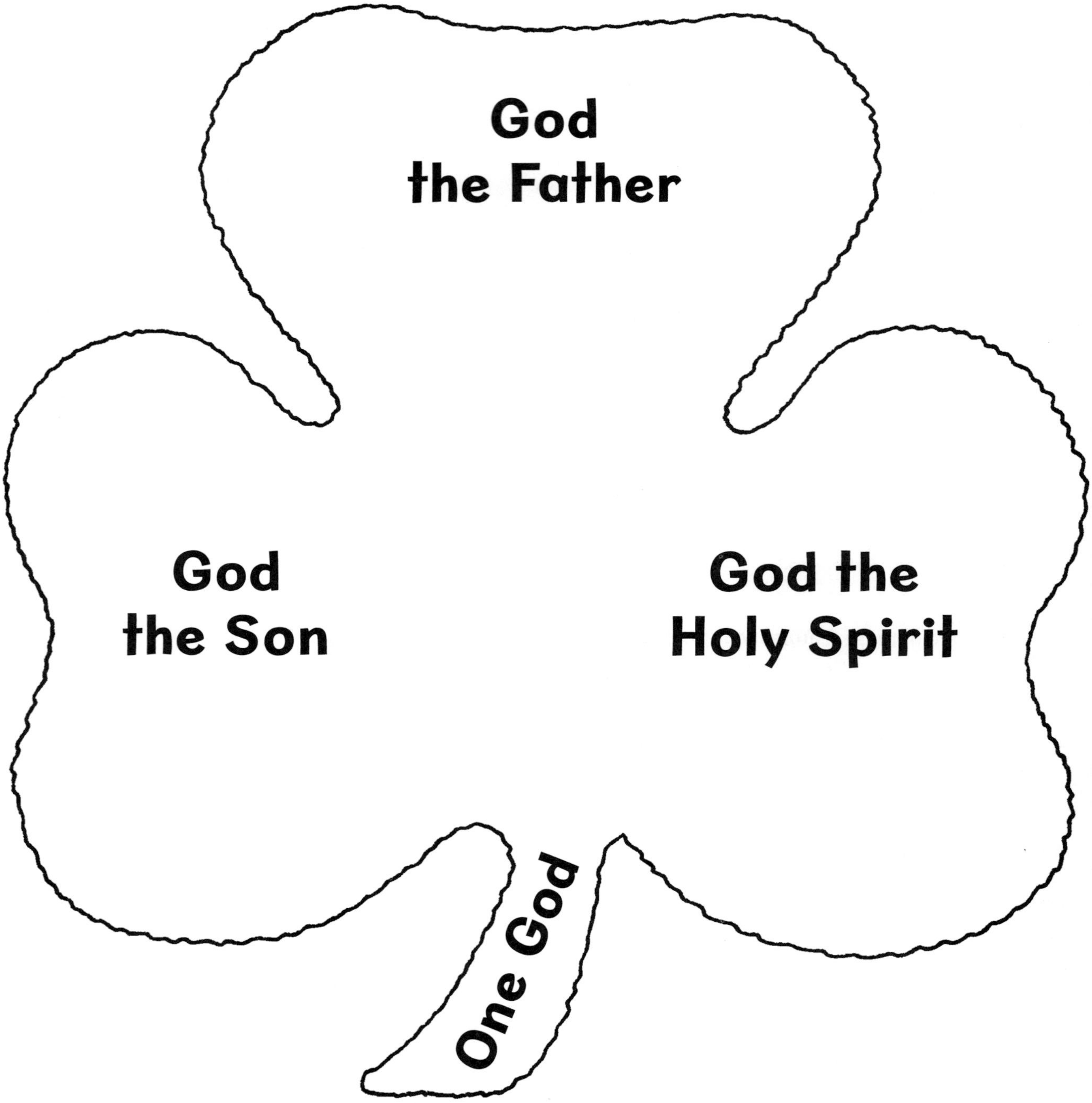

God the Holy Spirit

Let Us Pray

Leader: God, send us your Holy Spirit.

"May your kind spirit guide me." Psalm 143:10

All: Holy Spirit, be with us always. Amen.

God's Word

"And [behold] I am sending the promise of my Father upon you; but stay in the city until you are clothed with power from on high."

Luke 24:49

What Do You Wonder?

- What does the Holy Spirit look like?
- How do you know the Holy Spirit is with you?

Optional Activity

Chapter Story: "Wind" *Bodily/Kinesthetic, Visual/Spatial*

Use this story after the opening prayer, before talking to the children about the Holy Spirit.

- Discuss how every time we make good choices and show love for God, the Holy Spirit is present and working in us.
- Connect the effects of the wind with the effects of the Holy Spirit as you transition back to the lesson instruction.

Go to **aliveinchrist.osv.com** for Chapter Story.

Invite

Let Us Pray

Invite the children to gather in the prayer space and make the Sign of the Cross. Ask a volunteer to read aloud the leader's prayer, including the Psalm verse. Prompt the group's response.

Have the children move out of the prayer space and back to their seats.

Explain that Jesus promised the Apostles that God the Father would send them help.

Say: Let's listen to find out what Jesus said about the Holy Spirit.

God's Word

Guide the children through the process of Scripture reflection.

- Invite them to close their eyes, be still, and open their minds and hearts to what God is saying to them in this passage.
- Proclaim the Scripture.
- Maintain several moments of silence.
- *Ask:* What did you hear God say to you today?
- Invite volunteers to share.

What Do You Wonder?

Say: In today's passage, Jesus says he is sending the promise of his Father to give the Apostles "power from on high." He's talking about the Holy Spirit.

Invite the children to respond to the questions. Ask what else they might wonder about the Holy Spirit.

Discover

Objectives

- Define the Holy Trinity as one God in three Divine Persons
- Identify the Holy Spirit as the Third Divine Person of the Holy Trinity who helps and guides us
- Identify Jesus as the Second Divine Person of the Holy Trinity

One in Three

Ask a volunteer to read the question.

- List the children's answers on the board or on chart paper.

Read aloud the introduction.

- Stress that although you cannot see the Holy Spirit, you can see what the Holy Spirit does.

God's Word

Proclaim the Scripture story.

Ask: What did Jesus promise his followers? the Holy Spirit

- Discuss the question with the children.

Work with Words

Ask the children to name the two Catholic Faith Words in the box.

Ask: Which word is part of both new words? Holy Which words are different? Spirit and Trinity

Have the children write the definitions and practice reading them to a partner.

☆ Invite the children to color in the stained glass frame around the image of the Holy Spirit.

- Allow plenty of time for the children to color carefully.

Color in the stained glass frame around the image of the Holy Spirit.

One in Three

Who is the Holy Trinity?

You cannot see the wind, but you know that it is there. You cannot see the **Holy Spirit** either, but you can see what the Spirit does.

Catholic Faith Words

Holy Spirit the Third Divine Person of the Holy Trinity

Holy Trinity the one God in three Divine Persons—God the Father, God the Son, and God the Holy Spirit

God's Word

The Promise

Jesus knew he would be returning to his Father in Heaven. He wanted his followers to continue his work.

Jesus promised his followers, "The Advocate, the holy Spirit that the Father will send in my name—he will teach you everything and remind you of all that [I] told you." Based on John 14:15–26

Songs of Scripture

Holy Spirit

This simple song helps the children to understand the attributes of the Holy Spirit.

- The Holy Spirit gives us courage to stand up for others, teaches us about Jesus, guides us in making good decisions, and helps us pray.
- Teach the children the song "Holy Spirit."

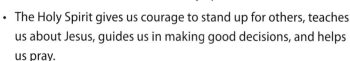

Use *Songs of Scripture*, Grades 1–3 CD, Track 12

Father, Son, and Holy Spirit

Jesus teaches you that God is the Father of all. Jesus is the Son of God. And the Holy Spirit, sent from the Father and the Son, is also God.

But there are not three gods. There is only one God, who is Father, Son, and Holy Spirit. The Church's name for the one God in three Divine Persons is the **Holy Trinity**.

God the Father is the First Person of the Holy Trinity. God the Son became man in Jesus Christ. He is the Second Person of the Holy Trinity. God the Holy Spirit is the Third Person of the Holy Trinity.

Believing in the Holy Trinity is the most important part of your faith and you show your belief when you make the Sign of the Cross.

Share Your Faith

Think Choose a color for each Person of the Holy Trinity, then color or decorate the circles using the colors you have chosen.

Share Talk about your picture with a partner.

Father, Son, and Holy Spirit

Explain to the children that what they are going to learn next is one of the most important parts of their faith.

- Read aloud the first paragraph. Stress that Father, Son, and Holy Spirit are one God.
- *Say:* Jesus' teachings helped us understand that there is one God in three Divine Persons.

Read aloud the remaining paragraphs.

- *Ask:* Who is the First Divine Person of the Holy Trinity? God the Father Who is the Second Divine Person of the Holy Trinity? God the Son Who is the Third Divine Person of the Holy Trinity? God the Holy Spirit
- Ask the children how we show our belief in the Trinity. by making the Sign of the Cross
- Have the children turn to Our Catholic Tradition, page 320, to read and pray together the Sign of the Cross.

Activity

Read aloud the directions.

- Allow the children time to color the circles.

Optional Activity

Activity Master 6: The Holy Trinity

Distribute copies of the activity found on catechist page 107E.

- Have the children draw or write about each Divine Person of the Holy Trinity.
- As an alternative, you may wish to send this activity home with the children.

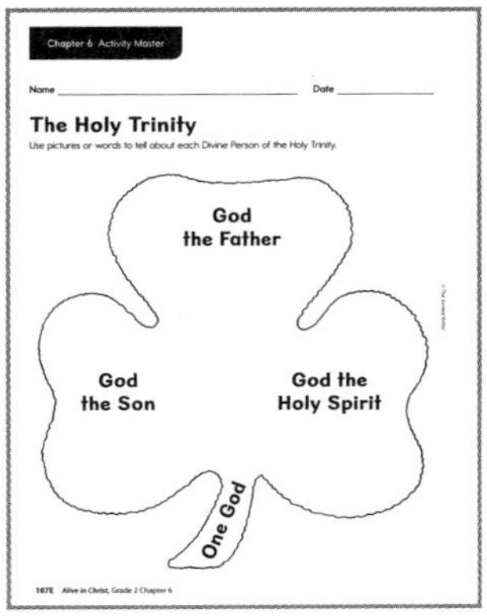

Chapter 6 Activity Master

Name ____________ Date ____________

The Holy Trinity

Use pictures or words to tell about each Divine Person of the Holy Trinity.

God the Father

God the Son

God the Holy Spirit

One God

107E Alive in Christ, Grade 2 Chapter 6

Quick Review

After Jesus' Ascension, God sent the Holy Spirit to Jesus' followers. The Holy Spirit is the Third Divine Person of the Holy Trinity and the guide that Jesus promised.

Discover

Objectives

- Recognize the Holy Spirit's role in helping the Apostles understand and spread the teachings of Jesus
- Understand that the Holy Spirit is with the Church today, helping us in many ways

Guided by the Spirit

Remind the children that before Jesus returned to Heaven, he made a special promise to the Apostles.

Have a volunteer read the question at the top of the page.

- Discuss with the children their responses.

God's Word

Proclaim the Scripture story.

- Ask the children what Jesus told the disciples to do. He told them to go to Jerusalem.
- Ask the children what happened when the disciples were waiting. There was a noise like a driving wind, and it filled the place where they were staying.
- ☆ Have the children underline the ways the Holy Spirit came to the disciples.
- Invite the children to describe what they see in the illustration.

Guided by the Spirit

How is the Holy Spirit with us today?

Before Jesus returned to Heaven, he told his **disciples** his plan for them.

God's Word

The Spirit Comes

Jesus told his disciples to wait for the promise of the Father that he had told them about. He said, "You will receive power when the holy Spirit comes upon you, and you will be my witnesses in Jerusalem . . . and to the ends of the earth."

The Twelve disciples and some other followers of Jesus stayed in Jerusalem and prayed. Soon the Holy Spirit came. Suddenly a noise like a strong driving wind came from the sky, and it filled the entire house in which they were gathered. Then tongues of fire appeared to them, which parted and came to rest on each one of them. This day is called Pentecost.

Based on Acts 1:4–5, 8; 2:2–3

☆ Underline the ways the Holy Spirit came to the disciples on the day of Pentecost.

Optional Activity

Disciple Collage *Visual/Spatial*

Tell the children they will be making a collage or a picture-story of how the disciples helped others.

- Provide poster board, pictures from magazines and newspapers, markers, construction paper, and other craft items.
- Invite the children to work in pairs to create a collage of things disciples do to help others.
- Ask the children to tell the group about their collages when they are completed.

The Holy Spirit Today

After the Holy Spirit came to them at **Pentecost**, Jesus' Twelve closest disciples were guided to continue his work. They became known as his **Apostles**.

The Holy Spirit comes today through the Church's Sacraments and prayer and in God's Word. The Holy Spirit guides the Church and makes Jesus' disciples holy. He helps you make good decisions and grow more loving.

Disciples of Jesus

Jesus' disciples are in every part of the world. The Holy Spirit teaches us all how to pray. The Spirit helps today's disciples remember and understand the stories of Jesus. You are learning to be a disciple of Jesus.

Catholic Faith Words

disciples followers of Jesus who believe in him and live by his teachings

Pentecost fifty days after the Resurrection when the Holy Spirit first came upon the Twelve disciples and the Church

Apostles the Twelve disciples Jesus chose to be his closest followers. After the coming of the Holy Spirit, they shared in his work and mission in a special way.

Connect Your Faith

Circle the Places Circle each place on the map where the Holy Spirit helps you be a disciple of Jesus.

The Holy Spirit Today

Ask a volunteer to read aloud the first paragraph to discover when the Holy Spirit came to the Apostles. Read the next paragraph and ask the children to listen closely to learn four things that the Holy Spirit does. The Holy Spirit guides the Church, helps you follow Jesus, guides you in the decisions you make, and helps you to become a more loving person.

Disciples of Jesus

Ask the children to read the paragraphs. Discuss the definition of *disciples*. Point out that all Christians are disciples of Jesus.

- Help the children identify ways they are becoming disciples.

Activity

Read aloud the directions for the Connect Your Faith activity.

- Help the children circle the places on the map where the Holy Spirit helps them be a disciple of Jesus.

Quick Tip

Love Your Neighbor

Jesus said that one of the greatest commandments was to "love your neighbor as yourself." This obligation is deeply rooted in both Jewish and Christian faith.

- Help the children identify people around and among them who are in need.
- Talk with them about simple ways they can share God's love with others.

Quick Review

The Holy Spirit came to the disciples of Jesus on Pentecost. We find the Holy Spirit in the Church's Sacraments, in prayer, and in God's Word. The Holy Spirit helped the Apostles and still guides the Church today.

Our Catholic Life

Begin by reading aloud the question.

- Write the children's responses on the board or on chart paper.

Invite a volunteer to read aloud both paragraphs.

Ways to Follow Jesus

Read aloud the heading and each entry in the chart. Ask the children to give specific examples of how to put each step into action.

- ☆ Direct the children to write or draw a way they can follow Jesus' example today.
- Give the children enough time to complete the activity.
- Allow the children to share with a partner what they wrote or drew.

Music Option: While the children work, play "The Sign of the Cross," "The Trinity," or "Come to Us, Spirit of Jesus," downloaded from **aliveinchrist.osv.com**.

Our Catholic Life

What does it mean to follow Jesus?

Jesus' first followers were his friends. They traveled with Jesus and listened to his stories. They saw how Jesus treated others. Jesus asked his Apostles and other disciples to help others learn about God's love.

You are Jesus' friend and follower, too. He wants you to listen to him and to live the way he lived. Being a disciple of Jesus means following his example.

Ways to Follow Jesus

- Pray to God the Father.
- Ask the Holy Spirit to guide you.
- Think of other people, not only of yourself.
- Be fair to your family members and friends.
- Help people who are in need.

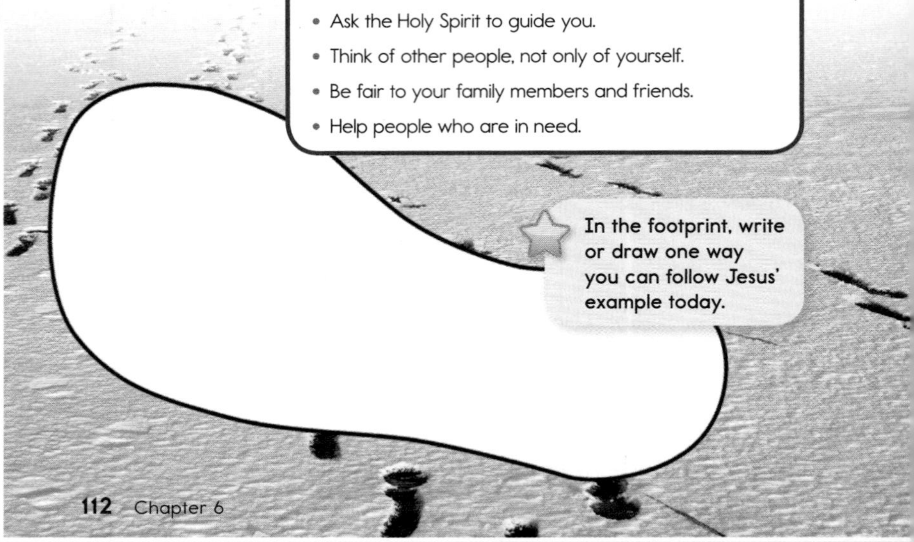

☆ In the footprint, write or draw one way you can follow Jesus' example today.

Catechist Background

Vocabulary: Disciple

Remind the children that the word *disciple* comes from a word that means "learner."

- Another word that comes from the same root is *discipline* (a lesson or a way of reinforcing learning).
- Sharing stories about the disciples is a good way to provide the children with examples of ways to follow Jesus.

People of Faith

Saint Arnold Janssen, 1837–1909

January 15

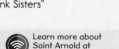

Saint Arnold Janssen was a German priest. He wanted everybody to know about Jesus. He helped priests and sisters, serving as missionaries, build churches all around the world. They went to faraway places like China. Saint Arnold prayed to the Holy Spirit to help with his work. He asked some religious sisters to help him pray. These sisters took turns praying all day and night for the missionaries. Today, sisters like these are sometimes called "Pink Sisters" because they wear pink habits.

Discuss: What do you pray to the Holy Spirit for?

Learn more about Saint Arnold at **aliveinchrist.osv.com**

Live Your Faith

Learn by Heart
Memorize the Prayer for the Holy Spirit.

Come, Holy Spirit, fill the hearts of your faithful.
And kindle in them the fire of your love.
Send forth your Spirit and they shall be created.
And you will renew the face of the earth.

113

People of Faith

Tell the children about Saint Arnold Janssen.

- Saint Arnold started a printing press to get funding for missionaries. Thousands of lay persons helped him distribute the magazines.
- His whole life, he constantly searched for God's will.
- The missionary communities he founded are active in 63 countries.
- Read aloud the paragraph on Saint Arnold.
- Discuss the final question.

Encourage the children to go to **aliveinchrist.osv.com** at home to learn more about Saint Arnold Janssen.

Activity

Read aloud the directions for the Live Your Faith activity.

- Have the children work in pairs as they read and then recite the prayer.
- When they are all finished, recite the prayer together as a group.

Catholic Social Teaching

Chapter Connections

To integrate Catholic Social Teaching into your lesson, choose one of the following features: Call to Community, pages 292–293; or Rights and Responsibilities, pages 294–295.

- Start the Live process by talking about Saint Arnold on page 113. Then move to the Catholic Social Teaching feature.
- Or, to expand the lesson, complete both pages 112 and 113, then move to the Catholic Social Teaching feature.
- Return to Chapter 6 for the prayer on page 114.

Let Us Pray

Prayer for the Holy Spirit

Prepare

Choose a leader for the prayer, and practice with him or her.

Have the children rehearse "The Holy Spirit," downloaded from **aliveinchrist.osv.com**.

Gather

Ask the children to join you in the prayer space. Have each child bring his or her book.

Pray

Begin by praying the Sign of the Cross.

Follow the order of prayer on the student page.

To extend the celebration, pray with the children the Prayer for the Holy Spirit that they memorized earlier.

Conclude by processing around the room with the children singing "The Holy Spirit."

Let Us Pray

Prayer for the Holy Spirit

Gather and begin with the Sign of the Cross.

Leader: Let us sing as we ask God to send the Holy Spirit to us each day.
In our family...

All: Send us your Spirit, O Lord.

Leader: With our classmates...

All: Send us your Spirit, O Lord.

Leader: In all that we say and do...

All: Send us your Spirit, O Lord.

Leader: We ask this in Jesus' name.

All: Amen.

Sing "The Holy Spirit"

The Holy Spirit, sent from God above.
The Holy Spirit, bringing peace and love.
Receive the power of the Holy Spirit today!

The Holy Spirit, giving strength each day.
The Holy Spirit, showing us the way.
Receive the power of the Holy Spirit today!

Liturgy Link

Sacred Music

Singing is a wonderful way for the children and adults to praise God.

- Sacred music has dignity and lovely melodies which embellish the voices of the Christian people who praise God.
- Its special power and excellence should lift the minds of the faithful to God. It should make the prayers of the Christian community more alive and fervent.

Go to **aliveinchrist.osv.com** for Sunday readings, Scripture background, questions of the week, and seasonal resources.

FAMILY + FAITH

LIVING AND LEARNING TOGETHER

YOUR CHILD LEARNED >>>

This chapter explains that Jesus promised to send the Holy Spirit to be our helper and guide.

God's Word

Read **Acts 2:1–4** to find out about the coming of the Holy Spirit on the first Pentecost.

Catholics Believe

- The Holy Spirit guides the Church and helps you to be a disciple.
- The Holy Trinity is one God in three Divine Persons.

To learn more, go to the *Catechism of the Catholic Church* #237, 243 at **usccb.org**.

People of Faith

This week, your child met Saint Arnold Janssen, a German priest with a special devotion to the Holy Spirit.

CHILDREN AT THIS AGE >>>

How They Understand God the Holy Spirit The Holy Spirit might still be difficult for your child to understand, but children this age are growing in their understanding that the Holy Spirit lives in their heart. Because cause and effect is so important to children this age, reflecting on the Gifts and Fruits of the Spirit can help second-graders see the work of the Holy Spirit in their own lives. Talk with your child about the Fruits and Gifts of the Spirit (See the We Live section in the back of your book.), and point out times when you see examples in their actions.

CONSIDER THIS >>>

Imagine being invited somewhere you really want to go.

The greatest invitation we ever get is the invitation to spend all of eternity with God. "'Heaven is the ultimate end and fulfillment of the deepest human longings, the state of supreme, definitive happiness' (CCC, no. 1024). This will be brought about by a perfect communion with the Holy Trinity, the Blessed Mother, the angels and saints. Jesus Christ opened heaven to us by his death and Resurrection" (*USCCA, p. 153*).

LET'S TALK >>>

- Have your child describe who the Holy Spirit is and what he does.
- Name some ways your family can be followers of Jesus.

LET'S PRAY >>>

Guard me, ... O Holy Spirit, that I always may be holy. (Prayer of Saint Augustine)

For a multimedia glossary of Catholic Faith Words, Sunday readings, seasonal and Saint resources, and chapter activities go to **aliveinchrist.osv.com**.

Family + Faith

Distribute the page to the children or parents/adult family members. Point out the chapter highlights, insights on how second graders understand concepts, the opportunity for the adults to reflect on their own experience and faith journey, and the family prayer.

Chapter 6 Review

A Work With Words Complete each sentence with the correct word or words from the Word Bank.

1. The Holy Spirit came to the disciples as [b].
2. The [d] is one God in three Divine Persons.
3. The Holy Spirit helps us make good [c].
4. The day the Holy Spirit came is called [e].
5. The disciples became known as Jesus' [a] after the Holy Spirit came to them.

Word Bank
a. Apostles
b. wind
c. decisions
d. Holy Trinity
e. Pentecost

B Check Understanding Fill in the circle beside the correct answer.

6. You show belief in the Holy Trinity when you make the ____.
   - ● Sign of the Cross ○ sign of love ○ sign of peace
7. Being a disciple of Jesus means following his ____.
   - ○ orders ○ directions ● example
8. To follow Jesus, you need to think of ____.
   - ● other people ○ yourself ○ only your friends
9. Jesus asked his Apostles to help others learn about ____.
   - ○ animals ○ creation ● God's love
10. The ____ guides the Church.
   - ○ Holy Friends ● Holy Spirit ○ Holy Week

Go to **aliveinchrist.osv.com** for an interactive review.

Chapter Review

Use Catechist Quick Reviews to highlight lesson concepts.

A Work with Words
Have the children write the letter that corresponds to the correct word in the Word Bank to complete each sentence.

B Check Understanding
Explain to the children that they will be filling in the circle of the correct answer.

Go to **aliveinchrist.osv.com** to prepare customized and downloadable assessments, send eAssessments, and assign interactive reviews.

UNIT 2

Unit Review

Use Catechist Quick Reviews in each chapter to highlight lesson concepts for this unit and prepare for the Unit Review.

Have the children complete the Review pages. Then discuss the answers as a group. Review any concepts with which the children are having difficulty.

A Work with Words Direct the children to complete each sentence with the correct word or words from the Word Bank.

B Check Understanding Tell the children to draw a line from the descriptions in Column A to the correct names in Column B.

Unit Review

UNIT 2

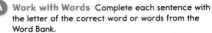

A Work with Words Complete each sentence with the letter of the correct word or words from the Word Bank.

Word Bank
- a. Holy Spirit
- b. disciples
- c. Holy Trinity
- d. Father
- e. prayer

1. People who follow Jesus are called b.
2. Jesus promised to send the a.
3. Listening and talking to God is called e.
4. Jesus taught us to call God d.
5. The one God in three Divine Persons is called the c.

B Check Understanding Draw a line from the descriptions in Column A to the correct names in Column B.

Column A	Column B
6. The Third Person of the Holy Trinity	Mary
7. The Mother of God's Son	John Bosco
8. The First Person of the Holy Trinity	God the Holy Spirit
9. A Saint who helped homeless boys	God the Son
10. The Second Person of the Holy Trinity	God the Father

UNIT 2

Unit Review

Fill in the circle beside the correct answer.

11. You can always ____ God to love you.

○ respect ● trust ○ know

12. After Jesus was ____ he traveled the country where he lived.

● baptized ○ older ○ risen

13. Jesus teaches today through the ____.

● Church ○ town ○ Earth

14. You can follow Jesus by ____ people.

○ mistreating ○ forgetting ● forgiving

15. A ____ of Jesus follows his example.

○ enemy ○ Saint ● disciple

C Make Connections Complete each sentence below.

16. A Saint is a holy person who **obeyed God**.

17. Prayer is talking to and **listening to God**.

18. To trust is to believe in and **depend on someone**.

19. Disciples are people who choose **to follow Jesus**.

20. The Apostles are the Twelve **disciples**.

Write the name or names that best answer the question.

21. I am the Mother of the Church. Who am I?

Mary

22. Once when my parents were looking for me they found me in the Temple talking to the wise teachers. Who am I?

Jesus

23. I baptized my cousin Jesus in the Jordan River. Who am I?

John the Baptist

24. You receive me in the Church's Sacraments and I help you pray. Who am I?

The Holy Spirit

25. Together we make up the Holy Family. Who are we?

Jesus, Mary, and Joseph

B Check Understanding

Have the children fill in the circle beside the correct answer.

C Make Connections

Instruct the children to complete each sentence for 16–20. Have them write the name or names that best answer the question for 21–25.

Go to **aliveinchrist.osv.com** to prepare customized and downloadable assessments, send eAssessments, and assign interactive reviews.

UNIT 3

Jesus Christ

Our Catholic Tradition

- God gave Moses the Ten Commandments to help us know how to live in love. (CCC, 2077)
- Jesus gave us a New Commandment to love as he loves us. (CCC, 1970)
- Our conscience is a gift from God that helps us make choices about right and wrong. (CCC, 1777–1778)
- Jesus teaches us that God our Father always offers forgiveness and shows us mercy. (CCC, 545)

Why do we depend on Jesus' promise for mercy and forgiveness?

Unit 3 Overview

The children will:

- describe the Ten Commandments as God's laws that teach us to love him and others
- relate the Great Commandment, which sums up all of God's laws, to our lives
- recognize that Jesus told The Parable of the Good Samaritan to help us understand that loving God means loving our neighbor
- relate the New Commandment, to love as Jesus loves, to our lives

Songs of Scripture
"LOVE God"

Catholic Social Teaching: Live Your Faith

- Rights and Responsiblities, Pages 294–295
- Option for the Poor, Pages 296–297

The children will:

- understand that when we make bad choices that hurt our relationship with God and others, God forgives us if we are truly sorry
- describe sin as a free choice to do what we know is wrong; discern mistakes and accidents as different from sins
- differentiate between venial sin and mortal sin and how each harms our relationship with God
- identify conscience as an ability given to us by God that helps us make choices about right and wrong

Catholic Social Teaching: Live Your Faith

- Rights and Responsibilities, Pages 294–295
- The Dignity of Work, Pages 298–299

The children will:

- explore God's mercy in the story of the Prodigal Son
- celebrate that God has mercy on us even though we are sinners
- recognize that virtues can help us say no to temptation and choose what is good
- understand the importance of asking God for forgiveness and being forgiving toward others

Catholic Social Teaching: Live Your Faith

- Call to Community, Pages 292–293
- Human Solidarity, Pages 300–301

Preview Unit Theme

Ask: What is the unit theme?

Affirm that the unit focus is on Jesus Christ.

Ask: Why do we depend on Jesus' promise for mercy and forgiveness? Encourage the children to share their thoughts.

Have four volunteers each read aloud one of the bullet points under the Our Catholic Tradition head.

Ask other volunteers to describe what they see in the photo and illustrations. Have them connect the images to the unit theme.

After some discussion, explain that the group will be exploring all of these things in the next three chapters.

Chapter 7 God's Commandments

KEY CONCEPT
The Ten Commandments are God's laws to his People. Jesus teaches you to love God above all things and love others as you love yourself.

DOCTRINAL CONTENT

- The Ten Commandments are God's laws that teach us to love him and others. (CCC, 1962)
- The Great Commandment sums up all of God's laws, telling us to love God above all else and others the way you love yourself. (CCC, 2055)
- Jesus told the parable of the Good Samaritan to help us understand that loving God means loving our neighbor. (CCC, 546, 1465)
- Jesus gave us a New Commandment to love as he loves. (CCC, 1970)

TASKS OF CATECHESIS
Helping children grow in a faith that is "known, celebrated, lived, and expressed in prayer" (NDC, 20).

This chapter focuses on the following tasks of catechesis:

- Promoting Knowledge of the Faith
- Moral Formation

Catechist Background

The LORD said to Moses: Come up to me on the mountain and, while you are there, I will give you the stone tablets on which I have written the commandments intended for their instruction. Exodus 24:12

➜ **Reflect** Does knowing how the Ten Commandments came to be affect the way you view them?

The Israelites sometimes lost their way on their forty-year journey through the desert. They worshipped false gods and lost faith when there was no food to eat or water to drink. They grumbled at Moses and Aaron and quarreled among themselves. God, through Moses, gave the Israelites the Ten Commandments to guide them. The people received his Commandments and laws with good intentions, responding with one voice, "All that the LORD has said, we will hear and do" (Exodus 24:7). The Israelites found that the promise was easier made than kept.

Reflect on your own journey of life. Like the Israelites, you may find yourself grumbling, too—"I'm tired; it's boring; life is hard." The Israelites were lost and in need of God's mercy. God responded by providing guidance in the form of the Ten Commandments, which he asked his People to follow. He asks you to do the same in your own faith journey.

Jesus summed up God's Commandments in one word, and that word is *love*. For Jesus, faithfulness to all God's Commandments could be shown in love of God and love of neighbor. Loving God and others is challenging. Exhaustion and ambivalence can cause you to steer off course and to fail to love with all your heart. Throughout the journey, it is important to stay focused on God for guidance. He is love, and that love is your strength as you journey with others to the Kingdom.

➜ **Reflect** How can you love more completely today?

Catechist's Prayer

Lord, help me take time to refocus my life and get more in touch with your Spirit within me. Nourish me, Lord. Fill me with your love, so that I can more fully give your love to others. Amen.

Lesson Plan

Objectives	Process	Materials
Invite, 10 minutes		
God's Commandments Page 121	**Psalm 119:18–19** Pray the opening prayer. **Exodus 24:12** Reflect prayerfully on the Word. • Discuss What Do You Wonder questions.	**Optional Activity** Chapter Story: "A Good Place"
Discover, 35 minutes		
The Ten Commandments Pages 122–123 • Describe the Ten Commandments as God's laws that teach us to love him and others • Relate the Great Commandment, which sums up all of God's laws, to our lives	• **Catholic Faith Words** Ten Commandments, Great Commandment • Discuss ways to live the Commandments. ☆ Indicate where more help is needed in living the Commandments. **Luke 10:29–37** Proclaim the Scripture passage. • Talk about how to show love for God. • **Share Your Faith Activity** Write ways to follow one Commandment.	☐ pencils or pens
The Ways of Love Pages 124–125 • Recognize that Jesus told The Parable of the Good Samaritan to help us understand that loving God means loving our neighbor • Relate the New Commandment, to love as Jesus loves, to our lives	• **Catholic Faith Words** parable, New Commandment • Discuss how Jesus helped people understand his teachings with parables. **John 10:11–14** Proclaim "The Parable of the Good Samaritan." • Name ways to show love for neighbors. • **Connect Your Faith Activity** Plan a skit.	☐ pencils or pens ☐ board or chart paper ☐ poster board ☐ markers
Live, 15 minutes		
Our Catholic Life Pages 126–127	• Read and discuss ways to live the Great Commandment and the New Commandment. • **People of Faith** Learn about Saint Elizabeth of Hungary. • **Live Your Faith Activity** Give examples of people who are neighbors.	☐ pencils or pens • **Optional Activity** Live the Commandments ☐ Activity Master 7 (Page 121E)
Prayer of Praise Page 128	• Practice the response with the children. Rehearse "Loving God." • Follow the order of prayer.	Download "Loving God."

Family + Faith Page 129

Point out that the Catholic Families page provides chapter highlights, information on how second graders understand faith concepts, and family prayer.

Chapter Review Page 130

aliveinchrist.osv.com

- Customize and Download Assessments
- Email Links to eAssessments
- Interactive Student Reviews

ONLINE RESOURCES

Go to **aliveinchrist.osv.com**

You will find:

- Interactive lesson planning with web specific content and additional activities
- Step by step lesson instruction from printed Catechist Edition for integrated lesson planning
- Custom-built assessments to download and eAssessment links
- Interactive reviews that provide scores and the option to review answers
- Sunday readings with background and questions of the week

Go to **osvparish.com**

You will find:

- Ask the Experts Q and A
- General Catechist Helps
- Community Connections and Blogs

Sharing the Message with Second Graders

The Great Commandment Second graders are just beginning to move out of the self-centered tendencies of earlier childhood. But in a society so focused on individual comfort and fulfillment, it can be counter-cultural to speak of putting God over everything else or loving others as much as one loves one's self. Second graders will need much guidance to understand how this translates into the practical decisions they make every day.

Teaching Tip: When discussing the Great Commandment and other guidelines for living, try to point to specific examples from the lives of second graders whenever possible. You might also wish to act out everyday situations that involve moral decision making, and encourage the children to demonstrate loving choices.

How Second Graders Understand

- Children this age need rules. Help them by setting clear limits so they know what to do.
- Second graders not only like to know the rules but they also like to help establish them.
- Children want others to play fair. They need to know that they are playing fair, too.

"Rules help me know what to do. Please make sure they are clear."

Chapter Connections

Chapter Story

Invite

"A Good Place"

Use this story to expand the chapter introduction.

- Pair the children together. Give them time to discuss the rules they would make for the playground.
- Have the partners share their ideas with the rest of the group.

Go to **aliveinchrist.osv.com** Lesson Planning section for this story.

NCEA IFG: ACRE Edition

Discover

Knowledge of the Faith

- Objective: To know and understand basic Catholic teaching about the Incarnate Word Jesus Christ as the way, truth, and life

Moral Formation

- Objective: To be knowledgeable about the teachings of Jesus and the Church as the basis of Christian morality and to understand Catholic Social Teaching

Catholic Social Teaching

Live

Use one of these features to introduce a principle and engage the children with an activity.

- Rights and Responsibilities, Pages 294–295
- Option for the Poor, Pages 296–297

Music Options

Use one or more of the following songs to enhance catechetical learning or for prayer.

- "Loving God," Live Prayer, Page 128
- "God's Good Rules," Discover, Page 124
- "Jesu, Jesu," Discover, Page 124
- "Love Like Jesus Did," Discover, Page 124

LECTIONARY CONNECTION

Chapter 7 highlights Lectionary-connected themes such as the Ten Commandments, the Great Commandment, and the New Commandment. If your parish aligns its curriculum to the liturgical year, you could use this chapter in connection with the following Sundays.

Year A

Twenty-third Sunday in Ordinary Time—Love Fulfills the Law

Thirtieth Sunday in Ordinary Time—The Greatest Commandment

Year B

Sixth Sunday in Ordinary Time—Love for Others

Seventh Sunday in Ordinary Time—Keep the Commandments

Year C

Fifth Sunday of Easter—Love One Another

Fifteenth Sunday in Ordinary Time—Great Commandments

Go to **aliveinchrist.osv.com** for a complete correlation ordered by the Sundays of the year and suggestions for how to integrate the Scripture readings into chapter lessons.

Name ______________________________ Date ______________

Live the Commandments

Read the sentences below. After each sentence, write the Commandment it describes. Use the Commandments listed in the tablets as a guide. Then write one way you can live the Commandment at home or at school.

1. I do not take what does not belong to me. ______________________

____

2. I always listen to my parents. ______________________

____

3. I do not use God's name in a bad way. ______________________

____

4. I praise and honor God on Sundays. ______________________

____

God's Commandments

Let Us Pray

Leader: Dear God, help us to know and follow your truth.

"Open my eyes to see clearly
the wonders of your law....
do not hide your commandments from
me." Psalm 119:18–19

All: Thank you, God, for showing us how to follow you. Amen.

God's Word

"The LORD said to Moses: Come up to me on the mountain and, while you are there, I will give you the stone tablets on which I have written the commandments intended for their instruction." Exodus 24:12

What Do You Wonder?

- Who gives you the rules to live by every day?
- Why do people need rules?

Optional Activity

Chapter Story: "A Good Place" *Verbal/Linguistic*

Use this story after the opening prayer, before explaining that God gives us rules.

- Ask the children what they do at recess. Then read "A Good Place."
- Have the children identify some rules they must follow on the playground. List responses on the board or on chart paper.
- Discuss why rules are important, then transition back to the lesson instruction.

Go to **aliveinchrist.osv.com** for Chapter Story.

Invite

Let Us Pray

Invite the children to gather in the prayer space and make the Sign of the Cross. Ask a volunteer to read aloud the leader's prayer and the Psalm verses. Prompt the children's response.

Have the children move from the prayer space back to their seats.

Explain that God gives us rules that help us to live as Jesus lived.

Say: Let's listen to what Jesus said about following God's rules.

God's Word

Guide the children through the process of Scripture reflection.

- Invite them to close their eyes, be still, and open their minds and hearts to what God is saying to them in this passage.
- Proclaim the Scripture.
- Maintain several moments of silence.
- *Ask:* What did you hear God say to you today?
- Invite volunteers to share.

What Do You Wonder?

Say: Jesus gives us rules for how to live each day as he did. We need rules or there would be no order. Jesus' rules help us to stay safe and guide us to be more loving toward our neighbors.

Invite the children to respond to the questions. Ask what else they might wonder about God's laws and why he shares them with us.

Discover

Objectives

- Describe the Ten Commandments as God's laws that teach us to love him and others
- Relate the Great Commandment, which sums up all of God's laws, to our lives

The Ten Commandments

Have a volunteer read aloud the question.

- Discuss possible responses with the children.

Read aloud the paragraph. Explain that God gave people laws called the Ten Commandments. These laws help us to know right from wrong and to make good choices.

☆ Tell the children that as the group reviews the chart, they should work on their own to check two things they need more help understanding.

- Read aloud each of the Commandments.
- Ask volunteers to respond with how we can live them.
- Take questions on anything the children would like more help in understanding.

The Ten Commandments

What can help me to make good choices?

God gave Moses and his Chosen People some laws to help them. These laws are called the **Ten Commandments**. God wants you to follow these laws, too. They help you make good choices about your friendship with God and others.

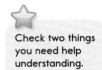

☆ Check two things you need help understanding.

The Ten Commandments		How You Can Live Them
1 I am the LORD your God: you shall not have strange Gods before me.	☐	Make God the most important thing in your life.
2 You shall not take the name of the LORD your God in vain.	☐	Use God's name in a reverent way.
3 Remember to keep holy the LORD'S Day.	☐	Attend Mass and rest on Sunday.
4 Honor your father and your mother.	☐	Love and obey your parents and guardians.
5 You shall not kill.	☐	Be kind to people and animals.
6 You shall not commit adultery.	☐	Be respectful in the things you do with your body.
7 You shall not steal.	☐	Don't take other people's things.
8 You shall not bear false witness against your neighbor.	☐	Tell the truth.
9 You shall not covet your neighbor's wife.	☐	Keep your thoughts and words clean.
10 You shall not covet your neighbor's goods.	☐	Be happy with the things you have; don't be jealous of what others have.

Catechist Background

Ten Commandments

The Ten Commandments are recorded in the Book of Exodus.

- God gave Moses the Ten Commandments as a sign of his love and friendship.
- Scripture tells us that Moses received the Commandments on two stone tablets when he was talking to God on top of a mountain.
- Moses then brought the Commandments to the people.

Jesus' Commands

Jesus learned and followed the Ten Commandments. When he grew up, Jesus taught a Commandment called the **Great Commandment**. It includes all the other Commandments and sums up God's laws.

Catholic Faith Words

Ten Commandments God's laws that tell people how to love him and others

Great Commandment the law to love God above all else and to love others the way you love yourself.

God's Word

"You shall love the Lord, your God, with all your heart, with all your being, with all your strength, and with all your mind, and your neighbor as yourself." Luke 10:27

God's Commandments teach us how to live and show love. Learning about his Commandments helps us grow closer to him. It also helps us prepare for the Sacrament of Penance and Reconciliation.

➔ How do you show love for God?

Share Your Faith

Think Pick one Commandment and write some ways you can follow it.

____

____

____

Share Talk about it in a small group.

Jesus' Commands

Ask the children to silently read the first paragraph.

- Explain that Jesus taught one Commandment that sums up all of the Ten Commandments.

God's Word

Proclaim the Scripture passage. Read aloud the last paragraph on the page.

- Have the children discuss the question.

Direct the children to page 317 in the Our Catholic Tradition section of their books, and discuss the importance of God's Laws.

Work with Words

Have a volunteer read aloud the highlighted words on pages 122 and 123.

- Ask the children to find the definitions of both words in the Catholic Faith Words box. Have them write them down and discuss with a partner how the definitions are alike and different.

Activity

Read aloud the directions for the Share Your Faith activity.

- Have the children work in groups.
- Ask someone from each group to share their written statement.

Songs of Scripture

LOVE God

The children should be familiar with this song as it is commonly sung in the primary grades.

- To help the children understand the words more deeply, have them think about the two important commands in this song: to love God and our neighbor.
- Teach the children the song "LOVE God."

Use *Songs of Scripture*, Grades 1–3 CD, Track 4

Quick Review

The Ten Commandments help us follow God. The Great Commandment tells us to love God above all else and to love others as we love ourselves.

Objectives

- Recognize that Jesus told The Parable of the Good Samaritan to help us understand that loving God means loving our neighbor
- Relate the New Commandment, to love as Jesus loves, to our lives

The New Commandment

Write the word *parable* on the board or on chart paper.

- Explain that Jesus liked to tell stories called *parables* because they taught people how to love God and others.
- Ask the children to recall other parables Jesus told, such as the story of the Good Shepherd.

God's Word

Invite the children to sit in a circle; have them bring their books with them.

- Proclaim "The Parable of the Good Samaritan."
- Remind the children to look at the pictures on both pages as they listen to the story.
- Ask the children if they can identify the people from the story in the illustrations.

Music Option: Have the children sing "God's Good Rules," "Jesu, Jesu," or "Love Like Jesus Did," downloaded from **aliveinchrist.osv.com**.

Go back up to the top of the page and read aloud the question. Based on the parable they heard, the children should be able to answer: love our neighbor.

The New Commandment

What does Jesus ask us to do?

Jesus told many stories, or parables, to teach his followers that loving God means loving our neighbor. Here is a **parable** he told.

Catholic Faith Words

parable a short story Jesus told about everyday life to teach something about God

New Commandment Jesus' command for his disciples to love one another as he has loved us

God's Word

The Parable of the Good Samaritan

Once a man asked Jesus, "Who is my neighbor?" Jesus told this story to answer him.

A man was going along a road alone. Robbers came and beat him up. They took everything he had and ran away, leaving him half-dead.

A Jewish priest was going down the same road. When he saw the man, he ignored him.

Later, someone who took care of the Temple came along. When he saw the man, he also ignored him.

Catechist Background

Parable

The word *parable* means "to compare beside." It denotes a story that draws a comparison. Jesus' parables convey religious messages. He could have simply told the questioner that everyone should be treated as a neighbor, but he chose instead to set his answer in a story that would invite the listener in, as well as lead to a specific conclusion.

Then a man from Samaria came along and saw the man lying on the roadside. He hurried over to help. The Samaritan bandaged the man's sores and took him to an inn. The Samaritan gave the innkeeper two silver coins to help take care of the man.

Then Jesus asked, "Which of the three was a neighbor to the robbers' victim?" The man said, "The one who treated him with mercy."

Jesus said, "Go and do likewise." Luke 10:29–37

This story shows that a neighbor is any person who is in need. The Samaritan saw a man who needed help. He showed him kindness and respect. Jesus tells us how we should treat each other. We are to love one another as he has loved us. This is called the **New Commandment**.

Connect Your Faith

Act It Out Plan a Good Samaritan skit.

1. Make notes for each part and include some props.
2. Take turns acting out different roles.

What good or bad choices were made in this story?

The Parable of the Good Samaritan

Ask the children to name the two people in the story who did not show love. the priest and temple worker

Ask: What better choice could the priest or temple worker have made?

- Allow the children to make some suggestions.
- Write *Jesus* in the center of a piece of poster board. Have the children take turns writing around Jesus' name some ways that they can be a "good samaritan" and show love for their neighbor.

Work with Words

Have the children place their finger on the Catholic Faith Words *New Commandment*.

Have them look at page 124 and silently read the definition.

Activity

Read aloud the directions for the Connect Your Faith activity.

- Help the children plan the words to be spoken by the "actors."
- Allow time for the children to rehearse their roles before presenting their skits to the group.
- Discuss the question with the children.

Quick Tip

Personal Safety

The story of the Good Samaritan might seem to contradict what the children have learned about not talking to strangers.

- Explain that they can be a neighbor to people their own age—perhaps by being kind on the playground.
- Remind the children that they should never put themselves at risk by helping someone else. This includes when an adult they do not know asks for help. They can report a troubling situation to a trusted adult instead.

Quick Review

Jesus used parables, or stories, to teach about love of God and neighbor. A neighbor is anyone in need of kindness and mercy. The New Commandment is Jesus' command on how to love.

Our Catholic Life

Ask: How can you be a good neighbor?

- Invite group discussion.

Read aloud the introductory paragraphs.

- Invite the children to name people who are their neighbors according to Jesus' definition.

Draw attention to the chart, and invite a child to read aloud "The Great Commandment" and another to read "The New Commandment."

- Ask one volunteer to read the three entries in the first column and another to read the three entries in the second column.
- Have the children work independently to fill in the blank under each column, writing one way they can show love for God and one way they can show love for a neighbor.
- *Ask:* What would you tell a preschooler about how to be a good neighbor?
- Have the children discuss possible answers with a partner.

Our Catholic Life

How can you be a good neighbor?

In the story of the Good Samaritan, Jesus taught that neighbors aren't just the people who live next door to you. All people are neighbors. A neighbor can be someone who is in need, like the man who was robbed. A neighbor can be someone who helps, like the Samaritan.

How do neighbors treat one another? The Great Commandment and Jesus' New Commandment tell us.

Write one way you love God and one way you can love your neighbor.

The Great Commandment	The New Commandment
"Love God above all things, and love your neighbor as you love yourself."	"Love one another as I have loved you."
Spend time with God every day in prayer.	Don't judge people by how they look or by how many things they have.
Thank him for all he has given us.	Reach out to people who are lonely.
Grow closer to him by learning more about him.	When someone asks you for forgiveness, give it gladly.
______________________	______________________

Optional Activity

Activity Master 7: Live the Commandments

Distribute copies of the activity found on catechist page 121E.

- Allow the children to work with a partner.
- As an alternative, you may wish to send this activity home with the children.

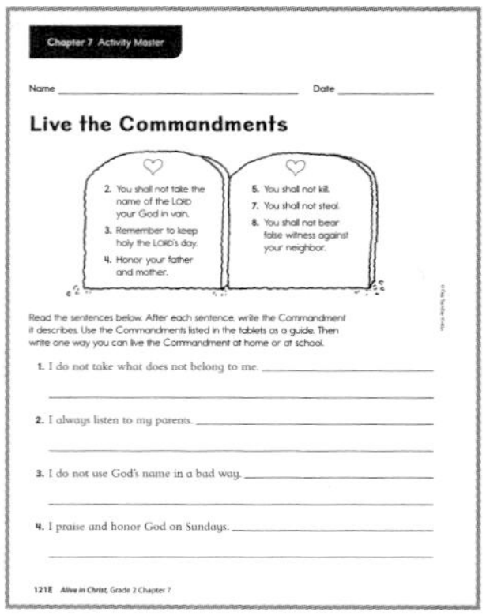

Chapter 7 Activity Master

Name ______ Date ______

Live the Commandments

2. You shall not take the name of the LORD your God in vain.
3. Remember to keep holy the LORD's day.
4. Honor your father and mother.
5. You shall not kill.
7. You shall not steal.
8. You shall not bear false witness against your neighbor.

Read the sentences below. After each sentence, write the Commandment it describes. Use the Commandments listed in the tablets as a guide. Then write one way you can live the Commandment at home or at school.

1. I do not take what does not belong to me. ______
2. I always listen to my parents. ______
3. I do not use God's name in a bad way. ______
4. I praise and honor God on Sundays. ______

121E Alive in Christ, Grade 3 Chapter 7

People of Faith

Saint Elizabeth of Hungary, 1207–1231

November 17

Saint Elizabeth was a princess of Hungary. Jesus' command to love one another was very important to Elizabeth. She spent her entire life caring for people who were poor and suffering. Elizabeth fed the hungry by giving them food at the castle gate. She sold her jewels and used the money to build hospitals. When her husband died, she was very sad. She worked hard to take care of her four children, but she kept helping the poor, too.

Discuss: What have you donated to those in need?

Learn more about Saint Elizabeth at **aliveinchrist.osv.com**

Live Your Faith

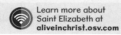

Love Others Give two examples of people who are your neighbors and how you help each other.

1. ______________________________

____

____

____

2. ______________________________

____

____

____

Catholic Social Teaching

Chapter Connections

To integrate Catholic Social Teaching into your lesson, choose one of the following features: Rights and Responsibilities, pages 294–295; or Option for the Poor, page 296–297.

- Start the Live process by talking about Saint Elizabeth of Hungary on page 127. Then move to the Catholic Social Teaching feature.
- Or, to expand the lesson, complete both pages 126 and 127, then move to the Catholic Social Teaching feature.
- Return to Chapter 7 for the prayer on page 128.

People of Faith

Tell the children about Saint Elizabeth of Hungary.

- Saint Elizabeth was the daughter of King Andrew II (the King of Hungary) and his wife Gertrude.
- Her marriage was planned when she was four years old; she went to live with and was raised by her future marital family. But her future husband died, so when she came of age, she married his brother.
- Saint Elizabeth was very religious and prayed often.
- She had a hospital built, which aided nine hundred poor people daily.
- Read aloud the paragraph on Saint Elizabeth.
- Have a volunteer read aloud the Discuss question. Invite the children to share their answers with the group.

Encourage the children to go to **aliveinchrist.osv.com** at home to learn more about Saint Elizabeth of Hungary.

Activity

Read aloud the directions for the Live Your Faith activity.

- Encourage the children to think about how they help their neighbors and how their neighbors help them.
- Allow the children to read their responses to the group.

Let Us Pray

Prayer of Praise

Explain to the children that praise means to give honor and thanks to God. In this prayer of praise, we are praising Jesus as we follow his example to love our neighbor and love the Lord with all our heart.

Prepare

Practice the response with the children. You will be the leader.

Rehearse with the children "Loving God," downloaded from **aliveinchrist.osv.com**.

Gather

Invite the children to assemble in the prayer space with their books

- Invite them to quiet themselves on the inside and outside for prayer.

Pray

Follow the order of prayer on the student page.

Conclude by processing around the room with the children singing "Loving God."

Let Us Pray

Prayer of Praise

Gather and begin with the Sign of the Cross.

Leader: Jesus, you tell us you are the Way,
the Truth, and the Life (See John 14:6).

All: we praise and honor you.

Leader: You show us the way to the Father,

All: we praise and honor you.

Leader: You teach us the truth about love,

All: we praise and honor you.

Leader: You give us hope and life,

All: we praise and honor you.

Leader: Help us, Lord, to love as you do,
fully and completely.

All: Amen.

Sing "Loving God"

Love the Lord, your God,
with all your heart,
with all your soul,
with all your mind,
and with all your strength.

Liturgy Link

The Word of the Lord

The Church has always venerated both Sacred Scripture and the Body and Blood of Christ as sources of Divine nourishment.

- Model how to listen attentively to what is read from the Bible.
- Explain that you proclaim what you believe about the Scriptures when you hear, "The Word of the Lord" and respond "Thanks be to God."

Go to **aliveinchrist.osv.com** for Sunday readings, Scripture background, questions of the week, and seasonal resources.

FAMILY + FAITH

LIVING AND LEARNING TOGETHER

YOUR CHILD LEARNED >>>

This chapter explains that the Ten Commandments teach us how to love God above all things and to love others. They are summed up in the Great Commandment.

God's Word

Read **Exodus 24:12** to learn what God said to Moses about the Ten Commandments.

Catholics Believe

- The Ten Commandments are God's laws to his People.
- Jesus teaches you to love God above all things and love others as you love yourself.

To learn more, go to the *Catechism of the Catholic Church* #830, 2053 at **usccb.org**.

People of Faith

This week, your child met Saint Elizabeth of Hungary, a princess who used her wealth to feed the hungry and build hospitals for the sick.

CHILDREN AT THIS AGE >>>

How They Understand the Great Commandment
Second-graders are just beginning to move out of the self-centered tendencies of earlier childhood. But in a society so focused on individual comfort and fulfillment, it can be counter-cultural to speak of putting God over everything else or loving others as much as one loves one's self. Your child will need much guidance to understand how this translates into the practical decisions he or she makes every day. Much of this guidance will come in the form of the example you provide of caring for others and prioritizing God over other things.

CONSIDER THIS >>>

How do the rules in your home help you to love each other?

Children might think that rules restrict our freedom, but in actuality they lead us to reap the benefits of a deeper love. "... God has given us the virtue of love, the very love that he has for us. Our Lord asks us to accept this love and respond to him with it. Jesus made the love of God the first of the two greatest Commandments: 'You shall love the Lord, your God, with all your heart, with all your soul, and with all your mind (Matthew 22:37)'" *(USCCA, p. 343).*

LET'S TALK >>>

- Talk about family rules and why they are important.
- Ask your child what rules God gives us (Ten Commandments) and what Jesus commands us to do (to love one another as he has loved us).

LET'S PRAY >>>

Saint Elizabeth, pray for us that we always love our neighbors as ourselves. Amen.

For a multimedia glossary of Catholic Faith Words, Sunday readings, seasonal and Saint resources, and chapter activities go to **aliveinchrist.osv.com**.

Family + Faith

Distribute the page to the children or parents/adult family members. Point out the chapter highlights, insights on how second graders understand concepts, the opportunity for the adults to reflect on their own experience and faith journey, and the family prayer.

Chapter 7 Review

A Work with Words Complete each sentence with the correct word from the Word Bank.

Word Bank
Love
neighbor
Forgive
Share
choices

1. **Love** God above all things.
2. The Ten Commandments help you make good **choices**.
3. The Great Commandment helps you know how to be a good **neighbor**.
4. **Share** what you have with others.
5. **Forgive** someone who asks you for forgiveness.

B Check Understanding Match the Commandment on the left with the correct action on the right.

Column A	Column B
6. You shall not kill.	Say God's name with care
7. You shall not take the name of the LORD your God in vain.	Do not harm yourself or others
8. Honor your father and your mother.	Go to Mass on Sunday
9. You shall not steal.	Obey your parents
10. Remember to keep holy the LORD'S day.	Do not take what belongs to another

Go to **aliveinchrist.osv.com** for an interactive review.

Chapter Review

Use Catechist Quick Reviews to highlight lesson concepts.

A Work with Words
Ask the children to use the words in the Word Bank to complete the sentences.

B Check Understanding
Have the children work to match the Commandments and actions. Tell them that each action can be used only once.

Go to **aliveinchrist.osv.com** to prepare customized and downloadable assessments, send eAssessments, and assign interactive reviews.

Chapter 8 Choose to Do Good

KEY CONCEPT
Conscience is the ability given to us by God that helps us make choices about right and wrong. Sin is a free choice to do what you know is wrong.

DOCTRINAL CONTENT

- When we make bad choices that hurt our relationship with God and others, God forgives us if we are truly sorry. (CCC, 1441)
- Sin is a free choice to do what we know is wrong. Mistakes and accidents are not sins. (CCC, 1849)
- Both venial and mortal sins harm our relationship with God, but in different ways. (CCC, 1854–1855)
- Conscience is an ability given to us by God that helps us make choices about right and wrong. We need to know God's laws and let the Holy Spirit guide us. (CCC, 1777–1778)

TASKS OF CATECHESIS
Helping children grow in a faith that is "known, celebrated, lived, and expressed in prayer" (NDC, 20).

This chapter focuses on the following tasks of catechesis:

- Promoting Knowledge of the Faith
- Moral Formation

Catechist Background

Then Peter remembered the word that Jesus had said to him, "Before the cock crows twice you will deny me three times." He broke down and wept. Mark 14:72

➔ **Reflect** In what ways do you deny Jesus' teachings?

Prior to finding the Promised Land, the Israelites wandered for forty years in the desert. Before Jesus began his public ministry, he was tempted in the desert. Today, some people feel as if they are wandering aimlessly in the desert. At times, the road of life can be lonely and frightening, barren, and empty. When things are difficult, it is easy to lose your way. At these times, it is good to remember that God does not abandon his People.

Let the difficult times be a reminder to you of how close God was to his Chosen People during their forty-year sojourn in the desert. It was there that God made his loving intentions clear to his People. "I will take you as my own people, and I will be your God" (Exodus 6:7).

The Creator intends for you to be his very own. Like the Israelites, your challenge is to not lose sight of God on the journey.

The Apostle Peter loved Jesus dearly, yet his love did not stop him from denying Jesus three times. Peter was devastated by his own actions, but Jesus did not abandon him. Jesus forgave Peter and called him to go forth to share the Good News. When you freely choose the wrong path, God will not abandon you. Sin is a choice, but so is your willingness to seek forgiveness. God is always ready to give you another chance and to forgive you, and that is truly good news.

➔ **Reflect** For what do you wish to be forgiven?

Catechist's Prayer

Lord, please help me teach the children about your love and forgiveness. Help me practice patience and understanding as I try to make each child feel loved. Amen.

Lesson Plan

Objectives	Process	Materials
Invite, 10 minutes		
Choose to Do Good Page 131	**Psalm 119:33** Pray the opening prayer **Mark 14:69–73** Reflect prayerfully on the Word. • Discuss What Do You Wonder questions.	**Optional Activity** Chapter Story: "New Friends"
Discover, 35 minutes		
A Hard Choice Pages 132–133 • Understand that when we make bad choices that hurt our relationship with God and others, God forgives us if we are truly sorry	• **Catholic Faith Words** free well • Discuss with the children ways they can show they are sorry for something. ☆ Underline Jesus' response to Peter. **John 18:17–18; 25–27** Proclaim "Peter Denies Jesus." • **Share Your Faith Activity** Think about ways to show you are sorry.	☐ pencils or pens ☐ construction paper • **Optional Activity** Jesus Forgives Peter ☐ Activity Master 8 (Page 131E)
God Helps You Choose Pages 134–135 • Describe sin as a free choice to do what we know is wrong; discern mistakes and accidents as different from sins • Differentiate between venial sin and mortal sin and how each harms our relationship with God • Identify conscience as an ability given to us by God that helps us make choices about right and wrong	• **Catholic Faith Words** mortal sin, venial sin, conscience • Discuss how to choose right from wrong. • Review definitions in the text. ☆ Circle the mistake and put an *X* over the picture that shows a sin. • **Connect Your Faith Activity** Look at the pictures and answer the questions.	☐ pencils or pens
Live, 15 minutes		
Our Catholic Life Pages 136–137	• Talk about making good choices. ☆ Write the correct step number next to the corresponding picture. • **People of Faith** Learn about Saint Thérèse of Lisieux. • **Live Your Faith Activity** Write a story and act it out.	☐ pencils or pens ☐ paper
Prayer of Petition Page 138	• Practice the leader and reader parts with the volunteers. Rehearse "C-H-O-I-C-E-S." • Follow the order of prayer.	Download "C-H-O-I-C-E-S."

Family + Faith Page 139

Point out that the Catholic Families page provides chapter highlights, information on how second graders understand faith concepts, and family prayer.

Chapter Review Page 140

aliveinchrist.osv.com

- Customize and Download Assessments
- Email Links to eAssessments
- Interactive Student Reviews

Teaching This Grade

ONLINE RESOURCES

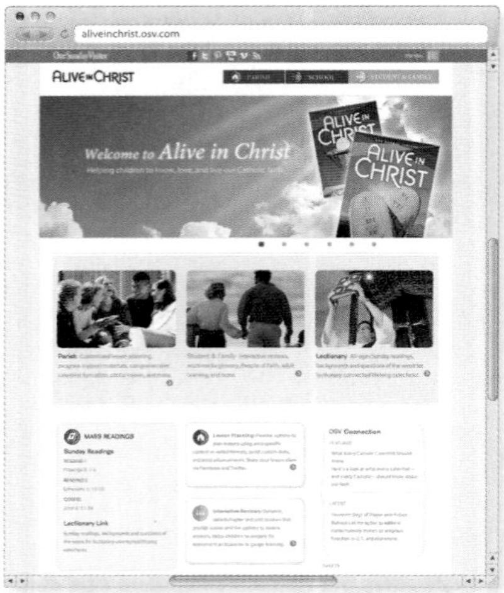

Go to **aliveinchrist.osv.com**

You will find:

- Interactive lesson planning with web specific content and additional activities
- Step by step lesson instruction from printed Catechist Edition for integrated lesson planning
- Custom-built assessments to download and eAssessment links
- Interactive reviews that provide scores and the option to review answers
- Sunday readings with background and questions of the week

Go to **osvparish.com**

You will find:

- Ask the Experts Q and A
- General Catechist Helps
- Community Connections and Blogs

Sharing the Message with Second Graders

Making Good Choices Children need and want limits and guidance. They get a sense of security from structure. But in a society that is increasingly unwilling to make value judgments, children can sometimes be at a loss to know right from wrong. Knowing the rules and understanding how things work are very important to second graders. Parents, teachers, and catechists serve as important mentors and examples to them.

Teaching Tip: Make rules explicit by putting them in written form and posting them in the room. Talk with the children about how they relate to love for God and others.

How Second Graders Understand

- Second graders like hearing the words "you made a good choice."
- When children this age choose to do wrong, teach them to say, "I am sorry," to anyone they hurt and to God.
- All children need to hear that they are loved and forgiven.

"When I choose to do wrong, teach me to say, 'I am sorry,' to anyone I hurt and to God."

Chapter Connections

Chapter Story

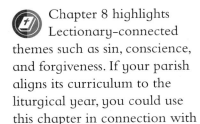

Invite

"New Friends"

Use this story to expand the chapter introduction.

- Have the children discuss what they think about what Tony did.
- Talk about how we should treat others, especially new friends.
- Encourage the children to share alternate endings to the story.

Go to **aliveinchrist.osv.com** Lesson Planning section for this story.

NCEA IFG: ACRE Edition

Discover

Knowledge of the Faith

- Objective: To know and understand basic Catholic teaching about the Incarnate Word Jesus Christ as the way, truth, and life

Moral Formation

- Objective: To be knowledgeable about the teachings of Jesus and the Church as the basis of Christian morality and to understand Catholic Social Teaching

Catholic Social Teaching

Live

Use one of these features to introduce a principle and engage the children with an activity.

- Rights and Responsibilities, Pages 294–295
- The Dignity of Work, Pages 298–299

Music Options

Use one or more of the following songs to enhance catechetical learning or for prayer.

- "C-H-O-I-C-E-S," Live Prayer, Page 138
- "Children of God," Discover, Page 132
- "Choices," Discover, Page 132
- "I'm Sorry," Live, Page 135

LECTIONARY CONNECTION

Chapter 8 highlights Lectionary-connected themes such as sin, conscience, and forgiveness. If your parish aligns its curriculum to the liturgical year, you could use this chapter in connection with the following readings.

Year A

Easter Sunday of the Resurrection of the Lord—Resurrection

Eleventh Sunday in Ordinary Time—Sinners Saved by Christ

Year B

Seventeenth Sunday in Ordinary Time—Sacraments

Thirty-second Sunday in Ordinary Time—Resurrection

Year C

Friday of the Passion of the Lord (Good Friday)—Jesus' Sacrifice

Holy Saturday—Resurrection

Go to **aliveinchrist.osv.com** for a complete correlation ordered by the Sundays of the year and suggestions for how to integrate the Scripture readings into chapter lessons.

Name ______________________________ Date ______________

Jesus Forgives Peter

Use the secret code to discover what Jesus said to Peter and what Peter said to Jesus.

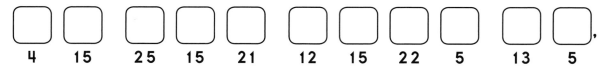

A = 1	B = 2	C = 3	D = 4	E = 5	F = 6	G = 7	H = 8	I = 9
J = 10	K = 11	L = 12	M = 13	N = 14	O = 15	P = 16	Q = 17	R = 18
S = 19	T = 20	U = 21	V = 22	W = 23	X = 24	Y = 25	Z = 26	

Jesus:

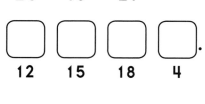

☐ ☐   ☐ ☐ ☐   ☐ ☐ ☐ ☐   ☐ ☐,
4 15   25 15 21   12 15 22 5   13 5

☐ ☐ ☐ ☐ ☐?
16 5 20 5 18

Peter:

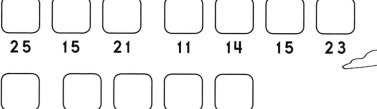

☐ ☐ ☐   ☐ ☐ ☐ ☐
25 15 21   11 14 15 23

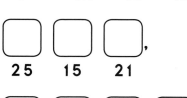

☐   ☐ ☐ ☐ ☐
9   12 15 22 5

☐ ☐ ☐,
25 15 21

☐ ☐ ☐ ☐.
12 15 18 4

Choose to Do Good

Let Us Pray

Leader: Lord, teach us how to make good choices.

"LORD, teach me the way of your statutes;
I shall keep them with care." Psalm 119:33

All: God, help us to follow your laws, with all our heart. Amen.

God's Word

The servant girl saw Peter and said, "This man is one of them!" "No, I'm not!" Peter replied. Later, some of the people said to Peter, "You certainly are one of them, you're a Galilean!" Once again Peter denied knowing Jesus. Right away a rooster crowed a second time. Then Peter remembered that Jesus had told him, "Before a rooster crows twice, you will say three times that you don't know me." So Peter started crying.

Based on Mark 14:69–72

What Do You Wonder?

- Why are God's rules or laws important?
- Who helps you make good choices?

Optional Activity

Chapter Story: "New Friends" *Verbal/Linguistic*

Use this story after the opening prayer, before explaining that we make decisions every day.

- Have the children silently read "New Friends."
- Ask why Paul was sad. because Tony went to play without him
- Have the children read the question. Discuss their responses, then transition back to the lesson instruction.

Go to **aliveinchrist.osv.com** for Chapter Story.

Invite

Let Us Pray

Invite the children to gather in the prayer space and make the Sign of the Cross. Read aloud the leader's prayer and the Psalm verse. Prompt the children's response.

Have the children move from the prayer space back to their seats.

Explain that each of us makes decisions every day.

Say: Let's listen to hear how Jesus asks us to make good choices by following God's laws.

God's Word

Guide the children through the process of Scripture reflection.

- Invite them to close their eyes, be still, and open their minds and hearts to what God is saying to them in this passage.
- Proclaim the Scripture.
- Maintain several moments of silence.
- *Ask:* What did you hear God say to you today?
- Invite volunteers to share.

What Do You Wonder?

Say: Like Peter, all people can make good choices to follow God's rules or bad choices to break God's rules. We want to make good choices and do what God says.

Invite the children to respond to the questions. Ask what else they might wonder about how to make good choices.

Discover

Objective

- Understand that when we make bad choices that hurt our relationship with God and others, God forgives us if we are truly sorry

A Hard Choice

Have a volunteer read the question.

- Discuss responses with the children.
- Explain to the children that, like Peter, everyone makes bad choices sometimes.
- Tell them that even the friends of Jesus did not always make the right choices.

God's Word

Proclaim the Scripture story.

- Point out the illustration and caption. Discuss what it means to deny someone.
- *Ask:* Why was it hard for Peter to say he was Jesus' friend?
- Invite the children to share their responses.

Direct the children's attention to page 314 in the Our Catholic Tradition section of the Student Book. Explain that the Sacrament of Penance and Reconciliation is one important way the Church provides us the opportunity to experience God's forgiveness.

Music Option: Have the children sing "Children of God" or "Choices," downloaded from **aliveinchrist.osv.com**.

A Hard Choice

How did Jesus respond to Peter?

God made us with **free will**. We are fee to choose how we act. Sometimes we make bad choices that do not show love. Peter, one of Jesus' closest friends, had a hard choice to make.

Catholic Faith Words

free will being able to choose whether to obey God or disobey God. God created us with free will because he wants us to make good choices.

God's Word

Peter Denies Jesus

The night before Jesus died on the Cross, soldiers took Jesus away. Peter followed them to a courtyard. The gatekeeper said to Peter, "You are not one of this man's disciples, are you?" He said, "I am not."

Later, Peter was standing around a fire to keep warm. And someone said to him, "You are not one of his disciples, are you?" Peter said, "I am not."

One of the slaves said, "Didn't I see you in the garden with him?" Again, Peter said no.

Based on John 18:17–18, 25–27

Jesus told Peter that he would deny him three times.

Scripture Background

John 18:17–18, 25–27

Earlier in that same evening, Peter had been willing to defend Jesus by cutting off the ear of one of the men who came to arrest Jesus.

- Why was Peter unafraid of defending Jesus first but later fearful of admitting that he knew Jesus?
- Explore with the children how Peter chose to act both fearlessly and cowardly on the same night.

Jesus Forgives

Peter did not tell the truth about being Jesus' follower. He did not show his love for Jesus. After Jesus was raised from the dead, he spoke to Peter.

Three times Jesus asked Peter if he loved him. Three times Peter said yes. Jesus believed Peter and asked him to take care of his followers.

Jesus forgave Peter because Peter was sorry for what he had done. Jesus gave us the the Sacrament of Penance so that we could know his forgiveness. If you tell God that you are truly sorry for the wrong you do, he will forgive you.

After his Resurrection, Jesus forgave Peter.

Underline what Jesus did when Peter said he was sorry.

One way we receive God's forgiveness is in the Sacrament of Penance.

Share Your Faith

Think How can you show you are sorry for something?

____

____

____

Share In a small group, talk about ways you respond to someone who tells you they are really sorry.

Jesus Forgives

Have the children silently read the three paragraphs to find out why Peter is sad and upset.

- Ask the children what Peter wanted to tell Jesus. He wanted to tell Jesus he was sorry for saying he did not know him.
- Instruct the children to underline what Jesus did when Peter said he was sorry.
- Have the children work in pairs. On a piece of construction paper, have them use markers to draw speech bubbles over the figures of Jesus and Peter. Write in the bubbles what they think Jesus and Peter said to each other. Have each pair present their speeches.

Activity

Read aloud the directions for the Share Your Faith activity.

- Have the children work independently at first.
- Invite the children to form small groups, and talk about ways they can respond to someone who says they are sorry.

Optional Activity

Activity Master 8: Jesus Forgives Peter

Distribute copies of the activity found on catechist page 131E.

- Tell the children they are going to decode a secret message to discover what Peter and Jesus said to one another.
- As an alternative, you may wish to send this activity home with the children.

Chapter 8 Activity Master

Name ______ Date ______

Jesus Forgives Peter

Use the secret code to discover what Jesus said to Peter and what Peter said to Jesus.

A=1 B=2 C=3 D=4 E=5 F=6 G=7 H=8 I=9 J=10 K=11 L=12 M=13 N=14 O=15 P=16 Q=17 R=18 S=19 T=20 U=21 V=22 W=23 X=24 Y=25 Z=26

Jesus: 4 15 / 25 15 21 / 12 15 22 5 / 13 5 / 16 5 20 5 18?

Peter: 25 15 21 / 11 14 15 23 / 9 / 12 15 22 5 / 25 15 21. 12 15 18 4.

131E Alive in Christ, Grade 2 Chapter 8

Quick Review

Jesus forgave Peter because he loved him. No matter what we do, God loves us and, if we are sorry, he will always forgive us.

Objectives

- Describe sin as a free choice to do what we know is wrong; discern mistakes and accidents as different from sins
- Differentiate between venial sin and mortal sin and how each harms our relationship with God
- Identify conscience as an ability given to us by God that helps us make choices about right and wrong

God Helps You Choose

Have volunteers read aloud the paragraphs.

- Invite the children to share their thoughts on choosing between right and wrong.
- Make sure they understand the differences between sins, accidents, and mistakes.

Work with Words

Have the children write out the definitions of *mortal sin* and *venial sin*. Have them work in pairs to decide what is alike and what is different about the definitions.

☆ Point out the pictures on the page. Instruct the children to circle the picture that shows a mistake and put an *X* over the picture that shows a sin.

God Helps You Choose

How do you know right from wrong?

A sin is a person's choice to disobey God on purpose and do what he or she knows is wrong. Accidents and mistakes are not sins.

An accident is something we do not do on purpose. We don't plan accidents or expect them to happen. A mistake is a misunderstanding or an incorrect answer or something we think is right but is not. A sin is a choice to do something we know is wrong. Sin hurts your friendship with God and others.

1. Circle the picture that shows a mistake and put an X over the picture that shows a sin.
2. Discuss what Marita should do next and what Arnie could have done differently.

Marita spilled her milk all over the kitchen counter.

Arnie teased Rachel for losing the game of freeze tag.

Catechist Background

Sin and Culpability

As the Church has always taught, sin has degrees of gravity. Sin is personal because a person is responsible for his or her actions. But one can be guilty of participating in the sins of others by failing to stop someone from doing something sinful or by participating in another's sin through approval or praise. (See *Catechism of the Catholic Church*, 1868.)

Types of Sin

Some choices lead to serious sins called mortal sins. A **mortal sin** is a serious sin that causes a person's relationship with God to be broken. It is a choice to turn completely away from God's love.

A less serious sin is called a **venial sin**. Venial sins hurt a person's relationship with God but do not completely remove him or her from God's life and love. They still matter, though, because they can lead to more serious sins.

God's love is always greater than sin. His mercy never ends.

Conscience

God helps you choose what is good. He gives you a **conscience**. This gift from God helps you know right from wrong. It is important for us to know God's laws so our conscience can help us make good decisions. The Holy Spirit guides you to listen to your conscience.

You know something is right when it follows God's law. You know it is wrong when it goes against one of the Ten Commandments.

Catholic Faith Words

mortal sin a serious sin that causes a person's relationship with God to be broken

venial sin a sin that hurts a person's friendship with God, but does not completely break it

conscience an ability given to us by God that helps us make choices about right and wrong

Connect Your Faith

Identify What are some choices children your age make? Choose one and talk about how God's Commandments can help you know what to do.

Type of Sin/Conscience

Ask volunteers to help you read aloud the text on the page.

Work with Words

Have the children place their finger on the word *conscience*.

- Ask a volunteer to read aloud the definition from the Catholic Faith Words box.
- Discuss how we are given choices and help with deciding what is right and wrong.
- *Ask:* Who helps us listen to our conscience? the Holy Spirit

Activity

Ask a volunteer to read the question.

- Read aloud the rest of the activity instructions.
- Invite the children to choose a partner and discuss their thoughts.

Music Option: Have the children sing "I'm Sorry," downloaded from **aliveinchrist.osv.com**.

Quick Tip

Conscience

Help the children understand that their conscience is a function of their common sense, not a literal voice they will hear.

- The word *conscience* means "with knowledge." Using our conscience means using what we know about right and wrong to make conscious choices.
- The Holy Spirit guides us in listening to our conscience.

Quick Review

Sin is a free choice to do what you know is wrong. There are two types of sin: venial sin and mortal sin. Conscience is a gift from God that helps us to know right from wrong.

Live

Our Catholic Life

Ask: How can you make good choices?

- Allow time for the children to respond.

Read aloud the paragraph.

- Remind the children that their conscience is a tool they can use to help them choose what is good and avoid what is not.

Steps for Making Good Choices

Have a volunteer read aloud the entire chart.

- Point out the illustrations below the chart.

☆ Have the children write the number of the step next to the image that fits with that action.

- Review the group's responses.

Our Catholic Life

How can you make good choices?

When you have to choose, you can remember what you know about being a follower of Jesus. Knowing the difference between right and wrong is not always easy. You can use your conscience, the ability from God to choose what is good and avoid what is not. Here are some steps to follow:

Steps for Making Good Choices

1. Stop what you are doing.
2. Look to what you have learned about the Commandments.
3. Imagine: How can I act like a follower of Jesus right now?
4. Stop and listen to what your conscience is saying, the gift from God to help you know right from wrong.
5. Pray to the Holy Spirit for help.

☆ Next to each picture, write the number of the step that it shows.

Catechist Background

Discerning What Is Right

Second graders may not be able to identify the process as discernment, but they are beginning to make moral choices. Reinforce their learning by

- reminding the children to take time to consider the consequences of their choices.
- noting good choices, and asking the children who make them to share the thinking that went into the choice.

People of Faith

Saint Thérèse of Lisieux, 1873–1897

Saint Thérèse of Lisieux lived in France. As a little girl, she sometimes did bad things. She would cry if she didn't get her own way. When her mother died, Thérèse was very sad and decided she would always choose to do what was good. When Thérèse joined the Carmelite convent she said she couldn't do big, important things for God. But she could do little things, like her chores. She offered them to God. She is known as the "Little Flower of Jesus."

October 1

Discuss: What is one little thing you can do for God today?

Learn more about Saint Thérèse at **aliveinchrist.osv.com**

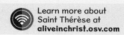

Live Your Faith

Plan a Skit With a partner, write a story about making a choice. Then together act it out.

1. What choice does the person have to make?

   ____

2. What things should the person think about before making the choice?

   ____

3. What will the person do?

   ____

4. Why is it important to think before making a choice to do something?

   ____

Catholic Social Teaching

Chapter Connections

To integrate Catholic Social Teaching into your lesson, choose one of the following features: Rights and Responsibilities, pages 294–295; or The Dignity of Work, pages 298–299.

- Start the process by talking about Saint Thérèse of Lisieux on page 137. Then move to the Catholic Social Teaching feature.
- Or, to expand the lesson, complete both pages 136 and 137, then move to the Catholic Social Teaching feature.
- Return to Chapter 8 for the prayer on page 138.

People of Faith

Tell the children about Saint Thérèse of Lisieux.

- She was the ninth child in her family of saintly parents.
- Saint Thérèse joined a convent at fifteen years of age.
- She performed many miracles, but considered small, simple duties important in her work, as a servant of God.
- Read aloud the paragraph on Saint Thérèse.
- Discuss the final question with the children.

Encourage the children to go to **aliveinchrist.osv.com** at home to learn more about Saint Thérèse of Lisieux.

Activity

Read aloud the directions for the Live Your Faith activity.

- When arranging partners for this activity, give some thought to balancing individual skills, pairing shyer children with more extroverted partners.
- Have the children answer the questions before beginning to write.
- Give them a separate sheet of paper to write out their stories.
- Allow the children to perform their skits.

Let Us Pray
Prayer of Petition

Remind the children that a petition is a request. In this prayer of petition, we are requesting that the Lord will hear us and help us.

Prepare

Choose volunteers for the leader part and the two reader parts.

- Practice the parts with the leader and readers.

Rehearse with the children "C-H-O-I-C-E-S," downloaded from **aliveinchrist.osv.com**.

Gather

Invite the children to come to the prayer space with their books.

Pray

Follow the order of prayer on the student page.

- If you use the stepping-stone idea from the Liturgy Link below, provide the leader with this one extra line to add to the beginning of the celebration: Thank you for those who teach us about you and lead us along the correct path.

Conclude by singing together "C-H-O-I-C-E-S."

Let Us Pray

Prayer of Petition

Gather and begin with the Sign of the Cross.

Leader: Our Father, thank you for helping us find the way to life with you and peace with others.

Reader 1: You gave us the Ten Commandments to guide us in our choices.

All: Show us the way, O Lord.

Reader 2: Jesus shows us the way to love and seek forgiveness.

All: Show us the way, O Lord.

Reader 1: The Holy Spirit brings us peace and a forgiving heart.

All: Show us the way, O Lord.

Reader 2: Our family and friends help us choose all that is good.

All: Show us the way, O Lord. Amen.

Sing "C-H-O-I-C-E-S"

C-H-O-I-C-E-S.

God gives us choices every day.

In every single way (repeat).

Liturgy Link

Lead Us in Right Paths

Have the children cut stepping-stone shapes from construction paper.

- On the stepping stones, have them write the names of people who help them learn about God.
- Place the stepping stones on the floor as a path leading to the prayer space.

Go to **aliveinchrist.osv.com** for Sunday readings, Scripture background, questions of the week, and seasonal resources.

FAMILY + FAITH

LIVING AND LEARNING TOGETHER

YOUR CHILD LEARNED >>>

This chapter explains making good choices, the difference between a sin, a mistake, or an accident, and God's willingness to forgive our sin.

God's Word

Read **Mark 14:69–72** to see how Peter denied knowing Jesus after his arrest.

Catholics Believe

- Conscience is the ability given to us by God that helps us make choices about right and wrong.
- Sin is a free choice to do what you know is wrong.

To learn more, go to the *Catechism of the Catholic Church* #1778, 1783–1784 at **usccb.org**.

People of Faith

This week, your child met Saint Thérèse of Lisieux, the Little Flower. She once said she wanted to take an elevator directly to God.

CHILDREN AT THIS AGE >>>

How They Understand Making Good Choices Children need and want limits and guidance. They get a sense of security from structure. But in a society that is increasingly unwilling to make value judgments, children can sometimes be at a loss to know right from wrong. Knowing the rules and understanding how things work are very important to second-graders. Parents, teachers, and catechists serve as important mentors and examples to them. Don't hesitate to tell your child how you feel about various moral issues and choices he or she may face. Children listen to their parents about these things and often internalize a parent's values even when we don't realize it.

CONSIDER THIS >>>

Can you recall a time you received undeserved forgiveness?

That experience leaves us feeling both humbled and grateful. Perhaps that is why we so identify with the people in the Scriptures who experience God's forgiveness. "When Peter asked the number of times a person should forgive, Jesus told him that there should be no limit to forgiving. Jesus forgave Peter his triple denial, showed mercy to the woman taken in adultery, forgave the thief on the cross, and continually witnessed the mercy of God...the Sacrament of Penance is God's gift to us so that any sin committed after Baptism can be forgiven" (*USCCA, p.243*).

LET'S TALK >>>

- Talk about the difference between a mistake and a sin.
- Ask your child to share a story from the Bible that talks about forgiveness. What did that story teach them?

LET'S PRAY >>>

Dear God, help us to do all the "little things" in our lives with love, like Saint Thérèse did. Amen.

For a multimedia glossary of Catholic Faith Words, Sunday readings, seasonal and Saint resources, and chapter activities go to **aliveinchrist.osv.com**.

Family + Faith

Distribute the page to the children or parents/adult family members. Point out the chapter highlights, insights on how second graders understand concepts, the opportunity for the adults to reflect on their own experience and faith journey, and the family prayer.

Chapter 8 Review

A Work with Words Fill in the circle beside the correct answer.

1. Your ____ helps you know right from wrong.
   ○ sin ● conscience
2. ____ is a free choice to do what you know is wrong.
   ○ An accident ● A sin
3. A ____ sin breaks a person's relationship with God.
   ● mortal ○ venial
4. A ____ sin hurts a person's friendship with God, but does not completely break it.
   ○ mortal ● venial
5. You must be ____ for your sins before you can ask God's forgiveness.
   ● sorry ○ scared

B Check Understanding The sentences below name the steps for making good choices. Use the numbers 1–5 to put the steps in order.

6. [4] Listen to your conscience.
7. [1] Stop and think.
8. [3] Ask yourself, "What would Jesus tell me to do?"
9. [5] Pray to the Holy Spirit for help.
10. [2] Remember what you have learned about the Commandments.

Go to **aliveinchrist.osv.com** for an interactive review.

Chapter Review

Use Catechist Quick Reviews to highlight lesson concepts.

A Work with Words
Tell the children to fill in the circle beside the correct answer.

B Check Understanding
Explain to the children that they will write the numbers 1–5 in the correct boxes to put the steps in order.

Go to **aliveinchrist.osv.com** to prepare customized and downloadable assessments, send eAssessments, and assign interactive reviews.

KEY CONCEPT

God is merciful and forgiving. God will always forgive you if you are truly sorry.

DOCTRINAL CONTENT

- We learn about God's mercy in the story of the Prodigal Son. (CCC, 1439)
- Mercy is kindness and concern for those who are suffering. God us has mercy on us even though we are sinners. (CCC, 270, 2447)
- The virtues can help us say no to temptation and choose what is good. (CCC, 1810)
- It's important to ask God and others for forgiveness, and to be forgiving. (CCC, 1459)

TASKS OF CATECHESIS

Helping children grow in a faith that is "known, celebrated, lived, and expressed in prayer" (NDC, 20).

This chapter focuses on the following tasks of catechesis:

- Moral Formation
- Education for Community Life

Catechist Background

Then Peter approaching asked him, "Lord, if my brother sins against me, how often must I forgive him? As many as seven times?" Jesus answered, "I say to you, not seven times but seventy-seven times." Matthew 18:21–22

→ **Reflect** How completely do you forgive people who have hurt you?

The word *mercy* is translated from the Hebrew word *hesed*, meaning "goodness," and the Greek word *eleos*, which captures the essence of God's will to save sinners.

Mercy and compassion are at the forefront of Jesus' ministry to save sinners. He calls his disciples to follow his example. In the Gospel according to Matthew, Jesus quotes the prophet Hosea, telling the people that he desires mercy and not sacrifice. To the Pharisees, Jesus says, "If you knew what this meant, 'I desire mercy, not sacrifice,' you would not have condemned these innocent men" (Matthew 12:7). In the Gospel according to Luke, Jesus tells the Parable of the Prodigal Son to reveal the greatness of God's mercy. Though the son had hurt his father deeply, his father declares, " . . . let us celebrate with a feast"(Luke 15:23). God the Father loves with such mercy and compassion that he not only takes you back when you are sorry for your sin, but celebrates your return.

After telling the story of the Good Samaritan, Jesus questioned a certain man, an expert in Jewish law. "Which of these three, in your opinion, was neighbor to the robbers' victim?" He answered, "The one who treated him with mercy." Jesus said to him, "Go and do likewise" (Luke 10:36–37). You have probably experienced the loving mercy of a parent, friend, or spouse. Jesus asks you, his follower by virtue of your Baptism, to show the same mercy and compassion that God has shown you.

→ **Reflect** How does mercy play a role in your decision making?

Catechist's Prayer

Lord, you taught us to say, "forgive us our trespasses as we forgive those who trespass against us." Help me to have a forgiving heart and spirit that I may better reflect your example. Amen.

Lesson Plan

Objectives	Process	Materials
Invite, 10 minutes		
God's Mercy Page 141	**Psalm 86:15** Pray the opening prayer. **Matthew 18:21–22** Reflect prayerfully on the Word. • Discuss What Do You Wonder questions.	**Optional Activity** Chapter Story: "Kim's Problem"
Discover, 35 minutes		
Jesus Teaches Forgiveness Pages 142–143 • Explore God's mercy in the story of the Prodigal Son • Celebrate that God has mercy on us even though we are sinners • Recognize that virtues can help us say no to temptation and choose what is good	• **Catholic Faith Words** virtues, temptation, mercy **Luke 15:11–32** Proclaim "The Prodigal Son." • Talk about how the father and son felt in the story. ☆ Draw the last part of the story. • **Share Your Faith Activity** Name people who help you make good choices.	☐ pencils or pens
Forgive One Another Pages 144–145 • Understand the importance of asking God for forgiveness and being forgiving toward others	• Discuss how to show God's love and mercy, even to those who have hurt us. ☆ Circle the names of those who need to ask for forgiveness. • **Connect Your Faith Activity** Write a new story ending that shows making good choices.	☐ pencils or pens ☐ crayons or markers • **Optional Activity** A Forgiveness Puzzle ☐ Activity Master 9 (Page 141E)
Live, 15 minutes		
Our Catholic Life Pages 146–147	• Talk about the importance of forgiveness. ☆ Write one more way to show and ask for forgiveness. • **People of Faith** Learn about Saint Jane Frances de Chantal. • **Live Your Faith Activity** Draw a way God's mercy was shown.	☐ pencils or pens ☐ board or chart paper
Prayer for Mercy Page 148	• Review with the children the definition of mercy. Rehearse "God of Mercy." • Follow the order of prayer.	Download "God of Mercy."

Family + Faith Page 149

Point out that the Catholic Families page provides chapter highlights, information on how second graders understand faith concepts, and family prayer.

Chapter Review Page 150

aliveinchrist.osv.com

- Customize and Download Assessments
- Email Links to eAssessments
- Interactive Student Reviews

ONLINE RESOURCES

Go to **aliveinchrist.osv.com**

You will find:

- Interactive lesson planning with web specific content and additional activities
- Step by step lesson instruction from printed Catechist Edition for integrated lesson planning
- Custom-built assessments to download and eAssessment links
- Interactive reviews that provide scores and the option to review answers
- Sunday readings with background and questions of the week

Go to **osvparish.com**

You will find:

- Ask the Experts Q and A
- General Catechist Helps
- Community Connections and Blogs

Sharing the Message with Second Graders

God's Mercy God loves us no matter what. A second grader's understanding of this will be influenced by his or her experience with love and forgiveness from significant adults. It's important that parents, teachers, and catechists do not overreact to accidents (which are not the same as bad choices unless a bad choice led to the accident). It's also important that when children this age make a purposeful wrong choice, they be given a way to help repair the damage that was done. Finally, adults should reassure children that they are loved, even when they make wrong choices.

Teaching Tip: Take care to deal with a conflict thoroughly, even if it pre-empts other activities. The lessons that children learn about resolving conflicts and the process of reconciliation will be well worth it.

How Second Graders Understand

- Some second graders like to play games that help them learn right from wrong.
- All children need to know they are loved even when they have made mistakes and chosen to do what they know is wrong.
- Children this age need to learn ways to say "I'm sorry" and "I forgive you."

"I like to play games that help me learn right from wrong."

Chapter Connections

Chapter Story

Invite

"Kim's Problem"

Use this story to expand the chapter introduction.

- Have the children work in pairs to create an ending to the story that would solve Kim's problem.
- Encourage the children to share their endings with the group.

Go to **aliveinchrist.osv.com** Lesson Planning section for this story.

NCEA IFG: ACRE Edition

Discover

Moral Formation

- Objective: To be knowledgeable about the teachings of Jesus and the Church as the basis of Christian morality and to understand Catholic Social Teaching

Communal Life

- Objectives: To know the origin, mission, structure, and communal nature of the Church; to know the rights and responsibilities of the Christian faithful

Catholic Social Teaching

Live

Use one of these features to introduce a principle and engage the children with an activity.

- Call to Community, Pages 292–293
- Solidarity of the Human Family, Pages 300–301

Music Options

Use one or more of the following songs to enhance catechetical learning for prayer.

- "The Supper of the Lamb," Live Prayer, Page 148
- "Behold the Lamb," Discover, Page 146
- "We Come to Worship You," Discover, Page 146

LECTIONARY CONNECTION

Chapter 9 highlights Lectionary-connected themes such as Holy Communion, Real Presence, reverence, and the Blessed Sacrament. If your parish aligns its curriculum to the liturgical year, you could use this chapter in connection with the following Sundays.

Year A

First Sunday of Lent—Unity

Second Sunday of Easter—Communal Life

Year B

Palm Sunday of the Passion of the Lord—Communion

Eighteenth Sunday in Ordinary Time—Communion

Year C

The Holy Family of Jesus, Mary, and Joseph—God's Children

Second Sunday of Easter—Great numbers were added.

Go to **aliveinchrist.osv.com** for a complete correlation ordered by the Sundays of the year and suggestions for how to integrate the Scripture readings into chapter lessons.

Name ______________________________ Date ______________

A Forgiveness Puzzle

Think about the story "The Prodigal Son." Read and answer the clues below, then fill in the letters for the words to complete the puzzle.

Clues

1. The person who forgave the son was his ________________.
2. The son lost all his ________________.
3. When the father saw his son, he ________________ to meet him.
4. The son had to get a job feeding the ________________.
5. The son went to a far away ________________.
6. The story of The Prodigal Son reminds us of our ________________ Father.
7. The father showed his forgiveness and ________________.

					F	☐	☐	☐	☐	☐
				☐	O	☐	☐	☐		
					R	☐	☐			
			☐	☐	G	☐				
				☐	I	☐	☐			
☐	☐	☐	☐	☐	V	☐	☐	☐		
				☐	E	☐	☐	☐		

CHAPTER 9

God's Mercy

Let Us Pray

Leader: Blessed be our loving God of Mercy.

You, Lord, are a merciful and gracious God,
slow to anger, most loving and true.
Based on Psalm 86:15

All: God of mercy and love, bless us and guide us. Amen.

God's Word

"Then Peter approaching asked him, 'Lord, if my brother sins against me, how often must I forgive him? As many as seven times?' Jesus answered, 'I say to you, not seven times but seventy-seven times.'"
Matthew 18:21–22

What Do You Wonder?

- Why does Jesus tell us to forgive?
- How is forgiving others connected to God forgiving us?

Optional Activity

Chapter Story: "Kim's Problem" *Verbal/Linguistic*

Use this story after the opening prayer, before you talk about God's mercy and love.

- Tell the children to silently read "Kim's Problem."
- Ask the children if something similar has ever happened to them and how they handled it.
- Remind them that God is merciful, and this shows us how to be merciful. At this point, transition back to the lesson instruction.

Go to **aliveinchrist.osv.com** for Chapter Story.

Invite

Let Us Pray

Invite the children to gather in the prayer space and make the Sign of the Cross. Read aloud the leader's prayer. Have the children pray the Psalm verse with you. Prompt the children's response.

Have the children move from the prayer space back to their seats.

Explain that when God shows us mercy and love, he gives us examples of being kind and forgiving.

Say: Let's listen to hear how many times Jesus wants us to forgive someone.

God's Word

Guide the children through the process of Scripture reflection.

- Invite them to close their eyes, be still, and open their minds and hearts to what God is saying to them in this passage.
- Proclaim the Scripture.
- Maintain several moments of silence.
- *Ask:* What did you hear God say to you today?
- Invite volunteers to share.

What Do You Wonder?

Say: Jesus tells us that we need to forgive each other often and always.

Invite the children to respond to the questions. Ask what else they might wonder about forgiveness.

Objectives

- Explore God's mercy in the story of the Prodigal Son
- Celebrate that God has mercy on us even though we are sinners
- Recognize that virtues can help us say no to temptation and choose what is good

Jesus Teaches Forgiveness

Have a volunteer read aloud the question.

- Tell the children that they will find out the answer after reading this page. God is always ready to forgive us when we are truly sorry.

God's Word

Tell the children that today's Scripture story is about a loving father.

Proclaim the first two paragraphs of the Scripture story.

- Ask the children how they think the father felt when his son went away.
- Have the children look at the first illustration at the bottom of the page. Invite a volunteer to describe what he or she sees and how it relates to the story.

Discover

Jesus Teaches Forgiveness

When does God forgive us?

Since the time of Adam and Eve, we've all been tempted to do what was wrong and choose sin. The **virtues** can help us say no to **temptation**. Even if we fail, and hurt our friendship with God, he is kind and full of **mercy**. He is always ready to forgive us when we are truly sorry.

God's Word

The Prodigal Son

Once, a father had two sons. The younger son did not want to stay home. "Give me my half of your money," the son said.

The father sadly gave the younger son the money. The son went to a city far away. He wasted all his money.

Scripture Background

Luke 15:11–32

The Scripture reading for this lesson is "The Prodigal Son."

- The younger son in this story offended his father by asking for his inheritance so that he could squander it on foolish, harmful things.
- He also offended his family by forsaking Israel, the land in which God had settled his Chosen People.
- However, despite his offenses, his father still forgave him and welcomed him home.
- Jesus knew that this story would powerfully show that God the Father is always willing to forgive sinners.

The son needed more money, so he got a job feeding pigs. He did not like his job. He was sad and cold and all alone.

He said, "I will go home to my father. I will beg him to give me a job as his servant." The son started to walk home.

One day, the father saw his son far away. The father ran to meet him. The son fell into his arms and cried, "I am sorry I have sinned. I am not good enough to be your son."

The father hugged his son. He threw a big party. The older son said, "That's not fair. He disobeyed you!" But the father said, "He has come home. We must welcome him." Based on Luke 15:11–32

Catholic Faith Words

virtues good habits that make you stronger and help you do what is right and good

temptation wanting to do something we should not, or not doing something we should

mercy kindness and concern for those who are suffering. God has mercy on us even though we are sinners.

Draw the last part of the story in the empty box.

Share Your Faith

Think Name two people in your life that help you make good choices.

1. ______________________

2. ______________________

Share Share with a partner.

Optional Activity

Forgiveness Chain *Visual/Spatial*

Prepare different colored construction paper strips. On some strips write *I forgave*, and on other strips write *I was forgiven*.

- Have the children write their names on the strips that correspond to their own experiences.
- Glue, tape, or staple the strips together to make a forgiveness chain.

The Prodigal Son

Continue reading the Scripture story on this page. Pause after the first paragraph and have the children look at the second illustration on page 142.

- *Ask:* How do you think the younger son felt?
- Finish reading the passage.
- ☆ Instruct the children to draw the last part of the story in the empty box.

Work with Words

Help the children sound out the Catholic Faith Words.

- Review the definitions with them.

Activity

Read aloud the directions for the Share Your Faith activity.

- Allow the children time to write their answers, then share them with a partner.
- Ask a few volunteers to share their work with the group.

Invite the children to go to page 326 in the Our Catholic Tradition section and read the last of the litanies "Lord, have mercy." Explain the nature of the repeated lines and how we plead for God's mercy.

Quick Review

God has mercy and forgives us when we are truly sorry. God showed us how to have mercy in the story of The Prodigal Son. Virtues can strengthen us to choose what is good.

Discover

Objective

- Understand the importance of asking God for forgiveness and being forgiving toward others

Forgive One Another

Read aloud the paragraphs.

- Ask the children to underline the sentences that tell what Jesus wants us to know about God and forgiveness. God our Father always forgives us if we are truly sorry. Jesus wants us to forgive others in the same way that the Father forgives us!
- Discuss the concept of God's love and mercy and how to show these same thing even to those who have hurt us.

A New Model

Invite a proficient reader to read aloud the story.

- *Ask:* How would you change this scene?
- Have groups role-play how they would change the story.

☆ Instruct the children to circle who needs to ask for forgiveness.

- *Ask:* How can they do that? What can the other people in the story say or do to show they forgive?

Discover

Forgive One Another

How can we forgive others?

☆ Read each story and circle who needs to ask for forgiveness. How can they do that? What can the other people in the story say or do to show they forgive?

God our Father always forgives us if we are truly sorry. He gives us the Sacrament of Penance so we can always have his forgiveness. And Jesus wants us to forgive others in the same way that the Father forgives us!

Sometimes it is not easy to forgive others. You want to stay angry. But, Jesus asks that you make the choice to love the person that hurt you the way that God loves you.

The following stories are about children who made wrong choices.

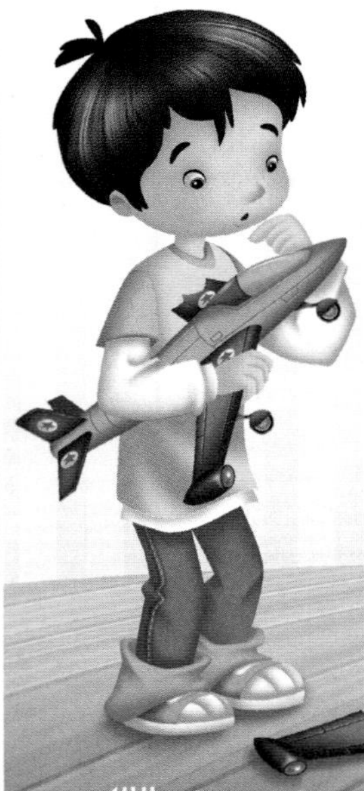

A New Model

Ethan crept into Michael's room to see his brother's new model airplane. As he picked it up, he broke the wing. Michael walked in and became angry.

Ethan apologized, but Michael screamed, "I will never forgive you!"

"Well, I'll never talk to you again," said Ethan as he stomped out of the room.

Quick Tip

Reconciling

Help the children see that forgiveness is an important part of bringing peace not only to relationships with family and friends, but also to the world. Remind them to look for peaceful, non-violent resolutions to conflicts, such as

- listening without interrupting someone while they are explaining what is concerning them.
- being willing to compromise and look for solutions that benefit everyone.

Putting Things Away

Chloe was supposed to put the balls away after recess. She forgot. The next day the balls were gone. Chloe told the teacher that it had been Alex's turn to put the balls away. Alex got in trouble because of Chloe's lie.

Jesus Asks Us to Forgive

Jesus wants you to ask forgiveness when you have done wrong. And Jesus asks you to be a forgiving person, too.

Connect Your Faith

Rewrite the Story Choose one of the stories and write a different ending to show good choices.

____

____

____

____

Putting Things Away

Have a volunteer read aloud the next story.

☆ Instruct the children to circle who needs to ask for forgiveness.

- Ask the same questions you asked after the story on page 144.

Jesus Asks Us to Forgive

Read aloud the paragraph.

- Explain that this means we are to forgive as we are forgiven by God. We should ask for forgiveness from those we have hurt, and we should forgive those who have hurt us.

Activity

Read aloud the directions for the Connect Your Faith activity.

- Encourage the children to share which story they chose and their new ending. Allow several volunteers to share with the group.

Quick Review

Ask for forgiveness from God and others, and forgive in the same way.

Optional Activity

Activity Master 9: A Forgiveness Puzzle

Distribute copies of the activity found on catechist page 141E.

- Tell the children they are to read the clues and use the answers to complete the puzzle.
- As an alternative, you may wish to send this activity home with the children.

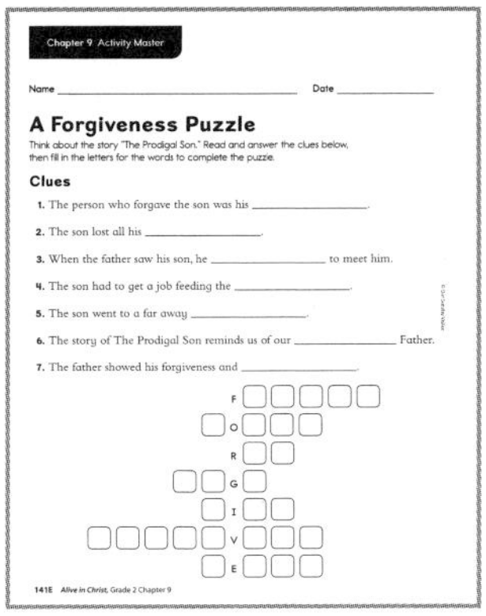

Chapter 9 Activity Master

Name ____________ Date ________

A Forgiveness Puzzle

Think about the story "The Prodigal Son." Read and answer the clues below, then fill in the letters for the words to complete the puzzle.

Clues

1. The person who forgave the son was his ____________.
2. The son lost all his ____________.
3. When the father saw his son, he ____________ to meet him.
4. The son had to get a job feeding the ____________.
5. The son went to a far away ____________.
6. The story of The Prodigal Son reminds us of our ____________ Father.
7. The father showed his forgiveness and ____________.

141E Alive in Christ, Grade 2 Chapter 9

Live

Our Catholic Life

Ask: How do people forgive one another?

- Encourage the children to discuss their ideas.

Have a volunteer read aloud both paragraphs.

- Ask another volunteer to read the "Show Forgiveness" box.
- Read aloud the "Ask Forgiveness" box.

Music Option: Have the children sing "Behold the Lamb" or "We Come to Worship You," downloaded from **aliveinchrist.osv.com**.

Direct the children to write in one more way they can show forgiveness and one more way they can ask for forgiveness.

- Allow volunteers to share their answers.

Live

Our Catholic Life

How do people forgive one another?

When someone has been unkind or unfair, you may be angry with that person. You may not want to talk to him or her. But Jesus asks you to do something very different. Jesus asks you to forgive.

Sometimes you are the person who does the hurting. You need to ask forgiveness if you have been unkind or unfair.

Write one more way you can show forgiveness and one more way you can ask forgiveness.

Show Forgiveness

- Be ready and willing to make things better.
- Listen to the person's apology.
- Say "I forgive you," and show it with a hug or a smile.
- Don't hold a grudge or pout.
- ______________________

Ask Forgiveness

- Imagine how it felt for the other person.
- Say "I'm sorry," and mean it.
- Do whatever you can to make up for the wrong you did.
- Pray for help to make better choices.
- ______________________

Optional Activity

Act of Contrition *Interpersonal*

The children may soon be preparing for the Sacrament of Penance and Reconciliation. This lesson on forgiveness is an important start.

- Have the children write a short prayer asking for God's mercy and forgiveness. They should acknowledge that they have done wrong, but they should not name their sins in the prayer.
- After they have written their own prayers, you might want to show them the Act of Contrition on page 323 in the Our Catholic Tradition section of the Student Book.

People of Faith

August 12

Saint Jane Frances de Chantal, 1572–1641

Saint Jane Frances de Chantal is one of the few saints who was a wife and mother. Jane was born in France. As she grew up, her parents helped her to grow in faith. When she was twenty years old, Jane married Christophe. The couple shared their love and their deep faith with their four children. One day, Christophe was killed in a hunting accident. Before he died, he forgave the man who shot him. Jane was heartbroken with grief. She struggled to forgive the man. She prayed to God to help her. Eventually, with God's help, she was able to forgive.

Discuss: How can you be forgiving?

Learn more about Saint Jane at **aliveinchrist.osv.com**

Live Your Faith

Draw one way someone has shown God's mercy to you.

Think of a way you can show mercy to someone this week.

Catholic Social Teaching

Chapter Connections

To integrate Catholic Social Teaching into your lesson, choose one of the following features: Call to Community, pages 292–293; or Solidarity of the Human Family, pages 300–301.

- Start the Live step of the process by talking about Saint Jane Frances de Chantal on page 147. Then move directly to the Catholic Social Teaching feature.
- Or, to expand the lesson, complete both pages 146 and 147, then move to the Catholic Social Teaching feature.
- Return to Chapter 9 for the prayer on page 148.

People of Faith

Tell the children about Saint Jane Frances de Chantal.

- At twenty-eight she became a widow with four children.
- Saint Francis de Sales was her spiritual director. Her oldest daughter married his brother.
- When she died, there were eighty six houses that she and Saint Frances de Sales had founded together.
- Read aloud the paragraph on Saint Jane.
- *Ask:* How can you be forgiving?
- Allow the children to respond.

Encourage the children to go to **aliveinchrist.osv.com** at home to learn more about Saint Jane Frances de Chantal.

Activity

Read aloud the directions for the Live Your Faith activity.

- Have the children brainstorm ideas and situations that require forgiveness or mercy.
- List these ideas and situations on the board or on chart paper, and discuss with the children ways they can practice forgiveness.
- Allow the children time to draw how God's mercy has been shown to them.
- When you ask the children to think of ways they can show mercy to someone, remind them that they do not have to share this information.

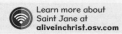

Let Us Pray

Prayer for Mercy

Explain that this prayer is prayed at Mass. It is a prayer for God's mercy. Have the children return to page 143 and reread the definition for *mercy*.

Prepare

Choose a volunteer for the leader part. Help the leader practice his or her parts.

Rehearse with the children "God of Mercy," downloaded from **aliveinchrist.osv.com**.

Gather

Invite the children to come to the prayer space with their books.

- Lead the children into the prayer space while playing or singing "God of Mercy."
- Have the children kneel around the prayer table.

Pray

Follow the order of prayer on the student page.

- Prompt the children to respond appropriately.

Conclude by processing around the room with the children singing "God of Mercy."

Let Us Pray

Prayer for Mercy

Gather and begin with the Sign of the Cross.

Leader: For the times when we were slow to forgive those who hurt us,

All: Lord, have mercy.

Leader: For the times when our words and actions have hurt others,

All: Christ, have mercy.

Leader: For the times we have not told the truth,

All: Lord, have mercy.

Leader: May God give us mercy and forgiveness.

All: Amen.

Sing "God of Mercy"

God of mercy, you are with us.
Fill our hearts with your kindness.
God of patience, strong and gentle,
fill our hearts with your kindness.
Lord, have mercy. Lord, have mercy.
Lord, have mercy upon us.

Repeat

Liturgy Link

Lord, Have Mercy

This is a prayer by which the faithful praise the Lord and ask for his mercy. It is usually prayed by the priest and the people alternating back and forth: *Lord, have mercy. Christ, have mercy. Lord, have mercy.*

- Remind the children that this prayer is prayed at Mass during the Penitential Act.

Go to **aliveinchrist.osv.com** for Sunday readings, Scripture background, questions of the week, and seasonal resources.

FAMILY + FAITH

LIVING AND LEARNING TOGETHER

YOUR CHILD LEARNED >>>

This chapter explains God's mercy and how important it is to show we are sorry and ask for the forgiveness of God and others.

God's Word

Read **Matthew 18:21–22** to find out how many times Jesus wants us to forgive someone.

Catholics Believe

- God is merciful and forgiving.
- God will always forgive you if you are truly sorry.

To learn more, go to the *Catechism of the Catholic Church* #1428, 1439 at **usccb.org**.

People of Faith

This week, your child met Saint Jane Frances de Chantal, a wife and mother who prayed to God to help her to forgive.

CHILDREN AT THIS AGE >>>

How They Understand God's Mercy God loves us no matter what. A second-grader's understanding of this will be influenced by his or her experience with love and forgiveness from significant adults. It's important that we not overreact to accidents (which are not the same as bad choices unless a bad choice led to the accident). It's also important that when children this age make a purposeful wrong choice, they be given a way to help repair the damage that was done. Finally, be sure to reassure your child of your love, even when he or she makes wrong choices.

CONSIDER THIS >>>

How important is being able to admit you are wrong?

As difficult as it may be to say those words, admitting that we are wrong is the necessary first step in the journey of forgiveness and reconciliation. "God's mercy makes possible the repentance of the sinner and the forgiveness of sin. Time and again in the Old Testament, the sins of the people are met with God's outreach of mercy and the invitation to be healed and return to a covenant relationship" *(USCCA, p. 235)*.

LET'S TALK >>>

- Ask your child what Jesus teaches us about forgiveness.
- Talk about a time when you needed forgiveness and received it. Share how it impacted you in some way.

LET'S PRAY >>>

God our Father, help us to be merciful and forgiving like Saint Jane Frances de Chantal. Amen.

For a multimedia glossary of Catholic Faith Words, Sunday readings, seasonal and Saint resources, and chapter activities go to **aliveinchrist.osv.com**.

Family + Faith

Distribute the page to the children or parents/adult family members. Point out the chapter highlights, insights on how second graders understand concepts, the opportunity for the adults to reflect on their own experience and faith journey, and the family prayer.

Chapter 9 Review

A Work with Words Complete each sentence with the correct word from the Word Bank.

Word Bank
sin
mercy
temptation
sorry
Virtues

1. God forgives when we are truly **sorry**.
2. **Virtues** are good habits that help us choose good.
3. We've all been tempted to choose **sin**.
4. God is kind and full of **mercy**.
5. Wanting to do something we should not do is a **temptation**.

B Check Understanding Fill in the circle beside the correct answer.

6. You show forgiveness when you listen to a person's ____.
   - ○ anger ● apology ○ stories
7. You need to ask forgiveness if you have been ____.
   - ○ unhappy ○ unloved ● unkind
8. You show forgiveness when you don't hold a ____.
   - ● grudge ○ party ○ sin
9. When you need forgiveness, you can say, "____."
   - ● I'm sorry ○ I'm angry ○ I'm hurt
10. Jesus asks you to ____ those who hurt you.
   - ○ hurt ○ ignore ● forgive

Go to **aliveinchrist.osv.com** for an interactive review.

Chapter Review

Use Catechist Quick Reviews to highlight lesson concepts.

A Work with Words
Review the Word Bank. Have the children write the correct word from the Word Bank to complete each sentence.

B Check Understanding
Direct the children to fill in the circle beside the correct answer.

Go to **aliveinchrist.osv.com** to prepare customized and downloadable assessments, send eAssessments, and assign interactive reviews.

UNIT 3

Unit Review

Use Catechist Quick Reviews in each chapter to highlight lesson concepts for this unit and prepare for the Unit Review.

Have the children complete the Review pages. Then discuss the answers as a group. Review any concepts with which the children are having difficulty.

A Work with Words

Instruct the children to find the words from the Word Bank in the word search.

Unit Review

UNIT 3

A Work with Words Find the words in Word Bank in the word search. Circle the word when you find it.

Word Bank

Commandments	forgives	mortal	love	sin
conscience	venial	mercy	accident	Jesus

1–10.

C	O	M	M	A	N	D	M	E	N	T	S
O	A	E	E	C	P	R	Z	O	S	T	M
N	F	S	R	C	Z	S	L	J	P	R	O
S	A	B	C	I	O	P	O	E	A	B	R
C	Q	N	Y	D	D	Z	V	S	Q	C	T
I	W	G	T	E	H	R	E	U	M	O	A
E	F	Y	H	N	V	Z	A	S	Y	H	L
N	Z	S	M	T	A	O	B	E	D	C	A
C	P	I	E	F	C	V	E	N	I	A	L
E	X	N	Y	F	O	R	G	I	V	E	S

UNIT 3

Unit Review

B Check Understanding Draw a line from each item in Column A to match the correct ending in Column B.

Column A	Column B
11. Jesus teaches that all people are	the way you want to be treated.
12. The Great Commandment tells you to treat others	is in need.
13. Jesus' New Commandment says, "Love one another as	your neighbors.
14. A neighbor can be someone who helps or	the ability God gave you to make choices about right and wrong.
15. Your conscience is	I have loved you."

Draw a line from each item in Column A to match the correct ending in Column B.

Column A	Column B
16. To make a good choice, you must	asks you to forgive.
17. When someone has been unkind or unfair, Jesus	that loving God means loving our neighbor.
18. To ask forgiveness, you should	listen to your conscience.
19. To help you make better choices, you can always	pray.
20. Jesus told a parable to teach his followers	do all you can to help make up for the wrong you did.

C Make Connections Write the word or name that best answers the question.

21. I am the ability given to you by God that helps you make choices. What am I?

    Conscience

22. I am the kind stranger who helped the injured man in one of Jesus' parables? Who am I?

    The Good Samaritan

23. I denied knowing Jesus three times but he forgave me and asked me to take care of his followers. Who am I?

    Peter

24. I returned home and my father forgave me for spending his money in one of Jesus' parables. Who am I?

    The Prodigal Son

25. I will always forgive those who are truly sorry. Who am I?

    God

B Check Understanding

Have the children draw a line from each item in Column A to match the correct ending in Column B.

C Make Connections

Instruct the children to write the word or name that best answers each question.

Go to **aliveinchrist.osv.com** to prepare customized and downloadable assessments, send eAssessments, and assign interactive reviews.

UNIT
4

The Church

Our Catholic Tradition

- God shares his life with the Church. Grace is sharing in God's life. (CCC, 1997)
- The Seven Sacraments are signs and celebrations of God's life. They give us grace. (CCC, 1131)
- The Seven Sacraments help us celebrate our friendship with Jesus. They help us to follow him. (CCC, 1123)
- The Church year celebrates the Incarnation, life, Death, Resurrection, and Ascension of Jesus. (CCC, 1171)

How does Jesus share his life with us in the Sacraments?

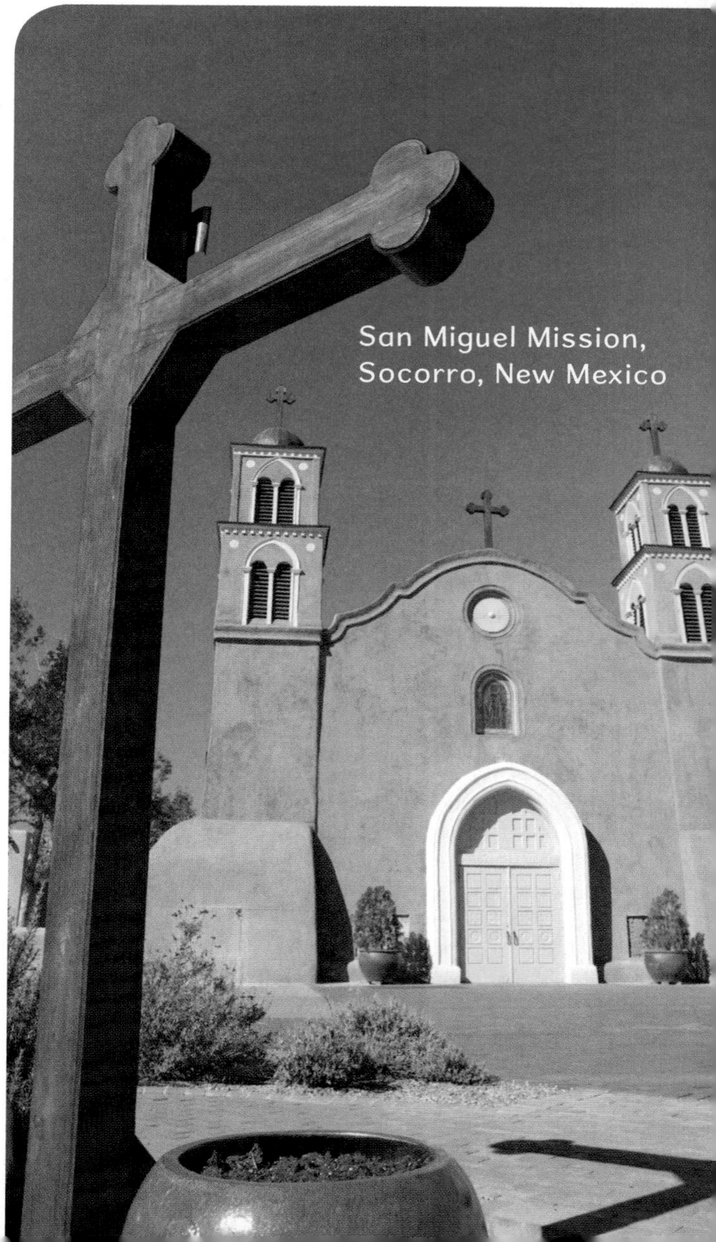

San Miguel Mission, Socorro, New Mexico

Unit 4 Overview

Chapter 10

The Sacraments 155

The children will:

- describe the Seven Sacraments as special signs and celebrations that come from Jesus and give us a share in God's life and work
- understand that Jesus continues to share his life and love with us through the Sacraments
- explore Baptism as the first Sacrament we receive that frees us from sin and makes us children of God
- learn that in the Seven Sacraments, we receive the gift of God's life and help, or grace
- identify the Sacraments of Initiation as the beginning of our life in the Church

Catholic Social Teaching: Live Your Faith

- Option for the Poor, Pages 296–297
- Care for Creation, Pages 302–303

Chapter 11

Seek Forgiveness 165

The children will:

- relate an examination of conscience to a prayerful way of looking at our lives
- identify the importance of expressing sorrow
- name the two parts of contrition—being sorry and wanting to live better
- understand that in the Sacrament of Penance and Reconciliation, God's forgiveness is given through the Church
- list the steps in the Sacrament of Penance and Reconciliation

Songs of Scripture
"How Many Times, Lord?"

Catholic Social Teaching: Live Your Faith

- Call to Community, Pages 292–293
- Human Solidarity, Pages 300–301

Chapter 12

The Church Year 175

The children will:

- identify liturgy as the public prayer of the Church
- recognize that the Church year celebrates the life, Death, Resurrection, and Ascension of Jesus
- review the sequence of the seasons of the Church year
- describe Holy Thursday, Good Friday, and Holy Saturday as the holiest days of the Church year
- recognize that Easter is the greatest feast of the Church year

Catholic Social Teaching: Live Your Faith

- Life and Dignity, Pages 290–291
- Solidarity of the Human Family, Pages 300–301

Preview Unit Theme

Ask: What is the unit theme?

Confirm that the unit focus is on the Church.

Have four volunteers each read aloud one of the bullets under Our Catholic Tradition.

Explain that they will learn more about all these things in the next three chapters.

Have the children study the photos. Ask volunteers to describe what they see and how these images connect to the unit theme.

Ask: How does Jesus share his life with us in the Sacraments?

After some discussion, point out that we will learn more in this unit.

KEY CONCEPT
Grace is a share in God's life and help. Sacraments are special signs and celebrations that come from Jesus and give grace.

DOCTRINAL CONTENT

- The Seven Sacraments are special signs and celebrations that Jesus gave his Church that allow us to share in God's life and work. (CCC, 1113, 1116)
- Jesus continues to share his life and love with us in the Sacraments. (CCC, 1127–1128)
- Baptism, the first Sacrament received, makes a person a child of God and member of the Church, taking away Original Sin and all personal sin. (CCC, 1213)
- The Sacraments of Initiation—Baptism, Confirmation, and Eucharist—celebrate our beginning, and membership into the Catholic Church. (CCC, 1212)

TASKS OF CATECHESIS
Helping children grow in a faith that is "known, celebrated, lived, and expressed in prayer" (NDC, 20).

This chapter focuses on the following tasks of catechesis:

- Promoting Knowledge of the Faith
- Liturgical Education

Catechist Background

Then Jesus stopped and ordered that he be brought to him; and when he came near, Jesus asked him, "What do you want me to do for you?" He replied, "Lord, please let me see." Jesus told him, "Have sight; your faith has saved you." Luke 18:40–42

➔ **Reflect** How do Jesus' actions reveal God's saving love? How do we ask for, and receive, God's help in the Seven Sacraments?

When anyone asks him why he heals, forgives, and brings new life, Jesus has the same answer: to reveal God's saving love. Jesus' miraculous actions are neither done to astonish a crowd nor to prove his own power.

They are the transformation of ordinary moments of human connection by the acknowledgment of God's presence. When we gather as Church to celebrate the Seven Sacraments, we are following in Jesus' footsteps, doing "the works of the Father." God uses the gifts of his creation—water, oil, bread, wine—and works through the ordinary gestures of human interaction—words, touch—to reveal his presence in our midst and to share grace with us.

There is a progression in the way we enter into the communal life of the Body of Christ. We die to our old selves (even if, as infants, our old selves are not that old) in Baptism, are sealed and strengthened by the Spirit in Confirmation, and are nourished by the Body and Blood of Christ in the Eucharist.

The Sacraments of Initiation are just the beginning of a lifelong process of receiving the Sacraments and coming to see signs of God's love in all the Sacraments and in our daily lives.

➔ **Reflect** When have you most movingly experienced God's presence in the Seven Sacraments?

Catechist's Prayer

Jesus, you taught your followers that everything you said and did was a sign of your Father's love. Help me use my words and actions to show God's love, so the children in my care will come to recognize and welcome the grace of the Seven Sacraments. Amen.

Lesson Plan

Objectives	Process	Materials
Invite, 10 minutes		
The Sacraments Page 155	**Psalm 66:5** Pray the opening prayer. **Luke 18:35–43** Reflect prayerfully on the Word. • Discuss What Do You Wonder questions.	**Optional Activity** Chapter Story: "My Abuela and Me"
Discover, 35 minutes		
Signs of God's Life Pages 156–157 • Describe the Seven Sacraments as special signs and celebrations that come from Jesus and give us a share in God's life and work • Understand that Jesus continues to share his life and love with us through the Sacraments • Explore Baptism as the first Sacrament we receive that frees us from sin and makes us children of God	• **Catholic Faith Words** Seven Sacraments, Baptism • Name things Jesus did to show others God's love. **Matthew 28:19–20** Proclaim "The Commissioning of the Apostles." • Name two things that happen at Baptism. • **Share Your Faith Activity** Write one way to walk in the light of Jesus.	☐ pencils or pens
The Seven Sacraments Pages 158–159 • Learn that in the Seven Sacraments, we receive the gift of God's life and help, or grace • Identify the Sacraments of Initiation as the beginning of our life in the Church	• **Catholic Faith Words** grace, Sacraments of Initiation • Explain that God's action we can't see, and our words and actions in the celebration, help his life in us grow. ☆ Circle Sacraments received; draw a square around those to receive soon. • **Connect Your Faith Activity** Make a card about Sacraments for new Church member.	☐ pencils or pens
Live, 15 minutes		
Our Catholic Life Pages 160–161	• Discuss what each Sacrament celebrates. ☆ Match the Sacrament to how it helps the Church. • **People of Faith** Learn about Saint Pius X. • **Live Your Faith Activity** Draw a way to make someone feel welcome.	☐ pencils or pens • **Optional Activity** Sacrament Match Up ☐ Activity Master 10 (Page 155E)
Remembering Baptism Page 162	• Choose volunteers for the two reader parts. • Follow the order of prayer. Sing "The Seven Sacraments."	☐ bowl of holy water Download "The Seven Sacraments."

Family + Faith Page 163

Point out that the Catholic Families page provides chapter highlights, information on how second graders understand faith concepts, and family prayer.

Chapter Review Page 164

aliveinchrist.osv.com

- Customize and Download Assessments
- Email Links to eAssessments
- Interactive Student Reviews

ONLINE RESOURCES

Go to **aliveinchrist.osv.com**

You will find:

- Interactive lesson planning with web specific content and additional activities
- Step by step lesson instruction from printed Catechist Edition for integrated lesson planning
- Custom-built assessments to download and eAssessment links
- Interactive reviews that provide scores and the option to review answers
- Sunday readings with background and questions of the week

Go to **osvparish.com**

You will find:

- Ask the Experts Q and A
- General Catechist Helps
- Community Connections and Blogs

Sharing the Message with Second Graders

The Sacraments It is a mystery to us, adults and children alike, that God invites us to participate with him in his work. The Seven Sacraments have human actions and divine actions—the things people say and do and what God does through the Sacrament. Second graders might tend to only focus on the human actions—the things they can see. It's important that parents and catechists direct them to the ways in which these visible signs help us understand the invisible reality—what God is doing in the Sacrament.

Teaching Tip: When you are doing something in the classroom that the children would not be able to do by themselves, ask a child to assist you. Point out that this invitation to share in your work is similar in some ways to how God invites us to participate in his work through the Sacraments.

How Second Graders Understand

- Knowing what things mean, at the right level, promotes a sense of belonging. However, many children in this age group have trouble grasping abstract ideas.
- Use simple language and concrete, practical examples to explain the sacramental symbols to second graders.
- Hearing their own stories about being welcomed into the Church builds children's sense of Catholic identity. Encourage the children to talk about their Baptism with their family.

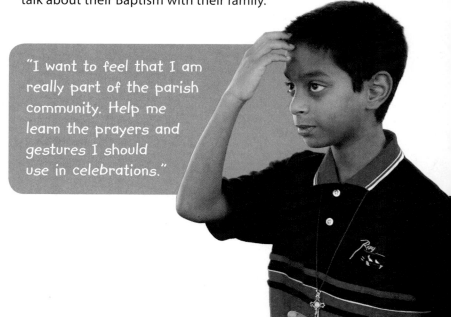

"I want to feel that I am really part of the parish community. Help me learn the prayers and gestures I should use in celebrations."

Chapter Connections

Chapter Story

Invite

"My Abuela and Me"

Use this story to expand the chapter introduction.

- Have the children name things that could be considered signs of love.
- Explain that *abuela* is the Spanish word for grandmother.
- *Ask:* What are the signs of love in this story?

Go to **aliveinchrist.osv.com** Lesson Planning section for this story.

NCEA IFG: ACRE Edition

Discover

Knowledge of the Faith

- Objective: To know and understand basic Catholic teaching about the Incarnate Word Jesus Christ as the way, truth, and life

Liturgical Life

- Objective: To know the Paschal Mystery of Jesus: in the Church's liturgical life—feast, seasons, symbols, and practices and in the Sacraments as signs and instruments of grace

Catholic Social Teaching

Live

Use one of these features to introduce a principle and engage the children with an activity.

- Option for the Poor, Pages 296–297
- Care for Creation, Pages 302–303

Music Options

Use one or more of the following songs to enhance catechetical learning or for prayer.

- "The Seven Sacraments," Live Prayer, Page 162
- "Belonging Through Baptism," Discover, Page 157
- "Share the Light," Live, Page 160
- "Through My Fault," Live, Page 160

LECTIONARY CONNECTION

Chapter 10 highlights Lectionary-connected themes such as Seven Sacraments, grace, Baptism, and Sacraments of Initiation. If your parish aligns its curriculum to the liturgical year, you could use this chapter in connection with the following Sundays.

Year A

Seventh Sunday of Easter—Grace

Eighteenth Sunday in Ordinary Time—Invitation to Grace

Year B

First Sunday of Lent—Grace

Fourth Sunday of Lent—We are saved by grace.

Year C

Trinity Sunday—We have access to grace through Christ.

Twenty-fourth Sunday in Ordinary Time—Grace

Go to **aliveinchrist.osv.com** for a complete correlation ordered by the Sundays of the year and suggestions for how to integrate the Scripture readings into chapter lessons.

Name ______________________________ Date ________________

Sacrament Match-Up

Six of the Seven Sacraments are pictured below. Draw lines to match the Sacrament names with the pictures that best tell about them.

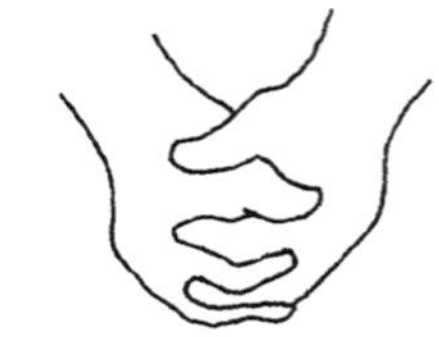 • • **Confirmation**

 • • **Eucharist**

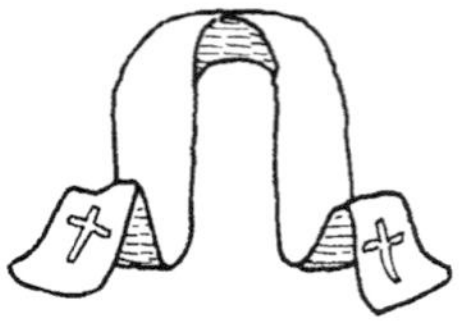 • • **Anointing of the Sick**

 • • **Reconciliation**

 • • **Holy Orders**

 • • **Matrimony**

Draw a picture of the missing Sacrament.
Label your picture with the Sacrament's name.

____

CHAPTER 10

The Sacraments

Let Us Pray

Leader: God, thank you for the blessings you give us.

"Come and see the works of God,
awesome in deeds before the
children of Adam." Psalm 66:5

All: Help us to see your gifts and fill our hearts with thanks. Amen.

God's Word

Jesus and his disciples were approaching a town called Jericho. A blind beggar was sitting by the road. When he heard the crowd, he began to shout, "Jesus, Son of David, have pity on me!" People told him to be quiet, but he shouted louder. Jesus stopped and asked that the beggar be brought to him. "What do you want me to do for you," Jesus asked? The blind man said, "Lord, please let me see." Jesus said, "Have sight; your faith has saved you." Immediately the blind man got back his sight and followed Jesus. And the people praised God.

Based on Luke 18:35–43

What Do You Wonder?

- Why did Jesus heal the sick?
- Why do we celebrate the Seven Sacraments?

Optional Activity

Chapter Story: "My Abuela and Me" *Verbal/Linguistic*

Use this story after the opening prayer, before you explain how people communicate.

- Ask the children to listen for signs of love as you read aloud the chapter story. Explain that *abuela* is a Spanish word for grandmother.
- Help the children see that signs can be words or actions, then transition back to the lesson instruction.

Go to **aliveinchrist.osv.com** for Chapter Story.

Invite

Let Us Pray

Invite the children to gather in the prayer space and make the Sign of the Cross. Read aloud the leader's prayer and the Psalm verse. Prompt the children's response.

Have the children move from the prayer space back to their seats.

Explain that people speak with words and actions, and tell us about themselves if we pay attention to what they say and do.

Say: Listen to this story about Jesus and pay attention to what we learn about him.

God's Word

Guide the children through the process of Scripture reflection.

- Invite them to close their eyes, be still, and open their minds and hearts to what God is saying to them in this passage.
- Proclaim the Scripture.
- Maintain several moments of silence.
- *Ask:* What did you hear God say to you today?
- Invite volunteers to share.

What Do You Wonder?

Say: God made us to be loved and to love others. But, no one loves us like God loves us. The Seven Sacraments are ways that God continues to share his love with us.

Invite the children to respond to the questions. Ask what else they might wonder about love and the Seven Sacraments.

Discover

Objectives

- Describe the Seven Sacraments as special signs and celebrations that come from Jesus and give us a share in God's life and work
- Understand that Jesus continues to share his life and love with us through the Sacraments
- Explore Baptism as the first Sacrament we receive that frees us from sin and makes us children of God

Discover

The Apostles gathering on the mountain where Christ sends them out to share the Good News and baptize in his name.

Signs of God's Love

What are the Sacraments?

Jesus' actions were signs of love that brought people closer to God the Father. Jesus welcomed people who felt alone. He fed people who were hungry. Jesus forgave and healed people. In these ways, Jesus shared God's life with others. Later, the Holy Spirit gave the Apostles the power to do what Jesus had done.

God's Word

The Commissioning of the Apostles

After his Resurrection, Jesus asked his Apostles to continue his work. "Go, therefore, and make disciples of all nations, baptizing them in the name of the Father, and of the Son, and of the holy Spirit, teaching them to observe all that I have commanded you." Matthew 28:19–20

➔ **What did Jesus ask the Apostles to do?**

➔ **Who has taught you about Jesus?**

Signs of God's Life

Have the children name some things Jesus did to show others God's love.

- Draw together the children's responses by summarizing the first paragraph.
- Invite the children to think of ways the disciples continued what Jesus had done.
- Ask the children how the Apostles found the courage and power to do the things Jesus had done.

God's Word

Proclaim the Scripture story.

- Ask the children what is happening in the fine art at the top of the student page.
- Explain that it is a picture of Jesus sending out the disciples.
- Discuss the questions at the bottom of the student page as a group.

Scripture Background

Matthew 28:19–20

This passage from the Gospel according to Matthew is often called "The Great Commission."

- Jesus sent his closest followers out to share the Good News and help others believe in him.
- In this passage Jesus clearly establishes the first Sacrament we receive—Baptism—and shows that we must continue to learn about him and live by his commands.

Signs and Celebrations

The Catholic Church shares God's life and love through special celebrations called Sacraments. The **Seven Sacraments** are special signs and celebrations that come from Jesus and allow us to share in God's life.

Baptism is the first Sacrament a person receives. Through Baptism, a person receives forgiveness and new life in Christ. He or she becomes a child of God and a member of Christ's Body, the Church.

In Baptism, a priest or deacon pours water over the head of the person being baptized and says, "I baptize you in the name of the Father, and of the Son, and of the Holy Spirit." The person is then anointed with oil and marked forever by God's love. Afterward, they receive a lit candle as a sign of walking in the light of Jesus.

Catholic Faith Words

Seven Sacraments special signs and celebrations that Jesus gave his Church. They allow us to share in God's life and work.

Baptism the Sacrament in which a person is immersed in water or has water poured on him or her. Baptism takes away Original Sin and all personal sin, and makes a person a child of God and member of the Church.

Share Your Faith

Think What is one way girls and boys your age can walk in the light of Jesus?

____

____

____

____

Share Take turns talking with a partner.

Signs and Celebrations

Read aloud the first paragraph. Remind the children that signs can be both words and actions.

- Invite the children to describe what is happening in the photograph on this page.

Read aloud the second and third paragraphs.

- Have the children name two things that happen at a Baptism.
- Invite volunteers to share what they know of their own Baptisms.

Work with Words

Point out the Catholic Faith Words.

- Have the children practice reading the words and definitions to a partner, with each reading at least once.

Activity

Read aloud the directions for the Share Your Faith activity.

- Have the children work independently to write their ideas. After a short time, have them discuss their ideas with a partner.

Music Option: Have the children sing "Belonging Through Baptism," downloaded from **aliveinchrist.osv.com**.

Optional Activity

Visit the Church *Bodily/Kinesthetic*

Arrange for the children to visit the parish church to see the font or pool used for Baptism.

- If possible, arrange for a priest or deacon to show the children what happens at a baptism.
- Ask them what we should do when we enter and leave the church. After volunteers share, explain that we bless ourselves with holy water, making the Sign of the Cross. It's a reminder of who we are: baptized Catholics blessed with God's life in us.

Quick Review

Jesus shares his life and love with us. Sacraments are special signs and celebrations that come from Jesus and allow us to share in God's life.

Discover

Objectives

- Learn that in the Seven Sacraments, we receive the gift of God's life and help, or grace
- Identify the Sacraments of Initiation as the beginning of our life in the Church

The Seven Sacraments

Use the opening question to begin discussion or direct the children's reading.

Read aloud the first paragraph.

Explain the key points in the second paragraph: The actions of the Holy Spirit, which we can't see, and our own words and actions in the celebration of the Sacraments, help God's life in us grow.

Have a volunteer read aloud the third paragraph.

- Explain to the children that the word *initiation* is also used to describe the process of becoming a part of a group.

Choose seven children to read aloud the names of the Seven Sacraments listed across pages 158 and 159.

- Have the rest of the group follow along by looking at the pictures.

☆ Instruct the children to circle the Sacraments they have already received and draw a square around the ones they will soon receive.

- After the children have finished, allow them to share their answers with a partner.

The Seven Sacraments

How do we become Church members?

In the Seven Sacraments, we receive the gift of God's life and help. This is called **grace**. Jesus is present in the Sacraments. He welcomes, heals, and feeds us.

In each Sacrament, the Holy Spirit does things that we can't see. But we are invited to cooperate with his work. We do this by things we can see: our words and actions in the celebration. When you receive the Sacraments, God's life in you grows. You grow in love for him and others.

Baptism, Confirmation, and Eucharist are the **Sacraments of Initiation**. Initiation means "beginning." These Sacraments welcome new members into the Catholic Church. Everyone is invited to follow Jesus and join the Church.

Catholic Faith Words

grace God's gift of a share in his life and help

Sacraments of Initiation the three Sacraments that celebrate membership in the Catholic Church: Baptism, Confirmation, and Eucharist

1. Circle the Sacraments you have already received.
2. Draw a square around the ones you will receive soon.

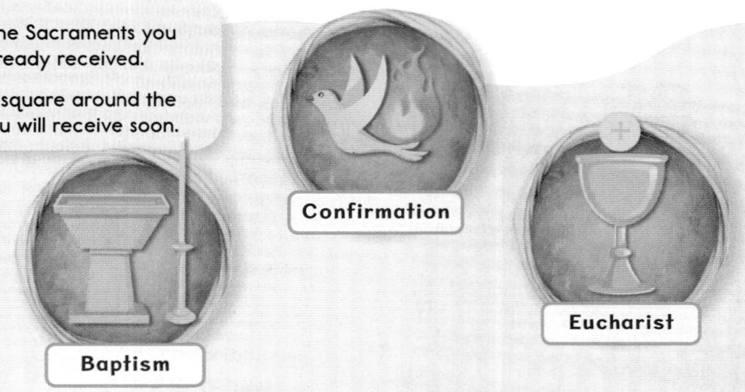

Catechist Background

Age of Reception

Unbaptized adults and children of catechetical age come into the Church through the RCIA—Rite of Christian Initiation of Adults. They receive the three Sacraments of Initiation in one celebration, usually at the Easter Vigil.

The Confirmation of previously baptized children takes place at different ages and times of the year. The candidates renew their baptismal promises and are usually confirmed during a Mass to show the connection among the three Sacraments.

The Sacraments of Initiation

- Through **Baptism**, a person is given new life in Christ.
- In **Confirmation**, a person is sealed with the Gifts of the Holy Spirit and strengthened to follow Jesus.
- In the **Eucharist**, the Body and Blood of Christ help disciples grow closer to him and others.

People of any age can become members of the Catholic Church. Sometimes all three Sacraments of Initiation are received in the same celebration. Other times, they are spread over many years.

Connect Your Faith

Make a Card Create a welcome message for a new Church member. Tell them something you think new Catholics need to know about the Sacraments and the Church.

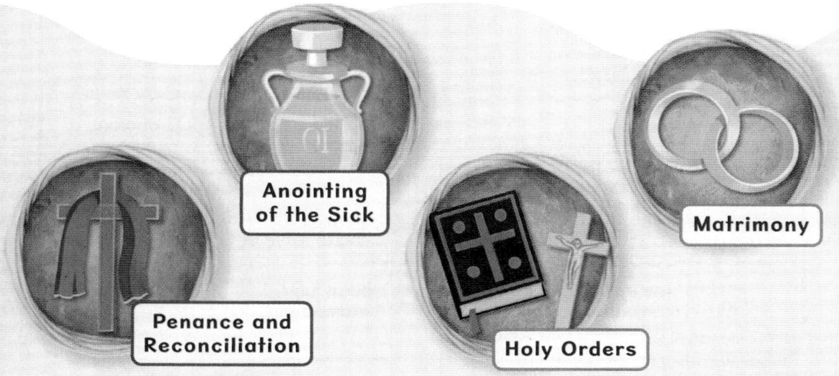

Teaching Tip

Talk with Candidates

Invite older children or adults who recently received or are preparing to celebrate Sacraments in your parish to talk with the children about their experience.

- With the permission of your director of faith formation, contact the RCIA coordinator of the parish for possible guest speakers.
- Ask guest speakers to share some of the experiences they had during their preparation.
- Invite the children to ask their own questions.

The Sacraments of Initiation

Explain that the Church celebrates Seven Sacraments. New members join the Church through the Sacraments of Initiation: Baptism, Confirmation, and Eucharist.

Ask three volunteers to each read aloud one of the bullet points.

- Summarize the last paragraph.

Activity

Explain the Connect Your Faith activity to the children.

- Help them brainstorm a list of things new Catholics should know.
- Allow time for the children to complete the activity.
- Collect the cards for delivery.

Invite the children to turn to page 307 in the Our Catholic Tradition section of the Student Book to review "The Seven Sacraments."

- Read aloud the paragraph below the chart.
- Have the children silently review the chart.
- Allow them to ask questions.

Quick Review

In the Seven Sacraments, we receive God's grace. The Sacraments of Initiation are the beginning of our life in the Church.

Live

Our Catholic Life

Summarize the introductory paragraph.

Review the chart with the group.

- Discuss with the children the explanation of what each Sacrament celebrates.
- ☆ Instruct the children to match the first three Sacraments on the left to how they help the Church on the right.
- Point out that the remaining four Sacraments already have the correct content next to them.
- As a group, go over the correct matches for each Sacrament. Explain as necessary, and ask if there are any questions.
- Remind the children that the grace received from the Sacraments not only helps individuals, but also helps the Church as a community.

Music Option: Have the children sing "Share the Light" or "Through My Fault," downloaded from **aliveinchrist.osv.com**.

Live

Our Catholic Life

How do the Sacraments help the Church?

Each of the Sacraments is sign and a celebration. In the Sacraments, you receive grace. God's life and love help you be more loving. The grace of the Sacraments helps the whole Church community, too.

☆ Match the first three Sacraments on the left to how they help the Church on the right.

What It Celebrates	How It Helps the Church
Baptism Becoming children of God and members of the Church	Feeds, heals, and unites the members of the Body of Christ
Confirmation Being sealed with the Gift of the Holy Spirit	Welcomes new members into the Catholic family
Eucharist Jesus' sacrifice and the gift of his Body and Blood received in Holy Communion	Gives members the strength to follow Jesus' example
Penance and Reconciliation God's forgiveness when we are sorry for and confess our sins	Brings people back into the Church and helps make peace
Anointing of the Sick God's healing love through prayer and anointing with oil	Gives support to people who are ill or elderly
Holy Orders The call of a man to be a deacon, priest, or bishop	Strengthens men to be leaders and to serve God and the Church
Matrimony The lifelong love of a baptized man and a baptized woman who become a new family	Builds family love and gives an example of loving care

Optional Activity

Activity Master 10: Sacrament Match-Up

Distribute copies of the activity found on catechist page 155E.

- Have the children draw lines to match the Sacrament names with the appropriate pictures.
- As an alternative you may wish to send this activity home with the children.

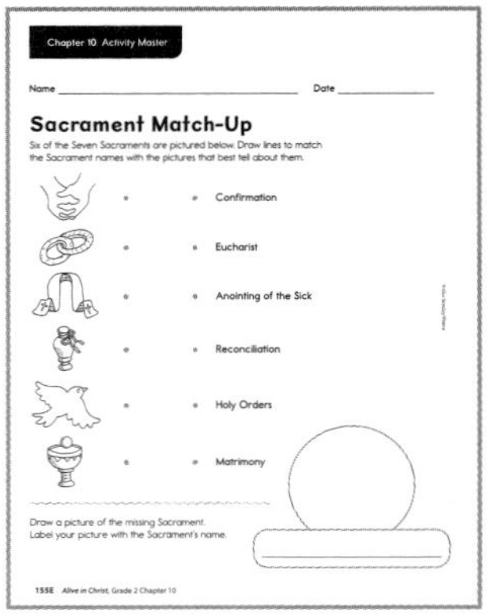
Chapter 10 Activity Master

Name ______ Date ______

Sacrament Match-Up

Six of the Seven Sacraments are pictured below. Draw lines to match the Sacrament names with the pictures that best tell about them.

Confirmation

Eucharist

Anointing of the Sick

Reconciliation

Holy Orders

Matrimony

Draw a picture of the missing Sacrament. Label your picture with the Sacrament's name.

155E Alive in Christ, Grade 2 Chapter 10

People of Faith

August 21

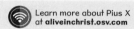

Saint Pius X (Giuseppe Sarto), 1835–1914

Giuseppe Sarto was born in Italy. He became a priest and a teacher. He loved children and wanted everyone to learn about Jesus and the Church. When he became Pope, he took the name Pius X. He did many things to show how important the Eucharist is. He encouraged Catholics to receive Holy Communion every day, even children. He knew the Sacraments help us stay close to God.

Discuss: When do you feel close to Jesus?

Learn more about Pius X at **aliveinchrist.osv.com**

Live Your Faith

Tell what is happening in the picture.

Draw one way you can make someone feel welcome and see God's love.

People of Faith

Tell the children about Saint Pius X.

- Explain that the *X* in his name is the Roman numeral for 10, meaning that Giuseppe was the tenth Pope to take the name Pius.
- Read aloud the paragraph.
- Share that Pope Pius X also encouraged use of beautiful Church music and clear simple homilies by the priests at Mass.
- *Ask:* When do you feel close to Jesus?
- Invite the children to respond.

Encourage the children to go to **aliveinchrist.osv.com** at home to learn more about Saint Pius X.

Activity

Explain the directions for the activity.

- Invite a volunteer to describe what is happening in the picture.
- Allow time for the children to complete the drawing part of the activity.
- Encourage the children to share their drawings with the group.

Catholic Social Teaching

Chapter Connections

To integrate Catholic Social Teaching into your lesson, choose one of the following features: Option for the Poor, pages 296–297, or Care for Creation, pages 302–303.

- Start the Live step of the process by talking about Saint Pius X on page 161. Then move directly to the Catholic Social Teaching feature.
- Or, to expand the lesson, complete both pages 160 and 161, then move to the Catholic Social Teaching feature.
- Return to Chapter 10 for the prayer on page 162.

Let Us Pray

Remembering Baptism

Prepare

Select two children, one for Reader 1 and one for Reader 2. Allow them to practice their parts.

Rehearse with the children "The Seven Sacraments," downloaded from **aliveinchrist.osv.com**.

Gather

Carry the bowl of holy water, leading the children in procession to the prayer space.

- Instruct the children on how they are to come forward when their name is called. Model by dipping your fingers in the holy water with your right hand, and bless yourself with the Sign of the Cross, saying "In the name of the Father, and of the Son, and of the Holy Spirit. Amen."
- Invite the children to quiet themselves for prayer and to be seated for the reading.

Pray

Follow the order of prayer on the student page.

- At the appropriate time, call each child by name and invite him or her to make the Sign of the Cross as you demonstrated.

Conclude by processing around the room with the children singing "The Seven Sacraments."

Let Us Pray

Remembering Baptism

Gather and begin with the Sign of the Cross.

Leader: Let us remember that we are God's children. We share in his life. We are disciples of Jesus.

Reader 1: Jesus sent his Apostles out to make disciples of others, to baptize them and teach them.

Reader 2: Paul wrote: You have been baptized. It does not matter who you are or where you come from. Baptism makes you a disciple of Jesus. Based on Galatians 3:27–28

Leader: When we were baptized, we were marked with the Sign of the Cross. Listen to what was said.

"My dear children, the Christian community welcomes you with great joy. In its name I claim you for Christ our Savior by the sign of the cross."
Rite of Baptism, 41

Child: Come forward when your name is called. Dip the fingers of your right hand in the water and bless yourself with the Sign of the Cross.

All: Sing "The Seven Sacraments"

The Sacraments, the Seven Sacraments.
Signs that come from Jesus and
give us grace.

The Sacraments, the Seven
Sacraments. Signs that
God is with us in
a special way.

Liturgy Link

Gathering Prayer

Our sacramental celebrations are communal. Even individual confession is celebrated in the name of the whole Church. These celebrations, including the Mass, all begin with gathering prayers.

- The first gesture of any sacramental liturgy is the Sign of the Cross, which recalls our Baptism and identifies us as members of the Body of Christ.

Go to **aliveinchrist.osv.com** for Sunday readings, Scripture background, questions of the week, and seasonal resources.

FAMILY + FAITH

LIVING AND LEARNING TOGETHER

YOUR CHILD LEARNED >>>

This chapter explains that Jesus shares his life with us in the Seven Sacraments. He welcomes, feeds, and heals us.

God's Word

Read **Luke 18:35–43** to learn about a man Jesus healed and how it changed the man's life.

Catholics Believe

- Grace is a share in God's life and help.
- Sacraments are special signs and celebrations that come from Jesus and give grace.

To learn more, go to the *Catechism of the Catholic Church* #1145–1152 at **usccb.org**.

People of Faith

This week, your child met Saint Pius X. He was elected Pope in 1903 and is sometimes called "The Pope of the Eucharist."

CHILDREN AT THIS AGE >>>

How They Understand the Sacraments It's a mystery to us, adults and children alike, that God invites us to communicate with him in his work. The Seven Sacraments have human actions and divine actions—the things people say and do and what God does through the Sacrament.

Your child might tend to only focus on the human actions—the things he or she can see. It's important that we direct children to the ways in which these visible signs help us understand the invisible reality—what God is doing in the Sacrament.

CONSIDER THIS >>>

Have you been a little overwhelmed lately? Do things sometimes seem out of control?

As Catholics, "We may recognize that many times in many ways God's special love is such that he offers us help to live in a way that leads to sharing his life... we face a struggle prompted by our culture's understanding that everything is within our human power." Learning to rely on "grace, the free and undeserved assistance from God" changes our lives (*USCCA, p. 329*).

LET'S TALK >>>

- Ask your child to name the first Sacrament we receive (Baptism).
- Share about your child's Baptism and how it was special.

LET'S PRAY >>>

Saint Pius X, pray to God for us that we may receive Jesus in Holy Communion with reverence. Amen.

For a multimedia glossary of Catholic Faith Words, Sunday readings, seasonal and Saint resources, and chapter activities go to **aliveinchrist.osv.com**.

Chapter 10 Review

A **Work with Words** Complete each sentence with the correct word or words from the Word Bank.

Word Bank
Sacraments
Holy Spirit
Baptism
love
grace
Initiation

1. Baptism and Eucharist are Sacraments of **Initiation**.
2. During **Baptism** water is poured over the person's head.
3. In Confirmation, you are made stronger by the **Holy Spirit**.
4. Sharing in God's life is called **grace**.
5. Each Sacrament is a sign of God's **love**.
6. Jesus is present in the **Sacraments**.

B **Check Understanding** Fill in the circle beside the correct answer.

7. The Seven Sacraments are ____.
   - ● holy signs
   - ○ holy days
8. ____ people are invited to follow Jesus and join the Church.
   - ● All
   - ○ Some
9. Jesus sent his Apostles out to ____ and baptize.
   - ○ eat
   - ● teach
10. At Baptism, a ____ is given to show the light of Jesus.
    - ○ white garment
    - ● candle

Go to **aliveinchrist.osv.com** for an interactive review.

Family + Faith

Distribute the page to the children or parents/adult family members. Point out the chapter highlights, insights on how second graders understand concepts, the opportunity for the adults to reflect on their own experience and faith journey, and the family prayer.

Chapter Review

Use Catechist Quick Reviews to highlight lesson concepts.

A **Work with Words**
Review the Word Bank with the children before having them complete the exercise.

B **Check Understanding**
Direct the children to fill in the circle beside the correct answer.

Go to **aliveinchrist.osv.com** to prepare customized and downloadable assessments, send eAssessments, and assign interactive reviews.

Chapter 11 Seek Forgiveness

KEY CONCEPT
In the Sacrament of Penance and Reconciliation, you receive God's forgiveness. This Sacrament also celebrates your friendship with God and the Church.

DOCTRINAL CONTENT
- An examination of conscience is a prayerful way of thinking about how we have followed the Ten Commandments, Beatitudes, and Church teachings. (CCC, 1779)
- Contrition is being sorry for your sins and wanting to live better. (CCC, 1432)
- In the Sacrament of Penance and Reconciliation, God's forgiveness for sin is given through the Church. (CCC, 1422)
- The Sacrament includes confession, penance, contrition, and absolution. (CCC, 1423–1424)

TASKS OF CATECHESIS
Helping children grow in a faith that is "known, celebrated, lived, and expressed in prayer" (NDC, 20).

This chapter focuses on the following tasks of catechesis:
- Liturgical Education
- Moral Formation

Catechist Background

[Jesus] said to them again, "Peace be with you. As the Father has sent me, so I send you.... Whose sins you forgive are forgiven them, and whose sins you retain are retained."
John 20:21, 23

➔ **Reflect** Do you find peace after forgiving or being forgiven?

When you hear that someone has had "a change of heart," your first response is most likely one of joy. The words typically signal that someone's hardness of heart has given way to compassion.

The burdens of life tend to cause a certain hardness of heart. Dealing daily with human weakness and insensitivity, your own and that of others, may sometimes prevent you from seeing the comfort and compassion that God is always extending to you. Take a moment to think about the things that prevent you from seeing God's love around you. You may feel trapped in poor relationships, caught up in an overwhelming desire for material possessions, or goaded by the wrong priorities. Yet, these very situations may also provoke a desire for change, a feeling that there must be a better way. At best, they become the Holy Spirit's way of helping you hear the call to conversion.

Jesus describes the process of conversion in the story of the woman who was sorry for her sins. In this story, a woman visits Jesus to tell him how sorry she is for what she has done. She actually washes Jesus' feet with her tears and dries them with her hair. Jesus is moved by her great love and sorrow and forgives her sins. She is finally at peace.

God the Father eagerly awaits your return and personally invites you to the Sacrament of Reconciliation.

➔ **Reflect** What in your life needs change?

Catechist's Prayer

Dear God, help me have faith in your willingness to love and forgive me, no matter what my failings. Give me a humble heart, open to receiving your love and forgiveness. Amen.

Lesson Plan

Objectives	Process	Materials
Invite, 10 minutes		
Seek Forgiveness Page 165	**Psalm 85:3** Pray the opening prayer. **Luke 20:21, 23** Reflect prayerfully on the Word. • Discuss What Do You Wonder questions.	**Optional Activity** Chapter Story: "New Again"
Discover, 35 minutes		
Making Things Right Pages 166–167 • Relate an examination of conscience to a prayerful way of looking at our lives • Identify the importance of expressing sorrow • Name the two parts of contrition—being sorry and wanting to live better	• **Catholic Faith Words** examination of conscience, contrition • Think about ways to express sorrow and ask for forgiveness. **Luke 7:36–39, 44–50** Proclaim "The Woman Who Was Forgiven." ☆ Underline what Jesus said to the woman after she washed his feet. • **Share Your Faith Activity** Share how you feel when you say you are sorry.	☐ pencils or pens ☐ board or chart paper
The Sacrament of Reconciliation Pages 168–169 • Understand that in the Sacrament of Penance and Reconciliation, God's forgiveness is given through the Church • List the steps in the Sacrament of Penance and Reconciliation	• **Catholic Faith Words** Sacrament of Penance and Reconciliation, confession, penance, absolution • Learn how the Church celebrates God's forgiveness. • Review the steps of the Sacrament of Penance and Reconciliation. • **Connect Your Faith Activity** Unscramble the words.	☐ pencils or pens • **Optional Activity** The Sacrament of Reconciliation ☐ Activity Master 11 (Page 165E)
Live, 15 minutes		
Our Catholic Life Pages 170–171	• Explain the meaning of the Act of Contrition. ☆ Match the words of the prayer to what they mean. • **People of Faith** Learn about Saint Benedict-Joseph Labré. • **Live Your Faith Activity** Draw one way you can show you are sorry.	☐ pencils or pens ☐ board or chart paper
Prayer for Forgiveness Page 172	• Teach the ASL signs for *Lord* and *Christ*. • Follow the order of prayer. Conclude with the song and a sign of peace.	☐ candle Download "Through My Fault."

Family + Faith Page 173

Point out that the Catholic Families page provides chapter highlights, information on how second graders understand faith concepts, and family prayer.

Chapter Review Page 174

aliveinchrist.osv.com

- Customize and Download Assessments
- Email Links to eAssessments
- Interactive Student Reviews

Teaching This Grade

ONLINE RESOURCES

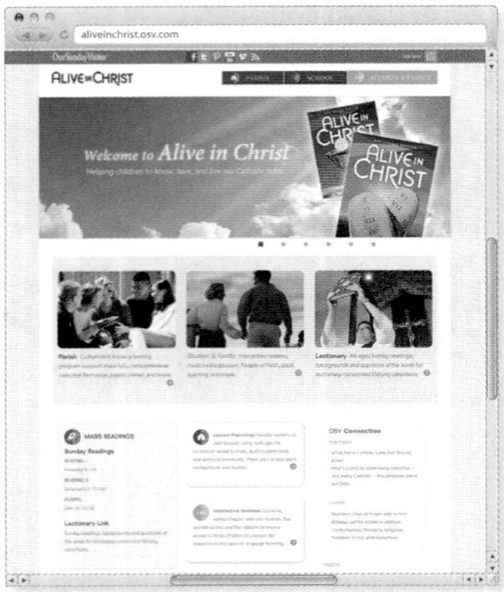

Go to **aliveinchrist.osv.com**

You will find:

- Interactive lesson planning with web specific content and additional activities
- Step by step lesson instruction from printed Catechist Edition for integrated lesson planning
- Custom-built assessments to download and eAssessment links
- Interactive reviews that provide scores and the option to review answers
- Sunday readings with background and questions of the week

Go to **osvparish.com**

You will find:

- Ask the Experts Q and A
- General Catechist Helps
- Community Connections and Blogs

Sharing the Message with Second Graders

Sacrament of Reconciliation Children in second grade might feel nervous about confessing their sins to a priest. They rarely speak alone with any adult, except for mom or dad. They might question why they have to confess their sins to a priest and be worried about what he will think of them. Kids this age need reassurance that the priest has likely heard every sin confessed (they won't shock him) and that the priest cannot talk to anyone about their confession. They also need to know that the priest is a visible sign of both Christ and the Church, and confession to a priest gives us a chance to experience God's forgiveness in a way that we can see.

Teaching Tip: Visit the reconciliation room as a group and discuss what you see (the chair where the priest and penitent sit, etc.). Talk through the rite while the children can see where it happens. This will bring a sense of familiarity that will dispel some unnecessary anxiety.

How Second Graders Understand

- When teaching second graders something serious, they may giggle because it makes them uncomfortable.
- Children this age need to know that God loves them always, even when they make a wrong choice.
- Help the children learn how to apologize if they hurt someone's feelings.

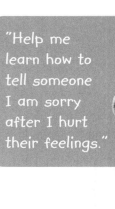

"Help me learn how to tell someone I am sorry after I hurt their feelings."

Chapter Connections

Chapter Story

Invite

"New Again"

Use this story to expand the chapter introduction.

- Arrange the children into small groups.
- Have them share a story about something broken that was fixed or something lost that was found.
- Have the children tell how they feel when broken things are fixed.

Go to **aliveinchrist.osv.com** Lesson Planning section for this story.

NCEA IFG: ACRE Edition

Discover

Liturgical Life

- Objective: To know the Paschal Mystery of Jesus: in the Church's liturgical life—feasts, seasons, symbols, and practices and in the Sacraments as signs and instruments of grace

Moral Formation

- Objectives: To be knowledgeable about the teachings of Jesus and the Church as the basis of Christian morality and to understand Catholic Social Teaching; to be aware of the importance of a well-formed conscience for decision making

Catholic Social Teaching

Live

Use one of these features to introduce a principle and engage the children with an activity.

- Call to Community, Pages 292–293
- Solidarity of the Human Family, Pages 300–301

Music Options

Use one or more of the following songs to enhance catechetical learning or for prayer.

- "Through My Fault," Live Prayer, Page 172
- "God of Mercy," Discover, Page 169

LECTIONARY CONNECTION

Chapter 11 highlights Lectionary-connected themes such as an examination of conscience, contrition, absolution, penance, and the Sacrament of Penance and Reconciliation. If your parish aligns its curriculum to the liturgical year, you could use this chapter in connection with the following Sundays.

Year A

Ninth Sunday in Ordinary Time—Justice Apart from the Law

Thirteenth Sunday in Ordinary Time—Death to Sin, Life in God

Year B

Second Sunday of Lent—Reconciliation

Twenty-sixth Sunday in Ordinary Time—Reconciliation

Year C

Baptism of the Lord—Conversion

First Sunday of Lent—Conversion

Go to **aliveinchrist.osv.com** for a complete correlation ordered by the Sundays of the year and suggestions for how to integrate the Scripture readings into chapter lessons.

Name ______________________________ Date ______________

The Sacrament of Reconciliation

Review the steps for the Sacrament of Reconciliation. Then use the words in the Word Bank to complete each sentence. You will use each word only once.

Word Bank

sins	conscience	pray	Bible
sorrow	sorry	absolution	penance

1. I ______________________ to God.
2. I examine my ______________________.
3. I tell God I am ______________________ for my sins.
4. I listen to the reading from the ______________________.

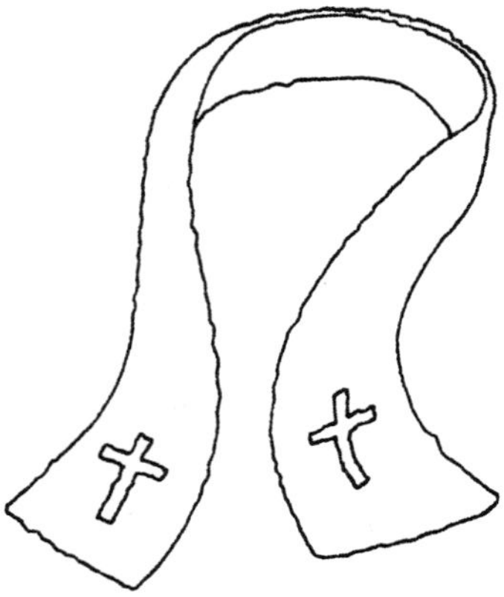

5. I confess my ______________________.
6. The priest gives me a ______________________.
7. I pray a prayer of ______________________.
8. The priest gives me ______________________.

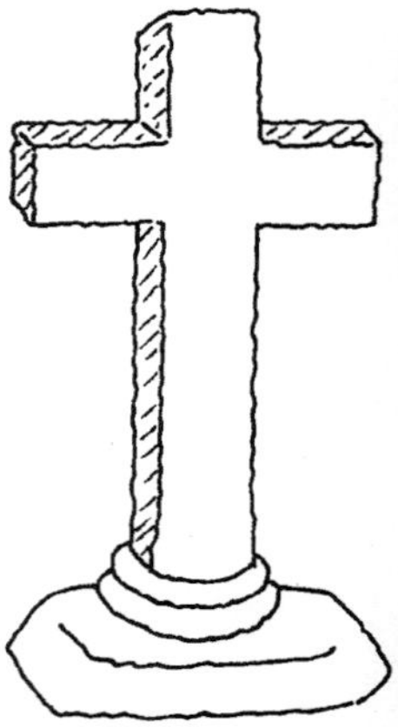

Seek Forgiveness

Let Us Pray

Leader: God, we thank you for your love and forgiveness.

You have forgiven your people's sins and all their wrongs. Based on Psalm 85:3

All: Thank you, God, for your forgiveness. Amen.

God's Word

After Jesus rose from the dead, he went to the disciples who were locked in a room because they were afraid. "Peace be with you," he said. "Whose sins you forgive are forgiven them..." Based on John 20:21, 23

What Do You Wonder?

- Do you think about what your actions say to others?
- Why is forgiveness so important to Jesus?

Optional Activity

Chapter Story: "New Again" *Verbal/Linguistic*

Use this story after the opening prayer, before you talk to the children about forgiveness.

- Have the children silently read "New Again."
- Ask them if something of theirs was ever broken and then fixed by someone. Possible responses: a toy truck, a deflated ball
- After explaining that today they will learn about repairing or fixing friendships, transition back to the lesson instruction.

Go to **aliveinchrist.osv.com** for Chapter Story.

Invite

Let Us Pray

Invite the children to gather in the prayer space and make the Sign of the Cross. Read aloud the leader's prayer. Have the children repeat the Psalm verse after you. Prompt the children's response.

Have the children move from the prayer space back to their seats.

Explain that we can always ask God for forgiveness.

Say: Let's listen to see what Jesus said about forgiveness.

God's Word

Guide the children through the process of Scripture reflection.

- Invite them to close their eyes, be still, and open their minds and hearts to what God is saying to them in this passage.
- Proclaim the Scripture.
- Maintain several moments of silence.
- *Ask:* What did you hear God say to you today?
- Invite volunteers to share.

What Do You Wonder?

Say: Jesus was inviting the disciples to look at how they forgive and pardon others.

Invite the children to respond to the questions. Ask what else they might wonder about forgiveness.

Discover

Objectives

- Relate an examination of conscience to a prayerful way of looking at our lives
- Identify the importance of expressing sorrow
- Name the two parts of contrition—being sorry and wanting to live better

Making Things Right

Ask a volunteer to read aloud the question.

- List the children's answers on the board or on chart paper.

Read aloud the introductory paragraph.

God's Word

Proclaim the Scripture story, and ask the children to listen for the words Jesus spoke to the woman. Your sins are forgiven. Your faith has saved you. Go in peace.

Have the children silently read the question at the bottom of the page.

- *Ask:* How did the woman show she was sorry for her sins? How do you show you are sorry?
- Encourage the children to give specific examples.

Discover

Making Things Right

How can you show you are sorry?

Sometimes we make choices that accidently hurt someone. Other times, we hurt others on purpose; we choose to sin. In this story, Jesus tells us how to show we are sorry and seek forgiveness.

Underline what Jesus said to the woman after she washed his feet.

God's Word

The Woman Who Was Forgiven

One day, Jesus was having dinner. An uninvited woman came into the room and knelt at Jesus' feet. She was sorry for her sins. Her tears fell on Jesus' feet. Then she dried his feet with her long hair and poured sweet-smelling ointment on his feet.

Jesus spoke up for the woman. "She has bathed [my feet] with her tears and. . . anointed my feet with ointment. So I tell you, her many sins have been forgiven; hence, she has shown great love."

Then Jesus said to the woman, "Your sins are forgiven. . .Your faith has saved you; go in peace." Based on Luke 7:36–39, 44–50

➔ **How did the woman show she was sorry for her sins?**

Songs of Scripture

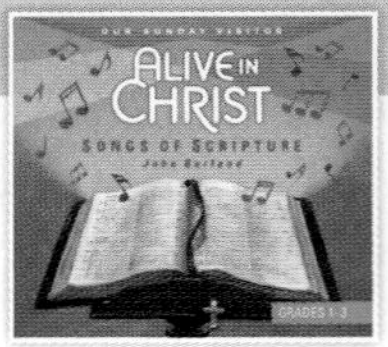

How Many Times, Lord?

Forgiveness is a true sign of holiness. However, while God asks us to forgive, we should always report actions that are harmful (bullying, inappropriate touching).

- With the Holy Spirit's help, we can make the choice to be like Jesus and forgive others.
- Teach the children the song, "How Many Times, Lord?"

Use *Songs of Scripture*, Grades 1–3 CD, Track 13

Examination of Conscience

You may sometimes choose not to obey God's laws. This hurts your friendship with God and others.

You can ask the Holy Spirit to help you see where you have made wrong choices. You can think about your thoughts, words, and actions. This prayerful way of looking at your life is called an **examination of conscience**, it helps us know whether what we've done is right or wrong.

Here are some questions you can think about to help you examine your conscience:

- Did I put God first in my life?
- Did I use God's name in a holy way?
- Did I keep Sunday a holy day?
- Did I obey my parents and teachers?

After you think about your sins, you can tell God that you are sorry. Then tell him you will try harder to live by his Commandments. This means you have **contrition** for your sins.

Catholic Faith Words

examination of conscience a prayerful way of thinking about how we have followed the Ten Commandments, Beatitudes, and Church teachings

contrition being sorry for your sins and wanting to live better

Share Your Faith

Think Write one more question you can use to examine your conscience.

____

____

Share Share your answer with a partner.

Examination of Conscience

Ask a volunteer to read aloud the first two paragraphs.

- Review with the children the questions they should reflect on when examining their conscience.

Read aloud the last paragraph.

- Discuss with the group ways to show contrition.
- Invite the children to turn to page 315 in the Our Catholic Tradition section of the Student Book to read more about making an Examination of Conscience.
- Allow time for discussion.

Activity

Read aloud the directions.

- Ask the children to work independently to answer the question, but then share it with a partner.

Quick Review

An examination of conscience is a prayerful way of looking at one's life in order to reflect on the choices we have made. Contrition is being sorry for one's sins and wanting to do better.

Optional Activity

Prayer of Sorrow *Verbal/Linguistic*

Give the children writing paper, and have them write a prayer that tells God about their sorrow. Provide the following formula.

- Tell God you are sorry for having sinned.
- Promise to do better.
- Ask God's forgiveness and help.
- Thank God for his love.

Tell the children that no one will read their prayers. Have them take the prayers home to pray before going to bed.

Objectives

- Understand that in the Sacrament of Penance and Reconciliation, God's forgiveness is given through the Church
- List the steps in the Sacrament of Penance and Reconciliation

The Sacrament of Reconciliation

Read aloud the question at the top of the student page.

- Tell the children that they will learn the answer to that question by studying the steps shown on page 169.

Read aloud both paragraphs.

Work with Words

Have the children place a finger on the words *Sacrament of Penance and Reconciliation.*

- Read the Catholic Faith Words definition.
- Explain that *penance*, *confession*, and *absolution* are parts of the celebration of the Sacrament of Reconciliation.
- Have volunteers read aloud the definitions.

The Sacrament of Reconciliation

How do we receive God's forgiveness?

After examining your conscience and being sorry for your sins, you are ready to celebrate the Church's **Sacrament of Penance and Reconciliation**. Each time you receive this Sacrament, you receive God's forgiveness and celebrate your friendship with him and the Church community.

You can participate in the Sacrament of Reconciliation individually or as part of a parish celebration. Either way, you always confess your sins privately to a priest, who grants forgiveness in God's name. The priest will help you if you forget a step.

Catholic Faith Words

Sacrament of Penance and Reconciliation the Sacrament in which God's forgiveness for sin is given through the Church

confession telling your sins to the priest

penance a prayer or an act to make up for sin

absolution words spoken by the priest during the Sacrament of Penance and Reconciliation to grant forgiveness of sins in God's name

Connect Your Faith

Unscramble the Words Find a phrase used during the Sacrament of Reconciliation.

SIH REYCM RNDEEUS OEFRVRE

H I S M E R C Y
E N D U R E S
F O R E V E R

Quick Tip

All Children May Not Be Ready

All second graders may not be ready to celebrate the Sacrament of Penance and Reconciliation.

- The parents—in consultation with a priest, the director of faith formation, the catechist, and child—are the ones who must decide upon the child's readiness for this Sacrament.
- If First Penance is delayed, so must be First Holy Communion. Through prayer, you can help guide the parents in making this important decision.

Steps in the Sacrament

1 Welcome Rites The priest greets you with the Sign of the Cross.

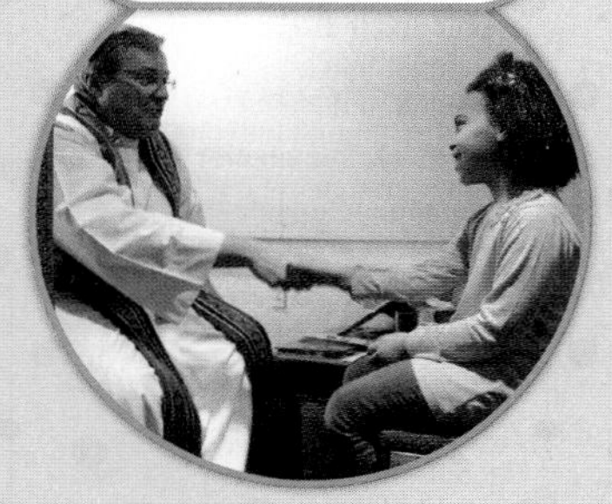

2 Scripture Reading Sometimes the priest reads, or you quietly read, a Bible passage about forgiveness.

3 Confession and Penance Next you tell your sins to the priest. This is called **confession**. He can never tell anyone your sins. He talks with you about ways you can do better. He gives you a **penance**.

4 Contrition You pray an Act of Contrition. (See page 170 for this prayer.)

5 Absolution The priest gives **absolution**, or forgiveness of your sins in the name of the Father, the Son, and the Holy Spirit. (See page 315 for the words of this prayer.)

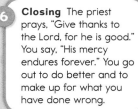

6 Closing The priest prays, "Give thanks to the Lord, for he is good." You say, "His mercy endures forever." You go out to do better and to make up for what you have done wrong.

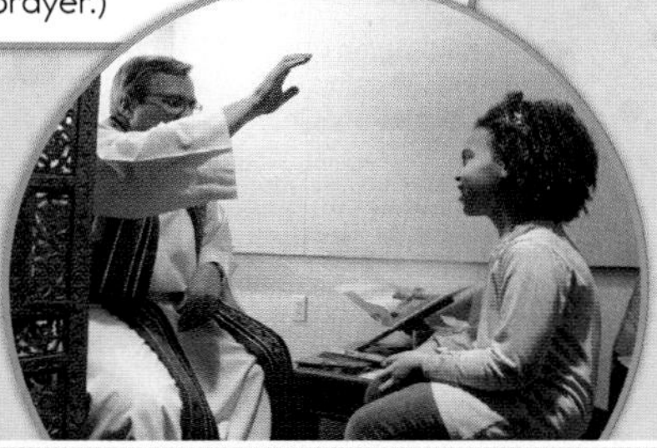

169

Steps in the Sacrament

Review each of the steps with the children by reading them yourself or asking volunteers to read them.

- Ask the children if they have questions on any of the steps. Discuss as needed.
- Discuss the types of penance the priest might give to the children.
- Tell them how important the words of absolution are and that they will make the Sign of the Cross as the priest prays these words. Point out that some priests may shake hands with them as they leave as a sign of the peace of Christ.

Music Option: Have the children sing, "God of Mercy," downloaded from **aliveinchrist.osv.com**.

Activity

Read aloud the directions on page 168.

- Give the children time to solve the puzzle.
- Ask a volunteer to share the answer.

Optional Activity

Activity Master 11: The Sacrament of Reconciliation

Distribute copies of the activity found on catechist page 165E.

- This activity helps the children learn the steps of receiving the Sacrament of Reconciliation.
- As an alternative, you may wish to send this activity home with the children.

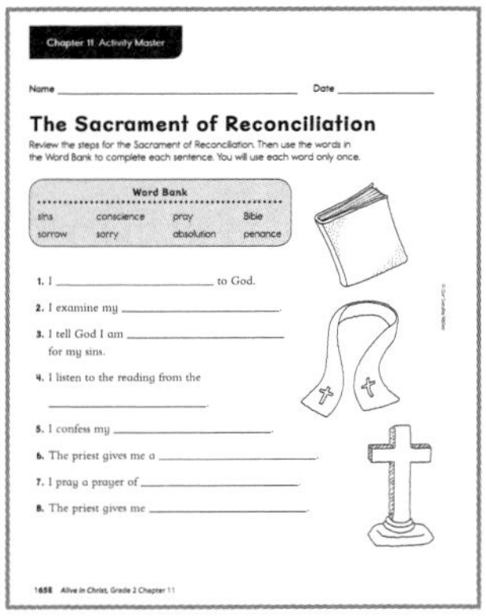

Chapter 11 Activity Master

Name ______ Date ______

The Sacrament of Reconciliation

Review the steps for the Sacrament of Reconciliation. Then use the words in the Word Bank to complete each sentence. You will use each word only once.

Word Bank			
sins	conscience	pray	Bible
sorrow	sorry	absolution	penance

1. I ______ to God.
2. I examine my ______.
3. I tell God I am ______ for my sins.
4. I listen to the reading from the ______.
5. I confess my ______.
6. The priest gives me a ______.
7. I pray a prayer of ______.
8. The priest gives me ______.

165E Alive in Christ, Grade 2 Chapter 11

Quick Review

The Sacrament of Penance and Reconciliation can be celebrated individually or as part of a parish or communal celebration with individual confession. It is the Church's Sacrament of forgiveness.

Live

Our Catholic Life

Invite a volunteer to read aloud the question at the top of the student page.

- Write the children's suggestions on the board or on chart paper.

Read aloud the first paragraph.

Act of Contrition

Read aloud all of the lines under *Words of the Prayer*.

- Instruct the children to match the words of the prayer on the left with what they mean on the right.
- Have the children sit in pairs and work together.
- Review the correct answers with the children by having seven volunteers each read aloud one of the matches.

Live

Our Catholic Life

How do you tell God you are sorry for sin?

In the Sacrament of Reconciliation, you pray an Act of Contrition. This prayer tells God that you are sorry for what you've done and that you need him to help you do better in the future.

Act of Contrition

Match the words of the prayer on the left with what they mean on the right.

Words of the Prayer	What They Mean
My God, I am sorry for my sins with all my heart.	Sometimes I have done wrong things on purpose. Sometimes I haven't done good things that I should have done.
In choosing to do wrong and failing to do good.	God I know I have done wrong, and I am very sorry.
I have sinned against you, whom I should love above all things.	God, you have asked me to love you with my whole heart, soul, mind, and strength, and I haven't done that.
I firmly intend, with your help, to do penance,	Jesus died on the Cross to save us from the power of sin.
to sin no more, and to avoid whatever leads me to sin.	I believe what Jesus taught us about you, his loving Father. Please forgive me.
Our Savior Jesus Christ suffered and died for us.	From now on, I will try harder to make better choices. I will stay away from people and things that lead me from you.
In his name, my God, have mercy.	God, I promise to do the actions and say the prayers that the priest gives me. I need your help.

Quick Tip

Getting Ready for Reconciliation

In order to help the children feel more at ease, it is advisable to take them into church to show them the reconciliation room or confessional.

- Show them how to wait their turn outside the room or confessional.
- Once inside, let them sit on the chair or kneel. Let them see where the priest will sit.
- If their penance is to pray a prayer, explain where they should go to pray their penance.
- Help them to feel comfortable and not afraid to receive this Sacrament.

People of Faith

Saint Benedict-Joseph Labré, 1748–1783

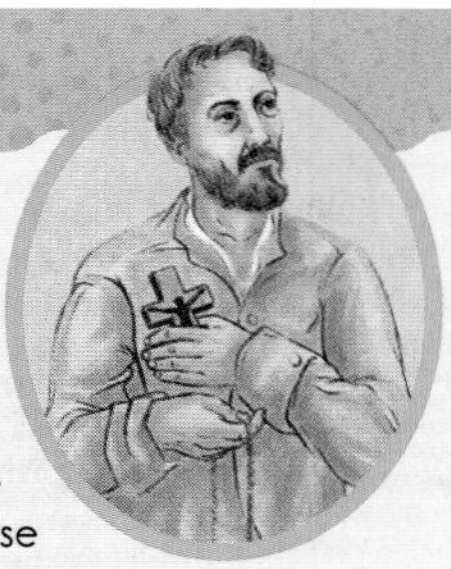

April 17

Saint Benedict-Joseph Labré wanted to be a priest, but he had a mental disease and couldn't go to a seminary. Instead, he became a beggar. From the time he was very young, Saint Benedict-Joseph confessed all of the wrong things he did. He would ask God to forgive him. Then he would promise God he would try very hard not to do anything wrong again. Sometimes people were afraid of Saint Benedict-Joseph because he wore rags and lived outside. After he died, people realized that he was a very holy man.

Discuss: How can you try harder to follow God's laws?

Learn more about Saint Benedict at **aliveinchrist.osv.com**

Live Your Faith

Tell what is happening in the picture.

Draw one way that you can show you're sorry.

Catholic Social Teaching

Chapter Connections

To integrate Catholic Social Teaching into your lesson, choose one of the following features: Call to Community, pages 292–293; or Human Solidarity, pages 300–301.

- Start the Live step of the process by talking about Saint Benedict-Joseph Labré on page 171. Then move directly to the Catholic Social Teaching feature.
- Or, to expand the lesson, complete both pages 170 and 171, then move to the Catholic Social Teaching feature.
- Return to Chapter 11 for the prayer on page 172.

People of Faith

Tell the children about Saint Benedict-Joseph Labré.

- He was the oldest of fifteen children.
- It is said that he didn't talk very much.
- When he traveled, Saint Benedict traveled by foot.
- Read aloud the paragraph on Saint Benedict.
- Encourage the children to discuss possible answers to the question.

Encourage the children to go to **aliveinchrist.osv.com** at home to learn more about Saint Benedict-Joseph Labré.

Activity

Read aloud the directions for the Live Your Faith activity.

- Invite volunteers to describe what is happening in the picture.
- Have the children draw how they can show they are sorry.
- Invite volunteers to share their drawings.

Let Us Pray

Prayer for Forgiveness

Prepare

Teach the ASL signs for *Lord* and *Christ* (go to **aliveinchrist.osv.com** for more information).

- Practice the signs to help the children become comfortable with them.
- Explain that they will use words and signs in their prayer asking for God's forgiving and reconciling mercy.
- Allow the children time to look over the prayer.
- Light the candle.

Rehearse with the children "Through My Fault," downloaded from **aliveinchrist.osv.com**.

Gather

Gather the children in the prayer space around the candle.

Pray

Follow the order of prayer on the student page.

- Help the children with their verbal and signing responses.

Conclude by processing around the room with the children singing the hymn refrain. When finished, invite the children to share a sign of peace.

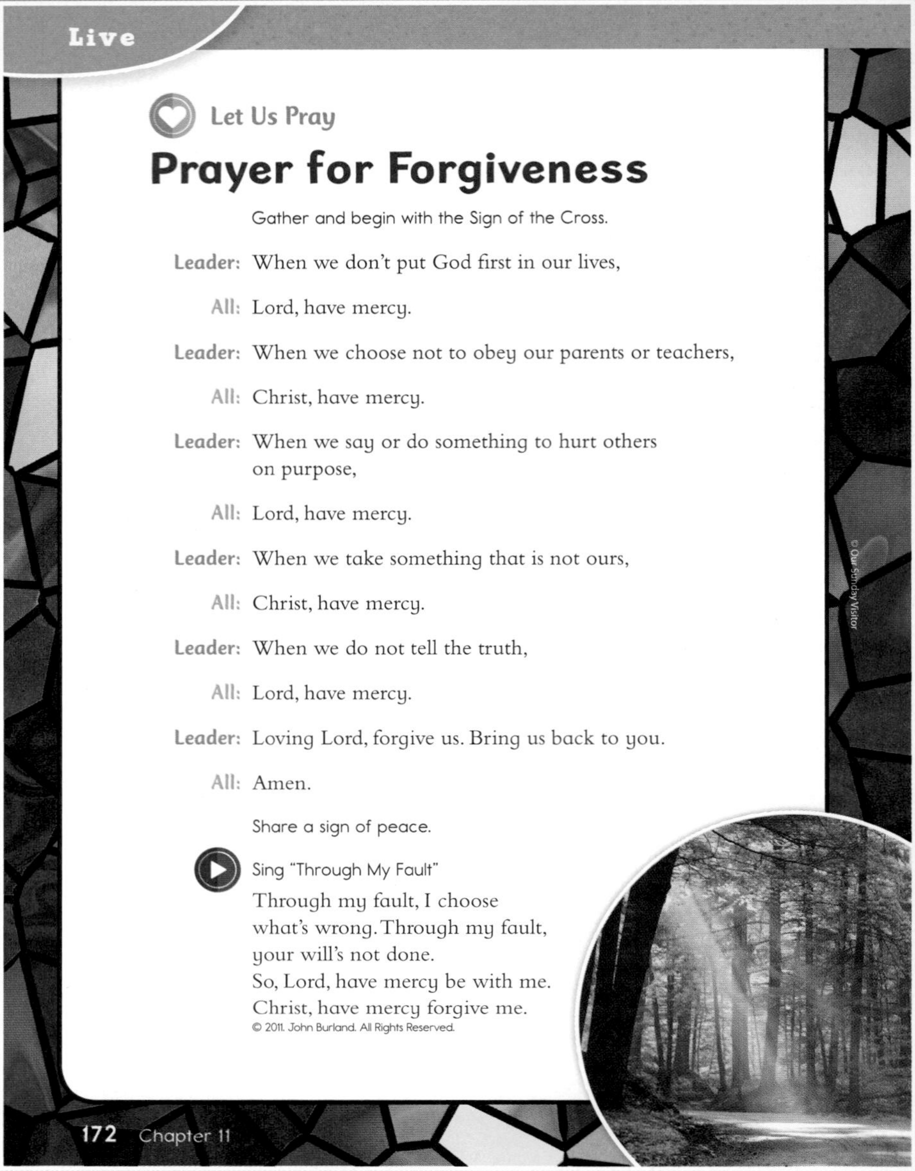

Live

Let Us Pray

Prayer for Forgiveness

Gather and begin with the Sign of the Cross.

Leader: When we don't put God first in our lives,

All: Lord, have mercy.

Leader: When we choose not to obey our parents or teachers,

All: Christ, have mercy.

Leader: When we say or do something to hurt others on purpose,

All: Lord, have mercy.

Leader: When we take something that is not ours,

All: Christ, have mercy.

Leader: When we do not tell the truth,

All: Lord, have mercy.

Leader: Loving Lord, forgive us. Bring us back to you.

All: Amen.

Share a sign of peace.

Sing "Through My Fault"

Through my fault, I choose
what's wrong. Through my fault,
your will's not done.
So, Lord, have mercy be with me.
Christ, have mercy forgive me.

172 Chapter 11

Liturgy Link

Prayer Services

Children enjoy prayer services because they give structure to their prayer. When the atmosphere and tone are properly set, the weekly prayer service is a beautiful experience.

- Children have to be taught attitudes of prayer and posture.
- The Prepare and Gather sections of the celebration help to create appropriate attitudes of prayer.

Go to **aliveinchrist.osv.com** for Sunday readings, Scripture background, questions of the week, and seasonal resources.

FAMILY + FAITH

LIVING AND LEARNING TOGETHER

YOUR CHILD LEARNED >>>

This chapter explains how we celebrate the Sacrament of Penance and Reconciliation and how forgiveness heals people and relationships with God and the Church.

God's Word

Read **Luke 7:36–39, 44–50** to learn more about how Jesus invites us to look at how we forgive.

Catholics Believe

- In the Sacrament of Penance and Reconciliation, you receive God's forgiveness.
- This Sacrament also celebrates your friendship with God and the Church.

To learn more, go to the *Catechism of the Catholic Church* #1422–1424 at **usccb.org**.

People of Faith

This week, your child met Saint Benedict-Joseph Labré, a homeless beggar who was a very holy man.

CHILDREN AT THIS AGE >>>

How They Understand the Sacrament of Reconciliation
Children at this age might feel nervous about confessing their sins to a priest. They might worry about what the priest will think of them. Tell them that the priest has likely heard every sin confessed and cannot talk to anyone about their confession. The priest is a visible sign of both Christ and the Church, and confession to a priest gives us a chance to experience God's forgiveness in a way that we can see. It's also helpful for children to see a parent receive this Sacrament.

CONSIDER THIS >>>

What makes you believe that someone is truly sorry?

How easy it is to tell "imperfect sorrow" when you have to direct your child to tell his sister he is sorry! In our adult lives it takes great trust to believe that who hurt you is truly sorry. "Contrition that arises from the love of God above all else is called 'perfect contrition.' This loving sorrow remits [forgives] venial sins and even mortal sins so long as we resolve to confess them as soon as possible. When other motives, such as the ugliness of sin or fear of damnation, brings us to confession, this is called 'imperfect contrition,' which is sufficient for forgiveness in the Sacrament" (*USCCA, p. 237–238*).

LET'S TALK >>>

- Ask your child to describe what happens in the Sacrament of Penance and Reconciliation (confession, penance, contrition, and absolution).
- Talk about ways your family asks for and gives forgiveness.

LET'S PRAY >>>

Dear God, we are sorry for all that we have done wrong, and with your help, we promise to do better in the future. Saint Benedict-Joseph Labré, pray for us. Amen.

For a multimedia glossary of Catholic Faith Words, Sunday readings, seasonal and Saint resources, and chapter activities go to **aliveinchrist.osv.com**.

Family + Faith

Distribute the page to the children or parents/adult family members. Point out the chapter highlights, insights on how second graders understand concepts, the opportunity for the adults to reflect on their own experience and faith journey, and the family prayer.

Chapter 11 Review

A Work with Words Complete each sentence with the correct word from the Word Bank.

Word Bank
- penance
- forgiveness
- Absolution
- Reconciliation

1. **Absolution** are the words spoken by the priest during the Sacrament of Penance to grant forgiveness of sins in God's name.
2. In the Sacrament of **Reconciliation**, forgiveness for sin is given through the Church.
3. A **penance** is a prayer or an act to make up for sin.
4. The Sacrament of Penance celebrates God's **forgiveness**.

B Check Understanding Put the steps of the Sacrament of Reconciliation in order using numbers 1 through 6.

5. Step **5** The priest forgives my sins in the name of the Father, the Son, and the Holy Spirit.
6. Step **2** I read or listen to a story of forgiveness.
7. Step **1** The priest greets me with the Sign of the Cross.
8. Step **6** I try to do better and make up for my sins.
9. Step **4** I pray an Act of Contrition.
10. Step **3** I confess to the priest and receive a penance.

Go to **aliveinchrist.osv.com** for an interactive review.

Chapter Review

Use Catechist Quick Reviews to highlight lesson concepts.

A Work with Words
Review the Word Bank with the children. Have them complete each sentence with a word from the Word Bank.

B Check Understanding
Have the children put the steps of the Sacrament of Reconciliation in the correct order.

Go to **aliveinchrist.osv.com** to prepare customized and downloadable assessments, send eAssessments, and assign interactive reviews.

Chapter 12 The Church Year

KEY CONCEPT

The Church year celebrates the life, Death, Resurrection, and Ascension of Jesus. The Resurrection is the mystery of Jesus being raised from the dead.

DOCTRINAL CONTENT

- The liturgy is the public prayer of the Church. (CCC, 1069–1070)
- The Church Year celebrates the life, Death, Resurrection, and Ascension of Jesus. (CCC, 1171)
- The seasons of the Church Year are Advent, Christmas, Ordinary Time, Lent, The Three Days (Triduum), and Easter. (CCC, 1163–1164)
- Easter celebrates Christ's Resurrection and is the greatest feast of the Church Year. (CCC, 1169)

TASKS OF CATECHESIS

Helping children grow in a faith that is "known, celebrated, lived, and expressed in prayer" (NDC, 20).

This chapter focuses on the following tasks of catechesis:

- Liturgical Education
- Education for Community Life

Catechist Background

Each year his parents went to Jerusalem for the feast of Passover, and when he was twelve years old, they went up according to festival custom. Luke 2:41–42

➔ **Reflect** Do you celebrate a Church custom with family or friends every year?

Saint Paul called on the Philippians to be ever joyful and with grateful hearts to call upon God in prayer. Today, God's people rejoice and call on God in and through the saving actions of Jesus in the liturgy. By actively participating in sacramental celebrations, particularly the Eucharist, they take part in the Incarnation, life, Death, Resurrection, and Ascension of Jesus. In addition, the Church celebrates the Paschal Mystery in and through the seasons of the liturgical year, as it slowly unfolds to reveal the message, mission, and meaning of Jesus Christ.

Reflect for a moment on the last time you truly rejoiced at a family celebration. Think about those who took part in it. Whether it was a birthday party or a wedding reception, the celebration most likely included festive decorations, music, and enthusiastic participation. The liturgical year celebrations are similar to family celebrations.

Celebration is the foundation of the Church year. Its six seasons—Advent, Christmas, Ordinary Time, Lent, Triduum, and Easter—celebrate the mystery of Jesus Christ. Readings at Mass center on events in the life of Jesus that are appropriate to the season, and many of the hymns echo his words. The church environment also reflects the seasons, using liturgical colors of purple, white, red, or green that are seen in vestments and banners proclaiming the season. The next time you are in church take note of the signs of the Church season being celebrated.

➔ **Reflect** How do you celebrate the seasons of the Church year?

Catechist's Prayer

Lord, help me learn more about your love for me each year as I recall and celebrate your birth, life, Death, and Resurrection. Amen.

Lesson Plan

Objectives	Process	Materials
Invite, 10 minutes		
The Church Year Page 175	**Psalm 9:2–3** Pray the opening prayer. **Luke 2:41–42** Reflect prayerfully the Word. • Discuss What Do You Wonder questions.	**Optional Activity** Chapter Story: "Puzzling Questions"
Discover, 35 minutes		
Celebrate the Seasons Pages 176–177 • Identify liturgy as the public prayer of the Church • Recognize that the Church year celebrates the life, Death, Resurrection, and Ascension of Jesus	• **Catholic Faith Words** liturgy, worship • Share that we celebrate the seasons by celebrating the events of Jesus' life throughout the year. ☆ Underline what the Church celebrates during Christmas. • **Share Your Faith Activity** Write one way to celebrate the current Church season.	☐ pencils or pens
Celebrating Jesus Pages 178–179 • Review the sequence of the seasons of the Church year • Describe Holy Thursday, Good Friday, and Holy Saturday as the holiest days of the Church year • Recognize that Easter is the greatest feast of the Church year	• **Catholic Faith Words** Resurrection • Review the different seasons of the Church year and what makes them different and special. • **Connect Your Faith Activity** Decorate a cross.	☐ pencils or pens • **Optional Activity** We Celebrate the Church Year ☐ Activity Master 12 (Page 175E)
Live, 15 minutes		
Our Catholic Life Pages 180–181	• Talk about the Church seasons. ☆ Fill in the blanks to complete the descriptions. • **People of Faith** Learn about Saint Victor. • **Live Your Faith Activity** Draw how your family celebrates a Church season.	☐ pencils or pens ☐ colored pencils or markers
Bless the God of Seasons Page 182	• Choose volunteers for the two reader parts. Rehearse "A Circle of Colors." • Follow the order of prayer.	Download "A Circle of Colors."

Family + Faith Page 183

Point out that the Catholic Families page provides chapter highlights, information on how second graders understand faith concepts, and family prayer.

Chapter Review Page 184

aliveinchrist.osv.com

- Customize and Download Assessments
- Email Links to eAssessments
- Interactive Student Reviews

Teaching This Grade

ONLINE RESOURCES

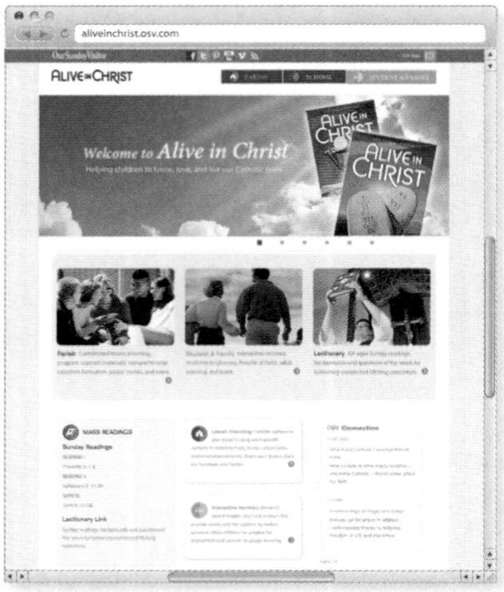

Go to **aliveinchrist.osv.com**

You will find:

- Interactive lesson planning with web specific content and additional activities
- Step by step lesson instruction from printed Catechist Edition for integrated lesson planning
- Custom-built assessments to download and eAssessment links
- Interactive reviews that provide scores and the option to review answers
- Sunday readings with background and questions of the week

Go to **osvparish.com**

You will find:

- Ask the Experts Q and A
- General Catechist Helps
- Community Connections and Blogs

Sharing the Message with Second Graders

The Church Year Children at this age have grown in their awareness of special seasons and times of year. They understand at what time of year they will have a birthday or celebrate Christmas or Easter. They might have missed some of the more subtle indicators of changes in the Church year (e.g., changes in color of vestments and Church décor, special Lectionary readings), but can begin to identify them with some help.

Teaching Tip: Use the colors and symbols of the liturgical season in your sacred space in the room, and enlist the help of the children when it's time to change them. Talk about why you are using these particular colors and symbols.

How Second Graders Understand

- Second graders are still trying to figure out many things. They may need help understanding why it is a good thing to give to the poor.
- Children this age often like to figure out patterns. Use puzzles with them.
- Young people usually love holidays. Help them see why we celebrate Christmas and Easter.

"I like to figure out patterns. I enjoy puzzles."

Chapter Connections

Chapter Story

Invite

"Puzzling Questions"

Use this story to expand the chapter introduction.

- Ask the children which season is their favorite.
- Have volunteers explain why they chose their favorite season.
- Emphasize to the children that there are different seasons in the Church year, too.

Go to **aliveinchrist.osv.com** Lesson Planning section for this story.

NCEA IFG: ACRE Edition

Discover

Liturgical Life

- Objective: To know the Paschal Mystery of Jesus: in the Church's liturgical life—feasts, seasons, symbols, and practices and in the Sacraments as signs and instruments of grace

Communal Life

- Objectives: To know the origin, mission, structure, and communal nature of the Church; to know the rights and responsibilities of the Christian faithful

Catholic Social Teaching

Live

Use one of these features to introduce a principle and engage the children with an activity.

- Life and Dignity, Pages 290–291
- Solidarity of the Human Family, Pages 300–301

Music Options

Use the following song in the celebration of the Live Prayer.

- "A Circle of Colors," Live Prayer, Page 182

LECTIONARY CONNECTION

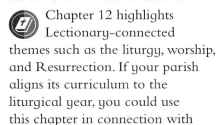

Chapter 12 highlights Lectionary-connected themes such as the liturgy, worship, and Resurrection. If your parish aligns its curriculum to the liturgical year, you could use this chapter in connection with the following Sundays.

Year A

Easter Sunday of the Resurrection of the Lord—Resurrection

Thirty-second Sunday in Ordinary Time—Resurrection

Year B

Easter Sunday of the Resurrection of the Lord—Resurrection

Second Sunday of Easter—Resurrection

Year C

Second Sunday of Advent—Church Year

Second Sunday of Lent—Resurrection

Go to **aliveinchrist.osv.com** for a complete correlation ordered by the Sundays of the year and suggestions for how to integrate the Scripture readings into chapter lessons.

Name ______________________________ Date ______________

We Celebrate the Church Year

Draw a line to the season of the Church year when we celebrate the event shown.

- Lent

- Christmas

- Advent

- The Three Days

- Easter

- Ordinary Time

CHAPTER 12

Invite

The Church Year

Let Us Pray

Leader: Giving Father, we thank you every day for all that you give us.

"I will praise you, LORD, with all my heart;
I will declare all your wondrous deeds.
I will delight and rejoice in you;
I will sing hymns to your name, Most High." Psalm 9:2–3

All: We praise you, Almighty God, forever and ever. Amen.

God's Word

"Each year his parents went to Jerusalem for the feast of Passover, and when he was twelve years old, they went up according to festival custom." Luke 2:41–42

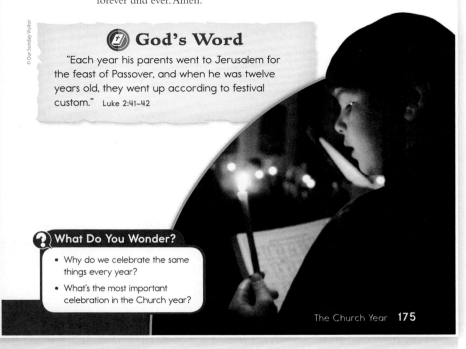

What Do You Wonder?

- Why do we celebrate the same things every year?
- What's the most important celebration in the Church year?

Optional Activity

Chapter Story: "Puzzling Questions" *Verbal/Linguistic*

Use this story after the opening prayer, before you talk about worshipping throughout the year.

- Read aloud "Puzzling Questions."
- Provide the children time to write their response to the question in the text.
- Have the children share their response with the group. When finished, transition back to the lesson instruction.

Go to **aliveinchrist.osv.com** for Chapter Story.

Invite

Let Us Pray

Invite the children to gather in the prayer space and make the Sign of the Cross. Have a volunteer read aloud the leader's prayer; you will pray the Psalm verse. Prompt the children's response.

Have the children move from the prayer space back to their seats.

Explain that we praise God in our prayer and in our worship throughout the year.

Say: Let's listen to hear what Jesus did as a young boy.

God's Word

Guide the children through the process of Scripture reflection.

- Invite them to close their eyes, be still, and open their minds and hearts to what God is saying to them in this passage.
- Proclaim the Scripture.
- Maintain several moments of silence.
- *Ask:* What did you hear God say to you today?
- Invite volunteers to share.

What Do You Wonder?

Say: Jesus went with his parents to the Jewish celebration of Passover.

We also celebrate the Church year with many feasts and celebrations.

Invite the children to respond to the questions. Ask what else they might wonder about Church celebrations.

Discover

Objectives

- Identify liturgy as the public prayer of the Church
- Recognize that the Church year celebrates the life, Death, Resurrection, and Ascension of Jesus

Celebrate the Seasons

Explain that just like the year has four seasons: spring, summer, fall, and winter, the Church year also has seasons. We celebrate the seasons by celebrating the events of Jesus' life throughout the year.

Work with Words

Have the children place their finger on the word *liturgy*. Invite a volunteer to read the definition.

Ask the children what they think *worship* means. Read aloud the definition and discuss what *adore* and *praise* mean.

Advent

Have a volunteer read aloud the text on Advent.

- Ask the children what color the Church uses for Advent. violet
- Tell the children that Advent is a time for everyone to grow closer to Jesus.
- Discuss the meaning of the Advent wreath shown in the picture.
- Ask another volunteer to read the caption. Discuss with the children what is happening in the photo.

Discover

Celebrate the Seasons

What seasons are celebrated in the Church year?

During the year, the Church's **liturgy** celebrates the events in the life of Jesus. In her **worship**, the Church celebrates the light of Jesus throughout the Church year.

Catholic Faith Words

liturgy the public prayer of the Church. It includes the Sacraments and forms of daily prayer.

worship to adore and praise God, especially in the liturgy and in prayer

Advent

During the four weeks of Advent, the Church gets ready to celebrate Jesus' birth. You tell God that you want to get better at loving him and others. Just as the seasons of the year have different colors, so do the Church's seasons. The color for Advent is violet. It is a sign of getting ready and change of heart.

Children celebrate the feast of Epiphany by dressing up as Mary, Joseph, and the three wise men.

176 Chapter 12

Catechist Background

The Liturgical Year

The mysteries of our faith unfold throughout the Church year.

- The key events are the prophecies and anticipation in Advent through the birth, life, Death, Resurrection, and Ascension of Jesus, and the sending of the Holy Spirit at Pentecost.
- Each year the Church relives these marvelous events so that every year people may praise God and grow in their spiritual journey.

Christmas

The three weeks of the Christmas season celebrate Jesus' presence in the world. The Son of God came so all people could know his Father's love. The Christmas celebrations help people love Jesus and other people more. White or gold are the colors for the Christmas season. It is a sign of great joy.

Underline what the Church celebrates during Christmas.

Ordinary Time

Ordinary Time comes twice during the Church year. The first time comes after the Christmas season. The second is after the Easter season. During these times, you learn more about Jesus and grow as his follower. Green is the season's color because it is the color of growth.

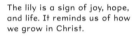

The lily is a sign of joy, hope, and life. It reminds us of how we grow in Christ.

Share Your Faith

Think What season is the Church in now? Write one way you will celebrate this season.

____

____

____

Share Talk about your answer with a partner.

Christmas

Have a volunteer read about Christmas.

- *Ask:* How long is the Christmas season? three weeks
- Tell the children that we celebrate Christmas because Jesus came so all people could know his Father's love.
- Have the children underline what the Church celebrates during Christmas.
- Then read the caption for the peace lily.

Ordinary Time

Read aloud the paragraph about Ordinary Time.

- *Ask:* What is the color for Ordinary Time? green Why? It is the color for growth How do we grow during Ordinary Time?
- Encourage the children to share their thoughts.

Activity

Read aloud the directions.

- Ask the children to think about what season of the Church we could be in right now.
- Have them write how they will celebrate it.
- Invite volunteers to share their responses.

Quick Tip

Vocabulary: Vestments

Explain to the children the meaning of the word *vestments.*

- The word *vestments* comes from a Latin word that means "clothing." Vestments are the special clothing worn by the priests and other ministers.
- To invest in a someone or something is to symbolically clothe the recipient with one's own authority or money.

Quick Review

Throughout the year, the Church celebrates the events in the life of Jesus in the liturgy.

Discover

Objectives

- Review the sequence of the seasons of the Church year
- Describe Holy Thursday, Good Friday, and Holy Saturday as the holiest days of the Church year
- Recognize that Easter is the greatest feast of the Church year

Celebrating Jesus

Ask a volunteer to read the question.

- Tell the children that we will find the answer in the reading.

Lent

Read aloud the paragraph.

- Explain to the children that the forty days of Lent symbolize the forty days Jesus spent in the desert.

The Three Days

Write *Holy Thursday*, *Good Friday*, *Holy Saturday*, and *Easter Sunday* on the board or on chart paper.

- Call on two volunteers to read aloud the paragraphs on pages 178 and 179.
- Ask the children which color is used for each day and what each symbolizes.

Volunteers show their love for God and neighbors by helping others during Lent.

Celebrating Jesus

What is the greatest feast of the year?

Lent

The Season of Lent is a preparation for the important feast of Easter. For forty days and six Sundays, the Church's color is violet. As during Advent, you are asked to make changes that will help you grow closer to Jesus. It's a special time to show God you are sorry and fully focused on him. You are to pray more often and help others.

The Three Days

The three days before Easter are the holiest days of the Church year. On Holy Thursday, the Church celebrates Jesus' gift of the Eucharist at the Last Supper. It is a happy occasion, a time of joy, so the color is white.

Catholic Faith Words

Resurrection the event of Jesus being raised from Death to new life by God the Father through the power of the Holy Spirit

Catechist Background

Tides of Time

People throughout history have thought of time as a vast sea, ebbing and flowing.

- Like the tides, seasons and events were described as having ebbs and flows.
- Feasts were described as seasons—Christmas became Yuletide, and so on with Shrovetide, and Eastertide.

On Good Friday, the Church gives thanks to Jesus as Savior. The color is red because Jesus died for all people. Holy Saturday evening begins the Easter celebration. For this joyous feast, the color is white.

Easter

Every Sunday, the Church celebrates the **Resurrection**, when Jesus was raised from the dead. But each year, the Church also celebrates the Resurrection of Jesus for fifty days from Easter to Pentecost. Easter is the greatest feast of the Church year. The color during this season is white.

The last ten days of this season celebrate Jesus' promise to send the Holy Spirit. Pentecost is the celebration of the Holy Spirit coming to the Apostles, Mary, and other disciples. For this feast, the color red is used as a sign of the power of the Holy Spirit.

➔ **Why do you think Easter is the greatest feast of the Church year?**

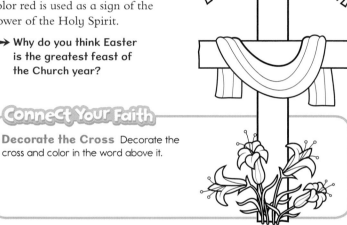

Connect Your Faith

Decorate the Cross Decorate the cross and color in the word above it.

Easter

Read aloud the first paragraph on Easter.

Then call on a volunteer to read the second paragraph about Pentecost.

- *Ask:* Why do you think Easter is the greatest feast of the Church year?
- Invite the children to share their responses.

Work with Words

Call the children's attention to the meaning of *Resurrection* in the Catholic Faith Words box on page 178. Have them silently read the definition.

Tell the children that the Resurrection is a very important event in the life of the Church.

Activity

Read aloud the directions.

- Provide the children with colored pencils or markers.
- Allow them enough time to color the illustration.
- To further review the Church seasons, invite the children to turn to pages 308–309 of the Our Catholic Tradition section in the back of the Student Book.
- Allow time for observations and discussion.

Optional Activity

Activity Master 12: We Celebrate the Church Year

Distribute copies of the activity found on catechist page 175E.

- This activity allows the children to match names of a season of the Church to a corresponding image.
- As an alternative, you may wish to send this activity home with the children.

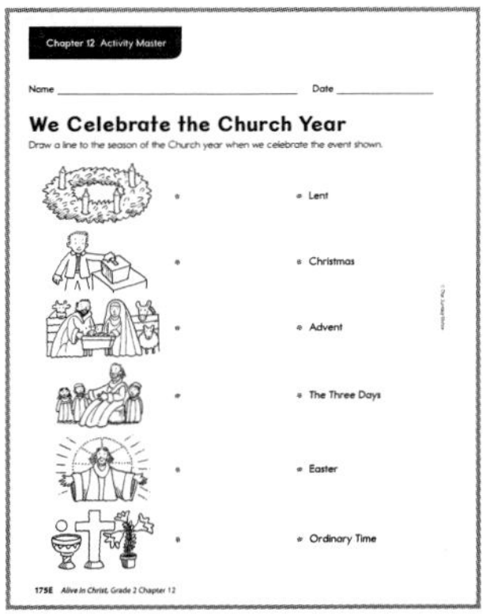
Chapter 12 Activity Master

Name ______________ Date ______

We Celebrate the Church Year

Draw a line to the season of the Church year when we celebrate the event shown.

- Lent
- Christmas
- Advent
- The Three Days
- Easter
- Ordinary Time

175E Alive in Christ, Grade 2 Chapter 12

Quick Review

Jesus' gift of the Eucharist and his Death are remembered during the Three Days before Easter. Easter is the greatest feast of the Church year.

Our Catholic Life

Read aloud the question.

- Ask a volunteer to read the paragraph.
- ☆ Have the children work in pairs to fill in the blanks to complete the descriptions of the words on the left.
- Review the answers with the help of several volunteers. Have one volunteer read aloud the word on the left, and another read aloud the completed description.
- Invite the other children to follow along to be sure everyone has the same answers.
- Have the children ask their families to help them obtain photos of these things from around your parish church. Invite them to bring these pictures to a later session to share.

Our Catholic Life

How do you know what Church season it is?

Your parish family uses colors to celebrate the Church's seasons and feasts, too. Here are some places you may see colors of the season used in your parish church.

Fill in the blanks to describe the words on the left.

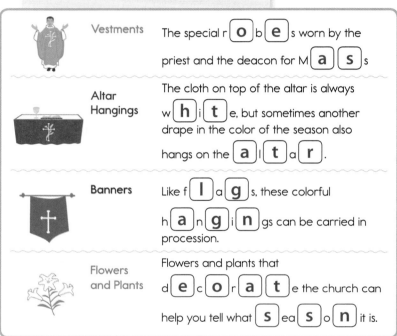

	Vestments	The special robes worn by the priest and the deacon for Mass
	Altar Hangings	The cloth on top of the altar is always white, but sometimes another drape in the color of the season also hangs on the altar.
	Banners	Like flags, these colorful hangings can be carried in procession.
	Flowers and Plants	Flowers and plants that decorate the church can help you tell what season it is.

Quick Tip

Celebrating

You can reinforce the children's participation in liturgical celebrations through room decorations.

- Use the appropriate liturgical colors and thematic symbols to decorate the prayer area.
- Display a color-coded liturgical calendar in the room.

People of Faith

Pope Saint Victor, d. 199

Pope Saint Victor was the first Pope from Africa. When he was Pope, people couldn't agree when to celebrate Easter. They needed to know the day of Easter to plan the seasons of the Church year. Pope Victor and the bishops decided that it must be celebrated on Sunday. He also knew it was important for people to be able to understand the Mass, which was only said in Latin. He declared that the Mass should be said in the language of the people, and today the Mass is said in many languages, including Latin.

July 28

Discuss: What languages have you heard at Mass?

Learn more about Saint Victor at **aliveinchrist.osv.com**

Live Your Faith

How Do You Celebrate the Church season? Choose a season and draw how your family celebrates it using the color of the season.

People of Faith

Tell the children about Saint Victor.

- He was a Roman soldier who worshipped the true God instead of the false idols of Roman gods.
- Saint Victor is often depicted as a soldier on a war horse.
- Read aloud the paragraph on Saint Victor.
- Have a volunteer read aloud the Discuss question.
- Invite the group to respond.

Encourage the children to go to **aliveinchrist.osv.com** at home to learn more about Saint Victor.

Activity

Read aloud the directions for the Live Your Faith activity.

- Give the children colored pencils or markers.
- Provide them with enough time to draw the family celebration of their favorite season of the Church year.

Catholic Social Teaching

Chapter Connections

To integrate Catholic Social Teaching into your lesson, choose one of the following features: Life and Dignity, pages 290–291; or Human Solidarity, pages 300–301.

- Start the Live step of the process by talking about Saint Victor on page 181. Then move directly to the Catholic Social Teaching feature.
- Or, to expand the lesson, complete both pages 180 and 181, then move to the Catholic Social Teaching feature.
- Return to Chapter 12 for the prayer on page 182.

Let Us Pray

Bless the God of Seasons

Explain to the children that they will be praying a blessing prayer. Remind them that the Sign of the Cross is also a blessing prayer.

Prepare

Choose two readers and let them have time to read and rehearse their parts.

- If necessary, offer help with words.

You will be the leader.

Rehearse with the children "A Circle of Colors," downloaded from **aliveinchrist.osv.com**.

If you are using the chapter song, you may wish to use white, gold, purple, red, or green streamers for the children to process with while singing.

Gather

Gather the children in the prayer space with their books.

- Invite them to quiet themselves.

Pray

Lead the children in the Sign of the Cross.

- Follow the order of prayer on the student page.

Conclude by processing around the room with the children singing "A Circle of Colors."

Let Us Pray

Bless the God of Seasons

Gather and begin with the Sign of the Cross.

Leader: God our Father, we thank you for all that is beautiful in the world and for the happiness you give us.

Reader 1: We praise you for your daylight and your word which gives light to our minds.

Reader 2: We praise you for our Earth and all the people on it.

All: We know that you are good.
You love us and do great things for us.

Sing "A Circle of Colors"

It's a circle of colors painting the Church year
with reminders of the love God has for you.
The white and golds of Christmas
and Easter. Pretty purples at
Advent and Lent.
Red at Pentecost and to honor
the Holy Spirit.
Ordinary Time's alive with greens.
Each color chosen for
a special reason.
A circle of colors through
the seasons.

Text and music by Chet A. Chambers.

Liturgy Link

Church Tour

Make arrangements with a parish staff member to take the children on a tour of the parish church.

- Visit the sacristy so that the children can see the different colored vestments. Talk about when each vestment is used.
- Tour the church, and point out the features such as statues or stained glass windows that are unique to your church.

Go to **aliveinchrist.osv.com** for Sunday readings, Scripture background, questions of the week, and seasonal resources.

Family + Faith

Distribute the page to the children or parents/adult family members. Point out the chapter highlights, insights on how second graders understand concepts, the opportunity for the adults to reflect on their own experience and faith journey, and the family prayer.

FAMILY + FAITH

LIVING AND LEARNING TOGETHER

YOUR CHILD LEARNED >>>

This chapter explores how the seasons of the Church year celebrate the life, Death, Resurrection, and Ascension of Jesus.

God's Word

Read **Luke 2:41–42** to see how people listened to what Jesus said.

Catholics Believe

- The Church year celebrates the life, Death, Resurrection, and Ascension of Jesus.
- The Resurrection is the mystery of Jesus being raised from the dead.

To learn more, go to the *Catechism of the Catholic Church* #1188–1195 at **usccb.org**.

People of Faith

This week, your child met Saint Victor. An early Pope, Victor determined that Easter must always be celebrated on a Sunday.

CHILDREN AT THIS AGE >>>

How They Understand the Church Year Children at this age have grown in their awareness of special seasons and times of year. They understand at what time of year they will have a birthday or celebrate Christmas or Easter. They might have missed some of the more subtle indicators of changes in the Church year, like changes in color of vestments and church decor, but can begin to identify them with some help. Point out to your child the times when something has changed in the church to mark a change in the Church year. See if your child can tell you what is different.

CONSIDER THIS >>>

Do you have family traditions in your home that celebrate the Church seasons?

All traditions give children and adults alike a deep sense of continuity and rootedness. Traditions that communicate God's presence in our lives draw us ever closer to God and our Church. "In the Liturgical Year, the Church celebrates the whole mystery of Christ from the Incarnation until the day of Pentecost and the expectation of Christ's second coming. . . The presence of the Risen Lord and his saving work permeates the entire Liturgical Year: Advent, the Christmas Season, Lent, the Easter Season, and Ordinary Time" (*USCCA p. 173*).

LET'S TALK >>>

- Ask your child to name one Church season and what we celebrate during that time.
- Share a special childhood memory about a season or feast day, and discuss some ways your family can celebrate the current season.

LET'S PRAY >>>

Saint Victor, help us to always remember the importance of Easter. Amen.

For a multimedia glossary of Catholic Faith Words, Sunday readings, seasonal and Saint resources, and chapter activities go to **aliveinchrist.osv.com**.

Chapter Review

Use Catechist Quick Reviews to highlight lesson concepts.

A Work with Words
Have the children match the season name to its description.

B Check Understanding
Explain that the children will be deciding if the statement is true or false and then writing a *T* or *F* in the box.

Go to **aliveinchrist.osv.com** to prepare customized and downloadable assessments, send eAssessments, and assign interactive reviews.

Chapter 12 Review

A Work with Words Write the letter of the correct season from the Word Bank next to the description of the season.

Word Bank
a. Advent
b. Christmas
c. Lent
d. Ordinary Time
e. Easter

1. **b** Three weeks of joy that celebrate Jesus' birth and presence in the world.
2. **d** The season that comes twice during the year.
3. **a** Four weeks of getting ready to celebrate Jesus' birth and presence with us.
4. **e** The season that celebrates Jesus' Resurrection.
5. **c** Forty days of praying and helping others as a way to prepare for Easter.

B Check Understanding Write T if the sentence is TRUE. Write F if the sentence is FALSE.

6. **F** Banners are special robes worn by the priest.
7. **T** The cloth on top of the altar is white.
8. **T** Flowers and plants that decorate the church can help you tell what season it is.
9. **T** The Church's seasons have different colors.
10. **F** Each year the Church celebrates Pentecost sixty days after Christmas.

Go to **aliveinchrist.osv.com** for an interactive review.

UNIT 4 Unit Review

Use Catechist Quick Reviews in each chapter to highlight lesson concepts for this unit and prepare for the Unit Review.

Have the children complete the Review pages. Then discuss the answers as a group. Review any concepts with which the children are having difficulty.

A Work with Words Instruct the children to complete each sentence with the correct word from the Word Bank.

B Check Understanding Have the children draw a line from the sentences in Column A to the correct answers in Column B for problems 6–10.

Unit Review (UNIT 4)

A Work with Words Complete each sentence with the correct word from the Word Bank.

Word Bank: Sacraments, Grace, liturgy, Absolution, Contrition

1. The **liturgy** is the public prayer of the Church.
2. **Sacraments** are special signs and celebrations from Jesus that give us life.
3. **Contrition** is being sorry for sin and wanting to live better.
4. **Grace** is sharing in the life and work of God.
5. **Absolution** are the words spoken by the priest during the Sacrament of Penance to grant forgiveness of sins in God's name.

B Check Understanding Draw a line from the sentences in Column A to the correct answers in Column B.

Column A	Column B
6. The word Resurrection means	God's forgiveness
7. Pentecost celebrates	Jesus' birth
8. The first Sacrament we receive is	Jesus rose from the dead
9. Reconciliation celebrates	the coming of the Holy Spirit
10. Christmas celebrates	Baptism

UNIT 4

Unit Review

Write the letter T if the sentence is TRUE. Write the letter F if the sentence is FALSE.

11. T In the Sacraments, you receive grace.
12. T Grace is a share in God's own life and help.
13. F Confirmation is the first Sacrament you receive.
14. F You can only receive the Sacrament of Penance and Reconciliation once.
15. T A priest cannot talk to anyone about your confession.

C **Make Connections** Unscramble the words to complete each sentence.

16. Baptism, Confirmation, and Eucharist are the Sacraments of IONITATNII.
    Initiation
17. Thinking about your thoughts, words, and actions is called an examination of SENOCECINC.
    Conscience
18. CAENPEN is a prayer or an act to make up for sin.
    Penance
19. Lent is a preparation for the important feast of RASETE.
    Easter

20. During DRNYOAIR ITME, you learn more about Jesus.
    Ordinary Time

Describe each of the things used in church during the Church year.

21. Colors: Celebrate the Church's season.
22. Vestments: Special robes worn by the priest and deacon for Mass.
23. Altar hangings: The cloth on top of the altar is always white.
24. Banners: Colorful hangings that can be carried in procession.
25. Flowers and plants: Decorate the church and help tell the season.

B Check Understanding

Have the children write the letter *T* if the sentence is true and the letter *F* if the sentence is false for problems 11–15.

C Make Connections

Direct the children to unscramble the words to complete each sentence for 16–20, and describe each of the things used in church during the Church year for 21–25.

Go to **aliveinchrist.osv.com** to prepare customized and downloadable assessments, send eAssessments, and assign interactive reviews.

UNIT 5

Morality

Our Catholic Tradition

- Jesus told us that all are welcome in the Kingdom of God—the world of love, peace, and justice that is in Heaven and is still being built on Earth. (CCC, 543, 2819)
- Jesus taught us to pray to the Father in the Lord's Prayer. (CCC, 2773)
- As Jesus' followers, we share in his life and work. We share the Good News with the world. (CCC, 897, 940)
- We can pray in many ways, for many reasons, at any time. (CCC, 2743)

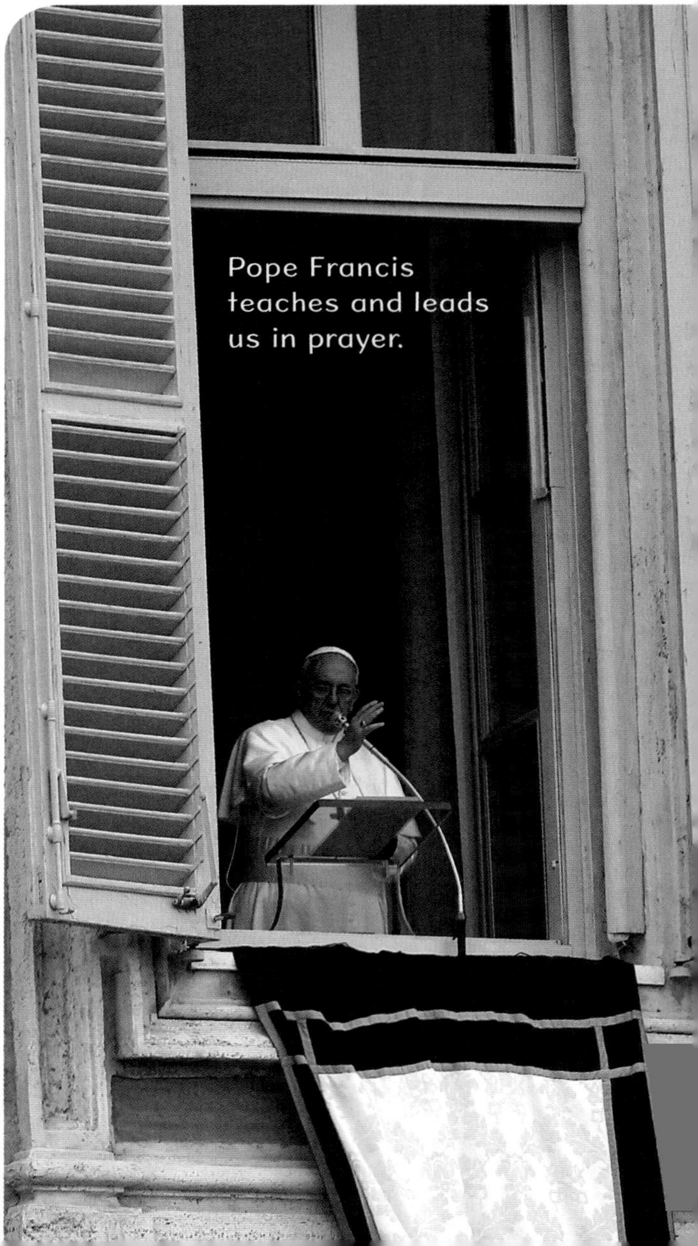

Pope Francis teaches and leads us in prayer.

What do we mean when we pray, "thy kingdom come, thy will be done on earth as it is in heaven"?

Unit 5 Overview

Chapter 13

Welcome in the Kingdom 189

Children will:

- identify how Jesus included those often left out and showed that God welcomes everyone
- discuss the faith of Zacchaeus and his willingness to repent
- recognize Jesus' great love for children and how he welcomes them and all others into his Kingdom
- understand that the Kingdom of God is the world of love, peace, and justice that God has in Heaven and wants for us on Earth

Songs of Scripture
"Zacchaeus"

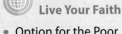

Catholic Social Teaching: Live Your Faith

- Option for the Poor, Pages 296–297
- The Dignity of Work, Pages 298–299

Chapter 14

Share the Good News 199

Children will:

- recognize that the Gospel message is the Good News of God's Kingdom and his saving love
- recall how in The Parable of the Vine and Branches, Jesus teaches us that we need to stay connected to him in order to have life
- discover that the Holy Spirit strengthened the Apostles to share what Jesus had taught them
- begin to develop a desire to share Jesus' message, and work together with God as he builds his Kingdom

Catholic Social Teaching: Live Your Faith

- Rights and Responsibilities, Pages 294–295
- The Dignity of Work, Pages 298–299

Chapter 15

Ways to Pray 209

Children will:

- recall Jesus' instruction to us to pray the Lord's Prayer, which we also call the Our Father
- identify the five basic forms of prayer: blessing, petition, intercession, thanksgiving, and praise
- understand that prayer is important to deepen our friendship with God
- discover that sacramentals are blessings, objects, and actions that remind us of God and are made sacred through the prayers of the Church

Catholic Social Teaching: Live Your Faith

- Human Solidarity, Pages 300–301
- Care for Creation, Pages 302–303

Preview Unit Theme

Ask: What is the unit theme?

Confirm that the unit focus is on Morality.

Ask: What do we mean when we pray, "thy kingdom come, thy will be done on earth as it is in heaven"?

Allow the children to share their thoughts.

Explain that they will learn about this in one of the following chapters.

Have the children study the photos and images. Ask volunteers to describe what they see, and what these images say about the unit theme.

Read aloud the bullet points under Our Catholic Tradition.

Explain to the group that they will be exploring these points in the next three chapters.

KEY CONCEPT
The Kingdom of God is the world of love, peace, and justice that is in Heaven and is still being built on Earth. Everyone is welcome in God's Kingdom and in the Catholic Church

DOCTRINAL CONTENT

- By the things he said and did, Jesus included those often left out and showed that God welcomes everyone. (CCC, 542–543)
- The story of Zacchaeus is an example of Jesus welcoming someone who had faith and was willing to repent. (CCC, 2412)
- Jesus has a great love for children, and welcomed them along with all others into his Kingdom. (CCC, 526, 559)
- The Kingdom of God is the world of love, peace, and justice that God has in Heaven and wants for us on Earth. (CCC, 2818–2819)

TASKS OF CATECHESIS
Helping children grow in a faith that is "known, celebrated, lived, and expressed in prayer" (NDC, 20).

This chapter focuses on the following tasks of catechesis:

- Promoting Knowledge of the Faith
- Education for Community Life

Catechist Background

People were bringing even infants to him that he might touch them, and when the disciples saw this, they rebuked them. Jesus, however, called the children to himself and said, "Let the children come to me ... for the kingdom of God belongs to such as these. Amen, I say to you, whoever does not accept the kingdom of God like a child will not enter it." Luke 18:15–17

➔ **Reflect** How do Jesus' actions reveal God's love? How do we ask for, and receive, God's help in the Seven Sacraments?

Jesus dined with tax collectors and sinners. Some Pharisees saw this and wondered why. Jesus said, "Those who are well do not need a physician, but the sick do. Go and learn the meaning of the words, 'I desire mercy, not sacrifice'" (Matthew 9:12–13). When children were brought to Jesus for a blessing, his disciples reprimanded their parents, but Jesus said, "Let the children come to me" (Matthew 19:14). Jesus showed merciful love toward those who were young, oppressed, and in need. His love knew no boundaries.

Responding with love, compassion, and hospitality to a family member going through a crisis, or a child who is fighting with a friend, or a person in the midst of a difficult time is fulfilling Jesus' command of love. Busy schedules and stressful situations may sometimes make it difficult for you to step out of your own daily life. Yet, you are called by your Baptism to do just that.

Jesus reached out to Zacchaeus, and Zacchaeus welcomed Jesus into his life, promising to share what he had with those who were poor and to make up for his sins. Jesus in return promised Zacchaeus salvation. (See Luke 19:9.) The joy that Zacchaeus had in knowing Jesus was the kind of joy that Christians come to know in God's great power of love.

➔ **Reflect** To whom can you pass on God's love today?

Catechist's Prayer

Lord Jesus, you taught that everyone is welcome in God's Kingdom. Help me create a loving environment in my room so that all feel welcome. Amen.

Lesson Plan

Objectives	Process	Materials
Invite, 10 minutes		
Welcome in the Kingdom Page 189	**Psalm 86:13** Pray the opening prayer. **Luke 18:15–17** Reflect prayerfully on the Word. • Discuss What Do You Wonder questions.	**Optional Activity** Chapter Story: "Come In"
Discover, 35 minutes		
Welcomed by Jesus Pages 190–191 • Identify how Jesus included those often left out and showed that God welcomes everyone • Discuss the faith of Zacchaeus and his willingness to repent	• **Catholic Faith Words** faith, peace **Luke 19:1–10** Proclaim "Zacchaeus the Tax Collector." ☆ Underline what the mumblers and grumblers said; circle what Jesus said. • Brainstorm with the children things they could do and say to make Jesus feel welcome in their homes. • **Share Your Faith Activity** Write the name of someone who makes people feel welcome.	☐ pencils or pens
All Are Invited Pages 192–193 • Recognize Jesus' great love for children and how he welcomes them and all others into his Kingdom • Understand that the Kingdom of God is the world of love, peace, and justice that God has in Heaven and wants for us on Earth	• **Catholic Faith Words** Kingdom of God • Stress that Jesus welcomes everyone. **Matthew 19:13–15** Proclaim "Blessing of the Children." ☆ Underline what greeters do. • **Connect Your Faith Activity** Complete the sentence about whom God welcomes.	☐ pencils or pens ☐ board or chart paper • **Optional Activity** Have Faith! ☐ Activity Master 13 (Page 189E)
Live, 15 minutes		
Our Catholic Life Pages 194–195	• Talk about who is welcome in God's Kingdom. ☆ Write how the people in the pictures help to be a sign of God's Kingdom. • **People of Faith** Learn about Saint Brigid of Kildare. • **Live Your Faith Activity** Write an invitation.	☐ pencils or pens ☐ crayons, markers, and art supplies
Prayer of Welcome Page 196	• Choose volunteers for the three reader parts. • Follow the order of prayer. Sing "Loving Others."	Download "Loving Others."

Family + Faith Page 197

Point out that the Catholic Families page provides chapter highlights, information on how second graders understand faith concepts, and family prayer.

Chapter Review Page 198

aliveinchrist.osv.com

- Customize and Download Assessments
- Email Links to eAssessments
- Interactive Student Reviews

Teaching This Grade

ONLINE RESOURCES

Go to **aliveinchrist.osv.com**

You will find:

- Interactive lesson planning with web specific content and additional activities
- Step by step lesson instruction from printed Catechist Edition for integrated lesson planning
- Custom-built assessments to download and eAssessment links
- Interactive reviews that provide scores and the option to review answers
- Sunday readings with background and questions of the week

Go to **osvparish.com**

You will find:

- Ask the Experts Q and A
- General Catechist Helps
- Community Connections and Blogs

Sharing the Message with Second Graders

Caring for Others Our secular society sometimes speaks of the "greater good"— which can mean sacrificing the few for the sake of the many, or violating a smaller principle for the sake of a larger one. Children today are often exposed to this concept. However, our Catholic Faith upholds the importance of the common good, the good of everyone, with particular attention to the poor, marginalized, and disadvantaged. Children will need much guidance from parents, teachers, and catechists to fully understand this concept and its implications.

Teaching Tip: Encourage ongoing awareness of the poor, disadvantaged, and marginalized. Include them in your prayers and in group discussions of service to others.

How Second Graders Understand

- Second graders are still learning right from wrong. Give them practice making choices.
- Children this age do not have a very long attention span. Give them a variety of activities to do.
- Help the children understand that the Kingdom of God is made up of different kinds of people from many cultures.

"Help me understand that the Kingdom of God is made up of different kinds of people from many cultures."

Chapter Connections

Chapter Story

Invite

"Come In"

Use this story to expand the chapter introduction.

- Tell the children that we use our words and gestures to show others that they are welcome.
- Ask the children to share words and gestures, such as handshakes or hugs, that they use to welcome others. Encourage children from other cultures to share welcoming words from the culture of their heritage.

Go to **aliveinchrist.osv.com** Lesson Planning section for this story.

NCEA IFG: ACRE Edition

Discover

Knowledge of the Faith

- Objective: To know and understand basic Catholic teaching about the Incarnate Word Jesus Christ as the way, truth, and life

Communal Life

- Objectives: To know the origin, mission, structure, and communal nature of the Church; to know the rights and responsibilities of the Christian faithful

Catholic Social Teaching

Live

Use one of these features to introduce a principle and engage the children with an activity.

- Option for the Poor, Pages 296–297
- The Dignity of Work, Pages 298–299

Music Options

Use one or more of the following songs to enhance catechetical learning or for prayer.

- "Loving Others," Live Prayer, Page 196
- "Allelu! Let the Children Come," Invite, Page 189
- "Act Justly" or "Raise Your Voice for Justice," Discover, Page 191
- "Building God's Kingdom" or "Seek Ye First," Discover, Page 192

LECTIONARY CONNECTION

Chapter 13 highlights Lectionary-connected themes such as faith, peace, welcome, and Kingdom of God. If your parish aligns its curriculum to the liturgical year, you could use this chapter in connection with the following Sundays.

Year A

Third Sunday in Ordinary Time—The Prince of Peace

Twenty-seventh Sunday in Ordinary Time—Joy and Peace through Christ

Year B

Twelfth Sunday in Ordinary Time—Kingdom of God

Nineteenth Sunday in Ordinary Time—Kingdom of God

Year C

First Sunday of Advent—Kingdom of God

Nineteenth Sunday in Ordinary Time—God's Kingdom

Go to **aliveinchrist.osv.com** for a complete correlation ordered by the Sundays of the year and suggestions for how to integrate the Scripture readings into chapter lessons.

Name ______________________________ Date ______________

Have Faith!

Jesus saw that Zacchaeus had faith in God. Color the sentences below that tell something about your faith in God.

God gives me a family who loves me.

God cares for me. His love never ends.

God is always willing to forgive me.

God loves only the members of the Catholic Church.

God wants me to be happy with him forever.

God gives me the Church to help me grow closer to him.

God sent his own Son to save me from sin.

God's love will leave me when I make wrong choices.

CHAPTER 13

Welcome in the Kingdom

Let Us Pray

Leader: Lord, we praise you for your love.

"Your mercy to me is great." Psalm 86:13

All: Lord, we praise you for your love. Amen.

God's Word

Some people brought their children for Jesus to bless. But when Jesus' disciples saw them doing this, they told the people to stop bothering Jesus. So Jesus called the children over to him, and said, "Let the children come to me and do not prevent them; for the kingdom of God belongs to such as these…whoever does not accept the kingdom of God like a child will not enter it." Based on Luke 18:15–17

What Do You Wonder?

- How are you like Jesus?
- Where do you share Jesus' love?

Optional Activity

Chapter Story: "Come In" *Verbal/Linguistic*

Use this story after the opening prayer, before you talk about God's love and care.

- Read aloud the story.
- Ask the children how Omar may have felt about going to the principal's office. Possible responses: nervous, anxious
- Give the children time to write their responses to the question.
- After sharing responses, transition back to the lesson instruction.

Go to **aliveinchrist.osv.com** for Chapter Story.

Invite

Let Us Pray

Music Option: Have the children sing "Allelu! Let the Children Come," downloaded from **aliveinchrist.osv.com**.

Invite the children to gather in the prayer space and make the Sign of the Cross. Read aloud the leader's prayer and the Psalm verse. Prompt the children's response.

Have the children move from the prayer space back to their seats.

Say: God's love and care show us how to love and care for everyone. Let's listen to what Jesus said about his love for children.

God's Word

Guide the children through the process of Scripture reflection.

- Invite them to close their eyes, be still, and open their minds and hearts to what God is saying to them in this passage.
- Proclaim the Scripture.
- Maintain several moments of silence
- *Ask:* What did you hear God say to you today?
- Invite volunteers to share.

What Do You Wonder?

Say: Jesus calls each of us to welcome others, to trust in his Father as children do, and to open our hearts to love.

Invite the children to respond to the questions. Ask what else they might wonder about welcoming others.

Objectives

- Identify how Jesus included those often left out and showed that God welcomes everyone
- Discuss the faith of Zacchaeus and his willingness to repent

Welcomed by Jesus

Tell the children that they are going to learn about Zacchaeus and how he showed his faith in God.

Have a volunteer read aloud the opening paragraph.

- Emphasize the importance of making others feel welcome.

God's Word

Proclaim the Scripture story.

- Be mindful that the story rhymes, so it will require careful cadence to accentuate the rhyming.
- You may want to complete the Scripture review before covering the Catholic Faith Words.

Work with Words

Have two volunteers read aloud the content of the Catholic Faith Words box.

- After each definition is read, ask the children for examples of the term.
- *Ask:* So, when do we need faith?
- *Ask:* When do you feel at peace?

Encourage the children to turn to page 324 of the Our Catholic Tradition section in the back of their books to pray the Act of Faith, Hope, and Love.

Welcomed by Jesus

How did Zacchaeus show his faith in God?

We feel happy when someone invites us to join a group. Being included on a team or in a club makes us feel welcome. By the things he said and did, Jesus showed us that God welcomes everyone.

Catholic Faith Words

faith believing in God and all that he helps us understand about himself. Faith leads us to obey God.

peace when things are calm and people get along with one another

God's Word

Zacchaeus the Tax Collector

The news went uphill and down
That Jesus was coming to Jericho town.

Zacchaeus, you know, was too short to see,
So he scurried right up a sycamore tree.

"Zacchaeus, come down, come down, I say.
Let's have dinner at your house today."

Songs of Scripture

Zacchaeus

Help the children to understand that God loves us just as we are but he wants us to turn away from the sin that causes us to be less than he created us to be.

- Explain that because we became part of Christ in Baptism, we should look at everyone through Jesus' eyes and see the best in each person.
- Have the children sing the song, "Zacchaeus."

Use *Songs of Scripture*, Grades 1–3 CD, Track 14

Jesus and Zacchaeus walked by the crowd
who grumbled and mumbled and said out loud:
"He is a sinner and he is a snitch.
He took our money. That's why he is rich."

Zacchaeus proclaimed in a loud, clear tone,
"To the poor I will give half of all that I own."

Then Jesus said, "God's love has no end.
My friend, Zacchaeus, is also God's friend.

Put away your frowns. Be full of cheer.
God's love and kindness are truly here.

God calls everyone, the small and the great.
So, come gather around. Come celebrate!"

Based on Luke 19:1–10

1. Underline what the mumblers and grumblers said.
2. Circle what Jesus said.

The Surprise Ending

Jesus saw that Zacchaeus had **faith**. Faith is a gift from God, but it's also something we choose. Zacchaeus wanted to follow Jesus. So Jesus surprised everyone. He welcomed Zacchaeus to share in God's love. Jesus wanted him to be at **peace**.

Share Your Faith

Think Write the name of someone who helps you feel welcome.

____

Share Share your answer with a partner.

Zacchaeus the Tax Collector

Finish sharing the Scripture story with the group.

- ☆ Have the children underline what the mumblers and grumblers said, and circle what Jesus said.

The Surprise Ending

Have a volunteer read aloud the paragraph.

- *Ask:* Why would Zacchaeus feel at peace after returning the money? knowing that he is doing the right thing relieves his conscience
- Explain that Jesus, by going to Zacchaeus' house, showed Zacchaeus that God loved him.
- Brainstorm with the children things they could do and say to make Jesus feel welcome in their homes.

Activity

Read aloud the directions.

- Arrange the children in pairs to share their answers.

Music Option: Have the children sing "Act Justly" or "Raise Your Voice for Justice," downloaded from **aliveinchrist.osv.com**.

Reaching All Learners

Accepting Ourselves

Use the Zacchaeus story as a way to help the children understand how we need to love others and ourselves as God loves us.

- This may be a good time to discuss the fact that Zacchaeus was short, so he had to climb up into a tree to see over the crowd. Even though he was a sinner, he wanted to see Jesus.
- Let the children know that, like Zacchaeus, some people may have to work a little harder than others to follow God's plan for them, but it is worth it.
- Remind the children that everyone is important to Jesus.

Quick Review

Jesus welcomes everyone into the Kingdom of God. Since Zacchaeus had faith and was willing to repent, he felt peace from his actions.

Discover

Objectives

- Recognize Jesus' great love for children and how he welcomes them and all others into his Kingdom
- Understand that the Kingdom of God is the world of love, peace, and justice that God has in Heaven and wants for us on Earth

All Are Invited

Ask a volunteer to read aloud the question.

- Invite the children to share their best guesses.

Read aloud the introductory paragraph.

- Stress that Jesus welcomes everyone.

God's Word

Proclaim the Scripture.

- *Ask:* How did Jesus treat the children? He welcomed them and blessed them.

Discuss the picture with the children.

Work with Words

Share with the children the meaning of the words *Kingdom of God* by reading aloud the definition from the Catholic Faith Words box.

- Remind the children that they can help God as he builds his Kingdom by welcoming others.

Music Option: Play or sing with the children "Building God's Kingdom" or "Seek Ye First," downloaded from **aliveinchrist.osv.com**.

All Are Invited

Who does Jesus invite to God's Kingdom?

It did not matter to Jesus how old a person was or how tall. Jesus welcomed everyone. Jesus teaches us that people of all ages and backgrounds are welcome in God's Kingdom.

Catholic Faith Words

Kingdom of God the world of love, peace, and justice that is in Heaven and is still being built on Earth

God's Word

Blessing of the Children

People often brought their children to Jesus. The disciples said, "Don't bother Jesus. He is too busy!" But Jesus said, "Let the children come to me. . .for the Kingdom of heaven belongs to such as these."

Jesus welcomed the children and blessed them. Then he went on his way. Based on Matthew 19:13–15

Scripture Background

Matthew 19:13–15

In Jesus' time, adults often saw children as insignificant.

- By welcoming and blessing the children, Jesus affirms children's value.
- His laying of hands on the children was both the traditional way of conveying a blessing in Judaism and a gesture of affection and acceptance.

In God's Kingdom

Another name for the Kingdom of Heaven is the **Kingdom of God**. Jesus invites everyone to enter the Kingdom, to live by God's love and seek his peace. Jesus knew how to make people feel welcome. Many people came to him for help and healing. Some people were like Zacchaeus. They thought Jesus wouldn't care about them. Jesus taught that all people are welcome in God's Kingdom.

Like Jesus, the Catholic Church welcomes all people. In some Catholic parishes there are people who welcome each Church member before Mass begins. These "welcomers" can be men, women, or children. Sometimes these people are called "greeters."

Underline what greeters do.

➔ How do others make you feel welcome?

Connect Your Faith

Fill It In Who does God welcome? Fill in the blanks to complete the statement.

G O D

W E L C O M E S

E V E R Y O N E

193

In God's Kingdom

Invite a volunteer to read aloud the first paragraph.

- *Ask:* How did Jesus make people feel welcome? People came to Jesus for healing and help and he did both. He didn't turn anyone away.
- Help the children understand that Jesus welcomes everyone to God's Kingdom.

Read aloud the last paragraph.

- Ask the children to think about how their parish community welcomes people.
- Discuss how all people come together in Church to worship God.
- ☆ Direct the children to underline what greeters do.

Ask: How do others make you feel welcome?

- Write the children's responses on the board or on chart paper.

Activity

Read aloud the directions.

- Allow the children to work in pairs to solve the statement. Review the answer when everyone is through.

Quick Review

Jesus loves and welcomes everyone, including children. The Kingdom of God is the world of love, peace, and justice.

Optional Activity

Activity Master 13: Have Faith!

Distribute copies of the activity found on catechist page 189E.

- Read aloud the directions, and help anyone having difficulty getting started.
- As an alternative, you may want to send this activity home with the children.

Chapter 13 Activity Master

Name ______________ Date ______________

Have Faith!

Jesus saw that Zacchaeus had faith in God. Color the sentences below that tell something about your faith in God.

God gives me a family who loves me.

God cares for me. His love never ends.

God is always willing to forgive me.

God loves only the members of the Catholic Church.

God wants me to be happy with him forever.

God gives me the Church to help me grow closer to him.

God sent his own Son to save me from sin.

God's love will leave me when I make wrong choices.

189E Alive in Christ, Grade 2 Chapter 13

Live

Our Catholic Life

Read aloud the question at the top of the student page.

- Invite the children to respond.

Ask three volunteers to each read aloud one paragraph.

- *Ask:* When will God's Kingdom be complete? at the end of time

☆ Direct the children to explain in two or three words how the people in the pictures are helping to build God's Kingdom.

- Let the children work in pairs to talk through the pictures and write their conclusions on the line below the images.
- Discuss their responses and reinforce those that are correct.

Our Catholic Life

What is God's Kingdom like?

Jesus told people about the Kingdom of God. Some people thought Jesus meant a king who lived in a castle. But Jesus was talking about a different kind of Kingdom.

God's Kingdom is filled with joy. Everyone puts God first and works with him to make sure every person has what they need. By his kindness and care, Jesus showed that everyone is welcome.

God's Kingdom will be complete at the end of time when Jesus returns in glory, but you have already recieved an invitation. When you were baptized, you were welcomed into God's Kingdom.

☆ How are the people in the pictures helping to build God's Kingdom?

Showing Love

Celebrating Mass

Quick Tip

Vocabulary: Kingdom

Some of the meanings of Kingdom are "realm, domain, government, and sphere." Use the following points to help explain the Christian meaning of Kingdom.

- Even in the last months of Jesus' ministry, the Apostles were still asking when Jesus was going to establish his Kingdom.
- Some Scripture passages suggest that the Apostles had difficulties understanding that Jesus did not come to set up an earthly Kingdom. After the experience of Pentecost, they understood more clearly the spiritual nature of the Kingdom proclaimed by Jesus.

People of Faith

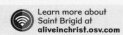

Saint Brigid of Kildare, c. 451–525

Saint Brigid was a religious sister who dedicated her life to God. Everywhere Brigid went, she spoke of God's love. She walked and traveled by horse and cart all around Ireland. She sailed in a boat on the Irish Sea. She was known for her kindness and mercy to everyone. She once said that she would like to turn a whole lake into something good to drink and have everyone share it. She wanted everyone to feel loved by God.

February 1

Discuss: How can you share God's kindness and mercy with your friends and family?

Learn more about Saint Brigid at **aliveinchrist.osv.com**

Live Your Faith

Write an Invitation Fill in the blanks to complete the invitation. Then decorate the invitation with colorful designs.

You Are Invited!

Jesus invites

____

to the Kingdom of

________________________.

Join us this Sunday at

______________________________.

Catholic Social Teaching

Chapter Connections

To integrate Catholic Social Teaching into your lesson, choose one of the following features: Option for the Poor, pages 296–297; or The Dignity of Work, pages 298–299.

- Start the Live step of the process by talking about Saint Brigid of Kildare on page 195. Then move directly to the Catholic Social Teaching feature.
- Or, to expand the lesson, complete both pages 194 and 195, then move to the Catholic Social Teaching feature.
- Return to Chapter 13 for the prayer on page 196.

People of Faith

Tell the children about Saint Brigid of Kildare.

- She refused many good offers of marriage, and chose to be a religious sister instead.
- Saint Brigid founded a school of art with metal work and illumination.
- She also founded two monasteries, one for men and one for women.
- Read aloud the paragraph on Saint Brigid.
- Discuss the question with the children.

Encourage the children to go to **aliveinchrist.osv.com** at home to learn more about Saint Brigid of Kildare.

Activity

Read aloud the directions for the Live Your Faith activity.

- Ask the children to think of someone they might invite to attend their parish church this Sunday.
- Provide crayons, markers, and art supplies so the children can complete and decorate the invitation.

Let Us Pray

Prayer of Welcome

Prepare

Choose volunteers for the three reader parts.

- Practice the parts with the readers.

Rehearse with the children "Loving Others," downloaded from **aliveinchrist.osv.com**.

Gather

With "Loving Others" playing in the background, invite the children to gather in the prayer space with their books.

Pray

Follow the order of prayer on the student page.

- Prompt the children's responses.

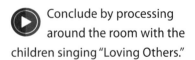

Conclude by processing around the room with the children singing "Loving Others."

When finished, invite the children to share a sign of peace.

Live

Let Us Pray

Prayer of Welcome

Gather and begin with the Sign of the Cross.

Leader: God our Father, we gather together in Jesus' name.

Reader 1: When we welcome a friend,

All: Jesus' love shows through us.

Reader 2: When we welcome a child who is left out,

All: Jesus' love shows through us.

Reader 3: When we take extra time to help,

All: Jesus' love shows through us.
Amen.

All: Sing "Loving Others"

Share the Good News of the Lord and sing.
Shout it out and make the church bells ring!
Show the people on Earth today.
Jesus' love is a better way!

You gotta be good to your neighbor
Good to your friends
Good to your family.
You gotta love one another
Like a sister or a brother
'cause Jesus loves you and me!

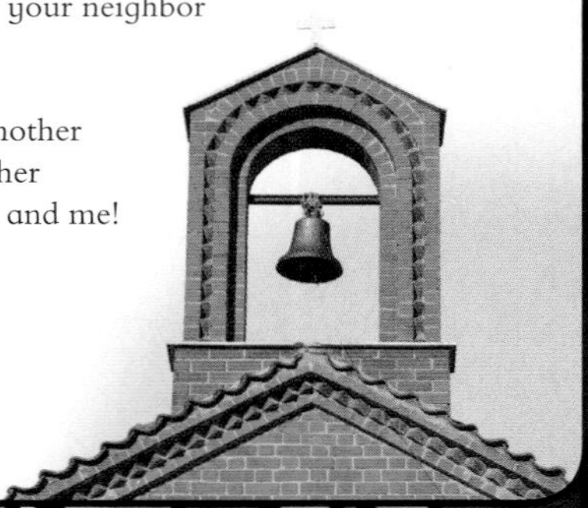

Liturgy Link

Ministers of Hospitality

Talk with the children about what being a minister of hospitality means.

- Ministers of hospitality, often referred to as ushers or greeters, are the visible sign of a parish community's hospitality.
- Their task is to greet people, to make them feel welcome, to assist individuals with disabilities, to help the assembly to gather together, and to take up the collection.

Go to **aliveinchrist.osv.com** for Sunday readings, Scripture background, questions of the week, and seasonal resources.

FAMILY + FAITH

LIVING AND LEARNING TOGETHER

YOUR CHILD LEARNED >>>

This chapter explains Jesus' teaching on the Kingdom and his desire for the Church to welcome and care for all people in his name.

God's Word

Read **Luke 18:15–17** to learn what Jesus says about children in God's Kingdom.

Catholics Believe

- The Kingdom of God is the world of love, peace, and justice that is in Heaven and is still being built on Earth.
- Everyone is welcome in God's Kingdom and in the Catholic Church.

To learn more, go to the *Catechism of the Catholic Church* #543, 544 at **usccb.org**.

People of Faith

This week, your child met Saint Brigid of Kildare. One of the patrons of Ireland, she is known for her kindness and mercy.

CHILDREN AT THIS AGE >>>

How They Understand Caring for Others Our secular society sometimes speaks of the "greater good"—which can mean sacrificing the few for the sake of the many, or violating a smaller principle for the sake of a larger one. Children today are often exposed to this concept. However, our Catholic faith upholds the importance of the common good, the good of everyone, with particular attention to the poor, marginalized, and disadvantaged. Your child will need guidance from you to fully understand this concept and what it means for his or her daily life. A good place to start is in the family, where everyone should be concerned about the good of all.

CONSIDER THIS >>>

How does your family welcome others into your home?

Hospitality is such an important value in the life of a family. When we welcome others into our families, we show love by including and accepting them. In this way the family is an example of the Church. "Church exists by the will of God the Father and his plan to gather all people under the Lordship of his Son. As Head of the Church, Jesus Christ continues to fill her with his life and saving grace, pouring into her the Holy Spirit with his gifts of unity, peace, and love" (*USCCA, p. 115*).

LET'S TALK >>>

- Ask your child what he or she learned about the Kingdom of God (the world of love, peace, and justice in Heaven and still being built on Earth).
- Together, name some ways to promote peace, fairness, and love in your family.

LET'S PRAY >>>

Saint Brigid, pray for us that we may be welcoming and kind to everyone we know. Amen.

For a multimedia glossary of Catholic Faith Words, Sunday readings, seasonal and Saint resources, and chapter activities go to **aliveinchrist.osv.com**.

Family + Faith

Distribute the page to the children or parents/adult family members. Point out the chapter highlights, insights on how second graders understand concepts, the opportunity for the adults to reflect on their own experience and faith journey, and the family prayer.

Chapter 13 Review

A Work with Words Fill in the blank with the correct word or words from the Word Bank.

Word Bank
- welcomes
- Kingdom of God
- Faith
- children
- Zacchaeus

1. ___Zacchaeus___ became Jesus' friend.
2. Jesus ___welcomes___ everyone.
3. Jesus blessed the ___children___.
4. Everyone is invited into the ___Kingdom of God___.
5. ___Faith___ is believing in God and all that he helps us understand about himself.

B Check Understanding Fill in the circle beside the correct answer.

6. The Kingdom of God is not about ____.
   ○ joy ● castles ○ love
7. Jesus showed that everyone is welcome in ____.
   ○ other countries ○ every club ● God's Kingdom
8. Your ____ welcomes you into God's Kingdom.
   ○ birthday ● Baptism ○ school
9. Mass celebrates the ____ of God's Kingdom.
   ● banquet ○ beginning ○ end
10. At Mass ____ welcome people as they arrive.
   ● greeters ○ readers ○ singers

Go to **aliveinchrist.osv.com** for an interactive review.

Chapter Review

Use Catechist Quick Reviews to highlight lesson concepts.

A Work with Words
Have the children fill in the blanks with the correct word or words from the Word Bank.

B Check Understanding
Explain to the children that they will be filling in the circle beside the correct answer.

Go to **aliveinchrist.osv.com** to prepare customized and downloadable assessments, send eAssessments, and assign interactive reviews.

Share the Good News

KEY CONCEPT

Jesus' disciples share in his life and in his work. The Holy Spirit helps us proclaim the Gospel in our words and actions.

DOCTRINAL CONTENT

- The Gospel message is the Good News of God's Kingdom and his saving love. (CCC, 541)
- In his parable of the Vine and Branches, Jesus teaches us that we need to stay connected to him in order to have life. (CCC, 787)
- The Holy Spirit strengthened the Apostles to share what Jesus had taught them. (CCC, 746–747)
- Many people in our parish share Jesus' message and work together with God as he builds his Kingdom. (CCC, 941–942)

TASKS OF CATECHESIS

Helping children grow in a faith that is "known, celebrated, lived, and expressed in prayer" (NDC, 20).

This chapter focuses on the following tasks of catechesis:

- Education for Community Life
- Missionary Initiation

Catechist Background

[Jesus told his disciples:] "Go into the whole world and proclaim the gospel to every creature. Whoever believes and is baptized will be saved ..." Mark 16:15–16

➔ **Reflect** How do you share the Good News?

In actions and words, Jesus taught lessons of love, mercy, and forgiveness to his disciples. He performed miracles and wonders out of compassion for those who suffered, and he gave the credit to his Father for his work. Jesus invites all his disciples to follow in his footsteps. In return, he asks his followers to invite him into their hearts.

By your Baptism, you inherit the responsibility to do what Jesus did. Family members love one another, support one another, and learn to take care of one another out of love for the family as a whole. As a member of God's family, you are called to help those in need and to serve as Christ served. There are many hats that you wear in a day: catechist, friend, sibling, spouse, parent. In each of these ways, you fulfill the call to serve as a member of God's Church.

Think for a moment about someone who may have been an answer to a prayer. This person's willingness to help you at your hour of need may have deepened your awareness of God's presence in your life. In a sense, that person became the hands of God. When you help another person, show compassion, mercy, and love for another in need, you too become God for others. Jesus is the vine and you are the branches. Jesus is present through you.

➔ **Reflect** Who has been a sign of God's presence for you recently?

Catechist's Prayer

Lord, please bless my efforts. Thank you for being with me always, in the presence of the Holy Spirit, and for sustaining me in all that I do, especially when I teach these children about you. Amen.

Lesson Plan

Objectives	Process	Materials
Invite, 10 minutes		
Share the Good News Page 199	**Psalm 100:1–2** Pray the opening prayer. **Mark 16:15–16** Reflect prayerfully on the Word. • Discuss What Do You Wonder questions.	**Optional Activity** Chapter Story: "Someone Special"
Discover, 35 minutes		
Someone Special Pages 200–201 • Recognize that the Gospel message is the Good News of God's Kingdom and his saving love • Recall how in The Parable of the Vine and Branches, Jesus teaches us that we need to stay connected to him in order to have life	• **Catholic Faith Words** Gospel • Allow the children to give examples of the good news they've shared. **John 15:4–5** Proclaim "The Vine and the Branches." Write names of people who are followers of Jesus. • **Share Your Faith Activity** Talk about the Good News to share.	☐ pencils or pens ☐ board or chart paper • **Optional Activity** Something Beautiful for God ☐ Activity Master 14 (Page 199E)
Taking Jesus' Message to Others Pages 202–203 • Discover that the Holy Spirit strengthened the Apostles to share what Jesus had taught them • Begin to develop a desire to share Jesus' message, and work together with God as he builds his Kingdom	• **Catholic Faith Words** proclaim, parish • Learn about the people who serve Jesus and share his love. • **Connect Your Faith Activity** Name two people who proclaim the Gospel.	☐ pencils or pens ☐ board or chart paper
Live, 15 minutes		
Our Catholic Life Pages 204–205	• Help the the children see that their actions can be ways of sharing Good News. Write one way you can share your time, talent, and treasure. • **People of Faith** Learn about Blessed Mother Teresa. • **Live Your Faith Activity** Answer questions about the Good Samaritan story.	☐ pencils or pens ☐ board or chart paper
Prayer of Thanksgiving Page 206	• Select a strong reader to be the leader. • Follow the order of prayer. Conclude by singing "Gifts."	Download "Gifts."

Family + Faith Page 207

Point out that the Catholic Families page provides chapter highlights, information on how second graders understand faith concepts, and family prayer.

Chapter Review Page 208

aliveinchrist.osv.com

- Customize and Download Assessments
- Email Links to eAssessments
- Interactive Student Reviews

Teaching This Grade

ONLINE RESOURCES

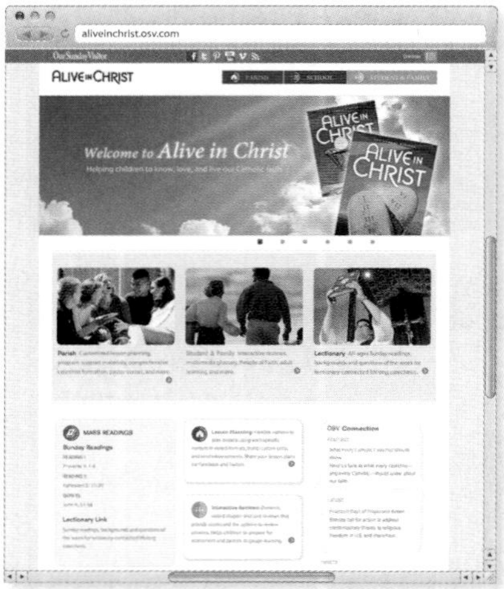

Go to **aliveinchrist.osv.com**

You will find:

- Interactive lesson planning with web specific content and additional activities
- Step by step lesson instruction from printed Catechist Edition for integrated lesson planning
- Custom-built assessments to download and eAssessment links
- Interactive reviews that provide scores and the option to review answers
- Sunday readings with background and questions of the week

Go to **osvparish.com**

You will find:

- Ask the Experts Q and A
- General Catechist Helps
- Community Connections and Blogs

Sharing the Message with Second Graders

Sharing the Good News Children in second grade may think of sharing the Good News of Jesus only as talking about God. While telling others about our faith is an important part of sharing the Gospel, the witness of our lives is the most powerful testimony we can give to our belief in Christ. Second graders can begin to understand this through the guidance of parents, catechists, and other teachers as they point out the many choices we make each day, often witnessed by other people. Even when we cannot preach with our words, our actions can say a lot about who we are and what we believe.

Teaching Tip: Make sure that you are sharing your faith through your actions and not by teaching one thing but doing another.

How Second Graders Understand

- Children this age like it when you welcome them by name.
- Second graders have many heroes, and they need to be free to give honor and respect to those who are wholesome and good for them.
- Young people often like learning. Praise them when they successfully complete an assignment.

"I have many heroes. Let me have fun trying to be like those who set good examples for me."

Chapter Connections

Chapter Story

Invite

"Someone Special"

Use this story to expand the chapter introduction.

- *Ask:* Who do you think of when you think of someone special?
- Have the children work in pairs to write a few sentences about someone they admire.

Go to **aliveinchrist.osv.com** Lesson Planning section for this story.

NCEA IFG: ACRE Edition

Discover

Community Life

- Objectives: To know the origin, mission, structure, and communal nature of the Church; to know the rights and responsibilities of the Christian faithful

Missionary Spirit

- Objectives: To recognize the centrality of evangelization as the Church's mission and identity embodied in vocation and service; to be aware of how cultures are transformed by the Gospel

Catholic Social Teaching

Live

Use one of these features to introduce a principle and engage the children with an activity.

- Rights and Responsibilities, Pages 294–295
- The Dignity of Work, Pages 298–299

Music Options

Use one or more of the following songs to enhance catechetical learning or for prayer.

- "Gifts," Live Prayer, Page 206
- "Jesu, Jesu," Discover, Page 202
- "Share the Light," Live, Page 205

LECTIONARY CONNECTION

Chapter 14 highlights Lectionary-connected themes such as the Gospel, gifts, and disciples. If your parish aligns its curriculum to the liturgical year, you could use this chapter in connection with the following readings.

Year A

First Sunday of Advent—Watchfulness

Fifth Sunday in Ordinary Time—The Disciples

Year B

Second Sunday in Ordinary Time—Disciples

Fifteenth Sunday in Ordinary Time—Apostles' Creed

Year C

Twelfth Sunday in Ordinary Time—Jesus and the Disciples

The Assumption of the Blessed Virgin Mary—Discipleship

Go to **aliveinchrist.osv.com** for a complete correlation ordered by the Sundays of the year and suggestions for how to integrate the Scripture readings into chapter lessons.

Name ____________________ Date ____________

Something Beautiful for God

A. Read each story. Circle the letter of the answer that gives the best way to show God's love.

1. A boy in your class drops his lunch tray. He is standing there with his lunch all over the floor. He begins to cry. What would you do?

a. Laugh and tell your friends that he is clumsy.

b. Help him clean up, and offer to share your lunch with him.

c. Pray that this never happens to you.

2. Your mom or dad comes home late from work, feeling very tired. You want to go to the mall to get things for an art project that is due in two weeks. What would you do?

a. Demand that Mom or Dad take you to the mall right away.

b. Tell your teacher that your parent would not help you with your project.

c. Wait until your mom or dad asks you about your day, and tell her or him about your art project.

B. Draw a picture about one of these stories, showing God's love.

Share the Good News

Let Us Pray

Leader: God, let us sing your songs.

"A psalm of thanksgiving.
Shout joyfully to the LORD, all you lands." Psalm 100:1–2

All: God, fill us with your joy and praise. Amen.

God's Word

Jesus told his disciples: "Go into the whole world and proclaim the gospel to every creature. Whoever believes and is baptized will be saved..." Mark 16:15–16

What Do You Wonder?

- Why does Jesus ask you to share the Good News with others?
- How do you share Jesus' Good News with your family?

Invite

Let Us Pray

Invite the children to gather in the prayer space and make the Sign of the Cross. Ask a volunteer to read aloud the first line of the leader's prayer, then you proclaim the Psalm verse. Prompt the group's response.

Have the children move from the prayer space back to their seats.

Explain that each of us is called to share the wonderful stories of God.

Say: Let's listen and hear what Jesus said about those who believe in him.

God's Word

Guide the children through the process of Scripture reflection.

- Invite them to close their eyes, be still, and open their minds and hearts to what God is saying to them in this passage.
- Proclaim the Scripture.
- Maintain several moments of silence.
- *Ask:* What did you hear God say to you today?
- Invite volunteers to share.

What Do You Wonder?

Say: Jesus tells us to preach the Good News by our lives. We can do this in many ways, with words and actions.

Invite the children to respond to the questions. Ask what else they might wonder about living the Good News.

Optional Activity

Chapter Story: "Someone Special" *Verbal/Linguistic*

Use this story after the opening prayer, before telling the children that we are to share stories of God.

- Invite the children to silently read "Someone Special."
- Ask them why Justin was proud of his uncle. Possible response: He was a good hockey player.
- After allowing the children time to write their response to the question, transition back to the lesson instruction.

Go to **aliveinchrist.osv.com** for Chapter Story.

Objectives

- Recognize that the Gospel message is the Good News of God's Kingdom and his saving love
- Recall how in The Parable of the Vine and Branches, Jesus' teaches us that we need to stay connected to him in order to have life

Someone Special

Read aloud the question at the top of the student page and allow the children to give examples of the types of good news they've shared.

Invite a volunteer to read aloud the definition of the word *Gospel*.

- *Ask:* Have you ever thought of the Bible stories in the Gospels as being good news? Why do you think we call them the Good News? because the stories tell about Jesus and his teachings and the sacrifice he made to save us

Ask a volunteer to read aloud the paragraph and the question that follows.

- Invite discussion.
- To share more about Jesus' teachings, have the children turn to page 318 of the Our Catholic Tradition section in the back of the Student Book and read "The Beatitudes."

Someone Special

When did you have good news to share?

Catholic Faith Words

Gospel a word that means "Good News." The Gospel message is the Good News of God's Kingdom and his saving love.

Gaby likes to share stories and pictures of her aunt and uncle. Aunt Jill and Uncle Todd spend a lot of time helping other people. On the weekends they help build houses for families who need a place to live. Last year, they spent their summer vacation in another country providing medical assistance to people who needed it. Gaby wants everyone to know about her aunt and uncle and the special things they do for others.

➔ **How do you think Gaby shares the news about her aunt and uncle?**

Live as Followers

Just like Gaby wants everyone to know about her aunt and uncle, Jesus wanted everyone to know about God his Father.

Optional Activity

Activity Master 14: Something Beautiful for God

Distribute copies of the activity found on catechist page 199E.

- Have the children draw one of the stories showing God's love.
- As an alternative, you may wish to send this activity home with the children.

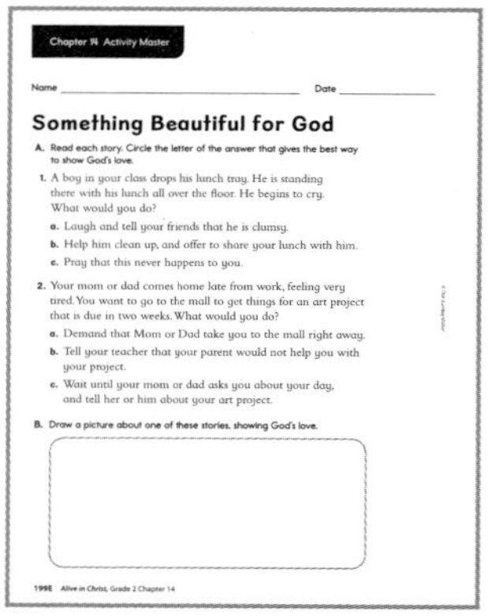

Chapter 14 Activity Master

Name ____ Date ____

Something Beautiful for God

A. Read each story. Circle the letter of the answer that gives the best way to show God's love.

1. A boy in your class drops his lunch tray. He is standing there with his lunch all over the floor. He begins to cry. What would you do?
   a. Laugh and tell your friends that he is clumsy.
   b. Help him clean up, and offer to share your lunch with him.
   c. Pray that this never happens to you.
2. Your mom or dad comes home late from work, feeling very tired. You want to go to the mall to get things for an art project that is due in two weeks. What would you do?
   a. Demand that Mom or Dad take you to the mall right away.
   b. Tell your teacher that your parent would not help you with your project.
   c. Wait until your mom or dad asks you about your day, and tell her or him about your art project.

B. Draw a picture about one of these stories, showing God's love.

199E Alive in Christ, Grade 2 Chapter 14

Jesus knew that the work of spreading the **Gospel** would be hard. His followers would need his help. He made a promise. If they stayed close to him, they would do many good things.

➔ **Name one way you can stay close to Jesus.**

God's Word

The Vine and the Branches

Jesus told his disciples "Remain in me, as I remain in you. Just as a branch cannot bear fruit on its own unless it remains on the vine, so neither can you unless you remain in me."

Jesus said, "I am the vine, you are the branches. Whoever remains in me and I in him will bear much fruit..." John 15:4–5

On the leaves, write your name and the names of people you know who are followers of Jesus.

Share Your Faith

Think What Good News about Jesus do you want share with others?

Share Talk about these things with a partner.

Live as Followers

Read aloud the paragraph on page 200.

Ask: How does Jesus tell about God his Father? in words and actions

Have a volunteer read aloud the paragraph at the top of page 201 and the statement that follows.

- Write the children's answers on the board or on chart paper.

God's Word

Proclaim the Scripture.

☆ Direct the children to write their own name and two other follower's names on the lines provided.

Activity

Read aloud the directions for the Share Your Faith activity.

- Let the children choose their own partners for this activity.

Quick Review

Stay close to Jesus like a branch to a vine. Share the Good News of God's Kingdom with loving words and actions.

Catechist Background

Followers of Jesus

The first followers of Jesus literally followed him around as he walked from town to town in Palestine.

- These followers listened as Jesus talked about God the Father and his Kingdom, and as he taught them how the Father wants people to treat other people.
- Today, Christian followers of Jesus try to act like him and serve others with love.

Discover

Objectives

- Discover that the Holy Spirit strengthened the Apostles to share what Jesus had taught them
- Begin to develop a desire to share Jesus' message, and work together with God as he builds his Kingdom

Taking Jesus' Message to Others

Read aloud the question. List the children's answers on the board or on chart paper.

- Ask a volunteer to read the paragraph.
- *Ask:* Where did they get their strength and courage? From the Holy Spirit

Work with Words

Have the children place their finger on the highlighted word, *proclaim*.

- Ask them to follow along as you read the definition from the box on page 203.
- Have the children work together in groups of four to list ways to proclaim the Good News with their actions.
- Ask the small groups to share their ideas with the larger group.

Music Option: Have the children sing "Jesu, Jesu," downloaded from **aliveinchrist.osv.com**.

Discover

Taking Jesus' Message to Others

How can we share Jesus' message of love?

The Holy Spirit guided Jesus' followers to places that they had never seen. The Spirit strengthened them to **proclaim** the Gospel. They shared everything that Jesus had taught them with others.

People Who Serve Jesus and Share His Love

Religious sisters and brothers teach children more about God the Father, God the Son, and God the Holy Spirit.

Catechists help children learn songs to sing to God.

Parents and grandparents show their children how to love God.

Optional Activity

Role Play *Interpersonal*

Invite the small groups to role play some of the ideas they came up with for ways to proclaim the Good News through their actions.

- Ask each group to vote on which idea they will enact.
- Allow time for the groups to practice and then present their dramatizations.

Jesus' Followers Today

Jesus' followers still bring his message to the world. People do this in different ways. There are many people in your **parish** that share Jesus' message. When we share the Good News, we work together with God as he builds his Kingdom.

Catholic Faith Words

proclaim to tell about Jesus in words and actions

parish the local community of Catholics that meets at a particular place

Priests are pastors who lead the parish, celebrate Mass, and bless people.

Deacons serve in the parish in many ways, including baptizing people.

Connect Your Faith

Proclaim the Gospel Name two people in your parish who proclaim the Gospel.

1. ______________________________

2. ______________________________

Jesus' Followers Today

Read aloud the paragraph.

- *Ask:* Who in your parish shares Jesus' message? anyone who uses loving words and actions to tell about Jesus

Point out the highlighted word and read aloud the definition for *parish*.

Invite volunteers to take turns reading aloud the captions for each of the photos on pages 202 and 203. After each caption is read,

- *Ask:* How is this an example of being a follower of Jesus?
- Discuss ways to follow Jesus by being a helper in the parish. Assist the children in coming up with other ways of helping in the parish that are not pictured on these pages, for example, director of religious education, reader, or altar server.
- Write the children's answers on the board or on chart paper.

Activity

Read aloud the directions for the Connect Your Faith activity.

- Allow the children to share some of the names they wrote down.

Quick Tip

Opportunities to Serve

If possible, invite a deacon or another member of the parish to come and talk to the children about the ways that they help in the church.

- It would help the children better connect with the lesson and the parish if your guest speaker were able to share opportunities for helping in the church that are open to the children's participation, such as being an altar server.

Quick Review

The Holy Spirit strengthened the Apostles to share the Good News. Members of our parish now share Jesus' message and work together with God to build his Kingdom.

Live

Our Catholic Life

Write on the board or on chart paper the words *Time*, *Talent*, and *Treasure*.

Read aloud the introductory paragraph.

- *Ask:* How is sharing your gifts a good way to share the Good News of Jesus?
- Help the the children see that their actions can be ways of sharing the Good News.

Share Your Gifts

Remind the children that everyone has time, talent, and treasures to share with the world.

☆ Tell the children that as you review each box, they will write in one way to share their time, talent, or treasure.

Invite a volunteer to read aloud the "Time" box.

- Allow time for the children to think and write their response on the line.

Invite another volunteer to read aloud the "Talent" box.

- Invite verbal responses so that the children can better determine what their talent is.
- Allow time for the children to think and write their response.

Invite one more volunteer to read aloud the "Treasure" box.

- Allow time for the children to think and write their response on the line.

Our Catholic Life

How can you share the Good News?

Jesus asked all of his followers to share the Good News. He told them to use the gifts God gave them to help them do this. God has given you gifts, too. You have the gifts of time, talent, and treasure to help you share the Good News.

Write in one way you can share your time, talent, and treasure.

Share Your Gifts

Time: All the minutes of your day, which you can choose to use generously or selfishly.

You can: Do extra chores at home or run errands for a neighbor.

____

Talent: All the things you like to do and things you do well, which you can use generously or selfishly.

You can: Teach someone to play your favorite game or read a story to a younger child.

____

Treasure: All the things you have, which you could use generously or selfishly.

You can: Let a friend borrow a toy or collect extra clothes and toys for people who have less.

____

Quick Tip

Identify Gifts

Young children sometimes have a difficult time recognizing their own gifts and talents.

- You can help by identifying and praising the wide range of gifts exhibited by the children in your group.
- Remind the children that everyone has time, talent, and treasure of some kind to share.

People of Faith

Blessed Mother Teresa of Calcutta, 1910–1997

September 5

Blessed Mother Teresa of Calcutta was born in Albania. She was named Agnes by her parents. When she grew up, she became a nun. Her new name was Mother Teresa. She worked in Calcutta, India, far from her home. She cared for the poor and dying. She began a new group of sisters called the Missionaries of Charity. When people asked, "What can we do to help the people who are poor?" Mother Teresa told them to use their gifts of time, talent, and treasure to build God's Kingdom. She said, "Do something beautiful for God."

Discuss: How can you do something beautiful for God?

Learn more about Blessed Mother Teresa at **aliveinchrist.osv.com**

Live Your Faith

Share the Good News With a partner, answer the questions about this story.

1. How did the Samaritan use his gifts?
2. What gifts could you use to bring the Good News to someone in need?

Catholic Social Teaching

Chapter Connections

To integrate Catholic Social Teaching into your lesson, choose one of the following features: Rights and Responsibilities, pages 294–295; or The Dignity of Work, pages 298–299.

- Start the Live step of the process by talking about Blessed Mother Teresa on page 205. Then move directly to the Catholic Social Teaching feature.
- Or, to expand the lesson, complete both pages 204 and 205, then move to the Catholic Social Teaching feature.
- Return to Chapter 14 for the prayer on page 206.

People of Faith

Tell the children about Blessed Mother Teresa.

- She listened to her conscience even if it was not the popular thing to do.
- Mother Teresa was petite, quiet, and shy.
- She heard the call to give up everything she had and follow Christ.
- Read aloud the paragraph on Blessed Mother Teresa.
- *Ask:* How can you do something beautiful for God?
- Allow the children to share their ideas.

Encourage the children to go to **aliveinchrist.osv.com** at home to learn more about Blessed Mother Teresa.

Activity

Read aloud the directions for the Live Your Faith activity.

- Remind the children that they heard the story of the good Samaritan in an earlier chapter.
- Ask the children to work with a partner as they answer the question and determine which gifts they could use to share the Good News and help someone in need.

Music Option: Have the children sing "Share the Light," downloaded from **aliveinchrist.osv.com**.

Let Us Pray

Prayer of Thanksgiving

Explain that this prayer is to tell God how thankful we are for all that we've been given in time, talent, and treasure and mostly, for his love.

Prepare

Select a strong reader and ask him or her to be the leader. Allow time for the leader to practice.

Rehearse with the children "Gifts," downloaded from **aliveinchrist.osv.com**.

Gather

Invite the children to come to the prayer space with their books.

- Lead the children into the prayer space while playing or singing "Gifts."

Pray

Follow the order of prayer on the student page.

Conclude by having the children process around the room singing "Gifts."

Let Us Pray

Prayer of Thanksgiving

Gather and begin with the Sign of the Cross.

Leader: We praise and thank you,
O Lord, for the many people
who share your Good News.
Blessed be the name of the Lord.

All: Now and forever.

Leader: We praise and thank you,
O Lord, for the people
who help in our parish.
Blessed be the name of the Lord.

All: Now and forever. Amen.

Leader: We praise and thank you,
O Lord, for giving gifts and talents
to us to serve others.
Blessed be the name of the Lord.

All: Now and forever. Amen.

Sing "Gifts"

We thank you, God,
for giving talents to us.
Now we use those gifts to serve others and you.
Singing and teaching, helping each other.
Caring for needs of our sisters and brothers.
We thank you, God,
as we give our talents back to you!

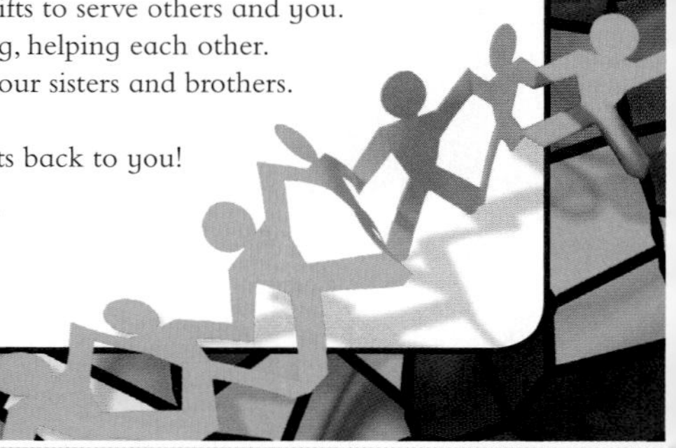

Liturgy Link

Singing and Prayer

Prayer takes on a nobler aspect when it is celebrated with singing.

- Help the children appreciate the fact that singing is also praying.
- Music enhances prayer, joining both voice and heart in praise of God.
- Encourage the children to sing whole-heartedly to God, especially during a prayer celebration.

Go to **aliveinchrist.osv.com** for Sunday readings, Scripture background, questions of the week, and seasonal resources.

FAMILY + FAITH
LIVING AND LEARNING TOGETHER

YOUR CHILD LEARNED >>>

This chapter teaches that we are all called as disciples to share the Good News of Jesus and that priests, deacons, and religious sisters and brothers serve the Church in many ways.

God's Word

Read **Mark 16:15–16** to find out who is saved through Jesus Christ.

Catholics Believe

- Jesus' disciples share in his life and in his work.
- The Holy Spirit helps us proclaim the Gospel in our words and actions.

To learn more, go to the *Catechism of the Catholic Church* #746–747, 900, 904, 905 at **usccb.org**.

People of Faith

This week, your child met Blessed Mother Teresa of Calcutta. Her work with others in need reminds us that there are many ways to serve God.

CHILDREN AT THIS AGE >>>

How They Understand Sharing the Good News Children in second grade may think of sharing the Good News of Jesus only as talking about God. While telling others about our faith is an important part of sharing the Gospel, the witness of our lives is the most powerful testimony we can give to our belief in Christ. Second-graders can begin to understand this through the guidance of parents and other teachers as they point out the many choices we make each day, often witnessed by other people. Even when we cannot preach with our words, our actions can say a lot about who we are and what we believe.

CONSIDER THIS >>>

Do you believe that your actions speak louder than your words?

Research tells us that people trust body language more than verbal language. Jesus offered us the perfect image of God, as his words and actions never contradict each other. "We are called in imitation of the Lord Jesus, to be people who offer ourselves willingly in service to others. Actions of such service can point to Christ's Kingdom of love, justice, mercy, and salvation to all persons, cultures, governments, and other structures of society. We are also called to a life of service to the Church herself" (*USCCA, p. 118*).

LET'S TALK >>>

- Talk about the talents of each member of your family and how they can be used to serve God and share his love with others.
- Name some people in your parish who spread Jesus' message to others.

LET'S PRAY >>>

Dear Jesus, help us use our gifts to do something beautiful for God, as Blessed Mother Teresa did. Amen.

For a multimedia glossary of Catholic Faith Words, Sunday readings, seasonal and Saint resources, and chapter activities go to **aliveinchrist.osv.com**.

Family + Faith

Distribute the page to the children or parents/adult family members. Point out the chapter highlights, insights on how second graders understand concepts, the opportunity for the adults to reflect on their own experience and faith journey, and the family prayer.

Chapter 14 Review

A Work with Words Fill in the blank with the correct word from the Word Bank to complete each sentence.

Word Bank: vine, talent, proclaim, baptize, disciples

1. Jesus said to make **disciples** of all nations.
2. The Holy Spirit was sent to help Jesus' disciples **proclaim** the Gospel.
3. Jesus told his followers to **baptize** all people everywhere.
4. Jesus is the **vine**, and we are the branches.
5. The gifts of time, **talent**, and treasure help you share the Good News.

B Check Understanding Write the letter T if the sentence is TRUE. Write the letter F if the sentence is FALSE.

6. **T** Jesus told his disciples to proclaim the Gospel.
7. **F** Jesus asked his followers to keep the Good News a secret.
8. **T** God gives us gifts to help us spread the Good News.
9. **T** We work together with God to build his Kingdom.
10. **F** The Holy Spirit strengthened Jesus' followers to proclaim the newspaper.

Go to **aliveinchrist.osv.com** for an interactive review.

Chapter Review

Use Catechist Quick Reviews to highlight lesson concepts.

A Work with Words
Have the children fill in the blank with the correct word from the Word Bank to complete each sentence.

B Check Understanding
Explain to the children that they will be writing a *T* for True and an *F* for False.

Go to **aliveinchrist.osv.com** to prepare customized and downloadable assessments, send eAssessments, and assign interactive reviews.

KEY CONCEPT
Prayer is being with God in your mind and heart. We pray in many ways, for many reasons. Jesus taught his followers the Lord's Prayer.

DOCTRINAL CONTENT
- Jesus' taught us to pray the Lord's Prayer, which we also call the Our Father. (CCC, 2759)
- There are five basic forms of prayer: blessing, petition, intercession, thanksgiving, and praise. (CCC, 2644)
- Prayer is important to deepen our friendship with God, and we can pray in many ways and at different times. (CCC, 2565)
- Sacramentals are blessings, objects, and actions that remind you of God and are made sacred through the prayers of the Church. (CCC, 1668, 1671)

TASKS OF CATECHESIS
Helping children grow in a faith that is "known, celebrated, lived, and expressed in prayer" (NDC, 20).

This chapter focuses on the following tasks of catechesis:
- Liturgical Education
- Teaching to Pray

Catechist Background

He was praying in a certain place, and when he had finished, one of his disciples said to him, "Lord, teach us to pray…." He said to them, "When you pray, say: Father, hallowed be your name, your kingdom come. Give us each day our daily bread and forgive us our sins for we ourselves forgive everyone in debt to us, and do not subject us to the final test." Luke 11:1–4

➔ **Reflect** How often do you pray? Do you pray in a certain place?

Jesus prayed often. He prayed when he was baptized, before beginning his public ministry and choosing his Apostles, on a mountaintop, and during his Agony in the Garden on the night before he died. When his disciples needed guidance, Jesus taught them the Lord's Prayer, which is recorded in the long passage in the Gospel according to Matthew during the Sermon on the Mount.

Reflect on your own prayer life. How do you open your heart and mind to God? Numerous things may keep you from sincere and vigilant prayer. Minimal time, unfruitful liturgical experiences, spiritual emptiness, and seemingly unanswered prayers may be obstacles for you. Even so, Jesus calls you to persevere in prayer. "And I tell you, ask and you will receive; seek and you will find; knock and the door will be opened to you" (Luke 11:9).

No matter what your situation, God tirelessly calls you to the mysterious encounter known as prayer. (See CCC, 2567.) When it is too difficult to pray or when you are at a loss for words, you can use the Lord's Prayer to help you begin your encounter with God. Jesus gives each of his followers an invitation to know him more completely; your response is your perseverance in prayer.

➔ **Reflect** When does it feel most natural for you to pray?

Catechist's Prayer

Lord Jesus Christ, help me show the children that prayer is vital to their lives. May I help them feel comfortable in praying so that they will always be ready to turn to you. Amen.

Lesson Plan

Objectives	Process	Materials
Invite, 10 minutes		
Ways to Pray Page 209	**Psalm 86:4** Pray the opening prayer. **Luke 11:1–4** Reflect prayerfully on the Word. • Discuss What Do You Wonder questions.	**Optional Activity** Chapter Story: "In Your Heart"
Discover, 35 minutes		
Talking with God Pages 210–211 • Recall Jesus' instruction to us to pray the Lord's Prayer, which we also call the Our Father	• **Catholic Faith Words** Lord's Prayer **Matthew 6:5–9** Proclaim "How to Pray." • Recognize the words Jesus asked his followers to pray. ☆ Underline what Jesus says about how we are to pray. • **Share Your Faith Activity** Write when to pray the Lord's Prayer.	☐ pencils or pens
Types of Prayer Pages 212–213 • Identify the five basic forms of prayer: blessing, petition, intercession, thanksgiving, and praise • Understand that prayer is important to deepen our friendship with God • Discover that sacramentals are blessings, objects, and actions that remind us of God and are made sacred through the prayers of the Church	• **Catholic Faith Words** blessing, petition, intercession, thanksgiving, praise, sacramentals • Talk about how prayer is a way to deepen our friendship with God. ☆ Write about one thing prayed for before going to bed. • Discuss sacramentals and how they help us pray. • **Connect Your Faith Activity** Memorize the Glory Be.	☐ pencils or pens ☐ crayons, colored pencils, or markers ☐ paper • **Optional Activity** Time to Pray ☐ Activity Master 15 (Page 209E)
Live, 15 minutes		
Our Catholic Life Pages 214–215	• Discuss the ways we can talk to God. ☆ Identify the five different prayer types. • **People of Faith** Learn about Saint Alphonsus Liguori. • **Live Your Faith Activity** Write a prayer.	☐ pencils or pens
The Lord's Prayer Page 216	• Explain the prayer. Rehearse "Open My Eyes." • Follow the order of prayer.	Download "Open My Eyes."

Family + Faith Page 217

Point out that the Catholic Families page provides chapter highlights, information on how second graders understand faith concepts, and family prayer.

Chapter Review Page 218

aliveinchrist.osv.com

- Customize and Download Assessments
- Email Links to eAssessments
- Interactive Student Reviews

Teaching This Grade

ONLINE RESOURCES

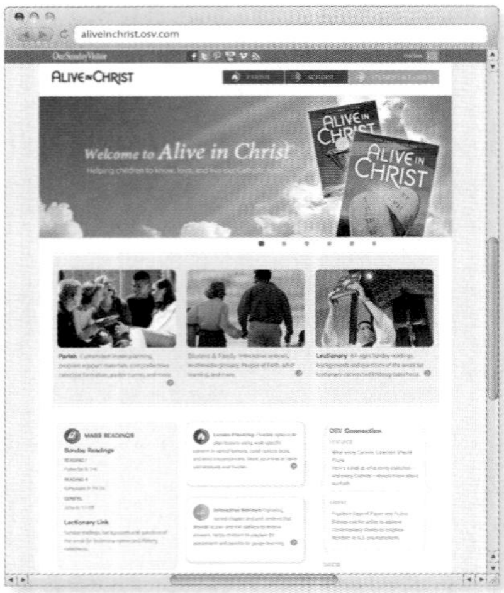

Go to **aliveinchrist.osv.com**

You will find:

- Interactive lesson planning with web specific content and additional activities
- Step by step lesson instruction from printed Catechist Edition for integrated lesson planning
- Custom-built assessments to download and eAssessment links
- Interactive reviews that provide scores and the option to review answers
- Sunday readings with background and questions of the week

Go to **osvparish.com**

You will find:

- Ask the Experts Q and A
- General Catechist Helps
- Community Connections and Blogs

Sharing the Message with Second Graders

Prayer Children may view prayer as "prayers:" memorized, recited words we say to God. These prayers can be important because they allow us to pray together with one voice, but prayer is conversation with God, in our hearts, minds, and with words. If they haven't already, children in second grade are old enough now to begin speaking to God in their own words. They can do this with some prompting and structure. Sacred spaces, at home and in the room where you meet, also provide a place for listening to God in quiet reflection.

Teaching Tip: Make some time for spontaneous prayer by forming a circle, having a theme for a type of prayer (thanksgiving, praying for others, etc.), and going around the circle giving each child an opportunity to say something relevant.

How Second Graders Understand

- Children this age are learning to express themselves. Prompt them with phrases such as "Tell me more about . . ."
- Second graders like to hear how they're doing. Give them positive, specific feedback.
- Often, children this age are still learning to follow directions. Help them understand each step before moving on to the next one.

"I like to hear how I'm doing. Give me positive, specific feedback."

Chapter Connections

Chapter Story

Invite

"In Your Heart"

Use this story to expand the chapter introduction.

- Discuss things that the children have in their homes that remind them to pray.
- Ask them if they have a cross or medal that they wear?
- Encourage the children to share with the group those things that remind them of God.

Go to **aliveinchrist.osv.com** Lesson Planning section for this story.

NCEA IFG: ACRE Edition

Discover

Liturgical Life

- Objective: To know the Paschal Mystery of Jesus: in the Church's liturgical life—feasts, seasons, symbols, and practices and in the Sacraments as signs and instruments of grace

Prayer

- Objective: To recognize and learn how to engage in Catholic forms of personal and communal prayer and ways of deepening one's spiritual life

Catholic Social Teaching

Live

Use one of these features to introduce a principle and engage the children with an activity.

- Solidarity of the Human Family, Pages 300–301
- Care for Creation, Pages 302–303

Music Options

Use the following song to enhance catechetical learning or for prayer.

- "Open My Eyes," Live Prayer, Page 216

LECTIONARY CONNECTION

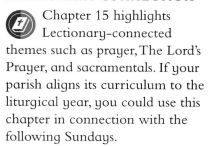

Chapter 15 highlights Lectionary-connected themes such as prayer, The Lord's Prayer, and sacramentals. If your parish aligns its curriculum to the liturgical year, you could use this chapter in connection with the following Sundays.

Year A

Second Sunday of Advent—Prayer of Encouragement

Twelfth Sunday in Ordinary Time—Faith in Crisis

Year B

First Sunday of Advent—Lord's Prayer

Third Sunday of Easter—Lord's Prayer

Year C

First Sunday of Advent—The Lord's Prayer

Thirtieth Sunday in Ordinary Time—Prayer

Go to **aliveinchrist.osv.com** for a complete correlation ordered by the Sundays of the year and suggestions for how to integrate the Scripture readings into chapter lessons.

Name ______________________________ Date ______________

Time to Pray

You know that there are many kinds of prayers. You can pray anytime and anywhere. Use the doorknob sign when you pray in your room. Color and decorate it before cutting it out.

CHAPTER 15

Ways to Pray

Let Us Pray

Leader: Lord, hear us when we pray.

"Gladden the soul of your servant;
to you, Lord, I lift up my soul." Psalm 86:4

All: Lord, hear us when we pray. Amen.

God's Word

When Jesus had finished praying, one of his disciples said to him, "Lord, teach us how to pray just as John taught his disciples."

So Jesus told them, "When you pray, say: 'Father, hallowed be your name, your kingdom come. Give us each day our daily bread and forgive us our sins as we forgive everyone who has done wrong to us. And keep us from being tempted.'" Based on Luke 11:1–4

What Do You Wonder?

- Why does Jesus teach us to pray?
- Can you pray by yourself?

Optional Activity

Chapter Story: "In Your Heart" *Verbal/Linguistic*

Use this story after the opening prayer, before telling the children how Jesus taught us to pray.

- Discuss how holy things remind us of God and his holy People, but it is not necessary to have them to pray.
- When finished with the discussion, transition back to the lesson instruction.

Go to **aliveinchrist.osv.com** for Chapter Story.

Invite

Let Us Pray

Invite the children to gather in the prayer space and make the Sign of the Cross. Ask the whole group to pray together the leader's prayer, including the Psalm verse and the response.

Have the children move from the prayer space back to their seats.

Explain that Jesus teaches us how to pray.

Say: Let's listen to how Jesus taught his disciples the Lord's Prayer.

God's Word

Guide the children through the process of Scripture reflection.

- Invite them to close their eyes, be still, and open their minds and hearts to what God is saying to them in this passage.
- Proclaim the Scripture.
- Maintain several moments of silence.
- *Ask:* What did you hear God say to you today?
- Invite volunteers to share.

What Do You Wonder?

Say: Jesus' taught his disciples and us how to approach God in prayer.

Invite the children to respond to the questions. Ask what else they might wonder about praying.

Discover

Objective

- Recall Jesus' instruction to us to pray the Lord's Prayer, which we also call the Our Father

Talking with God

Invite a volunteer to read aloud the introductory paragraph.

- Talk about times Jesus prayed to God the Father, such as at the Last Supper.

Read aloud the question at the top of the student page.

Tell the children they are going to learn how Jesus taught his followers to pray, and how we should pray.

God's Word

Proclaim the Scripture story.

- Ask the children if they recognize the words Jesus asked his followers to pray.
- ☆ Instruct the group to underline what Jesus says about how we are to pray.
- *Ask:* Where do you pray?
- Invite volunteers to share their responses.
- Direct the children's attention to the image on the page.
- Read aloud the caption. Ask them what they think Jesus might be praying about.

The Lord's Prayer

Read aloud the paragraph.

Ask for a volunteer to read aloud the Catholic Faith Word and its definition.

Talking with God

What does Jesus teach us about prayer?

When you pray, you talk to and listen to God. The Bible says that Jesus prayed often. He wanted his followers to pray often, too.

Catholic Faith Words

Lord's Prayer the prayer that Jesus taught his disciples to pray to God the Father

God's Word

How to Pray

Jesus said, "When you pray, go to your inner room, close the door, and pray to your Father in secret."

Jesus also told them, "Do not babble like the others, who think that they will be heard because of their many words . . . Your Father knows what you need before you ask him. This is how you are to pray: Our Father in Heaven, hallowed be your name." Based on Matthew 6:5–9

☆ Underline what Jesus says about how we are to pray.

The Lord's Prayer

The name of the prayer that Jesus taught his followers is the **Lord's Prayer**. It is also called the "Our Father." When we say the Lord's Prayer, we are talking directly to God our Father.

Jesus showed us to pray at all times.

Scripture Background

Matthew 6:5–9

The Lord's Prayer is a summary of Jesus' teachings. This prayer also appears in Luke 11:2:4 but it is not as developed or as long as the version in the Gospel according to Matthew.

- The Lord's Prayer, or Our Father, expresses Jesus' reverence for and confidence in his Father.
- If you'd like to review the Latin version of the Lord's Prayer with the children, you can find it on page 320 in the Our Catholic Tradition section of the Student Book.

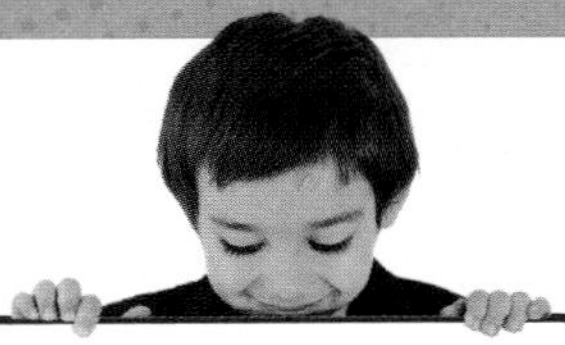

The Lord's Prayer

Words of the Prayer	What They Mean
Our Father, who art in heaven, hallowed be thy name;	We praise God the Father. We say his name with love and respect.
thy kingdom come,	We pray that all people will know God's justice and peace.
thy will be done on earth as it is in heaven.	We will do what God wants, not what we want.
Give us this day our daily bread;	We ask God to give us what we need for now.
and forgive us our trespasses as we forgive those who trespass against us;	We ask God to be as forgiving of us as we are of others.
and lead us not into temptation, but deliver us from evil.	We ask God to protect us from harm and keep us from sin.
Amen.	May it be so!

Share Your Faith

Think When do you pray the Lord's Prayer?

____

____

____

Share Talk about the times the Lord's Prayer is prayed.

The Lord's Prayer

Explain that the Lord's Prayer is sometimes referred to as the "Our Father."

Ask for two volunteers to read aloud the content of the chart.

- Have the first reader read a line from "Words of the Prayer," and the second reader, as an echo, read its meaning.
- Discuss any phrases the children might not understand.

Activity

Read aloud the directions for the Share Your Faith activity.

- Ask the children to think about the different times when they might pray the Lord's Prayer and write them down.
- Encourage volunteers to share their responses.

Quick Review

Jesus taught us to pray and showed us the many opportunities we have in our lives for prayer.

Optional Activity

Time to Pray *Verbal/Linguistic*

When Jesus was a little boy, he probably prayed at 9:00 a.m., noon, and 3:00 p.m., the appointed times of Jewish prayer.

- Give each child a paper plate, and have them mark these three times, as they would appear on a clock face.
- Have the children draw a line from each time to the center of the clock, and write a one-sentence prayer in each space.

Discover

Objectives

- Identify the five basic forms of prayer: blessing, petition, intercession, thanksgiving, and praise
- Understand that prayer is important to deepen our friendship with God
- Discover that sacramentals are blessings, objects, and actions that remind us of God and are made sacred through the prayers of the Church

Types of Prayer

Read aloud the question at the top of the student page, and encourage the children to share the words they use in prayer.

Invite a volunteer to read the paragraph.

Work with Words

Help the children sound out the words in the Catholic Faith Words box.

- As the words are sounded out, have the children circle familiar words and put question marks by unfamiliar words.
- Discuss the unfamiliar words.
- Have the children copy all the words and definitions on a separate piece of paper.
- ☆ Invite the children to share one thing they pray for before going to bed. Then have them color the picture.
- Provide crayons, colored pencils, or markers.

Discover

Types of Prayer

What is your favorite way to pray?

Prayer is a way to deepen your friendship with God. You can pray in many ways. You can say many things when you pray to God. Sometimes you can just be quiet and enjoy being with God.

Catholic Faith Words

blessing blessing God who is the source of everything that is good

petition asking God for what we need

intercession asking God to help others

thanksgiving giving thanks to God for all he has given us

praise giving God honor and thanks because he is God

☆ Color the picture. Then share one thing you pray for before you go to bed.

Optional Activity

Activity Master 15: Time to Pray

Distribute copies of the activity found on catechist page 209E.

- This activity allows the children to create a door hanging for their room.
- As an alternative, you may wish to send this activity home with the children.

Chapter 15 Activity Master

Name Date

Time to Pray

How to Pray

You can use your words to pray. You can also use prayers that the Church and some of the Saints have written. These prayers include the Hail Mary, the Glory Be, and prayers before meals. You can pray when you are happy, sad, alone, or with others.

You can also pray when you see pictures or objects that remind you that God is with you. Objects such as a crucifix, a rosary, or holy water are called **sacramentals**. Words of blessing and actions, such as the Sign of the Cross, are also sacramentals.

→ **What sacramentals do you see in church?**

→ **What sacramentals do you have in your home?**

Catholic Faith Words

sacramentals blessings, objects, and actions that remind you of God and are made sacred through the prayers of the Church

The crucifix is a sacramental that we see often on necklaces, walls, and in processions at church.

Connect Your Faith

Learn by Heart Memorize the words of the Glory Be.

Glory be to the Father,
and to the Son,
and to the Holy Spirit.
As it was in the beginning,
is now, and ever shall be,
world without end. Amen.

Quick Tip

Living Rosary

The Rosary is part of our Catholic Tradition and a prayer that is prayed often by many people around the world. If your parish celebrates a living Rosary, encourage the children to attend with their families.

- You may want to hold a simple living Rosary celebration with your group. Remind them that the rosary is a sacramental.
- Pray a decade of the Rosary with the children. Have one child represent each bead of the decade.

How to Pray

Invite a volunteer to read the first paragraph. Choose another volunteer to read the second paragraph.

Read aloud the questions that follow, one at a time.

- Pause after each for the children to share all the sacramentals they can recall seeing at church and at home.

Ask the children to place their finger on the highlighted word, *sacramentals*.

- Read aloud the definition in the Catholic Faith Words box.

Activity

Read aloud the directions for the Connect Your Faith activity.

- Have the children work in pairs to practice and memorize the Glory Be.
- Instruct the first reader of each pair to say one clause within punctuation marks, then let his or her partner repeat the phrase. Continue in this manner, one clause at a time, until the prayer has been completely prayed. Repeat the process with the second partner starting off the reading.

Quick Review

Prayer is necessary, and there are various forms of prayer: blessing, petition, intercession, thanksgiving, and praise. Sacramentals are blessings, objects, and actions that remind us of God.

Live

Our Catholic Life

Read aloud the question at the top of the student page, and tell the children that we will read the lesson and find out the answer.

Read aloud the first paragraph.

- *Ask:* What are the three ways we can talk to God? our own words, memorized prayers, and words from the Bible

Remind the children that there are five types of prayer.

Say: We covered these when we reviewed the Catholic Faith Words on page 212.

☆ Tell the children that they are going to fill in the blanks, or boxes, to identify each prayer type.

- Let the children work in pairs.
- Suggest they read the column titled "Words We Can Say" first to help them figure out the missing letters of the type of prayer.
- When finished, allow volunteers to share their answers.

Our Catholic Life

How can you talk to God?

Sometimes you talk to God using the words of prayers you have memorized, like the Lord's Prayer. Sometimes you pray in the words of the Bible, like the psalm verses. But you can use your own words, too, when you pray together with your family and by yourself.

➔ **What are some prayers you can pray?**

Fill in the blanks to identify the prayer type.

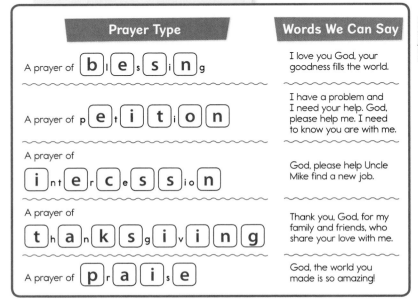

Prayer Type	Words We Can Say
A prayer of blessing	I love you God, your goodness fills the world.
A prayer of petition	I have a problem and I need your help. God, please help me. I need to know you are with me.
A prayer of intercession	God, please help Uncle Mike find a new job.
A prayer of thanksgiving	Thank you, God, for my family and friends, who share your love with me.
A prayer of praise	God, the world you made is so amazing!

Reaching All Learners

Nonverbal Learners

Allow children with visual or motor impairments, or those whose primary learning style is nonverbal, to complete the prayer activity on page 215 using one of these alternatives.

- Have the children speak or sing their prayers. If possible, help them record their prayers.
- Invite them to draw or sign their prayers.
- Help all the children develop spontaneous prayer, sung prayer, and prayerful movement.

People of Faith

Saint Alphonsus Liguori, 1696–1787

Saint Alphonsus Liguori was a very good lawyer. God wanted him to become a priest, so he did. He was an even better priest than he was a lawyer. Saint Alphonsus loved to pray. He wrote many different prayers. He wrote prayers of praise, thanksgiving, and petition. He especially loved to ask the Blessed Mother to pray for him. He was also a painter, poet, and musician. He even wrote a song to sing at Christmas!

August 1

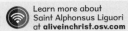

Discuss: What type of prayer do you like to pray?

Learn more about Saint Alphonsus Liguori at **aliveinchrist.osv.com**

Live Your Faith

Write a Prayer Write a short prayer of thanksgiving to God. Tell what you are thankful for and why.

____

____

____

____

____

____

____

Catholic Social Teaching

Chapter Connections

To integrate Catholic Social Teaching into your lesson, choose one of the following features: Human Solidarity, pages 300–301; or Care for Creation, pages 302–303.

- Start the Live step of the process by talking about Saint Alphonsus Liguori on page 215. Then move directly to the Catholic Social Teaching feature.
- Or, to expand the lesson, complete both pages 214 and 215, then move to the Catholic Social Teaching feature.
- Return to Chapter 15 for the prayer on page 216.

People of Faith

Tell the children about Saint Alphonsus Liguori.

- He suffered often with illness, and was given the Sacraments of the dying eight times in his long life.
- After a year-long case of rheumatic fever, he was paralyzed until his death.
- He lived another twelve years and died at ninety-one.
- Read aloud the paragraph on Saint Alphonsus.
- Discuss the question with the children.

Encourage the children to go to **aliveinchrist.osv.com** at home to learn more about Saint Alphonsus Liguori.

Activity

Ask a volunteer to read aloud the directions for the Live Your Faith activity.

- Have the children work alone to write their prayers.
- Circulate around the room to see if they need help with spelling.

Let Us Pray
The Lord's Prayer
Explain to the children that the prayer we are going to pray today is the prayer that Jesus taught his disciples.

Prepare
Tell the children to think about the meaning of each part of the prayer as they pray.

- You will be the leader.

Rehearse with the children "Open My Eyes," downloaded from **aliveinchrist.osv.com**.

Gather
Invite the children to come to the prayer space with their books.

- Lead them into the prayer space while playing or singing "Open My Eyes."

Pray
Follow the order of prayer on the student page.

Conclude by processing around the room with the children, singing "Open My Eyes."

Let Us Pray

The Lord's Prayer

Gather and begin with the Sign of the Cross.

Leader: Let us pray together the prayer that Jesus taught us.

All: Our Father, who art in heaven,
hallowed be thy name;
thy kingdom come,
thy will be done
on earth
as it is in heaven.
Give us this day our daily bread,
and forgive us our trespasses,
as we forgive those who trespass
against us;
and lead us not into temptation,
but deliver us from evil. Amen.

Sing "Open My Eyes"

Open my eyes, Lord.
Help me to see your face.
Open my eyes, Lord.
Help me to see.
Open my ears, Lord.
Help me to hear your voice.
Open my ears, Lord.
Help me to hear.

Liturgy Link
Sacred Music
The real solemnity of a celebration does not depend on the musical style but on it being a worthy and reverent celebration.

- Suitable melodies should be provided for the liturgy of the liturgical year.
- All music used at the liturgy has but one goal—to bring honor, praise, and glory to God.

Go to **aliveinchrist.osv.com** for Sunday readings, Scripture background, questions of the week, and seasonal resources.

FAMILY + FAITH

LIVING AND LEARNING TOGETHER

YOUR CHILD LEARNED >>>

This chapter explores the importance of prayer, the many ways we pray, and how we use sacramentals—sacred objects, actions, and words.

God's Word

Read **Luke 11:1–4** to learn what Jesus taught us about prayer and the words he used to pray.

Catholics Believe

- Prayer is being with God in your mind and heart. We pray in many ways, for many reasons.
- Jesus taught his followers the Lord's Prayer.

To learn more, go to the *Catechism of the Catholic Church* #2692–2696 at **usccb.org**.

People of Faith

This week, your child met Saint Alphonsus Liguori. He loved to pray to the Blessed Mother.

CHILDREN AT THIS AGE >>>

How They Understand Prayer Children may view prayer as "prayers:" memorized, recited words we say to God. These prayers can be important because they allow us to pray together with one voice, but prayer is a conversation with God, in our hearts, minds, and with words. If they haven't already, children in second grade are old enough now to begin speaking to God in their own words. Your child can do this with some prompting and structure. A sacred space in the home can also provide a place for listening to God in quiet reflection.

CONSIDER THIS >>>

Do you remember seeing sacred pictures and objects in the home where you were raised?

We are transformed by images. Whether it is a piece of great art or a picture of a suffering child we see on the news, images can change our minds and hearts. Faith-filled people can come to know the grace that flows from Christ through the use of sacramentals (blessings, objects, and actions that remind you of God and are made sacred through the prayers of the Church). "We use these signs and symbols to help us experience God's invisible presence" (*USCCA, p. 171*).

LET'S TALK >>>

- Invite your child to share one thing Jesus teaches us about prayer.
- Talk about some ways your family prays together and why.

LET'S PRAY >>>

Mary, I kneel here before you with my family and choose you for my Mother (Saint Alphonsus' family prayer of dedication).

For a multimedia glossary of Catholic Faith Words, Sunday readings, seasonal and Saint resources, and chapter activities go to **aliveinchrist.osv.com**.

Family + Faith

Distribute the page to the children or parents/adult family members. Point out the chapter highlights, insights on how second graders understand concepts, the opportunity for the adults to reflect on their own experience and faith journey, and the family prayer.

Chapter 15 Review

A Work with Words Unscramble the words to find five good reasons to pray.

1. To LEBSS God the Father. ___bless___
2. To ESIARP the Lord for his greatness. ___praise___
3. To KNATH Jesus for his gift of life. ___thank___
4. To KAS the Holy Spirit for what you need. ___ask___
5. To RPAY for someone else. ___pray___

B Check Understanding Draw a line from the prayers in Column A to the best description of that prayer in Column B.

Column A	Column B
6. Loving Father, you are the best!	prayer of thanksgiving
7. I bless you and love you, God.	prayer of blessing
8. Jesus help me today in school.	prayer of intercession
9. Please, Lord help Grandma get well.	prayer of praise
10. Thank you, God, for all my friends.	prayer of petition

Go to **aliveinchrist.osv.com** for an interactive review.

Chapter Review

Use Catechist Quick Reviews to highlight lesson concepts.

A Work with Words Have the children unscramble the words to find reasons to pray and write them on the line.

B Check Understanding Explain to the children that they will be drawing a line from the words of a prayer to the type of prayer.

Go to **aliveinchrist.osv.com** to prepare customized and downloadable assessments, send eAssessments, and assign interactive reviews.

UNIT 5

Unit Review

Use Catechist Quick Reviews in each chapter to highlight lesson concepts for this unit and prepare for the Unit Review.

Have the children complete the Review pages. Then discuss the answers as a group. Review any concepts with which the children are having difficulty.

A Work with Words

Instruct the children to complete each sentence with the correct word from the Word Bank.

B Check Understanding

Have the children circle the correct answer in problems 6–10.

Unit Review

UNIT 5

A Work with Words Complete each sentence with the correct word from the Word Bank.

Word Bank

- proclaim
- teachings
- Faith
- Kingdom of God
- Lord's

1. To **proclaim** Jesus is to tell about him in word and action.
2. Jesus taught us the **Lord's** Prayer.
3. **Faith** is believing in God and that he helps us understand about himself.
4. The **Kingdom of God** is in Heaven and is still being built on Earth.
5. Jesus' disciples believed in him and in his **teachings**.

B Check Understanding Circle the correct answer.

6. Who did Jesus call from the tree?
   Peter — John — **Zacchaeus** (circled)
7. Who does Jesus invite to the Kingdom of God?
   everyone (circled) — Saints — only children
8. Who is always guiding the Church's actions?
   Saints — **Holy Spirit** (circled) — disciples
9. What name do we give to rosaries and holy water?
   Sacraments — prayers — **sacramentals** (circled)
10. When will Jesus be with us?
    always (circled) — when we dream — when we sin

Morality 219

UNIT 5

Unit Review

Write the letter T if the sentence is TRUE. Write the letter F if the sentence is FALSE.

11. F Peace is when things are not calm and people do not get along.

12. T Intercession is a prayer in which we ask God to help others.

13. F A petition is a prayer in which we give God honor because he is God.

14. T Jesus asked all of his followers to share the Good News.

15. T Sometimes you can use memorized prayers to pray.

C Make Connections Circle the word or words below that tell something about God's Kingdom.

16–20.

justice (circled)	praying (circled)	stealing
ignoring someone	lying	being unfair
peace (circled)	love (circled)	kindness (circled)
sharing your gifts (circled)	being selfish	welcome (circled)

Complete each sentence below.

21. Jesus saw that Zaccheaus had **faith**.

22. God gave you time, talent, and treasure to help you share the **Good News**.

23. Prayer is a way to deepen your friendship with **God the Father, Son, and Holy Spirit**

24. Jesus taught that all people are welcomed in God's **Kingdom**.

25. When you thank God in a prayer it is called a prayer of **thanksgiving**.

B Check Understanding

Have the children write the letter *T* if the sentence is true and the letter *F* if the sentence is false for problems 11–15.

C Make Connections

Direct the children to circle the word or words that tell something about God's Kingdom for problems 16–20. Have them complete each sentence for problems 21–25.

Go to **aliveinchrist.osv.com** to prepare customized and downloadable assessments, send eAssessments, and assign interactive reviews.

UNIT
6

Sacraments

Our Catholic Tradition

- The Mass is another name for the celebration of the Eucharist. (CCC, 1332)
- The Mass has two parts: the Liturgy of the Word and the Liturgy of the Eucharist. (CCC, 1346)
- At every Mass, we hear God's Word from the Bible and pray for the Church and the needs of the world. (CCC, 1349)
- We remember Jesus' sacrifice and give thanks for it. (CCC, 1350)
- We receive Christ's Body and Blood in Holy Communion. (CCC, 1355)

How is the Mass both a holy meal and a sacrifice?

Unit 6 Overview

Chapter 16

Gather to Worship 223

The children will:

- define the Eucharist as the Sacrament in which Jesus Christ shares himself and the bread and wine become his Body and Blood
- describe the Mass as another name for the celebration of the Eucharist
- recognize that the assembly takes part in the Mass by praying, singing, and using actions to worship God
- examine the Introductory Rites of the Mass as that which gathers and unites us, preparing our hearts to hear God's Word

Catholic Social Teaching: Live Your Faith

- Call to Community, Pages 292–293
- The Dignity of Work, Pages 298–299

Chapter 17

Listen to God's Word 233

The children will:

- recognize Jesus' use of stories as a way to help us understand more about God and his Kingdom
- examine the components of the Liturgy of the Word, including readings from both the Old Testament and New Testament
- understand that the deacon or priest proclaims the Gospel reading and gives a homily to help us understand and apply God's Word to our lives
- identify that the Liturgy of the Word ends with the Creed and the Prayer of the Faithful

Catholic Social Teaching: Live Your Faith

- Call to Community, Pages 292–293
- Care for Creation, Pages 302–303

Chapter 18

Remembering Jesus' Sacrifice 243

The children will:

- explain the Mass as a memorial celebration of Jesus' Death, Resurrection, and Ascension
- describe Jesus' Death on the Cross as a sacrifice and a gift that saves all people from the power of sin and everlasting death
- appreciate the Liturgy of the Eucharist as the second main part of the Mass in which we receive Holy Communion
- discover how the gifts of bread and wine become the Body and Blood of Jesus Christ

Songs of Scripture
"The Rich Young Man"

Catholic Social Teaching: Live Your Faith

- Option for the Poor, Pages 296–297
- Human Solidarity, Pages 300–301

Preview Unit Theme

Point out that this unit focus is on Sacraments.

Ask five volunteers to each read aloud one of the bullet points under Our Catholic Tradition.

Explain that they will learn more about all of these things in the next three chapters.

Invite volunteers to describe what they see in the photos and illustration on this page. Ask them how these images connect to the unit theme.

Ask: How is the Mass both a holy meal and a sacrifice?

After some discussion, explain that the group will explore this question in the next three chapters.

KEY CONCEPT
Mass is another name for the celebration of the Eucharist. The assembly uses songs, prayers, and actions to worship God.

DOCTRINAL CONTENT

- The Eucharist is the Sacrament in which Jesus Christ shares himself and the bread and wine become his Body and Blood. (CCC, 1323–1324)
- The Mass is another name for the celebration of the Eucharist. (CCC, 1382)
- The assembly is all those gathered for Mass. We take part by praying, singing, and using actions to worship God. (CCC, 1346)
- The Introductory Rites gather and unite us, preparing our hearts to hear God's Word. (CCC, 1348–1349)

TASKS OF CATECHESIS
Helping children grow in a faith that is "known, celebrated, lived, and expressed in prayer" (NDC, 20).

This chapter focuses on the following tasks of catechesis:

- Education for Community Life
- Liturgical Education

Catechist Background

And it happened that, while he was with them at table, he took bread, said the blessing, broke it, and gave it to them. With that their eyes were opened and they recognized him, but he vanished from their sight. Then they said to each other, "Were not our hearts burning [within us] while he spoke to us on the way and opened the scriptures to us?" Luke 24:30–32

➔ **Reflect** Has your heart ever burned at the words in the Scripture?

The communal life was part of the Church, according to the Acts of the Apostles, from the very beginning. Those thousands of people baptized on Pentecost morning became the first Eucharistic assembly, gathering to share the Good News that they could not keep to themselves. So life-changing was this experience for many people that they gave up their jobs, their wealth, and their homes to become part of a community of faith.

Most of us are not called to so literal a life of community. We keep our daily lives, our ordinary jobs, our single-family homes. But every Sunday (or Saturday evening), we do what Christians have been doing since the first Lord's Day. We gather with our sisters and brothers to devote ourselves to prayer, the teaching of the Apostles, and the breaking of the bread. Mass can be celebrated, under certain circumstances, by a priest alone, but it is only in the presence of the full, active, celebrating assembly that the liturgy lives up to its name in the original Greek, "the work of the people."

➔ **Reflect** What do you value most about being part of the Eucharistic assembly?

Catechist's Prayer

Lord of the Sabbath, welcome me into the joyful assembly and grant me the rest that renews and refreshes. Help me serve as a living witness to the children of the blessings of full participation in the Mass. Amen.

Lesson Plan

Objectives	Process	Materials
Invite, 10 minutes		
Gather to Worship Page 223	**Psalm 92:2–3** Pray the opening prayer. **Luke 24:30–32** Reflect prayerfully on the Word. • Discuss What Do You Wonder questions.	**Optional Activity** Chapter Story: "The Invitation"
Discover, 35 minutes		
Celebrating the Eucharist Pages 224–225 • Define the Eucharist as the Sacrament in which Jesus Christ shares himself and the bread and wine become his Body and Blood • Describe the Mass as another name for the celebration of the Eucharist • Recognize that the assembly takes part in the Mass by praying, singing, and using actions to worship God	• **Catholic Faith Words** Eucharist, Mass, assembly ☆ Underline things that Jesus' followers did that parishes do now. **Acts 2:42–47** Proclaim "The Community Gathers." • Discuss taking part in the assembly. • Review definitions in the text. • **Share Your Faith Activity** Write one way to get ready to take part in the Mass.	☐ pencils or pens ☐ board or chart paper ☐ index cards, three per child
The Introductory Rites Pages 226–227 • Examine the Introductory Rite of the Mass as that which gathers and unites us, preparing our hearts to hear God's Word	• Learn what happens after the procession ends. ☆ Underline the assembly's responses at Mass. • Talk about when we sing the Gloria. • **Connect Your Faith Activity** Unscramble the words to find the name of a hymn.	☐ pencils or pens
Live, 15 minutes		
Our Catholic Life Pages 228–229	• Discover ways to join in the Mass. • **People of Faith** Learn about Saint Tarcisius. • **Live Your Faith Activity** Draw a picture of taking part in Mass.	☐ pencils or pens ☐ crayons, colored pencils, or markers • **Optional Activity** Match Words and Actions ☐ Activity Master 16 (Page 223E)
Prayer of Praise Page 230	• Divide larger group into three smaller groups. • Follow the order of prayer. Finish by singing "We Glorify You."	Download "We Glorify You."

Family + Faith Page 231

Point out that the Catholic Families page provides chapter highlights, information on how second graders understand faith concepts, and family prayer.

Chapter Review Page 232

aliveinchrist.osv.com

• Customize and Download Assessments
• Email Links to eAssessments
• Interactive Student Reviews

ONLINE RESOURCES

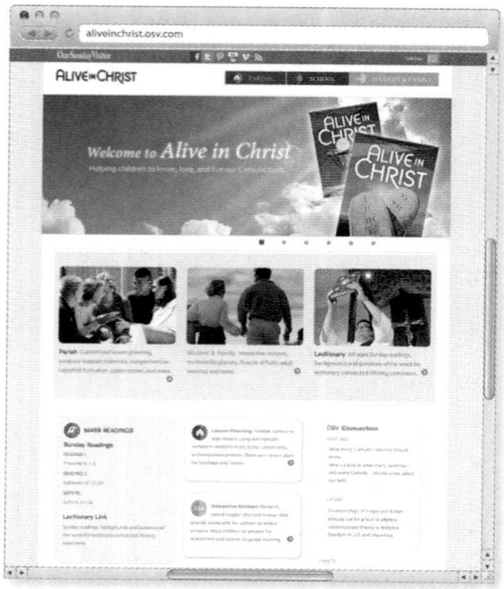

Go to **aliveinchrist.osv.com**

You will find:

- Interactive lesson planning with web specific content and additional activities
- Step by step lesson instruction from printed Catechist Edition for integrated lesson planning
- Custom-built assessments to download and eAssessment links
- Interactive reviews that provide scores and the option to review answers
- Sunday readings with background and questions of the week

Go to **osvparish.com**

You will find:

- Ask the Experts Q and A
- General Catechist Helps
- Community Connections and Blogs

Sharing the Message with Second Graders

The Mass Second graders may see the Mass as primarily an adult activity, but they are preparing to join together with the parish in the Eucharistic celebration on the day of their First Communion. It's important that they are able to really share in the celebration by being familiar with the liturgy and its meaning. They are ready to understand in more detail the parts of the Mass, their meanings, and how to participate fully.

Teaching Tip: Consider arranging an opportunity to meet and sit together for a Sunday Mass. Include whole families in this activity. Provide liturgical aids for the children, like a child-friendly missal, so they can follow along and participate.

How Second Graders Understand

- Second graders don't like to feel left out. Help them find ways to feel welcome at Mass.
- Children this age have their own gifts. Help them see how these might blossom into liturgical ministries.
- Older siblings can be good role models. Encourage them to help their younger siblings participate more fully at Mass.

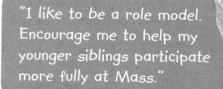

"I like to be a role model. Encourage me to help my younger siblings participate more fully at Mass."

Chapter Connections

Chapter Story

Invite

"The Invitation"

Use this story to expand the chapter introduction.

- Discuss how being welcomed makes one feel like part of a group.
- Have the children tell about a time when someone made them feel welcome.
- Have them share what they have learned about welcoming others.

Go to **aliveinchrist.osv.com** Lesson Planning section for this story.

NCEA IFG: ACRE Edition

Discover

Communal Life

- Objectives: To understand the origin, mission, structure, and communal nature of the Church; to know the rights and responsibilities of the Christian faithful

Liturgical Life

- Objective: To know the Paschal Mystery of Jesus in the Church's liturgical life—feasts, seasons, symbols, and practices and in the Sacraments as signs and instruments of grace.

Catholic Social Teaching

Live

Use one of these features to introduce a principle and engage the children with an activity.

- Call to Community, Pages 292–293
- The Dignity of Work, Pages 298–299

Music Options

Use one or more of the following songs to enhance catechetical learning or for prayer.

- "We Glorify You," Live Prayer, Page 230
- "We Come to Worship You," Discover, Page 225
- "And With Your Spirit," Discover, Page 226
- "We Gather Around Your Throne," Live, Page 229

LECTIONARY CONNECTION

Chapter 16 highlights Lectionary-connected themes such as the Eucharist, Mass, and assembly. If your parish aligns its curriculum to the liturgical year, you could use this chapter in connection with the following Sundays.

Year A

Twenty-fourth Sunday in Ordinary Time—Forgiveness and Mercy

Feast of All Saints—Triumph of the Elect

Year B

Seventeenth Sunday in Ordinary Time—Mass

Twentieth Sunday in Ordinary Time—Mass

Year C

The Most Holy Body and Blood of Christ—Mass

Twenty-second Sunday in Ordinary Time—Mass

Go to **aliveinchrist.osv.com** for a complete correlation ordered by the Sundays of the year and suggestions for how to integrate the Scripture readings into chapter lessons.

Name ______________________________ Date ______________

Match Words and Actions

Draw a line from the words in Column A to the correct action in Column B.

Column A	Column B
1. "In the name of the Father, and of the Son, and of the Holy Spirit."	Stand.
2. entrance procession	Sing.
3. gathering song	Give praise and honor to God.
4. "Lord, have mercy"	Make the Sign of the Cross.
5. "Glory to God in the highest"	Ask God's forgiveness.

Draw a picture that shows one of the Mass actions listed above.

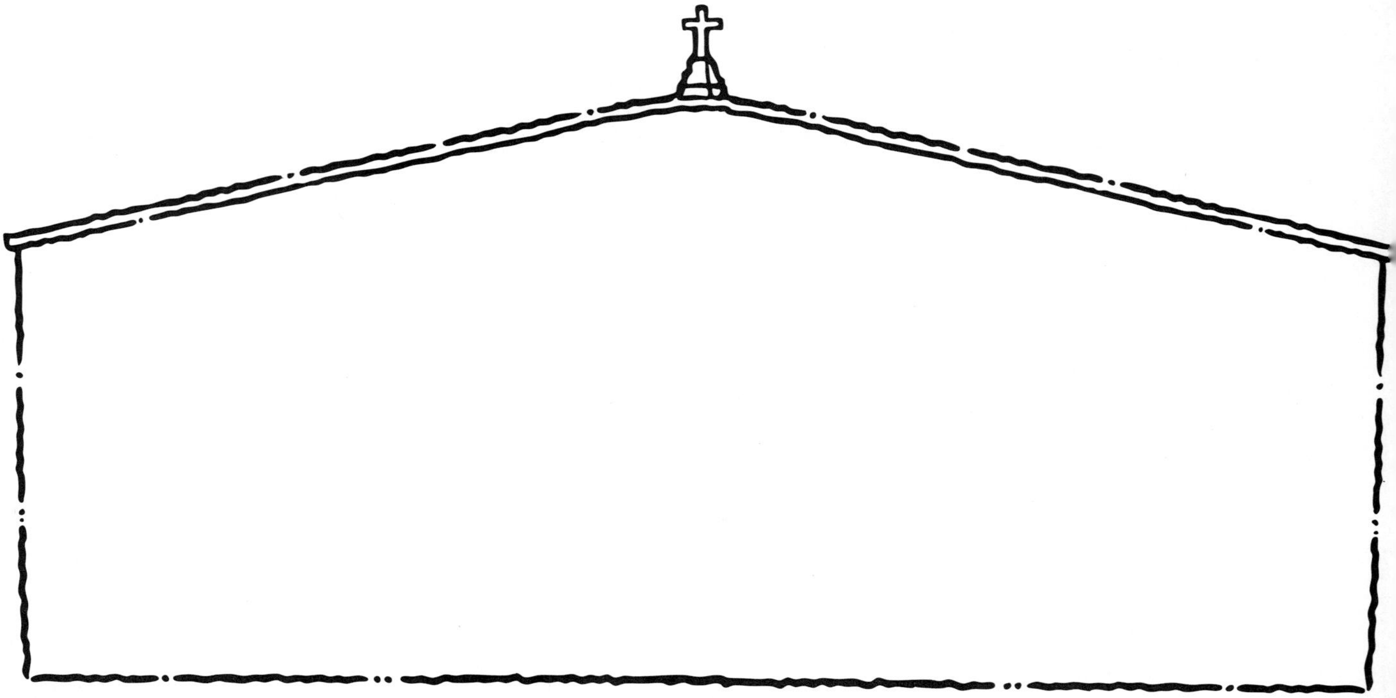

CHAPTER 16

Invite

Gather to Worship

Let Us Pray

Leader: God, we gather to worship with you.

"It is good to give thanks to the LORD…
To proclaim your love at daybreak,
your faithfulness in the night…" Psalm 92:2–3

All: Thank you, God, for being with us and filling us with your grace. Amen.

God's Word

And it happened that, while he was with them at table, he took bread, said the blessing, broke it, and gave it to them. With that their eyes were opened and they recognized him, but he vanished from their sight. Then they said to each other, "Were not our hearts burning [within us] while he spoke to us on the way and opened the scriptures to us?" Luke 24:30–32

What Do You Wonder?

- Where do you go to be fed by Jesus?
- How does Jesus feed you?

Optional Activity

Chapter Story: "The Invitation" *Verbal/Linguisitic*

Use this story after the opening prayer, before telling the children that Jesus invites us to gather and pray.

- Ask the children if they have ever received an invitation to a party or an event.
- Read aloud "The Invitation."
- After discussing being welcomed and welcoming others, transition back to the lesson instruction.

Go to **aliveinchrist.osv.com** for Chapter Story.

Invite

Let Us Pray

Invite the children to gather in the prayer space and make the Sign of the Cross. Pray aloud the leader's prayer and Psalm verse. Have a volunteer pray the verse a second time. Prompt the group to respond.

Have the children move from the prayer space back to their seats.

Explain that Jesus invites us to gather with each other to pray and worship our God.

Say: Let's listen to hear what happened when Jesus appeared to his friends after he rose from the dead.

God's Word

Guide the children through the process of Scripture reflection.

- Invite them to close their eyes, be still, and open their minds and hearts to what God is saying to them in this passage.
- Proclaim the Scripture.
- Maintain several moments of silence.
- *Ask:* What did you hear God say to you today?
- Invite volunteers to share.

What Do You Wonder?

Say: The disciples of Jesus invite us to gather to be fed by Jesus as they were.

Invite the children to respond to the questions. Ask what else they might wonder about gathering to worship together.

Discover

Objectives

- Define the Eucharist as the Sacrament in which Jesus Christ shares himself and the bread and wine become his Body and Blood
- Describe the Mass as another name for the celebration of the Eucharist
- Recognize that the assembly takes part in the Mass by praying, singing, and using actions to worship God

Celebrating the Eucharist

Read aloud the question at the top of the student page.

- Allow time for responses and discussion.

Ask two volunteers to read aloud the two paragraphs.

Write *Mass = Eucharist* on the board or on chart paper to show that these two names are interchangeable.

God's Word

Proclaim the Scripture passage from Acts.

- *Ask:* Why do you think the first followers gathered together? When does your parish community get together?
- Encourage the children to give examples.

☆ Instruct the children to underline the things that Jesus' first followers did that their parish community does also.

- Allow time for the children to reread or scan the text and underline their answers.

Celebrating the Eucharist

Who gathers for the Mass?

How much do you look forward to your birthday or Christmas? We gather with people we love to celebrate and share these important events.

Celebrations are an important part of Church life, too. The **Eucharist** is the Sacrament in which Jesus shares himself with us and the bread and wine become his Body and Blood. Since the beginning, followers of Jesus have come together to worship.

☆ Underline the things that Jesus' first followers did that your parish community does, too.

God's Word

The Community Gathers

After the Holy Spirit came, Jesus' followers met often to learn from the Apostles, to break bread together, and to pray. Some of the members sold what they had and gave the money to help the others. Still others shared their belongings with those who were in need. These followers of Jesus were very happy, and new members joined every day.

Based on Acts 2:42–47

Scripture Background

Acts 2:42–47

Many of the first followers of Jesus were Jews.

- They participated in the daily prayers at the synagogue, but celebrated the Lord's Supper in large home gatherings.
- Even when Christianity separated itself from Judaism, and the Mass began to be celebrated in churches, the order of the Liturgy kept elements from the Jewish service.

We Gather

Mass is another name for the celebration of the Eucharist. Every Sunday, people wave and greet each other as they walk toward their church. As we enter the church, we dip our hands in holy water and make the Sign of the Cross. This action reminds us of our Baptism.

All those gathered together make up the **assembly**. We take part in the Mass by praying, singing, and using actions to worship God.

As the Mass begins, the assembly stands. We all sing a gathering song. The altar servers enter carrying a cross in a procession. The readers, deacon, and priest follow. They are singing, too.

Catholic Faith Words

Eucharist the Sacrament in which Jesus shares himself, and the bread and wine become his Body and Blood

Mass the gathering of Catholics to worship God. It includes the Liturgy of the Word and the Liturgy of the Eucharist.

assembly the people gathered together for worship

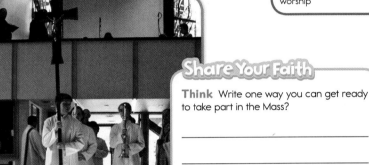

Share Your Faith

Think Write one way you can get ready to take part in the Mass?

____

____

Share Talk about what happens in your home or parish before Mass begins.

We Gather

Invite three volunteers to each read aloud one of the paragraphs.

Ask: When do we stand? when the Mass begins When do the altar servers enter? while we are singing the gathering song Do the readers, deacon, and priest sing the gathering song as they enter? yes

Work with Words

Help the children sound out the Catholic Faith Words.

- As the words are sounded out, have the children circle familiar words and put question marks by unfamiliar words.
- Ask where they heard the words that are familiar to them.
- Have the children write the words and definitions on index cards, which they can use as flash cards for chapter or unit reviews.

Music Option: Have the children sing "We Come to Worship You," downloaded from **aliveinchrist.osv.com**.

Activity

Read aloud the directions for the Share Your Faith activity.

- Allow the children time to write their responses.
- Ask volunteers to share what happens before the Mass.

Optional Activity

Liturgical Calendar *Mathematical/Logical*

Have the children make calendars for one or more months.

- Show the children how to calculate the dates for their calendars.
- Encourage the children to mark the Sundays with special signs; remind them to participate in the Mass.
- You might also want to provide them with any special feast days celebrated during those months that they can add to their calendars.

Go to **aliveinchrist.osv.com** for information regarding the Church year.

Quick Review

The Mass is another name for the celebration of Eucharist. The Eucharist is the Sacrament in which Christ shares himself and the bread and wine become his Body and Blood.

Discover

Objective

- Examine the Introductory Rites of the Mass as that which gathers and unites us, preparing our hearts to hear God's Word

The Introductory Rites

Tell the children that this section will focus on how the Mass begins.

Read aloud the two paragraphs. At the end of the second paragraph, encourage the group response after you read each line that is normally said by the priest.

Ask: What does the priest lead the assembly in making? The Sign of the Cross

Say: Let's demonstrate it.

- Lead the children in praying the Sign of the Cross.

Ask: What does the priest say when he greets the assembly? "The Lord be with you."

☆ Now ask the children to underline the responses that they say at Mass.

- Give the children time to reread the text and underline their responses.

Music Option: Have the children sing "And With Your Spirit," downloaded from **aliveinchrist.osv.com**.

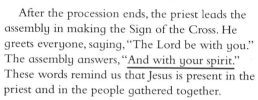

The Introductory Rites

What happens as Mass begins?

☆ Underline the responses that you say at Mass.

After the procession ends, the priest leads the assembly in making the Sign of the Cross. He greets everyone, saying, "The Lord be with you." The assembly answers, "And with your spirit." These words remind us that Jesus is present in the priest and in the people gathered together.

Next, the members of the assembly recall God's forgiveness. The priest asks us to think of times they may have hurt others. We ask for God's mercy and for him to forgive us for any wrong we have done during the week. We say together,

Priest: Lord, have mercy.
All: Lord, have, mercy.
Priest: Christ, have mercy.
All: Christ, have, mercy.
Priest: Lord, have mercy.
All: Lord, have, mercy.

Quick Tip

Keeping the Lord's Day

Remind the children that participating at Mass is only part of fulfilling the Commandment to keep the Lord's Day.

- Encourage the children to think of ways they can help older family members have time to rest on Sunday.
- Brainstorm ways that family members can relax, pray, and help others on Sunday.
- Remind the children that Sundays are also good days to enjoy nature and show our appreciation to the Creator.

Words of Praise

With God's forgiveness in your heart, you are better able to pray and take part in the Mass. Many times during the year, the Gloria is sung or prayed during Mass. This is a very old hymn that the Church prays to give praise and honor the Holy Trinity. The hymn begins with these words.

All: Glory to God in the highest, and on earth peace to people of good will.

After this song, the priest invites the people to pray. The priest and assembly are silent for a few moments. The priest then prays the opening prayer, and the people respond "Amen." The Introductory Rites have ended. All gathered are now ready for the first main part of the Mass.

Connect Your Faith

Unscramble the Words Find the name of the hymn that we sing during Mass.

LRGOY TO ODG IN HTE SEGHITH

G L O R Y
T O G O D
I N T H E
H I G H E S T

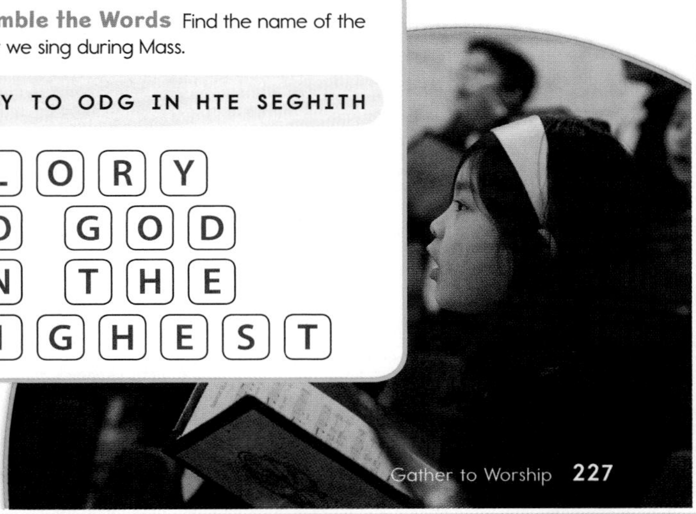

Words of Praise

Ask the children to silently read the paragraphs on this page.

- *Ask:* What helps us better participate in the Mass? forgiveness in our hearts

Have the children underline the words they say at Mass on this page also.

Activity

Read aloud the directions for the Connect Your Faith activity.

- Allow time for the children to solve the puzzle.
- Ask a volunteer to share the song title.

Ask the children to describe what they see and what is happening in the photograph on this page.

Quick Review

When the assembly gathers for Mass, we take part by praying, singing, and using actions to worship God. The Introductory Rites of the Mass gather and unite us, preparing our hearts to hear God's Word.

Catechist Background

Gloria

The *Gloria* begins with the words sung to the shepherds by the angels at the Nativity (Luke 2:14). The Student Book reflects the language change made when we began to implement the English translation of the Third Edition of *the Roman Missal* in November 2011.

- The prayer follows the form of many scriptural hymns.
- Review the words of the *Gloria*, helping the children identify the praises of Father, Son, and Holy Spirit. Invite them to turn to page 322 of the Our Catholic Tradition section in the back of their books and read the *Gloria*. Ask volunteers to each read a paragraph.

Our Catholic Life

Read aloud the question.

- Discuss the children's responses. Tell the children that they may discover more ways to participate after you have covered this page.

Ask a volunteer to read aloud the paragraphs.

- *Ask:* Who leads us in the celebration of the Mass?
  the priest

Ways to Join in the Mass

Ask a different volunteer to read aloud each bullet point on ways to join in the Mass.

- Have the children share the ways they like to join in the Mass. See if there are any other ideas that could be added to this list.

Help the children understand that participation in the Sunday Mass is required. However, don't put the children on the spot about individual attendance; instead, be general and inclusive when discussing participation.

Our Catholic Life

How can you take part in the celebration of the Mass?

The priest leads us in the celebration of the Mass. But he is not the only person celebrating. The whole assembly gathers to praise and give thanks to God.

You are part of the assembly. You don't go to Mass to watch but to take part in the celebration. Taking part in the Mass will help you grow closer to Jesus in the Eucharist.

Ways to Join In the Mass

- Get to know the parts of the Mass.
- Learn the prayers and responses.
- Arrive on time and ready to participate.
- Greet and be friendly to the other people in the assembly.
- Join in the singing.
- Follow the actions of the priest, deacon, and other ministers.
- Listen to all of the readings and the homily.
- Show respect in the way you stand, sit, and kneel.

Optional Activity

Activity Master 16: Match Words and Actions

Distribute copies of the activity found on catechist page 223E.

- Read aloud the directions, and have the children work in pairs.
- As an alternative, you may wish to send this activity home with the children.

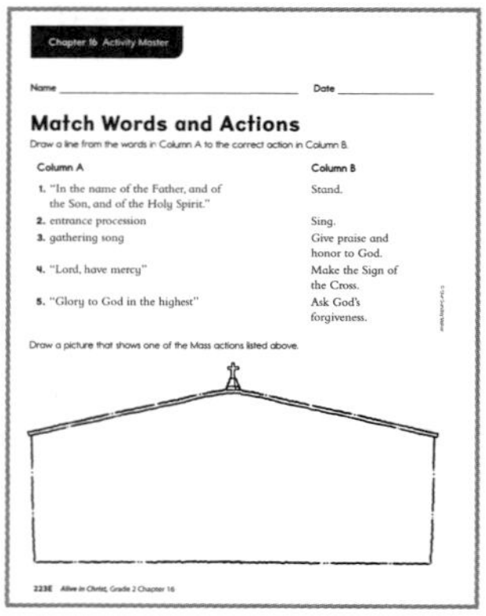

Chapter 16 Activity Master

Name ______ Date ______

Match Words and Actions

Draw a line from the words in Column A to the correct action in Column B.

Column A	Column B
1. "In the name of the Father, and of the Son, and of the Holy Spirit."	Stand.
2. entrance procession	Sing.
3. gathering song	Give praise and honor to God.
4. "Lord, have mercy"	Make the Sign of the Cross.
5. "Glory to God in the highest"	Ask God's forgiveness.

Draw a picture that shows one of the Mass actions listed above.

223E Alive in Christ, Grade 2 Chapter 16

People of Faith

Saint Tarcisius, third or fourth century AD

August 15

Saint Tarcisius lived in Rome. He loved Jesus very much. One day, he secretly carried the Eucharist to Christians who were jailed because of their faith in Jesus. Some people who were not Christians discovered what he did. They wanted to take the Eucharist from him. They threw stones at him and killed him. When they looked at his robes they saw that the Eucharist had disappeared! Saint Tarcisius reminds us to always respect the Eucharist because it is Jesus.

Discuss: How can you show respect for Jesus in the Eucharist?

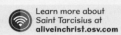

Learn more about Saint Tarcisius at **aliveinchrist.osv.com**

Live Your Faith

Picture Yourself Celebrating
Draw yourself taking part in the Mass with your family and with other members of the assembly.

Catholic Social Teaching

Chapter Connections

To integrate Catholic Social Teaching into your lesson, choose one of the following features: Call to Community, pages 292–293; or The Dignity of Work, pages 298–299.

- Start the Live step of the process by talking about Saint Tarcisius on page 229. Then move directly to the Catholic Social Teaching feature.
- Or, to expand the lesson, complete both pages 228 and 229, then move to the Catholic Social Teaching feature.
- Return to Chapter 16 for the prayer on page 230.

People of Faith

Tell the children about Saint Tarcisius.

- Tarcisius was a 12-year-old altar server during the Roman persecutions in the third century.
- Each day, after the Christians gathered in a secret place for Mass, a deacon would be sent to the prisons to carry the Eucharist to Christians who were sentenced to die.
- One day, there was no deacon to send, and so Saint Tarcisius was sent to deliver the Eucharist.
- On the way, he was stopped by boys his own age who were not Christians. Because Tarcisius would not show them the Christian "Mysteries," they turned on him. He later died from his injuries.
- Saint Tarcisius reminds us to always respect the Eucharist because it is Jesus.
- Allow volunteers to answer the Discuss question.

Encourage the children to go to **aliveinchrist.osv.com** at home to learn more about Saint Tarcisius.

Activity

Read aloud the directions for the Live Your Faith activity.

- Provide the children with crayons, colored pencils, or markers.
- Allow time for the children to draw.

Music Option: Have the children sing "We Gather Around Your Throne," downloaded from **aliveinchrist.osv.com**.

Live

Let Us Pray
Prayer of Praise

Prepare
Arrange the large group into three smaller groups.

- Assign each group a number.
- Allow time for each group to review their parts and remind them to carry their books with them into the prayer space.

Rehearse with the children "We Glorify You," downloaded from **aliveinchrist.osv.com**.

Gather
Lead the children in procession to the prayer space, singing together the refrain for "We Glorify You."

Pray
Follow the order of prayer on the student page.

Conclude by having the children process around the room and back to their seats, singing together "We Glorify You."

Let Us Pray

Prayer of Praise

Gather and begin with the Sign of the Cross.

All: In the name of the Father,

Group 1: the maker of stars and planets, oceans and mountains,

Group 2: who created all living things,

Group 3: who brought us to life and keeps us alive today and all our days.

All: And of the Son,

Group 1: God who became man,

Group 2: who taught us and celebrated with us,

Group 3: who died and rose to save us.

All: And of the Holy Spirit,

Group 1: who guides, strengthens, and helps us,

Group 2: who remains in our hearts,

Group 3: who will be with us to the end.

All: Amen.

Sing "We Glorify You"

God the Father, we praise you.
God the Father, we bless you.
God the Father, we adore you.
God the Father, we glorify you.
Jesus Christ, we praise you…
Holy Spirit, we praise you…

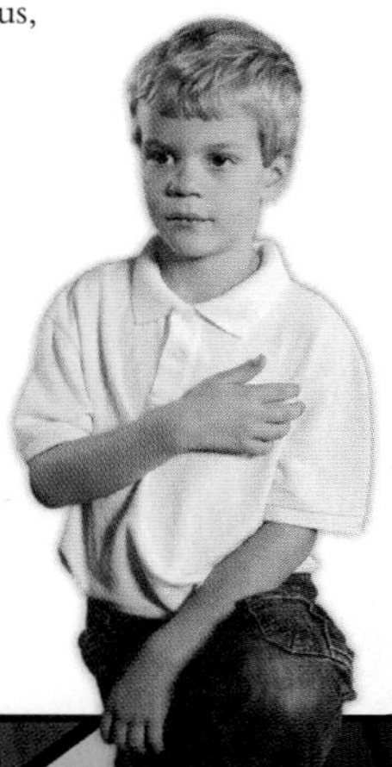

Liturgy Link

Ministers of Hospitality
Ministers of hospitality, often referred to as ushers or greeters, are the visible sign of a parish community's hospitality.

- Their task is to greet people, to make them feel welcome, to assist individuals with disabilities, to help the assembly to gather together, and to take up the collection.
- If possible, invite ministers of hospitality to speak with the children on becoming more involved in the liturgical celebration.

Go to **aliveinchrist.osv.com** for Sunday readings, Scripture background, questions of the week, and seasonal resources.

FAMILY+FAITH

LIVING AND LEARNING TOGETHER

YOUR CHILD LEARNED >>>

This chapter is about gathering as the Church at Mass to praise God and how our community takes part in the celebration.

God's Word

Read **Luke 24:30–32** to learn more about longing for Jesus in the Eucharist.

Catholics Believe

- Mass is another name for the celebration of the Eucharist.
- The assembly uses songs, prayers, and actions to worship God.

To learn more, go to the *Catechism of the Catholic Church* #1141–1142 at **usccb.org**.

People of Faith

This week, your child met Saint Tarcisius of Rome, who risked his life and was eventually killed while trying to bring the Eucharist to imprisoned Christians.

CHILDREN AT THIS AGE >>>

How They Understand the Mass Second-graders may see the Mass as primarily an adult activity, but they are preparing to join together with the parish in the Eucharistic celebration on the day of their First Communion. It's important that they are able to really share in the celebration by being familiar with the liturgy and its meaning. They are ready to understand in more detail the parts of the Mass, their meanings, and how to participate fully. A child-friendly missal can assist children in becoming more familiar with the Mass and following along with the prayers, responses, and readings.

CONSIDER THIS >>>

How important is it for you to gather with those you love to celebrate important moments?

There is a reason that the day before Thanksgiving and Christmas are peak travel times. Sitting at the table with those we love feeds our soul. At Mass, we gather in celebration to give thanks and praise for the love of our God. "The Christian community united by the Holy Spirit, gathers for worship in response to God's call. Jesus, our High Priest, is the principal agent of our celebration" (*USCCA, p. 218*).

LET'S TALK >>>

- Ask your child to explain what happens at the beginning of Mass.
- Talk about ways your family participates in the Mass and can serve in the celebration.

LET'S PRAY >>>

Almighty God, help us be generous in our gifts to the Church. Venerable Pierre Toussaint, pray for us. Amen.

For a multimedia glossary of Catholic Faith Words, Sunday readings, seasonal and Saint resources, and chapter activities go to **aliveinchrist.osv.com**.

Family + Faith

Distribute the page to the children or parents/adult family members. Point out the chapter highlights, insights on how second graders understand concepts, the opportunity for the adults to reflect on their own experience and faith journey, and the family prayer.

Chapter 16 Review

A Work with Words Circle the correct answer.

1. The ____ is the great celebration of the Church.
   (Eucharist) assembly procession
2. At Mass, the whole ____ gathers to praise God.
   class (assembly) neighborhood
3. The ____ is a very old hymn that the Church prays to give praise and honor to God.
   Amen opening prayer (Gloria)
4. As Mass begins the assembly sings the ____.
   (gathering song) Sign of the Cross Lord's Prayer
5. Taking part in the Mass helps us grow closer to ____.
   (Jesus) the priest the deacon

B Check Understanding Use the numbers 1 to 5 to put the actions in the order they happen at Mass.

6. [2] The altar servers, readers, deacon, and priest process into the church.
7. [3] The priest leads us in the Sign of the Cross.
8. [4] The priest says, "The Lord be with you."
9. [1] The assembly gathers.
10. [5] The priest and assembly say, "Lord, have mercy."

Go to **aliveinchrist.osv.com** for an interactive review.

Chapter Review

Use Catechist Quick Reviews to highlight lesson concepts.

A Work with Words
Have the children circle the correct answer.

B Check Understanding
Explain to the children that they will use numbers 1 through 5 to order the actions in Mass.

Go to **aliveinchrist.osv.com** to prepare customized and downloadable assessments, send eAssessments, and assign interactive reviews.

Listen to God's Word

KEY CONCEPT

In the Liturgy of the Word, God's living Word is read. We profess what we believe about God and pray for the needs of the Church and the world.

DOCTRINAL CONTENT

- Jesus used stories as a way to help us understand more about God and his Kingdom. (CCC, 2613)
- The first main part of the Mass is the Liturgy of the Word during which we hear readings from both the Old Testament and New Testament. (CCC, 1154)
- We listen to the deacon or priest proclaim the Gospel reading and give a homily to help us understand and apply God's Word to our lives. (CCC, 131–132, 1349)
- This part of the Mass ends with the Creed and Prayer of the Faithful. (CCC, 1184, 1346)

TASKS OF CATECHESIS

Helping children grow in a faith that is "known, celebrated, lived, and expressed in prayer" (NDC, 20).

This chapter focuses on the following tasks of catechesis:

- Promoting Knowledge of the Faith
- Liturgical Education

Catechist Background

Then he said, "What is the kingdom of God like? To what can I compare it? It is like a mustard seed that a person took and planted in the garden. When it was fully grown, it became a large bush and 'the birds of the sky dwelt in its branches.'"
Luke 13:18–19

➔ **Reflect** Do you feel that you are an active, working part of God's Kingdom?

Why do English translations of this passage from Luke retain the Old English word *dwelt*, instead of substituting *lived* or *resided*? Maybe it's because the particular combination of sounds in the word dwelt evokes a sense of home and comfort that is missing from the modern synonyms. Like the Colossians who were invited to let the word of God dwell in them (see Col. 3:16), we are invited to bring God's Word home with us and let it move in. If we allow the Word to dwell in us "richly," as Saint Paul suggests, it will put down roots in our hearts and bear fruit.

But we are also called to *dwell* in the Word—to find our own shelter and sustenance in the Scriptures, and to grow closer to the living Word of God, Jesus. Here's where it's important to remember a bit of trivia about the word *dwell*. Its original meaning was not "to make a home" but the very opposite—"to stray," "to wander away." Only over time did *dwell* come to mean "to tarry," "to spend time with." Our lives are full of distractions that cause us to stray and to wander from our true dwelling place in God's love. But if we take time to tarry with the Word, we will always find our way home.

➔ **Reflect** How can you invite the Word of God home with you and spend time with it this week?

Catechist's Prayer

Jesus, Word of God, be at home in my heart. Give me a listening spirit, a hungry mind, and a welcoming silence in which your Word can dwell. Amen.

Lesson Plan

Objectives	Process	Materials
Invite, 10 minutes		
Listen to God's Word Page 233	**Psalm 130:5** Pray the opening prayer. **Luke 13:18–21** Reflect prayerfully on the Word. • Discuss What Do You Wonder questions.	**Optional Activity** Chapter Story: "Story Time"
Discover, 35 minutes		
God's Word Proclaimed Pages 234–235 • Recognize Jesus' use of stories as a way to help us understand more about God and his Kingdom • Examine the components of the Liturgy of the Word, including readings from both the Old Testament and New Testament	• **Catholic Faith Words** Liturgy of the Word • Learn about Jesus' parables. ☆ Color the mustard bush. **Matthew 13:31–32** Proclaim "The Mustard Seed" ☆ Indicate where the readings of the Liturgy of the Word come from. • **Share Your Faith Activity** Complete the sentence on how to learn about God.	☐ pencils or pens ☐ crayons, colored pencils, or markers ☐ board or chart paper ☐ index cards, one per child
The Good News Pages 236–237 • Understand that the deacon or priest proclaims the Gospel reading and gives a homily to help us understand and apply God's Word to our lives • Identify that the Liturgy of the Word ends with the Creed and the Prayer of the Faithful	• **Catholic Faith Words** homily, creed, Prayer of the Faithful • Review the process of the Liturgy of the Word. • Talk about what the assembly does after after the homily. • Learn about the creed and the Prayer of the Faithful. • **Connect Your Faith Activity** Write prayers.	☐ pencils or pens ☐ board or chart paper ☐ index cards, three per child • **Optional Activity** The Liturgy of the Word ☐ Activity Master 17 (Page 233E)
Live, 15 minutes		
Our Catholic Life Pages 238–239	• Learn how Jesus used stories to teach. ☆ Match the story to the description. • **People of Faith** Learn about Saint Paul. • **Live Your Faith Activity** Plan a parable play.	☐ pencils or pens ☐ optional: props, headdresses, costumes, painted backdrop
Celebration of the Word Page 240	• Choose a leader and two readers. • Follow the order of prayer. Finish with "Gospel Acclamation/Alleluia."	☐ Bible and stand Download "Gospel Acclamation/Alleluia."

Family + Faith Page 241
Point out that the Catholic Families page provides chapter highlights, information on how second graders understand faith concepts, and family prayer.

Chapter Review Page 242
aliveinchrist.osv.com
- Customize and Download Assessments
- Email Links to eAssessments
- Interactive Student Reviews

ONLINE RESOURCES

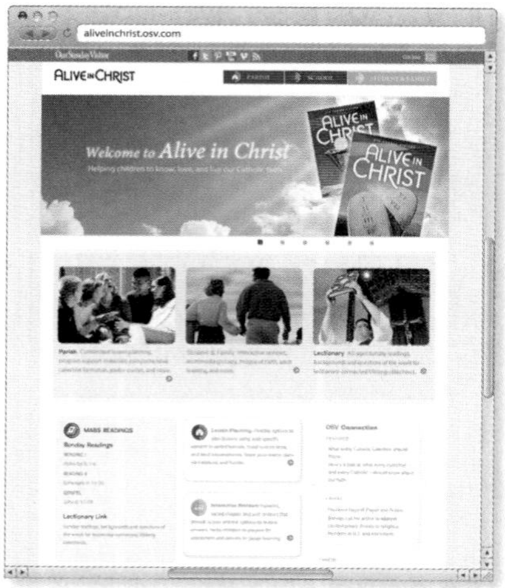

Go to **aliveinchrist.osv.com**

You will find:

- Interactive lesson planning with web specific content and additional activities
- Step by step lesson instruction from printed Catechist Edition for integrated lesson planning
- Custom-built assessments to download and eAssessment links
- Interactive reviews that provide scores and the option to review answers
- Sunday readings with background and questions of the week

Go to **osvparish.com**

You will find:

- Ask the Experts Q and A
- General Catechist Helps
- Community Connections and Blogs

Sharing the Message with Second Graders

The Liturgy of the Word Second graders might not have yet picked up the connection between the Lectionary readings in Mass. Paying attention to the relationship between each Sunday's passages from the Old Testament, Psalms, New Testament, and Gospel will help with their overall understanding of the Scriptures and will encourage more active participation in the Mass. Some discussion about the readings prior to Mass can help to facilitate this.

Teaching Tip: Spend a minute or two talking about the readings for the upcoming week. Prompt the children for something they could be listening for, and ask about it the next week.

How Second-Graders Understand

- Second graders love stories. Help them listen to and understand the stories from the Bible that they hear on Sunday morning.
- Children this age are learning the meaning of symbolic language, so help them practice by reading fables, riddles, and poems.
- Some children like to share the message of God's Word; give them opportunities to share the Word with younger children.

"I love stories. Help me listen to and understand the stories from the Bible that I hear on Sunday morning."

Chapter Connections

Chapter Story

Invite

"Story Time"

Use this story to expand the chapter introduction.

- Organize the children in several small groups.
- Have group members share and discuss their favorite story.
- Ask each group to choose one story to share with the class.

Go to **aliveinchrist.osv.com** Lesson Planning section for this story.

NCEA IFG: ACRE Edition

Discover

Knowledge of the Faith

- Objective: To know and understand basic Catholic teaching about the Incarnate Word Jesus Christ as the way, truth, and life

Liturgical Life

- Objective: To know the Paschal Mystery of Jesus in the Church's liturgical life—feasts, seasons, symbols, and practices and in the Sacraments as signs and instruments of grace

Catholic Social Teaching

Live

Use one of these features to introduce a principle and engage the children with an activity.

- Call to Community, Pages 292–293
- Care for Creation, Pages 302–303

Music Options

Use one or more of the following songs to enhance catechetical learning or for prayer.

- "Gospel Acclamation/Alleluia," Live Prayer, Page 240
- "Jesus' Stories," Discover, Page 234
- "Jesus Is the Word," Discover, Page 235
- "We Hear God's Word," Discover, Page 236

LECTIONARY CONNECTION

Chapter 17 highlights Lectionary-connected themes such as the Liturgy of the Word, creed, and Prayer of the Faithful. If your parish aligns its curriculum to the liturgical year, you could use this chapter in connection with the following readings.

Year A

Immaculate Conception of the Blessed Virgin Mary— Father's Plan

Fifth Sunday of Easter—Living Stones

Year B

Fourteenth Sunday in Ordinary Time—God's Word

Thirty-first Sunday in Ordinary Time—Liturgy of the Word

Year C

Third Sunday of Advent—Bible

Third Sunday of Easter—God's Word

Go to **aliveinchrist.osv.com** for a complete correlation ordered by the Sundays of the year and suggestions for how to integrate the Scripture readings into chapter lessons.

Name ______________________________ Date ______________

The Liturgy of the Word

Each dotted strip below has the name of a part of the Liturgy of the Word. Cut out the strips along the dotted lines. Put the parts in the correct order. Then have a partner check your answers.

Alleluia

Prayer of the Faithful

New Testament Letter

homily

Psalm

Old Testament reading

Creed

Gospel reading

CHAPTER 17 Invite

Listen to God's Word

Let Us Pray

Leader: Lord, your Word gives us hope.

"I wait for the LORD,
my soul waits
and I hope for his word." Psalm 130:5

All: God, open my ears so I can better hear your Word. Amen.

God's Word

Jesus said, "What is God's Kingdom like? What can I compare it with? It is like what happens when a woman mixes a tiny little bit of yeast into a batch of flour. The yeast makes the whole batch of dough rise."
Based on Luke 13:18–21

What Do You Wonder?

- How are the stories in the Bible different from other stories?
- Can the Word of God in the Bible really change my heart?

Optional Activity

Chapter Story: "Story Time" *Verbal/Linguistic*

Use this story after the opening prayer, before sharing with the children that God tells us about himself in the Bible.

- *Ask:* Do you like to go to the library? Do you enjoy stories?
- Invite the children to listen to "Story Time."
- After allowing the children to share their favorite stories with a partner, transition back to the lesson instruction.

Go to **aliveinchrist.osv.com** for Chapter Story.

Invite

Let Us Pray

Invite the children to gather in the prayer space and make the Sign of the Cross. Read aloud the leader's prayer; have the whole group read the Psalm verse. Prompt the children's response.

Have the children move from the prayer space back to their seats.

Explain that in the Bible, God tells us so much about himself. We learn how God wants to be with us.

Say: Let's listen to one parable Jesus told to help us understand life with God.

God's Word

Guide the children through the process of Scripture reflection.

- Invite them to close their eyes, be still, and open their minds and hearts to what God is saying to them in this passage.
- Proclaim the Scripture.
- Maintain several moments of silence.
- *Ask:* What did you hear God say to you today?
- Invite volunteers to share.

What Do You Wonder?

Say: Jesus told his disciples many parables. The stories he told are part of God's living Word. We read them today in the Bible.

Invite the children to respond to the questions. Ask what else they might wonder about the Word of God.

Discover

Objectives

- Recognize Jesus' use of stories as a way to help us understand more about God and his Kingdom
- Examine the components of the Liturgy of the Word, including readings from both the Old Testament and New Testament

God's Word Proclaimed

Point out that today's focus is on what we hear at Mass.

Ask a volunteer to read aloud both paragraphs.

God's Word

Proclaim the Scripture.

- Direct the children's attention to the illustration. Have the children locate the mustard seeds, the large tree, and the bird coming to nest.
- ☆ Have the children color in the picture and underline the name of the parable.
- *Ask:* What are some other stories Jesus teaches us?
- Write all appropriate responses on the board or on chart paper.

Music Option: Have the children sing "Jesus' Stories," downloaded from **aliveinchrist.osv.com**.

Work with Words

Read aloud the Catholic Faith Word.

- Pass out index cards. Ask the children to write the word on one side of the card and the definition on the other.
- Have them save the cards for future review.

Discover

God's Word Proclaimed

What do you hear at Mass?

Catholic Faith Words

Liturgy of the Word the first main part of the Mass during which we hear God's Word proclaimed

Jesus learned the stories of the Jewish people. He studied Scripture and talked about God's law with wise teachers. Jesus was a wonderful teacher, too.

He told many parables. Parables are stories about everyday life that Jesus told to help his followers learn how to love and follow God. Jesus wanted everyone to know that the Kingdom would grow with prayer and sharing in God's work of love, peace, and justice. Here is one parable Jesus told.

God's Word

The Mustard Seed

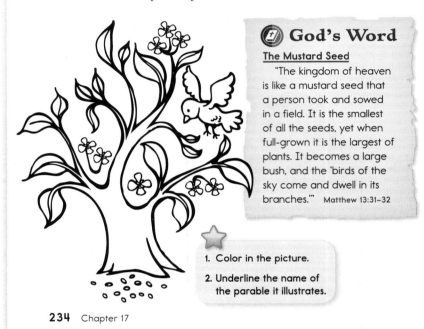

"The kingdom of heaven is like a mustard seed that a person took and sowed in a field. It is the smallest of all the seeds, yet when full-grown it is the largest of plants. It becomes a large bush, and the 'birds of the sky come and dwell in its branches.'" Matthew 13:31–32

1. Color in the picture.
2. Underline the name of the parable it illustrates.

Scripture Background

Matthew 13:31–32

Tell the children that mustard is made from the fruit of a spice bush.

- In the Palestine of Jesus' day, a tiny mustard seed might grow into a sprawling desert bush large enough for birds to nest in.
- Tell the children that the phrase "the birds of the sky come and dwell in its branches" is an old Jewish proverb used by the prophets to describe God's universal rule over all people.
- Explain that The Parable of the Mustard Seed illustrates the small beginnings of the Kingdom and its potential for expansion.

The Scripture Readings Begin

The first main part of the Mass is the **Liturgy of the Word**. The assembly listens to God's Word from the Bible.

- The reader steps forward to proclaim the first reading. It is usually from the Old Testament.
- Next, a singer, called a cantor, leads everyone in singing a psalm. Remember, psalms are prayers found in the Old Testament.
- Then, either another reader or the same reader stands and reads the second reading from one of the letters in the New Testament.
- At the end of each reading, the reader says, "The word of the Lord." The assembly answers, "Thanks be to God."

After each reading, everyone quietly thinks about what they have heard.

1. Circle the part of the Bible where the first reading comes from.
2. Underline the part of the Bible where the second reading comes from.

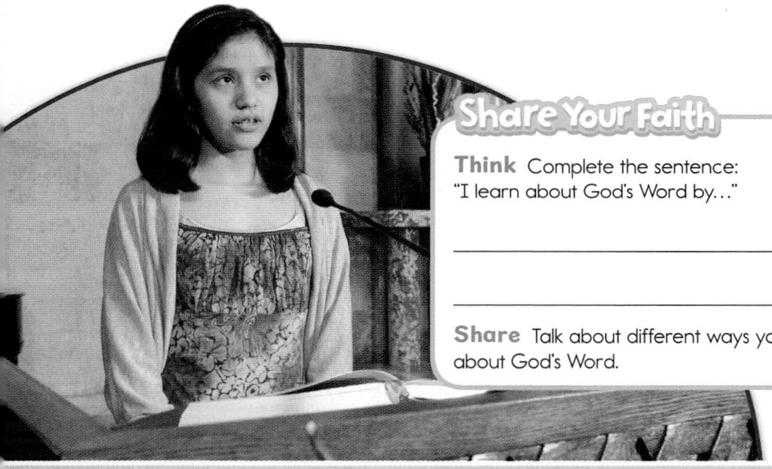

Share Your Faith

Think Complete the sentence: "I learn about God's Word by..."

____

____

Share Talk about different ways you learn about God's Word.

Quick Tip

Storytelling Helps

There are many ways to enhance storytelling.

- Stuffed toys—a stuffed sheep or dove can enhance stories of the Holy Spirit or the Good Shepherd.
- Props—enhance the story of the mustard seed by bringing in small seeds.
- Scenery—draw the scenery yourself or make the creation of scenery a group project.

The Scripture Readings Begin

Write the term *Liturgy of the Word* on the board or on chart paper.

- Invite the children to think about ways in which Jesus continues to teach us using stories today.

Read aloud the first paragraph.

- Ask five children to take turns reading aloud the bullet points and the last paragraph.
- List the parts of the Liturgy of the Word on the board or on chart paper.
- Read aloud the acclamation "The Word of the Lord," and have the children respond "Thanks be to God."
- Instruct the children to circle the part of the Bible where the first reading comes from and underline the part where the second reading comes from.

Music Option: Have the children sing "Jesus Is the Word," downloaded from **aliveinchrist.osv.com**.

Activity

Read aloud the directions.

- Have the children work in small groups to discuss the question and then complete their sentences.

Quick Review

Jesus used stories as a way to help us understand the Kingdom.The readings of the Liturgy are from both the Old Testament and New Testament.

Discover

Objectives

- Understand that the deacon or priest proclaims the Gospel reading and gives a homily to help us understand and apply God's Word to our lives
- Identify that the Liturgy of the Word ends with the Creed and the Prayer of the Faithful

Jesus' Good News

Read aloud the caption.

Ask a volunteer to read aloud the question at the top of the student page.

- Write the children's responses on the board or on chart paper.

Ask five volunteers to read aloud the five paragraphs.

Work with Words

Ask a volunteer to read aloud all three words and definitions in the Catholic Faith Words box.

- Pass out index cards, three per child.
- Have the children write the word on one side of the card and the definition on the other.
- Encourage the children to save the cards to use in a memory game or for further study.

Music Option: Have the children sing "We Hear God's Word," downloaded from **aliveinchrist.osv.com**.

Discover

A deacon crosses his forehead, lips, and chest before reading the Gospel.

Jesus' Good News

What happens after the First and Second Readings?

Now, everyone stands and sings "Alleluia!" It is time to hear the Good News of Jesus Christ.

"The Lord be with you," says the priest or deacon. The assembly immediately replies, "And with your spirit."

The priest or deacon announces what Gospel is going to be read. The Gospels contain stories about Jesus, the words of Jesus, and stories that Jesus told. The priest or deacon reads the Good News of Jesus from one of the Gospels.

At the end of the Gospel, the priest or deacon says, "The Gospel of the Lord." Everyone says, "Praise to you, Lord Jesus Christ."

After the reading of the Gospel, the priest gives a **homily**, a short talk about the readings that helps explain what it means to follow Jesus.

Catholic Faith Words

homily a short talk about the readings at Mass

creed a statement of the Church's beliefs

Prayer of the Faithful prayer at Mass for the needs of the Church and the world

---

Optional Activity

Activity Master 17: The Liturgy of the Word

Distribute copies of the activity found on catechist page 233E.

- Supply scissors, paper, and tape or glue, and have the children work on the activity.
- As an alternative, you may wish to send this activity home with the children.

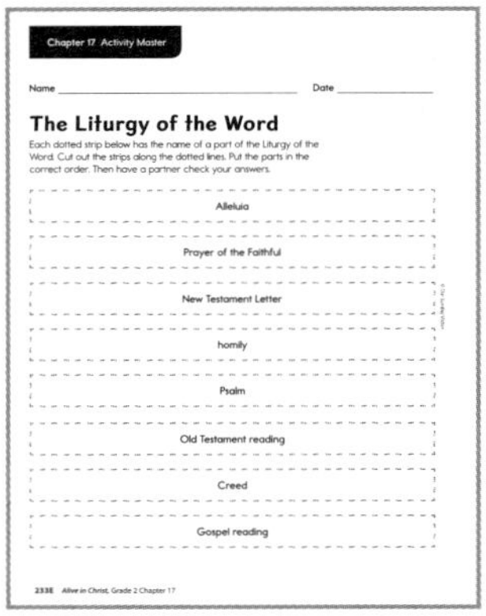
Chapter 17 Activity Master

Name ______ Date ______

The Liturgy of the Word

Each dotted strip below has the name of a part of the Liturgy of the Word. Cut out the strips along the dotted lines. Put the parts in the correct order. Then have a partner check your answers.

Alleluia

Prayer of the Faithful

New Testament Letter

homily

Psalm

Old Testament reading

Creed

Gospel reading

233E Alive in Christ, Grade 2 Chapter 17

The People Speak

The assembly then stands to pray the **creed**. We say proudly that we believe in God the Father, God the Son, and God the Holy Spirit. We say that you believe in the Church and her teachings.

Next, the assembly stands together and prays the **Prayer of the Faithful**.

As a leader says each prayer, we respond with our answer, such as "Lord, hear our prayer."

- We pray for the leaders of the Church and of our country.
- We pray for those who are sick and those who have died.
- We pray for people all around the world who have needs at this time.

Connect Your Faith

Write Prayers Think of things that are happening in your family or neighborhood. Fill in the blanks in these prayers.

For ________________, we pray to the Lord.

For ________________, we pray to the Lord.

The People Speak

Read aloud the first paragraph. Then have the children turn to page 304 in the Our Catholic Tradition section of the Student Book and silently read the Apostles' Creed.

Read aloud the next two sentences. Instruct the children to say "Lord, hear our prayer," after each bullet.

- Have three volunteers each read aloud one of the bullets.

Activity

Read aloud the directions.

- Allow time for the children to work independently on their prayers.
- Invite the children to pray aloud their petitions, and have the group respond "Lord, hear our prayer."

Quick Review

The deacon or priest proclaims the Gospel reading and gives a homily. The Liturgy of the Word ends with the Creed and Prayer of the Faithful.

Catechist Background

Praying for Others

Praying for others is an important part of being a Christian.

- Intercessory prayer is an ancient practice in Jewish and Christian tradition.
- We are called to feel such solidarity with all humans that we ask God's blessing without limits, including even our enemies and those who persecute us. (See *CCC*, 2634–2636.)

Our Catholic Life

Tell the children that this section will focus on how Jesus used stories to teach. Point out that we can still read his stories today in the Bible.

Read aloud the paragraph.

Parables You've Heard

☆ Instruct the children to match the story titles on the left to the correct description on the right.

- Allow the children to work in pairs.
- Ask three volunteers to each share their answer for one of the stories.

Help the children see that all three stories stress God's forgiving love.

- Discuss with the children the images in the chart and how they illustrate each parable.
- *Ask:* What is your favorite story Jesus told and why do you like it?
- Allow the children to share.

Our Catholic Life

How did Jesus use stories to teach?

Jesus was a great storyteller. He used lots of details and characters that were familiar to his listeners. Often his parables had surprise endings to make people think. Jesus' stories taught people how to show love for God and others. This year you have read or heard some of these parables.

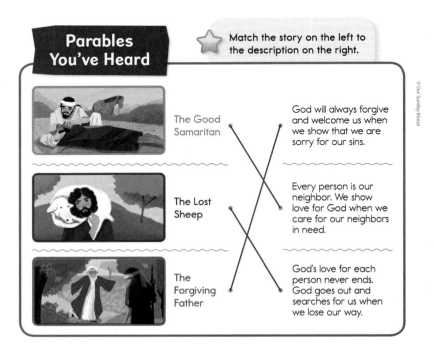

Parables You've Heard

☆ Match the story on the left to the description on the right.

The Good Samaritan — God will always forgive and welcome us when we show that we are sorry for our sins.

The Lost Sheep — Every person is our neighbor. We show love for God when we care for our neighbors in need.

The Forgiving Father — God's love for each person never ends. God goes out and searches for us when we lose our way.

Catechist Background

Parables

Help the children see that Jesus' stories used everyday situations that were familiar to people of his time, but he gave the stories a twist.

- Good Samaritan: The people who were expected to help didn't.
- The Forgiving Father: The father not only forgave his son, he welcomed him home with a celebration.
- Discuss with the children other ways Jesus' stories have had an unexpected ending.

People of Faith

July 25

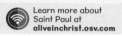

Saint Paul, first century

Saint Paul did not always like Christians. He helped put them in jail. Then one day, Paul heard a voice from above say, "Why do you persecute me?" It was Jesus. Paul realized that he had done wrong. That very minute, Paul stopped hurting Christians. Instead, he went everywhere telling people about Jesus. He started many churches. He traveled and wrote letters to teach about God. He gave people advice on how to love Jesus. Now we read his letters at Mass. They are called "Epistles."

Discuss: If you were writing a letter about Jesus, what would you write?

Learn more about Saint Paul at **aliveinchrist.osv.com**

Live Your Faith

Act It Out With a small group, choose one of Jesus' parables to act out. Use these steps to help you plan your play.

1. Choose one of Jesus' parables you have heard.
2. Make a list of the people and the animals in the story.
3. Decide who will play each part.

Talk It Over With your group, talk about ways people today can follow the message of this story.

Catholic Social Teaching

Chapter Connections

To integrate Catholic Social Teaching into your lesson, choose one of the following features: Call to Community, pages 292–293; or Care for Creation, pages 302–303.

- Start the Live step of the process by talking about Saint Paul on page 239. Then move directly to the Catholic Social Teaching feature.
- Or, to expand the lesson, complete both pages 238 and 239, then move to the Catholic Social Teaching feature.
- Return to Chapter 17 for the prayer on page 240.

People of Faith

Tell the children about Saint Paul.

- Saint Paul was born with the Jewish name of Saul, but as a Roman citizen, his Latin name was Paul.
- Saint Paul was blinded at his conversion on the road to Damascus, but regained his sight when he went where Jesus told him to go to be healed.
- Saint Paul experienced many miracles, including a rescue from jail after being arrested for preaching the Gospel.
- Read aloud the paragraph on Saint Paul.
- Ask the children to share their responses to the question.

Encourage the children to go to **aliveinchrist.osv.com** at home to learn more about Saint Paul.

Activity

Read aloud the directions for the Live Your Faith activity.

- Allow the children to work in groups of three or four.
- Each person can have more than one part, if necessary. Voice/head covering changes can denote the difference in character.
- Have the children write their plans on a separate piece of paper, assigning parts to each group member.
- Let them consider how to stage the play with props.
- Have the children perform their plays one at a time after allowing time for practice. You might even schedule the actual performances on a later date.

Let Us Pray

Celebration of the Word

Explain that this prayer is prayed as the Word of God is read.

Prepare

Choose volunteers for the leader part and the two reader parts.

- Help the children find the Scripture passages and practice reading them.
- Explain that the group's responses will be those said at Mass.

Rehearse with the children "Gospel Acclamation/Alleluia," downloaded from **aliveinchrist.osv.com**.

If this lesson is taught during the season of Lent, select the "Gospel Acclamation" track and do not sing "Alleluia."

Gather

Invite the children to gather in the prayer space. Have each child bring his or her book.

- Have the children bow before the Bible.

Pray

Follow the order of prayer on the student page.

Conclude by singing with the children the hymn refrain.

Live

Let Us Pray

Celebration of the Word

Gather and begin with the Sign of the Cross.

Leader: Gracious God, open our hearts and minds to hear your Word.

Reader 1: A reading from the First Letter of John.

Read 1 John 5:13–14.

The Word of the Lord.

All: Thanks be to God.

Sing together the refrain.

Reader 2: A reading from the holy Gospel according to Matthew.

Read Matthew 7:7–8.

The Gospel of the Lord.

All: Praise to you, Lord Jesus Christ.

Say together the Apostles Creed on page 304.

I believe in God,
the Father almighty,
Creator of heaven and earth,
and in Jesus Christ, his only Son,
our Lord...

Sing "Gospel Acclamation/Alleluia"

240 Chapter 17

Liturgy Link

The Cycle of Gospels

Explain to the children that the Church reads through the Gospels in a three-year cycle. The Church cycle begins on the First Sunday of Advent.

- The Sunday Gospels for Year A come primarily from Matthew, those for Year B from Mark, and those for Year C from Luke.
- Readings from the Gospel according to John are often proclaimed on special feast days.

Go to **aliveinchrist.osv.com** for Sunday readings, Scripture background, questions of the week, and seasonal resources.

FAMILY + FAITH
LIVING AND LEARNING TOGETHER

YOUR CHILD LEARNED >>>

This chapter focuses on the Liturgy of the Word, the first main part of Mass in which we hear God's Word in the Bible.

God's Word

Read **Luke 13:18–21** to find out what Jesus said about the Kingdom of God.

Catholics Believe

- In the Liturgy of the Word, God's living Word is read.
- We profess what we believe about God and pray for the needs of the Church and the world.

To learn more, go to the *Catechism of the Catholic Church* #1154, 1349 at **usccb.org**.

People of Faith

In this chapter, your child met the great Apostle, Saint Paul. He wrote many letters that are part of the New Testament.

CHILDREN AT THIS AGE >>>

How They Understand the Liturgy of the Word Second-graders might not have yet picked up the connection between the Lectionary readings in Mass. Paying attention to the relationship between each Sunday's passages from the Old Testament, Psalms, New Testament, and Gospel will help your child's overall understanding of the Scriptures and will encourage more active participation in the Mass. Some discussion about the readings prior to Mass can help to facilitate this. The readings for each Sunday can be found on the U.S. Bishops' site at **usccb.org/nab**.

CONSIDER THIS >>>

Do you long to hear God's voice?

Have you ever thought, "God, just tell me what to do?" Longing for God's presence is part of our human experience. "The desire for God is written in the human heart, because man is created by God and for God" (CCC, 27). "Every human person seeks to know the truth and to experience goodness. Moral goodness appeals to us… The more we become aware of these truths the more we are drawn to the reality of God who is the Supreme Good. These are the seeds of eternity within us that have their origins only in God" (*USCCA, p. 4*).

LET'S TALK >>>

- Ask your child to describe what happens in the Liturgy of the Word, the first main part of the Mass (readings, homily, creed, Prayer of the Faithful).
- Talk about times you have read the Bible as a family or when you were a child or adult.

LET'S PRAY >>>

Saint Paul, help us understand the Bible and listen carefully to the readings at Mass. Amen.

For a multimedia glossary of Catholic Faith Words, Sunday readings, seasonal and Saint resources, and chapter activities go to **aliveinchrist.osv.com**.

Family + Faith

Distribute the page to the children or parents/adult family members. Point out the chapter highlights, insights on how second graders understand concepts, the opportunity for the adults to reflect on their own experience and faith journey, and the family prayer.

Chapter 17 Review

A **Check Understanding** Match the description in Column A to the correct word or words in Column B.

Column A	Column B
1. Short stories about everyday life that Jesus told.	teach
2. The first main part of the Mass.	parables
3. Jesus used parables to do this.	homily
4. A short talk about the readings at Mass.	Liturgy of the Word
5. A statement of the Church's beliefs.	creed

B **Check Understanding** Circle the correct answer.

6. Jesus was a great ____.
   storyteller farmer follower
7. Jesus' stories had lessons about God's ____.
   family friends love
8. We say the Prayer of ____ together at Mass.
   contrition the Faithful the people
9. Jesus' parables teach you how to ____.
   go to Mass read follow God
10. The ____ is like a mustard seed.
   Kingdom of God land Bible

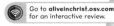

Go to **aliveinchrist.osv.com** for an interactive review.

Chapter Review

Use Catechist Quick Reviews to highlight lesson concepts.

A **Work with Words**
Have the children match the description in Column A to the correct word or words in Column B.

B **Check Understanding**
Explain to the children that they will circle the correct answer.

Go to **aliveinchrist.osv.com** to prepare customized and downloadable assessments, send eAssessments, and assign interactive reviews.

KEY CONCEPT
The Eucharist is a memorial of the sacrifice Jesus made. The Liturgy of the Eucharist is the second main part of the Mass.

DOCTRINAL CONTENT
- The Mass is a memorial celebration of Jesus' Death, Resurrection, and Ascension. (CCC, 1330)
- Jesus' Death on the Cross is a sacrifice and gift that saves all people from the power of sin and everlasting death. (CCC, 616–617)
- The Liturgy of the Eucharist is the second main part of the Mass in which Jesus gives us the gift of himself, and we receive his Body and Blood in Holy Communion. (CCC, 1408)
- In the consecration, through the power of the Holy Spirit and the words and actions of the priest, the gifts of bread and wine become the Body and Blood of Jesus Christ. (CCC, 1142, 1411)

TASKS OF CATECHESIS
Helping children grow in a faith that is "known, celebrated, lived, and expressed in prayer" (NDC, 20).

This chapter focuses on the following tasks of catechesis:
- Liturgical Education
- Education for Community Life

Catechist Background

"No one can serve two masters. He will either hate one and love the other, or be devoted to one and despise the other. You cannot serve God and mammon." Matthew 6:24

→ **Reflect** Do you have only one master?

The Sacrament of the Eucharist is so vital to the Church that the Second Vatican Council called it the "source and summit of the Christian life." To understand why the Eucharist is so important, it is helpful to understand what Christ himself, and the Church after him, have taught about the Sacrament.

Jesus taught that his flesh and blood were "true food." Our Lord, who frequently spoke in metaphors, seemed to go out of his way with repetition to emphasize the fact that he intended the Eucharist to be understood literally: he was giving himself to us as food and drink. This was difficult even for his followers to understand, and some left him, but Jesus did not try to stop them by offering an alternative explanation, an indication that they understood what he meant but could not accept it.

One key to understanding Jesus' offering of himself as food is the Passover celebration of the Old Testament. The Israelites were commanded to eat the flesh of the Passover lamb that was sacrificed to save them. Passover was intended to prepare God's People for Jesus, the "Lamb of God" who would be sacrificed to save us from the bondage of sin. In fact, Saint Paul calls Jesus "our Paschal Lamb." On the night he was betrayed, Jesus ate the Passover meal with his disciples, offering the bread and the cup with the words, "This is my body" and "This is my blood." He asked the disciples to do what he did in his memory, and the Church continues to celebrate this meal in the Mass.

→ **Reflect** How can you enlarge your understanding of Jesus' sacrifice, and help the children understand and participate in it?

Catechist's Prayer

Jesus, help me to follow your example of giving yourself lovingly and wholeheartedly for others. Guide me as I invite the children to share in your spirit of sacrifice and give thanks to your Father. Amen.

Lesson Plan

Objectives	Process	Materials
Invite, 10 minutes		
Remembering Jesus' Sacrifice Page 243	**Psalm 116:17** Pray the opening prayer. **Matthew 6:24** Reflect prayerfully on the Word. • Discuss What Do You Wonder questions.	**Optional Activity** Chapter Story: "Helping Others"
Discover, 35 minutes		
Making Sacrifices Pages 244–245 • Explain the Mass as a memorial celebration of Jesus' Death, Resurrection, and Ascension • Describe Jesus' Death on the Cross as a sacrifice and a gift that saves all people from the power of sin and everlasting death	• **Catholic Faith Words** sacrifice, Last Supper **Matthew 19:21–22** Proclaim "The Rich Young Man." ☆ Draw one thing to sacrifice. • Learn what the Mass celebrates. • **Share Your Faith Activity** Write about giving up something for someone else.	☐ pencils or pens ☐ colored pencils or markers ☐ index cards, two per child • **Optional Activity** My Prayer of Thanks ☐ Activity Master 18 (Page 243E)
Liturgy of the Eucharist Pages 246–247 • Appreciate the Liturgy of the Eucharist as the second main part of the Mass in which we receive Holy Communion • Discover how the gifts of bread and wine become the Body and Blood of Jesus Christ	• **Catholic Faith Words** Liturgy of the Eucharist, consecration • Learn about the second main part of the Mass. ☆ Underline the gifts brought forward during the Liturgy of the Eucharist. • Review how and what the assembly prays. • **Connect Your Faith Activity** Complete the find-a-word puzzle.	☐ pencils or pens ☐ crayons or markers ☐ board or chart paper ☐ index cards, two per child
Live, 15 minutes		
Our Catholic Life Pages 248–249	• Discuss the Mystery of Faith. ☆ Place a check mark next to recognized Mystery of Faith acclamations. • **People of Faith** Learn about Blessed Imelda. • **Live Your Faith Activity** Design a stained-glass window.	☐ pencils or pens ☐ crayons, colored pencils, or markers
Prayer of Remembrance Page 250	• Choose a reader and leader. Rehearse the song with the children. • Follow the order of prayer.	☐ Bible and stand ☐ crucifix Download "We Proclaim Your Death, O Lord."

Family + Faith Page 251
Point out that the Catholic Families page provides chapter highlights, information on how second graders understand faith concepts, and family prayer.

Chapter Review Page 252
aliveinchrist.osv.com
- Customize and Download Assessments
- Email Links to eAssessments
- Interactive Student Reviews

ONLINE RESOURCES

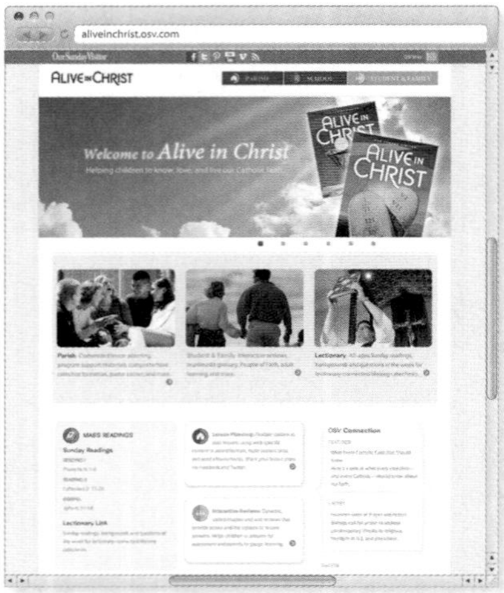
aliveinchrist.osv.com
Welcome to Alive in Christ
ALIVE IN CHRIST

Go to **aliveinchrist.osv.com**

You will find:

- Interactive lesson planning with web specific content and additional activities
- Step by step lesson instruction from printed Catechist Edition for integrated lesson planning
- Custom-built assessments to download and eAssessment links
- Interactive reviews that provide scores and the option to review answers
- Sunday readings with background and questions of the week

Go to **osvparish.com**

You will find:

- Ask the Experts Q and A
- General Catechist Helps
- Community Connections and Blogs

Sharing the Message with Second Graders

The Liturgy of the Eucharist Many second grade children have heard the words of the Liturgy of the Eucharist without fully realizing or understanding what they mean. It is hard for children this age to understand how and why Jesus gave himself as a sacrifice for all of humanity. The ritual form of this portion of the Mass will help second graders to continue to reflect upon and grow in their understanding of Christ's sacrifice and its meaning for each of us.

Teaching Tip: After checking with the director of faith formation, ask your parish priest if he would be available to provide a "walk through the Liturgy of the Eucharist" for the children, explaining what each part means. It's best if this occurs in the church, where they would experience the liturgy.

How Second Graders Understand

- Second graders are beginning to learn how to share with others out of love, and not because they're told to. Acknowledge them when they share spontaneously.
- Children this age want to be like Jesus. Help them see how they can give of themselves to others as he did.
- Remind the children that they will grow in understanding, but they can be attentive members of the assembly now.

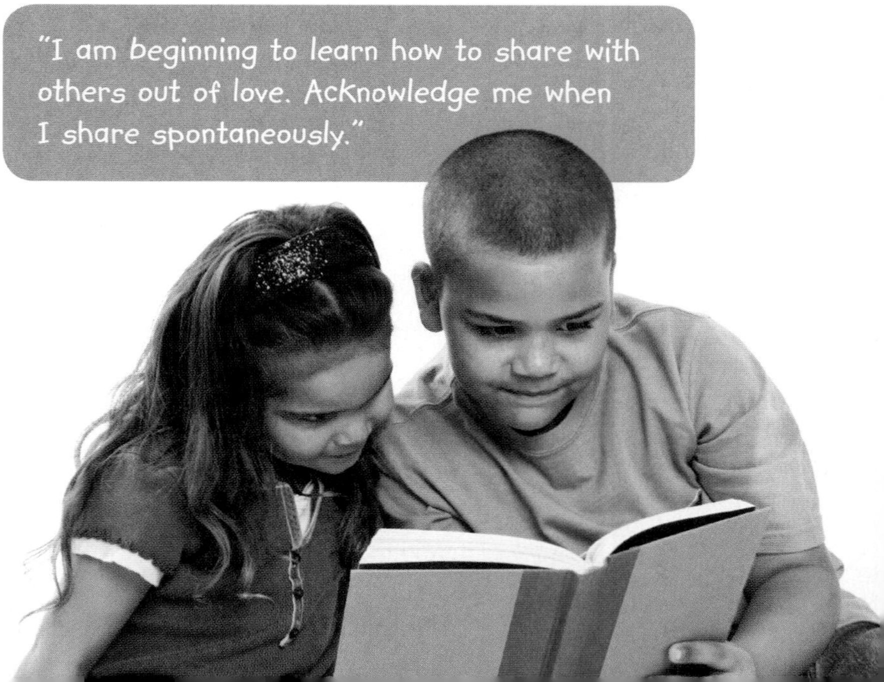
"I am beginning to learn how to share with others out of love. Acknowledge me when I share spontaneously."

Chapter Connections

Chapter Story

Invite

"Helping Others"

Use this story to expand the chapter introduction.

- Some children may not recognize the reference to the natural disaster of a hurricane.
- *Say:* Sometimes things happen that we don't always understand, so we need to trust God that he will take of us when bad things happen. We can live and love as Jesus taught us when we share what we have with those who need help.

Go to **aliveinchrist.osv.com** Lesson Planning section for this story.

NCEA IFG: ACRE Edition

Discover

Liturgical Life

- Objective: To know the Paschal Mystery of Jesus in the Church's liturgical life—feasts, seasons, symbols, and practices and in the Sacraments as signs and instruments of grace.

Communal Life

- Objectives: To understand the origin, mission, structure, and communal nature of the Church; to know the rights and responsibilities of the Christian faithful

Catholic Social Teaching

Live

Use one of these features to introduce a principle and engage the children with an activity.

- Option for the Poor, Pages 296–297
- Solidarity of the Human Family, Pages 300–301

Music Options

Use one or more of the following songs to enhance catechetical learning or for prayer.

- "We Proclaim Your Death, O Lord," Live Prayer, Page 250
- "Jesus, You Are Bread for Us," Discover, Page 246

LECTIONARY CONNECTION

Chapter 18 highlights Lectionary-connected themes such as the Eucharist, Eucharistic Prayer, consecration, sacrifice, and Last Supper. If your parish aligns its curriculum to the liturgical year, you could use this chapter in connection with the following Sundays.

Year A

The Most Holy Body and Blood of Christ—Living Bread

Tenth Sunday in Ordinary Time—Life in God

Year B

Sixth Sunday of Easter—Eucharist

The Most Holy Body and Blood of Christ—Eucharist

Year C

Twenty-first Sunday in Ordinary Time—Eucharist

Our Lord Jesus Christ, King of the Universe—Eucharist

Go to **aliveinchrist.osv.com** for a complete correlation ordered by the Sundays of the year and suggestions for how to integrate the Scripture readings into chapter lessons.

Name ______________________ Date ____________

My Prayer of Thanks

The Eucharistic Prayer is a prayer of thanksgiving. Finish the prayers below to write your own prayers of thanks.

Dear God, our Father,

Thank you for sending your Son, Jesus, to

____

____

____

Amen!

Dear Jesus,

Thank you for

____

____

____

Amen!

Holy Spirit,

Help me to show that I am thankful

____

____

____

Amen!

CHAPTER 18

Invite

Remembering Jesus' Sacrifice

Let Us Pray

Leader: God, we offer you our praise and thanks.

"I will offer a sacrifice of praise
and call on the name of the LORD."
Psalm 116:17

All: God, we offer you our praise and thanks. Amen.

God's Word

Jesus said to his followers, "You cannot serve two masters." He told them that God must be first in their lives, not money, not things that they own, or things that they want to get. Based on Matthew 6:24

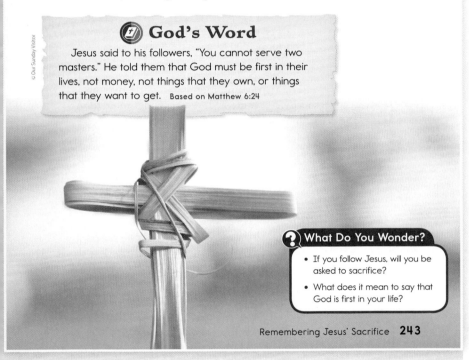

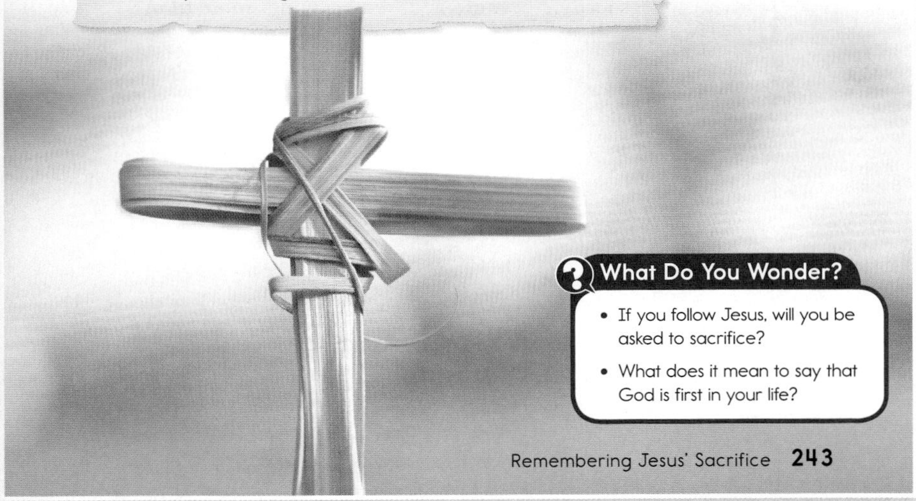

What Do You Wonder?

- If you follow Jesus, will you be asked to sacrifice?
- What does it mean to say that God is first in your life?

Optional Activity

Chapter Story: "Helping Others" *Verbal/Linguistic*

Use this story after the opening prayer, before you tell the children that God needs to be first in our lives.

- Invite the children to share what they know about the destruction brought by recent hurricanes or other natural disasters. (Be mindful that some children may have lost family members or property.)
- Ask a volunteer to read aloud the story. Then discuss the question. When finished, transition back to the lesson instruction.

Go to **aliveinchrist.osv.com** for Chapter Story.

Invite

Let Us Pray

Invite the children to gather in the prayer space and make the Sign of the Cross. Read aloud the leader's prayer and the Psalm verse. Prompt the children's response.

Have the children move from the prayer space back to their seats.

Explain that Jesus reminds us that God needs to be first in our lives.

Say: Let's listen to hear what Jesus tells us that we need to sacrifice in order to follow him.

God's Word

Guide the children through the process of Scripture reflection.

- Invite them to close their eyes, be still, and open their minds and hearts to what God is saying to them in this passage.
- Proclaim the Scripture.
- Maintain several moments of silence.
- *Ask:* What did you hear God say to you today?
- Invite volunteers to share.

What Do You Wonder?

Say: Sometimes the things that we have, like our games or our toys, can distract us from following Jesus. If we spend too much time playing, or wanting more things, we take time away from getting to know Jesus better.

Invite the children to respond to the questions. Ask what else they might wonder about keeping God first in their life.

Objectives

- Explain the Mass as a memorial celebration of Jesus' Death, Resurrection, and Ascension
- Describe Jesus' Death on the Cross as a sacrifice and gift that saves all people from the power of sin and everlasting death

Making Sacrifices

Read aloud the question at the top of the student page, and encourage the group to respond.

Have the children follow along as you read the definition of *sacrifice* from the Catholic Faith Words box.

Invite a volunteer to read the opening paragraph.

God's Word

Proclaim the Scripture story.

- Invite the children to explain why the young man went away sad.

Read aloud the last sentence.

- *Say:* Tell me about a time you had to give up something for someone else.
- Allow several volunteers to share.

☆ Direct the children to draw one thing they would give up to make a sacrifice.

- Pass out colored pencils or markers for children to make their drawings.

Making Sacrifices

What sacrifice did Jesus make for us?

Catholic Faith Words

sacrifice giving up something out of love for someone else or for the common good (good of everyone). Jesus sacrificed his life for all people.

Last Supper the meal Jesus shared with his disciples on the night before he died. At the Last Supper, Jesus gave himself in the Eucharist.

Making a **sacrifice** can be very difficult. Sacrifice takes love and courage. A rich young man found this out when he asked Jesus about life with God forever.

God's Word

The Rich Young Man

"Jesus said to him, 'If you wish to be perfect, go, sell what you have and give to [the] poor, and you will have treasure in heaven. Then come, follow me.'

When the young man heard this . . . he went away sad, for he had many possessions." Matthew 19:21–22

The rich young man could not make the sacrifice because he loved his things more than he loved God.

Draw one thing you would give up to make a sacrifice.

Songs of Scripture

The Rich Young Man

This song, based on Matthew's Gospel, tries to help children understand that like the rich young man, Jesus asks us to place God first in our lives. Help them understand the difference between want and need.

- Ask various questions like "Is having two coats too much?"
- Teach the children the song "The Rich Young Man."

Use *Songs of Scripture*, Grades 1–3 CD, Track 15

The Greatest Gift

People sometimes make sacrifices, but Jesus chose to make the greatest sacrifice of all. Jesus' sacrifice is that he freely gave up his life on a Cross to save all people from the power of sin and everlasting death. He made this sacrifice so that you would have new life with God forever.

God the Father rewarded Jesus for his loving choice. Through God's loving power, Jesus overcame death and was raised to new life.

The Mass is a memorial celebration of Jesus' Death, Resurrection, and Ascension. Jesus' great sacrifice is celebrated at every Mass when we follow his command to do what he did at the **Last Supper**.

Share Your Faith

Think Write about a time when you gave up something for someone else or when someone else gave up something for you.

____

____

____

Share Share your answer with a partner.

The Greatest Gift

Ask the children what a crucifix helps us remember. Discuss their responses.

Read aloud the first two paragraphs.

- Invite the children to describe the wonderful thing that happened to Jesus three days after his Death.

Read aloud the last paragraph.

- Ask the children how we remember and celebrate Jesus' Death and Resurrection. If the children mention Easter, explain to them that we celebrate a "little Easter" every Sunday at Mass.

Work with Words

Pass out two index cards per child.

- Have the children write the Catholic Faith Words from page 244 on one side of the card and the definitions on the other.
- Encourage them to use the cards to help them become more familiar with the terms.

Activity

Read aloud the directions.

- Have the children share their stories with a partner.

Optional Activity

Activity Master 18: My Prayer of Thanks

Distribute copies of the activity found on catechist page 243E.

- Read aloud the directions, and have the children compose their prayers.
- As an alternative, you may wish to send this activity home with the children.

Chapter 18 Activity Master

Name ______ Date ______

My Prayer of Thanks

The Eucharistic Prayer is a prayer of thanksgiving. Finish the prayers below to write your own prayers of thanks.

Dear God, our Father, Thank you for sending your Son, Jesus, to

Amen!

Dear Jesus, Thank you for

Amen!

Holy Spirit, Help me to show that I am thankful

Amen!

243E Alive in Christ, Grade 2 Chapter 18

Quick Review

The Mass is a memorial celebration of Jesus' Death, Resurrection and Ascension. Jesus' great sacrifice saves us from the power of sin and everlasting death.

Objectives

- Appreciate the Liturgy of the Eucharist as the second main part of the Mass in which we receive Holy Communion
- Discover how the gifts of bread and wine become the Body and Blood of Jesus Christ

Liturgy of the Eucharist

Ask a volunteer to read the question.

- List the children's answers on the board or on chart paper.

Read aloud the first paragraph.

Have the children place their finger on the words *Liturgy of the Eucharist*.

- Read aloud the definition.

Invite another volunteer to read the second paragraph.

- *Ask:* Who prepares the gifts? the priest

Begin reading aloud the third paragraph.

- Ask the children to read together the "All" parts after you read the parts for the "Priest."

☆ Have the children underline the gifts that are brought forward during the Liturgy of the Eucharist.

Music Option: Invite the children to sing "Jesus, You Are Bread for Us," downloaded from **aliveinchrist.osv.com**.

Members of the assembly bring forward the gifts of bread and wine during the Liturgy of the Eucharist.

Liturgy of the Eucharist

What will the gifts of bread and wine become during the Mass?

The second main part of the Mass is called the **Liturgy of the Eucharist**. Those gathered remember in a special way Jesus' Death, Resurrection, and Ascension.

The Liturgy of the Eucharist begins when members of the assembly bring forward the gifts of bread and wine. The people offer these gifts to God as a sign of their love. The priest prepares the gifts. He asks God to bless them. They will become the Body and Blood of Jesus Christ.

Now, another important part of the celebration begins. The priest leads the assembly in prayer.

Priest: "The Lord be with you."
All: "And with your spirit."
Priest: "Lift up your hearts."
All: "We lift them up to the Lord."
Priest: "Let us give thanks to the Lord our God."
All: "It is right and just."

Catholic Faith Words

Liturgy of the Eucharist the second main part of the Mass that includes Holy Communion

☆ Underline the gifts that are brought forward during the Liturgy of the Eucharist.

Catechist Background

Giving Thanks

Remind the children that the word *Eucharist* means "thanksgiving."

- Ask them to list ways they can show they are thankful for Jesus' sacrifice.
- Have the children practice ways of showing gratitude and appreciation to family members, teachers, friends, and the people of their parish.
- At the next session, allow the children to share some of the responses they got from their attitude of gratitude.

246 Chapter 18

The Eucharistic Prayer

The priest now begins the Eucharistic Prayer. He gives praise and thanks to God. He asks the Father to send the Holy Spirit. The priest repeats what Jesus said at the Last Supper:

Priest: FOR THIS IS MY BODY,
WHICH WILL BE GIVEN UP FOR YOU . . .
FOR THIS IS THE CHALICE OF MY BLOOD, . . .
WHICH WILL BE POURED OUT FOR YOU AND
FOR MANY FOR THE FORGIVENESS OF SINS.
DO THIS IN MEMORY OF ME.

This is called the **consecration**. The bread and wine are now the Body and Blood of Christ. The assembly prays the Mystery of Faith:

All: We proclaim your Death, O Lord, and profess your Resurrection until you come again.

The assembly recalls all that Jesus did and offers the Father the gift of his Son. The prayer ends with everyone saying or singing the "Great Amen."

Catholic Faith Words

consecration through the power of the Holy Spirit and the words and actions of the priest, the gifts of bread and wine become the Body and Blood of Jesus

Connect Your Faith

Find the Word Color each X with one color and each O with a different color to find the word you say at the end of the Eucharistic Prayer.

The Eucharistic Prayer

Write the term *Eucharistic Prayer* on the board or on chart paper.

- Remind the children that the word *Eucharist* means "thanksgiving." Ask the children what we are giving thanks for when we celebrate the Eucharist. Jesus' sacrifice

Have the children follow along with you as you read aloud the text on this page.

- Remind them that we give thanks to God for sending Jesus, whose Body and Blood become present.

Work with Words

Have the children place their finger on the word *consecration*. Read aloud the definition from the Catholic Faith Words box.

Pass out two index cards. Have the children write the words and definitions from pages 246 and 247 on the index cards for future review.

Activity

Read aloud the directions for the Connect Your Faith activity.

- Provide the children with crayons or markers so they can color by symbol to find the word.

Quick Review

The Liturgy of the Eucharist is the second main part of the Mass in which Jesus gives us the gift of himself, and we receive his Body and Blood in Holy Communion.

Reaching All Learners

Children with Learning Disabilities or Vision Impairments

Many children with vision impairments (including color blindness) or learning disabilities can have difficulty with hidden word or object puzzles such as the activity on this page. Adapt the activity to the children's needs by

- supplying crayons with marked contrast in color, or having the children color only the X spaces with black;
- having the children work with partners who can help them distinguish colors and recognize letters.

Our Catholic Life

Tell the children to think about the question at the top of the page as you read aloud the first paragraph.

- Now ask the question. by praying or singing the Mystery of Faith

Read aloud the second paragraph.

- Be sure the children understand the sense in which we use the word *mystery* at Mass. See the Quick Tip box below.

The Mystery of Faith

Direct the children's attention to the chart. Invite them to join you in reading aloud each version of the Mystery of Faith.

Ask the children to place a check mark next to the version they have sung during Mass.

Ask: Why should you join in proclaiming the Mystery of Faith at Mass? Possible response: to say aloud what we believe about Jesus' sacrifice

If time permits, invite the children to turn to page 311 in the Our Catholic Tradition section of their books and view The Order of Mass.

- Read aloud the Introductory Rites.
- Have one side of the room find and read aloud what takes place in the Liturgy of the Word.
- Have the other side of the room find and read the Liturgy of the Eucharist and what takes place.
- Ask the children to find the Mystery of Faith and when it happens in the Order of Mass.
- Read aloud the Concluding Rites.

Our Catholic Life

How do you remember Jesus' sacrifice at Mass?

At Mass, the priest prays the Eucharistic Prayer. After he consecrates the bread and wine he invites everyone to say aloud what we believe about Jesus' sacrifice. He says to the assembly, "The Mystery of Faith." We answer the priest by praying or singing a Mystery of Faith.

The Mystery of Faith is not a puzzle or a riddle. It is God's love for us, which is greater than we can ever understand completely. So, we simply say what we believe and thank God in our hearts.

Place a check mark next to one you've sung during Mass.

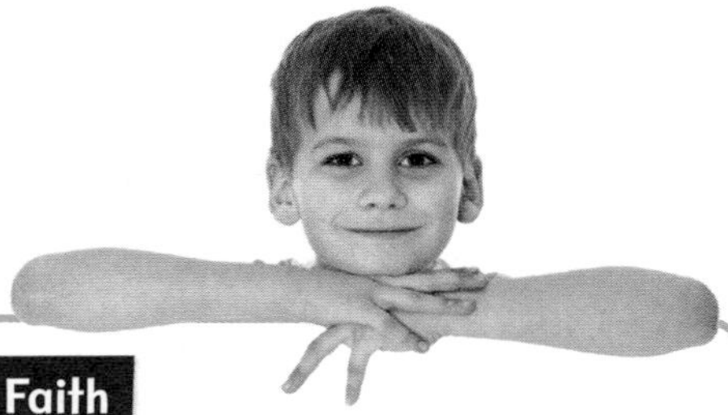

The Mystery of Faith

- [ ] 1. We proclaim your Death, O Lord, and profess your Resurrection until you come again.
- [ ] 2. When we eat this Bread and drink this Cup, we proclaim your Death, O Lord, until you come again.
- [ ] 3. Save us, Savior of the world, for by your Cross and Resurrection, you have set us free.

Quick Tip

Mystery of Faith

Give the children further insight into this term.

- The word *mystery* comes from the Greek word *mysterion*, which means "a truth whispered."
- In the Church, it is used to describe truths of faith that are beyond human understanding.

People of Faith

Blessed Imelda Lambertini, 1322–1333

Blessed Imelda Lambertini lived at a time when children couldn't receive Holy Communion until they were twelve. She was too young to receive Communion but she would pray at Mass and make a "spiritual communion." Jesus would come into her heart, but she still wanted to receive the Body of Christ in the Eucharist. One day, she was praying at Mass and a beautiful light with a host in it appeared over her head. Blessed Imelda is the patron Saint of children receiving their First Communion.

May 13

Discuss: What is one message about Jesus you can share with someone?

Learn more about Blessed Imelda at **aliveinchrist.osv.com**

Live Your Faith

Design A Window Choose one of the three Mysteries of Faith and design your own stained glass window using symbols and pictures that remind people of this statement of faith.

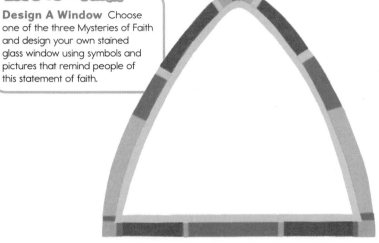

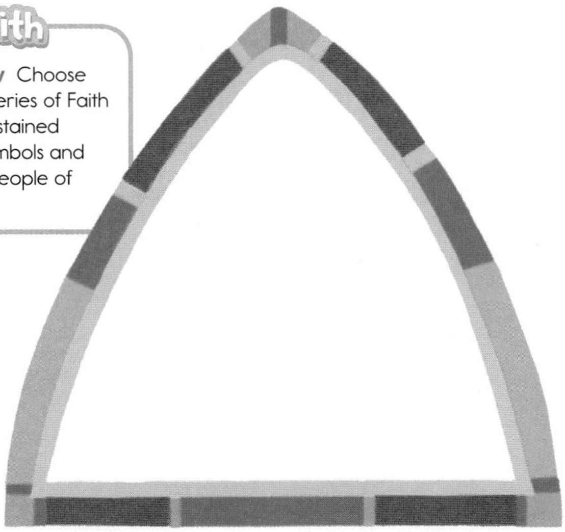

People of Faith

Tell the children about Blessed Imelda Lambertini.

- Imelda took delight in prayer and she would often slip off to a quiet corner of the house to pray.
- She adorned her prayer space with flowers and pictures.
- When she was nine, she was placed, at her own wish, in a Dominican convent, to be trained there by the religious sisters.
- Read aloud the paragraph on Blessed Imelda.
- Discuss the question.

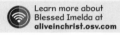

Encourage the children to go to **aliveinchrist.osv.com** at home to learn more about Blessed Imelda Lambertini.

Activity

Read aloud the directions for the Live Your Faith activity.

- Provide crayons, colored pencils, or markers.
- Allow the children time to be creative and finish coloring their designs.
- Ask volunteers to share their work with the group and explain how it reminds them of their favorite Mystery of Faith acclamation.

Catholic Social Teaching

Chapter Connections

To integrate Catholic Social Teaching into your lesson, choose one of the following features: Option for the Poor, pages 296–297; or Human Solidarity, pages 300–301.

- Start the Live process by talking about Blessed Imelda Lambertini on page 249. Then move directly to the Catholic Social Teaching feature.
- Or, to expand the lesson, complete both pages 248 and 249, then move to the Catholic Social Teaching feature.
- Return to Chapter 18 for the prayer on page 250.

Let Us Pray

Prayer of Remembrance

Explain that this prayer is a reminder that Jesus sacrificed his life to save us.

Prepare

Choose volunteers for the leader and the reader roles. Allow them to rehearse their parts.

- Help the reader find the Scripture and practice reading it.

Rehearse with the children "We Proclaim Your Death, O Lord," downloaded from **aliveinchrist.osv.com**.

Gather

Lead the children in procession to the prayer space, carrying a Bible and singing together "We Proclaim Your Death, O Lord."

- Invite the children to come forward individually and bow with respect before the crucifix.

Pray

Follow the order of prayer on the student page.

Conclude by processing around the room with the children, singing the song refrain.

Let Us Pray

Prayer of Remembrance

Gather and begin with the Sign of the Cross.

Leader: God our Father, your Son Jesus gave his life for us. Be with us as we pray.

Reader: A reading from the First Letter of Paul to the Corinthians.

Read 1 Corinthians 11:23–26.

The Word of the Lord.

All: Thanks be to God.

Sing "We Proclaim Your Death, O Lord"

We proclaim your Death, O Lord.
Jesus died for us.
We profess your Resurrection.
Jesus lives with us.
Until you come again,
we wait in joyful hope!

Liturgy Link

The Mass Around the World

Although the Mass has been celebrated in the vernacular since the 1960s, the order of Mass in the Roman Rite is the same in every place around the world.

- One can go to a Mass anywhere in the world and the Scripture and rituals are the same as they are everywhere on that day. All profess the Death and celebrate the Resurrection of Jesus Christ.

Go to **aliveinchrist.osv.com** for Sunday readings, Scripture background, questions of the week, and seasonal resources.

FAMILY+FAITH

LIVING AND LEARNING TOGETHER

YOUR CHILD LEARNED >>>

This chapter discusses how we celebrate Jesus' sacrifice and gift of himself in the Eucharist at Mass.

God's Word

Read **Matthew 6:24** to see what Jesus says about sacrifice and serving God.

Catholics Believe

- The Eucharist is a memorial of the sacrifice Jesus made.
- The Liturgy of the Eucharist is the second main part of the Mass.

To learn more, go to the *Catechism of the Catholic Church* #1356–1358 at **usccb.org**.

People of Faith

This week, your child met Blessed Imelda Lambertini, the patron Saint of children receiving First Communion.

CHILDREN AT THIS AGE >>>

How They Understand the Liturgy of the Eucharist Many second-grade children have heard the words of the Liturgy of the Eucharist without fully realizing or understanding what they mean. It is hard for children this age to understand how and why Jesus gave himself as a sacrifice for all of humanity. The ritual form of this portion of the Mass will help your child to continue to reflect upon and grow in his or her understanding of Christ's sacrifice and its meaning for each of us.

CONSIDER THIS >>>

What have you sacrificed for your children as a gift of love?

Becoming a parent sets one on a lifelong journey of sacrifice—sacrifices that come from love. This love gives us a glimpse of the love and sacrifice of Jesus. "In a self-centered culture where people are taught to extend themselves only for something in return, the sacrifices each of us make, following the example of Jesus, who freely sacrificed his life in love for all, point to the reality and power of God's love for us" (*USCCA, p. 221*).

LET'S TALK >>>

- Have your child explain what a sacrifice is and how Jesus sacrificed for us.
- Talk with your child about when he or she will have First Communion.

LET'S PRAY >>>

Blessed Imelda Lambertini, pray to God for us that we may receive Holy Communion with reverence. Amen.

For a multimedia glossary of Catholic Faith Words, Sunday readings, seasonal and Saint resources, and chapter activities go to **aliveinchrist.osv.com**.

Family + Faith

Distribute the page to the children or parents/adult family members. Point out the chapter highlights, insights on how second graders understand concepts, the opportunity for the adults to reflect on their own experience and faith journey, and the family prayer.

Chapter 18 Review

A Work with Words Write the letter of the correct word or words from the Word Bank to complete each sentence.

Word Bank
a. memory
b. sacrifice
c. Amen
d. The Mass
e. bread and wine

1. Jesus' great [b] was his Death on the Cross.
2. The [e] become the Body and Blood of Jesus.
3. Jesus said, "Do this in [a] of me."
4. At the end of the Eucharistic Prayer, the people say, [c].
5. [d] is a memorial of Jesus' Death, Resurrection, and Ascension.

B Check Understanding Draw a line to complete the sentences in Column A with the correct words in Column B.

Column A	Column B
6. At Mass, the priest prays the	Eucharistic Prayer.
7. We remember what Jesus said at	God's love for us.
8. The second main part of the Mass is the	the Last Supper.
9. The mystery of faith is	Liturgy of the Eucharist.
10. The Eucharistic Prayer ends with the	Great Amen.

Go to **aliveinchrist.osv.com** for an interactive review.

Chapter Review

Use Catechist Quick Reviews to highlight lesson concepts.

A Work with Words
Have the children write the letter that corresponds to the correct word in the Word Bank.

B Check Understanding
Tell the children to draw a line from Column A to Column B to complete each sentence.

Go to **aliveinchrist.osv.com** to prepare customized and downloadable assessments, send eAssessments, and assign interactive reviews.

Unit Review

Use Catechist Quick Reviews in each chapter to highlight lesson concepts for this unit and prepare for the Unit Review.

Have the children complete the Review pages. Then discuss the answers as a group. Review any concepts with which the children are having difficulty.

A Work with Words
Have the children complete each sentence with the correct word from the Word Bank.

B Check Understanding
Instruct the children to draw a line from the description in Column A to the correct word or words in Column B for problems 6–10.

Unit Review

UNIT 6

A Work with Words Complete each sentence with the correct word from the Word Bank.

Word Bank
Eucharist
Word
assembly
Mass
creed

1. **Mass** is another name for the celebration of the Sacrament of the Eucharist.
2. In the Liturgy of the **Word**, stories from the Bible are read.
3. The people gathered together at Mass make up the **assembly**.
4. The Liturgy of the **Eucharist** is the second main part of the Mass.
5. A **creed** is a statement of the Church's beliefs.

B Check Understanding Draw a line from the description in Column A to the correct word or words in Column B.

Column A	Column B
6. This is said at the end of the Eucharistic Prayer.	Jesus' Sacrifice
7. The bread and wine become this.	Homily
8. A short talk about Scripture readings.	"Great Amen"
9. The priest or deacon reads this.	Christ's Body and Blood
10. The Mass celebrates this.	The Gospel

UNIT 6

Unit Review

Write T if the sentence is TRUE. Write F if the sentence is FALSE.

11. T The priest leads the assembly in celebrating the Mass.
12. F At Mass you do not take part in the celebration.
13. T Jesus' stories are called parables.
14. T Jesus' parables teach us about God's love.
15. F The Mass is a memorial celebration of Peter's birth, life, and death.

C Make Connections Circle the correct answer.

16. As Mass begins, the assembly ____.
    sits   kneels   (stands and sings)
17. A ____ is giving up something out of love.
    (sacrifice)   celebration   trade
18. At the ____ Jesus shared a meal with his disciples.
    Resurrection   (Last Supper)   Ascension
19. Jesus' stories always had lessons about ____.
    history   animals   (God's love)
20. The Mass celebrates Jesus' death and ____.
    family   (Resurrection)   Father

Write about parts of the Mass that remind you of each of the parts of a family meal described below.

21. Your cousins come for Sunday dinner.
    The assembly gathers to celebrate the Mass.
22. Your family welcomes everyone once they are together.
    The priest greets everyone, saying "The Lord be with you."
23. Family members tell stories during the meal.
    The assembly listens to stories from the Bible.
24. Family members bring food and drink to share.
    The assembly brings up gifts of bread and wine as a sign of their love.
25. Your family shares a meal of food and drink.
    The parish family shares a holy meal that is the Body and Blood of Jesus.

B Check Understanding

Have the children write the letter *T* if the sentence is true and the letter *F* if the sentence is false for problems 11–15.

C Make Connections

Tell the children to circle the correct answer for problems 16–20. Then have them write about parts of the Mass that remind them of each of the parts of a family meal described in 21–25.

Go to **aliveinchrist.osv.com** to prepare customized and downloadable assessments, send eAssessments, and assign interactive reviews.

UNIT 7

Kingdom of God

Our Catholic Tradition

- The Eucharist unites us with Jesus and with one another. We share the same mission to love the way Jesus did. (CCC, 1396)
- Jesus, the Lamb, is truly present in Holy Communion. We call this Real Presence. (CCC, 1380)
- The Eucharist is a sign of what Heaven will be like—happiness forever with God. We spread the news of the Kingdom to everyone. (CCC, 562, 1419)

Christ the Redeemer Statue, Rio de Janerio, Brazil

How does receiving Holy Communion help us on our journey to Heaven?

Unit 7 Overview

Chapter 19

The children will:

- compare the story of the Loaves and the Fish to what Jesus gives us in Holy Communion
- recognize the value of praying together the Lord's Prayer and offering each other a sign of peace before receiving Communion
- understand that through the Eucharist, Jesus' followers are united with him and one another
- appreciate that through the Eucharist, Jesus Christ is really and truly present with us, so we receive Holy Communion with reverence and adore him in the reserved Blessed Sacrament

Catholic Social Teaching: Live Your Faith

- Call to Community, Pages 292–293
- Option for the Poor, Pages 296–297

Chapter 20

The children will:

- understand that in the Concluding Rites of the Mass, we are blessed and sent out to proclaim the Good News and give honor to God by the way we live
- examine the Apostles' call to share the Good News
- identify the Church's mission as sharing Jesus' message of love and the Kingdom
- recognize that all members of the Church share in her mission, and some serve as missionaries who travel far away to spread the Good News

Catholic Social Teaching: Live Your Faith

- Life and Dignity, Pages 290–291
- The Dignity of Work, Pages 298–299

Chapter 21

The children will:

- define Heaven as life and happiness forever with God
- relate the story of the Wedding Feast to God's invitation and our response
- describe the Eucharist as the spiritual food that helps us to live with Jesus forever
- recognize the need to say "yes," daily to God

Songs of Scripture
"The Great Feast"

Catholic Social Teaching: Live Your Faith

- Option for the Poor, Pages 296–297
- The Dignity of Work, Pages 298–299

Preview Unit Theme

Ask: What is the unit theme?

Confirm that the unit focus is on the Kingdom of God.

Ask: How does receiving Holy Communion help us on our journey to Heaven?

Point out that the children will learn more about this in the next three chapters.

Have volunteers read aloud each of the bullet points under Our Catholic Tradition.

Have the children study the photos. Ask volunteers to describe what they see. Ask them what the images say about the unit theme.

After some discussion, explain that the group will be exploring all of these questions/comments in the next three chapters.

KEY CONCEPT
Through the Eucharist, Jesus' followers are united with him and one another. The gift of Holy Communion is received with reverence.

DOCTRINAL CONTENT

- The story of the Loaves and the Fish helps us understand what Jesus gives us in Holy Communion. (CCC, 1335)
- Before receiving Communion, we pray together the Lord's Prayer and offer each other a sign of peace. (CCC, 1365)
- Through the Eucharist, Jesus' followers are united with him and one another. (CCC, 1369–1370)
- Jesus Christ is really and truly present with us in the Eucharist, so we receive Holy Communion with reverence and adore him in the reserved Blessed Sacrament. (CCC, 1374)

TASKS OF CATECHESIS
Helping children grow in a faith that is "known, celebrated, lived, and expressed in prayer" (NDC, 20).

This chapter focuses on the following tasks of catechesis:

- Liturgical Education
- Moral Formation

Catechist Background

So they said to him, "What sign can you do, that we may see and believe in you? What can you do? Our ancestors ate manna in the desert, as it is written: 'He gave them bread from heaven to eat.'" John 6:30–31

➔ **Reflect** How do you receive the bread of life from God?

Every human needs food and nourishment to survive. Jesus knew this well. In the Gospels, there are many examples of Jesus eating a meal with friends. Jesus also knew that people could not survive on bread alone, and he said so.

After Jesus fed the 5,000, crowds continued to follow him. He told his followers that the food they sought would disappear, but the food he offered would never run out, because the food he gave was the Bread of Life. Jesus told them that anyone who comes to him will never go hungry and will have eternal life.

Think of a time when you felt very hungry or thirsty. The sensation of an empty stomach may have driven you to the vending machine. Or your thirst may have caused you to head for the nearest drinking fountain. Now think of a time when you felt emotionally hungry or spiritually thirsty. What did you reach for—a moment of prayer, a spiritual friend, or nothing at all?

Jesus knew the significance of sharing a meal. In his culture, eating together was a sign of deep intimacy. He celebrated a meal at a wedding feast in Cana. He shared the Jewish Passover meal with his Apostles. The Eucharistic Meal is the reality of spiritual nourishment, given under the sign of physical nourishment. The Eucharist is your spiritual nourishment needed for survival. All those who receive Jesus in the Eucharist become one with him.

➔ **Reflect** How does the Eucharist nourish you?

Catechist's Prayer

Lord Jesus, help me find ways to nourish my soul. Teach me how to help others, especially the children, to draw upon your love. Help me serve as a wonderful example of your love for them. Amen.

Lesson Plan

Objectives	Process	Materials
Invite, 10 minutes		
Supper of the Lamb Page 257	**Psalm 67:7** Pray the opening prayer. **John 6:30–35** Reflect prayerfully on the Word. • Discuss What Do You Wonder questions.	**Optional Activity** Chapter Story: "Antonio's Feast"
Discover, 35 minutes		
Jesus Feeds Us Pages 258–259 • Compare the story of the Loaves and the Fish to what Jesus gives us in Holy Communion • Recognize the value of praying together the Lord's Prayer and offering each other a sign of peace before receiving Communion	• **Catholic Faith Words** Holy Communion **Luke 9:10–17** Proclaim "The Feeding of the Five Thousand." ☆ Color the baskets of loaves and fish. • Explain that the Mass is the Supper of the Lamb. • **Share Your Faith Activity** Talk about how Jesus feeds believers.	☐ pencils or pens ☐ board or chart paper ☐ index cards, one per child
Holy Communion Pages 260–261 • Understand that through the Eucharist, Jesus' followers are united with him and one another • Appreciate that through the Eucharist, Jesus Christ is really and truly present with us, so we receive Holy Communion with reverence and adore him in the reserved Blessed Sacrament	• **Catholic Faith Words** Real Presence, reverence, Blessed Sacrament, Tabernacle • Discuss what happens after the Lord's Prayer. ☆ Underline who is present in Holy Communion. • Teach that the Blessed Sacrament is reserved in the Tabernacle. • **Connect Your Faith Activity** Write one good action to show reverence.	☐ pencils or pens ☐ index cards, four per child • **Optional Activity** Receiving Jesus ☐ Activity Master 19 (Page 257E)
Live, 15 minutes		
Our Catholic Life Pages 262–263	• Discuss the work of extraordinary ministers of Holy Communion. ☆ Draw a box around the word *Tabernacle*. • **People of Faith** Learn about Venerable Pierre Toussaint. • **Live Your Faith Activity** Decorate a prayer card.	☐ pencils or pens ☐ art supplies
Prayer of Petition Page 264	• Select two readers. Rehearse "The Supper of the Lamb." • Follow the order of prayer.	Download "The Supper of the Lamb."

Family + Faith Page 265

Point out that the Catholic Families page provides chapter highlights, information on how second graders understand faith concepts, and family prayer.

Chapter Review Page 266

aliveinchrist.osv.com

- Customize and Download Assessments
- Email Links to eAssessments
- Interactive Student Reviews

ONLINE RESOURCES

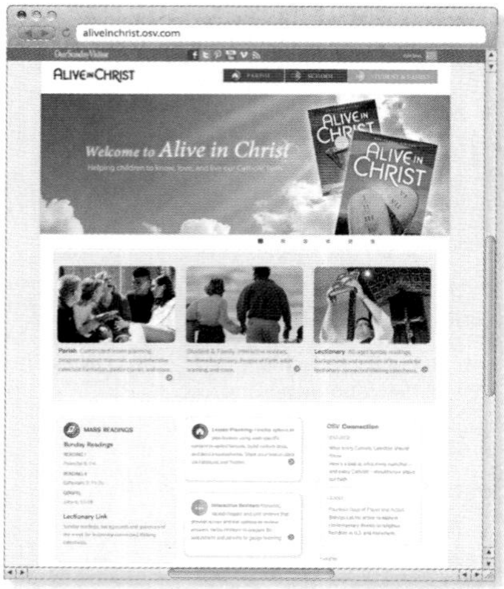

Go to **aliveinchrist.osv.com**

You will find:

- Interactive lesson planning with web specific content and additional activities
- Step by step lesson instruction from printed Catechist Edition for integrated lesson planning
- Custom-built assessments to download and eAssessment links
- Interactive reviews that provide scores and the option to review answers
- Sunday readings with background and questions of the week

Go to **osvparish.com**

You will find:

- Ask the Experts Q and A
- General Catechist Helps
- Community Connections and Blogs

Sharing the Message with Second Graders

The Real Presence of Jesus Christ in the Eucharist Transubstantiation, the transformation of the bread and wine in Mass to the Body and Blood of Jesus Christ, seems like a very difficult concept to impart to children. However, many children's stories and movies have examples of things or people that have taken the form of something else (shape shifters, etc.). Therefore, they are capable of understanding that the Eucharist still looks and tastes like bread and wine but is Jesus himself. Jesus has taken the form of bread and wine in order to be food for our souls.

Teaching Tip: Ask the children about stories they have heard or movies they have seen in which something or someone takes the form of something else.

How Second Graders Understand

- Second graders sometimes understand things better than they can express. Help them find the right words to tell what they know.
- The children know that their words and actions show their love for God. Help them develop self-discipline to control both of these things.
- Children this age understand concrete experiences best. Include stories, activities, and songs in the lessons.

"I understand concrete experiences best. Include stories, activities, and songs in our lessons."

Chapter Connections

Chapter Story

Invite

"Antonio's Feast"

Use this story to expand the chapter introduction.

- Have the children think of the kinds of things they would want someone to share with them.
- Ask them to brainstorm things they would like to share with someone who is sick.

Go to **aliveinchrist.osv.com** Lesson Planning section for this story.

NCEA IFG: ACRE Edition

Discover

Liturgical Life

- Objective: To know the Paschal Mystery of Jesus: in the Church's liturgical life—feasts, seasons, symbols, and practices and in the Sacraments as signs and instruments of grace

Moral Formation

- Objective: To be knowledgeable about the teachings of Jesus and the Church as the basis of Christian morality and to understand Catholic Social Teaching

Catholic Social Teaching

Live

Use one of these features to introduce a principle and engage the children with an activity.

- Call to Community, Pages 292–293
- Option for the Poor, Pages 296–297

Music Options

Use one or more of the following songs to enhance catechetical learning or for prayer.

- "The Supper of the Lamb," Live Prayer, Page 264
- "Behold the Lamb," Discover, Page 258
- "We Come to Worship You," Discover, Page 260

LECTIONARY CONNECTION

Chapter 19 highlights Lectionary-connected themes such as the Holy Communion, Real Presence, reverence, and Blessed Sacrament. If your parish aligns its curriculum to the liturgical year, you could use this chapter in connection with the following Sundays.

Year A

First Sunday of Lent—Unity

Second Sunday of Easter—Communal Life

Year B

Palm Sunday of the Passion of the Lord—Communion

Eighteenth Sunday in Ordinary Time—Communion

Year C

The Holy Family of Jesus, Mary, and Joseph—God's Children

Second Sunday of Easter—Great numbers were added.

Go to **aliveinchrist.osv.com** for a complete correlation ordered by the Sundays of the year and suggestions for how to integrate the Scripture readings into chapter lessons.

Name ______________________________ Date ______________

Receiving Jesus

We receive Jesus himself when we receive Holy Communion.
Draw a picture of you and your family receiving Holy Communion.

CHAPTER 19

Supper of the Lamb

Let Us Pray

Leader: We praise you God, for you are good and holy.

"The earth has yielded its harvest;
God, our God, blesses us." Psalm 67:7

All: O God, we thank you for sharing your harvest with us in Holy Communion. Amen.

God's Word

Once, the people wanted a sign from Jesus so that they could better see and believe in him. They said, "Our ancestors ate manna in the desert, as it is written: 'He gave them bread from heaven to eat.'" Jesus said to them, "Amen, amen, I say to you, it was not Moses who gave the bread from heaven; my Father gives you the true bread from heaven. For the bread of God is that which comes down from heaven and gives life to the world. I say to you, I am the bread of life; whoever comes to me will never hunger, and whoever believes in me will never thirst."
Based on John 6:30–35

What Do You Wonder?

- How does Jesus feed us today?
- How does the Father take care of us?

Optional Activity

Chapter Story: "Antonio's Feast" *Verbal/Linguistic*

Use this story after the opening prayer, before talking to the children about wheat and grapes.

- Have the children silently read the story.
- Ask them at what special gatherings food is important. birthdays, weddings, holidays
- After discussing the importance of feasts, transition back to the lesson instruction.

Go to **aliveinchrist.osv.com** for Chapter Story.

Invite

Let Us Pray

Invite the children to gather in the prayer space and make the Sign of the Cross. Read aloud the leader's prayer and the Psalm verse. Prompt the children's response.

Have the children move from the prayer space back to their seats.

Explain that a wonderful part of God's gift to us in the harvest is wheat and grapes. From those, we make bread and wine.

Say: Let's listen with our hearts to this story about bread.

God's Word

Guide the children through the process of Scripture reflection.

- Invite them to close their eyes, be still, and open their minds and hearts to what God is saying to them in this passage.
- Proclaim the Scripture.
- Maintain several moments of silence.
- *Ask:* What did you hear God say to you today?
- Invite volunteers to share.

What Do You Wonder?

Say: Jesus was telling his disciples that he is the bread that comes from Heaven. He gives us life. He is the Bread of Life. And so we can always have that life, Jesus Christ gives himself to us in the Eucharist.

Invite the children to respond to the questions. Ask what else they might wonder about how Jesus feeds us.

Discover

Objectives

- Compare the story of the Loaves and the Fish to what Jesus gives us in Holy Communion
- Recognize the value of praying together the Lord's Prayer and offering each other a sign of peace before receiving Communion

Jesus Feeds Us

Invite a volunteer to read aloud the question.

- Write the children's responses on the board or on chart paper.

Invite another volunteer to read the first paragraph.

God's Word

Proclaim the Scripture.

- Have the children role-play this story. Tell them to imagine themselves in the crowd that day, and then ask them to share what they might have said and done.

Music Option: Have the children sing "Behold the Lamb," downloaded from **aliveinchrist.osv.com**.

Work with Words

Read aloud the Catholic Faith Word and its definition.

- Provide one index card per child.
- Have the children write the word on one side of the card and the definition on the other.
- Encourage the children to use their cards for chapter or unit review.

Jesus Feeds Us

How does Jesus provide for us?

Jesus knew how important food was for life. The Gospels have many stories of Jesus sharing meals with his friends.

Catholic Faith Words

Holy Communion receiving Jesus' Body and Blood in the celebration of the Eucharist

God's Word

The Feeding of Five Thousand

One day, Jesus was speaking to a crowd of five thousand people. Late in the day, the Apostles told Jesus to send the crowds away to nearby villages to find food.

Jesus told the Apostles to feed the people themselves. "How can we do that?" they asked. "We have only five loaves of bread and two fish."

Scripture Background

Luke 9:10–17

In "The Feeding of the Five Thousand," also known as "The Loaves and the Fish," the disciples saw the crowd as a bother, but Jesus saw the people's need for love, care, and compassion.

- Jesus wanted to minister not only to their spiritual needs, but also to their physical needs.
- This Scripture helps us to see that Jesus can and does care about both our physical and spiritual needs.

Jesus told them to have the people sit down. He took the bread and fish, looked up to Heaven, and blessed the food. He broke it into pieces and gave the pieces to his followers to pass out among the people.

Everyone had enough to eat. The leftovers filled twelve straw baskets. Based on Luke 9:10–17

The Lord's Prayer

When Jesus fed the people, they felt his love and care. Jesus continues to care for us. In the Mass, he gives us his Body and Blood. The Mass is the Supper of the Lamb. Jesus is the Lamb of God because of his sacrifice for us. He invites us to his supper where he feeds us in the Eucharist.

As we prepare to receive **Holy Communion**, we stand to say the Lord's Prayer. We praise the Father and ask that he reign in our hearts and lives. We show our trust in him for all we need now and to be with him forever.

Color the baskets of loaves and fish below.

Share Your Faith

Think What did Jesus feed the crowd in the story? How does Jesus feed us in the Mass?

Share Break into two groups and talk about it.

The Feeding of the Five Thousand

Continue proclaiming the Scripture.

- *Ask:* How did Jesus take care of the people? Possible responses: He didn't send them away; he performed a miracle; he fed them.
- Write all responses on the board or on chart paper.

The Lord's Prayer

Have the children read this section with a partner.

- Explain that before people receive Jesus in Holy Communion, they share a sign of peace and they pray the prayer Jesus taught.
- ☆ Direct the children to color the baskets of loaves and the fish.
- Allow enough time for the children to color the illustration.

Activity

Read aloud the directions for the Share Your Faith activity.

- Arrange the children into two groups to discuss the question.
- Ask volunteers to share their answers.

Catechist Background

Proper Disposition

Explain to the children the following regulations for the reception of Holy Communion.

- Before receiving Holy Communion, one must be free of serious sin and observe the required fast of not eating or drinking anything except water or medicine for an hour before Holy Communion.
- Encourage them to celebrate the Sacrament of Reconciliation often and to attend Mass every Sunday and on Holy Days of Obligation.
- Share in an appropriate way with the children that it is the desire of the Church that Catholics meet these dispositions.

Quick Review

The story of the Loaves and the Fish is comparable to Holy Communion because Jesus continues to feed his followers at Mass. The Eucharist is the Supper of the Lamb.

Discover

Objectives

- Understand that through the Eucharist, Jesus' followers are united with him and one another
- Appreciate that through the Eucharist, Jesus Christ is really and truly present with us, so we receive Holy Communion with reverence and adore him in the reserved Blessed Sacrament

Holy Communion

Read aloud the question.

- Invite the children to respond.
- Tell the children that they will find the answer as they silently read the text.
- *Ask:* What happens after the Lord's Prayer? We exchange the sign of peace and then receive Holy Communion.
- Read aloud the definition of *Real Presence*.
- Ask the children to underline, in the text, who is really and truly present in Holy Communion.
- *Ask:* What does the sign of peace remind us of? that we share with others the peace, love, and goodwill that comes from Christ and unites us
- Point out the photo where the sign of peace is being offered.

Music Option: Have the children sing "We Come to Worship You," downloaded from **aliveinchrist.osv.com**.

Discover

Holy Communion

What happens after the Lord's Prayer?

Catholic Faith Words

Real Presence the teaching that Jesus is really and truly with us in the Eucharist. We receive Jesus in his fullness.

Underline who is really and truly present in Holy Communion.

After praying to our Father, we offer the peace of Christ to one another. This sign of peace is a reminder that we share with others the peace, love, and goodwill that comes from Christ and unites us.

After the sign of peace, the priest breaks the Host that is the Body of Christ before he eats and shares it. This is what Jesus did at the Last Supper. The priest's action again reminds the assembly that Jesus died and was raised from the dead for all people. If you are free from serious sin, you are welcome at the Lord's table. Jesus is really and truly present in Holy Communion. We call this **Real Presence**. When you receive Holy Communion, you become one with Jesus and all his Church.

We offer the sign of peace during Mass by shaking hands or hugging one another.

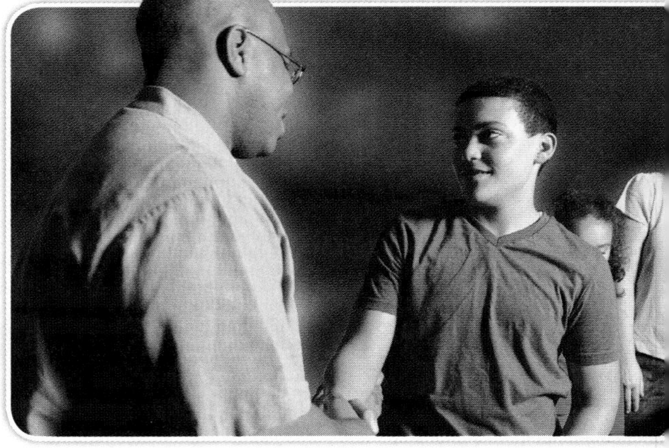

Optional Activity

Activity Master 19: Receiving Jesus

Distribute copies of the activity found on catechist page 257E.

- Provide supplies for the children to draw the picture.
- As an alternative, you may wish to send this activity home with the children.

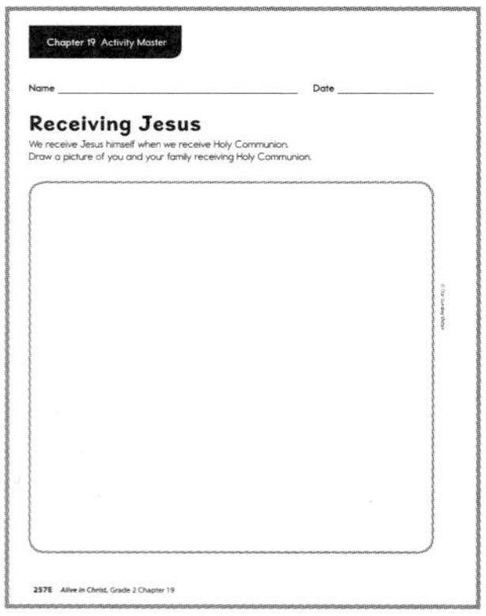

Chapter 19 Activity Master
Name
Date
Receiving Jesus
We receive Jesus himself when we receive Holy Communion.
Draw a picture of you and your family receiving Holy Communion.
257E Alive in Christ, Grade 2 Chapter 19

Receiving Communion

The Body and Blood of Jesus is a great gift. When you receive it, you show **reverence**, or care and respect. You walk to the altar prayerfully. As the person in front of you receives the Eucharist, you bow slightly. When it is your turn, the priest, deacon, or an extraordinary minister of the Holy Communion says, "The Body of Christ," and you say, "Amen." You receive the Body of Christ in your hand or on your tongue. You may also receive the Blood of Christ from the chalice.

Afterward, you go back to your place and sing with everyone. Then you pray in silence.

The Blessed Sacrament

Any Hosts reserved, or left over, after Mass are stored in a beautiful cabinet or container called the **Tabernacle**. Jesus remains present in the reserved Hosts, which are also called the **Blessed Sacrament**.

Catholic Faith Words

reverence the care and respect you show to God and holy persons and things

Blessed Sacrament a name for the Holy Eucharist, especially the Body of Christ kept in the Tabernacle

tabernacle the special place in the church where the Blessed Sacrament is reserved after Mass for those who are ill or for Eucharistic Adoration

Connect Your Faith

Show Reverence Write one good action that you can do to show reverence during Mass.

____

____

____

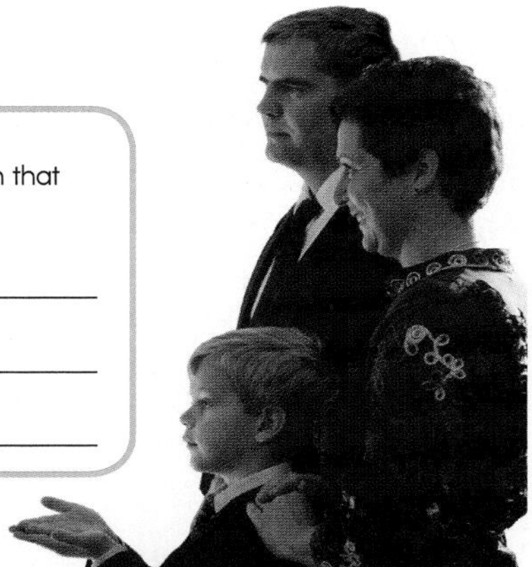

Receiving Communion

Have a volunteer read aloud the paragraphs.

- Demonstrate how the children are to hold their hands to receive the Body of Christ. (See the Quick Tip box below.)
- Tell them that Catholics who receive Holy Communion in a state of grace become one with Jesus and his Church.
- Remind them that the priest asks God to bless everyone and to give them peace so that they can go forth to love others as Jesus did.

The Blessed Sacrament

Read aloud the paragraph.

Work with Words

Ask volunteers to read the Catholic Faith Words and definitions on both pages.

- Distribute four index cards per child and have them create flash cards to use in chapter and unit reviews.

Activity

Read aloud the directions.

- Allow time for the children to write an action they can do.

Quick Tip

Receiving Holy Communion

Here is an easy way to teach the children the proper way to receive Holy Communion in the hand.

- Tell right-handed children to place the hand with which they write underneath their other hand. Left-handed children can do the opposite.
- In this way, they always have the correct hand ready to take the host. Tell them that they may reverently chew the host.
- Tell them to hold the cup with both hands while they take a tiny sip.

Quick Review

In the Eucharist, Jesus Christ is truly present. He unites us with himself and one another. We should receive the Eucharist with reverence.

Our Catholic Life

Ask: How do we honor Jesus in the Eucharist outside of Mass?

- Allow the children to share their ideas.

Read aloud the first paragraph.

- Pause to discuss the work of extraordinary ministers of Holy Communion in your parish.

Ask a volunteer to read the second paragraph.

- Direct the group's attention to the photograph, and ask the children if they have ever seen the Tabernacle in their parish.
- Invite those who have to describe it.
- ☆ Direct the children to draw a box around the word *Tabernacle*.
- After the children have found the word, ask them if they know what is kept inside the Tabernacle. the Blessed Sacrament, or the Body of Christ

Ask: How can we respect Jesus' presence in the Eucharist?

- Invite the children to discuss the question.

Point out that the Tabernacle is listed among several other special Church objects on page 313 in the Our Catholic Tradition section in the Student Book.

Our Catholic Life

How do we honor Jesus in the Eucharist outside of Mass?

Some people cannot join the community at Mass. They may be sick at home or in the hospital. Some elderly people are too weak to travel. All these people are still a part of the assembly. They are still joined to the community in prayer. After Mass, they may be visited by the priest, a deacon, or an extraordinary minister of Holy Communion who brings Holy Communion to them and prays with them.

Any other Hosts reserved after Mass are placed in the Tabernacle. A lamp or candle always burns near the Tabernacle to remind people that Jesus is present.

Draw a box around the word "Tabernacle." What is kept inside the Tabernacle?

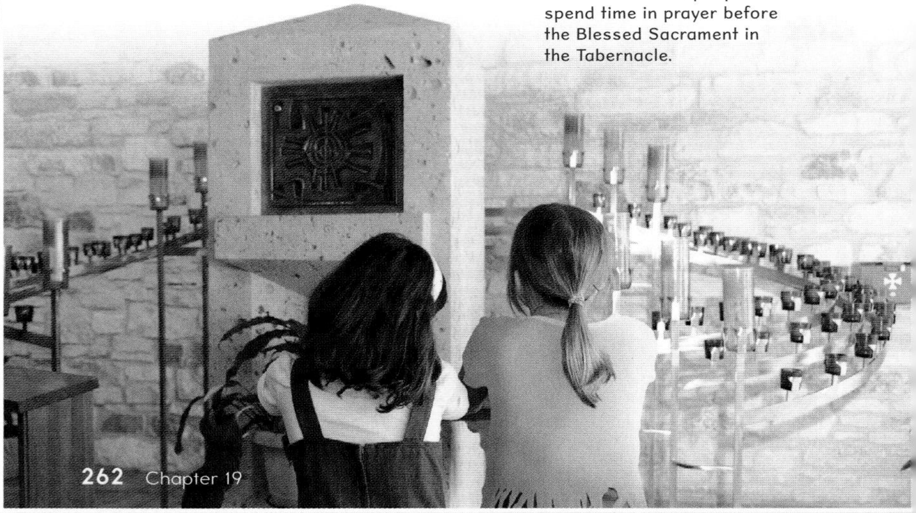

Outside of Mass, people can spend time in prayer before the Blessed Sacrament in the Tabernacle.

Catechist Background

Tabernacle

The word *Tabernacle* means "meeting place."

- In the Old Testament, the Book of Exodus describes the tent of meeting in which the tablets of the Law were kept in the ark of the covenant. Moses entered into the tent of meeting to speak with God as he led the Israelites in the wilderness.
- Today we meet with Jesus in the Blessed Sacrament when we pray before the Tabernacle.
- If possible, arrange for your group to spend time in prayer before the Blessed Sacrament.

People of Faith

Venerable Pierre Toussaint, 1766–1853

Venerable Pierre Toussaint was a slave born in Haiti. His owner taught him to read and write. When his owner's family moved to New York City, they brought Pierre with them. Pierre became a barber and helped support his owner's family after the man died. He and his wife raised his niece and Pierre often took her for walks in the city. He was well known for his generosity and aid to the poor. He attended daily Mass and had a great love for Jesus in Holy Communion. He helped build St. Patrick's Old Cathedral in New York.

July 25

Discuss: How can you show respect for Jesus in the Eucharist?

Learn more about Venerable Pierre Toussaint at **aliveinchrist.osv.com**

Live Your Faith

Make a Prayer Card Decorate the front of the prayer card and write a prayer for parish members who cannot be present at Mass.

Catholic Social Teaching

Chapter Connections

To integrate Catholic Social Teaching into your lesson, choose one of the following features: Call to Community, pages 292–293; or Option for the Poor, pages 296–297.

- Start the Live step of the process by talking about Venerable Pierre Toussaint on page 263. Then move directly to the Catholic Social Teaching feature.
- Or, to expand the lesson, complete both pages 262 and 263, then move to the Catholic Social Teaching feature.
- Return to Chapter 19 for the prayer on page 264.

People of Faith

Tell the children about Venerable Pierre Toussaint.

- After Pierre married, he and his wife adopted his orphaned niece, and opened their home to orphans.
- They also helped people, black and white, suffering from yellow fever.
- Pierre never allowed his slavery to make him bitter. He knew God's grace would free him, and it did.
- Read aloud the paragraph on Venerable Pierre.
- Discuss the question at the end of the story.

Encourage the children to go to **aliveinchrist.osv.com** at home to learn more about Venerable Pierre Toussaint.

Activity

Read aloud the directions for the Live Your Faith activity.

- Provide plenty of art supplies so that the children may be creative with their prayer card decorations.
- Assist the children as needed with writing their prayers.

Let Us Pray

Prayer of Petition

Tell the children that they will be praying a Prayer of Petition, which means that they will be asking God for something. In this case, it will be for God to stay with them always.

Prepare

Ask the children to pause briefly between each of the petitions that begin "Stay with me, . . ." and consider the meaning of the words during the pause.

- Select two readers. You will be the leader.

Rehearse with the children "The Supper of the Lamb," downloaded from **aliveinchrist.osv.com**.

Gather

Invite the children to come to the prayer space with their books.

- Lead the children into the prayer space while playing or singing "The Supper of the Lamb."

Pray

Follow the order of prayer on the student page.

Conclude by processing around the room with the children singing the hymn refrain.

Let Us Pray

Prayer of Petition

Gather and begin with the Sign of the Cross.

Leader: Let's pray the words of Saint Padre Pio, to ask Christ to be with us always.

Reader 1: Stay with me, Lord, for it is necessary to have you present so that I do not forget you. You know how easily I abandon you.

Stay with me, Lord, because I am weak and I need your strength, that I may not fall so often.

Stay with me, Lord, for you are my life...

Reader 2: Stay with me, Lord, for you are my light and without you I am in darkness.

Stay with me, Lord, to show me your will.

Stay with me, Lord, so that I hear your voice and follow you.

All: Stay with me, Lord, for I desire to love you very much and always be in your company...Amen.

Saint Padre Pio, Prayer After Communion

Sing "The Supper of the Lamb"

The Supper of the Lamb
The Body of our Lord
The Blood of Christ outpoured
The Supper of the Lamb
The gift of life anew
A gift of love for you
For you are called to the
Supper of the Lamb

Tabernacle

Liturgy Link

The Sign of Peace

The sign of peace is an expression of our unity and mutual respect.

- The priest, extending and then joining his hands, gives the greeting of peace: "The peace of the Lord be with you always." The people answer: "And with your spirit."
- Then the priest or deacon says: "Let us offer each other the sign of peace." The people exchange a sign of God's peace and love, according to local custom.

Go to **aliveinchrist.osv.com** for Sunday readings, Scripture background, questions of the week, and seasonal resources.

FAMILY + FAITH
LIVING AND LEARNING TOGETHER

YOUR CHILD LEARNED >>>
This chapter explains how we are united with Jesus and with one another when we reverently receive Holy Communion.

God's Word
Read **Matthew 14:15–21** to learn about the multiplication of the loaves and fishes.

Catholics Believe
- Through the Eucharist, Jesus' followers are united with him and one another.
- The gift of Holy Communion is received with reverence.

To learn more, go to the *Catechism of the Catholic Church* #319, 256, 454 at **usccb.org**.

People of Faith
This week, your child met Venerable Pierre Toussaint, a former slave who was well known for his love of the Eucharist and care for the poor.

CHILDREN AT THIS AGE >>>
How They Understand the Real Presence of Jesus Christ in the Eucharist Transubstantiation, the transformation of the bread and wine during Mass to the Body and Blood of Jesus Christ, seems like a very difficult concept to impart to children. However, many children's stories and movies have examples of things or people that have taken the form of something else (shape shifters, etc.). Therefore, they are capable of understanding that the Eucharist still looks and tastes like bread and wine but is Jesus himself.

CONSIDER THIS >>>
Have you ever wondered why we call Jesus' Body and Blood, "Communion"?

Communion is another name for Eucharist because the word describes an effect of Eucharist. When we receive the gift of Jesus' Body and Blood, we enter into communion with him. In Christ we are then made one with each other. "We testify in faith that God as Trinity wants to relate to us and to be engaged in our world. . .love within the Trinity makes possible a divine closeness to us. Love preserves the mystery and yet overcomes what might have been a gulf between us and God. Unity and communion with God in the Church also calls us to become a source of unity for all people" (*USCCA, p. 119*).

LET'S TALK >>>
- Have your child show you the way to receive Holy Communion. Ask children what they do (bow, hold out cupped hands, etc.) and what they say (Amen).
- Talk about why your family would stay after Mass to say a prayer in front of the Tabernacle.

LET'S PRAY >>>
Venerable Pierre, pray for us that we may help others see the presence of Jesus in the Eucharist. Amen.

For a multimedia glossary of Catholic Faith Words, Sunday readings, seasonal and Saint resources, and chapter activities go to **aliveinchrist.osv.com**.

Family + Faith

Distribute the page to the children or parents/adult family members. Point out the chapter highlights, insights on how second graders understand concepts, the opportunity for the adults to reflect on their own experience and faith journey, and the family prayer.

Chapter 19 Review

A Work with Words Use the word or words from the Word Bank to complete the sentences.

Word Bank: Reverence, Tabernacle, Holy Communion, Blessed Sacrament, Presence

1. Real __Presence__ is Jesus really and truly with us in the Eucharist.
2. __Holy Communion__ is the Body and Blood of Christ.
3. All Hosts reserved after Mass are placed in the __Tabernacle__.
4. __Reverence__ is the care and respect you show to God and holy persons and things.
5. The __Blessed Sacrament__ is the name we give to the Hosts kept in the Tabernacle.

B Check Understanding Use the numbers 1 to 5 to put the sentences in the order they happen at Mass.

6. [3] The priest breaks the bread.
7. [1] All stand to pray the Lord's Prayer.
8. [5] After Communion the people continue to sing and then pray in silence.
9. [2] The people offer the sign of peace.
10. [4] The people receive Holy Communion.

Go to **aliveinchrist.osv.com** for an interactive review.

Chapter Review

Use Catechist Quick Reviews to highlight lesson concepts.

A Work with Words
Review the Word Bank with the children. Have them write the word or words to complete each sentence.

B Check Understanding
Explain to the children that they will be using numbers to put the sentences in the correct order.

Go to **aliveinchrist.osv.com** to prepare customized and downloadable assessments, send eAssessments, and assign interactive reviews.

KEY CONCEPT
The Church's mission is to share Jesus' love and to announce the Good News of the Kingdom of God. All members of the Church share in her mission.

DOCTRINAL CONTENT

- In the Concluding Rites of the Mass, we are blessed and sent out to proclaim the Good News and give honor to God by the way we live. (CCC, 1332)
- As the Apostles were called to share the Good News, the Church's mission is to share Jesus' message of love and the Kingdom. (CCC, 849)
- All members of the Church share in her mission, and some serve as missionaries who travel far away to spread the Good News. (CCC, 851–852)

TASKS OF CATECHESIS
Helping children grow in a faith that is "known, celebrated, lived, and expressed in prayer" (NDC, 20).

This chapter focuses on the following tasks of catechesis:

- Education for Community Life
- Missionary Initiation

Catechist Background

[Paul] remained for two full years in his lodgings. He received all who came to him, and with complete assurance … he proclaimed the kingdom of God and taught about the Lord Jesus Christ. Acts 28:30–31

→ **Reflect** How do you, as a catechist, teach about the Kingdom of God?

Jesus commanded his Apostles to go forth and make disciples of all nations. In essence, he was asking his Apostles to bring the Good News to everyone everywhere, to call all people to conversion, and to baptize them in the name of the Holy Trinity. At first, members of the early Church were unsure as to whether or not persons had to be Jewish before they could be called to salvation in Christ. The Council of Jerusalem, recorded in Acts, Chapter 15, was a meeting of the leaders of the Church at that time, presided over by Peter. There, it was ultimately decided that one did not have to be Jewish to be saved. Indeed, Saint Paul, once a Jewish persecutor of Christians, chose to focus his missionary work on the Gentiles, while Peter preached to the Jews.

Where is the focus of your missionary work? While you may not have the opportunity to travel throughout the world to evangelize others, as a person in relationship with many people, you have the potential to bring the Christian message to all those you meet. Reflect for a moment on your own call to evangelize. How do you bring the Gospel message to others, including those you teach?

Jesus was a master teacher. While relying on Scripture, he taught the Good News most effectively through his words and actions, setting an example for future evangelizers. What do your words and actions teach? Do they show your love and respect for all people, no matter who or where they are?

→ **Reflect** In what way can you share God's message today?

Catechist's Prayer

Holy Spirit, thank you for being with me. Help me accomplish the mission you have entrusted to me. Amen.

Lesson Plan

Objectives	Process	Materials
Invite, 10 minutes		
Go Forth! Page 267	**Psalm 67:2–3** Pray the opening prayer. **Acts 28:30–31** Reflect prayerfully on the Word. • Discuss What Do You Wonder questions.	**Optional Activity** Chapter Story: "Good News Gazette"
Discover, 35 minutes		
Live the Gospel Pages 268–269 • Understand that in the Concluding Rites of the Mass, we are blessed and sent out to proclaim the Good News and give honor to God by the way we live • Examine the Apostles' call to share the Good News • Identify the Church's mission as sharing Jesus' message of love and the Kingdom	• **Catholic Faith Words** mission, missionaries • Explain that the final part of the Mass is known as the Concluding Rites. **Acts 10:42–48** Proclaim "Peter Preaches." • Discuss how most Church members share Jesus' message right where they are. • **Share Your Faith Activity** Talk about ways to bring Jesus' message to others.	☐ pencils or pens ☐ board or chart paper ☐ index cards, two per child
An Example for All Pages 270–271 • Recognize that all members of the Church share in her mission and some serve as missionaries who travel far away to spread the Good News	• Talk about how everyone has gifts and talents. • Learn how Frances Xavier Cabrini started her own community. ☆ Connect the dots on the map. • **Connect Your Faith Activity** Choose a place on the map to go to tell the Good News.	☐ pencils or pens ☐ maps or globes • **Optional Activity** The Good News ☐ Activity Master 20 (Page 267E)
Live, 15 minutes		
Our Catholic Life Pages 272–273	• Make flash cards of faith guides. ☆ Write how to teach others about God's love. • **People of Faith** Learn about Saint Anthony Claret. • **Live Your Faith Activity** The children will draw themselves teaching someone else about Jesus.	☐ pencils or pens ☐ board or chart paper ☐ index cards, five per child
Blessing Prayer Page 274	• Teach the children to bless their forehead, lips, and heart when the Gospel is proclaimed. • Follow the order of prayer. Finish by singing "Share the Light."	Download "Share the Light."

Family + Faith Page 275

Point out that the Catholic Families page provides chapter highlights, information on how second graders understand faith concepts, and family prayer.

Chapter Review Page 276

aliveinchrist.osv.com

- Customize and Download Assessments
- Email Links to eAssessments
- Interactive Student Reviews

Teaching This Grade

ONLINE RESOURCES

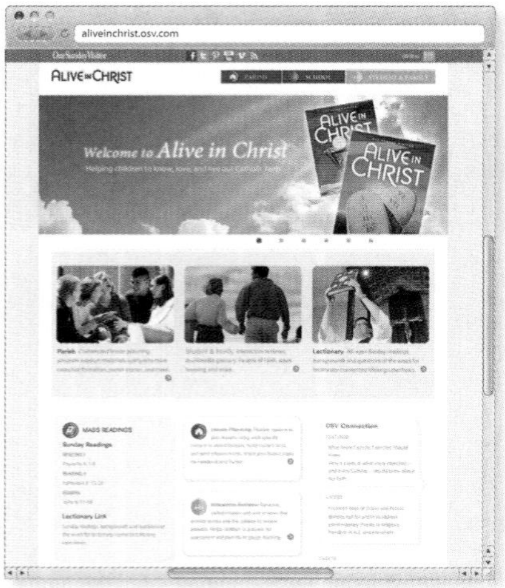

Go to **aliveinchrist.osv.com**

You will find:

- Interactive lesson planning with web specific content and additional activities
- Step by step lesson instruction from printed Catechist Edition for integrated lesson planning
- Custom-built assessments to download and eAssessment links
- Interactive reviews that provide scores and the option to review answers
- Sunday readings with background and questions of the week

Go to **osvparish.com**

You will find:

- Ask the Experts Q and A
- General Catechist Helps
- Community Connections and Blogs

Sharing the Message with Second Graders

Living as a Eucharistic People Children have sometimes been told "you are what you eat" as a way of helping them understand that they should eat healthy things that will help them grow and stay away from too much junk food. They should be prepared for the idea that as they nourish themselves with Jesus himself in the form of the Eucharist, God will help them to become more like Christ in their daily lives. In fact, we are sent forth after the Eucharistic celebration to be the hands and feet of Christ in the world.

Teaching Tip: Prompt the children to reflect on how they think they might change as they receive Christ in the Eucharist and grow in grace.

How Second Graders Understand

- Don't always try to do things for second graders. Suggest some ways for them to work out their own problems.
- Compliment the children on their work and problem-solving skills.
- Children this age enjoy stories. Read stories that teach them about the values and actions being covered in the lessons.

"Compliment me on my work and problem-solving skills."

Chapter Connections

Chapter Story

Invite

"Good News Gazette"

Use this story to expand the chapter introduction.

- Have the children write down some of their good deeds.
- Organize the children in pairs to share with one another how their good deeds helped others.
- Discuss with the children how good deeds make us feel.

Go to **aliveinchrist.osv.com** Lesson Planning section for this story.

NCEA IFG: ACRE Edition

Discover

Communal Life

- Objectives: To know the origin, mission, structure, and communal nature of the Church; to know the rights and responsibilities of the Christian faithful

Missionary Spirit

- Objective: To recognize the centrality of evangelization as the Church's mission and identity embodied in vocation and service

Catholic Social Teaching

Live

Use one of these features to introduce a principle and engage the children with an activity.

- Life and Dignity, Pages 290–291
- The Dignity of Work, Pages 298–299

Music Options

Use one or more of the following songs to enhance catechetical learning or for prayer.

- "Share the Light," Live Prayer, Page 274
- "Take the Word of God with You," Discover, Page 269
- "Malo, Malo, Thanks Be to God," Discover, Page 271

LECTIONARY CONNECTION

Chapter 20 highlights Lectionary-connected themes such as mission and missionaries. If your parish aligns its curriculum to the liturgical year, you could use this chapter in connection with the following Sundays.

Year A

The Epiphany of the Lord—Commission to Preach God's Plan

Twenty-fifth Sunday in Ordinary Time—Spreading the Gospel

Year B

Fourth Sunday of Advent—Mission

The Epiphany of the Lord—Commission to Preach God's Plan

Year C

The Epiphany of the Lord—Commission to Preach God's Plan

Twenty-eighth Sunday in Ordinary Time—Mission

Go to **aliveinchrist.osv.com** for a complete correlation ordered by the Sundays of the year and suggestions for how to integrate the Scripture readings into chapter lessons.

Name ______________________________ Date ______________

The Good News

Answer the questions by filling in the missing words.

1. How do we begin our prayers?

   With the Sign of the ______________________

2. Who were Jesus' special helpers?

   The ______________________.

3. Who preached to the people of Jerusalem?

   ______________________.

4. Who sent Jesus to save us?

   God the ______________________.

5. Sharing the Good News of Jesus and God's Kingdom is

   the Church's ______________________.

CHAPTER 20

Invite

Go Forth!

Let Us Pray

Leader: God, as we go forth, be with us.

May God be merciful to us and bless us…
so that the whole world may know your will.
Based on Psalm 67:2–3

All: Thank you, God, for going with us as we share you with others. Amen.

God's Word

"[Paul] remained for two full years in his lodgings. He received all who came to him, and with complete assurance…he proclaimed the kingdom of God and taught about the Lord Jesus Christ." Acts 28:30–31

What Do You Wonder?

- Why is the mission of Jesus important to us today?
- How do you tell others about Jesus' mission?

Optional Activity

Chapter Story: "Good News Gazette" *Verbal/Linguistic*

Use this story after the opening prayer, before you tell the children we are called to share God's Word and life.

- Ask volunteers to take turns reading as if they are TV anchors.
- Discuss with the children how good news makes them feel. Share some good news from your parish or your community.
- Connect our good news with the Good News of Jesus, then transition back to the lesson instruction.

Go to **aliveinchrist.osv.com** for Chapter Story.

Invite

Let Us Pray

Invite the children to gather in the prayer space and make the Sign of the Cross. Ask a volunteer to read aloud the leader's prayer and the Psalm verse. Prompt the group's response.

Have the children move from the prayer space back to their seats.

Explain that we are each called to share God's Word and Jesus' love with others.

Say: Let's listen to hear how Saint Paul taught about Jesus.

God's Word

Guide the children through the process of Scripture reflection.

- Invite them to close their eyes, be still, and open their minds and hearts to what God is saying to them in this passage.
- Proclaim the Scripture.
- Maintain several moments of silence.
- *Ask:* What did you hear God say to you today?
- Invite volunteers to share.

What Do You Wonder?

Say: Just as Saint Paul told everyone about Jesus Christ, we, too, are called to do the same.

Invite the children to respond to the questions. Ask what else they might wonder about the mission of the Church.

Discover

Objectives

- Understand that in the Concluding Rites of the Mass, we are blessed and sent out to proclaim the Good News and give honor to God by the way we live
- Examine the Apostles' call to share the Good News
- Identify the Church's mission as sharing Jesus' message of love and the Kingdom

Live the Gospel

Begin by reading aloud the question at the top of the student page.

- Write the children's responses on the board or on chart paper.
- Tell the children that as the group covers the text on the next two pages, they will discover more about this.

Ask the children to silently read the two paragraphs.

- *Ask:* What is the final part of the Mass called? Concluding Rites
- *Ask:* When you leave, what should you do next? proclaim the Good News and give honor to God by the way you live

God's Word

Proclaim the Scripture story.

Live the Gospel

How do we share the Good News?

After receiving Holy Communion, we may hear some announcements. Then, the priest or deacon blesses us and says the Mass has ended. He dismisses us to, "Go in peace." We respond, "Thanks be to God." This final part of the Mass is called the Concluding Rites.

We are sent to proclaim the Good News and give honor to God by the way we live. Jesus' first followers took his Good News to people everywhere.

Catholic Faith Words

mission a job or purpose. The Church's mission is to announce the Good News of God's Kingdom.

missionaries people who answer God's call to bring the message of Jesus and announce the Good News of his Kingdom to people in other places

God's Word

Peter Preaches

Peter told the people of Jerusalem that Jesus sent the Apostles to preach to all people.

The Apostles shared the Good News of God's Kingdom. Peter told the people that Jesus wanted everyone to believe in him. If they believed, they would receive forgiveness through Jesus' name.

Scripture Background

Acts 10:42–48

This passage from Acts shows that Jesus' message is meant for all people.

- The Holy Spirit came upon Jews and Gentiles alike as Peter spoke.
- The Gentiles were baptized and spent time learning from Peter.

After listening to Peter, many people from faraway places asked to be baptized. Peter told the crowd that anyone who was moved by the Spirit could be baptized. Based on Acts 10:42–48

Missionaries travel to countries around the world and help people meet their basic needs.

The Church's Mission

Peter and the other Apostles shared Jesus' Good News and led the Church. The Pope and bishops follow the Apostles in this role. They lead the Church in her work to spread the Good News of Jesus and God's Kingdom throughout the world. This work is called the Church's **mission**. All her members share this responsibility.

Most Church members share Jesus' message right where they are. Others bring the message of Jesus to faraway places. They are called **missionaries**.

Share Your Faith

Think What can you do to bring Jesus' message of love to others?

1. Encourage those who are afraid.

 ______________________________.

2. Trust in God the Father's love.

 ______________________________.

Share With a partner, talk about your responses.

Peter Preaches

Continue proclaiming the Scripture story.

- *Ask:* Who did Peter say could be baptized? anyone moved by the Spirit

The Church's Mission

Invite two volunteers to read aloud the two paragraphs.

Work with Words

Invite two more volunteers to read aloud the Catholic Faith Words and their definitions on page 268.

- Distribute two index cards per child.
- Have the children write the words on one side of the card and the definitions on the other.
- Encourage them to use the cards for chapter and unit reviews.

Activity

Read aloud the directions for the Share Your Faith activity.

- Allow the children to choose a partner to work with.
- Ask volunteers to share their work.

Music Option: Have the children sing "Take the Word of God with You," downloaded from **aliveinchrist.osv.com**.

Quick Tip

Working in Pairs

Children working in pairs are more apt to focus on the exercise when working as half of a team.

- Each child has to make a contribution and is challenged by the other to perform well.
- Rotate the children so that the same children are not paired each week.
- Sometimes you can arrange the pairs and sometimes you can let the children select a partner.

Quick Review

The Church's mission is to share Jesus' message of love and the Kingdom. It is the mission of all her members to share in this same mission that the Apostles had.

Discover

Objective

- Recognize that all members of the Church share in her mission, and some serve as missionaries who travel far away to spread the Good News

An Example for All

Tell the children that, in this section, they will learn about Mother Cabrini.

Summarize the first paragraph.

Saint Frances Xavier Cabrini

Invite two volunteers to each read aloud one of the paragraphs.

- *Ask:* Why did Frances Cabrini start her own community of sisters? she was thought too sickly to join any group
- *Ask:* What did Pope Leo XIII suggest to her? that she go to the United States to help Italian immigrants that had just arrived

Have the children turn to page 306 in the Our Catholic Tradition section of their books. Read aloud both paragraphs under "Her Mission."

An Example For All

What did Mother Cabrini do?

Everyone has different gifts. We can use those talents to spread Jesus' message in different ways.

Saint Frances Xavier Cabrini

Frances Xavier Cabrini was born in a small village in Italy. She was sickly throughout her life, but this did not stop her from doing God's work.

After hearing stories about the Saints, Frances wanted to be a missionary in China. She wanted to be a religious sister, but was thought too sickly to join any group. So she started her own community. Pope Leo XIII suggested Frances go to the United States to help Italian immigrants that had just arrived.

Catechist Background

Following a Dream

Mother Cabrini and six of her sisters did their work in Chinatown and fast-growing Little Italy on New York's East Side.

- Her first meeting with Archbishop Corrigan did not go well. He told her that an orphanage was out of the question and to go home.
- In the end, Mother Cabrini won him over. He made peace with her, by personally delivering to her a palm he carried on Palm Sunday.

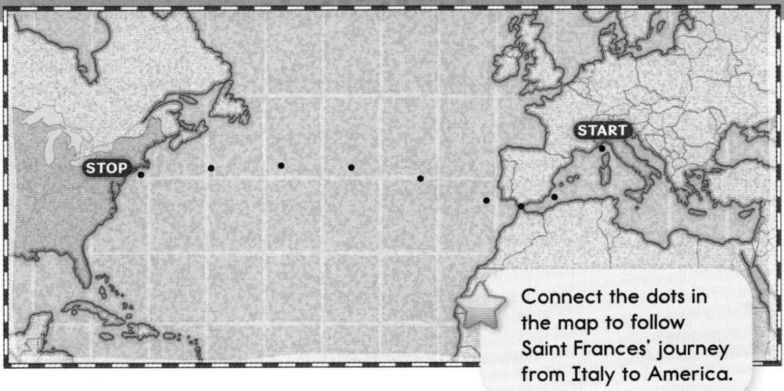

Connect the dots in the map to follow Saint Frances' journey from Italy to America.

Although she had a great fear of water, she crossed the ocean to New York. There she set up a home for orphaned Italian girls and other services for those who were poor.

By the time she was sixty-seven years old, Frances had set up over sixty schools, hospitals, orphanages, and convents throughout the world. In 1917 she died. In 1946, Frances became the first United States citizen to be named a Saint of the Catholic Church. She had carried out the Church's mission, bringing the love of Jesus to those in need.

Connect Your Faith

Spread the Good News If you could go anywhere in the world to tell others about Jesus' love, where would you go?

____

____

Saint Frances Xavier Cabrini,

continued

Invite two volunteers to read the remaining paragraphs.

- Have the children discuss the things Frances Cabrini did to help those who were poor.
- Remind the children that Frances Cabrini carried out the Church's mission by working to build orphanages, schools, convents, and hospitals to help people.
- ☆ Have the children connect the dots in the map to follow Saint Frances' journey.
- Allow time for the children to follow the dots.

Activity

Ask a volunteer to read aloud the directions for the Connect Your Faith activity.

- Allow the children to look at a map or globe so they can decide where they might like to go to spread the Good News.

Music Option: Have the children sing "Malo, Malo, Thanks Be to God," downloaded from **aliveinchrist.osv.com**.

Optional Activity

Activity Master 20: The Good News

Distribute copies of the activity found on catechist page 267E.

- Have a volunteer read aloud the directions.
- As an alternative, you may wish to send this activity home with the children.

Chapter 20 Activity Master

Name ____________ Date ________

The Good News

Answer the questions by filling in the missing words.

1. How do we begin our prayers?
   With the Sign of the ____________
2. Who were Jesus' special helpers?
   The ____________
3. Who preached to the people of Jerusalem?
   ____
4. Who sent Jesus to save us?
   God the ____________
5. Sharing the Good News of Jesus and God's Kingdom is the Church's ____________

267E Alive in Christ, Grade 2 Chapter 20

Quick Review

Everyone has different gifts. We can all use our talents to serve as missionaries of the Church.

Live

Our Catholic Life

Ask: Who can help you learn about Jesus?

- Write the children's answers on the board or on chart paper.

Read aloud the first paragraph.

- Tell the children that there are several guides listed on this page who can help them grow in faith.

Pass out five index cards.

- Have the children write the title of the faith guide on one side of the card and what they do on the other side.
- Allow time for children to write out the bullet points.
- ☆ Have the children write down one way they can teach others about God's love in the coming week.
- Ask volunteers to share their ideas with the group.

Our Catholic Life

Who can help you learn about Jesus?

Learning about Jesus is a journey that lasts your whole life. There is always more to learn. It's a good thing there are many people who can help you. They are your guides on the journey, helping you grow in faith.

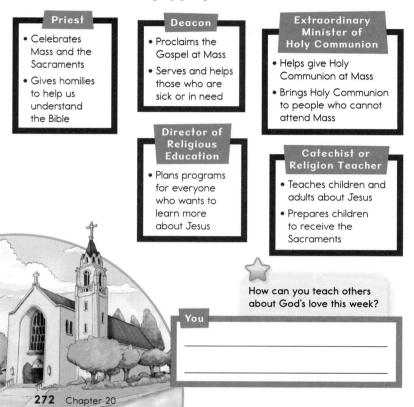

Priest
- Celebrates Mass and the Sacraments
- Gives homilies to help us understand the Bible

Deacon
- Proclaims the Gospel at Mass
- Serves and helps those who are sick or in need

Extraordinary Minister of Holy Communion
- Helps give Holy Communion at Mass
- Brings Holy Communion to people who cannot attend Mass

Director of Religious Education
- Plans programs for everyone who wants to learn more about Jesus

Catechist or Religion Teacher
- Teaches children and adults about Jesus
- Prepares children to receive the Sacraments

☆ How can you teach others about God's love this week?

You

____

____

Quick Tip

Invite Guests

When discussing the roles of those involved in Christian education, you may wish to invite representatives of these parish ministries to visit the group and answer the children's questions.

- Ask visitors to give concrete examples of how they help people learn about Jesus.
- Help the children develop questions for the visitors ahead of time.

People of Faith

Saint Anthony Claret, 1807–1870

Saint Anthony Mary Claret was born in Spain. His father taught him to weave and make designs. He also learned how to print books. Later, he became a priest and then a bishop. Saint Anthony used his skills to spread the message of Jesus. He went to Cuba as a missionary. He also started a company that printed religious books. He wrote more than 100 books himself. He started an order of priests called the Claretians. They continue his work today.

October 24

Discuss: What skills can you use to help others learn about Jesus?

Learn more about Saint Anthony at **aliveinchrist.osv.com**

Live Your Faith

Tell what is happening in the picture?

Draw a picture of yourself teaching someone else about Jesus.

People of Faith

Tell the children about Saint Anthony Claret.

- He was the confessor for Queen Isabella of Spain.
- He participated in the First Vatican Council.
- He had the gift of prophecy and performed many miracles.
- Read aloud the paragraph on Saint Anthony.
- Ask the children to share skills they can use to help others learn about Jesus.

Encourage the children to go to **aliveinchrist.osv.com** at home to learn more about Saint Anthony Claret.

Activity

Read aloud the directions for the Live Your Faith activity.

- Invite the children to volunteer what they see in the illustration.
- Allow time for the children to draw their own pictures.
- Encourage volunteers to share their picture with the rest of the group.

Catholic Social Teaching

Chapter Connections

To integrate Catholic Social Teaching into your lesson, choose one of the following features: Life and Dignity, pages 290–291; or The Dignity of Work, pages 298–299.

- Start the Live step of the process by talking about Saint Anthony Claret on page 273. Then move directly to the Catholic Social Teaching feature.
- Or, to expand the lesson, complete both pages 272 and 273, then move to the Catholic Social Teaching feature.
- Return to Chapter 20 for the prayer on page 274.

Let Us Pray
Blessing Prayer

Explain that this prayer is a blessing prayer that includes praying the Sign of the Cross with each blessing.

Prepare

Have the children rehearse "Share the Light," downloaded from **aliveinchrist.osv.com**.

Gather

Invite the children to gather in the prayer space. Tell them they will not need their books, as their only response to each part of the prayer is "Amen."

Pray

Follow the order of prayer on the student page.

- Prompt the children to sign themselves as you pray each blessing.

Conclude the celebration by processing around the room with the children, singing the refrain for "Share the Light."

Let Us Pray

Blessing Prayer

Gather and begin with the Sign of the Cross.

Leader: Make a Sign of the Cross on your forehead.
May you always remember to follow Jesus.

All: Amen.

Leader: Make a Sign of the Cross over your closed eyes.
May you learn to see Jesus in all whom you meet.

All: Amen.

Leader: Make a Sign of the Cross on your lips.
May all your words show respect.

All: Amen.

Leader: Make a Sign of the Cross over your heart.
May love move you to action and may God
give you strength to carry on the work of Jesus.

All: Amen.

Sing "Share the Light"

Share the light of Jesus.
Share the light that shows the way.
Share the light of Jesus.
Share God's spirit today.
Share God's spirit today.

Repeat Verse

Share the word…
Share the love…
Share the smile…
Share the light…

Liturgy Link

Sign of the Cross

The Sign of the Cross is used in many ways.

- During Mass, the celebrant makes a small cross on his forehead, lips, and heart before the Gospel reading. We are invited to do the same.
- Prayers often begin with the Sign of the Cross.
- It is a sacred gesture and a reminder of both the Holy Trinity and Jesus' saving Death on the Cross.

Go to **aliveinchrist.osv.com** for Sunday readings, Scripture background, questions of the week, and seasonal resources.

FAMILY + FAITH

LIVING AND LEARNING TOGETHER

YOUR CHILD LEARNED >>>

This chapter explains how we are sent from the Mass to live out the Church's mission of sharing Jesus' message of love and the Kingdom of God.

God's Word

Read **Acts 28:30–31** to learn more about Saint Paul and his mission.

Catholics Believe

- The Church's mission is to share Jesus' love and to announce the Good News of the Kingdom of God.
- All members of the Church share in her mission.

To learn more, go to the *Catechism of the Catholic Church* #900–905 at **usccb.org**.

People of Faith

This week, your child met Saint Anthony Mary Claret, the founder of the Claretians. He used his skills as a printer to produce books about the Catholic faith.

CHILDREN AT THIS AGE >>>

How They Understand Living as a Eucharistic People
Children have sometimes been told "you are what you eat" as a way of helping them understand that they should eat healthy things that will help them grow and stay away from too much junk food. They should be prepared for the idea that as they nourish themselves with Jesus himself in the form of the Eucharist, God will help them to become more like Christ in their daily lives. In fact, we are sent forth after the Eucharistic celebration to be the hands and feet of Christ in the world.

CONSIDER THIS >>>

How hard is it to keep good news to yourself?

We use the phrase, "bursting with good news" because it describes how difficult it is to keep good news to ourselves. The Good News that changed all of humanity was the life, Death, and Resurrection of Jesus. And we should be simply bursting with that Good News. "It is the Good News that results in love, justice, and mercy for the whole world. The Kingdom is realized partially on earth and permanently in heaven. We enter this Kingdom through faith in Christ, baptismal initiation into the Church, and life in communion with all her members" (*USCCA, p. 79-80*).

LET'S TALK >>>

- Have your child explain the Church's mission (spreading the Good News and working for the Kingdom).
- Share how God nourishes you through the Sacraments, your family, prayer, art, and so on.

LET'S PRAY >>>

Saint Anthony, pray for us that we may use our skills to teach others about Jesus. Amen.

For a multimedia glossary of Catholic Faith Words, Sunday readings, seasonal and Saint resources, and chapter activities go to **aliveinchrist.osv.com**.

Family + Faith

Distribute the page to the children or parents/adult family members. Point out the chapter highlights, insights on how second graders understand concepts, the opportunity for the adults to reflect on their own experience and faith journey, and the family prayer.

Chapter 20 Review

A Work with Words Write the letter of the correct words from the Word Bank to complete each sentence.

Word Bank
a. mission
b. Frances Cabrini
c. missionary
d. Church
e. Good News

1. Saint [b] was a missionary who worked in the United States.
2. Jesus' message of God's saving love is called the [e].
3. The Church's [a] is to spread the Good News.
4. A [c] is a person sent to bring the Good News of Jesus to people in faraway places.
5. All the members of the [d] share in its mission.

B Check Understanding Draw a line from the roles in Column A to the correct descriptions in Column B.

Column A	Column B
6. Director of Religious Education	serves and proclaims the Gospel at Mass
7. Catechist	celebrates Mass and the Sacraments
8. Extraordinary Minister	teaches about Jesus
9. Deacon	plans programs to help others learn about Jesus
10. Priest	distributes Holy Communion

Go to **aliveinchrist.osv.com** for an interactive review.

Chapter Review

Use Catechist Quick Reviews to highlight lesson concepts.

A Work with Words
Have the children write the letter of the correct words from the Word Bank to complete each sentence.

B Check Understanding
Direct the children to draw a line from the roles to the correct descriptions.

Go to **aliveinchrist.osv.com** to prepare customized and downloadable assessments, send eAssessments, and assign interactive reviews.

A Feast for Everyone

KEY CONCEPT
Heaven is the full joy of living with God forever. The Eucharist is a sign of joy and of what Heaven will be like.

DOCTRINAL CONTENT
- Heaven is life and happiness forever with God. (CCC, 326)
- The story of the Wedding Feast is compared to God's invitation and our response. (CCC, 1329)
- The Eucharist is spiritual food that helps us to live with Jesus forever. (CCC, 1391)
- We are called to say "yes" daily to God. (CCC, 143)

TASKS OF CATECHESIS
Helping children grow in a faith that is "known, celebrated, lived, and expressed in prayer" (NDC, 20).

This chapter focuses on the following tasks of catechesis:
- Promoting Knowledge of the Faith
- Moral Formation

Catechist Background

"Behold, I stand at the door and knock. If anyone hears my voice and opens the door, [then] I will enter his house and dine with him, and he with me." Revelation 3:20

➔ **Reflect** Have you heard God's call? Have you answered?

Jesus used The Parable of the Wedding Feast to show that everyone is invited to God's great feast, a metaphor for eternal life with God in Heaven. Those who are ready to accept his invitation, whenever it comes, are the ones who will be with God at the feast.

Think about the things that fill your day. Are they activities that enable you to respond to God or do they keep you from fulfilling the New Commandment? Do they help or hinder your willingness to reach out to a neighbor in need or to do a favor for a family member? People in need are always there, but too often we fail to see them. When we ignore them, we ignore God's outstretched invitation to the Kingdom of Heaven. Yet, Jesus continues to invite us, over and over again.

God wants everyone to have eternal life. He sent his Son, Jesus, to show us the way, and the way of Jesus is unfailing love. As a follower of Jesus, love of God and love of neighbor are the means by which you show your readiness to accept God's invitation to the heavenly banquet. We experience the sign of this heavenly banquet today in the Eucharist. As members of Christ's Body, we become one with him in and through the Eucharist, the Sacrament of love and unity and the pledge of future glory.

➔ **Reflect** How are you preparing to share in the happiness of Heaven?

Catechist's Prayer

Lord, thank you for being with me as I taught these children this year. Keep them safe and always in your love. Amen.

Lesson Plan

Objectives	Process	Materials
Invite, 10 minutes		
A Feast for Everyone Page 277	**Psalm 23:6** Pray the opening prayer. **Revelation 3:20** Reflect prayerfully on the Word. • Discuss What Do You Wonder questions.	**Optional Activity** Chapter Story: "A Family Picnic"
Discover, 35 minutes		
All Are Invited Pages 278–279 • Define Heaven as life and happiness forever with God • Relate the story of the Wedding Feast to God's invitation and our response	• **Catholic Faith Words** Heaven • Explain that God invites everyone to the happiness on this Earth and in Heaven forever. **Matthew 22:2–10; Luke 14:16–23** Proclaim "The Wedding Feast." • **Share Your Faith Activity** Discuss who the king is meant to portray.	☐ pencils or pens ☐ index cards, one per child
With God Now and Always Pages 280–281 • Describe the Eucharist as the spiritual food that helps us to live with Jesus forever • Recognize the need to say "yes" daily to God	• Teach that receiving Holy Communion at Mass helps you live forever in Jesus Christ. ☆ Underline how the Eucharist is a reminder of Heaven. • Discuss ways to say "yes" to God. • **Connect Your Faith Activity** Draw a picture of someone who says "yes" to God.	☐ pencils or pens ☐ colored pencils or markers ☐ board or chart paper • **Optional Activity** Say "Yes" to God ☐ Activity Master 21 (Page 277E)
Live, 15 minutes		
Our Catholic Life Pages 282–283	• Learn about and pray the Hail Mary. • **People of Faith** Learn about Saint Mary Magdalene de Pazzi. • **Live Your Faith Activity** Write a story about saying "yes" to God.	☐ pencils or pens ☐ board or chart paper
Pray with God's Word Page 284	• Choose a leader and reader. • Follow the order of prayer. Finish by singing "All That God Wants You to Be."	☐ Bible ☐ Bible stand Download "All That God Wants You to Be."

Family + Faith Page 285

Point out that the Catholic Families page provides chapter highlights, information on how second graders understand faith concepts, and family prayer.

Chapter Review Page 286

aliveinchrist.osv.com

- Customize and Download Assessments
- Email Links to eAssessments
- Interactive Student Reviews

Teaching This Grade

ONLINE RESOURCES

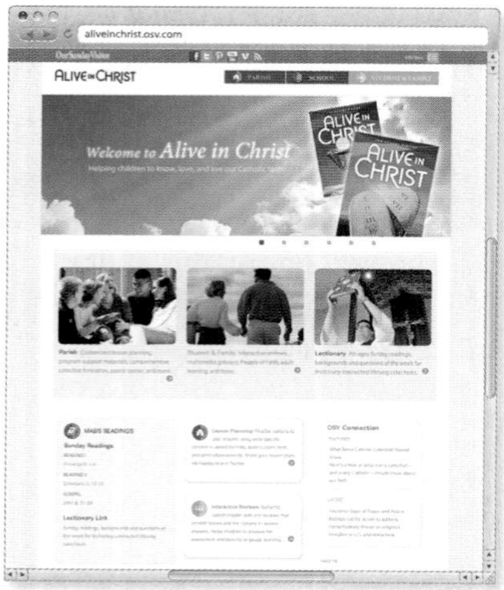

Go to **aliveinchrist.osv.com**

You will find:

- Interactive lesson planning with web specific content and additional activities
- Step by step lesson instruction from printed Catechist Edition for integrated lesson planning
- Custom-built assessments to download and eAssessment links
- Interactive reviews that provide scores and the option to review answers
- Sunday readings with background and questions of the week

Go to **osvparish.com**

You will find:

- Ask the Experts Q and A
- General Catechist Helps
- Community Connections and Blogs

Sharing the Message with Second Graders

Eternal Life in Heaven Second graders often have some limited experience with death. Perhaps a pet or a distant relative has died. This is often difficult for them, but they are comforted by the idea that their loved one is with God in Heaven. Their idea of Heaven may be influenced by what they have seen in cartoons or other media. For example, they might think people in Heaven live on clouds, have wings, and play harps. It is helpful for them to hear that we are not sure what Heaven looks like, but God promises that everyone there is happy—that it is a place of peace and love.

Teaching Tip: Encourage the children to create a visual depiction of their idea of Heaven. It might include personalized details or be more general.

How Second Graders Understand

- Second graders have a basic understanding of right and wrong. Let them make choices to deepen their understanding.
- Children this age sometimes have difficulty accepting criticism, even if they know they've made a poor choice. Be gentle with your words.
- Help the children understand that poor choices affect their relationship with God.

"Help me understand that poor choices affect my relationship with God."

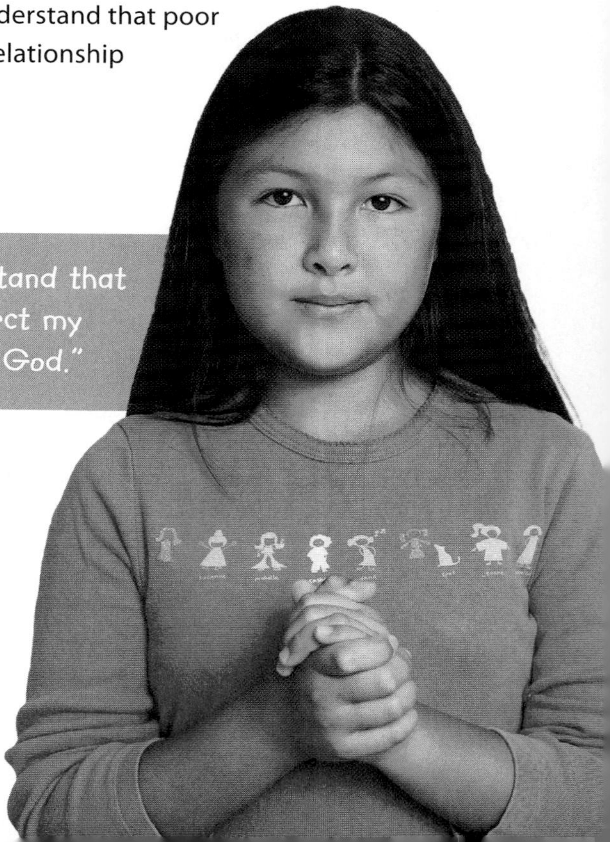

Chapter Connections

Chapter Story

Invite

"A Family Picnic"

Use this story to expand the chapter introduction.

- Brainstorm with the children a list of activities or things that they wish could last forever.
- Ask volunteers to tell what these activities have in common.

Go to **aliveinchrist.osv.com** Lesson Planning section for this story.

NCEA IFG: ACRE Edition

Discover

Knowledge of the Faith

- Objective: To know and understand basic Catholic teaching about the Incarnate Word Jesus Christ as the way, truth, and life

Moral Formation

- Objective: To be knowledgeable about the teachings of Jesus and the Church as the basis of Christian morality and to understand Catholic Social Teaching

Catholic Social Teaching

Live

Use one of these features to introduce a principle and engage the children with an activity.

- Option for the Poor, Pages 296–297
- The Dignity of Work, Pages 298–299

Music Options

Use one or more of the following songs to enhance catechetical learning or for prayer.

- "All That God Wants You to Be," Live Prayer, Page 284
- "Hail Mary," Live, Page 282

LECTIONARY CONNECTION

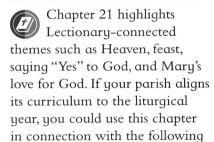

Chapter 21 highlights Lectionary-connected themes such as Heaven, feast, saying "Yes" to God, and Mary's love for God. If your parish aligns its curriculum to the liturgical year, you could use this chapter in connection with the following Sundays.

Year A

Palm Sunday of the Passion of the Lord—Salvation through the Lord's Servant

Twenty-eighth Sunday in Ordinary Time—Feast

Year B

Tenth Sunday in Ordinary Time—Heaven

Thirteenth Sunday in Ordinary Time—Heaven

Year C

Thirty-second Sunday in Ordinary Time—Heaven

Thirty-third Sunday in Ordinary Time—Heaven

Go to **aliveinchrist.osv.com** for a complete correlation ordered by the Sundays of the year and suggestions for how to integrate the Scripture readings into chapter lessons.

Name ______________________________ Date ______________

Say “Yes” to God

Color only the balloons that show a way to say “yes” to God.

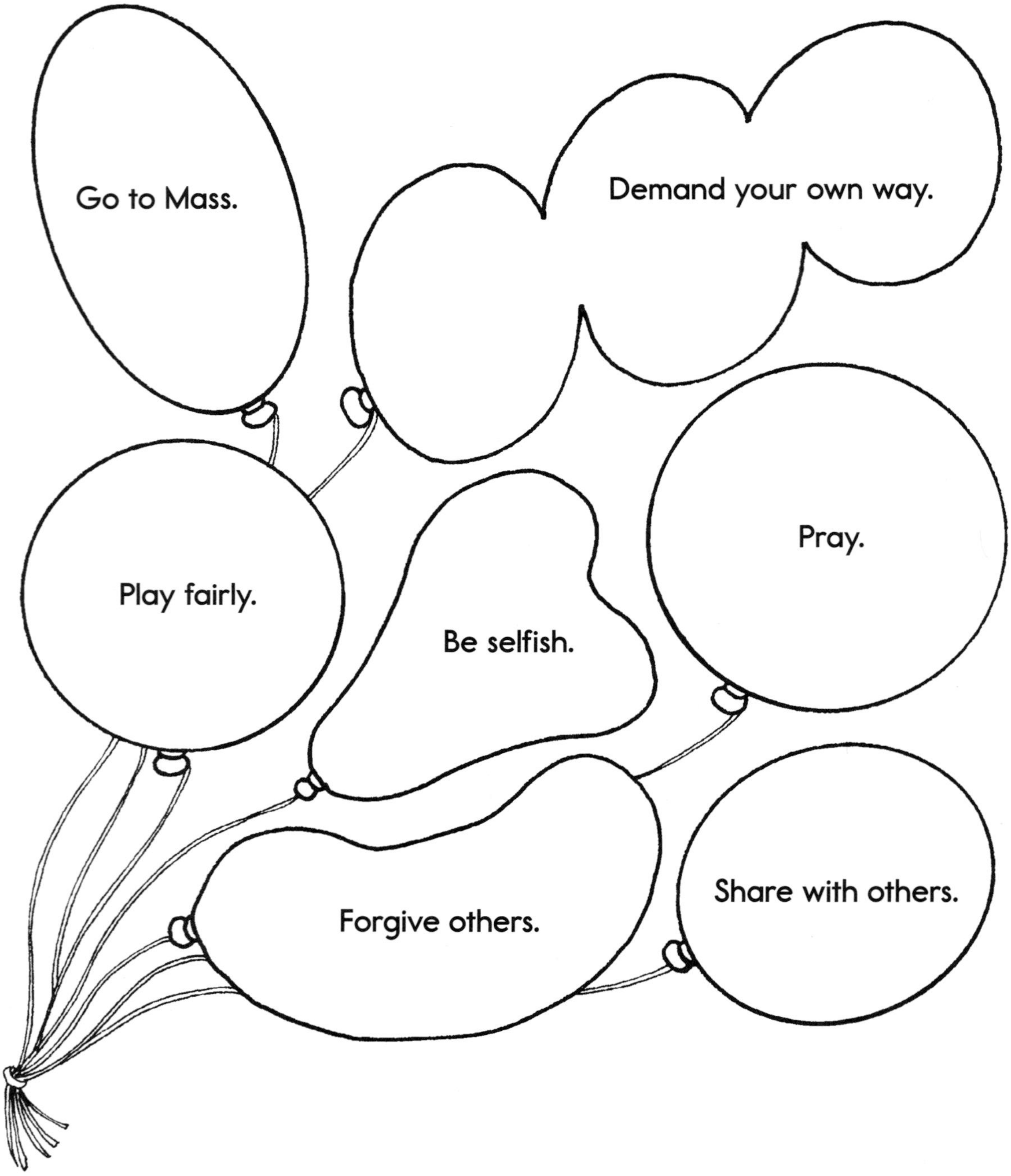

A Feast for Everyone

Let Us Pray

Leader: Dear God, we know you will be with us always.

Indeed, goodness and mercy will be with me
all the days of my life. Based on Psalm 23:6

All: Thank you, God, for guiding and directing us all our life. Amen.

God's Word

"Behold, I stand at the door and knock. If anyone hears my voice and opens the door, [then] I will enter his house and dine with him, and he with me."
Revelation 3:20

What Do You Wonder?

- How is Jesus with us in our home?
- How can I hear Jesus knocking?

Optional Activity

Chapter Story: "A Family Picnic" *Verbal/Linguistic*

Use this story after the opening prayer, before pointing out that Jesus tells us what we need to do to follow his call.

- Read aloud "A Family Picnic."
- Discuss with the children times when they have wanted a celebration to go on forever. Ask them why they felt this way.
- After discussing the question, transition back to the lesson instruction.

Go to **aliveinchrist.osv.com** for Chapter Story.

Invite

Let Us Pray

Have the children gather in the prayer space and make the Sign of the Cross. Read aloud the leader's prayer. Invite the children to pray the Psalm verse and the response with you.

Have the children move from the prayer space back to their seats.

Say: God is always there to guide and direct us. Let's listen as Jesus tells us how to invite him into our lives.

God's Word

Guide the children through the process of Scripture reflection.

- Invite them to close their eyes, be still, and open their minds and hearts to what God is saying to them in this passage.
- Proclaim the Scripture.
- Maintain several moments of silence.
- *Ask:* What did you hear God say to you today?
- Invite volunteers to share.

What Do You Wonder?

Say: Jesus is reminding us to listen for God's invitation to be his disciples. He calls each one of us.

Invite the children to respond to the questions. Ask what else they might wonder about inviting Jesus into our homes.

Discover

Objectives

- Define Heaven as life and happiness forever with God
- Relate the story of the Wedding Feast to God's invitation and our response

All Are Invited

Ask: What does God want for each of us?

- Tell the children to listen to the text.

Ask a volunteer to read aloud the text.

- Ask the question at the top of the page again. He wants us to enjoy happiness with him forever, on Earth and in Heaven.

Work with Words

Ask a volunteer to read aloud the Catholic Faith Word and its definition.

- Have the children create a flash card that they can use, with others they have created, for use in memory games or chapter and unit reviews.

God's Word

Select children for the reading parts of the Storyteller, the Servants, the Three People, and the King.

- Have them proclaim the Scripture story.

Discover

All Are Invited

What does God want for each of us?

Catholic Faith Words

Heaven the full joy of living with God forever

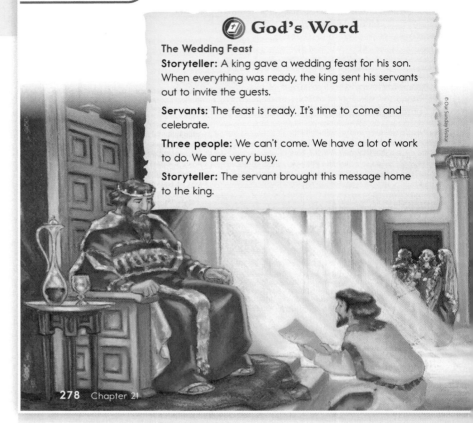

God the Father invites everyone to the happiness of his great love on this Earth and in **Heaven** forever. Jesus told this story to help people understand that God the Father wants everyone to enjoy this happiness.

God's Word

The Wedding Feast

Storyteller: A king gave a wedding feast for his son. When everything was ready, the king sent his servants out to invite the guests.

Servants: The feast is ready. It's time to come and celebrate.

Three people: We can't come. We have a lot of work to do. We are very busy.

Storyteller: The servant brought this message home to the king.

Songs of Scripture

The Great Feast

Responding to God's invitation to our Sunday Eucharistic feast is the focus of this parable.

- Be sensitive to the fact that children this age do not decide whether or not to attend Mass on their own.
- Discuss the reasons why God wants them to be there.
- Teach the children "The Great Feast."

Use *Songs of Scripture*, Grades 1–3 CD, Track 16

King: Go out to the highways and byways. Search all the paths and alleys. Tell everyone to come. I want my house bursting with people.

Storyteller: The servants did just as the king commanded. They invited everybody to come to the banquet. And many people came. Young and old people came. People who were blind came. People who were strong helped people with crutches. Soon the house was full." Based on Matthew 22:2–10 and Luke 14:16–23

Share Your Faith

Think 1. Who did the king invite to the party?

Everyone

2. Who does the king in this story remind you of?

God

Share Share your answers with a partner.

The Wedding Feast

Continue with the Scripture story.

- Point out that God wants everyone to come to the feast; in other words, to have happiness with him in Heaven.

Activity

Invite a volunteer to read aloud the directions for the Share Your Faith activity.

- Ask the children to work in pairs and write their answers.
- Tell the children that in this story, the king reminds us of God the Father, and the son that the feast is for reminds us of Jesus. The guests remind us of everyone in the world.

Quick Review

Heaven is life and happiness forever with God. The story of the Wedding Feast is similar to God's invitation and our response.

Optional Activity

Invitations *Visual/Spatial*

Share with the children that invitations welcome people to special events.

- Have the children design an invitation that God might extend to people to join him in the happiness of Heaven.
- You may want to show the children examples of invitations to help them get started.
- While the children are working on their invitations, discuss other events that they may have received an invitation to attend.

Objectives

- Describe the Eucharist as the spiritual food that helps us to live with Jesus forever
- Recognize the need to say "yes" daily to God

With God Now and Always

Read aloud the question.

- Write the children's responses on the board or chart paper.

Ask three volunteers to read aloud the three paragraphs.

- Tell the children that every time they receive Jesus in Holy Communion, they are preparing for the great feast of Heaven.
- ☆ Have the children underline what the Eucharist is a sign of.
- Allow time for the children to reread the text as needed and underline the sentence.

Say "Yes" to God!

Read aloud the paragraph.

- *Ask:* What does God call us to do? to know, love, and serve him How will you answer him?

With God Now and Always

How can you accept God's invitation?

Underline what the Eucharist is a sign of.

God invites you to share in the great feast in Heaven. In Heaven, you will see God face to face.

Until you see him face to face, God gives you the great gift of the Eucharist. The Eucharist is a sign of joy and of what Heaven will be like. Receiving the Eucharist helps you look forward to the day when you will be with God in Heaven.

Every time you receive Holy Communion at Mass, you receive the food that helps you live forever in Jesus Christ.

Say "Yes" to God!

God calls you to know, love, and serve him. You are like the guests in the Bible story. God invites you to share in a great feast. You could refuse to come. Or you can joyfully accept.

Catechist Background

Jesus' Body and Blood

The Eucharistic sacrifice of Jesus' Body and Blood is a memorial of his Death and Resurrection.

- The Eucharist is the sacrament of love, a sign of unity, a bond of charity, and the Paschal banquet in which Christ is consumed.
- In the Eucharist, we receive grace and a pledge of future glory. (CCC, 1323)

God invites you to say "yes" each day. Here are some ways you say "yes" to God.

- Obey the Commandments.
- Listen to God's Word in the Bible.
- Take part in Mass and receive Holy Communion.
- Seek God's forgiveness in the Sacrament of Penance and Reconciliation.
- Forgive and love other people.
- Help people in need.
- Pray to God each day.

Connect Your Faith

Answering God's Call
Draw a picture of a person you know who says "yes" to God.

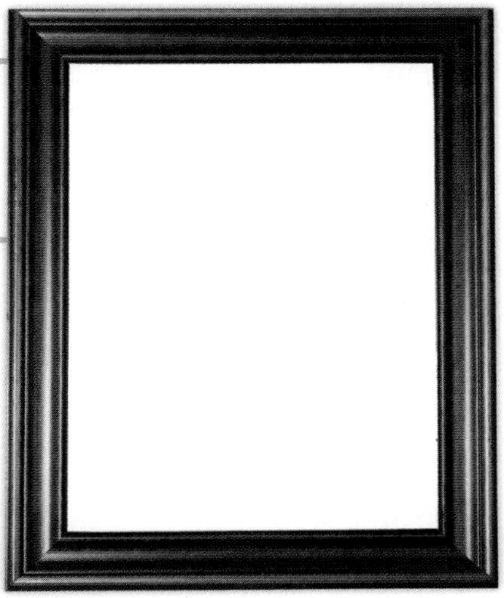

Say "Yes" to God!,

continued

Read aloud the first two sentences.

- Invite a different volunteer to read aloud each bullet.
- After each bullet is read, brainstorm with the children some ideas on how to do each thing.
- Encourage the children to incorporate some of the ideas the group comes up with in the coming week.

Activity

Read aloud the directions for the Connect Your Faith activity.

- Provide the children with colored pencils or markers.
- Allow time for them to think of and draw that person who says "yes."

Quick Review

The Eucharist is the spiritual food that helps us to live with Jesus forever. There are various ways to respond to God's invitation to know, love, and serve him.

Optional Activity

Activity Master 21: Say "Yes" to God

Distribute copies of the activity found on catechist page 277E.

- Tell the children to color each balloon that shows a way that they can say "yes" to God.
- As an alternative, you may want to send this activity home with the children.

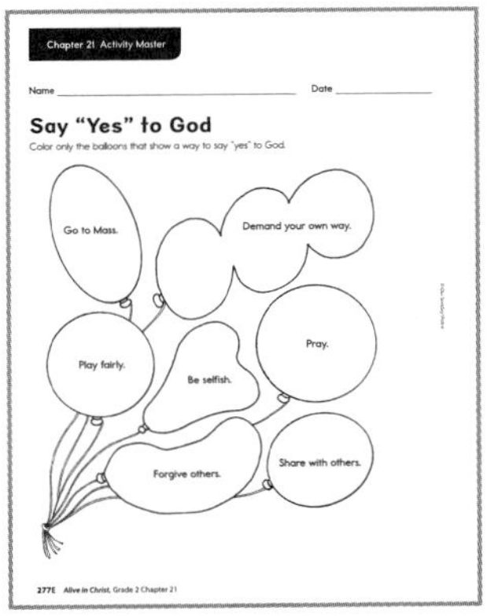

Chapter 21 Activity Master

Name ______ Date ______

Say "Yes" to God

Color only the balloons that show a way to say "yes" to God.

Go to Mass.
Demand your own way.
Play fairly.
Be selfish.
Pray.
Forgive others.
Share with others.

277E Alive in Christ, Grade 2 Chapter 21

Live

Our Catholic Life

Ask the children if they remember some of the ways Mary showed love for God.

- Write their responses on the board or on chart paper.
- Tell the children that we will read some more ways Mary showed love to God.

Read aloud both paragraphs.

The Hail Mary

Arrange the group into two sides.

- Have one side read the first line of "Words of the Prayer" in unison.
- Then have the other side read in unison, as an echo, the first line of "What They Mean."
- Continue this process through the remainder of the chart.
- Point out to the children that the Hail Mary is also provided on page 321 in the Our Catholic Tradition section at the back of their books. You might want to pray the Latin version of the Hail Mary (Ave, Maria) slowly and thoughtfully with them.

Music Option: Have the children sing "Hail Mary," downloaded from **aliveinchrist.osv.com**.

Our Catholic Life

How did Mary show love for God?

God calls each person to share his love. She gladly said "yes" when God asked her to be Jesus' Mother, even though she knew it would not be easy. You can learn from Mary how to show love for God in your own life.

We honor Mary for saying "yes" to God with all her heart, soul, and mind. Praying the Hail Mary is a way to honor Mary.

The Hail Mary

Words of the Prayer	What They Mean
Hail, Mary, full of grace,	Mary, you are filled with God's own life, help, and love.
the Lord is with thee.	You are very close to God.
Blessed art thou among women	God chose you for a very important mission.
and blessed is the fruit of thy womb, Jesus.	The baby that grew inside you is holy and very special.
Holy Mary, Mother of God,	Your child is the Son of God!
pray for us sinners,	Please pray for us, because we don't always say "yes" to God.
now and at the hour of our death.	Be with us now and all through our lives.
Amen.	Yes, we believe this!

Quick Tip

Gestures in Praying

People have many ways of praying. Jesus often prayed with outstretched arms.

- Muslims often pray kneeling on a prayer rug.
- Orthodox Jews bow at the waist and bend up and down while reading Scripture.
- At Mass the priest extends his arms during prayer.
- Tell the children that sometimes we kneel and sometimes we stand when we pray, but we should always show reverence.

People of Faith

Saint Mary Magdalene de Pazzi, 1566–1607

Saint Mary Magdalene de Pazzi was a nun from Italy who spent her whole life in prayer. She thought about Heaven a lot, even when she was sewing. Once, when her friend died, she saw her going into Heaven. Saint Mary Magdalene said that her friend looked like a white bird flying into a beautiful big house. She said that Heaven is beautiful, more beautiful than anything any of us have ever seen.

July 22

Discuss: What do you think Heaven looks like?

Learn more about Saint Mary Magdalene at **aliveinchrist.osv.com**

Live Your Faith

Write a Story Write a story about a time you or someone you know said "yes" to God.

____

____

____

____

____

____

____

____

People of Faith

Tell the children about Saint Mary Magdalene de Pazzi.

- She was named Caterina at Baptism.
- She felt great charity for the poor.
- She had an intense attraction toward the Blessed Sacrament, and longed to receive it.
- When she became a Carmelite nun, she took the name of Maria (Mary) Magdalene.

Read aloud the paragraph on Saint Mary Magdalene.

- Discuss the question at the end of the story with the group.

Encourage the children to go to **aliveinchrist.osv.com** at home to learn more about Saint Mary Magdalene de Pazzi.

Activity

Read aloud the directions for the Live Your Faith activity.

- Allow time for the children to write their story.
- Invite volunteers to share their story with the group.

Catholic Social Teaching

Chapter Connections

To integrate Catholic Social Teaching into your lesson, choose one of the following features: Option for the Poor, pages 296–297; or The Dignity of Work, pages 298–299.

- Start the Live step of the process by talking about Saint Mary Magdalene de Pazzi on page 283. Then move directly to the Catholic Social Teaching feature.
- Or, to expand the lesson, complete both pages 282 and 283, then move to the Catholic Social Teaching feature.
- Return to Chapter 21 for the prayer on page 284.

Let Us Pray

Pray with God's Word

Explain that this prayer is prayed with a reading from the Word of God.

Prepare

Choose a leader and a reader.

- Help the reader find the Scripture and rehearse it.
- Allow the leader to practice his/her parts as well.
- Tell the children to think about God's invitation to Heaven as they listen to the Gospel reading.

Rehearse with the children "All That God Wants You to Be," downloaded from **aliveinchrist.osv.com**.

Gather

Invite the children to come to the prayer space with their books.

- Have them bow before the Bible.

Pray

Follow the order of prayer on the student page.

Leader's concluding prayer (share this prayer with the leader): God the Father, because of your Son, Jesus, we have the hope of being with you forever. Thank you for this wonderful gift.

Sing with the children "All That God Wants You to Be" as they process from the prayer space back to their seats.

Live

Let Us Pray

Pray with God's Word

Gather and begin with the Sign of the Cross.

Leader: We rejoice that God invites us to Heaven.
He sent Jesus to show us the way.

Reader 1: A reading from the holy Gospel according to John.

Read John 3:16.

The Gospel of the Lord.

All: Praise to you, Lord Jesus Christ.

Leader: Let us pray.

Bow your heads as the leader prays.

All: Amen.

Leader: Go forth and share God's love with one another.

All: Thanks be to God.

Sing "All That God Wants You to Be"

You can become all that God wants you to be!
Here am I, O Lord! I come to do your will.
Help me become all that you want me to be!

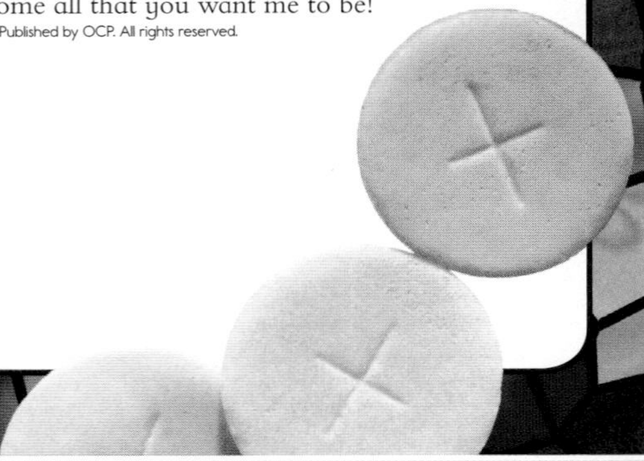

284 Chapter 21

Liturgy Link

Prayer Celebrations

The prayer celebrations this year have given the children opportunities to experience different types of prayer and to appreciate many ways to pray.

- "The *catechesis* of children, young people, and adults aims at teaching them to meditate on The Word of God in personal prayer, practicing it in liturgical prayer, and internalizing it at all times in order to bear fruit in a new life." (CCC, 2688)

Go to **aliveinchrist.osv.com** for Sunday readings, Scripture background, questions of the week, and seasonal resources.

FAMILY + FAITH

LIVING AND LEARNING TOGETHER

YOUR CHILD LEARNED >>>

This chapter explains that the Eucharist is a taste of the great feast of love and happiness we will have with God in Heaven.

God's Word

Read **Revelation 3:20** to find out how Jesus seeks us and responds when we accept his invitation.

Catholics Believe

- Heaven is the full joy of living with God forever.
- The Eucharist is a sign of joy and of what Heaven will be like.

To learn more, go to the *Catechism of the Catholic Church* #1023–1030 at **usccb.org**.

People of Faith

This week, your child met Saint Mary Magdalene de Pazzi. She said that Heaven is more beautiful than anything ever seen.

CHILDREN AT THIS AGE >>>

How They Understand Eternal Life in Heaven Second-graders often have some limited experience with death. Perhaps a pet or a distant relative has died. This is often difficult for them, but they are comforted by the idea that their loved one is with God in Heaven. Their idea of Heaven may be influenced by what they have seen in cartoons or other media. For example, they might think people in Heaven live on clouds, have wings, and play harps. It is helpful for them to hear that we are not sure what Heaven looks like, but God promises that everyone there is happy—that it is a place of peace and love.

CONSIDER THIS >>>

Have you ever wondered why God created you?

You might even wonder if God has a plan for your life. "We come to know God's plan for us not only through an understanding of our human nature and his created order but also because he speaks directly to us." We must make time to pay attention to God's direction (*USCCA, p. 328*).

LET'S TALK >>>

- Ask your child to share one thing they learned about Heaven.
- Talk about loved ones who have died and how your family remembers and celebrates them.

LET'S PRAY >>>

Dear God, help us to think about Heaven, like Saint Mary Magdalena, and to want to be with you there forever. Amen.

For a multimedia glossary of Catholic Faith Words, Sunday readings, seasonal and Saint resources, and chapter activities go to **aliveinchrist.osv.com**.

Family + Faith

Distribute the page to the children or parents/adult family members. Point out the chapter highlights, insights on how second graders understand concepts, the opportunity for the adults to reflect on their own experience and faith journey, and the family prayer.

Chapter 21 Review

A Work with Words Fill in the blank with the correct word from the Word Bank.

Word Bank: feast, happy, Eucharist, serve

1. God wants people to be **happy**.
2. God calls us to **serve**.
3. The **Eucharist** is a sign of the joy of Heaven.
4. The Kingdom of Heaven is like a **feast**.

B Check Understanding Write the letter T if the sentence is TRUE. Write the letter F if the sentence is FALSE.

5. **T** Heaven is the full joy of living with God forever.
6. **F** God calls only some people to share his love.
7. **T** Mary gladly said "yes" to God's call to be the Mother of his Son, Jesus.
8. **T** You honor Mary when you show love for God in your own life.
9. **F** The Lord's Prayer is about Mary.
10. **T** When your mother asks you to clean your room, and you do it, you are saying "yes" to God.

Go to **aliveinchrist.osv.com** for an interactive review.

Chapter Review

Use Catechist Quick Reviews to highlight lesson concepts.

A Work with Words
Review the Word Bank. Have the children write the correct word from the Word Bank to complete each sentence.

B Check Understanding
Explain to the children that they will be writing a *T* for each true statement and an *F* for each false statement.

Go to **aliveinchrist.osv.com** to prepare customized and downloadable assessments, send eAssessments, and assign interactive reviews.

UNIT 7

Unit Review

Use Catechist Quick Reviews in each chapter to highlight lesson concepts for this unit and prepare for the Unit Review.

Have the children complete the Review pages. Then discuss the answers as a group. Review any concepts with which the children are having difficulty.

A Work with Words

Have the children complete each sentence with the letter of the correct word from the Word Bank for problems 1–5. For 6–10, have them circle the correct answer.

UNIT 7

Unit Review

A Work with Words Complete each sentence with the letter of the correct word from the Word Bank.

Word Bank

a. Heaven
b. Lamb
c. serve
d. mission
e. Reverence

1. Jesus is the b of God.
2. e is the care and respect you show to God and holy persons and things.
3. A d is a job or purpose.
4. God calls you to know, love, and c.
5. God wants you to be with him forever in a.

Circle the correct answer.

6. A person who brings the message of Jesus and announces the Good News to people in other places is a ____.
   missionary catechist teacher
7. The Body of Christ received at Mass is ____.
   wine Holy Communion a mission
8. The first American Saint was ____.
   Frances Cabrini Saint Peter Pope Leo XIII
9. When you receive Holy Communion, you are one with ____.
   missionaries priests the Church
10. Jesus teaches that Heaven is like a great ____.
   feast fish book

UNIT 7

Unit Review

B Check Understanding Unscramble the words to complete each sentence.

11. Hosts placed in the Tabernacle after Mass are called the Blessed **CRAMENSAT**. SACRAMENT

12. People at home or in the hospital are still joined to the community in **YAERPR**. PRAYER

13. After Mass, people who are ill may be visited by a priest, a deacon, or an extraordinary minister of Holy Communion who brings the **HUISECTRA**. EUCHARIST

C Make Connections Write the letter T if the sentence is TRUE. Write the letter F if the sentence is FALSE.

14. T Jesus is really and truly present in the Eucharist.

15. T At the end of Mass we are sent out to "Go in peace," and proclaim the Good News.

16. F Jesus sends you on a mission to teach other people about yourself.

17. T Mary always said "yes" to God.

18. T Praying the Lord's Prayer is one way you praise the Father and ask for his help.

19. F We offer each other the Sign of Peace after we receive Holy Communion.

20. F God calls only priests and missionaries to share his love.

Complete each sentence below with the correct answer.

21. Walking to the altar prayerfully is showing reverence.

22. The Holy Communion that you receive at Mass is the Body and Blood of Christ.

23. Sharing the Good News of Jesus and God's Kingdom throughout the world is the Church's mission.

24. A catechist or religion teacher helps children by teaching them about Jesus.

25. Praying the Hail Mary is a way to honor Mary.

B Check Understanding

Have the children unscramble the words to complete each sentence

C Make Connections

For problems 14–20, tell the children to write the letter *T* if the sentence is true or *F* if the sentence is false. Have them complete each sentence for 21–25.

Go to **aliveinchrist.osv.com** to prepare customized and downloadable assessments, send eAssessments, and assign interactive reviews.

Live Your Faith
&
Our Catholic Tradition
Reference Section

Live Your Faith/Our Catholic Tradition at a Glance

Live Your Faith

"Let us keep a place for Christ in our lives, let us care for one another and let us be loving custodians of creation."

—Pope Francis via Twitter, March 19, 2013

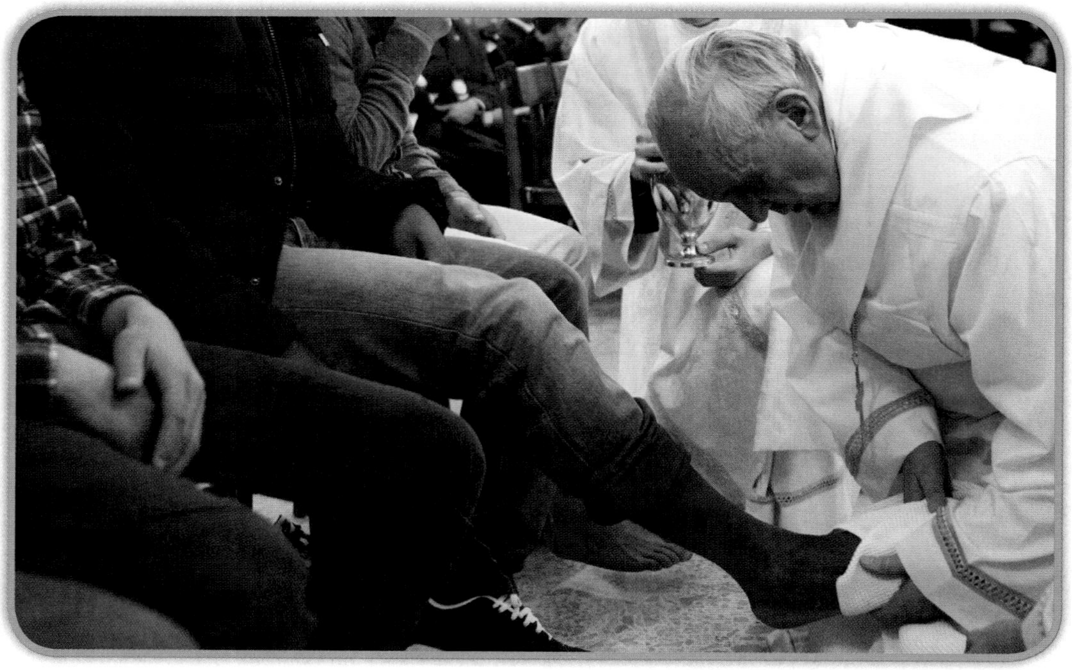

The Seven Themes of Catholic Social Teaching

The Catholic Church's Social Teaching helps build a just society and shows us how to live lives of holiness amidst the challenges of modern society. The wisdom of this tradition can be understood best through a direct reading of Church documents, but here is a synopsis of each of the seven key themes that are part of our Catholic Social Tradition.

Life and Dignity of the Human Person
Each person is created in God's image and all people have rights that flow from their human dignity. The equal dignity of all people means we must work to eliminate social and economic inequalities. We strive to value all people over our personal wealth or possessions.

Call to Family, Community, and Participation
In order for our society to be healthy, we must all make positive contributions to it, bringing to it the light of the Gospels. We can do this by finding practical ways to participate more fully in our own families, in our parishes, and in our communities.

Rights and Responsibilities of the Human Person
Every person has a right to life and the rights needed to live in dignity. The fundamental rights of all people are freedom, justice, and the basic necessities of everyday life. As individuals and as a society, we must work to protect these rights for all people.

Option for the Poor and Vulnerable
God loves all people, and he calls us to love one another as he loves us. In a world where many people live in

great poverty while others enjoy great wealth, we must pay special attention to the needs of the poor and reach out to them in Christian charity.

The Dignity of Work and the Rights of Workers

Through labor all people participate in the work of creation and all workers have the following rights that must be protected: the right to productive work, to fair wages, and to pursue economic opportunity. Catholics believe that our work can be a valuable way to serve God and others.

Solidarity of the Human Family

All people—rich and poor, young and old, weak and strong—have equal dignity and rights that flow from that dignity. As part of one human family, we are all dependent on one another and responsible for one another, and must work to reduce social inequalities and provide for one another's needs.

Care for God's Creation

God is the Creator of all people and all that exists in nature. He has given us the bounty of the Earth and its resources and has entrusted us with its care. We are called to respond by protecting and caring for all God's creation for generations to come.

Go to **aliveinchrist.osv.com** for a complete listing of chapters and Church year lessons correlated to the themes of Catholic Social Teaching.

About This Principle This section presents an overview of the theological foundation of the theme so that catechists have background information at point of use.

Wrap Instruction An easy to follow side column provides catechists with directions and activities for presenting the Catholic Social Teaching in developmentally appropriate ways.

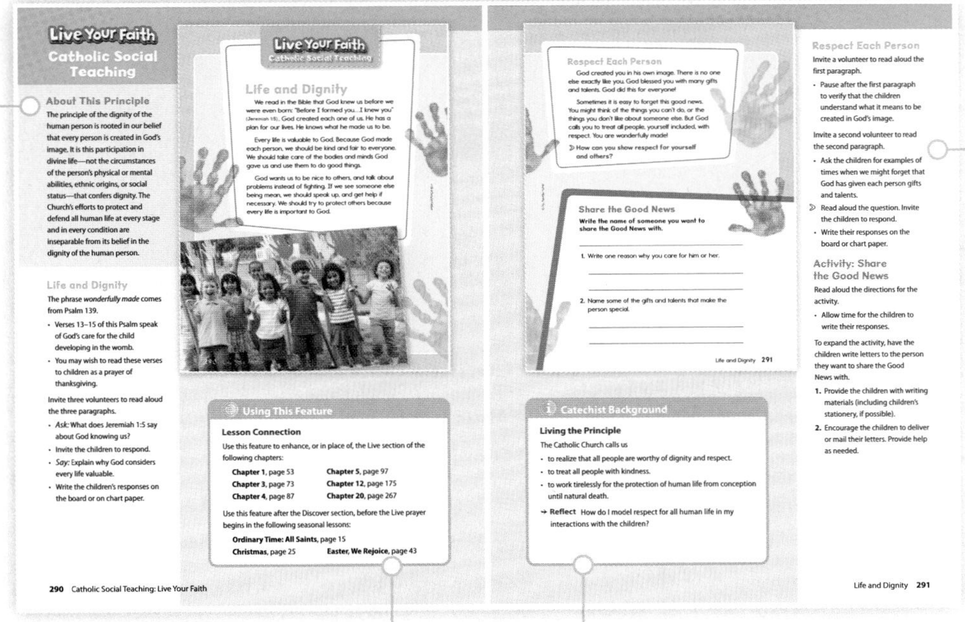

Live Your Faith
Catholic Social Teaching

About This Principle
The principle of the dignity of the human person is rooted in our belief that every person is created in God's image. It is this participation in divine life—not the circumstances of the person's physical or mental abilities, ethnic origins, or social status—that confers dignity. The Church's efforts to protect and defend all human life at every stage and in every condition are inseparable from its belief in the dignity of the human person.

Life and Dignity
The phrase *wonderfully made* comes from Psalm 139.

- Verses 13–15 of this Psalm speak of God's care for the child developing in the womb.
- You may wish to read these verses to children as a prayer of thanksgiving.

Invite three volunteers to read aloud the three paragraphs.

- *Ask:* What does Jeremiah 1:5 say about God knowing us?
- Invite the children to respond.
- *Say:* Explain why God considers every life valuable.
- Write the children's responses on the board or on chart paper.

Live Your Faith
Catholic Social Teaching

Life and Dignity
We read in the Bible that God knew us before we were even born: "Before I formed you...I knew you" (Jeremiah 1:5). God created each one of us. He has a plan for our lives. He knows what he made us to be.

Every life is valuable to God. Because God made each person, we should be kind and fair to everyone. We should take care of the bodies and minds God gave us and use them to do good things.

God wants us to be nice to others, and talk about problems instead of fighting. If we see someone else being mean, we should speak up, and get help if necessary. We should try to protect others because every life is important to God.

Using This Feature

Lesson Connection
Use this feature to enhance, or in place of, the Live section of the following chapters:

Chapter 1, page 53	**Chapter 5**, page 97
Chapter 3, page 73	**Chapter 12**, page 175
Chapter 4, page 87	**Chapter 20**, page 267

Use this feature after the Discover section, before the Live prayer begins in the following seasonal lessons:

Ordinary Time: All Saints, page 15
Christmas, page 25 **Easter, We Rejoice**, page 43

290 Catholic Social Teaching: Live Your Faith

Respect Each Person
God created you in his own image. There is no one else exactly like you. God blessed you with many gifts and talents. God did this for everyone!

Sometimes it is easy to forget this good news. You might think of the things you can't do, or the things you don't like about someone else. But God calls you to treat all people, yourself included, with respect. You are wonderfully made!

How can you show respect for yourself and others?

Share the Good News
Write the name of someone you want to share the Good News with.

1. Write one reason why you care for him or her.
2. Name some of the gifts and talents that make the person special.

Life and Dignity 291

Catechist Background

Living the Principle
The Catholic Church calls us

- to realize that all people are worthy of dignity and respect.
- to treat all people with kindness.
- to work tirelessly for the protection of human life from conception until natural death.

→ **Reflect** How do I model respect for all human life in my interactions with the children?

Respect Each Person
Invite a volunteer to read aloud the first paragraph.

- Pause after the first paragraph to verify that the children understand what it means to be created in God's image.

Invite a second volunteer to read the second paragraph.

- Ask the children for examples of times when we might forget that God has given each person gifts and talents.
- Read aloud the question. Invite the children to respond.
- Write their responses on the board or chart paper.

Activity: Share the Good News
Read aloud the directions for the activity.

- Allow time for the children to write their responses.

To expand the activity, have the children write letters to the person they want to share the Good News with.

1. Provide the children with writing materials (including children's stationery, if possible).
2. Encourage the children to deliver or mail their letters. Provide help as needed.

Life and Dignity 291

Using This Feature This box identifies core chapters and seasonal lessons to which the Live Your Faith feature is connected.

Catechist Background This box identifies ways the Church calls us to practice the principle and includes a question for catechist reflection.

Live Your Faith

Catholic Social Teaching

About This Principle

The principle of the dignity of the human person is rooted in our belief that every person is created in God's image. It is this participation in divine life—not the circumstances of the person's physical or mental abilities, ethnic origins, or social status—that confers dignity. The Church's efforts to protect and defend all human life at every stage and in every condition are inseparable from her belief in the dignity of the human person.

Life and Dignity

The phrase *wonderfully made* comes from Psalm 139.

- Verses 13–15 of this Psalm speak of God's care for the child developing in the womb.
- You may wish to read these verses to children as a prayer of thanksgiving.

Invite three volunteers to read aloud the three paragraphs.

- *Ask:* What does Jeremiah 1:5 say about God knowing us?
- Invite the children to respond.
- *Say:* Explain why God considers every life valuable.
- Write the children's responses on the board or on chart paper.

Live Your Faith

Catholic Social Teaching

Life and Dignity

We read in the Bible that God knew us before we were even born: "Before I formed you...I knew you" (Jeremiah 1:5). God created each one of us. He has a plan for our lives. He knows what he made us to be.

Every life is valuable to God. Because God made each person, we should be kind and fair to everyone. We should take care of the bodies and minds God gave us and use them to do good things.

God wants us to be nice to others, and talk about problems instead of fighting. If we see someone else being mean, we should speak up, and get help if necessary. We should try to protect others because every life is important to God.

Using This Feature

Lesson Connection

Use this feature to enhance, or in place of, the Live section in the following chapters:

Chapter 1, page 59
Chapter 3, page 79
Chapter 4, page 93
Chapter 5, page 103
Chapter 12, page 181
Chapter 20, page 273

Use this feature after the Discover section, before the Live Prayer begins in the following seasonal lessons:

Ordinary Time: All Saints, page 16
Christmas, page 28
Easter, page 44

Respect Each Person

God created you in his own image. There is no one else exactly like you. God blessed you with many gifts and talents. God did this for everyone!

Sometimes it is easy to forget this good news. You might think of the things you can't do, or the things you don't like about someone else. But God calls you to treat all people, yourself included, with respect. You are wonderfully made!

≫ How can you show respect for yourself and others?

Share the Good News

Write the name of someone you want to share the Good News with.

____

1. Write one reason why you care for him or her.

____

____

2. Name some of the gifts and talents that make the person special.

____

____

Catechist Background

Living the Principle

The Catholic Church calls us

- to realize that all people are worthy of dignity and respect.
- to treat all people with kindness.
- to work tirelessly for the protection of human life from conception until natural death.

→ **Reflect** How do I model respect for all human life in my interactions with the children?

Respect Each Person

Invite a volunteer to read aloud the first paragraph.

- Pause after the first paragraph to verify that the children understand what it means to be created in God's image.

Invite a second volunteer to read the second paragraph.

- Ask the children for examples of times when we might forget that God has given each person gifts and talents.

≫ Read aloud the question. Invite the children to respond.

- Write their responses on the board or on chart paper.

Activity: Share the Good News

Read aloud the directions for the activity.

- Allow time for the children to write their responses.

To expand the activity, have the children write letters to the person they want to share the Good News with.

1. Provide the children with writing materials (including children's stationery, if possible).
2. Encourage the children to deliver or mail their letters. Provide help as needed.

Live Your Faith
Catholic Social Teaching

About This Principle

The call to community is inherent in our humanity. In the Book of Genesis, the Creator sees that "it is not good for the man to be alone." Out of that observation came the first human relationships, with all their potential for joy and grief. No matter how complicated and tangled our relationships with one another become, the Church reminds us that we live in relationship with all members of the human family.

Call to Community

Invite two volunteers to each read aloud one of the paragraphs.

- *Ask:* Why does God give us families?
- Invite the children to respond.
- Write the children's responses on the board or on chart paper.

Recognize that the children in your group come from families of all kinds.

- Emphasize the love and support family members give one another, not the composition of the individual family.
- Remind the children that no family is perfect, but all families are called by God to share love the best way they know how.

Ask: How does our parish community help us learn about God?

- Discuss with the children.

Live Your Faith
Catholic Social Teaching

Call to Community

God gives us families and communities because he knows it would not be good for us to live our lives alone. In fact, the Bible says that this is why God created Eve to be a companion and friend to Adam, the first human being. (See Genesis 2:18.)

The Church teaches that God gives us families to help us learn who God is and how to love one another. Our parish community also helps us to learn about God. In families and in parish communities, we work together to take care of one another and to become the people God made us to be.

Using This Feature

Lesson Connection

Use this feature to enhance, or in place of, the Live section in the following chapters:

Chapter 2, page 69
Chapter 6, page 113
Chapter 9, page 147
Chapter 11, page 171
Chapter 16, page 229
Chapter 19, page 267

Use this feature after the Discover section, before the Live Prayer begins in the following seasonal lessons:

Advent, page 22
Holy Week, page 40
Pentecost, page 48

Get Involved!

LIGHT OF CHRIST

God made people to live in families and communities to share God's love. You are part of your own family, and part of the family of all God's people. You are part of many communities—your neighborhood, your school, your parish, and the Church around the world.

The gifts of family and community come with responsibilities, too. God calls everyone to help others so no one is left out, and no one feels alone.

A Catholic emblem of faith for Tiger and Wolf Cub Scouts

What are some things that you could do with your family to help in your community?

Draw a Picture

Draw one way you take part in the life of your family and your community.

Catechist Background

Living the Principle

The Catholic Church calls us

- to recognize that we live in relationship with all members of the human family.
- to break down walls of selfishness, isolation, and apathy.
- to become fully involved in family, community, and the world.

➔ **Reflect** How are you answering the call to be fully involved in your family, your community, and the world?

Get Involved

Ask the children to think about all the ways they are called to be involved with others.

Invite volunteers to read the two paragraphs.

Read aloud the question.

- Invite the children to respond.
- Write their responses on the board or on chart paper.

Read aloud the caption for the emblem.

- Invite volunteers to interpret its meaning.
- *Ask:* How is the Light of Christ and getting involved connected?
- Write the children's responses on the board or on chart paper.

Activity: Draw a Picture

Read aloud the directions for the activity.

- Provide the children with crayons, colored pencils, or markers.
- Allow time for them to draw.
- Encourage the children to share their finished artwork with the group.

To expand the activity, hang the children's drawings around the room and invite the parents/guardians to peruse the gallery.

Live Your Faith
Catholic Social Teaching

About This Principle

Slavery is one of the greatest institutional threats to human rights. As Americans, we still struggle with the legacy of slavery in our country, although it has technically been outlawed for more than a century. Slavery continues as a way of life in many parts of the world. The freedom that we claim as a human right comes from the responsibility as Catholics to work for the freedom of all.

Rights and Responsibilities

Read aloud the first paragraph.

Ask: What is the difference between a right and responsibility?

- Invite the children to respond.
- Write the children's responses on the board or on chart paper.
- Add the phrase *human rights* to the board or chart paper.

Invite a volunteer to read aloud the second paragraph.

- Ask a volunteer to summarize what it means to be responsible.

Direct the children's attention to the photo. Ask them to describe what is going on in the picture and how the people might be fulfilling their responsibility to protect human rights. the photo refers to the right to medical care

Live Your Faith
Catholic Social Teaching

Rights and Responsibilities

Because God made every person, everyone has rights and responsibilities. Rights are the freedoms or things every person needs and should have. Responsibilities are our duties, or the things we must do.

Jesus said, "You should love your neighbor as yourself" (Mark 12:31). Following this command means making sure everyone's rights are protected. We also have a responsibility to treat others well and work together for the good of everyone.

Using This Feature

Lesson Connection

Use this feature to enhance, or in place of, the Live section in the following chapters:

Chapter 3, page 79
Chapter 6, page 113
Chapter 7, page 127
Chapter 8, page 137
Chapter 14, page 205

Use this feature after the Discover section, before the Live Prayer begins in the following seasonal lesson:

Advent, page 22

Having the Things We Need

Humans need many things to live happy and healthy lives: a safe place to live, clothes, food, clean water, and medical care. These important things are called human rights. All people deserve to have these needs met.

The Church teaches that humans have rights because they are made in God's image. Each person has the responsibility to make sure other people get what they need. We are called to protect the human rights of all people.

How can we help others get what they need?

Make a List

List three ways you can be responsible at home and at school. What are some things you can do that will help others?

1. ______________________________

____

2. ______________________________

____

3. ______________________________

____

Catechist Background

Living the Principle

The Catholic Church calls us

- to recognize and respect God's image in each person.
- to take responsibility for our actions.
- to work for an end to conditions that enslave people.

→ **Reflect** How do I exercise my responsibility to work for the rights of others?

Having the Things We Need

Some children in your group may be living in poverty or may be experiencing other circumstances that keep them from having their basic needs met.

- Be sensitive to the range of economic and social circumstances represented in your group.
- Make sure not to ask the children to disclose personal information about their family circumstances.

Read aloud the question.

- Allow the children to discuss possible answers with a partner.
- Encourage volunteers to share some of the ideas they came up with.

Activity: Make a List

Ask a volunteer to read aloud the directions for the activity.

- Arrange the children in small groups and allow them to brainstorm answers together.
- Invite volunteers to share some of the ideas the group came up with.

To expand the activity, choose one of the ideas presented as something that can be done to help others. As a group, make a commitment to carry the action out.

Live Your Faith
Catholic Social Teaching

About This Principle

At first glance, the Church's longstanding practice of an option for the poor may seem "unfair" to young children, who are used to defining justice in terms of strict equality. We adults sometimes have as much difficulty with this concept as the children do. The justice of God's Kingdom calls us to redress the injustices of this world, which means tilting the scales in favor of those most in need.

Option for the Poor

Read aloud the first paragraph.

Ask: What does Matthew 25:40 say about helping the poor and needy?

- Invite the children to respond.
- Write the children's responses on the board or on chart paper.

Read aloud the second paragraph.

Ask: What does Saint Rose of Lima mean when she says we serve Jesus when we serve the poor and sick?

- Invite the children to discuss.

Remind them that when we find ways to help the poor, God will bless us.

Live Your Faith
Catholic Social Teaching

Option for the Poor

In Scripture, Jesus says that whatever we have done for people who are poor or needy, we have also done for him. (See Matthew 25:40.) We should treat people the same way we would treat Jesus himself. When people need food, drink, clothing, housing, or medical care, or when they are lonely, we should try extra hard to help.

Saint Rose of Lima said, "When we serve the poor and the sick, we serve Jesus." Our Church teaches that we should have special love and care for those who are poor and put their needs first. When we do this, God will bless us.

Using This Feature

Lesson Connection

Use this feature to enhance, or in place of, the Live section in the following chapters:

Chapter 7, page 127	**Chapter 18**, page 249
Chapter 10, page 161	**Chapter 19**, page 267
Chapter 13, page 195	**Chapter 21**, page 283

Use this feature after the Discover section, before the Live Prayer begins in the following seasonal lessons:

Ordinary Time: Mary, page 12 **Lent**, page 34

Those Most in Need

One day Jesus was talking with his disciples. They asked him how they could follow him more closely. Jesus told them,

"Whatever you do for your brothers and sisters who are most in need, you do for me. When you care for them, you care for me. When you turn your back on them, you turn your back on me" (Based on Matthew 25:31–46).

Jesus asks us to use the same message. "Look for those who need your care the most," Jesus says. "When you reach out to help them, you will find me."

Who are the people in your community who are most in need?

Make a Collage

Glue a picture of Jesus in the space below. Find pictures of people helping others and glue them around Jesus.

Catechist Background

Living the Principle

The Catholic Church calls us

- to recognize that all of life's blessings are gifts from God.
- to work for the just distribution of those blessings.
- to defend those whose vulnerabilities deprive them of a voice.

➔ **Reflect** Who are the poorest and most vulnerable people in my life, and how can I reach out to them?

Those Most in Need

Invite three volunteers to each read aloud one of the paragraphs.

- Ask the children to explain in their own words what Jesus meant.

Read aloud the question.

- Invite the children to respond.
- Write their responses on the board or on chart paper.

Activity: Make a Collage

Read aloud the directions for the activity.

- Provide safety scissors and glue, pictures of Jesus (old cards, magazines, flyers), and pictures of people helping others (magazines, newspapers).
- Encourage the children to share their art and explain their choices and what each picture means to them.

To expand the activity, create a larger, group collage.

1. Run a long sheet of parchment paper across one of the walls.
2. Have the children glue images of Jesus and people helping others all across the paper.
3. Encourage them to also write in words of hope and help around the images.

Live Your Faith
Catholic Social Teaching

About This Principle

In our society, people are often distanced from the workers who make their lives comfortable and convenient. Millions of workers in factories, on farms, and in service jobs provide Americans with a full range of both necessities and luxuries. We don't always stop to think who and where these workers are, what conditions they work under, and what their lives are like. But the Church has traditionally stood on the side of workers, promoting their dignity and securing their rights.

The Dignity of Work

Invite two volunteers to each read aloud one of the paragraphs.

- *Ask:* What does Deuteronomy 24:14 say about being treated fairly?
- Invite the children to respond.
- Write the children's responses on the board or on chart paper.

Say: Scripture teaches that workers should be treated fairly and be given fair pay. Unfortunately, that doesn't always happen.

Explain to the children that work is one of the ways in which humans share in the life of God, our Creator.

Live Your Faith
Catholic Social Teaching

The Dignity of Work

The different jobs people have help them earn money to buy food and other things they need to live. Jobs also allow people to work together with God and his creation. Work is part of God's plan for people, and everyone should work, either in the home or in a job outside the home.

All adults should be able to have a job if they want one. Scripture teaches that workers should be treated fairly by their bosses. (See Deuteronomy 24:14.) They should be given fair pay for their work. (See Leviticus 19:13 and Deuteronomy 24:15.) If workers are unhappy, they should be able to speak up and talk about it with their bosses.

298 Live Your Faith

Using This Feature

Lesson Connection

Use this feature to enhance, or in place of, the Live section in the following chapters:

Chapter 8, page 137
Chapter 13, page 195
Chapter 14, page 205
Chapter 16, page 229
Chapter 20, page 273
Chapter 21, page 283

Use this feature after the Discover section, before the Live Prayer begins in the following seasonal lesson:

Ordinary Time: All Saints, page 16

The Value of Work

Work is an important part of life. People work to earn money for both the things they need and want. Many workers take pride in doing their jobs well.

Jesus learned about work from his foster father, Joseph, a carpenter who made beautiful and useful things from wood. And Mary worked hard to teach Jesus and make a loving home.

All kinds of work are important. Workers and bosses have to treat one another with respect. Everyone who works deserves to be paid fairly. No one should work in unsafe conditions.

> **Who are some of the workers who help make your life safe, comfortable, and interesting?**

Write a Class Letter

With your catechist's help, write a class letter to the President or to your state senators. Ask elected leaders to help pass stronger laws that protect the health and safety of workers of all ages.

Catechist Background

Living the Principle

The Catholic Church calls us

- to respect the dignity of all work.
- to help secure adequate employment for all.
- to protect children from the need to go to work prematurely.

→ **Reflect** How can I learn more about, and show appreciation for, the workers who supply my needs?

The Value of Work

Ask the children what kinds of work they might want to do when they grow up.

- Invite them to share.
- Remind the children that God has given us different gifts and talents. It's natural that different people will be interested in different jobs.

Invite volunteers to read the paragraphs.

- Have the children pause after reading each paragraph to invite questions and comments from the rest of the group.

> Read aloud the question.

- Invite the children to respond.
- Write their responses on the board or on chart paper.

Be aware that children whose families are business owners may have different perspectives than those whose families are union members or who have had experience with long-term unemployment.

- Remind the children to listen to one another with openness and respect.

Activity: Write a Class Letter

Read aloud the directions.

- Help the children obtain the names of their congressional representatives.
- Guide them in researching issues facing U.S. workers.
- Help the children agree on issues to address, compose a group letter, and mail the letter to the state senators or the President.

Live Your Faith
Catholic Social Teaching

About This Principle

At the base of all our outreach as Catholics, to others, whether at home or around the world, it is the belief that we are all members of one human family, children of one God. That principle is sometimes obscured by international conflicts, racial and ethnic tensions, and religious divisions. Only solidarity can give us the energy and drive to work for the justice, love, and peace of God's Kingdom.

Human Solidarity

Invite volunteers to read aloud the paragraphs.

Ask: What are some of the ways that people around the world are different?

- Invite the children to respond.
- Write the children's responses on the board or on chart paper.

Ask: How are we all the same?

- Invite the children to circle the answer in the text. Confirm that everyone circled "God made us."

Remind the children that it is important for us to pray for members of our families as well as others.

- *Say:* Remember, each person is a part of the family of God.

Live Your Faith
Catholic Social Teaching

Human Solidarity

People around the world are different in many ways. Our hair, eyes, and skin are many different colors. There are people who are rich, people who are poor, and people who are in-between. People believe different things about how we should live.

But one way we are all alike is that God made us. We are one human family. (See Galatians 3:28.) God calls everyone to be his children. Because God made everyone, we should treat everyone with love, kindness, and fairness. In the Beatitudes, Jesus says, "Blessed are the peacemakers" (Matthew 5:9). Treating others fairly will help us to live in peace with one another.

300 Live Your Faith

Using This Feature

Lesson Connection

Use this feature to enhance, or in place of, the Live section in the following chapters:

Chapter 2, page 69
Chapter 5, page 103
Chapter 9, page 147
Chapter 11, page 171
Chapter 12, page 181
Chapter 18, page 249

Use this feature after the Discover section, before the Live Prayer begins in the following seasonal lessons:

Lent, page 34
Holy Week, page 40
Pentecost, page 48

One Human Family

The members of the human family, like the members of your family, may not all look alike. People have different skin colors. They may speak different languages and live in different places. But we are all part of one human family.

Just as you care for your brothers and sisters at home, Jesus wants us to care for our brothers and sisters around the world. One way we can do this is to pray for them.

How can you care for members of the human family?

Learn about the Human Family

Choose a country, find out about the people there, and answer the questions.

1. How are the people are like you?

____

2. How are the people different from you?

____

3. What could you learn from the people?

____

Catechist Background

Living the Principle

The Catholic Church calls us

- to recognize that we are all created in the image of God.
- to share in the joys/sorrows of the human condition.
- to do what we can to extend God's healing love to all.

➔ **Reflect** How can I help the children feel connected to people around the world?

One Human Family

Read aloud both paragraphs.

Direct the children's attention to the illustration on the page, and ask them to describe how it illustrates the idea that each person is a part of the human family.

Ask a volunteer to read aloud the question.

- Invite the children to share some ideas with the group.
- Write their responses on the board or on chart paper.

Activity: Learn about the Human Family

Have children form small groups.

- Read aloud the directions for the activity, including the questions.
- Invite each group to choose a country or culture to research.
- Provide the groups with lists of or access to appropriate resources.
- Allow time for groups to complete the research and answer the questions. If children will be doing some of the work from home, have each child in their group answer one of the questions.

To expand the activity, invite children who have lived in or visited other countries to talk about that experience.

1. Ask the children to identify similarities and differences in the places they have lived and the people they have encountered.
2. Mark a wall map to show the various countries in which children have lived or visited.

Live Your Faith

Catholic Social Teaching

About This Principle

The need to conserve and protect the Earth's resources increases annually. Communities across the world are working to battle the effect of pollution, global warming, waste landfills, and more. As Catholics, we have a responsibility to care for God's creation.

Care for Creation

Read aloud the first paragraph.

Ask: What does Genesis 1:31 say about God's work? It is "very good."

- Invite the children to respond.

Ask: What does God want us to do with the things he has made? enjoy and take care of them

- Invite the children to share some ways that we can enjoy creation.

Invite a volunteer to read aloud the second paragraph.

- Ask the children why we need to protect the gifts God has given us.

Live Your Faith
Catholic Social Teaching

Care for Creation

God created the whole world—the Earth and sky, the mountains and deserts, and all of the plants, animals, and people. When God made these things, he called them "very good" (Genesis 1:31). God put people in charge of the "fish of the sea, the birds of the air, and all the living things that crawl on the earth" (Genesis 1:28). God wants us to enjoy and take care of everything he has made.

Our Church teaches us that God gave the plants and animals for the good of all people. We need to work to take care of the plants and animals and the places where they live, so everyone can enjoy them now and in the future. We should also be kind to animals, because they are God's creatures.

302 Live Your Faith

Using This Feature

Lesson Connection

Use this feature to enhance, or in place of, the Live section in the following chapters:

Chapter 1, page 59
Chapter 4, page 93
Chapter 10, page 161
Chapter 15, page 215
Chapter 17, page 239

Use this feature after the Discover section, before the Live Prayer begins in the following seasonal lessons:

Ordinary Time: Mary, page 12
Christmas, page 28
Easter, page 44

God's Gifts

God calls you to protect his gifts and to use them wisely. You show God respect when you take care of the planet and all that is in it.

God wants people to have clean water, air, and the food they need to live. The things people do today can help save God's gifts for people to use many years from now.

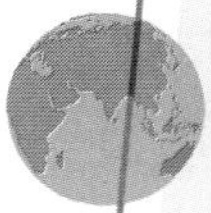

What are some ways you can care for God's creation?

Plan a Garden

Imagine that you are planting a garden. Work with a partner to make your plans.

1. What are two things you would like to grow?

   ____

2. What are some things you need for the garden?

   ____

3. What does the garden need to keep growing?

   ____

4. How would you share your garden?

   ____

Catechist Background

Living the Principle

The Catholic Church calls us

- to show respect for the Creator by caring for creation.
- to live our faith in relationship with all of God's creation.
- to take an active role in caring for the environment.

Reflect What can you do to promote respect for the environment?

God's Gifts

Invite two volunteers to each read aloud one of the paragraphs.

- Have the children circle the items in the text that God wants people to have.

Read aloud the question.

- Invite the children to respond.
- Write their responses on the board or on chart paper.
- *Ask:* How does what we do today affect people and their lives in the future?
- Discuss as a group.

Activity: Plan a Garden

Read aloud the instructions

- Help the children brainstorm things they would like to plant and what they might need to do this.
- Then have them work with partners to complete the activity.

To extend the activity, encourage the children to create a visual representation of their garden.

1. Let the children draw their gardens or cut out images from gardening magazines, or both.
2. Provide them with sheets of paper; crayons, colored pencils, or markers; scissors; glue; and old magazines.
3. Allow the children to work individually or with the partner that they brainstormed their garden with.

Creeds

The Creed tells the faith of the Church. It brings together the Church's most important beliefs about the Holy Trinity and our Catholic faith.

- God the Father, the Creator of all that is.
- Jesus, God's Son and the Savior.
- God the Holy Spirit, helps and guides us as Jesus promised.
- The Church, the Body of Christ in this world.

Apostles' Creed

This creed gives a summary of the Apostles' beliefs. It is often used at Mass during the season of Easter and in Masses with children. This creed is part of the Rosary.

I believe in God,
the Father almighty,
Creator of heaven and earth,
and in Jesus Christ, his only Son, our Lord,

At the words that follow, up to and including the Virgin Mary, all bow.

who was conceived by the Holy Spirit,
born of the Virgin Mary,
suffered under Pontius Pilate,
was crucified, died and was buried;
he descended into hell;
on the third day he rose again from the dead;
he ascended into heaven,
and is seated at the right hand of God the Father almighty;
from there he will come to judge the living and the dead.

I believe in the Holy Spirit,
the holy catholic Church,
the communion of saints,
the forgiveness of sins,
the resurrection of the body,
and life everlasting. Amen.

Nicene Creed

This creed which is prayed at Mass was written nearly two thousand years ago by leaders of the Church who met at a city named Nicaea. Christians over the centuries have prayed this creed.

I believe in one God,
the Father almighty,
maker of heaven and earth,
of all things visible and invisible.

I believe in one Lord Jesus Christ,
the Only Begotten Son of God,
born of the Father before all ages.
God from God, Light from Light,
true God from true God,
begotten, not made, consubstantial with the Father;
through him all things were made.
For us men and for our salvation
he came down from heaven,

At the words that follow, up to and including and became man, all bow.

and by the Holy Spirit was incarnate of the Virgin Mary, and became man.

For our sake he was crucified under Pontius Pilate,
he suffered death and was buried,
and rose again on the third day
in accordance with the Scriptures.
He ascended into heaven
and is seated at the right hand of the Father.
He will come again in glory
to judge the living and the dead
and his kingdom will have no end.

I believe in the Holy Spirit, the Lord, the giver of life,
who proceeds from the Father and the Son,
who with the Father and the Son is adored and glorified,
who has spoken through the prophets.

I believe in one, holy, catholic and apostolic Church.
I confess one Baptism for the forgiveness of sins
and I look forward to the resurrection of the dead
and the life of the world to come. Amen.

Optional Activity

Solve the Puzzle

The wording of the Apostles' Creed in the Student Edition reflects the translation, which was revised when we began to implement the Third Edition of the *Roman Missal*. To help children become more familiar with the Apostles' Creed, make the words of the prayer into a jigsaw puzzle.

- Before the group meets, duplicate the prayer so that each child will have his or her own copy.
- Cut each prayer into jigsaw shapes, and place the pieces into a plastic storage bag.
- Distribute the jigsaw puzzles, and challenge the children to put the pieces together to form the Apostles' Creed.
- Read aloud the Apostles' Creed.

Optional Activity

Nicene Creed

Help the children connect the Nicene Creed with their participation in the Liturgy. Explain that some of the language in the Creed changed when we began to implement the English translation of the Third Edition of the *Roman Missal* in November 2011.

- Explain to the children when the Nicene Creed is prayed (after the homily), and then read the first few lines aloud to them.
- Give each child a prayer card on which is printed: *I believe in one God, the Father almighty, maker of heaven and earth.*
- Encourage the children to bring their prayer cards to Mass and to pray the first lines of the Creed with the rest of the assembly.

The Church

The Church is the community of the People of God. She has many parts that form one body. Christ is her head, and all Catholics are her members. That is why the Church is called the Body of Christ.

Her Mission

Jesus chose Twelve Apostles to share in his work and ministry in a special way. Before his Ascension, Jesus told his Apostles to take his message everywhere.

Pope Francis

The Twelve Apostles

Peter	Philip	Thaddeus
Andrew	Bartholomew	Thomas
James	Matthew	James
John	Simon	Judas

The Church is led by the Pope and bishops, who continue the Apostles' work to spread the Good News of Jesus and God's Kingdom throughout the world. The Church is also a sign of the glory of Heaven meant for everyone.

Mary and the Saints

Mary is the greatest of the Saints because she said "yes" to being the Mother of God. Other holy people are also recognized as Saints. They are remembered on special feast days in the Church year.

The Seven Sacraments

Sacraments of Initiation	The three Sacraments that celebrate membership into the Catholic Church.	• Baptism • Confirmation • Eucharist
Sacraments of Healing	In these Sacraments, God's forgiveness and healing are given to those suffering physical and spiritual sickness.	• Penance and Reconciliation • Anointing of the Sick
Sacraments at the Service of Communion	These Sacraments celebrate people's commitment to serve God and the community and help build up the People of God.	• Holy Orders • Matrimony (Marriage)

The Seven Sacraments are special signs and celebrations that Jesus gave his Church. They allow us to share in God's life and work. The Sacraments are divided into three groups.

Gestures and Actions

To worship means to adore and honor God, especially in the celebration of the Eucharist (Mass) and in prayer. There are certain actions we do during worship. Here are some of them.

- A bow, a bending at the waist of the upper part of your body, or a reverent nod of your head is a gesture of reverence and worship.
- Folded hands is a traditional prayer posture. It is a sign of prayerfulness, humility, and attentiveness to the presence of God.
- When you kneel, you are in a posture of adoration or repentance. When you stand, you are showing respect.

Optional Activity

Learning About the Saints

Read aloud the paragraph on page 306 on "Mary and the Saints." Next, read a few Saint stories to the children or show a video on the life of a Saint.

- Choose a Saint whose life will speak to second grade children, such as Saint Francis of Assisi or Saint Katharine Drexel.
- Distribute a *People of Faith Saint Card* (Our Sunday Visitor) to each child.
- Encourage the children to ask their family members to help them find a book or story online about the Saint on their card that they can read together as a family.
- Allow time at a future lesson for volunteers to share what they learned about their Saint.

Optional Activity

Invite a Speaker

Invite a parish priest or other parish staff member to speak to the children about the Seven Sacraments. Be sure to invite them well in advance of the scheduled session.

- Before the speaker comes, review the text on page 307 with the children.
- Encourage the speaker to use pictures and other visuals, such as a priest's stole, a cross, a bowl of holy water, sacred oils, and other meaningful items.
- Help the children to prepare appropriate questions ahead of time. If time permits, allow them to ask the speaker their questions.

The Church's Seasons

The Church year is a celebration of events in the lives of Jesus, Mary, and the Saints. Every season of the Church's year has special feasts, colors, and symbols.

Advent

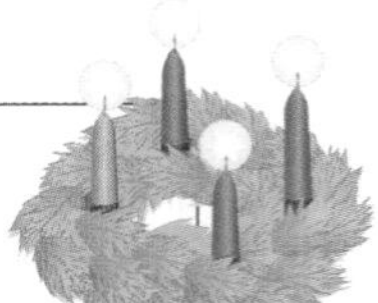

We prepare to celebrate God's coming in time through Jesus, and we await Christ's coming at the end of time.

Feasts: Immaculate Conception, Our Lady of Guadalupe

Color: violet

Symbols: Advent wreath, figure of John the Baptist

Christmas

The Church remembers the birth of Jesus and celebrates the coming in time of the Son of God.

Feasts: Christmas, Nativity of the Lord, Epiphany, Baptism of Jesus

Colors: white or gold

Symbols: manger scenes, star of Bethlehem, Jesse tree

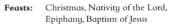

Ordinary Time

The Church celebrates the words and works of Jesus. Ordinary Time occurs twice in the year.

Feasts: Corpus Christi, Transfiguration, Solemnity of Christ the King

Color: green

Symbols: vine and branches, Good Shepherd

Lent

We recall our baptismal promises to change our lives through prayer, fasting, and good works.

Feasts: Ash Wednesday, Palm Sunday

Colors: violet (reddish-purple); red on Palm Sunday

Symbols: ashes, Stations of the Cross, palms

Easter Triduum

The three most holy days of the Church, when we remember Jesus' passing from Death to new life.

Feasts: Holy Thursday, Good Friday, Holy Saturday, Easter

Colors: white or gold and red (Good Friday)

Symbols: feet washing, veneration of cross, lighting the Paschal Candle

Easter

The Church celebrates Jesus' Resurrection and the new life that it brings to all.

Feasts: Ascension, Pentecost

Colors: white or gold, red for Pentecost

Symbols: Alleluia, Easter lilies

Optional Activity

Show a Video

There are many videos on the Church year for children of this age. Choose one that fits with the current Church season.

- Ask the director of faith formation in your parish or contact the diocesan religious education office to find a suitable video.
- Show the video to the children and invite their responses.
- To extend the activity, review with the children the feasts, colors, and symbols of the season from pages 308 and 309.

Optional Activity

Easter Triduum

These special days of the Church year are filled with drama and emotion. However, young children may be left out of the parish's observances due to working parents or the length of the services. Make these three holy days real for the children by staging a "walk-through."

- In advance, set up three stations in different parts of the room, and arrange objects of each day of the Triduum.
- Place cutout footprints on the floor leading to each station. "Walk" the children through the Triduum, stopping at each station to discuss what they find there.

Sacrament of Eucharist

The Eucharist is a Sacrament of Initiation. It is the great thanksgiving prayer of Jesus and the Church. It is a Catholic's greatest act of worship and prayer to God. The Eucharist is also a sign of the heavenly feast that all are invited to at the end of time. In the celebration, Jesus is fully present with us.

The celebration of the Eucharist is also called the Mass. It has two main parts. The Liturgy of the Word is the first great part of the Mass. During it, the assembly listens to and responds to God's Word written in the Bible. The second main part is the Liturgy of the Eucharist. During it, the priest leads us in offering thanks and praise to God, and we receive Holy Communion.

The Mass always includes:

- the proclamation of the Word of God.
- thanksgiving to God for all his gifts.
- the consecration of bread and wine.
- receiving Christ's Body and Blood in Holy Communion.

Holy Days of Obligation

Because the Mass is so important, Catholics are required to attend Mass on Sundays (or Saturday evening) and Holy Days of Obligation. The United States celebrates six Holy Days of Obligation.

- Christmas, December 25
- Solemnity of Mary, Mother of God, January 1
- Ascension of the Lord, 40 days after Easter or the Seventh Sunday of Easter
- Assumption of Mary, August 15
- All Saints Day, November 1
- Solemnity of the Immaculate Conception, December 8

The Order of Mass

Introductory Rites

1. Entrance Chant
2. Greeting
3. Rite for the Blessing and Sprinkling of Water
4. Penitential Act
5. Kyrie
6. Gloria
7. Collect

Liturgy of the Word

1. First Reading (usually from the Old Testament)
2. Responsorial Psalm
3. Second Reading (from New Testament letters)
4. Gospel Acclamation (Alleluia)
5. Gospel Dialogue
6. Gospel Reading
7. Homily
8. Profession of Faith (Creed)
9. Prayer of the Faithful

Liturgy of the Eucharist

1. Preparation of the Gifts
2. Invitation to Prayer
3. Prayer over the Offerings
4. Eucharistic Prayer
   - Preface Dialogue
   - Preface
   - Preface Acclamation
   - Consecration
   - Mystery of Faith
   - Concluding Doxology
5. Communion Rite
   - The Lord's Prayer
   - Sign of Peace
   - Lamb of God
   - Invitation to Communion
   - Communion
   - Prayer After Communion

Concluding Rites

1. Greeting
2. Blessing
3. Dismissal

Optional Activity

Picture It!

Help the children assimilate all they have learned about the correct reception of the Eucharist by having them draw themselves receiving the Body and Blood of Christ.

- Provide the children with drawing paper and crayons or markers. Have them fold the paper in half.
- Instruct them to draw a picture of themselves receiving the host at Mass on one half of the paper. On the other half, tell them to draw themselves receiving from the cup.

Optional Activity

Learn the Gestures and Postures

Take time to instruct the children in some of the various gestures and postures Catholics use during the Mass.

- Young children need direction and practice in the following Mass gestures: making the Sign of the Cross, extending hands for the reception of Communion, tapping the chest during the *Confiteor*, bowing during the Creeds, kneeling, and offering others a sign of peace.
- Take a few moments each day to demonstrate these and other Mass gestures. Allow the children to practice the gestures.

We Worship

Receiving Holy Communion

When you receive Jesus in Holy Communion, you welcome him by showing reverence. These steps can help you.

- Fold your hands and join in the singing as you wait in line.
- Bow slightly as the person before you is receiving.
- When it is your turn, you can receive the Body of Christ in your hand or on your tongue.
- The person who offers you Communion will say, "The Body of Christ." You say, "Amen." Step aside, and chew and swallow the host.
- You may choose to drink from the cup. When the cup is offered to you, the person will say, "The Blood of Christ." You say, "Amen." Take a small sip.
- Return to your place in church.
- Pray quietly in your own words, thanking Jesus for always being with you.

Because it is so important to have Jesus in your life through Holy Communion, the Church tells you to receive Communion frequently. In fact whenever you go to Mass, you should receive Jesus in Holy Communion, but all Catholics are required to at least once a year.

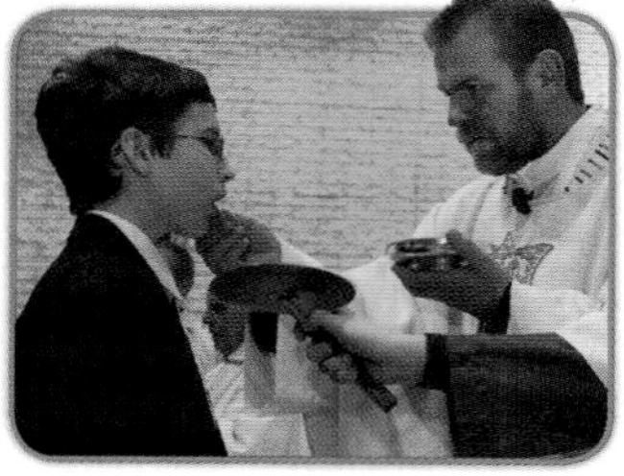

Special Church Objects

Altar The table where the Eucharist is celebrated.

Chalice The cup for the Blood of Christ.

Lectern (ambo) A stand for announcing God's Word in the readings at Mass.

Ciborium The special container placed in the Tabernacle that holds the Eucharistic Hosts, the Body of Christ.

Cruets Small bottles of water or wine.

Lectionary A special book used at Mass that contains readings from the Old and New Testament.

Tabernacle A special place in the church where the Blessed Sacrament is reserved after Mass for those who are ill or for Eucharistic Adoration.

Paten The small plate, usually made of silver or gold, used to hold the Body of Christ.

Book of Gospels The special book that contains the Gospel readings used at Mass.

Roman Missal The special book that contains the prayers of the Mass.

Candles Candles lit during Mass are usually beeswax pillars. They show that Christ, the light of the world, is present.

Optional Activity

Visit the Tabernacle

If feasible, take the children on a church tour, and be sure to visit the chapel or other designated area in your parish church where the Eucharist is reserved in the Tabernacle.

- Teach the children that Jesus is present in the Tabernacle in a very special way. The Body of Christ remaining from Mass is stored in the Tabernacle.
- Emphasize that whenever anyone comes before the Blessed Sacrament in the Tabernacle, they should show reverence for Jesus' presence there.
- Teach them to genuflect by having them bend on their right knee facing the Tabernacle.

Optional Activity

Special Church Objects

To help the children learn how various church objects are used, create a matching game.

- Write the names of the objects shown on page 313 on blank index cards. Create several sets.
- Next, write a description of how each object is used on blank index cards, once again creating several sets.
- Arrange the children in several small groups. Give each group a set of the words and a set of the descriptions.
- Have the children work together to match up all of the cards correctly.

Penance and Reconciliation

Even though we try, we do not always live as God wants us to live. Sometimes we need healing and forgiveness. So Jesus gives us the opportunity to experience God's love, mercy, and forgiveness in the Sacrament of Reconciliation. In this Sacrament, if you are truly sorry, God forgives any sins you have committed. Below are the steps of the Sacrament when it's celebrated with several penitents, the people who confess their sins to the priest. All steps but Step 4 are communal.

Step 1: Introductory Rites

Step 2: Reading from Scripture

Step 3: Examination of conscience, litany of contrition (Sometimes an Act of Contrition, which can be found on pages 170 and 323), the Lord's Prayer

Step 4: Each penitent meets individually with a priest for confession, penance, and absolution by the priest

Prayer of Absolution

God, the Father of mercies,
through the death and resurrection of his Son
has reconciled the world to himself
and sent the Holy Spirit among us
for the forgiveness of sins;
through the ministry of the Church
may God give you pardon and peace,
and I absolve you from your sins
in the name of the Father, and of the Son,
and of the Holy Spirit.

Step 5: Closing

Examination of Conscience

God's gift of conscience helps you choose right from wrong. His gift of grace, God's life within, gives you the strength to do what is right. For more on conscience and to learn more about conscience formation, see page 319.

We prepare for the Sacrament of Penance by thinking about how we have followed the Ten Commandments, Beatitudes, and other Church teachings. Questions like the ones below help us know whether what we've done is good or bad, right or wrong. Remember, mistakes and accidents are not intentional. They are not things done on purpose. They are not sins.

- Did I always use God's name with respect?
- Did I show my love for God and others in some way?
- Did I usually say my daily prayers?
- Did I always obey my mother and father?
- Was I kind to those around me, or was I mean?
- Was I fair in the way that I played and worked with others?
- Did I share my things with others?
- Did I avoid taking what belongs to someone else?
- Did I care for my own things and others' things?
- Did I hurt others by calling them names or telling lies about them?
- Did I go to Mass and take part in the celebration?

Optional Activity

Make Up Forgiveness Stories

Engage the children in making up stories about forgiveness.

- Allow the children to work in small groups.
- Have each group write a story that tells how two or more people are not at peace with one another. Then have the story evolve into a story of forgiveness.
- Walk around and assist the children as needed.
- Allow time for the groups to share their stories with the rest of the children.

Optional Activity

Examination of Conscience

Invite the children to experience an examination of conscience.

- Have them find a comfortable place to sit where they can listen and reflect on the questions by themselves.
- Read aloud the questions. Pause after each question to give the children time to think about their behavior over the past week.
- Remind them that they are responsible for their behavior and should not use the questions on page 315 to judge others.
- They should understand that no one is perfect and all we can do is try our best every day. This is not a tool for discouragement but to remember and appreciate God's grace.

Sacramentals

The Church has special signs and symbols to remind us of God. They are called sacramentals. A sacramental can be an object, words, gestures, or actions. They are made sacred through the prayers of the Church.

Words	blessings litanies other prayers	
Actions	Sign of the Cross Sign of Peace genuflection procession	
Objects	crucifix statues holy water candles	palms rosary images medals

The Rosary

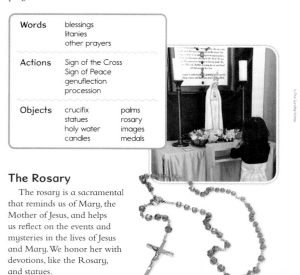

The rosary is a sacramental that reminds us of Mary, the Mother of Jesus, and helps us reflect on the events and mysteries in the lives of Jesus and Mary. We honor her with devotions, like the Rosary, and statues.

God's Laws

God desires you to be in relationship with him. To help you do this and to know what is right, he has given you laws.

The Ten Commandments	What They Mean
1 I am the Lord your God: you shall not have strange gods before me.	Make God the most important thing in your life.
2 You shall not take the name of the Lord your God in vain.	Always use God's name in a reverent way.
3 Remember to keep holy the Lord's Day.	Attend Mass and rest on Sunday.
4 Honor your father and your mother.	Love and obey your parents and guardians.
5 You shall not kill.	Be kind to the people and animals God made; care for yourself and others.
6 You shall not commit adultery.	Be respectful of your body.
7 You shall not steal.	Don't take other people's things.
8 You shall not bear false witness against your neighbor.	Always tell the truth.
9 You shall not covet your neighbor's wife.	Keep your thoughts and words clean; don't be jealous of other people's friendships.
10 You shall not covet your neighbor's goods.	Be happy with the things you have; don't be jealous of what other people have.

The Great Commandment

"You shall love the Lord, your God, with all your heart, with all your being, with all your strength, and with all your mind, and your neighbor as yourself." Luke 10:27

Optional Activity

Display Sacramentals

Provide the children with an experience of sacramentals by making a display of them in the prayer space.

- Collect a large variety of sacramentals. Include sacramentals that the children may not have come into contact with previously, such as palms, medals, and images of the Saints.
- Display the sacramentals in the prayer space, and allow the children to touch the items carefully and respectfully.

Optional Activity

Make Commandment Tablets

Engage the children in the making of their own Commandment tablets.

- Read a child's version of the story of Moses and the Ten Commandments.
- Provide the children with heavy construction paper or tag board cut into the shape of stone tablets.
- Have the children use pens or felt-tip markers to write simplified versions of the Commandments on each side of the tablets.

The Law of the Gospel

The Beatitudes

Blessed are the poor in spirit,
for theirs is the kingdom of heaven.
Blessed are they who mourn,
for they will be comforted.
Blessed are the meek,
for they will inherit the land.
Blessed are they who hunger and thirst for righteousness,
for they will be satisfied.
Blessed are the merciful,
for they will be shown mercy.
Blessed are the clean of heart,
for they will see God.
Blessed are the peacemakers,
for they will be called children of God.
Blessed are they who are persecuted for the sake of righteousness,
for theirs is the kingdom of heaven.
Matthew 5:3–10

Jesus' New Commandment

"This is my commandment: love one another as I have loved you."
John 15:12

Divine Help

What God commands us to do, he makes possible by his grace. (See Catechism, 2082.) God's grace is his life and help within you. It helps you grow in virtue. Virtues are good spiritual habits that strengthen you and enable you to do what is right and good.

These three virtues of faith, hope, and charity (love) are gifts from God that help us know and love him.

Gifts of the Holy Spirit

- Wisdom helps you see yourself and others as God sees you.
- Understanding helps you get along with others.
- Counsel (right judgment) helps you make good choices.
- Fortitude (courage) helps you act bravely.
- Knowledge helps you know God better.
- Piety (reverence) helps you pray every day.
- Fear of the Lord (wonder and awe) helps you understand how great and powerful God is.

Forming Your Conscience

Our conscience is the God-given ability that helps us judge whether our actions are right or wrong. It is important for us to know God's laws so our conscience can help us make good decisions.

It is your job to strengthen, or form, your conscience. This is something you will do throughout your life. We continue to educate our conscience as we grow older. Strengthening your conscience helps your heart be peaceful and loving. It is also necessary for making good choices.

But you cannot do this alone. God's Word is a very important guide for forming your conscience. When you read, pray, and study Scripture, you strengthen your conscience.

Ways to Form Your Conscience

The Holy Spirit strengthens you to make good choices.

Prayer and study help you think things through.

Sacred Scripture and Church teaching guide your decisions.

Parents, teachers, and wise people give you advice.

Optional Activity

Grow in Virtue

Read aloud "Divine Help" from page 318. Draw on the board or on chart paper the symbols for the virtues of faith, hope, and love (a cross, an anchor, and a heart).

- Provide the children with modeling clay, and ask them to make these symbols of our faith.
- Have them bring the symbols home and ask their parents if they can display them on the table or place them close to where the families eat their meals.
- Encourage the children to explain to their family members what each symbol stands for.

Optional Activity

Strengthening Your Conscience

Stress to the children that forming and strengthening our conscience, the ability to judge right from wrong, is something we will work on our whole lives.

- Provide the children with pencils and paper.
- Review with them some of the things they can do to strengthen their conscience: read God's Word, pray for guidance from the Holy Spirit, study Scripture, talk to wise counselors (parents/teachers), and spend time with others who use right judgment.
- Encourage the children to create a weekly "workout" plan to exercise and strengthen their conscience.

Basic Prayers

These are essential prayers that every Catholic should know. Latin is the official, universal language of the Church. No matter what language is someone's first or they speak daily, these prayers are prayed in common in Latin.

Sign of the Cross

In the name of the Father,
and of the Son,
and of the Holy Spirit.
Amen.

Signum Crucis

In nómine Patris
et Fílii
et Spíritus Sancti.
Amen.

The Lord's Prayer

Our Father, who art in heaven,
hallowed be thy name;
thy kingdom come,
thy will be done
on earth, as it is in heaven.
Give us this day our daily bread,
and forgive us our trespasses,
as we forgive those who trespass
against us;
and lead us not into temptation,
but deliver us from evil.

Pater Noster

Pater noster qui es in cælis:
santificétur Nomen Tuum;
advéniat Regnum Tuum;
fiat volúntas Tua,
sicut in cælo, et in terra.
Panem nostrum
cotidiánum da nobis hódie;
et dimítte nobis débita nostra,
sicut et nos
dimíttmus debitóribus nostris;
et ne nos indúcas in tentatiónem;
sed líbera nos a Malo.

The Hail Mary

Hail, Mary, full of grace,
the Lord is with thee.
Blessed art thou among women
and blessed is the fruit of thy womb,
Jesus.
Holy Mary, Mother of God,
pray for us sinners,
now and at the hour of our death.
Amen.

Ave, Maria

Ave, María, grátia plena,
Dóminus tecum.
Benedícta tu in muliéribus,
et benedíctus fructus ventris
tui, Iesus.
Sancta María, Mater Dei,
ora pro nobis peccatóribus,
nunc et in hora mortis nostræ.
Amen.

Glory Be

Glory be to the Father
and to the Son
and to the Holy Spirit,
as it was in the beginning
is now, and ever shall be
world without end.
Amen.

Gloria Patri

Gloria Patri
et Fílio
et Spíritui Sancto.
Sicut erat in princípio,
et nunc et semper
et in sæcula sæculorem.
Amen.

Optional Activity

Pray the Sign of the Cross

To reinforce its importance, always begin and end group prayer with the Sign of the Cross.

- Bring a bowl of holy water to the area.
- Have the children come up, one at a time, lightly dip the tips of their fingers in the holy water, and make the Sign of the Cross, praying it first in English and then again in Latin.
- Explain that using holy water when praying this prayer re-affirms our baptismal commitment.

Optional Activity

Glory Be Sentence Strips

Probably adapted from Jewish blessings, the "Glory Be" was influenced by the Trinitarian baptismal formula. It is often said at the end of Psalms in the Liturgy of the Hours.

- Write the prayer in English on a poster board and display it.
- Create a sentence strip for each line of the prayer.
- Have one child shuffle the paper strips.
- Then have small groups take turns working together to put the strips in the correct order.

Prayers from the Sacraments

I Confess/Confiteor

I confess to almighty God
and to you, my brothers and sisters,
that I have greatly sinned,
in my thoughts and in my words,
in what I have done and in what I
have failed to do,

Gently strike your chest with a closed fist.

through my fault, through my fault,
through my most grievous fault;

Continue:

therefore I ask blessed Mary
ever-Virgin,
all the Angels and Saints,
and you, my brothers and sisters,
to pray for me to the Lord our God.

The Apostles' Creed

See page 304 for this prayer.

The Nicene Creed

See page 305 for this prayer.

Gloria

Glory to God in the highest,
and on earth peace to people of
good will.

We praise you, we bless you, we adore
you, we glorify you, we give you
thanks for your great glory,
Lord God, heavenly King, O God,
almighty Father.

Lord Jesus Christ,
Only Begotten Son,
Lord God, Lamb of God,
Son of the Father,
you take away the sins of the world,
have mercy on us;
you take away the sins of the world,
receive our prayer;
you are seated at the right hand of
the Father, have mercy on us.

For you alone are the Holy One,
you alone are the Lord,
you alone are the Most High,
Jesus Christ, with the Holy Spirit,
in the glory of God the Father.
Amen.

Holy, Holy, Holy Lord

Holy, Holy, Holy Lord God of hosts.
Heaven and earth are full of your glory.
Hosanna in the highest.
Blessed is he who comes in the name of the Lord.
Hosanna in the highest.

Act of Contrition

(From Rite of Penance)

Often used at night after a brief examination of conscience.

My God, I am sorry for my sins
with all my heart.
In choosing to do wrong
and failing to do good,
I have sinned against you
whom I should love above all things.
I firmly intend, with your help,
to do penance, to sin no more,
and to avoid whatever leads me to sin.
Our Savior Jesus Christ
suffered and died for us.
In his name, my God, have mercy.

The Jesus Prayer

Lord Jesus Christ, Son of God,
have mercy upon me, a sinner.

Optional Activity

Add Gestures

Involve the whole child in learning prayers of our faith by adding gestures to some of the prayers.

- Work with the children in developing appropriate gestures for the Gloria prayer.
- Take time to include these gestures in appropriate group prayer celebrations.
- You might consider having your group share and teach the gestures with a younger group.

Optional Activity

The Jesus Prayer

Teach the children to pray this prayer as it was prayed by Greek and Russian mystics in the Middle Ages.

- Have the children sit quietly, close their eyes, and time their silent repetition of the prayer to their breathing in this way:

  Lord Jesus Christ, (breathe in)
  Son of God, (breathe out)
  Have mercy upon me, (breathe in)
  A sinner. (breathe out)
- Encourage them to repeat this exercise several times and then sit quietly, reflecting on God and his mercy.

Personal and Family Prayers

Grace Before Meals

Bless us, O Lord, and these thy gifts
which we are about to receive
from thy bounty, through
Christ our Lord. Amen.

Grace After Meals

We give you thanks, Almighty God,
for all these gifts
which we have received from thy
bounty,
through Christ our Lord. Amen.

Angel Guardian

An angel is a spiritual being that is a messenger of God. Angels are mentioned nearly 300 times in the Bible. Three important angels are Gabriel, Michael, and Raphael.

Angel of God,
my Guardian dear,
to whom his love commits
me here,
ever this day (night)
be at my side,
to light and guard,
to rule and guide.

Act of Faith, Hope, and Love

Often prayed in the morning to remind us that all gifts come from God, and that he can help us believe, trust, and love.

My God, I believe in you, I hope in
you,
I love you above all things, with all
my mind
and heart and strength.

Morning Prayer

Blessed are you, Lord, God of all
creation:
you take the sleep from my eyes
and the slumber from my eyelids.
Amen.

Evening Prayer

Protect us, Lord, as we stay awake;
watch over us as we sleep,
that awake, we may keep watch with
Christ,
and asleep, rest in his peace.
Amen.

Bedtime Prayer

Dear God, as this day comes to
an end,
bless my family and my friends.

Thank you for my happy day,
filled with laughter, learning,
and play.

Stay with me while I sleep tonight,
and wake me with your morning light.

Good night, God.
Amen.

Birthday Blessing

Loving God,
you created all the people of the world,
and you know each of us by name.
We thank you for N.,
who celebrates his/her birthday.
Bless him/her with your love and friendship
that he/she may grow in wisdom, knowledge,
and grace.
May he/she love his/her family always
and be ever faithful to his/her friends.
Grant this through Christ our Lord.
Amen.

Optional Activity

Make Guardian Angel Pins

Talk to the children about the role of a guardian angel and the role of angels in general. Explain that these special beings are messengers of God. Guardian angels are assigned to each person when he or she is born; they watch over us and keep us safe.

- Beforehand, make simple outlines of an angel from foam sheets.
- Give each child an image to cut out.
- You could also provide them with art supplies to decorate their angels.
- Use safety pins to fasten the angels to the children's clothing.

Optional Activity

Birthday Blessing

God made each of us, and he made us special and unique. Although we share similarities, even the same birthdays sometimes, none of us is exactly the same as another. Celebrating our birthdays is one way to thank God for creating not only our physical bodies, but also our hearts and souls.

- Each month, gather the children together, insert the individual names of the children celebrating their birthdays that month, and have the group pray the blessing over each birthday-child.

Praying with the Saints

When we pray with the Saints, we ask them to pray with us and for us. The Saints are with Christ. They speak for us when we need help.

A litany is a prayer with one line that is meant to be repeated so that those praying are caught up in the prayer itself. Some litanies are to Jesus; others are known as Litanies of the Saints.

Mary, Help of Those in Need

Holy Mary,
help those in need,
give strength to the weak,
comfort the sorrowful,
pray for God's people,
assist the clergy,
intercede for religious.
Mary, all who seek your help
experience your unfailing protection.
Amen.

Prayer for Saint Joseph's Day

Almighty God,
in your wisdom and love
you chose Joseph to be the husband
of Mary, the mother of your Son.
As we enjoy his protection on earth
may we have the help of his prayers
in Heaven.
We ask this through Christ our Lord.
Amen.

Litanies

Christ, hear us.
Christ, graciously hear us.
Lord Jesus, hear our prayer.
Lord Jesus, hear our prayer.

Holy Mary, Mother of God,
pray for us
Saint John the Baptist, **pray for us**
Saint Joseph, **pray for us**
Saint Peter and Saint Paul,
pray for us

Lord, have mercy.
Lord, have mercy.
Christ, have mercy.
Christ, have mercy.
Lord, have mercy.
Lord, have mercy.

Prayer for Saint Valentine's Day

God our Creator,
bless the love that brings people together
and grows ever stronger in our hearts.
May all the messages that carry the name
of your holy Bishop Valentine
be sent in good joy
and received in delight.
We ask this through Christ our Lord.
Amen.

Prayer of Saint Francis

Lord, make me an instrument of your peace;
where there is hatred, let me sow love;
where there is injury, pardon;
where there is doubt, faith;
where there is despair, hope;
where there is darkness, light;
and where there is sadness, joy.

Prayer of Petition

Lord God, you know our weakness.
In your mercy grant that the example
of your Saints may bring us back to
love and serve you through Christ
our Lord.
Amen.

Optional Activity

Communion of Saints

At each session, talk with the children about the Saints whose feast days are celebrated on the Church's calendar for that day or week.

- Assign each child to a different week. Ask him or her to find a story about a Saint whose feast day is celebrated during that week.
- Have the children share their stories with the rest of the group at the designated times.

Optional Activity

Peace Prayer

As Christians we are supposed to forgive those who hurt us and pray for everyone. Explain to the children that forgiving others and offering peace is something we must do for friends as well as people who may not be our friends.

- Obtain a recording of the hymn version of the Prayer of Saint Francis. One suggestion is "Make Me a Channel of Your Peace" (available from Oregon Catholic Press).
- Write the lyrics on the board or on chart paper and review them with the group.
- Encourage the children to sing the song with feeling.

Catholic Faith Words

A

absolution words spoken by the priest during the Sacrament of Penance and Reconciliation to grant forgiveness of sins in God's name **(169)**

angel a type of spiritual being that does God's work, such as delivering messages from God or helping to keep people safe from harm **(98)**

Apostles the Twelve disciples Jesus chose to be his closest followers. After the coming of the Holy Spirit, they shared in his work and mission in a special way. **(111)**

assembly the people gathered together for worship **(225)**

B

Baptism the Sacrament in which a person is immersed in water or has water poured on him or her. Baptism takes away Original Sin and all personal sin, and makes a person a child of God and member of the Church. **(157)**

Bible the Word of God written in human words. The Bible is the holy book of the Church. **(75)**

Blessed Sacrament a name for the Holy Eucharist, especially the Body of Christ kept in the Tabernacle **(261)**

blessing blessing God who is the source of everything that is good **(212)**

C

confession another name for the Sacrament of Penance and Reconciliation; an essential element of the Sacrament when you tell your sins to the priest **(169)**

conscience an ability given to us by God that helps us make choices about right and wrong **(134)**

consecration through the power of the Holy Spirit and the words and actions of the priest, the gifts of bread and wine become the Body and Blood of Jesus **(247)**

contrition being sorry for your sins and wanting to live better **(167)**

creation everything made by God **(55)**

creed a statement of the Church's beliefs **(236)**

D – F

disciples followers of Jesus who believe in him and live by his teachings **(111)**

Eucharist the Sacrament in which Jesus shares himself, and the bread and wine become his Body and Blood **(225)**

examination of conscience a prayerful way of thinking about how we have followed the Ten Commandments, Beatitudes, and Church teachings **(167)**

faith believing in God and all that he helps us understand about himself. Faith leads us to obey God. **(190)**

G

God the Father the First Divine Person of the Holy Trinity **(88)**

Gospel a word that means "Good News." The Gospel message is the Good News of God's Kingdom and his saving love. **(200)**

grace God's gift of a share in his life and help **(158)**

Great Commandment the law to love God above all else and to love others the way you love yourself **(123)**

H

Heaven the full joy of living with God forever **(278)**

Holy Communion receiving Jesus' Body and Blood in the celebration of the Eucharist **(258)**

Holy Family the name for the human family of Jesus, Mary, and Joseph **(100)**

Holy Spirit the Third Divine Person of the Holy Trinity **(108)**

Holy Trinity the one God in three Divine Persons—God the Father, God the Son, and God the Holy Spirit **(108)**

homily a short talk about the readings at Mass **(236)**

I

intercession asking God to help others **(212)**

K

Kingdom of God the world of love, peace, and justice that is in Heaven and is still being built on Earth **(192)**

L

Last Supper the meal Jesus shared with his disciples on the night before he died. At the Last Supper, Jesus gave himself in the Eucharist. **(244)**

liturgy the public prayer of the Church. It includes the Sacraments and forms of daily prayer. **(176)**

Liturgy of the Eucharist the second main part of the Mass that includes Holy Communion **(246)**

Liturgy of the Word the first main part of the Mass during which we hear God's Word proclaimed **(234)**

Lord's Prayer the prayer that Jesus taught his disciples to pray to God the Father **(210)**

M

Mary the Mother of Jesus, the Mother of God. She is also called "Our Lady" because she is our Mother and the Mother of the Church. **(98)**

Mass the gathering of Catholics to worship God. It includes the Liturgy of the Word and the Liturgy of the Eucharist. **(225)**

mercy kindness and concern for those who are suffering. God has mercy on us even though we are sinners. **(143)**

mission a job or purpose. The Church's mission is to announce the Good News of God's Kingdom **(268)**

missionaries people who answer God's call to bring the message of Jesus and announce the Good News of his Kingdom to people in other places **(268)**

mortal sin a serious sin that causes a person's relationship with God to be broken **(135)**

N – O

New Commandment Jesus' command for his disciples to love one another as he has loved us **(124)**

New Testament the second part of the Bible about the life and teachings of Jesus, his followers, and the early Church **(77)**

Old Testament the first part of the Bible about God and his People before Jesus was born **(75)**

Original Sin the first sin committed by Adam and Eve and passed down to everyone **(65)**

P

parable a short story Jesus told about everyday life to teach something about God **(124)**

parish the local community of Catholics that meets at a particular place **(203)**

peace when things are calm and people get along with one another **(190)**

penance a prayer or an act to make up for sin **(169)**

Pentecost Fifty days after the Resurrection when the Holy Spirit first came upon the Twelve disciples and the Church **(111)**

petition asking God for what we need **(212)**

praise giving God honor and thanks because he is God **(212)**

prayer talking to and listening to God **(91)**

Prayer of the Faithful prayer at Mass for the needs of the Church and the world **(236)**

proclaim to tell about Jesus in words and actions **(203)**

psalms poems and prayers from the Bible; they can be said or sung **(55)**

R

Real Presence the teaching that Jesus is really and truly with us in the Eucharist. We receive Jesus in his fullness. **(261)**

Resurrection the event of Jesus being raised from Death to new life by God the Father through the power of the Holy Spirit **(178)**

reverence the care and respect you show to God and holy persons and things **(261)**

S

Sacrament of Penance and Reconciliation the Sacrament in which God's forgiveness for sin is given through the Church **(169)**

sacramentals blessings, objects, and actions that remind you of God and are made sacred through the prayers of the Church **(213)**

Sacraments of Initiation the three Sacraments that celebrate membership in the Catholic Church: Baptism, Confirmation, and Eucharist **(158)**

sacrifice giving up something out of love for someone else or for the common good (good of everyone). Jesus sacrificed his life for all people. **(244)**

Saint a hero of the Church who loved God very much, led a holy life, and is now with God in Heaven **(88)**

Savior a title for Jesus, who was sent into the world to save all people lost through sin and to lead them back to God the Father **(66)**

Seven Sacraments special signs and celebrations that Jesus gave his Church. They allow us to share in God's life and work. **(157)**

sin a person's choice to disobey God on purpose and do what he or she knows is wrong. Accidents and mistakes are not sins. **(56)**

Son of God a name for Jesus that tells you God is his Father. The Son of God is the Second Divine Person of the Holy Trinity. **(56)**

T

temptation wanting to do something we should not, or not doing something we should **(143)**

Ten Commandments God's laws that tell people how to love him and others **(123)**

thanksgiving giving thanks to God for all he has given us **(212)**

trust to believe in and depend on someone **(91)**

V – W

venial sin a sin that hurts a person's friendship with God, but does not completely break it **(135)**

virtues good habits that make you stronger and help you do what is right and good **(143)**

worship to adore and honor God, especially at Mass and in prayer **(176)**

Index

Boldfaced numbers refer to pages on which the terms are defined.

H

I

J

K

L

Index

T

V

W

Y

Z

The Subcommittee on the Catechism, United States Conference of Catholic Bishops, has found this catechetical series, copyright 2014, to be in conformity with the *Catechism of the Catholic Church*.

Nihil Obstat
Rev. Fr. Jeremiah L. Payne, S.Th.L.
Censor Librorum, Diocese of Orlando

Imprimatur
✠ Most Rev. John Noonan
Bishop of Orlando
March 26, 2013

Write:
Our Sunday Visitor Curriculum Division
Our Sunday Visitor, Inc.
200 Noll Plaza, Huntington, Indiana 46750

Additional acknowledgments appear on page 336.

Alive in Christ Parish Grade 2 Student Book
ISBN: 978-1-61278-048-1
Item Number: CU5250

1 2 3 4 5 6 7 8 015016 17 16 15 14 13
Webcrafters, Inc.; Madison, WI; USA; June 2013; Job# 105389

Photo Credits

v Our Sunday Visitor; **vii** Our Sunday Visitor; **viii** Our Sunday Visitor; **1** Stockbyte/Thinkstock; **2** iStockphoto.com/Mike Sonnenberg; **3** Bill & Peggy Wittman; **5** iStockphoto.com/Skip ODonnell; **6** Ocean/Corbis; **7** (bg) Image Copyright Joan Kerrigan, 2012 Used under license from Shutterstock.com; **7** (inset) Image Copyright Zvonimir Orec, 2012 Used under license from Shutterstock.com; **10** Hemera/Thinkstock; **11** Digital Vision/Thinkstock; **13** Image Copyright Philip Meyer, 2012 Used under license from Shutterstock.com; **14** (t) Alan Spence/age fotostock; **14** (b) Digital Vision/Thinkstock; **15** Bill & Peggy Wittman; **16** Bill & Peggy Wittman; **17** Image Copyright Philip Meyer, 2012 Used under license from Shutterstock.com; **18** (t) Robert Harding Picture Library Ltd/Alamy; **18** (b) Bill & Peggy Wittman; **20** David Young-Wolff/Alamy; **22–23** Image Copyright Philip Meyer, 2012 Used under license from Shutterstock.com; **24** (t) David Young-Wolff/Alamy; **24** (b) Thomas Northcut/Photodisc/Thinkstock; **25** Photo by Janet Jensen/Tacoma News Tribune/MCT via Getty Images; **26** Image Copyright djem, 2012 Used under license from Shutterstock.com; **28–29** (bg) Image Copyright Philip Meyer, 2012 Used under license from Shutterstock.com; **30** Image Copyright Artisticco, 2012 Used under license from Shutterstock.com; **31** Image Copyright CREATISTA, 2012 Used under license from Shutterstock.com; **32** M.T.M. Images/Alamy; **33** Bill & Peggy Wittman; **34–35** (bg) Image Copyright Philip Meyer, 2012 Used under license from Shutterstock.com; **36** (t) Universal Images Group/DeAgostini/Alamy; **36** (b) Bill & Peggy Wittman; **38** Bill & Peggy Wittman; **40–41** (bg) Image Copyright Philip Meyer, 2012 Used under license from Shutterstock.com; **42** Stockbyte/Thinkstock; **43** Stockbyte/Thinkstock; **44** iStockphoto/Thinkstock; **45** (bg) Image Copyright Philip Meyer, 2012 Used under license from Shutterstock.com; **46** (t) Image Copyright Keith McIntyre, 2012 Used under license from Shutterstock.com; **46** (b) Stockbyte/Thinkstock; **49** (bg) Image Copyright Philip Meyer, 2012 Used under license from Shutterstock.com; **50** Image Copyright Bocman1973, 2012 Used under license from Shutterstock.com; **52** (t) Phillipe Lissac/Godong/Corbis; **52** (b) PhotoAlto/Laurence Mouton/Getty Images; **53** iStockphoto.com/Jani Bryson; **54** (br) Kayte Deioma/PhotoEdit; **54** (bc) Superstock; **54–55** (bg) iStockphoto.com/Robert Churchill; **56** Carlos's Pemium Images/Alamy; **57** SuperStock/Glowimages; **58** Carlos's Pemium Images/Alamy; **60** (bg) Image Copyright Joan Kerrigan, 2012 Used under license from Shutterstock.com; **60** (inset) iStockphoto/Thinkstock; **61** SuperStock/Glowimages; **63** iStockphoto.com/Shawn Gearhart; **64** IMAGEZOO/SuperStock; **68** Tuan Tran/Flickr/Getty Images; **69** (l) Photos.com/Thinkstock; **69** (c) Brand X Pictures/Thinkstock; **69** (r) iStockphoto.com/Jaren Wicklund; **70** (bg) Image Copyright Joan Kerrigan, 2012 Used under license from Shutterstock.com; **70** (inset) Godong/Robert Harding World Imagery/Getty Images; **71** iStockphoto.com/Shawn Gearhart; **73** Yousuke Tanaka/Aflo/Corbis; **76** Image Copyright magicinfoto, 2012 Used under license from Shutterstock.com; **77** iStockphoto.com/Nicole S. Young; **78** Digital Vision/Thinkstock; **80** (bg) Image Copyright Joan Kerrigan, 2012 Used under license from Shutterstock.com; **80** (inset) iStockphoto.com/Jason Doiy; **81** iStockphoto.com/Nicole S. Young; **86** (t) iStockphoto.com/Andrew Howe; **86** (b) Our Sunday Visitor; **87** iStockphoto/Thinkstock; **88** Exactostock/SuperStock; **90** iStockphoto/Thinkstock; **91** The Crosiers/Gene Plaisted, OSC; **94** (bg) Image Copyright Joan Kerrigan, 2012 Used under license from Shutterstock.com; **94** (inset) SuperStock/Ken Seet/Corbis; **95** The Crosiers/Gene Plaisted, OSC; **97** (l) iStockphoto/Thinkstock; **97** (r) Image Copyright Sergii Figurny, 2012 Used under license from Shutterstock.com; **98** (l) Image Copyright Zvonimir Atletic, 2012 Used under license from Shutterstock.com; **98** (r) Image Copyright Zvonimir Atletic, 2012 Used under license from Shutterstock.com; **98** (inset) iStockphoto/Thinkstock; **101** Sean Justice/Corbis; **102** JGI/Jamie Grill/Blend Images/Corbis; **104** (bg) Image Copyright Joan Kerrigan, 2012 Used under license from Shutterstock.com; **104** (inset) PhotoSpin/age fotostock; **107** iStockphoto.com/Hallgerd; **109** iStockphoto.com/Jaren Wicklund; **112** iStockphoto/Thinkstock; **113** Ingram Publishing/Thinkstock; **114** (bg) Image Copyright Joan Kerrigan, 2012 Used under license from Shutterstock.com; **114** (inset) FogStock LLC/SuperStock; **120** (c) iStockphoto/Thinkstock; **120** (b) The Crosiers/Gene Plaisted; **121** iStockphoto.com/Patrick Herrera; **126** Stockbyte/Thinkstock; **128** (bg) Image Copyright Joan Kerrigan, 2012 Used under license from Shutterstock.com; **128** (inset) Image Copyright Zvonimir Atletic, 2012 Used under license from Shutterstock.com; **129** iStockphoto.com/Patrick Herrera; **132** Photoservice Electa/Universal Images Group/Getty Images; **133** (t) Brooklyn Museum/Corbis; **133** (b) Myrleen Ferguson Cate/PhotoEdit; **134** (l) Image Copyright Ilike, 2012 Used under license from Shutterstock.com; **134** (r) Somos Images/age fotostock; **138** (bg) Image Copyright Joan Kerrigan, 2012 Used under license from Shutterstock.com; **138** (inset) Photos.com/Thinkstock; **141** (c) Fancy Collection/SuperStock; **146** Odilon Dimier/PhotoAlto/Corbis; **148** (bg) Image Copyright Joan Kerrigan, 2012 Used under license from Shutterstock.com; **148** (inset) Our Sunday Visitor; **149** Fancy Collection/SuperStock; **154** (c) Bill & Peggy Wittman; **154** (b) Jim West/age fotostock; **155** (b) Image Copyright Valua Vitaly, 2012 Used under license from Shutterstock.com; **156** (t) Photo by Alinari/Alinari Archives, Florence/Alinari via Getty Images; **156** (b) Ryan McVay/Photodisc/Thinkstock; **157** David Young-Wolff/PhotoEdit; **159** (t) Bill & Peggy Wittman; **162** (bg) Image Copyright Joan Kerrigan, 2012 Used under license from Shutterstock.com; **162** (inset) Design Pics Inc./Alamy; **163** David Young-Wolff/PhotoEdit; **166** zatletic/Bigstock.com; **169** (t) Our Sunday Visitor; **169** (c) Our Sunday Visitor; **169** (b) Our Sunday Visitor; **172** (bg) Image Copyright Joan Kerrigan, 2012 Used under license from Shutterstock.com; **172** (inset) Image Copyright Zack Clothier, 2012 Used under license from Shutterstock.com; **173** Our Sunday Visitor; **175** david sanger photography/Alamy; **176–177** (bg) Adrian Sherratt/Alamy; **176** (inset) iStockphoto/Thinkstock; **177** (c) iStockphoto/Thinkstock; **178** Jim West/Alamy; **182** (bg) Image Copyright Joan Kerrigan, 2012 Used under license from Shutterstock.com; **182** (inset) laurentiu iordache/Alamy; **183** iStockphoto/Thinkstock; **188** (t) Bill & Peggy Wittman; **188** (b) Photo by Joe Raedle/Getty Images; **189** (bg) Image Copyright Frannyanne, 2012 Used under license from Shutterstock.com; **189** (l) Our Sunday Visitor; **189** (r) Our Sunday Visitor; **192** Comstock/Thinkstock; **193** (t) Image Copyright Maria Dryfhout, 2012 Used under license from Shutterstock.com; **193** (b) Our Sunday Visitor; **196** (bg) Image Copyright Joan Kerrigan, 2012 Used under license from Shutterstock.com; **196** (inset) Image Copyright Kaetana, 2012 Used under license from Shutterstock.com; **197** Comstock/Thinkstock; **199** iStockphoto.com/Pathathai Chungyam; **200** Jim West/age fotostock; **202** (tl) P Deliss/GODONG; **202** (cr) Blend Images/SuperStock; **202** (bl) Our Sunday Visitor; **203** (l) Mario Ponta/age fotostock; **203** (r) Our Sunday Visitor; **206** (bg) Image Copyright Joan Kerrigan, 2012 Used under license from Shutterstock.com; **206** (inset) Creatas/Thinkstock; **207** Jim West/age fotostock; **209** Our Sunday Visitor; **209**; **210** Christie's Images Ltd./SuperStock; **211** Image Copyright Zurijeta, 2012 Used under license from Shutterstock.com; **215** iStockphoto.com/Maria Pavlova; **216** (bg) Image Copyright Joan Kerrigan, 2012 Used under license from Shutterstock.com; **216** (inset) mandy godbehear/Bigstock.com; **217** Our Sunday Visitor; **222** (t) Our Sunday Visitor; **222** (b) Corbis/SuperStock; **225** Our Sunday Visitor; **226** Our Sunday Visitor; **227** Our Sunday Visitor; **228** (t) Bill & Peggy Wittman; **228** (b) Caro/Alamy; **230** (bg) Image Copyright Joan Kerrigan, 2012 Used under license from Shutterstock.com; **230** (inset) Our Sunday Visitor; **231** Caro/Alamy; **233** Alex Mares-Manton/Asia Images/Corbis; **235** Our Sunday Visitor; **236** Our Sunday Visitor; **237** Bill & Peggy Wittman; **239** Kayte Deioma/PhotoEdit; **240** (bg) Image Copyright Joan Kerrigan, 2012 Used under license from Shutterstock.com; **240** (inset) Bill & Peggy Wittman; **241** Our Sunday Visitor; **243** iStockphoto.com/dtimiraos; **245** (t) PoodlesRock/Corbis; **245** (b) Myrleen Ferguson Cate/PhotoEdit; **246** Bill & Peggy Wittman; **247** Our Sunday Visitor; **248** Image Copyright Sergii Figurny, 2012 Used under license from Shutterstock.com; **250** (bg) Image Copyright Joan Kerrigan, 2012 Used under license from Shutterstock.com; **250** (inset) Robert Harding Picture Library/age fotostock; **251** Our Sunday Visitor; **256** (t) Peter Mather/First Light/Corbis; **256** (b) Istockphoto.com/g01xm; **257** Our Sunday Visitor; **260** Our Sunday Visitor; **261** Our Sunday Visitor; **262** Our Sunday Visitor; **264** (bg) Image Copyright Joan Kerrigan, 2012 Used under license from Shutterstock.com; **264** (inset) David Young-Wolff/PhotoEdit; **265** Our Sunday Visitor; **268** Our Sunday Visitor; **269** Joseph Project - Malawi/Alamy; **270** (l) Folio/Alamy; **270** (r) iStockphoto.com/Kim Gunkel; **270** (inset) iStockphoto/Thinkstock; **274** (bg) Image Copyright Joan Kerrigan, 2012 Used under license from Shutterstock.com; **275** iStockphoto.com/Kim Gunkel; **277** Our Sunday Visitor; **280** iStockphoto.com/Glenda Powers; **281** (t) Bill & Peggy Wittman; **281** (b) iStockphoto/Thinkstock; **280** Our Sunday Visitor; **284** iStockphoto.com/Magdalena Kucova; **284** (bg) Image Copyright Joan Kerrigan, 2012 Used under license from Shutterstock.com; **285** iStockphoto.com/Glenda Powers; **290** (cl) iStockphoto.com/blackred; **290–291** (cr) iStockphoto.com/blackred; **290** (bl) Ariel Skelley/Blend Images/Getty; **290–291** (br) iStockphoto.com/blackred; **291** (tr) iStockphoto.com/blackred; **291** (cr) iStockphoto.com/blackred; **292** (l) Dennis MacDonald/Alamy; **292** (r) Raymond Forbes/age fotostock; **294** iStockphoto.com/Steve Debenport; **296** Ton Koene/age fotostock; **298** PhotoAlto/SuperStock; **299** iStockphoto.com/Blend_Images; **300** Tim Gainey/Alamy; **302** John Lund/Sam Diephui/age fotostock; **305** The Crosiers/Gene Plaisted, OSC; 306 FILIPPO MONTEFORTE,FILIPPO MONTEFORTE/AFP/Getty Images; **312** Our Sunday Visitor; **314** Our Sunday Visitor; **316** (t) Our Sunday Visitor; **316** (b) Stockbyte/Thinkstock; **317** (t) Our Sunday Visitor; **319** Our Sunday Visitor

Acknowledgements:

For permission to reprint copyrighted material, grateful acknowledgment is made to the following sources:

International Consultation on English Texts: English translation of Glory Be (the *Gloria Patri*), Lord, have mercy, Apostles' Creed, Nicene Creed, the Lord's Prayer, and Lamb of God (*Agnus Dei*) by the International Consultation on English Texts (ICET). All rights reserved.

The English translation of the Confiteor, Order of Mass, Holy, Holy, Holy, Lord (*the Sanctus*), and Angel Guardian from *The Roman Missal* © 2010, International Commission on English in the Liturgy Corporation (ICEL): All rights reserved.

The English translation of the Act of Contrition from the *Rite of Penance* © 1974, ICEL: English translation. All rights reserved.

"Bedtime Prayer" from *My Book of Prayers* © 2010, Our Sunday Visitor, Inc. All rights reserved.

The Liturgical Conference: Adapted from "February 14, St. Valentine's Day" (Retitled: "Prayer for St. Valentine's Day") in *Major Feasts and Seasons*.

Liturgy Training Publications, 1800 North Hermitage Avenue, Chicago Il 60622, 1-800-933-1800, www.ltp.org: From "Meal Prayer for Harvest Time" (Retitled: "Grace Before Mealtime") in *Blessings and Prayer through the Year: A Resource for School and Parish* by Elizabeth McMahon Jeep. Text © 2004 by Archdiocese of Chicago.

Twenty-Third Publications, A Division of Bayard: "Grace After Meals" (Retitled: "Grace After Mealtime") from *500 Prayers for Catholic Schools and Parish Youth Groups* by Filomena Tassi and Peter Tassi. Text copyright © Filomena Tassi and Peter Tassi.

United States Conference of Catholic Bishops, Inc., Washington, D.C.: "At Bedside" (Retitled: "Evening Prayer") and "Washing and Dressing" (Retitled: "Morning Prayer") from *Catholic Household Blessings and Prayers*. Translation copyright © 1989 by United States Catholic Conference, Inc. From English translation of "Blessing on Birthdays or the Anniversary of Baptism" (Retitled: "Birthday Blessing") in *Book of Blessings*. Translation copyright © 1988 by United States Catholic Conference, Inc.

Activity Master Answer Keys

Activity Master Answer Key Preview

Activity Master Answer Keys

Chapter 1 Activity Master, p. 53E

Answers will vary, but should include variations of the following: nature, animals, plants, trees, mountains; Jesus; fish, whales, ocean life, birds; families, people.

Chapter 2 Activity Master, p. 63E

Chapter 3 Activity Master, p. 73E

W	R	T	Y	B	I	B	L	E	N	O	Q
O	L	D	T	E	S	T	A	M	E	N	T
R	G	O	S	P	E	L	S	R	W	T	X
D	B	L	S	C	R	I	P	T	U	R	E
O	Q	L	P	U	B	V	D	L	E	L	P
F	M	J	K	L	G	B	F	R	S	M	N
G	O	W	R	T	I	P	G	H	T	L	P
O	Z	H	G	F	D	S	A	K	L	P	B
D	Q	A	D	S	Z	R	T	P	M	Y	T
N	E	W	T	E	S	T	A	M	E	N	T

Chapter 4 Activity Master, p. 87E

Answers will vary, but the six answers will each begin with a letter that spells out F-A-T-H-E-R.

Chapter 5 Activity Master, p. 97E

Answers will vary. Pictures or words are acceptable.

Chapter 6 Activity Master, p. 107E

Answers will vary. Pictures or words are acceptable.

Chapter 7 Activity Master, p. 121E

1. 7, Answers will vary.
2. 4, Answers will vary.
3. 2, Answers will vary.
4. 3, Answers will vary.

Chapter 8 Activity Master, p. 131E

Jesus: Do you love me, Peter?
Peter: You know I love you, Lord.

Chapter 9 Activity Master, p. 141E

1. Father
2. Money
3. Ran
4. Pigs
5. City
6. Forgiving
7. Mercy

Chapter 10 Activity Master, p. 155E

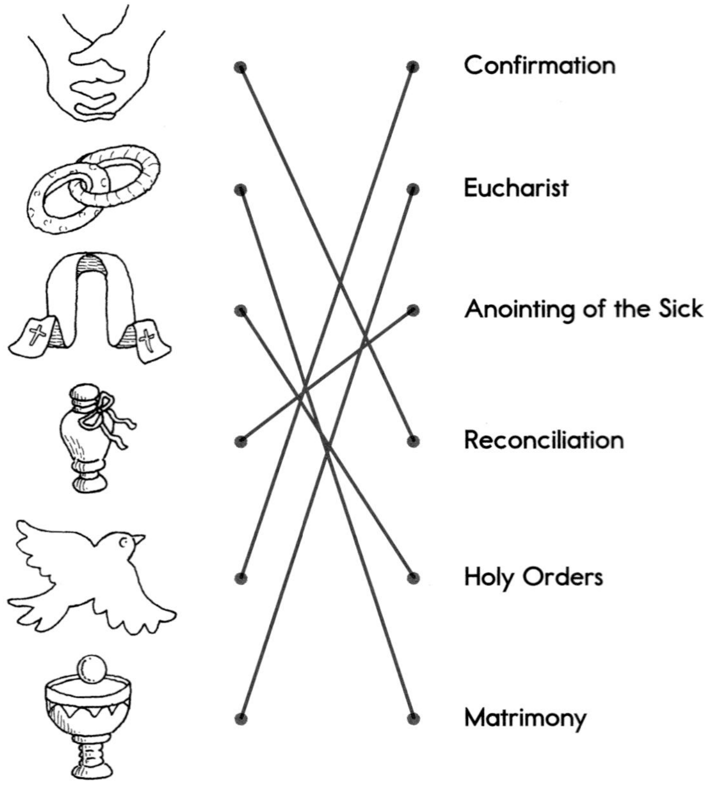

Sacrament's Name: Baptism
Drawing: Children should draw an appropriate symbol for Baptism.

Chapter 11 Activity Master, p. 165E

1. pray
2. conscience
3. sorry
4. Bible
5. sins
6. penance
7. sorrow
8. absolution

Chapter 12 Activity Master, p. 175E

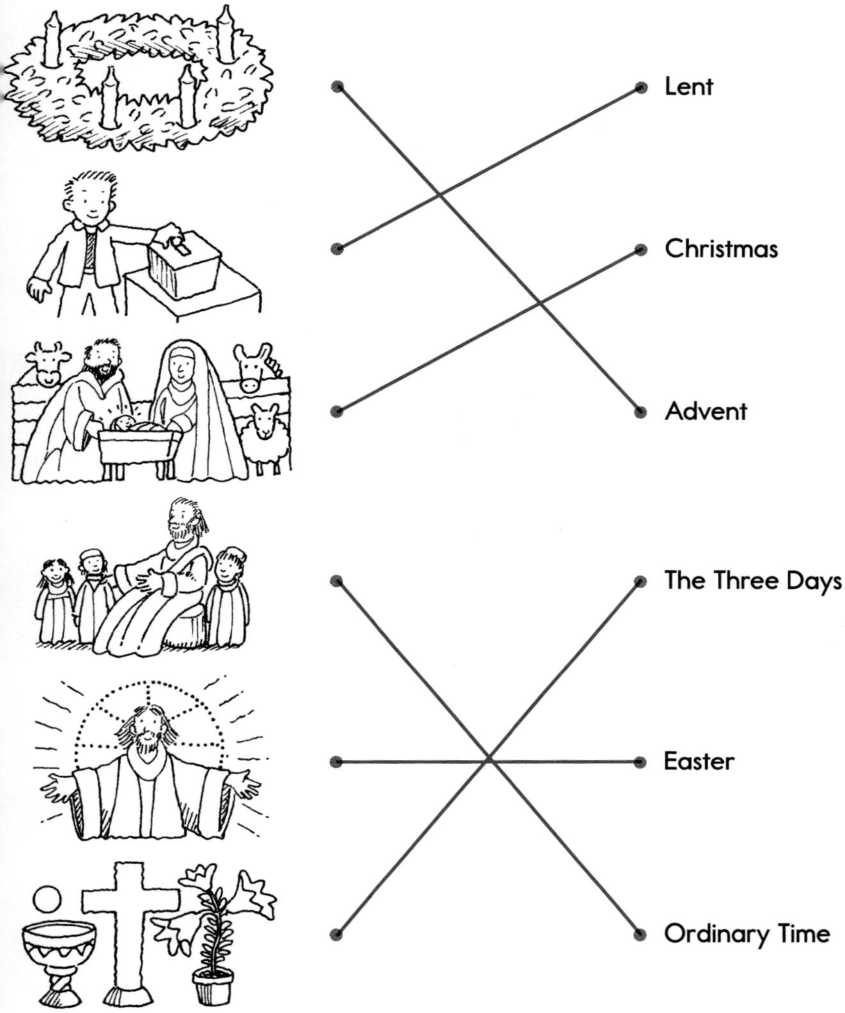

Chapter 13 Activity Master, p. 189E

Chapter 14 Activity Master, p. 199E

A1. b
A2. c
B. Drawings will vary.

Chapter 15 Activity Master, p. 209E

Children will color the doorknob sign.

Chapter 16 Activity Master, p. 223E

1. d
2. a
3. b
4. e
5. c

Chapter 17 Activity Master, p. 233E

4 Alleluia
8 Prayer of the Faithful
3 New Testament Letter
6 homily
2 Psalm
1 Old Testament reading
7 Creed
5 Gospel reading

Chapter 18 Activity Master, p. 243E

Answers will vary. Children will complete/write poems.

Chapter 19 Activity Master, p. 257E

Answers will vary. Check that drawings show family receiving Holy Communion.

Chapter 20 Activity Master, p. 267E

1. cross
2. Apostles
3. Peter
4. Father
5. mission

Chapter 21 Activity Master, p. 277E

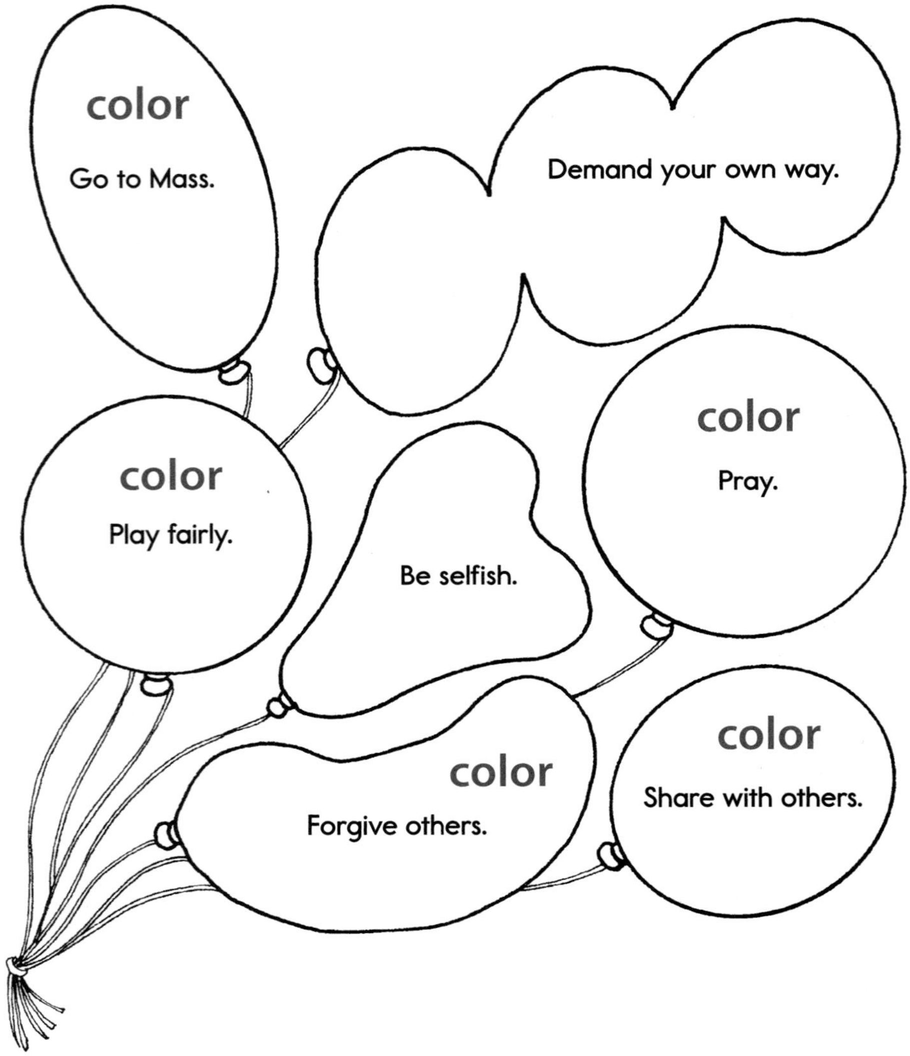
color
Go to Mass.
Demand your own way.
color
Play fairly.
Be selfish.
color
Pray.
color
Forgive others.
color
Share with others.

Photo Credits:

CE4 Our Sunday Visitor; **CE5** Our Sunday Visitor; **CE6** Our Sunday Visitor; **CE7** (t) SuperStock; **CE9** (cl) iStockphoto.com/laflor; **CE9** (c) iStockphoto.com/huronphoto; **CE9** (bl) Our Sunday Visitor; **CE9** (bcl) iStockphoto.com/redhumv; **CE9** (bcr) iStockphoto.com/Erdosain; **CE9** (br) Our Sunday Visitor; **CE11** iStockphoto.com/loops7; **CE12** Goodshoot/Thinkstock; **CE13** Sebastien Desarmaux/Corbis; **CE14** (t) United States Conference of Catholic Bishops; **CE14** (b) Our Sunday Visitor; **CE15** iStockphoto.com/asiseeit; **CE16** The Crosiers/Gene Plaisted, OSC; **CE17** Our Sunday Visitor; **CE22** Our Sunday Visitor; **CE23** United States Conference of Catholic Bishops; **CE26** (cl) Image Copyright Richard Paul Kane, 2012 Used under license from Shutterstock.com; **CE26** (cr) The Sacred Heart of Jesus, end of nineteenth century (mixed media), European School, (19th century)/Private Collection/Archives Charmet/The Bridgeman Art Library; **CE29** Hemera/Thinkstock; **CE30** Our Sunday Visitor; **CE52** Osservatore Romano/Reuters; **53C** Image Copyright Pete Pahham, 2012 Used under license from Shutterstock.com; **63C** Gabe Palmer/Alamy; **73C** Ron Chapple Studios/Thinkstock; **87C** Image Copyright Kiselev Andrey Valerevich, 2012 Used under license from Shutterstock.com; **97C** iStockphoto/Thinkstock; **107C** Radius Images/Alamy; **121C** Brian Summers/age fotostock; **131C** iStockphoto/Thinkstock; **141C** iStockphoto/Thinkstock; **155C** Bill & Peggy Wittman; **165C** Steve Gorton/Dorling Kindersley/Getty Images; **175C** Jose Luis Pelaez/Iconica/Getty Images; **189C** Hemera/Thinkstock; **199C** Hill Street Studios/age fotostock; **209C** Jupiterimages/Brand X Pictures/Thinkstock; **223C** John McInnes/age fotostock; **233C** Image Copyright Gordana Sermek, 2013 Used under license from Shutterstock.com; **243C** iStockphoto/Thinkstock; **257C** iStockphoto.com/princessdlaf; **267C** Image Copyright Anton Albert, 2012 Used under license from Shutterstock.com; **277C** Myrleen Pearson/PhotoEdit